The Psychobiology of the Depressive Disorders

Implications for the Effects of Stress

PERSONALITY AND PSYCHOPATHOLOGY

A Series of Monographs, Texts, and Treatises

David T. Lykken, Editor

1. The Anatomy of Achievement Motivation, *Heinz Heckhausen*. 1966*

2. Cues, Decisions, and Diagnoses: A Systems-Analytic Approach to the Diagnosis of Psychopathology, *Peter E. Nathan*. 1967*

3. Human Adaptation and Its Failures, *Leslie Phillips*. 1968*

4. Schizophrenia: Research and Theory, *William E. Broen, Jr.* 1968*

5. Fears and Phobias, *I. M. Marks*. 1969

6. Language of Emotion, *Joel R. Davitz*. 1969

7. Feelings and Emotions, *Magda Arnold*. 1970

8. Rhythms of Dialogue, *Joseph Jaffe* and *Stanley Feldstein*. 1970

9. Character Structure and Impulsiveness, *David Kipnis*. 1971

10. The Control of Aggression and Violence: Cognitive and Physiological Factors, *Jerome L. Singer* (Ed.). 1971

11. The Attraction Paradigm, *Donn Byrne*. 1971

12. Objective Personality Assessment: Changing Perspectives, *James N. Butcher* (Ed.). 1972

13. Schizophrenia and Genetics, *Irving I. Gottesman* and *James Shields*, 1972*

14. Imagery and Daydream Methods in Psychotherapy and Behavior Modification, *Jerome L. Singer*. 1974

15. Experimental Approaches to Psychopathology, *Mitchell L. Kietzman, Samuel Sutton,* and *Joseph Zubin* (Eds.). 1975

16. Coping and Defending: Processes of Self-Environment Organization, *Norma Haan*. 1977

17. The Scientific Analysis of Personality and Motivation, *R. B. Cattell* and *P. Kline*. 1977

18. The Determinants of Free Will: A Psychological Analysis of Responsible, Adjustive Behavior, *James A. Easterbrook*.

19. The Psychopath in Society, *Robert J. Smith*.

20. The Fears of Adolescents, *J. H. Bamber*.

21. Cognitive–Behavioral Interventions: Theory, Research, and Procedures, *Philip C. Kendall* and *Steven D. Hollon* (Eds.).

22. The Psychobiology of the Depressive Disorders: Implications for the Effects of Stress, *Richard A. Depue* (Ed.).

*Titles initiated during the series editorship of Brendan Maher.

The Psychobiology of
the Depressive Disorders

Implications for the Effects of Stress

EDITED BY

Richard A. Depue

Department of Psychology
State University of New York at Buffalo
Buffalo, New York

 1979

ACADEMIC PRESS

A Subsidiary of Harcourt Brace Jovanovich, Publishers

New York   London   Toronto   Sydney   San Francisco

ACADEMIC PRESS, INC.
111 Fifth Avenue, New York, New York 10003

United Kingdom Edition published by
ACADEMIC PRESS, INC. (LONDON) LTD.
24/28 Oval Road, London NW1 7DX

Library of Congress Cataloging in Publication Data
Main entry under title:

The Psychobiology of the depressive disorders.

    (Personality and psychopathology)
    Includes bibliographies.
    1. Depression, Mental——Physiological aspects.
2. Stress (Psychology) 3. Stress (Physiology)
I. Depue, Richard A. [DNLM: 1. Depression——Psychology.
2. Stress, Psychological W1 PE861 / WM171 P974]
RC537.P73   616.8'52   79—51676
ISBN 0—12—211650—X

PRINTED IN THE UNITED STATES OF AMERICA

79 80 81 82   9 8 7 6 5 4 3 2 1

Contents

PART *II*
Distinctions within the Topic

PART III
The Interaction of Stress and Biologic
Variables in the Depressive Disorders

PART *IV*
Psychosocial Aspects of Stress and the Depressive Disorders

PART **V**

Models of Stress–Biology Interactions: Theoretical and Research Strategies

CHAPTER **17**

Advantages of a Behavior–Genetic Approach to Investigating Stress in the Depressive Disorders   **391**

L. Erlenmeyer-Kimling

CHAPTER **18**

A Biobehavioral Approach to Depression   **409**

Hagop S. Akiskal

List of Contributors

Numbers in parentheses indicate the pages on which the authors' contributions begin.

Hagop S. Akiskal (409), Mood Clinic and Affective Disorders Program, Department of Psychiatry, University of Tennessee Center for the Health Sciences, Memphis, Tennessee 38103

James R. Averill (365), Department of Psychology, University of Massachusetts, Amherst, Massachusetts 01002

William H. Bailey (125), The Rockefeller University, New York, New York 10021

Joseph Becker (317), Department of Psychiatry and Behavioral Sciences, University of Washington School of Medicine, Seattle, Washington 98195

George W. Brown (263), Department of Sociology and Social Research Unit, Bedford College, University of London, London, England W1

Monte S. Buchsbaum (221), Section on Clinical Psychophysiology, Biological Psychiatry Branch, Division of Clinical and Behavioral Research, National Institute of Mental Health, Bethesda, Maryland 20014

Richard A. Depue (3, 23, 177), Department of Psychology, Bioclinical

Training Program, State University of New York at Buffalo, Buffalo, New York 14226

Bruce P. Dohrenwend (105), Department of Psychiatry, Columbia University College of Physicians and Surgeons, New York, New York 10032

Barbara Snell Dohrenwend (105), Division of Sociomedical Sciences, Columbia University School of Public Health, New York, New York 10032

L. Erlenmeyer-Kimling (391), Department of Medical Genetics, New York State Psychiatric Institute, New York, New York 10032

Don C. Fowles (55, 81), Department of Psychology, University of Iowa, Iowa City, Iowa 52242

Judy Garber (335), Department of Psychology, University of Minnesota, Minneapolis, Minnesota 55455

Frank S. Gersh* (55, 81), Division of Behavioral Neurology, Department of Neurology, University of Iowa Hospitals and Clinics, Iowa City, Iowa 52242

Howard I. Glazer (125), The Rockefeller University, New York, New York 10021

Sally J. Grosscup† (291), Department of Psychology, University of Oregon, Eugene, Oregon 97403

Ross M. Kleiman (177), Department of Psychology, Bioclinical Training Program, State University of New York at Buffalo, Buffalo, New York 14226

Peter M. Lewinsohn (291), Department of Psychology, University of Oregon, Eugene, Oregon 97403

James W. Maas (161), Department of Psychiatry, Yale University School of Medicine, New Haven, Connecticut 06511

William R. Miller (335), Marriage Council of Philadelphia, Department of Psychiatry, University of Pennsylvania, Philadelphia, Pennsylvania 19104

Scott M. Monroe‡ (3, 23), Department of Psychology, Bioclinical Training Program, State University of New York at Buffalo, Buffalo, New York 14226

Bruce C. Nisula (205), National Institute of Child Health and Human Development, National Institute of Health, Bethesda, Maryland 20014

E. S. Paykel (245), Department of Psychiatry, University of London, St. George's Hospital Medical School, London, England SW 17

* PRESENT ADDRESS: Department of Medical Psychology, University of Oregon Health Sciences Center, Portland, Oregon 97201

† PRESENT ADDRESS: Lane County Mental Health Clinic, Eugene, Oregon 97403

‡ PRESENT ADDRESS: Department of Psychology, University of Pittsburgh, Pittsburgh, Pennsylvania 15260

Larissa A. Pohorecky* (125), The Rockefeller University, New York, New York 10021

Linda H. Schneider (125), The Rockefeller University, New York, New York 10021

Stephen F. Seaman (335), Department of Psychology, University of Pennsylvania, Philadelphia, Pennsylvania 19104

Susan L. Shackman (3), Department of Psychology, State University of New York at Buffalo, Buffalo, New York 14226

Jon M. Stolk† (205), Departments of Psychiatry and Pharmacology, Dartmouth Medical School, Hanover, New Hampshire 03755

Donald R. Sweeney‡ (161), Department of Psychiatry, Yale University School of Medicine, New Haven, Connecticut 06511

Jay M. Weiss (125), The Rockefeller University, New York, New York 10021

Mary Ann Youngren§ (291), Department of Psychology, University of Oregon, Eugene, Oregon 97403

* PRESENT ADDRESS: Center for Alcohol Studies, Rutgers University, New Brunswick, New Jersey 08903

† PRESENT ADDRESS: Neuro Science Program, Maryland Psychiatric Research Center, Box 3235, Baltimore, Maryland 21228

‡ PRESENT ADDRESS: Fair Oaks Hospital, Summit, New Jersey 07901

§ PRESENT ADDRESS: Psychology Faculty at Portland State University, Portland, Oregon 97207

Preface

As stated later in this volume, in the past decade, conceptualizations of human disorders have undergone gradual yet highly significant modifications. The impetus for these modifications arises from the rapid development in two distinct, but nevertheless conceptually related, areas of inquiry concerned with human disease and man's well-being. The first area comprises that body of literature concerned with the impact of the physical and psychosocial environment on man's biologic and psychologic functioning. The second area involves the conceptualization of disease that has arisen from developments in theoretical biology concerning models of human biological systems. Unfortunately, development of a complete theory of human disorders is greatly impeded by the fact that the above two areas are seldom integrated theoretically or empirically.

The same problem is paralleled in conceptualizations of the depressive disorders. Biologic research has proliferated since 1965 when the catecholamine hypothesis of depressive disorders was first formulated. More recently, researchers have been calling for a shift in biologic research, from sole examination of pathophysiology to investigation of biological predisposition in high-risk individuals. But, in general, there has been little concern in the biologic "camp" for studying relevant biologic variables as a function of stress or specific stimulus conditions. And yet it is exactly this form of research that will illuminate the manner in which biologic predispositions become "activated" and result in the onset of disorder. The problem is equally serious with researchers interested in the initiating role of psychosocial factors in the depressive disorders. Both their theories and their research are generally devoid of biologic notions and measures.

A complete theory of depressive disorders needs to explain who is at risk for disorder and when and under what circumstances the person at risk is likely to develop disturbances. Clearly, such a theory is far from our current grasp, but it is equally clear that its development will require integrative stress–biology models and research strategies.

In view of the lack of any other book that attempts to stimulate stress–biology interactional thinking and research in the depressive disorders, this volume was developed to initiate the process of integration. Both biologic and psychosocial researchers who have pioneered an interactive approach have contributed their latest notions and research. For purposes of clarity, the volume has been divided into several parts.

Although the issues in each major part are enunciated in separate introductions to each part, some of the general topics are worth emphasizing here. Part I provides a conceptual framework for the many issues and variables inherent in a comprehensive theory of human disorders. The three major issues discussed are (a) the nature of a predisposition to disease, both psychological and biologic, (b) the initiation of disease by psychosocial factors, and (c) the mediation processes that relate the psychosocial and biologic influences on disorders. Overall, there is an attempt to relate issues in the stressful life events research with notions developed in theoretical biology.

Part II provides a framework for clinical distinctions in the depressive disorders which may prove meaningful in the investigation of more specific stress–biology pathways. A genetic taxonomy for unipolar and bipolar disorders is presented, and implications for differential stress factors are noted. Moreover, a comprehensive overview of neurotic depressions is presented, including an entire chapter on anxious depression. In chapters 3 and 4, the status of the notion that stress is an important contributor to neurotic-reactive depressions is discussed. This section concludes with an overview of the important distinctions and issues in the stress area. This overview helps to clarify discussions of stress in subsequent sections.

Part III provides a framework from several different vantage points for examining biologic variables, found to be relevant to the depressive disorders. Animal research on the relationship of psychological parameters to brain catecholamine metabolism initiates the discussion and is followed by clinical research that investigates the effects of stress and anxiety on peripheral indexes of central catecholamine activity. Beginning work with persons at-risk for depressive disorders is also discussed from a Stress–

Biology interaction viewpoint. The catecholamine discussion concludes with an examination of the implications for stress factors in relation to genetic influences on catecholamine metabolism. Part III closes with a look at recent, stimulus intensity modulation data in polar disorders, interpreted within a stress framework for the first time.

Part IV provides the latest statements on two issues by prominent researchers: (a) the role of psychosocial events, social support, and chronic stressors in the initiation of depressive disorders, and how that role is to be conceived; and (b) what psychological factors may serve to predispose individuals to depressive episodes. When the data from these chapters are considered together with the notions from Chapter 1 in this volume, a definite role, and its nature, begins to emerge for psychosocial factors in the initiation and predisposition to depressive disorders.

Finally, Part IV provides two creative discussions on the manner in which Stress–Biology interactions may be conceptualized and studied. These chapters provide an integration that is novel yet testable, and that embodies the major goal of this book: to stimulate thinking and research on the nature of Psychosocial–Biologic interactions in the depressive disorders.

Acknowledgments

Many people contributed to the completion of this volume, and unfortunately I could not begin to list them all. Most of all, I wish to acknowledge the encouragement and valuable suggestions of Brendan Maher during the initial phases of developing this book. Very helpful comments on different aspects of the book were also offered by Hagop Akiskal, Don Fowles, Ed Katkin, and Murray Levine. In addition, the bulk of editorial and secretarial assistance was provided by Gloria Aniebo, Carole Orsolits, Mary Lou Luehrsen, and Lee Ann Pawlick. Finally, I can not adequately express my appreciation to Wendy, Sean, and Brendan, whose unselfish encouragement and support helped me to complete the book.

PART I

Conceptual Overview of Stress and Disease

In the past decade, concepts of human disease have undergone gradual, yet highly significant, modifications. The impetus for these modifications arises from the rapid development in two distinct, but nevertheless conceptually related, areas of inquiry concerned with human disease and man's well-being. The first area comprises that body of literature concerned with the impact of the physical and psychosocial environment on man's biologic and psychologic functioning. The second area involves the conceptualization of disease that has arisen from developments in theoretical biology concerning models of human biological systems.

There has been little attempt to integrate the findings and notions arising from these two areas. Therefore, this section provides an organizational framework for such an integration. It is the Editor's belief that conceptualization of stress–biology interactions in depressive disorders discussed throughout this volume will acquire greater meaning when they are viewed within a larger framework of current models of human disease.

CHAPTER 1

The Psychobiology of Human Disease: Implications for Conceptualizing the Depressive Disorders

Richard A. Depue, Scott M. Monroe, and
Susan L. Shackman

INTRODUCTION

The rapid development of the body of literature devoted to human disease and man's well-being as they relate to his physical and psychosocial environment has provided the stimulus for modifications of our concepts of disease processes. Although not generally recognized, much of the stimulus for focusing on the environment as it relates to health is due to the changing patterns of disease over the past century. With the decline in major diseases resulting from exogenous sources, it gradually became evident that major health problems were due to the high prevalence of chronic disorders (e.g., coronary heart disease) that are not explained by an exogenous or infectious model of disease alone. Indeed, because epidemiologic research began to indicate that the prevalence of chronic diseases varied as a function of the type of setting (e.g., industrial–nonindustrial society, urban–rural lifestyle), it appeared that the incidence of chronic diseases might be influenced by the nature of the physical and psychosocial environments.

That man's biologic and psychological well-being could be threatened by

3

The Psychobiology of the Depressive Disorders:
Implications for the Effects of Stress

the environment enhanced interest in the "stressful" dimensions of psychosocial and physical stimuli, in the moderating effects of psychosocial assets (e.g., social support), and in personal factors that alter one's perception of the environment. Moreover, the effects of more global environmental variables (e.g., rapid population increases, urbanization, and poverty) on man's health status has become an international concern. For instance, a recent World Health Organization conference on the human environment stressed the importance of all aspects of the human environment, including psychosocial and socioeconomic factors, for human health, as well as the need for a reorientation of medical education as it relates to environment–disease conceptions (Levi & Andersson, 1975).

Changing concepts of disease, however, have not been stimulated solely by an increasing awareness of the importance of the psychosocial determinants in the initiation of disease. A second impetus has arisen in the biomedical camp itself (Engel, 1977). Part of the problem with biomedical concepts of disease results from historical influences. In its early stages of development, medicine adopted the basic scientific principle of reductionism, as enunciated by prominent people such as Newton. The major approach to researchable topics was analytical, where entities were resolved into isolable, causal chains or units and from which it was assumed that the whole could be understood, both materially and conceptually, by reconstituting the parts. Within a philosophic framework of mind–body dualism, early medical science readily fostered the notion of the body as a machine and of disease as a consequence of a breakdown of the machine. "Thus, the scientific approach to disease began by focusing in a fractional analytic way on biological (somatic) processes and ignoring the behavioral and psychosocial [Engel, 1977, p. 131]."

Although the analytic approach to disease has been fruitful, it has also led to a limited view of the nature and significance of biologic variables in human disorders. Most of the specific limitations of this approach are noted in our discussion in the next section of this chapter, however, there are two more general, but highly important, limitations worth noting briefly. The first is now well-known to all researchers in psychopathology: Even in genetically transmitted disorders, biologic factors clearly cannot be considered sufficient causes of disease. The second limitation is less well-known but is at the core of conceptualizing human biology and disease. Theoretical biology has emphasized a systems-theory framework for understanding the nature of human biology. As systems theory holds that all levels of organization (from molecules, cells, organs, the organism, the person, the family, the society, to the biosphere) are linked to each other in a hierarchical relationship so that change in one affects change in the others, the reductionistic conception of human biology would not be viewed as providing by itself an adequate framework for developing nor testing comprehensive theories of disease. This is not merely a theoretical issue, for a systems-theory concept of disease has implications for what are to be considered the relevant psychosocial and biologic parameters in disease (see our discussion on pages 6–14) as well as for research strategies for investigating disease (see Chapter 8 by Depue and Kleiman, this volume).

Strangely enough, there have been few attempts to integrate the notions developed in research on the psychosocial environment with the more recent concepts of human biology and disease (Weiner, 1977). Therefore, we attempt to provide this integration in this chapter. Because of the preliminary nature of development in each of the areas just mentioned, our discussion is necessarily speculative, and it is vague with respect to specific mechanisms. However, we believe that the framework developed will serve a heuristic purpose in stimulating new approaches to conceptualizing and investigating stress–biology interactions in the depressive disorders.

CONCEPTIONS OF DISEASE PARAMETERS: IMPLICATIONS FOR STRESS–BIOLOGY INTERACTIONS

The major portion of research on human diseases, including both medical and psychopathologic disorders, has focused on determining the mechanisms involved in the pathophysiology underlying their signs and symptoms. Although such work is important and may generate hypotheses about the etiologic role of certain variables in a disorder, explanations of disease which are derived from this research are essentially functional in nature. Unfortunately, an understanding of the functional relationship between signs and symptoms and their underlying pathophysiology does not provide information concerning that which we most want to know: who is at risk for the disease in question. Nor does such an understanding elucidate how the factors placing an individual at risk come about. As Weiner (1977) has noted, a complete theory of disease must be able to predict who is at risk for a particular disease and when and under what circumstances the person at risk is likely to develop it. In other words, a complete theory of disease must be based not only on functional explanations, but also on predictive and historical explanations.

Generally, a comprehensive theory of disease may be viewed as incorporating three main foci: (a) predisposition to disease, (b) initiation of disease, and (c) mediation processes. Each of these foci is exceedingly complex when considered individually, and researchers have only recently begun to study the nature of their interaction. Hence, we shall treat them separately in the following discussion.

The Nature of Predisposition to Disease

The enterprise of deriving predictive explanations of disease is basically one of exploring the nature of predisposition. It has long been assumed that predisposing factors may be either biologic or psychological in nature and contrary to common misconception, Alexander (1950) emphasized the interactional nature of biologic and psychological factors in accounting for the predisposing variance of certain "psychosomatic" disorders. However, little firm evidence exists demonstrating predispositional power with respect to psychological variables and, with only a few exceptions, the case is similar for biologic variables (Weiner, 1977).

It appears that the major reason for the inability to demonstrate predispositional power for either type of variable is due to the complex nature of predisposition itself. Earlier attempts to identify predisposing factors often operated under the notion that a particular disease would be associated with a particular predisposition. This notion of homogeneity of predisposition to (or etiology of) disease simply cannot account for the variety of findings that have emerged. For example, it is known that one factor may predispose to several different diseases. Conversely, different factors may predispose to the same disease. Such findings have led to the concept of a final common pathway, a biologic pathway through which the various predisposing variables produce a common outcome (see Chapter 18 in this volume for an application of this concept to depressive disorders). Moreover, some individuals in whom the predisposition is observable (or evocable) do not develop the disease, suggesting that in such cases one factor is not etiologically sufficient for disease production or that protective factors have altered the person's vulnerability.

All three of the preceding examples suggest that predisposition to disease is heterogeneous in nature. There are probably numerous factors that predispose to any particular disease, and these factors are likely to combine in varying numbers in different persons having a disease. With these issues in mind, a closer look at the nature of biologic and psychological predisposition is in order.

BIOLOGIC PREDISPOSITION

The significance of biologic predisposing variables lies in the fact that these variables determine "choice" of disease, that is, which particular disease a person will develop. Hence, from the standpoint of predicting who is at risk for certain disorders, a determination of the biologic predisposing variables greatly increases the specificity of outcome predictions, although here too, the concept of multiple predisposition seems to apply. The constellation of biologic predisposing variables will vary from individual to individual, making it difficult to account for large proportions of the predisposing variance (e.g., the attempts to identify significant predictors of coronary heart disease, Weiner, 1977).

Despite these difficulties, it seems fruitful to generally consider the manner in which biologic factors might predispose an individual to disease. In doing so, a useful strategy would be to outline the major characteristics of normal biologic processes and then to note their implications for conceptualizing the nature of biologic predispositions. Developments in theoretical biology provide the initial framework. In extending Cannon's notion of homeostasis of fluid compartments, Schoenheimer (1942) put forth the concept of the "dynamic steady state." The "dynamic steady state" represents a dynamic equilibrium of constantly interacting and inherently unstable biochemical systems. Within all of the body's tissues, there is a constant process of turnover, change, and replacement. Every metabolic activity within the organism, and every transaction between the organism and its environment, results in biologic variation within tissues. If the "dynamic steady state" is to be restored, some adaptive reaction is required.

Such adaptive reactions to changing biologic conditions are the responsibility of the body's major regulatory systems, of which we will discuss three. The first is the self-regulatory system which operates at the cellular level. This form of regulation involves the modulation of the activity of enzymes, two examples of which are end-product inhibition and rate-limiting characteristics. Both examples are evident in the biosynthetic pathways for monoamine neurotransmitters. For instance, in the biosynthesis pathway for norepinephrine, the initial enzyme (tyrosine hydroxylase) is regulated by its rate-limiting properties, as well as the inhibiting effects of norepinephrine as an end product.

The second regulatory system is the external regulatory system. Because enzymes are usually inactive, they are subject to an inducing regulation by substrate, hormone, or transmitter substance. External regulation by inducement generally involves the modulatory activity of the autonomic nervous system, neuroendocrine system, and the immune system. The neuroendocrine system is of particular importance in this respect, for there is no cellular mechanism nor general metabolic process that cannot be influenced by neuroendocrine mechanisms. This becomes readily apparent when one surveys the effects of some of the hypothalamic, anterior pituitary hormones, as shown in Table 1.1. In addition to the examples used with self-regulation in Table 1.1, the external regulatory adrenocortical hormone cortisol is known to induce the activity of tyrosine hydroxylase in certain norepinephrine pathways involved in the feedback modulation of cortisol production itself (see Chapter 8 of this volume). This example also illustrates the interaction of several modulatory inputs to tyrosine hydroxylase from different regulation systems (the self- and external-regulatory systems) for the purpose of regulating norepinephrine metabolism.

The third form of regulation involves the modulation of the external

Table 1.1

SOME EFFECTS OF THE HYPOTHALAMIC ANTERIOR PITUITARY SYSTEM

Hormone	Effect
Cortisol	Increases carbohydrate metabolism (gluconeogenesis)
	Increases mobilization of fatty acids
	Regulates enzyme activity
	Alters electrolyte metabolism
	Increases concentration of free amino acids in brain
	Increases brain excitability
	Alters monoamine uptake and synthesis
	Decreases activity of inhibitory neurotransmitters
	Suppresses immunologic response
	Permissive role for action of other hormones
Thyroxin	Increases turnover of carbohydrates, fats, cholesterol
	Increases heart rate, heart contractility, peripheral resistance
	Increases cortisol and growth hormone secretion
	Increases sensitivity of some tissues to catecholamines
Growth hormone	Increases protein synthesis via promotion of amino acids absorption into cells
	Conserves carbohydrates
	Increases mobilization of fats
Aldosterone	Alters metabolism of minerals and water

regulatory systems by the brain. This, of course, places central regulatory systems in the significant position of coordinating the operation of all of the body's major regulatory systems.

It should be clear from the above discussion that adaptive reactions aimed at restoring the "dynamic steady state," and hence at maintaining tissue integrity itself, are heavily dependent on the smooth operation of the body's regulatory systems. In view of the significance of regulatory systems, consideration of their functional characteristics might shed light on the nature of biologic predispositions. Although it is clear that physiologic functions are regulated by a dynamic interplay of excitatory and inhibitory influences, recent concepts of regulation have particularly emphasized the importance of inhibitory processes. For instance, Roberts (1972) and Delgado (1975) have proposed models of the central nervous system (CNS) based largely on disinhibition. These models suggest that genetically preprogrammed circuits are released to function at varying rates and in various combinations by the inhibition of inhibitory neurons that are tonically holding excitatory command neurons in check. Moreover, in reviewing the functions of the central sympathetic nervous system, Sigg (1975) emphasized that sympathetic efferent activity is subject to inhibitory modulation of areas in the brainstem and the diencephalon. Similarly, but in a more poetic vain, Eccles (1977) likened the excitatory pathways of the brain to a raw piece of marble, and the inhibitory pathways to a sculptor: the inhibitory pathways progressively determine the form of the information to be transmitted.

In each of these concepts, the central theme is that the fine tuning and the adaptive reactivity of biochemical systems in the human body depend largely on the modulatory action of inhibitory influences. The modulation of cortisol release again represents a perfect example (see Chapter 8 of this volume). Release of cortisol is generally due to an excitatory command pathway. Modulation of cortisol release is regulated by either disinhibiting or activating an inhibitory pathway that chronically holds the excitatory command pathway in check. If one extends the characteristics of the cortisol release system to other regulatory systems, one may infer an elaborate inhibitory network in the central nervous system which is responsible, in interaction with a remarkably complex system of buffers and feedback mechanisms, for the modulation (regulation) of all external regulatory systems and, hence, all biochemical–physiological processes in the human body.

This discussion would appear to have direct relevance for conceptualizing the nature of biologic predisposition. In as much as the "dynamic steady state," and, hence, tissue integrity, is dependent on the effective operation of regulatory systems, biologic predisposition may involve the introduction of a bias in a regulatory system. Such a bias may represent a potential for a distorted balance of regulatory mechanisms or, more simply, a potential for dysregulation (Schwartz, 1977; Weiner, 1977; Wolf, 1975). The implications of the concept of dysregulation are that predisposition and disease may be viewed, not as qualitatively different phenomena, but as quantitative variations in what are essentially malfunctioning normal bodily processes, exaggerated or insufficient in some way (Wolf, 1975). If we extend these models of regulatory systems one step further, such exaggerations or insufficiencies of physiologic processes would most likely correspond to functional alterations in inhibitory influences involved in regulatory systems. As suggested in Table 1.2, at face value, the functional biologic alterations that characterize many diseases are concordant with a notion of quantitative deviation in regulatory systems.

In major psychopathologic disorders, such as depressive disorders, the primary source of biologic predisposition is likely to be genetic, although other sources are possible (see Chapter 18 in this volume). Because genes express themselves in terms of enzyme and protein characteristics (Heston, 1973), the study of these latter variables should help to clarify the nature of biologic predisposing variables. Of course, a bias may be identified at other levels of analysis, such as the biochemical or hormonal (see Chapter 8 in this volume), however, at any level, the manifestation of the bias need not be expressed simply in terms of chronic increases or decreases in levels or activity. Rather, more subtle alterations may be involved, such as the balance between regulatory substances. Moreover, as biases may likely be

Table 1.2

DISEASE AS QUANTITATIVE DEVIATION IN BODILY PROCESSES

Disease	Functional biologic alteration
Exaggerations	
Rheumatic fever	Excess of tissue immunity
Peptic ulcer	Excessive excretion of acid and pepsin
Cancer	Cell replication that will not quit
Graves' disease	Excessive elaboration of thyroxin
Cushing's syndrome	Excessive elaboration of cortisol
Mania	Excessive catecholaminergic activity
Essential hypertension	Excessive constriction of arterioles
Ulcerative colitis	Sustained posture of transport
Connective-tissue diseases	Exaggerated immune behavior
Duodenal ulcer	Excessive gastric secretion of HCl
Insufficiencies	
Hypothyroidism	Reduced elaboration of thyroxin
Primary depression	Functional deficiency of monoamine activity
Infectious diseases	Reduced immunologic response

found in regulatory systems, identification and study of biologic predisposition might best be accomplished under stimulus conditions that tax the modulatory activity of a particular biologic system. (This point is discussed further in Chapter 8 of this volume.)

Whatever the nature of biologic predisposition, it is generally accepted that biologic factors, while necessary for the occurrence of most diseases, are not sufficient in and of themselves to account for the total variance in vulnerability to disease. Several theorists have posited interesting contributory roles for psychological variables in predisposition, and it is to these notions that we now turn.

PSYCHOLOGICAL PREDISPOSITION

The notion that the predisposition to, and the initiation of, disease is exclusively "psychogenic" has been extant for some time. Although Alexander (1950) is often cited as providing one of the main foundations for such a position, he quite explicitly stated that, given the activation of specific psychological conflicts, there must be predisposing bodily factors that determine the "choice" of disease. Other researchers interested in the psychosocial factors that predispose to disease have argued strongly in a similar vein (Engel, 1967; Mirsky, 1957, 1958; Wolf, 1975). Moreover, recent extensive reviews of this topic do not support an exclusively "psychogenic" determination of disease (Lipowski, Lipsitt, & Whybrow, 1977; Weiner, 1977). So as not to extend what appears to us to be an oversimplified and fruitless debate, we wish to assert quite categorically that the concept of "psychogenicity" is not adequate to explain the predisposing and initiating variances involved in most diseases. The more fruitful questions concern the nature and relative contribution of psychosocial variables within the concept of multiple factors predisposing to disease.

Two of the clearest proponents of a contributory role for psychological predisposing factors are Alexander and Engel. Although there is some overlap in their arguments, their ideas do provide distinctly different perspectives on the issue. A comparison of their notions may help to generate more comprehensive conceptions of the role of psychological factors in predisposition.

Alexander (1950, 1968) believed that there are specific psychological predispositions for specific diseases. He suggested that specific, unconscious conflicts (but not specific personality types) sensitized a person to respond to specific life experiences in a particular way. The life experience was made particularly poignant by the conflict, and the conflict, in turn, sensitized the person to perceive and interpret the social situation in terms of his individual predisposition. Activated by the experience, the conflict elicited strong emotions—particularly anger, anxiety, and depression. These emotions are mediated by autonomic and neuroendocrine mechanisms that, in interaction with biologic predispositions (biases), serve to initiate the disease process.

Alexander's specificity hypothesis has not received general support. Studies of several disorders, such as ulcerative colitis (Engel, 1955), bronchial asthma (Knapp & Nemetz, 1960), and duodenal ulcer (de M'Uzan & Bonfils, 1961; Weisman, 1956), have reached the similar conclusion that typically there is no single and central predisposing conflict, but rather several conflicts in individual patients, or across patient groups. Moreover, Alexander's own predictive data (Alexander et al., 1968) suggest that specific conflicts occur only in about one-half of the patients having a particular disease. Although it has been suggested that the low, specific-conflict-specific-disease concordance may be due to the heterogeneity of the specific disease, and that subgrouping patients within a disease category might improve concordance, this is as yet an untested proposition. Even if subgrouping were to improve results, the major problem with this research approach is that patients are assessed for conflicts after the disease onset. Without a prospective design, it is impossible to state irrefutably that certain conflicts—whether observed or inferred—existed in an individual prior to the disease onset.

Engel (1968) presents a more generalized view of psychological predisposition. His central thesis is that personal loss and bereavement provide the general setting in which many diseases are initiated. The likelihood of disease onset in such a setting is increased in the psychologically predisposed person. Dependency is viewed as the prime, psychological predisposing factor, for dependent people will respond to loss and bereavement by perceiving and interpreting it as a threat to their personal security. Dependent, insecure, and "abandoned," the person develops feelings of helplessness and hopelessness—essentially giving up altogether. In effect, an adaptive psychological failure occurs, and this failure (or the emotion it engenders) presumably has physiological concomitants which initiate disease onset in the biologically predisposed person.

Though there exist some very interesting data supporting Engel's notions (Engel, 1955, 1968; Schmale, 1958), the generality of the hypotheses have not been borne out by the findings. For example, helplessness and hopelessness have not been consistently found to be antecedents nor correlates of disease onsets. Additionally different kinds of settings, alone or in combination with bereavement, may antecede different disorders.

As diverse as the details of the formulations of Alexander and Engel appear, at a broader level there are some significant similarities. First, the studies generated by their notions illustrated that both personal and–or socioenvironmental determinants of particular diseases are heterogeneous (i.e., apparently psychological predispositions toward, and the environmental settings for, disease are neither singular nor specific for particular disorders). This suggests that the action of heterogeneous psychological predispositions cannot be accounted for by specific psychological–biologic interactions. Rather, a more general mechanism through which a variety of psychological predispositions exert their influence must be operative.

A second point of similarity is that, although both Alexander and Engel emphasize the interactive nature of environmental events and psychological predisposition, both do not consider the events themselves to be of central importance. The importance of events derives from their perceived symbolic significance, and from the emotional and biologic responses thereby engendered, rather than from any nonspecific impact on the organism (as in Selyé's conception of stressors; Selyé, 1976). This suggests that psychological predispositions and events operate interactively and, perhaps as both theorists suggest, specifically in some cases (i.e., dependence–loss; specific, psychological conflict–specific, instigative event).

When one considers both of these points—a general mechanism for the action of heterogeneous psychological predispositions, and the role of personal perception in determining the importance of environmental events—the nature of psychological predispositions, as viewed by Alexander and Engel, is clarified. The first point suggests that the biologic notion of a final common pathway may be profitably applied to the psychosocial area where psychological predispositions are viewed as exerting their influence through a common pathway. The second point suggests that the final common pathway is cognitive in nature. The characteristics of such a pathway overlap greatly with Lazarus' (1966) concepts of the appraisal process. Within a disease model framework, a host of psychological predispositions, and the developmental variables underlying them, might be viewed as having the common effect, via the appraisal process, of altering at least two factors: (*a*) the perception of events, and (*b*) quantitative and qualitative dimensions of adaptive coping patterns.

It is readily conceivable that specific events may acquire symbolic significance due to specific psychological predisposing "traits" or conflicts, as suggested by Alexander and Engel. But, Engel's notion, for example, that the psychological predisposition of dependency interacts particularly with loss and bereavement may be unnecessarily restrictive. A more general effect of psychological predispositions on the appraisal process is possible. For instance, one can imagine that high dependency may result in the general attribution that others do one's coping (which may actually be the case for dependent individuals) and that, therefore, one is deficient in coping skills. Such a "cognitive schema" would render, by operating on the appraisal process, a relatively large class of events as potentially threatening.

The latter example suggests that, in some cases, psychological predisposing factors may not alter the perception of specific events via a direct effect on the appraisal process. In this example, a particular psychological characteristic (dependency) contributes to the development of a more general "cognitive schema," which in turn may alter the perception of a larger range of events than those just related to loss or bereavement. Hence, it is possible to think of psychological predisposition at several levels. At a specific level, certain psychological characteristics (e.g., dependency) may operate directly on the appraisal process and may predispose the individual to perceive a particular class of events (e.g., loss) as highly threatening to personal security. At a more general level, certain psychological characteristics may lead to the development of a more general "cognitive schema," predisposing the individual to appraise a wider range of events as threatening.

It may well be that the more general psychological predisposing factors (e.g., cognitive schemas) have the greatest power in initiating disease owing to their more pervasive influence on appraisal and coping behavior. For instance, one variable that would be congruent with the notion of a general psychological predisposing factor is that of self-efficacy. Bandura (1977) views self-efficacy as a cognitive process which determines the expectation that one can or cannot successfully execute certain behaviors required to produce certain outcomes. In this conceptual system, expectations of personal mastery are viewed as affecting both the appraisal of the potential threat inherent in events, as well as the initiation and persistence of coping behavior. Bandura *et al.* (1977) have demonstrated that self-efficacy expectations can have a pervasive effect on a range of coping behaviors. Additionally, Chapters 12, 13, and 15 discuss the possibly significant role that this variable, or others conceptually similar to it, may play in increasing the vulnerability to depressive disorders.

Whether one is considering more specific psychological characteristics (e.g., dependency) or more general cognitive expectancy schemas (e.g., self-efficacy expectations) as psychological predisposing factors, viewing their influence as operating on the appraisal of life events places these factors in a central position with respect to modulating the impact of the environment on individuals. By increasing the potential threat of psychosocial stimuli, psychological predisposing variables may play a key role in exacerbating the emotional–biologic mediators that serve to "activate" biologic predisposing biases. We shall discuss this point further in the next section.

CONCLUSIONS

In addition to the complexity inherent in the nature of both biologic and psychological predisposition, one other point seems significant concerning predisposition. Predisposition to disease is rarely a univariate phenomenon. The predictive power of any single predisposing factor is likely to be relatively small. As the goal of the study of predisposition is to derive predictive explanations of disease (Weiner, 1977), we must begin to seriously assess predisposition within a multidimensional framework, where several biologic and psychological variables are explored simultaneously. But even then, we will still need to consider disease onset as a function of additional factors—in particular, initiating factors.

Initiation of Disease

The problem of when, and under what circumstances, disease onset or reoccurrence appears in individuals having a constellation of biologic and psychological predisposing factors is a major concern. Indeed, the very concept of predisposition suggests that other factors are necessary for initiating the disease. The rapidly expanding area of life events research, of course, has attempted to elucidate the dimensions of the psychosocial environment that are most closely related to the occurrence of disease. However, a general review of that area is beyond the scope of this chapter, and the literature relating to the initiation of depressive disorders is reviewed elsewhere in this volume (see Chapters 11 and 12). Therefore, we will address only some of the more relevant issues for our discussion.

Particularly in considering the initiation of disease, one issue relating to the impact of psychosocial stimuli concerns whether qualitative distinctions ought to be made between types of events. Evolving from Selyé's (1976) conception of stressors, some life-events investigators feel that events vary quantitatively in the demands they place on an organism's adaptive behavior. However, distinguishing between classes of events by their qualitatively different effects on an organism is not considered meaningful in a predictive sense. Conversely and following the lead of Mason (1975a) and

Lazarus (1977), other researchers do propose qualitative distinctions. In particular, psychosocial stimuli viewed as undesirable and psychologically threatening by the individual are considered to be the most "significant" stimuli for initiating a disease process. This position may be restated from a quantitative perspective, so that undesirable and threatening events would be viewed as placing greater, but qualitatively similar, demands on an organism's adaptive behavior. However, the truly qualitative model would hold that undesirable events result in qualitatively different mediating responses when compared to desirable events.

Although this issue has yet to be settled (and any solution will likely be more complex than current formulations suggest), there exists an important point of convergence between the qualitative conception of the psychosocial environment and the views of psychological predisposition held by Alexander and Engel. For both groups of theorists, it is not the event per se that is of central importance. Rather, it is the degree of threat as perceived by the individual that renders an event significant. This is a crucial assumption, for it not only places the appraisal process in a central position in the initiation of disease, but also suggests that emotions, as responses to threats, play a key role in mediating the effects of the environment. We shall discuss this latter point in another area.

We, as well as other theorists concerned with disease models (Hinkle, 1977; Lipowski et al., 1977; Weiner, 1977), adopt the qualitative position with respect to psychosocial stimuli. Moreover, there is increasing empirical support for this position in the life-events literature using both normal populations (see Mueller, Edwards, & Yarvis, 1977, for a review) and depressed patient samples (see Chapters 11 and 12 of this volume). By placing the appraisal process in a central position in the initiation of disease, the qualitative model also provides a unifying framework for conceptualizing the role of other variables that have been under examination in the life-events literature. For instance, several studies have shown that the variable of "social support" modifies the impact of psychosocial stimuli (Cobb, 1976; Kaplan, 1977). When present and satisfactory, social support appears to decrease the impact of life events on an individual whereas low or nonexistent social support appears to increase an individual's vulnerability to dysfunction (Brown, Chapter 12 of this volume; Cobb, 1976). The mechanisms by which social support operates to modify the impact of the environment are unclear, however, one reasonable possibility is that social support may be considered by people in weighing their weaknesses, strengths, and resources during their appraisal of the threat of life circumstances.

Other factors may operate in a similar fashion. The appraisal of life events, for instance, may be modified by the presence of already existing and ongoing difficulties or chronic stressors (Chapter 12 this volume; Ilfeld, 1977). Moreover, personal factors such as developmental history, psychobiologic "traits" (including those involved in psychological predisposition), and the current psychobiologic state of the individual, may all modify the impact of the environment by influencing the appraisal process.

Therefore, the appraisal process may provide the final common pathway for a host of person and psychosocial variables that modify the impact of the psychosocial environment. In applying this model to the initiation of disease, the factor unifying all of these variables is the appraisal process as it modifies the intensity and duration of the psychological response to a threat to the environment. The unifying factor is viewed in terms of psychological threat as it is this response that initiates what is, for some theorists, the major mediator of the psychosocial environment—emotions and their biological concomitants. Moreover, the degree of threat experienced may effect whether coping behavior is initiated, and, if it is, its form (direct and intrapsychic) and its persistence. A diagrammatic representation of the interaction of all these variables may be viewed in the upper two-thirds of Figure 1.1. The main purpose of Figure 1.1 is to serve as an organizational framework for the host of variables previously discussed rather than as a framework for defining specific mechanisms. The mediational pathways in the figure will be discussed only briefly due to their highly speculative nature.

Mediation Processes

Concepts regarding the significance of the psychosocial environment and that emphasize appraisal and psychological threat generally view emotions, and their biologic concomitants, as the major mediator of the impact of the environment. At a general level of conceptualization, the rationale for postulating emotional mediation rests on the fact that the autonomic and neuroendocrine concomitants of emotions have the capacity to influence practically every biochemical-physiological process in the human body. This influence is particularly pervasive for the neuroendocrine system (e.g., Table 1.1). Under highly threatening environmental conditions, biologic variation within the organism places heavy adjustive demands on the body's regulatory systems if the "dynamic steady state" is to be restored and maintained. Because the external neuroendocrine regulatory system plays a key role in modulating regulation of practically all biochemical processes, if a biological predisposition (bias or diathesis) exists within a regulatory pathway, it may be "activated" by the neuroendocrine hormones.

The probability of such "activation" of a bias might be seen as a function of the adjustive demand placed on regulatory systems. Adjustive demands, of course, will vary as a function of the perceived strength of threat in the psychosocial situation. Although it is not clear which dimensions of the threat will be important, the intensity and, perhaps particularly, the duration of the threat and the emotional arousal will be relevant parameters. One can

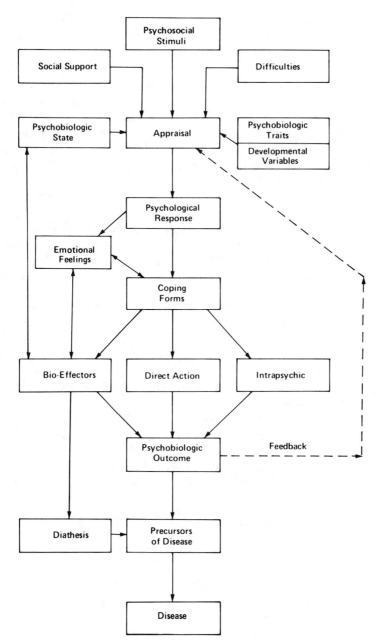

Figure 1.1. An organizational framework for the variables involved in initiation and mediation of disease.

imagine that the more intense and prolonged the threat, the greater will be the adjustive demands made on regulatory systems as they endeavor to maintain a dynamic equilibrium of biologic processes.

Figure 1.1 illustrates a simple, linear model for the initiation of disease. The action of a host of variables operates via the final common pathway of appraisal to elicit a psychological threat response. The threat response is mediated by emotions and their biologic concomitants, and a diathesis or bias is directly "activated" by these biologic concomitants. Precursors of disease may develop as a result, and, if the initiating circumstances intensify or continue for prolonged periods, actual disease may develop.

There has been little or no specificity defined in this mediation scheme with respect to the mechanisms or pathways involved (Mason, 1975a; Weiner, 1977). The only specific position concerns emotional mediation. However, not all emotions are considered etiologically significant, rather the unpleasant emotions are particularly emphasized. This position rests on the assumption that the various emotions are associated with different hormonal patterns, and evidence indicates that this may be the case (Mason, 1975b). Such evidence illustrates the primary importance of investigating the psychobiology of emotions as it relates to stress and disease interactions. However, as Hinkle (1977) has emphasized, nonspecific theories that postulate general mediators to account for the initiation of many different diseases may no longer be useful. Instead, the theory that the mediational pathway is different for each disorder, depending on the nature of the biologic predisposition for the disease in question, may better fit our current understanding of the disease process.

A final point related to Hinkle's notions concerning mediation is important. Mediation of the environment may not operate via a single pathway under any circumstances or for any disease, rather a collateral model of mediation may hold (Weiner, 1977). This model suggests the possibility that the brain abstracts different elements of environmental stimuli, and that each element is mediated via different pathways or mechanisms. Hofer and Weiner (1975), for instance, found that certain stimulus components of maternal deprivation resulted in behavioral disorganization in rat pups, whereas other stimulus components caused physiological disruption, but not vice versa. This suggests that psychological and physiological responses may be correlated, but may not "cause" each other.

CONCLUDING REMARKS

This chapter attempted to provide a general framework for three major issues in models of disease: predisposition, initiation, and mediation. Research on psychosocial and biologic aspects of depressive disorders can also be viewed within this framework. The rest of this volume addresses the previously mentioned three issues as they relate to the depressive disorders or to variables highly relevant to understanding stress–biology interactions in these disorders. Although chapters have been clustered into biologic and psychosocial sections, it will become apparent that all three of the major issues are addressed in Parts 3 and 4 of this volume.

The integration of the notions expressed in Parts 3 and 4 of this volume in future research is, of course, required if we are to achieve a comprehensive theory about the development of depressive disorders. Such integration in depression research is noticeably lacking at present. This situation may result largely from the lack of integrative models that delineate testable hypotheses. Most chapters in this volume contribute to working models of stress–biology interactions. However, Part 5 of this volume specifically attempts to stimulate thinking on integrative research strategies and models. This is an arduous task, and it is to the credit of Erlenmeyer-Kimling and Akiskal for accomplishing it so creatively.

In keeping with the thrust of this chapter, stress–biology interactions are probably more meaningfully considered when the heterogeneity of the depressive disorders is clarified. It may be that different types of depressive disorder respond differentially to stress as a function of differences in psychological and–or biologic characteristics. Therefore, several initial chapters attempt to delineate the heterogeneous clinical picture found in the depressive disorders.

REFERENCES

Alexander, F. *Psychosomatic medicine*. New York: Norton, 1950.

Alexander, F., French T., & Pollock, G. H. *Psychosomatic specificity*. Chicago: Univ. Chicago Press, 1968.

Bandura, A. Self-efficacy: Toward a unifying theory of behavioral change. *Psychological Review*, 1977, 84, 191–215.

Bandura, A., Adams, N., & Beyer, J. Cognitive processes mediating behavioral change. *Journal of Personality and Social Psychology*, 1977, 35, 125–139.

Cobb, S. Social support as a moderator of life stress. *Psychosomatic Medicine*, 1976, 38, 300–314.

Delgado, J. M. R. Inhibitory systems and emotions. In L. Levi (Ed.), *Emotions: Their parameters and measurement*. New York: Raven Press, 1975.

de M' Uzan, M. & Bonfils, S. Étude et classification des aspects psychosomatiques de l'ulcere gastroduodénal en milieu hospitalier. *Review of French Clinical Biology*, 1961, 6, 46–55.

Eccles, J. *Understanding the brain*. New York: McGraw-Hill, 1977.

Engel, G. L. Studies of ulcerative colitis. III. The nature of psychologic processes. *American Journal of Medicine*, 1955, 19, 231–240.

Engel, G. L. *Psychological development in health and disease*. Philadelphia: Saunders, 1967.

Engel, G. L. A life setting conducive to illness: The giving-up, given-up complex. *Archives of Internal Medicine*, 1968, 69, 293–305.

Engel, G. L. The need for a new medical model: A challenge for biomedicine. *Science*, 1977, 196, 129–136.

Heston, L. Genes and psychiatry. In J. Mendels (Ed.), *Biological psychiatry*. New York: Wiley, 1973.

Hinkle, L. The concept of "stress" in the biological and social sciences. In L. Lipowski, D. Lipsitt, & P. Whybrow (Eds.), *Psychosomatic medicine*. New York: Oxford Univ. Press, 1977.

Hofer, M., & Weiner, H. Physiological mechanisms for cardiac control by nutritional intake after maternal separation in the young rat. *Psychosomatic Medicine*, 1975, 37, 8–23.

Ilfeld, F. Current social stressors and symptoms of depression. *American Journal of Psychiatry*, 1977, 134, 161–166.

Kaplan, B. Social support and health. *Medical Care*, 1977, 15, 47–58.

Knapp, P. H. & Nemetz, S. J. Acute bronchial asthma-concomitant depression with excitement and varied antecedent patterns in 406 attacks. *Psychosomatic Medicine*, 1960, 22, 42–53.

Lazarus, R. S. *Psychological stress and the coping process*. New York: McGraw-Hill, 1966.

Lazarus, R. Psychological stress and coping in adaptation and illness. In Z. Lipowski, D. Lipsitt, & P. Whybrow (Eds.). *Psychosomatic medicine*. New York: Oxford Univ. Press, 1977.

Levi, L. & Andersson, L. *Psychosocial stress: Population, environment and quality of life*. New York: Wiley, 1975.

Lipowski, Z. J., Lipsitt, D. R., & Whybrow, P. C. (Eds.). *Psychosomatic medicine*. New York: Oxford Univ. Press, 1977.

Mason, J. A historical review of the stress field. Parts I and II. *Journal of Human Stress*, 1975, 1, 6–12, 22–36. (a)

Mason, J. Emotion as reflected in patterns of endocrine integration. In L. Levi (Ed.), *Emotions: Their parameters and measurement*. New York: Raven Press, 1975. (b)

Mirsky, I. A. The psychosomatic approach to the etiology of clinical disorders. *Psychosomatic Medicine*, 1957, 19, 424–435.

Mirsky, I. A. Physiologic, psychologic, and social determinants in the etiology of duodenal ulcer. *American Journal of Digestive Disorders*, 1958, 3, 285–293.

Mueller, D. P., Edwards, D. W., & Yarvis, R. M. Stressful life events and psychiatric symptomatology: Change or undesirability? *Journal of Health and Social Behavior*, 1977, 18, 307–317.

Roberts, E. An hypothesis suggesting that there is a defect in the GABA system in schizophrenia. *Neurosciences Research Program Bulletin*, 1972, 10, 468–482.

Schmale, A. H., Jr. Relation of separation and depression to disease. I. A report on a hospitalized medical population. *Psychosomatic Medicine*, 1958, 20, 259–268.

Schoenheimer, R. *Dynamic steady state of body constituents*. Cambridge, Massachusetts: Harvard Univ. Press, 1942.

Schwartz, G. E. Psychosomatic disorders and biofeedback: A psychobiological model of disregulation. In J. D. Maser & M. E. P. Seligman (Eds.), *Psychopathology: Experimental models*. San Francisco: W. H. Freeman, 1977.

Selyé, H. *The stress of life*. New York: McGraw-Hill, 1976.

Sigg, E. B. The organization and functions of the central nervous system. In L. Levi (Ed.), *Emotions: Their parameters and measurement*. New York: Raven Press, 1975.

Weiner, H. *Psychobiology and human disease*. New York: Elsevier, 1977.

Weisman, A. A study of the psychodynamics of duodenal ulcer exacerbations with special reference to treatment and the problem of specificity. *Psychosomatic Medicine*, 1956, 18, 2–13.

Wolf, S. Regulatory mechanisms and tissue pathology. In L. Levi (Ed.), *Emotions: Their parameters and measurement*. New York: Raven Press, 1975.

PART II

Distinctions within the Topic

One of the more difficult problems for both clinicians and researchers concerns the fact that most human diseases are heterogeneous with respect to their clinical picture. One major research effort in human disorders involves the attempt to delimit this phenotypic heterogeneity by evolving classification systems that posit various subgroups within larger categories. Delimitation of clinical heterogeneity by subgrouping is not only important for diagnostic concerns, but may also increase the homogeneity of each subgroup with respect to psychosocial, biologic, and treatment response variables. Derivation of subgroups that are more homogeneous with respect to the latter variables would appear to be a crucial initial step in studying stress–biology interactions in human diseases.

As was implied in our Chapter 1 discussion and as was emphasized by Hinkle (1977), a full understanding of stress–biology interactions in human disorders will not evolve until researchers look more closely at specific psychobiologic pathways which are thought to be involved in the predisposition to specific disease subgroups. This is, of course, a relevant point in relation to the depressive disorders. Such disorders are enormously heterogeneous (Depue & Monroe, 1978a, b) and it may be that different types of depressive disorders respond differentially to stress as a function of variations in psychological and–or biologic characteristics.

The first three chapters of this part attempt to delineate the heterogeneous clinical picture found in the depressive disorders. Depue and Monroe provide the latest view of a genetic taxonomy for the unipolar and bipolar disorders, and discuss several potentially important differences between the polar disorders that may have significance for the effects of stress. Fowles and Gersh present a comprehensive overview of neurotic depression, including an entire chapter on anxious depression. In both of their chapters, they discuss the status of the notion that stress is an important contributor to neurotic, reactive depressions. The area of stressful life events is probably as heterogeneous in its notions as is the clinical picture of the depressive disorders. The Dohrenwends provide an overview of important distinctions and issues in the stress area which helps to clarify discussions of stress in subsequent parts of this volume.

REFERENCES

Depue, R. A., & Monroe, S. M. The unipolar-bipolar distinction in the depressive disorders. *Psychological Bulletin*, 1978, 85, 1001–1029. (a)

Depue, R. A., & Monroe, S. M. Learned helplessness in the perspective of the depressive disorders: Conceptual and definitional issues. *Journal of Abnormal Psychology*, 1978, 87, 3–21. (b)

Hinkle, L. The concept of "stress" in the biological and social sciences. In Z. Lipowski, L. Lipsitt, & P. Whybrow (Eds.), *Psychosomatic medicine*. New York: Oxford Univ. Press, 1977.

CHAPTER 2

The Unipolar–Bipolar Distinction in the Depressive Disorders: Implications for Stress—Onset Interaction

Richard A. Depue and Scott M. Monroe

INTRODUCTION

In his most comprehensive treatment of the depressive disorders, Kraepelin (1921) subsumed most major forms of depression under the general rubric of "manic–depressive illness." Under this diagnostic approach, patients with recurrent depressions and patients with depressions plus manic episodes are both classified as experiencing manic–depressive illness. This classificatory scheme is still embraced in the current diagnostic manual of the American Psychiatric Association (DSM-II), where only involutional melancholia, psychotic depressive reaction, and depressive neurosis are differentiated from manic–depressive illness.

This continued lack of differentiation among patients classified as manic–depressive illness is surprising in light of the research amassed in the last two decades. As early as 1957, Leonhard suggested that patients having depressions and manic episodes (bipolar) should be distinguished from patients who exhibit only recurrent depressions (unipolar) on the basis of differences along various clinical dimensions. Since that time, a growing

23

body of evidence has illuminated numerous other differences between unipolar and bipolar depressives, including genetic, behavioral, clinical, and
treatment response factors. We have previously provided a comprehensive
discussion of this evidence (Depue & Monroe, 1978a, b). Therefore, this
chapter will present a more brief, integrated view of the findings and address
the issue of stress and polar disorders more directly.

Traditionally, the distinction between unipolar and bipolar disorders has
been made on the basis of phenotypic (observable) behavior. In its simplest
form, a differential diagnosis is determined on the basis of whether or not a
patient has exhibited a personal history of manic episodes. However, it has
become increasingly clear that such a diagnostic practice does not do justice
to the variety of phenotypic forms and familial patterns existing within both
of the larger polar groups.

Accordingly, and in keeping with recent advances in biologic and genetic
findings, many investigators have adopted a genetic taxonomy of unipolar
and bipolar disorders (Akiskal & McKinney, 1975; Fieve, 1975; Mendlewicz,
Fieve, Rainer, & Fleiss, 1972; Winokur, Cadoret, Dorzab, & Baker, 1971).
This system employs a familial definition of polarity, where family history
for affective disorder serves as one index of classification. Thus, along with
phenotypic behavior, the family history of the individual (i.e., presence or
absence of manic or hypomanic disorder in first-degree relatives) becomes
the determining criterion on which polarity is based. Phenotypic expression
by itself is, therefore, not the determining factor and may, in fact, be
variable within a polar group.

When such a system is applied to individuals requiring treatment, several
unipolar and bipolar subgroups may be formed on the basis of the severity of
the illness (i.e., the severity of manic or depressive symptoms) as well as a
family history of affective disorder. Patients with a personal and–or family
history of mania or hypomania may be separated into five bipolar sub-
categories: bipolar I, unipolar mania, bipolar II, bipolar III, and bipolar
Other. Bipolar I patients are characterized by both manic and depressive
episodes that require treatment and usually hospitalization. If the patient
has a positive family history of bipolar disorder, admissions for mania are
more frequent and severe than depressive admissions, whereas the reverse is
true for patients with a negative family history (Mendlewicz, et al., 1972).
Generally, bipolar I patients show intervals of relatively normal mood and
function (lasting from weeks to years) between episodes of depression and mania;
but when these intervals do not occur, the diagnosis of circular bipolar
disorder is used.

Unipolar manic patients have at least one hospitalization for mania but no
episodes of depression. Despite traditional beliefs of its rarity, this group
may comprise as much as 28% of patient samples selected on the basis of a
current manic episode (Abrams & Taylor, 1974). Recent evidence indicates
that these patients should be included within the bipolar disorder category

because, when they have been compared to bipolar manics matched for age of onset, the two groups have not differed significantly in terms of manic symptomatology, demographic and characterologic data, *family history* of affective disorder or alcoholism, and response to "doctor's choice" treatment—mainly lithium carbonate (Abrams & Taylor, 1974; Chopra, 1975; Perris, 1966). The only difference between the two types of mania appears to be that unipolar manics have a significantly later, mean age of onset of their first episode (10–12 years later). Because Abrams and Taylor have not reported follow-up data on these patients, it is still possible that some or all of these patients will show a depressive episode (although 86% had had three or more separate attacks of mania). Therefore, the question of unipolar mania remains an area in need of longitudinal analysis.

Bipolar II patients have a family history of mania or hypomania and require treatment and usually hospitalization for depressive episodes. However, manic or hypomanic symptoms have never led to hospitalization although outpatient drug treatment is often necessary (Fieve, 1975). *Bipolar Other* patients are treated on an outpatient basis for depressive and hypomanic symptoms, but are never hospitalized.

Bipolar III cases have at least one hospitalization for depression, no personal history of mania or hypomania, but *do* have a family history of mania or hypomania. It must be emphasized that, lacking of a personal history of mania or hypomania, it is unclear as to which polar group these patients are more closely related. Indeed, Fieve (1975) places this group within unipolar disorder (referred to as unipolar II) but distinguishes it from other unipolar cases with no family history of mania or hypomania. However, genetic researchers separate the former group out of unipolar samples in their studies (Winokur *et al.*, 1971), and it is more in keeping with a genetic taxonomy to refer to these cases as bipolar. Only future research will be able to provide more reliable evidence as to which polar group bipolar III cases belong.

The *unipolar group* represents all or most of the remaining, recurrent depressions lumped together in a single heterogeneous group, including the traditional involutional, neurotic, and psychotic reactive types. This group includes patients of varying onset ages, symptomatology patterns, severity, and (most probably) etiologies. A crude subclassification of unipolar cases includes unipolar I and unipolar Other.

Unipolar I patients have at least one hospitalization for depression and neither personal nor family history of mania or hypomania. *Unipolar Other* patients have sought help or been treated, but not hospitalized, for depression.

There have been numerous schemes put forth to delimit the heterogeneity of the unipolar group. Although beyond the scope of this review, one scheme involves a psychotic–neurotic distinction, which is reviewed extensively in Chapters 3 and 4 of this volume. This distinction is based not only on the severity of the depression, but also on the presence of neurotic symptoms and traits, and has gained credence on the basis of phenomenologic and pharmacological criteria. Although the more severe unipolar cases are somewhat less heterogeneous than the neurotic group and make up the majority of unipolar cases in the studies reviewed, no well-defined, clinical boundaries exist between these groups so that as much as a 15% overlap may exist (Akiskal & McKinney, 1975, p. 288; Chapters 3 and 4 of this volume).

Even within the more severe group of unipolar cases, Winokur *et al.* (1971, 1975) have suggested that patients varying in onset age form different groups with respect to familial disorder: (*a*) *pure depressive disease*, where the patient is a late onset (>40) male with a positive family history of depression in first-degree relatives of both sexes; and (*b*) *depressive spectrum disease*, where the patient is an early-onset (<40) female with depression in female first-degree relatives, and alcoholism and sociopathy in male, first-degree relatives.

One additional attempt to delimit the heterogeneity of unipolar samples has involved the use of selection criteria aimed at excluding patients who will later develop bipolar disorder. In order to obviate this problem, Perris (1973) has suggested the criterion of three depressive episodes with no manic episodes be used in defining unipolar cases. However, in a large bipolar I sample, Dunner, Fleiss, and Fieve (1976) have shown that almost 80% of bipolar I patients are either hospitalized for mania, or develop mania in the hospital or shortly after their first hospitalization. The remaining 20% are misdiagnosed as bipolar II or unipolar, and the majority of these patients show mania before the third episode and/or within 10 years. Because a sufficient number of cases did show manic attacks shortly after their initial hospitalization for depression, the authors suggested that, for research purposes, patients not be considered unipolar until they had been followed for about 6 months after their initial depression to ensure that this episode is not a pre-manic–depressive attack.

In another sample, Dunner, Fleiss, and Fieve (1976) illustrated that, if bipolar II patients are separated out of unipolar groups (because of their familial and biologic relationship to bipolar disorder and because some of these patients have manic episodes later), the probability that a unipolar group will be "contaminated" with patients who later develop bipolar disorder is .05 or less. These data taken together suggest that Perris' criterion may be unnecessarily stringent and outweighed by the loss of sample size necessary to achieve the criterion of three episodes.

The previous discussion serves to illustrate the taxonomic and diagnostic issues embodied in the unipolar–bipolar distinction. Unfortunately, several of these issues cannot be resolved in the literature currently available due to their relatively recent appearance, plus the fact that most available studies on the unipolar–bipolar distinction have only compared bipolar I cases with more severe, hospitalized unipolar patients. Only a few studies have looked systematically at bipolar II patients, and none have done so for bipolar III cases. Thus, most unipolar samples have undoubtedly combined unipolar I with bipolar III cases, and in many instances bipolar II cases. However, sufficient evidence does exist to characterize differences between the poorer differentiated, polar groups, as well as to propose hypotheses and needed research on the finer subgroup issues.

The remainder of our discussion will attempt to illustrate the importance of viewing some forms of unipolar and bipolar depression as distinct disorders. We do not wish to imply, however, that only two disorders are involved in the distinction. There may well be several disorders within each of the larger polar groups, and we shall return to this issue later. In any case, demonstration of differences between psychopathologic disorders may be accomplished best by demonstrating differences in (a) symptomatic behavior, (b) clinical course, (c) familial and genetic factors, and (d) pharmacological response. It is to these areas that we now turn our attention. We will conclude with a discussion of stress and polar disorders.

SYMPTOMATIC BEHAVIOR

As may have already become evident from the prior discussion, a problem inherent in the unipolar–bipolar distinction is its dependence on personal and–or familial history of mania or hypomania for an accurate diagnosis. Although the Dunner, Fleiss, and Fieve (1976) data indicate that this issue is of less concern in the diagnosis of bipolar I disorder, more refined differential diagnoses become problematic among cases not showing clear signs of mania (i.e., unipolar I, bipolar III, and bipolar II cases). The problem becomes most difficult with these groups when no previous episodes have occurred, or when reliable episodic and–or familial data are unavailable.

In light of these difficulties, the existence of reliable behavioral differences between bipolar and unipolar groups would be of high diagnostic value. Moreover, investigation of the degree of concordance in behavioral profiles across bipolar I, II, and III patients (in contrast to unipolar I patients) might serve as one type of evidence of a relationship between the three former groups. Unfortunately, the available literature does not allow for an evaluation along these lines because bipolar II and III patients have not been subject to separate behavioral assessment. However, it does appear that several behavioral differences do exist between less finely distinguished but severely depressed unipolar and bipolar I groups, although these are not generally recognized (Fieve, 1975). Thus, this evidence will be presented to serve as a stimulus for further studies using more refined polar subgroups.

The available evidence comparing psychotic (i.e., severe) unipolar and bipolar I patients in the depressed phase has demonstrated two somewhat different behavioral profiles for these groups, although significant overlap exists on some variables. If one considers only those variables that sufficiently differentiate polar groups to be of clinical utility, four behavior patterns are noteworthy. The most differentiating behavior is psychomotor activity, which refers to spontaneous and evoked motor activity. There are numerous studies that have consistently found bipolar I patients to exhibit psychomotor retardation in the depressed phase. This pattern has been observed clinically so consistently in bipolar depressives, that several authors have emphasized this clinical impression (Bunney & Murphy, 1973; Himmelhoch, Coble, Kupfer, & Ingenito, 1976; Kotin & Goodwin, 1972). Empirical studies have confirmed these clinical impressions using 24-hour behavior ratings over a 2-week period (Beigel & Murphy, 1971) or telemetric activity recordings for four consecutive 24-hour periods (Kupfer, Weiss, Foster, Detre, Delgado, & McPartland, 1974). Conversely, these same studies have found unipolar patients to be significantly more active and agitated than bipolar patients in terms of psychomotor behavior. With improvement in their clinical condition, bipolar patients have shown nearly a 50% increase in activity, whereas unipolars have exhibited a 12% decrease in activity. Although these differences in psychomotor patterns are themselves important from a diagnostic standpoint, they acquire additional significance in that a retarded pattern may be related to reduced turnover rates of dopamine in the extrapyramidal nigrostriatal pathway, whereas an agitated pattern may be related to dopaminergic hyperactivity in this pathway (Depue & Evans, 1979; Depue & Monroe, 1978a). If the two motor patterns do correspond to differences in dopaminergic metabolism, this would be one line of evidence suggesting biochemical differences between polar groups.

Differences in sleep disturbance patterns represent the second most discriminating behavioral pattern for polar groups. Generally, bipolar I patients exhibit hypersomnia (> 8 hours at night) and restfulness during sleep, whereas hyposomnia (< 6 hours) is more characteristic of the unipolar depressed phase (Detre, Himmelhoch, Swartzburg, Anderson, Byck, & Kupfer, 1972; Hartmann, 1968; Kupfer, Himmelhoch, Swartzburg, Anderson, Byck, & Detre, 1972). The increased sleep in bipolar patients is evident in all sleep stages and is associated with self-reports of feeling worse in the morning and an increase in weight. Hyposomnia is associated with self-reports of trouble falling asleep, and more awakenings during the night and early morning. Also, self-report of hypersomnia by patients and close relatives reaches 95% agreement, suggesting that this symptom may be reliably assessed in interviews. Finally, these and other studies (Kupfer *et al.*, 1974) have shown that changes in the sleep patterns accompanying recovery in unipolar and bipolar patients are inversely related to changes in telemetrically-recorded motor activity. This relationship would be expected given the respective deviations in motor activity and sleep patterns in unipolar and bipolar depressed patients.

Two final behaviors that differentiate psychotic unipolar and bipolar I groups, although less reliably than the previously mentioned behaviors, are somatic complaints and anger. Bipolar patients complain of somatic problems much less than unipolar cases, and bipolar patients are passive and show less anger toward themselves and others (Beigel & Murphy, 1971).

The behavioral profiles for unipolar and bipolar depressives have been assembled on the basis of too few studies to consider them as established. However, the existing data are encouraging in that differential diagnosis of well-defined unipolar and bipolar patients on the basis of psychomotor and–or sleep patterns may be accurate in as much as 85% of the cases. This possibility requires further testing. Regarding other behaviors studied, their discriminative power appears to be too low to be diagnostically useful. Thus, more studies are required to verify the existing behavioral data and to delineate further the nature of the behavioral heterogeneity in the polar groups.

In undertaking further studies, two relatively neglected distinctions should be made: Bipolar II patients should be distinguished from bipolar I patients and bipolar III patients should be differentiated from unipolar I patients. This practice may help to reduce the heterogeneity within polar groups, and may shed light on the potential behavioral similarity of bipolar I, II, and III patients, as might be predicted on the basis of the similarity in family history for bipolar disorders. That is, by virtue of similarity in genotype, these groups may share a psychobiologic dysfunction which is expressed behaviorally as psychomotor retardation and hypersomnia (as is found in bipolar I patients).

CLINICAL COURSE

In judging the significance of a distinction between psychopathologic groups, one becomes concerned with whether the purported differences between groups of patients are meaningfully related to clinical aspects of the disorder. Regarding the unipolar–bipolar distinction, several differences have been noted. In terms of clinical course, the only major difference is that bipolar patients are typically first hospitalized at an earlier median age (early thirties) than unipolar depressives (early forties) (Angst, Baastrup, Grof, Hippius, Poldinger, & Weis, 1973; Perris, 1968; Winokur, Clayton, & Reich, 1969). Dunner, Gershon, and Goodwin (1976) found that bipolar II patients also have an earlier age of onset of symptoms than unipolar patients, but the sample was small and differences were not significant. Finally, Mendlewicz et al. (1972) showed that when bipolar patients with a positive family history of affective disorder were compared with bipolar depressives with a negative family history, age of first hospitalization was quite similar. However, more patients (60%) with a positive family history exhibited mood disturbances sufficiently severe to necessitate medical intervention (but not hospitalization) at or before the age of 25 years than those patients with negative family histories (30%). In spite of this earlier dysfunction in "positive history" cases, more bipolar patients without a family history (33%) were hospitalized at first episode than were bipolar patients with a positive family history (7%) (Mendlewicz et al., 1972). These latter results may indicate that families "exposed" to bipolar disorder may have a somewhat greater initial tolerance of its presence in offspring.

Concerning number of episodes, although Angst et al. (1973) reported that there was great interindividual variability in the number of episodes, there appeared to be a general trend in both unipolar and bipolar patients to show an increase in the number of episodes over the first 10 years of the disorder. Thereafter, the median number of episodes reached a certain, limiting value so that the mean number of episodes of patients under observation for 40 years was not significantly higher than that of patients observed for 15 years. The limiting value for bipolar patients was 7–9, whereas for unipolar depressives it was 4–6. Overall, the majority of patients showed the recurrence of episodes to be limited to the first 20 years of the disorder.

Another aspect of clinical course characteristics is prognosis. There are several indexes of prognosis that have been compared across unipolar and bipolar groups. Although most studies find that depressives recover from initial episodes, short-term follow-up studies have shown that the majority of depressive patients do exhibit problems *after* leaving the hospital. For example, whereas 7–14% of bipolar I patients remain completely well after an episode, generally from one-third to one-half suffer either chronic illness or achieve only partial remission, and the majority of all patients suffer from significant depressive symptoms (Bratfos & Haug, 1968; Carlson, Kotin, Davenport, & Adland, 1974; Morrison, Winokur, Crowe, & Clancy, 1973; Shobe & Brion, 1971; Winokur et al., 1969). The situation is somewhat better for unipolar patients as 34% remained well after 6 years (Bratfos & Haug, 1968), but 25% were chronically ill and 41% experienced one or more relapses.

These studies and Angst's data indicate that bipolar cases suffer from a greater, total number of episodes and somewhat more intermorbid impairment than unipolar patients. Other studies offer support of this view, although comprehensive comparisons of intermorbid functioning in unipolar and bipolar groups are lacking. For instance, Brodie and Leff (1971) followed 30, unipolar I–bipolar I pairs of patients who were matched on age and sex and found that, whereas only 8% of the unipolar cases had marriages ending in divorce, 57% of the bipolar group experienced marital failure ($p < .01$). No difference in patient's age at time of marriage was found. In view of these findings, the authors suggested the possibility that manic symptoms may be incompatible with stable marriage. Indeed, it was found that divorce occurred only after a manic attack and never before a bipolar patient had experienced at least one period of mania.

The notion that mania, in particular, may be important for impaired intermorbid functioning is congruent with other studies showing that alcohol abuse is most highly associated with manic, rather than depressive, symptomatology (Mayfield & Coleman, 1968; Reich, Davies & Himmelhoch, 1974; Winokur *et al.*, 1969). Reich *et al.* (1974) suggested that the more severe the mania, the more likely the patient will abuse alcohol, either in an attempt at self-medication or due to poor judgment and impulsivity. Consequently, alcohol-related, work and interpersonal impairment may be one factor accounting for the somewhat poorer intermorbid adjustment of bipolar I than unipolar patients.

One final index suggestive of a poorer, long-term prognosis in bipolar patients is suicide rate. Dunner, Gershon, and Goodwin (1976) found that the rate of *completed* suicide was significantly higher in bipolar than unipolar patients, and that the rate was particularly high in bipolar II cases. The rate of *attempted* suicide showed even more pronounced differences between bipolar and unipolar patients (bipolar attempts were higher), and again bipolar II cases had the highest rate. Moreover, several researchers have found higher rates of suicide in the first-degree relatives of bipolar patients (Dunner, Gershon, & Goodwin, 1976; Leonhard, Korff, & Schulz, 1962; Perris, 1966), but only the Leonhard results reached statistical significance. However, Gershon *et al.* (1971) did not find a difference in family rates, and Perris (1969) found male unipolar patients to have a higher family rate than male bipolar cases. A further complication is posed by the finding of higher family rates in female than male bipolar cases by Perris (1969) and Winokur *et al.* (1969). It is difficult to ascertain the nature of these inconsistencies, but both patient and familial suicide rates will vary as a function of size, mean age, severity, and chronicity of the patient samples, as well as the thoroughness of the methodology used in first-degree relative studies.

FAMILIAL AND GENETIC FACTORS

The issues inherent in familial and genetic factors are complex, and space limitations preclude their discussion here. Therefore, we shall only briefly discuss the data and suggest that the reader consult more extensive reviews for more detailed discussion (e.g., Depue & Monroe, 1978a). In the following text, we shall focus particularly on findings from familial and linkage studies as they relate to unipolar–bipolar comparisons.

Familial studies have addressed three basic issues: (*a*) the degree to which polar groups "breed true," (*b*) sex ratios, and (*c*) twin concordance. Studies have consistently shown a higher frequency of affective disorders among relatives of bipolar I probands as compared to unipolar probands. More specifically, the family pedigrees of bipolar patients reveal a higher incidence of bipolar disorder than do the pedigrees of unipolar patients (Angst, 1966; Perris, 1966; Winokur et al., 1969). Yet, these disorders do not necessarily "breed true," for, although conflicting findings exist (Perris, 1966, 1968), unipolar disorder among relatives of bipolar patients is generally the more commonly found affective disorder (Helzer & Winokur, 1974; James & Chapman, 1975; Loranger, 1975; Reich, Clayton, & Winokur, 1969). Relatives of well-defined unipolar patients, however, are seldom found to exhibit bipolar disorder (Gershon et al., 1971; Perris, 1966, 1968; Winokur et al., 1969). Thus, within a family informative for bipolar disorder, there appears to be a significant overlap between the two affective disorders.

Along similar lines, bipolar I patients have a greater tendency to be members of families in which successive generations of affective disorders are found (positive family history), whereas unipolar patients are more likely to be members of families without a history of affective disorder (negative family history) (Winokur & Clayton, 1967). Such findings have yielded different morbidity risk percentage estimates for the two disorders; Leonhard (1969) recently estimated the morbidity risk for bipolar I and unipolar probands' siblings at 10.6% and 4.6%, and parents at 9.5% and 5.3%, respectively (in contrast to the general population rate of about 2–4%; Fieve, 1975). Among other investigators reporting similar differences, Angst (1966) and Perris (1966) have concluded that unipolar and bipolar disorders should be viewed consequently as separate entities.

For affective disorders in general, females have been found to outnumber males (Weissman & Klerman, 1977) both in familial investigations (Cadoret, Winokur, & Clayton, 1970; Perris, 1966; Reich et al., 1969) and in population studies (Helgason, 1964). Moreover, Winokur and colleagues have reported a female–male ratio of approximately 2 : 1 for bipolar I groups, whereas Perris (1966, 1968, 1973) and others (Goetzl, Green, Whybrow, & Jackson, 1974) have found parity for bipolar I sex ratios. In contrast, Perris (1973) reported a 2 : 1 female–male ratio for unipolar disorders. These discrepant results only suggest that different sex ratios for unipolar and bipolar disorders may exist. Such a possibility is theoretically provocative and highlights the necessity of further research in this area (Weissman & Klerman, 1977).

Allen (1976) reviewed the extant twin literature on affective illness and separated the previous studies into unipolar and bipolar I groups. When it was possible to classify polarity, he found a significant difference between the concordance rates for monozygotic, unipolar (40%) and bipolar I (72%) twins. For dizygotic probands, concordance rates of unipolar (11%) and bipolar (14%) twins did not differ significantly, yet both were significantly lower than the concordance rates for their monozygotic counterparts. Not only do Allen's results support other evidence that the unipolar–bipolar distinction is useful, but they also suggest that, because bipolar, monozygotic concordance (72%) is significantly greater than unipolar concordance (40%), "genetic factors may be more important in the occurrence of bipolar illness than in unipolar illness [Allen, 1976, p. 1478]."

Regarding mode of transmission studies, major lines of evidence have recently emerged supporting two different modes of transmission for affective disorders: (a) an X-linked, dominant gene inheritance, and (b) a form of polygenic inheritance. Definitions of, and data related to, each type of transmission follow.

Mode of Transmission: Dominant X-Linked

In dominant, X-linked genetic transmission, phenotypic expression of a trait results from the presence of a particular dominant gene present on the X chromosome of the individual under observation. When the requisite gene is present, the trait will eventually become manifest; when it is absent, the trait will not appear. Owing to the sex-linked locus of the gene on the X chromosome, it may be transmitted to female offspring by either or both parents, but to males only by the mother. Therefore, theoretically, father-to-son inheritance of the trait should not be found.

In order to support the dominant X-linked hypothesis, several additional requirements must be met:

1. Women should outnumber men with the disorder about 2 to 1 in both the general population and within the afflicted family.
2. Female probands should have equal numbers of afflicted male and female parents and children.
3. Male probands, however, should have only afflicted mothers and daughters, with no father-to-son transmission occurring.
4. Female probands should have about three times as many affected sisters as brothers, whereas male probands should have an equal number afflicted (Cadoret & Winokur, 1975; Mendlewicz & Fleiss, 1974).

Although controversy exists (Goetzl et al., 1974; James & Chapman, 1975; Loranger, 1975; Perris, 1973), support for these corollaries of the X-linkage hypothesis in bipolar I disorders has generally been found (Cadoret & Winokur, 1975; Cadoret et al., 1970; Helzer & Winokur, 1974; Mendlewicz & Rainer, 1974; Winokur et al., 1969). In addition to the previously cited discrepancy in sex-ratio incidence rates (where Perris found parity between male and female bipolar patients in contrast to the general trend for a greater incidence in females), the major point of contention has been the reported discoveries of father-to-son transmission of bipolar disorders. As the father cannot pass an X-linked gene to a son, but only to a daughter, such findings are incompatible with the theory of X-linkage being the only etiologic basis for bipolar disorders. Many studies have reported a substantial incidence of this familial pairing (Dunner & Fieve, 1975; Goetzl et al., 1974; Hays, 1976; James & Chapman, 1975; Loranger, 1975; Mendlewicz & Rainer, 1974), whereas others have found it less frequently, if at all (Helzer & Winokur, 1974; Taylor & Abrams, 1973; Winokur, 1970). Proposed alternative hypotheses have included questionable paternity and undetected affective disorders on the maternal side but have subsequently been discounted as satisfactory explanations (Cadoret & Winokur, 1975; Goetzl et al., 1974).

Presently, the most viable solution to these discrepant data is a theory of involvement of different genes resulting in similar phenotypes—genetic heterogeneity for bipolar disorders (Hays, 1976; Loranger, 1975; Taylor & Abrams, 1973). Winokur (1975) noted that such an interpretation appears reasonable as other illnesses (such as retinitis pigmentosa or Hunter-Hurler syndrome) may be inherited in some families via an X-linked gene, and in others through an autosomal (nonsex-linked chromosome) form of transmission.

Additional work by Winokur's group deserves some elaboration, especially with respect to their attempts to account for the overlap of unipolar and bipolar disorder in families having a positive bipolar history. To explicate the less than 50% morbidity risk in first-degree proband relatives, Winokur and his colleagues have postulated that either two genes may be necessary for the phenotypic expression of bipolar disorder, or that diminished penetrance may be involved. Although they did not rule out the latter possibility, the two gene theory (one gene locus being sex linked) appeared to fit the data better (Reich et al., 1969; Winokur, 1970, 1971), particularly with reference to the issue of unipolar disorders being the most commonly found affective disorder among bipolar patients' relatives. More specifically, they have proposed that, for bipolar pedigrees, affective disorders (both unipolar and bipolar) may be associated with an X-linked dominant gene which manifests itself in a unipolar phenotype when present alone, and in a bipolar phenotype when accompanied by a second gene that is most probably autosomally dominant (Winokur, 1970, 1971).

Other investigations have invoked environmental variables, rather than further genetic involvement, to explain the phenotypic overlap of unipolar and bipolar disorders within families having bipolar histories (Fieve, 1975; Mendlewicz et al., 1972). According to this hypothesis, environmental factors may determine whether or not a bipolar genotype is expressed in either a bipolar or unipolar phenotype. Consistent with this conjecture, a bipolar disorder (or genotype) may actually be manifested as a unipolar phenotype, depending upon certain environmental contingencies.

There is no evidence supporting an X-linkage hypothesis for unipolar disorders based on familial data. This is, in part, due to the selection criteria employed by researchers in this area. Based on ideas similar to the two-gene theory espoused by Winokur, these researchers are reluctant to include unipolar patients with a positive familial history of bipolar disorder in the unipolar study group. Hence, the unipolar sample is typically restricted to only unipolar patients without familial histories of bipolar disorder. Few, if any, of the requisite, X-linkage familial patterns have been found in these unipolar I groups.

In summary, the studies reviewed so far indicate unipolar and bipolar disorders may be distinguished on familial criteria that are supportive of genetic differences existing between, and possibly within, each category. However, in order to prove conclusively that these disorders differ with respect to genetic etiology, other, more direct assessments of the genetics involved are necessary. Linkage studies have proven fruitful in this respect and have provided more conclusive evidence for the separation of unipolar and bipolar disorders.

In one of the earlier linkage studies, Winokur and Tanna (1969) reported results of 2 family pedigrees that suggested a linkage between bipolar disorders and the loci for the Xg blood system, although these findings were not statistically significant. More recently, Mendlewicz and Fleiss (1974) have combined these data with 11 pedigrees from a previous investigation (Mendlewicz, Fleiss, & Fieve, 1975) and 10 new informative pedigrees. The combined analysis led Mendlewicz and Fleiss to conclude that there is statistical evidence of a measurable linkage between bipolar illness and the Xg blood group.

Even stronger support for the X-linkage hypothesis has been found by Mendlewicz and Fleiss (1974) in studies measuring the linkage between color blindness (both deutan and protan) and bipolar disorder. Again, by combining the data from previous studies (Mendlewicz, Fleiss, & Fieve, 1972; Reich et al., 1969) with new findings, these investigators were able to replicate and extend previously reported positive findings. They also found evidence of a relatively stronger linkage of deutan color blindness with bipolar disorder than of protan color blindness (the odds favoring protan color blindness occurring with bipolar disorder are 30,000 to 1, whereas deutan color blindness shows a 5000 to 1 ratio, based on the combined studies' data). These authors suggested that their data for linkage between bipolar disorder and both color blindness and the Xg blood group are consistent with other findings indicating that the loci for the Xg blood group and for color vision are far apart on the X chromosome (Renwick & Schulze, 1964). Furthermore, they postulated that the bipolar disorder gene locus is somewhere between these established loci and is probably closest to the color blindness loci.

Mendlewicz and Fleiss (1974) also explored the possibility of linkage between the Xg blood system and–or color blindness with unipolar disorders, but the results were negative in both cases. The authors concluded that whereas X-linked inheritance may be excluded as the mode of transmission for unipolar disorders, the positive evidence of X linkage within certain bipolar groups "represents the first known instances, aside from certain mental deficiency syndromes, of a Mendelian inheritance mechanism in psychiatric disorders [p. 292]."

An important implication of the linkage data is that unipolar I cases may be genetically different from unipolar cases within bipolar pedigrees (i.e., bipolar III cases). The evidence supporting this viewpoint is derived from the fact that although there are no data supporting X linkage for unipolar I cases, bipolar III cases are included in the analysis supporting X linkage for bipolar disorders.

Although these data are the most cogent indicators of an etiological difference between at least certain subgroups of the unipolar–bipolar population, some discretion is warranted in their interpretation. Some members of these family pedigrees have not passed through the age-of-risk for affective disorders, consequently later development of an affective disorder in some of these members could change the ratio of recombinants to nonrecombinants and weaken the evidence for linkage. In addition, Becker (1974) pointed out several methodological difficulties, such as the fact that certain tests for color vision may not be "optimally reliable (Thuline, Hodgkin, Fraser, & Motulsky, 1969)," and that there is still some question about the location of both the protan color blindness and Xg blood group genes (Cadoret & Winokur, 1975; Race & Sanger, 1969). Finally the unipolar group employed in the Mendlewicz and Fleiss (1974) study may not have been a homogeneously defined subgroup (Perris, 1973; Winokur et al., 1971), thereby limiting the generalizability of the conclusion that X linkage is not operative in any unipolar disorder. However, it is hard to account for the data by such discrepancies alone. Thus, one might tentatively conclude that different etiological predispositions exist for, at least, certain subgroups of unipolar and bipolar disorders.

Mode of Transmission: Polygenic

Polygenic inheritance involves the summation of many different genes, normally distributed in the population, which contribute in either positive or negative increments to the phenotypic expression of a trait. It is difficult, however, to distinguish this form of inheritance from that of a dominant, major gene with diminished penetrance. Various methods have been developed to help distinguish between these two possibilities in the transmission of affective disorders.

Based on the assumption that a genetic component exists for affective disorders, a computational model was devised by Slater (1966) to test whether polygenic or dominant X-linked transmission might be involved. The model entails the analysis of pairs of ancestral secondary cases of the disorder in a proband's pedigree. Polygenic theory predicts approximately twice as many unilateral pairs (two relatives with the disorder on the same side of the family) as bilateral pairs (two relatives on opposite sides of the family with the disorder). Dominant gene transmission, in contrast, predicts an even greater proportion of unilateral pairs.

It will be remembered that Perris (1966, 1968) reported equal proportions of bipolar I males and females, when all cases are considered, as well as different morbidity risks among first-degree relatives of patients having a bipolar disorder. These results, incompatible with dominant X-linked transmission, led him to propose polygenic inheritance for bipolar disorders. Employing Slater's computational model with his data, Perris found results that were congruent with a polygenic hypothesis (Perris, 1971). Similar results were found for bipolar I disorders using this model (Slater, Maxwell, & Price, 1971) as well as a different computational method (James & Chapman, 1975), although these findings have not been uniformly positive (Mendlewicz & Rainer, 1974).

Using Slater's (1966) computational model, Perris (1971) also found that his data for unipolar cases were more congruent with polygenic transmission. As the number of cases was small in Perris' study, a replication was undertaken by Baker, Dorzab, Winokur, and Cadoret (1972). Their data favored a polygenic transmission as opposed to a dominant gene transmission for various unipolar subgroups (depressive spectrum disease and pure depressive disease) as well as for the unipolar group as a whole.

All of the computational studies are subject to the criticism that they do not demonstrate the validity of polygenic transmission for either bipolar or unipolar disorders, but only indicate compatibility with polygenic theory provided certain assumptions are met. For example, one assumption is that the disorders have a genetic basis but the computational studies alone do not prove this. Consequently, without direct evidence of a genetic basis, these studies cannot exclude the effects of a common family environment in accounting for their results (James & Chapman, 1975). Additionally, Slater et al., (1971), in their study of polygenic transmission for bipolar disorders, have cited several biases that are potentially operative in these studies. In particular, if assortative mating is a factor in affective disorders, the results from their computational model would bias the data against dominant gene theory and for polygenic inheritance. Gershon, Dunner, Sturt, and Goodwin (1973) have questioned such an assumption, based on their findings of assortative mating in affective disorders. Should this or other assumptions prove to be inappropriate, the validity of conclusions drawn from the computational studies will be weakened.

Genetic and Environmental Heterogeneity

Recently, it has been suggested that polygenic and X-linkage theories are not necessarily mutually exclusive. This notion of genetic heterogeneity suggests that both unipolar and bipolar classifications may be amenable to further differentiation within each group in order to obtain more homogeneous groupings (Cadoret & Winokur, 1975; Gershon et al., 1971; Mendlewicz et al., 1972). The possibility of genetic heterogeneity in unipolar disorders has been demonstrated by the early and late onset subgroups proposed by Winokur and his colleagues. Similarly, genetic heterogeneity within bipolar disorders is illustrated by the two-gene theory and may account for the problematic occurrence of father-to-son transmission. Moreover, the application of Slater's (1966) computational model suggested that a single dominant-gene transmission may operate in bipolar patients having a positive family history of bipolar disorder, whereas polygenic transmission was implicated for bipolar probands with a negative family history of bipolar disorder (Mendlewicz, Fieve, Rainer, & Cataldo, 1973).

Environmental factors, usually overlooked in these studies, may still play an important role in unipolar and bipolar disorders (Allen, 1976; Hays, 1976). Genetic functions and the environment are inseparable, and environmental variables are particularly crucial in polygenic inheritance. Some investigators have proposed that environmental factors may determine the phenotypic expression of a bipolar genotype. However, little effort has been focused on how environmental contingencies might interact with a given genotype or, more important for the unipolar–bipolar distinction, how these two groups may each react to similar harmful or beneficial environments. The greater discordance in unipolar monozygotic twins suggests that environmental factors may play a decisive role in this group's phenotypic expression and illness onset.

PHARMACOLOGICAL RESPONSE

We will focus on the major drugs employed with unipolar and bipolar patients—lithium carbonate and tricyclic antidepressants (most typically imipramine and amitriptyline). Conclusions from studies of the efficacy of other antidepressant drugs suggest that the monoamine oxidase inhibitors are useful primarily in "atypical" depressed patients but not very·useful for patients with typical "endogenous" depression (Sack & Goodwin, 1974). Therefore, these latter drugs shall not be included in our discussion. The efficacy of lithium and tricyclic antidepressants in relation to the unipolar–bipolar distinction has been reviewed (Depue & Monroe, 1978a) and, therefore, we shall only summarize conclusions and incorporate the most recent data in more detail.

Lithium Carbonate

THERAPEUTIC EFFECT AGAINST DEPRESSION

Mendels (1976) recently reviewed 10 controlled studies assessing the therapeutic effect of lithium carbonate against depression and noted that of these, 3 studies claimed lithium did not produce a significant effect. These latter double-blind trials employed a total of 152 hospitalized, bipolar and unipolar depressed patients who exhibited moderate to severe depression. Additionally all of these studies, with the exception of the Mendels, Secunda, and Dyson (1972) study, used a placebo substitution design. Not only were these reports in agreement that a group of depressed patients responded satisfactorily to lithium carbonate, but also that the majority of the responders (approximately 80%) were bipolar depressives. However, equally consistent was the finding that not all bipolar depressives showed improvement when receiving lithium carbonate, and additionally, that a smaller proportion of unipolar depressives responded well to the drug. The reason for a lack of response to lithium carbonate in 20% of the bipolar depressives is not clear, but research has indicated that insufficient dosage levels, rapid cycling (i.e., four or more affective episodes per year, see Dunner & Fieve, 1974; Dunner, Stallone, & Fieve, 1976), and negative family history (Mendlewicz, Fieve, & Stallone, 1973) are related to a poor response to lithium carbonate.

Two possibly related explanations might be posited to account for the varied response of unipolar patients to lithium carbonate. First, there may be various subgroups of unipolar depressives, each characterized by different psychobiologic dysfunctions, that respond to different pharmacological agents. Indeed, several studies have suggested the presence of at least two "biochemical" subtypes of hospitalized unipolar depressives: (a) possibly characterized by a dysfunction in central noradrenergic activity, and (b) possibly characterized by a dysfunction in central serotonergic activity (Asberg, Thoren, Traskman, Bertilsson, & Ringberger, 1976; Depue & Evans, 1979; Maas, 1975). As lithium carbonate has been found to increase tryptophan levels (the amino acid precursor of serotonin) and the synthesis of serotonin in the brain (Tagliamonte, Tagliamonte, Perez-Cruet, Stern, & Gressa, 1971), and as reduced pretreatment accumulation of cerebrospinal fluid 5-Hydroxy-indoleacidic acid (5-HIAA) (the major metabolite of serotonin) during probenecid administration is related to a positive response to lithium carbonate (Goodwin, Post, Dunner, & Gordon, 1973), further research might profitably examine the response to lithium carbonate of the unipolar group possibly characterized by serotonergic dysfunction.

A second, but potentially related, alternative is that the unipolar patients responsive to lithium carbonate are related to bipolar patients (perhaps misdiagnosed bipolar II and–or bipolar III cases). Owing to this possibility,

Kupfer, Pickar, Himmelhoch, and Detre (1975) compared three groups of depressed patients: Unipolar (tricyclic responders), unipolar (tricyclic non-responders but lithium carbonate responders), and bipolar (lithium carbonate responders). None of the unipolar patients had a clinical history of hypomania and–or mania, but all had at least two previous episodes of depression which were severe enough to warrant medication. The three groups did not differ in age, number of prior depressive episodes, incidence of suicide attempts, use of alcohol or other drugs, or severity of depression. In addition to the congruence of response to lithium carbonate in the bipolar, and unipolar, lithium carbonate groups, these two groups had a significantly higher proportion of patients with a positive family history of "mood swings" (bipolar, lithium carbonate responders—50% positive; unipolar, lithium carbonate responders—42% positive) than did the unipolar, tricyclic group (14% positive). In addition, there were significantly more family members with a history of mood swings in both the bipolar, and unipolar, lithium carbonate groups than in the unipolar, tricyclic group.

Although these results are subject to criticism on the basis of the retrospective method employed, reliance on patient self-reports, and the lack of precise family-study methodology, they do provide preliminary support for the notion that *some* lithium carbonate-responsive, unipolar patients may be related to bipolar disorder. In this study the unipolar, lithium carbonate group might well qualify for a diagnosis of bipolar III. The potential relationship of this hypothesis to the theory of differing psychobiologic dysfunction mentioned earlier lies in the suggestion that mania (Mendels & Frazer, 1975), as well as bipolar depression (Depue & Evans, 1979; Prange, Wilson, Lynn, Alltop, & Stikeleather, 1974), is characterized, in part, by reduced, central, serotonergic activity. To test these two alternatives, future research needs to assess the biochemical functioning *and* family history of unipolar patients who respond to lithium carbonate (as compared to unipolar and bipolar depressed patients who do not respond to lithium carbonate).

PROPHYLACTIC EFFECT AGAINST DEPRESSION

Quitkin, Rifkin, and Klein (1976) reviewed the controlled, double-blind, prophylaxis studies employing either a discontinuation or prospective design up to 1975. We shall summarize these and add more recent trials. Of those studies with sufficiently large samples and with specification of type of relapse reviewed by Quitkin *et al.* (1976), a prophylactic effect of lithium carbonate against depressive relapses in bipolar I patients was found in three studies. Not included in the review is another study reported by Prien, Klett, and Caffey (1974) which was directed at the inconsistent findings of lithium carbonate prophylaxis against depressive episodes. This multihospital collaborative project clearly revealed a prophylactic effect of lithium carbonate against depressive episodes in bipolar I patients. More recently, in a double-blind prospective study, Fieve, Kumbaraci, and Dunner (1976) found lithium carbonate to be superior to a placebo for bipolar I patients in terms of the mean number of depressive episodes per patient-year and the mean number of months in the study.

In realizing that many of the patients involved in research on lithium carbonate prophylaxis drop out of the study because of manic rather than depressive attacks, Dunner, Stallone, and Fieve (1976) suggested that the evaluation of prophylaxis of bipolar depression might be more properly assessed by studying patients who would be less likely to have severe manic episodes during the trial. Therefore, the authors conducted a double-blind prospective trial employing bipolar II patients. No significant differences in the rates of depressive episodes per patient-year were found between groups receiving lithium carbonate or a placebo. However, 33% of the placebo-receiving group who exhibited depressive episodes were hospitalized for these attacks, whereas the corresponding figure for the lithium carbonate-receiving group was 11% (a nonsignificant trend). Moreover, 67% of the placebo-receiving group who were subject to depressive episodes dropped out of the study, whereas only 22% of the comparable, lithium carbonate-receiving group did so. Dunner et al. (1976) interpreted these data as representing a greater severity of depressive episodes in the placebo-receiving group, which is consistent with the findings of Fieve, Platman, and Plutchik (1968).

Recently, Fleiss, Dunner, Stallone, and Fieve (1976) supported these findings in a double-blind study of bipolar II patients, but the sample was too small for statistical analyses (lithium carbonate = 7, placebo = 11). The group receiving lithium carbonate showed approximately half the frequency of depressive episodes, shorter duration of depressions (lithium carbonate = 57 days, placebo = 194 days), and reduced severity of depressions in terms of fewer dropouts due to depressive illness than the group receiving a placebo. The presence of fewer dropouts is consistently associated with lithium carbonate prophylaxis, and in this study 57% of the patients receiving lithium carbonate versus 18% of the group receiving a placebo remained in the research protocol until the end of the 4-year trial.

The Dunner et al. (1976) and Fieve et al. (1976) studies come from the same research group. Across the two studies it becomes evident that bipolar II patients randomized into the study later, and participating for a shorter time period (included in the Dunner et al. study) show less of a prophylactic effect. Although it is possible that the smaller Fieve et al. (1976) bipolar II sample is comprised of less severe cases, it is equally possible that it may take a long time to demonstrate lithium carbonate prophylaxis in bipolar II depressions. Fieve (1975) has found that a decisive prophylactic effect of lithium carbonate against depressions often take a year or more with bipolar I patients, and this figure may be longer with bipolar II cases (Dunner, Stallone, & Fieve, 1976).

Turning to lithium carbonate's prophylactic effect against depression in unipolar patients, Quitkin *et al*. (1976) showed that lithium carbonate significantly reduced the frequency of depressive episodes in unipolar patients. Additionally, in a controlled study, Fieve *et al*. (1976) supported these earlier trials and showed that lithium carbonate use resulted in a significantly lower number of episodes per patient-year, fewer severe episodes, and a greater mean number of months in the study than use of a placebo in treating patients experiencing recurrent unipolar I disorders.

Tricyclic Antidepressants

Numerous studies and reviews have appeared documenting the therapeutic efficacy of the various tricyclic antidepressants with depressed patients (Bielski & Friedel, 1976; Klein & Davis, 1969). However, as was the case for lithium carbonate, significant variation in drug response is a common finding among depressed patients (e.g., approximately 30% do not respond to imipramine-like compounds, Klein & Davis, 1969), once again suggesting the existence of potentially important subdivisions within the depressive population. Although variation in patient response to lithium carbonate stimulated investigation into the predictive power of the unipolar–bipolar distinction, an equivalent research trend has not developed to delimit the variability in response to tricyclics (Bielski & Friedel, 1976), even though Bunney, Brodie, and Murphy (1970) reported a better response to tricyclics in unipolar than in bipolar depressed patients.

Thus, there is little data available from which to draw any firm conclusions concerning similarities or differences in the therapeutic response to tricyclic antidepressants of unipolar and bipolar depressed or manic patients (Mendels & Frazer, 1975). The situation is not very different when one considers the prophylactic effects of tricyclic antidepressants against depression. Quitkin *et al*. (1976) reviewed the five studies that employed proper controls and concluded that, on the basis of these trials involving 400–500 unipolar depressed patients, continuation therapy with tricyclics reduced the risk of relapse in unipolar patients by approximately 20–50%. However, if all patients were to receive continuation therapy, anywhere from 30 to 70% (those receiving placebo without relapse) would receive antidepressants unnecessarily. The problem exists in the fact that it is not currently possible to predict those patients who will or will not benefit from continuation therapy. The predictive power of the unipolar–bipolar distinction should be tested against this problem.

It must be emphasized that the previously mentioned trials examined the efficacy of continuation therapy, which is not a completely adequate test of tricyclic prophylaxis. With the exception of the Prien, Klett, and Caffey (1973) study, these trials did not follow patients longer than seven months, hardly long enough to test long-term prophylaxis. Therefore, the prospective, 2-year follow-up trials by Prien, Klett, and Caffey (1973, 1974) stand as the most definitive tests of tricyclic prophylaxis. In this project, 78 unipolar, and 44 bipolar, depressed patients (under 60 years of age) were randomly assigned to either an imipramine, lithium carbonate, or placebo receiving group (Prien *et al.*, 1974). Imipramine had a strong prophylactic effect against depressive episodes for both unipolar and bipolar patients, but this antidepressant effect was not significantly greater than that of lithium carbonate in either the unipolar or bipolar groups. On the other hand, imipramine was significantly inferior to lithium carbonate in "preventing" manic episodes.

Examining both the lithium carbonate and tricyclic research, the pharmacologic findings of greatest relevance for the unipolar–bipolar distinction are those showing significant similarity in drug response for the polar groups. Although the overlap of polar groups in their *therapeutic* response to lithium carbonate may be viewed as a misdiagnosis of bipolar II and III cases as unipolar patients, such an hypothesis is unlikely to apply to the general concordance in *prophylactic* response to lithium carbonate for the polar groups. Prien's study also suggests the inadequacy of a misdiagnosis hypothesis in accounting for the general similarity between the response of unipolar and bipolar depressed patients to tricyclic prophylaxis. Thus, it seems clear that even if some forms of unipolar and bipolar disorders are genetically different, at least with respect to lithium carbonate, polar groups either share common psychobiologic dysfunctions, or have different pathophysiologies, which respond well to the action of the lithium ion.

STRESS FACTORS

Direct comparisons of unipolar and bipolar groups with respect to the relationship of various stress factors to the onset of disease are essentially nonexistent. Therefore, we can only suggest some potential differences between these groups in the hope that they will promote empirical investigations. One framework for comparing these groups is suggested in the first chapter of this volume. Hence, we will discuss environmental variables, personality variables, and one biologic process, and conclude with a suggestion for investigating the effects of stress in polar disorders.

In terms of the initiation of episodes by psychosocial events, we were not able to locate one study systematically comparing unipolar and bipolar samples. Most life-event studies have employed unipolar patients almost solely (Brown, personal communication; Lewinsohn, personal communication), and often these samples are of "neurotic" (i.e., less intense) levels of severity (e.g., Lewinsohn, personal communication; some of Paykel's samples). In addition, because of the tremendous heterogeneity of the unipolar group, it is not clear from existing data whether the effects of stress demonstrated in terms of overall sample statistics would vary according to unipolar subgroups. For instance, Cadoret, Winokur, Dorzab, and Baker (1972) showed that loss (of person, home, job, etc.) prior to onset characterized the "depressive spectrum" unipolar group much more than the "pure depressive" unipolar group. Because the "spectrum" group may well define a group with nonaffective primary disorder accompanied by secondary depression which reflects various character disturbances (particularly sociopathy and hysteroid features, see Akiskal, Bitar, Puzantian, Rosenthal, & Walker, 1978), a portion of the variance attributed to the effects of events on the onset of unipolar depression might be more accurately interpreted as the generation of events by the maladaptive life-styles associated with patients having various character disorders and secondary depression. In any case, the important point is that derivation of general mechanistic theories of the effects of stress on the onset of unipolar episodes seems premature and perhaps unwarranted as the environment–onset pathways may differ radically as a function of unipolar subgroup.

There are other psychosocial factors outside of discrete events that, although not systematically assessed in relation to episodic onset, suggest that individuals having bipolar disorder accompanied by manic or more intense hypomanic phases (e.g., bipolar I and II) are subject to more intense chronic stress than unipolar cases. This is suggested in part by the higher divorce rate for bipolar cases discussed earlier. The higher divorce rate may not only reflect more chronic interpersonal conflict, but it also indicates that loss of social support is an important stress-producing factor for bipolar patients. Another chronic stressor discussed earlier which may be more prominent in bipolar cases is the alcohol-related work and interpersonal impairment accompanying manic phases; the latter outcome, of course, interacts with divorce rates and loss of social support. An additional stressor in bipolar cases is the high incidence of interepisodic, chronic symptomatic impairment relative to unipolar cases. If this form of impairment reflects an aspect of bipolar disorder that is independent of other chronic stressors, an impaired condition may well alter the perception of stressors as well as the ability to mobilize adequate coping behavior. Indeed, Ilfeld (1977) found this to be the case for the development of depressive symptoms in general. Thus, considering the above stressors together, they may place the individual with bipolar disorder at particularly high risk for stress-initiated recurrences of disorder over time.

Differences between polar groups with respect to the relationship of personality variables to episodic onset have not been studied. Indeed, these variables have been neglected generally in the study of stress and episodic onset. This is unfortunate, for as Chapter 1 of this volume suggests, psychological characteristics may play an important role in modifying an individual's vulnerability to psychosocial circumstances.

One potentially important difference in personality factors between unipolar and bipolar cases has been emphasized with some consistency in the literature. Many studies have found that unipolar patients are characterized by chronic anxiety, obsessiveness, insecurity, social anxiety, life dissatisfaction, and a fear of losing control, both in the depressive episode (see reviews by Kupfer et al., 1975; Nystrom & Lindegard, 1975) as well as in symptom-free periods (Perris, 1966, 1971). On the one hand, the generality of these findings, even in Perris' relatively severe unipolar groups, suggests that they are not limited to "depressive spectrum" cases or other anxiety disorders with secondary depression only. On the other hand, in a 3–4-year prospective study of depressed patients characterized by the neurotic traits mentioned above, 50% were found to be secondary depressive conditions, whereas only 20% were found to have a stable diagnosis of primary unipolar disorder (Akiskal et al., 1978). Moreover, the findings suggested that neurotic character "traits" did not characterize unipolar or bipolar cases in particular, but that these types of personality variables are best viewed as independent of depressive diagnosis. If this view is correct, these types of personality variables might be independent of the unipolar–bipolar distinction and therefore may be found to be distributed evenly across the polar groups. Until these issues are resolved, it is difficult to posit differential psychological predispositions for the polar disorders.

There are two additional related lines of evidence which suggest that personality variables may be particularly important in relation to the onset of unipolar disorders, although neither provide any insight into which variables may attain significance. First, as noted in the earlier genetics discussion, a polygenic mode of transmission appears to "fit" the unipolar data best. A polygenic model, of course, carries the implication that the onset of a disorder may, in large part, be accounted for by personality variables and environmental initiating factors. Support for this notion is provided by the larger discordance rates for unipolar, as compared to bipolar, monozygotic twins. The higher discordance rates for unipolar disorder may be interpreted as indicative of a greater role for psychosocial factors in the development of unipolar disorders.

A final variable that has been discussed with respect to bipolar vulnerability to environmental impact is a biologic process. Post and Kopanda (1976) recently reviewed a large body of pharmacologic evidence which suggested that repeated pharmacologic stimulation (amphetamine or cocaine) results in functional alterations in catecholamine limbic system pathways, and that these alterations are paralleled by a progressive disorganization of emotional and cognitive behavior, ending in a paranoid psychotic state. The functional alteration in catecholaminergic activity appears to involve increased recep-

tor site sensitivity, due either to reduced availability of a transmitter substance, alteration of receptor conformation, or some other unknown process.

These theories are of interest with respect to bipolar disorder because one
model that attempts to account for the onset of both depressive and manic
episodes posits oscillating neuronal receptor sensitivity (Pert, Rosenblatt,
Sivit, Pert, & Bunney, 1978). This model suggests that receptor sensitivity is
unstable in bipolar disorder, ranging from subsensitivity in the depressive
phase to supersensitivity in the manic phase. Pert *et al.* (1978) provided
some support for this model by illustrating that lithium carbonate stabilizes
neuronal receptor sensitivity under various conditions which normally alter
receptor sensitivity. Combining these notions, Post and Kopanda (1976) and
Goodwin and Bunney (1973) speculated that alterations in functional aspects of neuronal systems may occur as a result of recurrent environmental
stimulation, and that persons with predispositional biases in neuronal variables (e.g., unstable receptor sensitivity) may be more vulnerable to these
environmentally induced alterations.

Regardless of the exact mechanisms involved, if the oscillating behavioral
phases characterizing bipolar disorder are related to instability of some
aspect of neurotransmitter functioning, environmental events could play a
role in "activating" that instability, perhaps via a mechanism proposed by
Post and Kopanda. An important point illustrated by the latter authors was
that "activation" of altered behavioral patterns does not require awesome
stimulus conditions. Repetitive stimulation appeared to be the important
dimension. It may be that chronic stressors or less threatening, but repetitive, discrete, undesirable events may be effective in initiating disease onset
under such biologic conditions as unstable neurotransmitter functioning.

In conclusion, a more comprehensive understanding of the respective
power of the different factors potentially related to episodic onset, including
psychological and psychosocial variables, requires that future comparisons
of unipolar and bipolar groups (*a*) investigate onset within a multivariate
research design, where a variety of stress factors are assessed, and (*b*)
subcategorize the polar groups, particularly the unipolar group, as not all
subgroups may be characterized by similar stress–onset relationships. In
addition, the clearest demonstration for the effects of "stress" on episodic
onset probably relates most meaningfully to the degree to which stress
reduces the time from one episode to the next episode. That is, if stress
initiates onset by "activating" a bias in a biologic system (see the discussion
in the first chapter of this volume), then the major effect of stress on
episodic onsets should be to initiate onsets sooner than if stress were absent
or less intense. Brown (Chapter 12 of this volume) has provided one strategy
for assessing this effect of stress.

An alternative strategy, which appeals to us more, would be to follow unipolar and bipolar patients selected for their likelihood of experiencing a relapse within a reasonable time period, and to assess psychosocial variables (and biologic variables) periodically. Subgroups of patients will relapse, at varying rates, while others will not relapse during the prescribed follow-up period, thus forming naturally occurring, differential outcome groups which can be compared in terms of stress factors. To assess the relationship of stress to time-to-onset, the life-table method may be used to analyze stress–onset relationships as a function of time (Fleiss *et al.*, 1976).

CONCLUDING REMARKS

The power of the unipolar–bipolar distinction lies in its research generating potential for delimiting the heterogeneity of depressive disorders and for predictive studies of subtype correlates. This review indicates clearly that when the depressive disorders are differentiated into larger polar groups, *some* forms of unipolar and bipolar disorders differ with respect to behavioral, clinical, genetic, and pharmacologic patterns. Furthermore, the larger polar groups have exhibited differences in terms of 24-hour urinary 17-hydroxycorticosteroids (OHCS) secretion rates (bipolars lower; Dunner, Goodwin, Gershon, Murphy, & Bunney, 1972); visual evoked, cortical response patterns, which are partially under genetic influence (bipolars = augmentors, unipolars = reducers; Chapter 9 of this volume); cerebrospinal fluid accumulations of the major metabolite of dopamine (Depue & Evans, 1979); and response to lithium carbonate. In spite of these gains, the variability in results has required further subdivisions within the larger polar groups. A genetic taxonomy has consequently evolved and now stands as the most elaborate classification system of a major "functional" psychosis (Akiskal & McKinney, 1975). But, for the most part, both the clinical and research utility of this system *in its most complex form* remain to be proven.

Most comparisons of the genetic system's subtypes have focused on bipolar I and II groups and, though findings have posed interesting questions, examination of this research indicates that clear answers are not likely to be arrived at easily. For instance, a review of bipolar I–II comparisons suggests that these subtypes are similar in that both have higher familial rates of bipolar disorder, cyclothymic personality, and suicide than unipolar cases; both have earlier onset-of-symptoms and higher, personal suicide rates than unipolar patients; both show an augmented visual evoked, cortical response pattern as opposed to the unipolar reduction pattern; and both exhibit an activation response to L-DOPA, while unipolar cases show no such response (Dunner, Gershon, & Goodwin, 1976). Conversely, bipolar II cases have shown greater similarity to unipolar than bipolar I patients with respect to urinary 17-OHCS secretion rates and blood platelet, monoamine oxidase activity (Dunner *et al.*, 1976). Thus, while concordant results suggest that these bipolar subtypes may be conceived as related disorders falling along a severity continuum, the discordant findings indicate that they may be viewed to some extent as different disorders. Only additional research can clarify these alternative conceptions.

Where bipolar III cases might fall within these comparisons is unclear, but Kupfer *et al.*'s (1975) unipolar and bipolar I lithium carbonate analyses discussed earlier provide an exciting stimulus for exploring this group's relation to bipolar disorder further. Bipolar III cases should be studied more extensively because of the high potential for misclassification of these patients as unipolar cases, although in the end result it may be that they are more properly subsumed within unipolar disorder.

With respect to heterogeneity in unipolar disorder, subtyping of these cases is less well developed than for bipolar disorder. Indeed, the nonspecific polygenic results for unipolar disorder may simply reflect an averaging of the various genetic and environmental factors represented in this undifferentiated, diverse group. We have noted recent attempts at biochemically defined, unipolar, subtypes, but this research is in only an initial stage of development (Maas, 1975). Also, a psychotic–neurotic distinction and an anxious depression subtype within unipolar disorder appear to be promising, and recent reviews have offered numerous suggestions as to how research in these areas might proceed (see Chapters 3–4 of this volume).

Finally, two issues which have received inadequate attention in relation to the unipolar–bipolar distinction deserve brief mention. First, whereas numerous hypotheses concerning the differences between polar disorders have been put forth, rarely are similarities emphasized. The findings suggesting lithium carbonate prophylaxis in both unipolar and bipolar patients represent one very important example possibly indicative of a similar biologic dysfunction that is responsive to the action of the lithium ion. Therefore, serious consideration must be given to models of congruence of polar groups in future research.

Second, and perhaps most neglected, is the issue concerning the relative contribution of psychosocial factors to the development and onset of the polar disorders. It is quite possible that these factors may substantially account for the development and–or the form of some polar disorders (a point we emphasized in the genetics section with reference to the phenotypic expression of a bipolar genotype). At the least, these factors may contribute to the initiation of both polar forms of disorder. Clearly, if we are to achieve a fuller understanding of the polar disorders, we will need to broaden our perspective and entertain more encompassing biobehavioral models similar to that formulated by Akiskal and McKinney (1975) and by Akiskal (Chapter 18, this volume).

REFERENCES

Abrams, R. & Taylor, M. A. Unipolar mania: A preliminary report. *Archives of General Psychiatry*, 1974, 30, 441–443.

Akiskal, H. S. & McKinney, W. T., Jr. Overview of recent research in depression: Integration of ten conceptual models into a comprehensive clinical frame. *Archives of General Psychiatry*, 1975, 32, 285–305.

Akiskal, H. S., Bitar, A. H., Puzantian, V. R., Rosenthal, T. L., & Walker, P. W. The nosological status of neurotic depression. *Archives of General Psychiatry*, 1978, 35, 756–766.

Allen, M. G. Twin studies of affective illness. *Archives of General Psychiatry*, 1976, 33, 1476–1478.

Angst, J. *Zur Atiologie und Nosologie endogener depressiveo Psychosen.* Berlin: Springer Verlag, 1966.

Angst, J., Baastrup, P., Grof, P., Hippius, H., Poldinger, W., & Weis, P. The course of monopolar depression and bipolar psychoses. *Psychiatrica, Neurologica, et Neurochirurgia*, 1973, 76, 489–500.

Asberg, M., Thoren, P., Traskman, L., Bertilsson, L., & Ringberger, V. "Serotonin depression"—A biochemical subgroup within the affective disorders? *Science*, 1976, 191, 478–480.

Baker, M., Dorzab, J., Winokur, G., & Cadoret, R. Depressive disease: Evidence favoring polygenic inheritance based on an analysis of ancestral cases. *Archives of General Psychiatry*, 1972, 27, 320–327.

Becker, J. *Depression: Research and theory.* New York: Halsted, 1974.

Beigel, A. & Murphy, D. L. Unipolar and bipolar affective illness: Differences in clinical characteristics accompanying depression. *Archives of General Psychiatry*, 1971, 24, 215–220.

Bielski, R. J. & Friedel, R. O. Prediction of tricyclic antidepressant response: A critical review. *Archives of General Psychiatry*, 1976, 33, 1479–1489.

Bratfos, O. & Haug, J. O. The course of manic-depressive psychosis. *Acta Psychiatrica Scandinavica*, 1968, 44, 89–112.

Brodie, H. K. H. & Leff, M. J. Bipolar depression—A comparative study of patient characteristics. *American Journal of Psychiatry*, 1971, 127, 1086–1090.

Bunney, W. E., Jr., Brodie, H. K. H., & Murphy, D. L. Psychopharmacological differentiation between two subgroups of depressed patients. Paper presented at the *78th Annual Meeting of the American Psychological Association*, Miami, Florida, September 1970.

Bunney, W. E., Jr. & Murphy, D. L. The behavioral switch process and psychopathology. In J. Mendels (Ed.), *Biological psychiatry.* New York: Wiley-Interscience, 1973.

Cadoret, R. J. & Winokur, G. X-linkage in manic-depressive illness. *Annual Review of Medicine*, 1975, 26, 21–25.

Cadoret, R. J., Winokur, G., & Clayton, P. J. Family history studies: VII. Manic depressive disease versus depressive disease. *British Journal of Psychiatry*, 1970, 116, 625–635.

Cadoret, R. J., Winokur, G., Dorzab, J., & Baker, M. Depressive disease: Life events and the onset of illness. *Archives of General Psychiatry*, 1972, 26, 133–136.

Carlson, G. A., Kotin, J., Davenport, Y. B., & Adland, M. Follow-up of 53 bipolar manic-depressive patients. *British Journal of Psychiatry*, 1974, 124, 134–139.

Chopra, H. D. Family psychiatric morbidity, parental deprivation and socioeconomic status in cases of mania. *British Journal of Psychiatry*, 1975, 126, 191–192.

Depue, R. A. & Evans, R. The psychobiology of the depressive disorders. In B. A. Maher (Ed.), *Progress in experimental personality research* (Vol. 9). New York: Academic Press, 1979.

Depue, R. A. & Monroe, S. M. The unipolar–bipolar distinction in the depressive disorders. *Psychological Bulletin*, 1978, 85, 1001–1029. (a)

Depue, R. A. & Monroe, S. M. Learned helplessness in the perspective of the depressive disorders: Conceptual and definitional issues. *Journal of Abnormal Psychology*, 1978, 87, 3–21. (b)

Detre, T., Himmelhoch, J., Swartzburg, M., Anderson, C. M., Byck, R., & Kupfer, D. J. Hypersomnia and manic-depressive disease. *American Journal of Psychiatry*, 1972, 128, 1303–1305.

Dunner, D. L. & Fieve, R. R. Clinical factors in lithium carbonate prophylaxis failure. *Archives of General Psychiatry*, 1974, 30, 229–233.

Dunner, D. L. & Fieve, R. R. Psychiatric illness in fathers of men with bipolar primary affective disorder. *Archives of General Psychiatry*, 1975, 32, 1134–1137.

Dunner, D. L., Fleiss, J. L., & Fieve, R. R. The course of development of mania in patients with recurrent depression. *American Journal of Psychiatry*, 1976, 133, 905–908.

Dunner, D. L., Gershon, E. S., & Goodwin, F. K. Heritable factors in the severity of affective illness. *Biological Psychiatry*, 1976, 11, 31–42.

Dunner, D. L., Goodwin, F. K., Gershon, E. S., Murphy, D. L., & Bunney, W. E., Jr. Excretion of 17-OHCS in unipolar and bipolar depressed patients. *Archives of General Psychiatry*, 1972, 26, 360–363.

Dunner, D. L., Stallone, F., & Fieve, R. R. Lithium carbonate and affective disorders. V: A double-blind study of prophylaxis of depression in bipolar illness. *Archives of General Psychiatry*, 1976, 33, 117–125.

Fieve, R. R. New perspectives on an old problem. In S. Arieti & G. Chranowski (Eds.), *New dimensions in psychiatry: A world view*. New York: Wiley 1975.

Fieve, R. R., Kumbaraci, T., & Dunner, D. L. Lithium prophylaxis of depression in bipolar I, bipolar II, and unipolar patients. *American Journal of Psychiatry*, 1976, 133, 925–929.

Fieve, R. R., Platman, S. R., & Plutchick, R. R. The use of lithium in affective disorders. *American Journal of Psychiatry*, 1968, 125, 492–498.

Fleiss, J. L., Dunner, D. L., Stallone, F., & Fieve, R. R. The life table. *Archives of General Psychiatry*, 1976, 33, 107–112.

Gershon, S. Lithium salts in the management of the manic-depressive syndrome. *Annual Review of Medicine*, 1972, 23, 499–512.

Gershon, E., Dunner, D., & Goodwin, F. K. Toward a biology of affective disorders: Genetic contributions. *Archives of General Psychiatry*, 1971, 25, 1–15.

Gershon, E. S., Dunner, D. L., Sturt, L., & Goodwin, F. K. Assortative mating in the affective disorders. *Biological Psychiatry*, 1973, 7, 63–74.

Goetzl, U., Green, R., Whybrow, P., & Jackson, R. X linkage revisited: A further family study of manic-depressive illness. *Archives of General Psychiatry*, 1974, 31, 665–672.

Goodwin, F. K. & Bunney, W. E., Jr. Psychobiological aspects of stress and affective illness. In J. P. Scott & E. C. Senay (Eds.), *Separation and depression: Clinical and research aspects*. Washington, D. C.: American Association for the Advancement of Science, 1973.

Goodwin, F. K., Post, R. M., Dunner, D. L., & Gordon, E. K. Cerebrospinal fluid amine metabolites in affective illness: The probenecid technique. *American Journal of Psychiatry*, 1973, 130, 73–79.

Hartmann, E. Longitudinal studies of sleep and dream patterns in manic-depressive patients. *Archives of General Psychiatry*, 1968, 19, 312–329.

Hays, P. Etiological factors in manic-depressive psychoses. *Archives of General Psychiatry*, 1976, 33, 1187–1188.

Helgason, T. Epidemiology of mental disorders in Iceland. *Acta Psychiatrica Scandinavica*, 1964, 40 (Supplement no. 1973), 1–258.

Helzer, J. E. & Winokur, G. A family interview study of male manic-depressives. *Archives of General Psychiatry*, 1974, *31*, 73–77.

Himmelhoch, J. M., Coble, P., Kupfer, D. J., & Ingenito, J. Agitated psychotic depression associated with severe hypomanic episodes: A rare syndrome. *American Journal of Psychiatry*, 1976, *133*, 765–771.

Ilfeld, F. W. Current social stressors and symptoms of depression. *American Journal of Psychiatry*, 1977, *134*, 161–166.

James, N. M. & Chapman, C. J. A genetic study of bipolar affective disorder. *British Journal of Psychiatry*, 1975, *126*, 449–456.

Klein, D. & Davis, J. M. *Diagnosis and drug treatment of psychiatric disorders*. Baltimore, Md.: Williams & Wilkins, 1969.

Kotin, J. & Goodwin, F. K. Depression during mania: Clinical observations and theoretical implications. *American Journal of Psychiatry*, 1972, *129*, 679–686.

Kraepelin, E. *Manic-depressive insanity and paranoia*. Edinburgh: Livingstone, 1921.

Kupfer, D. J., Himmelhoch, J. M., Swartzburg, M., Anderson, C., Byck, R., & Detre, T. P. Hypersomnia in manic-depressive disease. *Disorders of the Nervous System*, 1972, *33*, 720–724.

Kupfer, D. J., Pickar, D., Himmelhoch, J. M., & Detre, T. P. Are there two types of unipolar depression? *Archives of General Psychiatry*, 1975, *32*, 866–871.

Kupfer, D. J., Weiss, B. L., Foster, G., Detre, T. P., Delgado, J., & McPartland, R. Psychomotor activity in affective states. *Archives of General Psychiatry*, 1974, *30*, 765–768.

Leonhard, K. *Aufteilung der Endogenen Psychosen* (1st ed.). Berlin: Akademieverlag, 1957.

Leonhard, K. *Aufteilung der Endogenen Psychosen* (4th ed.). Berlin: Akademieverlag, 1969.

Leonhard, K., Korff, I., & Schulz, H. Temperaments in the families of monopolar and bipolar phasic psychoses. *Psychiatria et Neurologia*, 1962, *143*, 416–434.

Loranger, A. W. X-linkage and manic-depressive illness. *British Journal of Psychiatry*, 1975, *127*, 482–488.

Maas, J. W. Biogenic amines and depression: Biochemical and pharmacological separation of two types of depression. *Archives of General Psychiatry*, 1975, *32*, 1357–1361.

Mayfield, D. C. & Coleman, L. L. Alcohol use and affective disorder. *Diseases of the Nervous System*, 1968, *29*, 467–474.

Mendels, J. Lithium in the treatment of depression. *American Journal of Psychiatry*, 1976, *133*, 373–378.

Mendels, J. & Frazer, A. Reduced central serotonergic activity in mania: Implications for the relationship between depression and mania. *British Journal of Psychiatry*, 1975, *126*, 241–248.

Mendels, J., Secunda, S. K., & Dyson, W. C. A controlled study of the antidepressant effects of lithium carbonate. *Archives of General Psychiatry*, 1972, *26*, 154–157.

Mendlewicz, J., Fieve, R. R., Rainer, J. D., & Cataldo, M. Affective disorder on paternal and maternal sides: Observations in bipolar (manic-depressive) patients with and without a family history. *British Journal of Psychiatry*, 1973, *122*, 31–34.

Mendlewicz, J., Fieve, R. R., Rainer, J. D., & Fleiss, J. L. Manic-depressive illness: A comparative study of patients with and without a family history. *British Journal of Psychiatry*, 1972, *120*, 523–530.

Mendlewicz, J., Fieve, R. R., & Stallone, F. Relationship between effectiveness of lithium therapy and family history. *American Journal of Psychiatry*, 1973, *130*, 1011–1013.

Mendlewicz, J. & Fleiss, J. L. Linkage studies with X-chromosome markers in bipolar (manic-depressive) and unipolar (depressive) illnesses. *Biological Psychiatry*, 1974, *9*, 261–294.

Mendlewicz, J., Fleiss, J. L., & Fieve, R. R. Evidence for X-linkage in the transmission of manic-depressive illness. *Journal of the American Medical Association*, 1972, *222*, 1624–1627.

Mendlewicz, J., Fleiss, J. L., & Fieve, R. R. Linkage studies in affective disorders: The Xg blood group and manic-depressive illness. In R. R. Fieve, D. Rosenthal, & H. Brill (Eds.), *Genetic research in psychiatry*. Baltimore, Maryland: Johns Hopkins Univ. Press, 1975.

Mendlewicz, J. & Rainer, J. D. Morbidity risk and genetic transmission in manic-depressive illness. *American Journal of Human Genetics*, 1974, 26, 692–701.

Morrison, J., Winokur, G., Crowe, R., & Clancy, J. The Iowa 500: The first follow-up. *Archives of General Psychiatry*, 1973, 29, 678–682.

Nystrom, S. & Lindegard, B. Depression: Predisposing factors. *Acta Psychiatrica Scandinavica*, 1975, 51, 77–87.

Paykel, E. S. & Weissman, M. M. Social adjustment and depression. *Archives of General Psychiatry*, 1973, 28, 659–663.

Perris, C. A study of bipolar (manic-depressive) and unipolar recurrent depressive psychoses. *Acta Psychiatrica Scandinavica*. 1966, 42 (Supplement 194), 1–188.

Perris, C. Genetic transmission of depressive psychoses. *Acta Psychiatrica Scandinavica*, 1968, 44, 238–248.

Perris, C. The separation of bipolar (manic-depressive) from unipolar recurrent depressive psychoses. *Behavioral Neuropsychiatry*, 1969, 1, 17–25.

Perris, C. Abnormality on paternal and maternal sides: Observations in bipolar (manic-depressive) and unipolar depressive psychoses. *British Journal of Psychiatry*, 1971, 118, 207–210.

Perris, C. The genetics of affective disorders. In J. Mendels (Ed.), *Biological psychiatry*. New York: Wiley-Interscience, 1973.

Pert, A., Rosenblatt, J. E., Sivit, C., Pert, C. B., & Bunney, W. E., Jr. Long term treatment with lithium prevents the development of dopamine receptor supersensitivity. *Science*, 1978, 201, 171–173.

Post, R. M. & Kopanda, R. T. Cocaine, kindling, and psychosis. *American Journal of Psychiatry*, 1976, 133, 627–633.

Prange, A. J., Wilson, I. C., Lynn, C. W., Alltop, L. B., & Stikeleather, R. A. L-tryptophan in mania. *Archives of General Psychiatry*, 1974, 30, 56–62.

Prien, R. F., Klett, C. J., & Caffey, E. M., Jr. Lithium carbonate and imipramine in prevention of affective episodes. *Archives of General Psychiatry*, 1973, 29, 420–425.

Prien, R. F., Klett, C. J., & Caffey, E. M., Jr. Lithium prophylaxis in recurrent affective illness. *American Journal of Psychiatry*, 1974, 131, 198–203.

Quitkin, F., Rifkin, A., & Klein, D. F. Prophylaxis of affective disorders: Current status of knowledge. *Archives of General Psychiatry*, 1976, 33, 337–341.

Race, R. R. & Sanger, R. Xg and sex chromosome abnormalities. *British Medical Bulletin*, 1969, 25, 99–103.

Reich, T., Clayton, P. J., & Winokur, G. Family history studies: V. The genetics of mania. *American Journal of Psychiatry*, 1969, 125, 1358–1369.

Reich, L. H., Davies, R. K., & Himmelhoch, J. M. Excessive alcohol use in manic-depressive illness. *American Journal of Psychiatry*, 1974, 131, 83–89.

Renwick, J. H. & Schulze, J. An analysis of some data on the linkage between the Xg blood group and color blindness in man. *American Journal of Human Genetics*, 1964, 16, 410–418.

Sack, R. & Goodwin, F. K. The "pharmacological bridge": A view from the clinical shores. *Psychopharmacology Bulletin*, 1974, 10, 52–53.

Shobe, F. O. & Brion, P. Long-term prognosis in manic-depressive illness. *Archives of General Psychiatry*, 1971, 24, 334–337.

Slater, E. Expectation of abnormality on paternal and maternal sides: A computational model. *Journal of Medical Genetics*, 1966, 3, 159–161.

Slater, E., Maxwell, J., & Price, J. S. Distribution of ancestral secondary cases in bipolar affective disorders. *British Journal of Psychiatry*, 1971, 118, 215–218.

Tagliamonte, A., Tagliamonte, P., Perez-Cruet, J., Stern, S., & Gressa, G. L. Effect of psychotropic drugs on tryptophan concentration in the rat brain. *Journal of Pharmacology and Experimental Therapeutics*, 1971, *177*, 475–480.

Taylor, M. & Abrams, R. Manic states: A genetic study of early and late onset affective disorders. *Archives of General Psychiatry*, 1973, *28*, 656–658.

Thuline, H. C., Hodgkin, W. E., Fraser, G. R., & Motulsky, A. G. Genetics of protan and deutan color vision anomalies: An instructive family. *American Journal of Human Genetics*, 1969, *21*, 581–592.

Weissman, M. M., Kasl, S. V., & Klerman, G. L. Follow-up of depressed women after maintenance treatment. *American Journal of Psychiatry*, 1976, *133*, 757–759.

Weissman, M. & Klerman, G. Sex differences and the epidemiology of depression. *Archives of General Psychiatry*, 1977, *34*, 98–111.

Winokur, G. Genetic findings and methodological considerations in manic depressive disease. *British Journal of Psychiatry*, 1970, *117*, 267–274.

Winokur, G. The genetics of manic-depressive illness. In R. R. Fieve (Ed.), *Depression in the 1970's: Modern theory and research*. The Hague: Excerpta Medica, 1971.

Winokur, G. The Iowa 500: Heterogeneity and course in manic-depressive illness (bipolar). *Comprehensive Psychiatry*, 1975, *16*, 125–131.

Winokur, G., Cadoret, R., Baker, M., & Dorzab, J. Depression spectrum disease versus pure depressive disease: Some further data. *British Journal of Psychiatry*, 1975, *127*, 75–77.

Winokur, G., Cadoret, R., Dorzab, J., & Baker, M. Depressive disease: A genetic study. *Archives of General Psychiatry*, 1971, *24*, 135–144.

Winokur, G. & Clayton, P. Family history studies: I. Two types of affective disorders separated according to genetic and clinical factors. In J. Wortis (Ed.), *Recent advances in biological psychiatry* (Vol. 9). New York: Plenum, 1967.

Winokur, G., Clayton, P. J., & Reich, T. *Manic depressive disease*. Saint Louis, Missouri: Mosby, 1969.

Winokur, G. & Tanna, V. L. Possible role of X-linked dominant factor in manic depressive disease. *Diseases of the Nervous System*, 1969, *30*, 89–94.

CHAPTER 3

Neurotic Depression: The Endogenous–Neurotic Distinction

Don C. Fowles and Frank Gersh

INTRODUCTION

In this chapter and the one that follows our concern will be with the diagnosis of neurotic depression. This diagnosis has been applied to an increasing number of patients over the years. During an examination of the discharge records of patients hospitalized at the Massachusetts Mental Health Center during the first 6 months of the years 1945, 1955, and 1965, Rosenthal (1966) found that psychoneurotic depressive reactions increased from 5 to 69% of all depressions, whereas psychotic depressions decreased from 95 to 31%. A similar preponderance of neurotic depressions was reported by Paykel, Klerman, and Prusoff (1974). Despite the large numbers of patients involved, neurotic depression has been a neglected topic. As Paykel (1972a) has noted, the current formal diagnostic schema provide multiple categories for psychotic depressives, but only one for neurotic depressives. A review of textbooks of psychiatry and abnormal psychology reveals a highly variable and inconsistent formulation of neurotic depression.

55

The Psychobiology of the Depressive Disorders:
Implications for the Effects of Stress

In this chapter we will focus on the distinction between neurotic depression, on the one hand, and endogenous or psychotic depression, on the other hand. In so doing, we will be concerned with tracing the evolution of the concept and evaluating the evidence for its validity. In the following chapter we will be concerned with the question of whether finer subdivisions than the gross endogenous–neurotic distinction result in a more adequate conceptualization of the depressions. We will particularly emphasize the concept of anxious depression and its relationship to both neurotic and endogenous depression and to anxiety neurosis.

HISTORICAL OVERVIEW

The roots of the distinction between psychotic and neurotic depression date back to the theoretical formulations of Kraepelin and other early investigators. Several historical themes have coalesced into the more recent concept of endogenous versus neurotic depression, which many investigators treat as the equivalent of endogenous versus reactive, or of psychotic versus neurotic, depression. Although there clearly are conceptual differences in the meaning of endogenous–reactive as opposed to psychotic–neurotic depression (Rosenthal & Klerman; 1966; Mendels & Cochrane, 1968), in practice they have been used interchangeably by many authors (Kendell, 1976). We will use endogenous–neurotic, the most often used combination, except where an author's own usage or an emphasis on a particular conceptualization dictates otherwise.

The rich history of debate on endogenous–neurotic depression is important both because it has subsumed many basic issues and because there appears to be an impressive amount of data supporting the validity of this distinction. A review of this literature will serve to clarify the nature and status of this dichotomy and to provide a background against which to evaluate recent studies of finer subdivisions of depression. We are indebted to Rosenthal and Klerman (1966), Mendels and Cochrane (1968), and Klerman (1972) for their reviews of the early history of endogenous–neurotic depression, to which the interested reader is referred for a more extensive coverage.

The seeds of this debate were sown in 1893 when Mobius first introduced the etiologic distinction between endogenous and reactive disorders (Becker, 1974). Applying a similar division within the affective disorders, Kraepelin distinguished between psychogenic and endogenous depression on the basis of emotional reactivity during the illness. Endogenous depressions were alleged to be nonreactive to external events and were viewed as psychotic, implying an organic etiology, whereas psychogenic depressions were believed to be emotionally affected by events and were not psychotic.

Hence, Kraepelin equated reactivity to the environment during the depression with a psychogenic etiology and nonreactivity with an organic etiology.

Gillespie (1929) argued that, in terms of presenting symptoms, depressions could be divided into those which are autonomous (showing no emotional response to changes in the environment) versus those which are reactive. Although Gillespie did not attribute etiologic significance to this distinction, others saw a parallel with Kraepelin's classification and viewed autonomous depression as having an endogenous etiology, whereas reactive patients were assumed to have a psychogenic etiology (Mendels & Cochrane, 1968). Gillespie (1926), as well as many other authors, emphasized the presence of normal, well-adjusted, premorbid personalities among his autonomous (or endogenous) depressions as contrasted with a range of "personality defects" in the premorbid personalities among the reactive depressions (Rosenthal & Klerman, 1966). The latter included neurotic personalities, alcoholism, hysterical and hypochondriacal symptoms, worrying, shyness, and emotionality. Other authors have used the term psychoneurotic rather than reactive to designate the type of depression associated with a poor premorbid personality.

In a classic paper, Mapother (1926) assaulted the endogenous–neurotic distinction and took the position that it reflects only differences in severity. In one of the few, early empirical studies, Lewis (1934, 1938) evaluated these arguments by examining the symptoms of hospitalized depressed patients. He concluded that it was impossible to distinguish two discrete groups of depressed patients on the basis of the presence of a precipitating event, emotional reactivity during the depression, or outcome, thereby supporting Mapother's position.

Thus debate has flared sporadically between the dualists, who maintain that there are two forms of affective disorder, and the monists, who argue that there is essentially a single disorder varying only in severity. In the dualist view the two forms of depression differ in terms of etiology (psychogenic versus organic), reactivity to environmental events during depression, and premorbid personality. The monists, on the other hand, emphasized the greater severity of endogenous depression. Differences have also been noted in clinical symptomatology. Although the symptoms which discriminate vary somewhat according to author, Rosenthal and Klerman (1966) listed the following (in addition to reactivity and severity already mentioned) as representative of those believed to characterize endogenous depression:

1. Feelings of guilt, remorse, and unworthiness (in contrast to self-pity and blaming the environment)
2. Insomnia, especially with middle of the night and early morning awakening
3. Depression which is worse in the morning

4. Retardation
5. Agitation
6. Visceral symptoms
7. Decreased sexual potency and desire, loss of menses
8. Weight loss
9. Loss of interest and general lassitude

Although the endogenous–neurotic debate has focused primarily on the relationship of neurotic and endogenous depression, that is, on whether the differences are qualitative or only quantitative—similar questions have been raised concerning the degree to which neurotic depression may be separated from anxiety neurosis. Thus the monist–dualist debate has been extended into the anxiety-based disorders, particularly in England where some professionals consider anxiety neurosis to be an affective disorder. Here again, the issue is whether anxiety and depression are qualitatively different syndromes, or whether they lie on a single continuum of severity. Mapother (1926) argued that anxiety neurosis was a point on the continuum running from normal adjustment to psychotic depression. Garmany (1956, 1958), on the other hand, characterized the two conditions as similar but distinct syndromes. More recently, Derogatis, Klerman, and Lipman (1972) have summarized evidence in support of both positions. They concluded that it is clear that a distinction can be made between anxiety and depression, but that the pivotal question is "whether differences observed are of a magnitude to be clinically significant [p. 392]."

The distinction between anxiety and depression involves a question as to the nature of the motor symptom of agitation, which has been viewed as both an indication of anxiety and as a symptom of depression. In the official nomenclature used in the United States, it is included as an important symptom of involutional melancholia, placing it among the depressive psychoses. It is mentioned at this point because agitation sometimes is included in the concept of endogenous depression, but it may also be associated with the anxious depression discussed in the next chapter. Thus the relationship between agitation and endogenous depression will be mentioned throughout this chapter, and the topic of anxiety and agitation will be discussed more fully in the following chapter.

The earlier literature provided little definitive evidence on these issues, with the result that interest in them waned. In the late 1950s and early 1960s, however, three developments converged to enhance interest in, and facilitate research on, subtypes of depression. The primary factors increasing interest in diagnosis were the already widespread use of electroconvulsive therapy (ECT) and the introduction of antidepressant drugs coupled with clinical observations that these treatments were more effective with some patients than with others. At the same time, the increased availability of high-speed computers facilitated the use of factor analysis and other multivariate statistical techniques for examining symptom clusters with the promise of more accurate subtype diagnosis.

Electroconvulsive therapy and antidepressant drugs were alleged to be most effective with depressed patients who had severely depressed mood, diurnal mood fluctuations, insomnia, retardation and–or agitation, and normal adjustment during nondepressed periods. These patients were characterized as experiencing endogenous depressions, despite the lack of any clear-cut evidence regarding etiology. The belief that the endogenous depressions responded best to biologic treatments nicely complemented the earlier view that only reactive depressions responded well to psychotherapeutic intervention, and served to strengthen the hypothesis that a psychogenic versus organic dichotomy was involved. It also added the response to biologic treatments to the list of criteria which were brought to bear on the classification of depressive subtypes.

FACTOR-ANALYTIC STUDIES OF ENDOGENOUS AND NEUROTIC DEPRESSION

The application of factor-analytic techniques to the study of endogenous and neurotic depression has played a major role in the modern studies of the classification of depression. A key concern in many of these studies has been the monist–dualist debate over whether there are two types of depression or a single type differing only along a dimension of severity. In addition, such studies provide information concerning the characteristics and correlates of this major subdivision of depression. Our major interest in briefly reviewing these studies is to clarify the meaning of endogenous and neurotic depression and to point out ambiguities which are relevant to more recent studies of depression subtypes. The reader is referred to several more extensive reviews of this area (Beck, 1967; Becker, 1974; Eysenck, 1970; Kendell, 1976; Kiloh & Garside, 1963; Mendels & Cochrane, 1968; Paykel, Prusoff, & Klerman, 1971; Rosenthal & Klerman, 1966).

In view of the importance of factor-analytic studies in the development of subtypes of depression, several comments are in order before proceeding further. First, in many studies the primary data have been clinicians' ratings of symptoms. As pointed out by several investigators (Kendell, 1976; Mendels & Cochrane, 1968; McConaghy, Joffe, & Murphy, 1967; Pilowsky, Levine, & Boulton, 1969), one must always be concerned that the resulting factors may reflect only the raters' biases and implicit theories, as opposed to the patients' symptoms. Second, the results of factor-analytic studies vary from study to study as a result of differences in methodology and the particular statistical techniques involved. These methodological issues can be quite esoteric, making it difficult to evaluate the results of such studies in the absence of a degree of consensus which is rare in this literature. Moreover, the investigators employing these statistical techniques often have not been fully aware of their limitations (Kendell, 1976). Third, the application of factor-analytic techniques necessitates certain assumptions about nature (e.g., a hierarchical model without interaction terms) which may well be false (Lykken, 1971). In view of this, Lykken (1971) argues that factor analysis be viewed as generating hypotheses and a means of operationalizing them, but that factors are to be taken seriously only when they have been validated by demonstrating important, external correlates.

Finally, it is important to keep in mind that a factor is a dimension rather than a diagnostic type. In clinical studies, a factor reflects an intercorrelation among symptoms within the population being studied. The demonstration that two or more factors are necessary to account for symptom variance means that two or more symptom clusters can be identified, not necessarily that subtypes should be created to correspond to the factors. The ease with which a factor can be translated into a diagnostic type depends on how patients are distributed in factor space (i.e., on the distributions obtained when patients are plotted as a function of their scores on each factor). When this is done, it may turn out that there are areas of low density, as in the middle portion of a bimodal distribution. If this is the case, the clinician is likely to think in terms of a subtype (perhaps, though not necessarily, corresponding to the factor dimension). Alternatively, patients may be continuously distributed in factor space, making it difficult (and possibly arbitrary) to determine the cut-off points necessary for the creation of diagnostic categories. These and other important problems concerning the application of factor analysis are discussed by Eysenck (1970), who is often credited with clarifying the issues in the endogenous–reactive literature. Hamilton (1967) and Paykel, Prusoff, & Klerman (1971) also include a sophisticated treatment of some of these issues.

At the very least, the factor-analytic studies of endogenous and reactive depression provide a systematic investigation of how these diagnostic labels are used by clinicians, and the extent to which there is a consensus about their meaning. In addition, insofar as rater bias is minimal, these studies offer valuable information about the varied clinical pictures to be found among patients diagnosed as depressed. That this may be the case is indicated by one study which obtained similar results using patients' self-reports (Pilowsky, Levine, & Boulton, 1969) and by a number of studies demonstrating that the endogenous–reactive (or psychotic–neurotic) distinction predicts response to treatment.

Results of Factor-Analytic Studies

Mendels and Cochrane (1968) reviewed seven factor-analytic studies (Carney, Roth, & Garside, 1965; Hamilton & White, 1959; Hordern, 1965;

Kiloh & Garside, 1963; Mendels & Cochrane, 1967; Rosenthal & Gudeman, 1967; Rosenthal & Klerman, 1966) which extracted a factor corresponding to endogenous depression. They tabulated the number of studies in which a given symptom showed a significant loading either in the negative or positive direction on the endogenous factor. There was said to be *perfect agreement* across studies when all studies rating a symptom found it to be significantly loaded on endogenous depression in the same direction and *fair agreement* when at least 75% of the studies agreed. Eight items were found in the perfect agreement category, all of them loading positively on the endogenous end: (*a*) retardation; (*b*) depth of depression; (*c*) lacking in reactivity to environmental changes; (*d*) loss of interest in life; (*e*) visceral symptoms; (*f*) absence of a precipitating stress; (*g*) middle of the night insomnia; and (*h*) not showing self-pity. The nine fair agreement items were (*a*) older age; (*b*) previous episodes; (*c*) weight loss; (*d*) early morning waking; (*e*) self-reproach or guilt; (*f*) suicidal thoughts; (*g*) suicidal attempts; and (*h*) not showing hysterical traits or inadequate personality. Finally, there are a number of items which, although they failed to meet the criterion of being rated in four or more studies, nevertheless load only on endogenous depression. These included delusions, hallucinations, and a previous manic attack. Agitation was not consistently associated with endogenous depression. In a similar review of six factor-analytic studies, Costello (1970) pointed out that only the symptom of retardation was found to be significantly associated with endogenous depression in all studies.[1]

These results showed considerable consensus that a severe, retarded, psychotic depression exemplifies endogenous depression. What other psychotic depressions might be subsumed by the term is far less clear. Agitated psychotic depression is not unanimously included in the concept of endogenous depression. Hamilton and White (1959) even suggest that agitated depression corresponds to reactive depression. Similarly, it is not clear how reactive psychotic depression (e.g., Kaplan & Sadock, 1972) would be classified on this dimension: It might be endogenous because many clinicians equate endogenous and psychotic, or it might be grouped with many neurotics at the reactive end. These ambiguities undoubtedly reflect, at least in part, variations in the view of endogenous depression among clinicians. As Kendell (1976) has pointed out, he and numerous other writers have treated endogenous—reactive depressions as the equivalent of psychotic—neurotic depressions. Other clinicians, particularly in North America, have defined endogenous—reactive depressions primarily in terms of whether or not the depression was preceded by an obvious stressor. It is probably safe to conclude from the factor-analytic studies that in terms of presenting symptoms, a retarded, psychotic depression would be viewed as endogenous by

[1] There is no contradiction between this statement by Costello (1970) and Mendels and Cochrane's (1968) perfect agreement list. An item which was not rated in all studies would not meet Costello's requirements but would meet Mendel's and Cochrane's as long as it was associated with endogenous depression in those studies in which it was rated.

both groups. On the other hand, for many authors endogenous is the same as psychotic, and several of the factor-analytic studies have been consistent with this view.[2] Which view is supported by the results of a factor analysis probably depends on methodological variables such as the patients and symptoms included and the particular orientation of the factor.

A special comment is needed with respect to the association of reactive depression with precipitating events and reactivity during depression. As mentioned above, lack of precipitating event and lack in reactivity to environmental changes were both in Mendels and Cochrane's perfect agreement list for endogenous depression. However, there seems to be a notable difference in the degree of association: as seen in their Table 1, "reactivity of depression" had loadings of $-.60$, $-.26$, $-.67$, and $-.57$ in the various studies, whereas the factor loadings for "precipitants" were lower ($-.48$, $-.29$, $-.23$, $-.40$, and $-.35$). This suggests that reactivity during depression is more closely associated with reactive depression than is the presence of a precipitating event, a conclusion which is consistent with historical views of endogenous depression that place primary emphasis on a lack of reactivity and acknowledge that precipitants may be found (Rosenthal & Klerman, 1966).

An inspection of the data on the neurotic subgroup in the seven studies examined by Mendels and Cochrane (1968) revealed that, except for reactivity and the presence of a precipitating event, items rarely loaded as highly on the neurotic factor as on the endogenous factor. This observation led several investigators to suggest that reactive depression seems to be even more loosely defined than endogenous depression. Mendels and Cochrane (1968) speculate that it may involve depression as a symptom in a variety of other disorders. Another possible explanation was proposed by Kiloh, Andrews, Neilson, and Bianchi (1972), who suggested that the diagnosis of neurotic depression is based primarily on the absence of endogenous depression and, consequently, consists of a heterogeneous group of patients. In their view, the factor-analytic evidence that neurotic depression is a distinct syndrome is an artifact which masks several distinct subtypes. Both of these concepts of neurotic depression suggest that the disorder may be composed of a heterogeneous group of patients, and that it remains to be determined empirically whether the group can be differentiated into distinct subgroups. Heterogeneity would explain low factor loadings as well as the lack of consistency across studies.

All of the studies just reviewed depended on the clinicians' ratings of symptoms as the primary data and thus are subject to bias on the basis of theoretical preconceptions. Paykel, Prusoff, and Klerman (1971) attempted

---

[2] As these studies predated the current interest in unipolar and bipolar depression, that distinction was not taken into account. All that can be said is that previous manic attacks were associated with the endogenous end (though not strongly), indicating that bipolar patients would be included.

to minimize this effect by having a research assistant assess precipitating events and the patient fill out the Maudsley Personality Inventory (MPI), both after the patient had recovered from the depression. Any bias on the part of the psychiatrist rating the symptoms (at the time of hospitalization) could not influence these additional sources of information. Since both precipitating events and MPI Neuroticism were associated with the neurotic end of the endogenous–neurotic factor, the symptom ratings on this factor cannot be attributed primarily to rater bias.

Another study (Pilowsky, Levine, & Boulton, 1969) eliminated rater bias by employing patients' self-ratings, taking care to obtain them prior to any interviews with the hospital psychiatric staff, and found support for an endogenous depression which resembled the results of the factor-analytic studies reviewed. In this study, a numerical clustering technique was used to develop a classificatory system, and thus diagnostic subtypes, rather than factors, were defined. Two depressive subtypes emerged, one of which (Class B) was described as corresponding to endogenous depression. These patients were characterized as showing "constant depression, retardation, loss of libido, loss of appetite, general insomnia, dry mouth, loss of interest, and poor concentration [p. 942]." Items which differentiated them from the other depressive group were retardation, poor appetite with weight loss, poor sleep, and dry mouth. The other depressive subtype (Class A) was less clearly defined. They were younger and reported more financial and housing problems, an absence of sleep disturbance, diurnal variation with depression worse in the evening, greater irritability, concern over bodily health, guilt, self-depreciation, and paranoid trends. The authors suggest that this group represents a nonspecific stress reaction of a depressive type that is not limited to neurotic patients.

The similarities between this study and those using clinicians' ratings include an endogenous depressive group that is relatively well-defined and characterized by a psychotic retarded depression and a second, more loosely defined, depressive group which appears to be more reactive to the environment. It should be stressed, on the other hand, that the match with hospital diagnosis was far from dramatic: Of the 51 patients in the Class B subtype, only 18 were diagnosed as having an endogenous depression, 12 were diagnosed as having a neurotic depression, 10 were diagnosed as exhibiting other illnesses with depressive features, 8 were diagnosed as having nondepressive neuroses, and 3 were diagnosed as having nondepressive psychoses. The source of this diagnostic heterogeneity is unclear. It could reflect the unreliability of self-reports or hospital diagnosis, problems with the rules for assigning patients to classes, the use of a primarily outpatient sample, or a host of other variables.

In summary, it can be seen that a large number of factor-analytic studies and one self-report study provide evidence for the existence of a fairly well-defined, endogenous symptom cluster and a vaguer, neurotic symptom cluster. The traditional criteria for distinguishing the two types of depression—presence or absence of a precipitating stress, presence or absence of reactivity to the environment and a good, versus a poor, premorbid personality—appear to be of value in classifying patients as exhibiting endogenous or reactive depression. Endogenous depressives are lacking in reactivity to the environment, have fewer precipitants, and do not have hysterical or neurotic traits or an inadequate personality, whereas neurotic depressives are thought to show the converse. At the same time, it should be stressed that there is a lot of variability from study to study. Therefore, while the endogenous–neurotic factor is readily identifiable in these studies, its precise definition is not consistent across studies. Furthermore, it accounts for a modest portion of the variance (Paykel, Prusoff, & Klerman, 1971) and, as would be expected for any diagnostic system involving a single dichotomy, it "does not do justice to the variety and diversity of depressive illness [Kendell, 1976, p. 19]."

Conceptualizations of the Endogenous–Reactive Dichotomy

The conclusion that an endogenous–neurotic factor can be demonstrated says little about how to interpret these results. As indicated in the historical section, much discussion has centered on the monist versus dualist question of whether one or two dimensions are necessary to account for the endogenous–neurotic concept. There has also been controversy over whether a dimensional or categorical view is more appropriate, operationally defined in terms of whether or not discontinuities (e.g., bimodal distributions) can be demonstrated when patients are plotted as a function of their factor scores. Eysenck (1970) summarized these issues and adopted the dualist view that two factors, or dimensions, are necessary to account for the results, but that no decision can be made as to the distribution of patients in factor space because it is impossible to obtain an unbiased sample. Most studies have reported two orthogonal factors, one termed a "general" factor reflecting severity and the other, a bipolar endogenous–neurotic factor. Rotation of these factors produces separate (and orthogonal) endogenous and neurotic factors. According to Eysenck, the choice of rotated or unrotated factors is a matter of theoretical preference, not an issue determined by the data of factor analyses. Either version produces a two-dimensional space which distinguishes both severity and endogenous versus neurotic symptoms. This conclusion, that there is a bipolar factor orthogonal to severity, may require a slight modification in view of data presented by Paykel, Prusoff, and Klerman (1971). They found that the endogenous and neurotic items were not quite bipolar and that severity was fairly highly correlated with endogenous depression. Thus both the bipolarity and the orthogonality appear to be somewhat forced.

Kendell (1968, 1969, 1976; Kendell & Gourlay, 1970) has offered a compromise between the monist and dualist positions in his psychotic–neurotic continuum formulation. In his most recent treatment of this topic (Kendell, 1976), he emphasizes that the differences between psychotic and neurotic depressions are not merely a function of severity, but that there is no basis for establishing a boundary between them (i.e., patients are distributed continuously on the psychotic–neurotic dimension). This acceptance of qualitative differences between neurotic and psychotic depression is very close to the dualist view, and it indicates a growing consensus on this point. In fact, the addition of a dimension of severity would bring Kendell very close to the dualist position adopted by Eysenck (1970). Kendell (1976) has noted that the failure to take into account differences in severity, as well as type of depression, is a weakness of his model. Thus, there is some agreement on the importance of severity, even though Kendell has not incorporated this into his own position. There does remain a continuing debate over the nature of the distribution on the endogenous–neurotic dimension.[3] As noted above, an ultimate answer to the distribution question will be extremely difficult to achieve because psychiatric patients may represent a biased sample from the general population of depressed individuals. However, the evidence strongly favors a continuum at the present (Paykel, Prusoff, & Klerman, 1971).

PREDICTION OF RESPONSE TO SOMATIC TREATMENT

It was stated on pages 59–60 that the results of factor analyses need to be supported by external validity data. Studies of response to treatment by electroconvulsive therapy (ECT) and antidepressant drugs have met this need in the case of the endogenous–neurotic distinction. In these studies, as in many of the factor-analytic studies, the term neurotic was used instead of reactive.

Electroconvulsive Therapy

There has been a long-standing belief among clinicians that endogenous depressions respond well to ECT but that neurotic depressions do not. Several studies have provided partial or full support for this belief. Generally

---

[3] The "Newcastle School," consisting of Roth and his colleagues, have reported a bimodal distribution over the endogenous–neurotic dimension (Carney *et al.*, 1965).

speaking, these studies have either diagnosed patients as endogenous or neurotic, or they have empirically determined which individual symptoms predict response to ECT.

Five studies (Carney, Roth, & Garside, 1965; Carney & Sheffield, 1972; Carney & Sheffield, 1974; Kendell, 1968; Mendels, 1965b) have made explicit the symptoms used to diagnose endogenous versus neurotic depression, and all five have found that patients with endogenous depressions respond better to ECT than do patients with neurotic depressions. Two studies (Hamilton & White, 1960; Rose, 1963) used only the presence or absence of precipitating events to distinguish between endogenous and reactive depressions; one of these (Rose, 1963) found a significantly better outcome for endogenous patients at 1 month after treatment but only marginally so at 3 months, whereas the other (Hamilton & White, 1960) failed to find a difference. However, Hamilton and White (1960) also reported that there were no differences clinically between the nine doubtful endogenous patients who did poorly and the eleven clearly endogenous patients who responded well to ECT. They suggest that perhaps their results are divergent because their sample is more severely ill. Another possibility is the large number of patients with paranoid symptoms (11 out of 49) as they found that these symptoms predicted poor response to ECT. Additionally, the use of a single symptom to determine a diagnosis in both studies may be questioned as single symptoms do not predict as well as scores based on groups of symptoms (e.g., Mendels, 1965a). Moreover, the symptom used may have been poorly chosen: most authors agree that precipitants may be associated with endogenous depression (Rosenthal & Klerman, 1966), and Mendels (1967) reported that the presence of a precipitant was not included as one of the predictors of response to ECT. Whatever the reason for the discrepant results in these two studies, there seems to be strong evidence that a differential response to ECT is associated with the endogenous–neurotic distinction if an adequate number of symptoms are used to make the diagnosis.

Three empirically derived scales have been developed by combining individual symptoms which were associated with a positive response to ECT. The earliest scale was the Hobson Score (Hobson, 1953), which was cross-validated by Roberts (1959) and Mendels (1965a). A second scale was the ECT prediction scale developed by Carney, Roth, & Garside (1965) and cross-validated by Carney and Sheffield (1972). Along the same lines, Mendels (1965c) developed a criterion-keyed scale using a sample of 50 patients and later modified the scale (Mendels, 1967) on the basis of a larger sample of 100 patients (which included the original 50). One study (Abrams, Fink, & Feldstein, 1973) rated 76 inpatients on many of the items used by Mendels (1967) and Carney et al. (1965) and evaluated their response to treatment using the Hamilton Scale 24 hr after the last ECT treatment. In contrast to the other studies, Abrams, Fink, and Feldstein (1973) did not find variables to correlate with changes in the Hamilton Scale scores. As the length of time between ECT and follow-up differed from all previous studies, the negative results may possibly be attributed to this variable.

All of these scales overlap considerably with the endogenous–neurotic dichotomy. Roberts (1959) showed that the Hobson Score was highly correlated with clinical diagnoses of neurotic versus psychotic depression, and Mendels (1965a) commented that the Hobson Score corresponded to the endogenous–reactive dimension. Similarly, while Carney et al. (1965) and Carney and Sheffield (1972) found that their ECT prediction scale predicted outcome slightly better (no tests of significance were reported) than ratings of the endogenous–neurotic dimension using the Newcastle Scale, the correlation between these two scores was just over .60 (Carney et al., 1965, p. 666). Furthermore, when the magnitude of the loadings for individual symptoms on the endogenous–neurotic factor and the correlations of those symptoms with ECT outcome at 6 months were compared, the pattern of correlations–loadings was essentially identical. This was shown by a correlation of .96 between the magnitude of the correlations and factor loadings (p. 663). Finally, Mendels (1967) stresses that, in his ECT prediction scale, neurotic traits are associated with a poor response whereas symptoms usually viewed as characteristic of manic-depressive psychosis or endogenous depression predicted a good response.

These studies, then, have provided a substantial amount of evidence that the endogenous–neurotic distinction is significantly associated with response to ECT. They have also provided a more positive definition of the neurotic or reactive end of the dimension than did the factor-analytic studies, and the prominence of neurotic symptoms justifies a preference for the term neurotic rather than reactive. For example, Mendels' (1967) ECT prediction scale included the following as poor prognostic features: neurotic traits in childhood or adulthood, "inadequate personality," hypochondriasis, and hysterical attitude to illness. The poor prognostic items in the Carney et al. (1965) ECT prediction scale were hypochondriasis, hysterical features or attitude, depression worse in P.M., anxiety, and self-pity; anxiety and blaming others were the negatively loaded (i.e., neurotic) items on their endogenous–neurotic diagnostic scale. In Hobson's Score, as used by Mendels (1965a), the poor prognostic items were neurotic symptoms in childhood or adult life, hypochondriasis, depersonalization, emotional lability, fluctuating course, ill-adjusted previous personality, and a hysterical attitude toward illness. As in the factor-analytic studies, there is considerable variation from study to study, but items recognizable as characteristic of neurotic depression occur frequently.

There is also some indication that agitation belongs in the endogenous group of symptoms where response to ECT is concerned. This evidence comes primarily from Carney and his colleagues, who included agitation as well as retardation in the symptom of "depressive psychomotor activity

(Carney *et al.*, 1965, p. 661)" as part of their endogenous–neurotic diagnostic scale. As this diagnosis was associated with a positive response to ECT in three studies and the authors did not suggest that the inclusion of agitation was inappropriate, this symptom appears to be predictive of a good response to ECT. Moreover, this conclusion is supported by strong clinical impressions that involutional depression (in which agitation is often prominent) responds particularly well to ECT (Slater & Roth, 1969, p. 232).

Finally, the positive results regarding ECT should not be presented without also noting the rampant methodological problems. In all studies, the patients chosen were those judged suitable for ECT by the clinical staff, thus producing a population selected on the basis of variables that were not made explicit. It is likely that there is some selection for severity and against milder, neurotic depressions. Placebo and no-treatment controls are missing and often other treatments are not controlled or not discussed. Consequently, improvement could possibly be confounded with "spontaneous" recovery and–or the effects of concurrent treatments. Blind ratings of improvement are often absent, raising the question of rater bias. The Newcastle group has been particularly sensitive to these issues and has attempted to minimize them by, for example, requiring that improvement be time-locked to ECT in order to avoid spontaneous changes (Carney *et al.*, 1965, pp. 662, 663). They also used raters not involved in treatment, and they found that patients' self-reports of improvement produced similar results (Carney & Sheffield, 1974). These procedures are reassuring although they do not, of course, eliminate all methodological problems. The interested reader is referred to the paper by Costello and Belton (1970) for a critique of the methodological problems in ECT studies.

Antidepressant Drug Therapy

As with response to ECT, patient response to antidepressant drug therapy is believed by many clinicians to be superior in endogenous as compared to neurotic depression. To some extent, there is empirical support for this belief, though there are enough inconsistent findings to at least require qualification. Interpretation of this literature is made difficult by large differences in methodology and procedures from study to study. Nevertheless, a recent comprehensive review of this area reached the conclusion that there is "pharmacological support for the division of depression into endogenous and neurotic types (Bielski & Friedel, 1976, p. 1487)." We tend to agree with this statement, though with the qualifications discussed in the following paragraphs.

The early literature has been reviewed by Raskin (1968), who should be consulted for a more detailed analysis; we will simply highlight the material here. Kuhn (1958) was one of the first to note that patients with endogenous depressions showed a better clinical response to imipramine than other depressive patients, including patients exhibiting reactive depression. Since 1958, numerous reports have confirmed Kuhn's initial observation (Blair, 1960; Delay & Deniker, 1959; Friedman, deMowbray, & Hamilton, 1961; Keup, Apolito, Olinger, Schwartz, & Yachnes, 1960; Kiloh & Garside, 1963). There have also been instances in which investigators have failed to replicate Kuhn's findings (Abraham, Kanter, Rosen, & Standen, 1963; Fleminger & Groden, 1962; Lemere, 1959; Spear, Hall, & Stirland, 1964). These studies are difficult to evaluate as many are impressionistic and either do not present quantitative results, or do not analyze the results statistically. Some include too few patients to perform a statistical analysis or do not employ double-blind control procedures.

One early study (Ball & Kiloh, 1959; Kiloh, Ball, & Garside, 1962) and two later investigations (Deykin & DiMascio, 1972; Raskin, Schulterbrandt, Reatig, & McKeon, 1970) were more careful and supported Kuhn's observation. They employed double-blind treatment (except for Deykin & DiMascio in which all patients received the same drug) with blind rating procedures and presented quantitative results on sufficiently large numbers of patients to allow adequate statistical analysis. These three studies also assessed a wide range of patient characteristics (pre- and posttreatment), permitting more objective assessment and prediction-of-change than the global ratings in early studies. Despite these controls, findings of no differential response to antidepressant drugs by endogenous versus neurotic depressed patients persist in the literature (Greenblatt, Grosser, & Wechsler, 1964; Hordern, Burt, & Holt, 1965; Paykel, 1972b; Raskin & Crook, 1976). In reviewing these more carefully controlled studies, we will summarize those which yielded positive results and then discuss factors which may have contributed to the inconsistent findings of other studies.

An important early study, which used a sample composed entirely of outpatients, found a superior response to imipramine among endogenous as compared with neurotic depressed patients. Kiloh *et al.* (1962) rated 97 depressive outpatients (59 neurotic and 38 endogenous cases) on 60 clinical items, and treated them with imipramine in a double-blind design (see Ball & Kiloh, 1959, for details of the original design). The results of treatment were assessed at 4 weeks and at 6 months. A good result was considered to be a patient who was asymptomatic or whose symptoms were mild enough to permit a full range of activities. Endogenous depressions had a good outcome significantly more frequently than neurotic depressions. Ten features were negatively correlated with improvement: the presence of a precipitating event, self-pity, hypochondriacal features, hysterical features, intensity of depression, suicidal attempts, subjective retardation, irritability, failure of concentration, and restless sleep. The first four of these features appear to be related to neurotic depression. Although, in general, the features associated with good response to imipramine were those characteristic of endogenous depression, there were two major exceptions. Depth of depression and subjective retardation, two of the major symptoms characterizing endogenous depression, were associated with a poor outcome with imipramine.

Kiloh et al. (1962) explained these divergent results by noting that subjective retardation, defined as the patient feeling that his thinking and movements are slowed, is not necessarily the same as true psychomotor retardation. With regard to depth of depression, they point out that there is a widely held clinical impression that the main value of antidepressant drugs is in the milder forms of depression. This belief is also supported by Mendels, who reviews three studies (including Kiloh et al., 1962) reporting a negative correlation between the response to antidepressant drugs and the severity of the illness "as reflected in depressive affect, delusions, suicidal tendencies, and possibly retardation (Mendels, 1967, p. 157)." At the same time, Mendels argues that the response to ECT is positively correlated with severity. Thus it appears that tricyclic antidepressants may work well for patients exhibiting endogenous depression only if their symptoms are not too severe.[4] It should be noted that only outpatients were used in the Kiloh et al. (1962) study, implying a possibly reduced effectiveness of antidepressants with the more severe symptomatology encountered with inpatient populations.

Raskin, Schulterbrandt, Reatig, and McKeon (1970) found a superior response to imipramine among patients with a diagnosis (by the project staff) of psychotic depression, including involutional psychotic reaction, psychotic depressive reaction, or manic-depressive reaction, depressed type. This was a major, multihospital collaborative study sponsored by the National Institute of Mental Health that provided a sample including 395 female and 160 male patients admitted to one of ten hospitals. Admission to the study required moderate depression, though not necessarily a primary diagnosis of depression. Patients were randomly assigned to double-blind treatment with imipramine, chlorpromazine, and a placebo for 5 weeks. They were assessed with eight rating scales and self-report instruments prior to their assignment to treatment and then at 1, 2, 3, 5, and 7 weeks after the start of treatment. Relevant results were that patients with psychotic depressions responded much better to imipramine than to chlorpromazine or a placebo, whereas patients with neurotic depressions showed no difference in their response to chlorpromazine, imipramine, or a placebo. An important aspect of these findings is that the neurotic depressed patients did as well as the psychotic depressed patients who received imipramine. That is, it was the response to

[4] A number of authors (Hordern, 1965; Klein & Davis, 1969; Deykin & DiMascio, 1972; Bielski & Friedel, 1976) have discussed the possibility that amitriptyline is superior to imipramine in the treatment of severe depression, raising the possibility that this generalization may apply more to imipramine than to amitriptyline. However, this superiority of amitriptyline for severe depression cannot be regarded as firmly established (Bielski & Friedel, 1976).

imipramine as compared to a placebo that distinguished the psychotic depressives, rather than a better response in absolute terms. By implication, there would have been no differences in the rate of improvement if only those psychotic and neurotic depressed patients who received imipramine had been compared. Thus, the inclusion of a placebo control may be essential in order to see the differential response to imipramine. Otherwise, the response of neurotic depressed patients to nonspecific (i.e., placebo) treatment factors will obscure a specific drug effect.

One study (Deykin & DiMascio, 1972) is of interest because it attempted to reduce the number of placebo responders by excluding from the major analysis all patients who responded to an active drug within one week. The subjects were 163 women having neurotic or psychotic depressions. The vast majority were outpatients and all of them received amitriptyline. For the 114 patients who were not excluded because of a large response during the first week, there was a strong negative association between their response to amitriptyline and both a history of neurotic symptoms and a clinical diagnosis of neurotic depression. A better outcome was associated with a diagnosis of psychotic depression and an absence of a history of neurotic symptoms. This study supports the suggestions of Raskin et al. (1970) and Kiloh et al. (1962) that a differential response to tricyclic antidepressants may be seen especially with outpatients and with some attempt to eliminate placebo responders.

In contrast to the positive studies just described, several double-blind studies showed no differential response to antidepressants for the two groups of depressives (Burt, Gordon, Holt, & Hordern, 1962; Greenblatt et al., 1964; Hordern et al., 1965; Paykel, 1972b; Raskin & Crook, 1976). Additionally, Wittenborn (1969) found a superior response among patients having reactive depressions as compared with those having involutional and manic-depressive psychoses. The report by Raskin and Crook (1976) requires special comment, as it was based on the same patients as the Raskin et al. (1970) study discussed earlier and yielded, at best, modest results for the endogenous–neurotic distinction. As opposed to the clinical diagnoses used in the earlier report, Raskin and Crook developed a four-group typology based on a Q-technique, or inverse factor analysis. A two-factor solution was stated to provide the best separation among patient types, and these two bipolar factors were used to define four patient types. The attempts to discover differential response to drugs for the four groups were disappointing. The most that could be said was that the Type 3 patients, who were termed as having endogenous depressions, showed the greatest active drug–placebo differences, though this effect was by no means large. The two active drugs, which were equally effective for the Type 3 patients, were imipramine and chlorpromazine.

Numerous possible explanations can be offered for these negative results. One is that the inclusion of depressed patients with a primary diagnosis of schizophrenia or "other neurosis" may have influenced the derivation of patient types: Of the 555 patients in the imipramine–chlorpromazine–placebo study, 82 carried a diagnosis of schizophrenia and 41 were "other neurotic reactions" (Raskin et al., 1970, p. 165). A second possibility is that the use of bipolar factors may have allowed the precise orientation of factors to be determined by characteristics of patients at the nonendogenous end of the factor. Finally, whatever the cause, the Type 3 patients were described as older and severely ill with high scores on the "core symptoms of depression, but they did not score particularly high on the symptoms of anergia and motor retardation (Raskin & Crook, 1976, p. 69)."

Raskin (1974) argued that imipramine is particularly effective for the symptoms of anergia and retardation, and Raskin and Crook suggested that these symptoms account for the differences in the results for the two analyses (i.e., psychotic depressives in the 1970, Raskin et al. study were high on anergia and retardation, whereas Type 3 "endogenous" patients were not in the Raskin and Crook paper). To this, one can add Mendels' (1967) comment that depressive delusions correlated positively with older patient age and the severity of the illness. Given the possibility already discussed that both delusions and the severity of the illness predict a poor response to treatment, the characterization of Type 3 patients as older and severely ill suggests that they may not have been the best candidates for drug therapy. Finally, 21% of the Type 3 patients were schizophrenic and another 32% were neurotic, neither of which would be expected to show a particularly good response to imipramine.[5] It appears, therefore, that this study has defined a somewhat atypical group of patients having "endogenous" depressions, at least when that term is used in the sense of contrasting it with neurotic depression.

One apparently negative study (Greenblatt et al., 1964) involving severely depressed inpatients failed to examine the data in terms of an interaction between drug–placebo and psychotic–neurotic diagnosis as required by the findings from Raskin et al. (1970). Although Greenblatt et al. seemed to find little specificity for treatments as a function of diagnosis, an examination of their Table 3 reveals that the effect of imipramine was superior to that of a placebo (in terms of percentage of patients showing marked improvement) for both manic-depressive, depressed (59 versus 37%) and involutional psychotic depressed patients (42 versus 25%), while it was inferior to the placebo for neurotic depressed patients (71 versus 83%). Although it is not clear that this interaction would be significant because of the small numbers of patients, these results are in the direction of supporting, rather than contradicting, the hypothesis that imipramine is more effective with psychotic rather than with neurotic depressed patients.

Another study (Burt et al., 1962; Hordern, Holt, Burt, & Gordon, 1963;

---

[5] See Table 2 of Raskin and Crook (1970) study.

Hordern et al., 1965) failed to find a better outcome for endogenous versus reactive depressive female inpatients when treated with either imipramine or amitriptyline. However, this study used inpatients and did not include a placebo control, making it impossible to distinguish between a placebo response and true drug response among the reactive depressive patients. It was found that amitriptyline was superior to imipramine among patients having an endogenous depression, especially those over 50 years of age, but apparently not for patients having a reactive depression (Hordern et al., 1963). This suggests that drug effects were more important for patients having endogenous rather than neurotic depressions, which is consistent with the results from Raskin et al. (1970). These investigators seem to have used the terms endogenous—reactive as the equivalent of psychotic—neurotic (Burt et al., 1962, p. 714).

Two studies by Wittenborn (Wittenborn, 1969; Wittenborn, Kiremitci, & Weber, 1973) report a poor response to imipramine and amitriptyline for a combined group of female inpatient depressives with (a) a history of schizophrenic symptoms, (b) at least one manic episode and a prior hospitalization for depression, or (c) an "involutional" picture defined as first hospitalization after age 45. A good response was reported for the "other depressions" to both drugs and, in the imipramine study, patients having "reactive" depressions (first episode with a clear precipitant) were separated from patients having "other depressions" who were found to show a good response. The problems with these studies center on the inappropriateness of the groupings for an endogenous—neurotic comparison, at least in the sense of psychotic—neurotic, and the absence of placebo controls. It would have been better not to include patients with a history of schizophrenia among the poor responders, and the good responders presumably include a heterogeneous group of both neurotic and psychotic depressed patients. A placebo comparison was provided for a small sample of the poor versus good responder groups as a whole, and the results were interpreted as showing that nonspecific factors were not involved in the differences between the good and poor responders to imipramine (Wittenborn, 1969). No placebo comparisons were possible for individual groups because of the small numbers of patients. This somewhat indirect method of controlling for placebo effects with a small sample is not sufficient to raise serious doubts as to the validity of Raskin et al. (1970) finding that many good imipramine responders were also good placebo responders. At the same time, the poor response of the bipolar patients to imipramine and, presumably, amitriptyline is worth noting. Whether the poor response of bipolar patients is to be interpreted as indicating that they should be excluded from a concept of endogenous depression, or whether it reflects a limited effectiveness of the drugs, as in the poor response of older, severely depressed patients, is unclear.

Finally, two studies by Paykel (Paykel, 1972b; Paykel, Klerman, & Prusoff,

1974) call attention to another apparently important variable, the duration of follow-up. In the first study (Paykel, 1972b), a group of 85 female depressed patients, most of whom were outpatients, were given amitriptyline and their response was assessed at 4 weeks. No differences in outcome were found for neurotic and psychotic groups defined by routine clinical diagnosis (DSM-II). Like most studies, the lack of placebo control rendered the negative results ambiguous. Of much greater interest were the results of the second study involving a 10-month follow-up of 190 depressed patients from a variety of sources (outpatient, daypatient, inpatient). Treatment was "uncontrolled and quite diverse (p. 63)." The major systematic predictor of outcome was the endogenous–neurotic distinction based on scores from a factor analysis. A better outcome at 10 months was associated with endogenous depression as indicated by a lower-rated depression, fewer relapses, and fewer suicide attempts. Of particular importance was the finding that the endogenous–neurotic factor predicted the speed of remission. Remission in endogenous depressions tended to require at least 1 month but less than 3 months; patients remitting in less than 1 month or more than 3 months tended to have neurotic depressions. Moreover, for the patients having neurotic (but not the endogenous) depressions, there was a relationship between the initial severity and the time required for remission: Mildly ill neurotic patients tended to remit in less than a month, whereas the patients requiring more than 3 months were moderately or severely ill neurotic depressives. The importance of this study is enhanced by the similarity of the outcome data to the results of an earlier 5–7 year retrospective (i.e., diagnosis was based on case records) follow-up (Kay, Garside, Roy, & Beamish, 1969).

Based on these studies, then, it appears that the good prognosis without relapse for patients having endogenous depressions can be seen with a follow-up of 10 months or longer. What will be seen with shorter follow-ups will depend on the time period involved (e.g., 1 month will minimize the recovery of the endogenous patients) and the composition of the neurotic depressive group (patients with mild neurotic depressions will show a rapid improvement within the first month, patients with severe neurotic depressions will not). How much these patterns might be altered by specific treatments cannot be determined as the treatments were uncontrolled in the Paykel et al. (1974) study. The strong placebo response of neurotic depressives already discussed presumably applies to the milder neurotics, suggesting that this group will recover quickly, regardless of the type of treatment.

The importance of the initial severity of the depression in predicting the speed of remission for patients having a neurotic depression offers an answer to an apparent contradiction between the drug and ECT studies. That is, if a placebo is necessary in order to control for high rates of spontaneous remission among patients experiencing neurotic depressions in these drug studies, why is the same not true of ECT studies? The answer would seem to be that the patients referred for ECT are almost universally described as severely depressed. According to Paykel *et al.* (1974) this should produce a group of neurotic depressed patients who do not show rapid recovery.

Summarizing this section, some portion of the endogenous, or psychotic, depressed patients show a good response to tricyclics as compared to their response when a placebo was prescribed. This effect is complicated by a possible negative correlation between patient response to imipramine, and possibly amitriptyline, and such variables as age, severity, presence of delusions, and suicidal tendencies. Patients exhibiting neurotic depressions show either less response, or no response to tricyclic therapy versus placebo therapy, but some of them show a rapid and marked improvement regardless of treatment. Follow-up studies of 10 months or longer find that endogenous depressed patients have a more complete recovery without relapse, whereas neurotic depressed patients tend to have a more chronic course marked by relapses.

SUMMARY AND CONCLUSIONS

This review of the endogenous–neurotic distinction has been primarily concerned with factor analyses and response to somatic treatments. The factor-analytic studies showed that a large majority of such studies support the dualist position by yielding two orthogonal factors. These factors can be identified, depending on the rotation, as either severity plus a bipolar endogenous–neurotic factor, or as separate endogenous and neurotic factors. The bulk of the evidence has also supported the dimensional view, showing that patients are continuously distributed in this two-dimensional factor space so that many patients show a mixed clinical picture. In terms of the symptoms associated with the endogenous–neurotic distinction, there appeared to be a consensus that a severe retarded depression would be viewed as endogenous, however, there was less agreement concerning other types of depression. At the neurotic end of the continuum, the pattern was even less clearly defined. Anxiety was frequently associated with neurotic or reactive depression and hysterical traits, neurotic traits, or an inadequate premorbid personality also appeared to be characteristic. Reactivity to the environment and presence of precipitants were reported to correlate with the endogenous–neurotic distinction.

The response to ECT studies provided surprisingly consistent results indicating a more positive patient response for endogenous rather than for neurotic depressions. They also supported the interpretation of the endogenous–reactive dichotomy as strongly parallel to a psychotic–neurotic dichotomy corresponding to the dominant British usage. Thus agitated psychotic depression would be included under the heading of endogenous.

Studies of patient response to tricyclic antidepressants also supported the validity of the endogenous–neurotic distinction in the sense that some patients with endogenous depressions show a specific response to these drugs, whereas patients with neurotic depressions tended to show a good response regardless of the treatment. Exactly which patients with endogenous depression respond well to tricyclics is far from clear, but it would appear to be especially those showing psychomotor retardation who are not too severely depressed. Severe delusions, suicidal tendencies, and increasing age may predict a poor response to tricyclic antidepressant therapy. An important 10-month follow-up of depressed patients receiving tricyclics by Paykel et al. (1974) replicated an earlier retrospective study in demonstrating a more positive outcome for patients exhibiting endogenous depressions, thereby supporting the validity of the distinction in terms of course and outcome. It also pointed to important differences in the time course of recovery and to an influence of severity on the speed of remission in patients having neurotic depression. Thus the severity of the symptoms of the patient having a neurotic depression and the duration of the assessment of the response to treatment with tricyclics may be critical factors which influence the results obtained.

Having emphasized the positive aspects of these findings, we should also stress their tentativeness. The problems of method variance and the unreliability of symptom ratings could hardly be exaggerated. This has resulted in different symptoms being used to define the endogenous–neurotic distinction in different studies. Thus, while one can recognize rather large sets of symptoms and characteristics that are associated with this distinction, it is difficult to predict which ones will be found in any given study. It has yet to be determined whether this situation can be remedied by increasing the number of symptoms used for the ratings, on the assumption that individual symptoms are unreliable, or whether what is needed is a careful selection of a small set of key discriminators.

A second problem is that the definition of endogenous–neurotic may well vary as a function of the specific criterion being applied. Differences between the ECT and antidepressant studies have already been noted. In part, this is to be expected, as diagnostic systems developed for a specific purpose are not likely to be identical to those with more general applications (Sokal, 1974). Nevertheless, it remains to be demonstrated whether a single diagnostic system can, in fact, be made consistent with different applications.

Finally, we should make clear that while we have tried to argue that the endogenous–neurotic distinction is valid and predicts clinically important phenomena, it is at best an approximation of an adequate classificatory system. Our intention has been only to demonstrate that this area merits continued attention, with the goal of more clearly defining the clinically important relationships which underlie the results reviewed earlier. We would anticipate that much finer distinctions would have to be made. The problem is to determine which distinctions increase the magnitude of the predictions based on the endogenous–neurotic dimension and in attempt to do so, based on currently available evidence, is the subject of the next chapter.

REFERENCES

Abraham, H. C., Kanter, V. B., Rosen, I., & Standen, J. L. A controlled clinical trial of imipramine (Tofranil) with out-patients. *British Journal of Psychiatry*, 1963, *109*, 286–293.
Abrams, R., Fink, M., & Feldstein, S. Prediction of clinical response to ECT. *British Journal of Psychiatry*, 1973, *122*, 457–460.
Ball, J. R. B. & Kiloh, L. G. A controlled trial of imipramine in treatment of depressive states. *British Medical Journal*, 1959, *2*, 1052–1055.
Beck, A. T. *Depression: Causes and treatment*. Philadelphia: Univ. Pennsylvania Press, 1967.
Becker, J. *Depression: Theory and research*. Washington, D. C.: Winston, 1974.
Bielski, R. J. & Friedel, R. O. Prediction of tricyclic antidepressant response. *Archives of General Psychiatry*, 1976, *33*, 1479–1489.
Blair, D. Treatment of severe depression by imipramine (Tofranil). *Journal of Mental Science*, 1960, *106*, 891–905.
Burt, C. G., Gordon, W. F., Holt, N. F., & Hordern, A. Amitriptyline in depressive states: A controlled trial. *Journal of Mental Science*, 1962, *108*, 711–730.
Carney, M. W. P., Roth, M., & Garside, R. F. The diagnosis of depressive syndromes and the prediction of E.C.T. response. *British Journal of Psychiatry*, 1965, *111*, 659–674.
Carney, M. W. P. & Sheffield, B. F. Depression and the Newcastle scales—their relationship to Hamilton's scale. *British Journal of Psychiatry*, 1972, *121*, 35–40.
Carney, M. W. P. & Sheffield, B. F. The effects of pulse ECT in neurotic and endogenous depression. *British Journal of Psychiatry*, 1974, *125*, 91–94.
Costello, C. G. Classification and psychopathology. In C. G. Costello (Ed.), *Symptoms of psychopathology*. New York: Wiley, 1970.
Costello, C. G. & Belton, G. P. Depression: Treatment. In C. G. Costello (Ed.), *Symptoms of psychopathology*. New York: Wiley, 1970.
Delay, J. & Deniker, P. Efficacy of Tofranil in the treatment of various types of depression: A comparison with other antidepressant drugs. *Canadian Psychiatric Association Journal*, 1959, *4*, S100–S112.
Derogatis, L. R., Klerman, G. L., & Lipman, R. S. Anxiety states and depressive neuroses. *Journal of Nervous and Mental Disease*, 1972, *55*, 392–403.
Deykin, E. Y. & DiMascio, A. Relationship of patient background characteristics to efficacy of pharmacotherapy in depression. *Journal of Nervous and Mental Disease*, 1972, *155*, 209–215.
Eysenck, H. J. The classification of depressive illnesses. *British Journal of Psychiatry*, 1970, *117*, 241–250.
Fleminger, J. J. & Groden, B. M. Clinical features of depression and the response to imipramine ("Tofranil"). *Journal of Mental Science*, 1962, *108*, 101–104.
Friedman, C., deMowbray, M. S., & Hamilton, U. Imipramine (Tofranil) in depressive states. *Journal of Mental Science*, 1961, *107*, 948–953.
Garmany, G. Anxiety states. *British Medical Journal*, 1956, *1*, 943–946.
Garmany, G. Depressive states: Their aetiology and treatment. *British Medical Journal*, 1958, *2*, 341–344.
Gillespie, R. D. Discussion on manic-depressive psychoses. *British Medical Journal*, 1926, *2*, 872–879.

Gillespie, R. D. The clinical differentiation of types of depression. *Guy's Hospital Reports*, 1929, 79, 306–344.

Greenblatt, M., Grosser, G. H., & Wechsler, H. Differential response of hospitalized depressed patients to somatic therapy. *American Journal of Psychiatry*, 1964, 120, 935–943.

Hamilton, M. Development of a rating scale for primary depressive illness. *British Journal of Social and Clinical Psychology*, 1967, 6, 278–296.

Hamilton, M. & White, J. M. Clinical syndromes in depressive states. *Journal of Mental Science*, 1959, 105, 985–998.

Hamilton, M. & White, J. M. Factors related to the outcome of depression treated with E.C.T. *Journal of Mental Science*, 1960, 106, 1031–1041.

Hobson, R. F. Prognostic factors in electric convulsive therapy. *Journal of Neurology, Neuro-surgery and Psychiatry*, 1953, 16, 275–281.

Hordern, A., Holt, N. F., Burt, C. G., & Gordon, W. F. Amitriptyline in depressive states. *British Journal of Psychiatry*, 1963, 109, 815–825.

Hordern, A. The antidepressant drugs. *The New England Journal of Medicine*, 1965, 272, 1159–1169.

Hordern, A., Burt, C. G., & Holt, N. F. *Depressive states: A pharmacotherapeutic study.* Springfield, Illinois: Thomas, 1965.

Kaplan, H., & Sadock, B. J. The psychotic depressive: A clarified psychiatric syndrome with a good treatment prognosis. *Psychosomatics*, 1972, 13, 34–40.

Kay, D. W. K., Garside, R. F., Roy, J. R., & Beamish, P. "Endogenous" and "neurotic" syndromes of depression: A 5- to 7-year follow-up of 104 cases. *British Journal of Psychiatry*, 1969, 115, 389–399.

Kendell, R. E. *The classification of depressive illnesses.* Maudsley Monograph No. 18. London: Oxford Univ. Press, 1968.

Kendell, R. E. The continuum model of depressive illness. *Proceedings Royal Society of Medicine*, 1969, 62, 335–339.

Kendell, R. E. The classification of depressions: A review of contemporary confusion. *British Journal of Psychiatry*, 1976, 129, 15–28.

Kendell, R. E. & Gourlay, J. The clinical distinction between psychotic and neurotic depressions. *British Journal of Psychiatry*, 1970, 117, 257–266.

Keup, W., Apolito, A., Olinger, L., Schwartz, M., & Yachnes, E. Tofranil (imipramine) in the treatment of depressive states. *Journal of Nervous and Mental Disease*, 1960, 130, 146–150.

Kiloh, L. G., Ball, J. R. B., & Garside, R. F. Prognostic factors in treatment of depressive states with imipramine. *British Medical Journal*, 1962, 1, 1225–1227.

Kiloh, L. G. & Garside, R. F. The independence of neurotic depression and endogenous depression. *British Journal of Psychiatry*, 1963, 109, 451–463.

Kiloh, L. G., Andrews, G., Neilson, M., & Bianchi, G. N. The relationship of the syndromes called endogenous and neurotic depression. *British Journal of Psychiatry*, 1972, 121, 183–196.

Klein, D. F., & Davis, J. M. *Diagnosis and drug treatment of psychiatric disorders.* Baltimore: Williams & Wilkins, 1969.

Klerman, G. L. Clinical phenomenology of depression: Implications for research strategy in the psychobiology of the affective disorders. In T. A. Williams, M. M. Katz, & J. A. Shield, Jr. (Eds.), *Recent advances in the psychobiology of the depressive illnesses* (DHEW Publication No. (HSM) 70-9053). Washington, D. C.: U. S. Govt. Printing Office, 1972.

Kuhn, R. The treatment of depressive states with G22355 (imipramine hydrochloride). *American Journal of Psychiatry*, 1958, 115, 459–464.

Lemere, F. Negative results in the treatment of depression with imipramine hydrochloride (Tofranil). *American Journal of Psychiatry*, 1959, 116, 258–259.

Lewis, A. J. Melancholia: A clinical survey of depressive states. *Journal of Mental Science*, 1934, 80, 277–378.

Lewis, A. J. States of depression: Their clinical and aetiological differentiation. *British Medical Journal*, 1938, 2, 875–878.
Lykken, D. T. Multiple factor analysis and personality research. *Journal of Experimental Research in Personality*, 1971, 5, 161–170.
Mapother, E. Discussion on manic-depressive psychosis. *British Medical Journal*, 1926, 2, 872–879.
McConaghy, N., Joffe, A. D., & Murphy, B. The independence of neurotic and endogenous depression. *British Journal of Psychiatry*, 1967, 113, 479–484.
Mendels, J. Electroconvulsive therapy and depression. I. The prognostic significance of clinical factors. *British Journal of Psychiatry*, 1965, 111, 675–681. (a)
Mendels, J. Electroconvulsive therapy and depression. II. Significance of endogenous and reactive syndromes. *British Journal of Psychiatry*, 1965, 111, 682–686. (b)
Mendels, J. Electroconvulsive therapy and depression. III. A method for prognosis. *British Journal of Psychiatry*, 1965, 111, 687–690. (c)
Mendels, J. The prediction of response to electroconvulsive therapy. *American Journal of Psychiatry*, 1967, 124, 153–159.
Mendels, J. & Cochrane, C. The nosology of depression: The endogenous–reactive concept. *American Journal of Psychiatry*, 1968, 124, 1–11.
Mendels, J. & Cochrane, C. Depressive factors and the response to electroconvulsive therapy. In preparation, 1967. Cited by Mendels and Cochrane (1968).
Paykel, E. S. Correlates of a depressive typology. *Archives of General Psychiatry*, 1972, 27, 203–210. (a)
Paykel, E. S. Depressive typologies and response to amitriptyline. *British Journal of Psychiatry*, 1972, 120, 147–156. (b)
Paykel, E. S., Klerman, G. L. & Prusoff, B. A. Treatment setting and clinical depression. *Archives of General Psychiatry*, 1970, 22, 11–21.
Paykel, E. S., Klerman, G. L., & Prusoff, B. A. Prognosis of depression and the endogenous–neurotic distinction. *Psychological Medicine*, 1974, 4, 57–64.
Paykel, E. S., Prusoff, B., & Klerman, G. L. The endogenous–neurotic continuum in depression: Rater independence and factor distributions. *Journal of Psychiatric Research*, 1971, 8, 73–90.
Pilowsky, I., Levine, S., & Boulton, D. M. The classification of depression by numerical taxonomy. *British Journal of Psychiatry*, 1969, 115, 937–945.
Raskin, A. The prediction of antidepressant drug effects: Review and critique. In D. H. Efron, J. O. Cole, J. Levine, & J. R. Wittenborn (Eds.), *Psychopharmacology; a review of progress, 1957–1967*. Public Health Service Publication No. 1836, 1968.
Raskin, A. A guide for drug use in depressive disorders. *American Journal of Psychiatry*, 1974, 131, 181–185.
Raskin, A. & Crook, T. H. The endogenous–neurotic distinction as a predictor of response to antidepressant drugs. *Psychological Medicine*, 1976, 6, 59–70.
Raskin, A., Schulterbrandt, J. G., Reatig, N., & McKeon, J. J. Differential response to chlorpromazine, imipramine, and placebo. *Archives of General Psychiatry*, 1970, 23, 164–173.
Roberts, J. M. Prognostic factors in the electroshock treatment of depressive states. I. Clinical features from history and examination. *Journal of Mental Science*, 1959, 105, 693–702.
Rose, J. T. Reactive and endogenous depressions—response to E.C.T. *British Journal of Psychiatry*, 1963, 109, 213–217.
Rosenthal, S. H. Changes in a population of hospitalized patients with affective disorders. *American Journal of Psychiatry*, 1966, 6, 671–681.
Rosenthal, S. H. & Gudeman, J. E. The endogenous depressive pattern—an empirical investigation. *Archives of General Psychiatry*, 1967, 16, 241–249.
Rosenthal, S. H. & Klerman, G. L. Content and consistency in the endogenous depressive pattern. *British Journal of Psychiatry*, 1966, 112, 471–484.

Slater, E. & Roth, M. *Clinical psychiatry* (3rd ed.). Baltimore, Maryland: Williams & Wilkins, 1969.

Sokal, R. R. Classification: Purposes, principles, progress, prospects. *Science*, 1974, *185*, 1115–1123.

Spear, F. G., Hall, P., & Stirland, P. A comparison of subjective responses to imipramine and tranylcypromine. *British Journal of Psychiatry*, 1964, *110*, 53–55.

Wittenborn, J. R. Diagnostic classification and response to imipramine. In P. R. A. May & J. R. Wittenborn (Eds.), *Psychotrophic drug response; advances in prediction.* Springfield, Illinois: Thomas, 1969.

Wittenborn, J. R., Kiremitci, N., & Weber, E. S. P. The choice of alternative antidepressants. *Journal of Nervous and Mental Disease*, 1973, *156*, 97–108.

CHAPTER 4

Neurotic Depression: The Concept of Anxious Depression

Frank S. Gersh and Don C. Fowles

INTRODUCTION

Although the endogenous–neurotic studies reviewed in the preceding chapter provide a first step in the classification of depressive disorders, it is likely that further subdivisions will prove useful. A number of attempts to accomplish this for psychotic depressives are well-known. The Diagnostic & Statistical Manual of Mental Disorders (DMS-II) listed several subtypes within the psychotic group of affective disorders. More recently, there has been a growing interest in, and literature about, unipolar and bipolar subtypes of psychotic depression (see Chapter 1 in this volume). Similarly, other investigators have argued for the importance of distinguishing between agitated and retarded depressions (e.g., Hamilton, 1967; Lader, 1975). By contrast, relatively few investigators have attempted to subtype neurotic depression, a state of affairs undoubtedly attributable, in part, to the general neglect of this group of patients (Paykel, 1972a). Fortunately, there are a handful of studies that attempt to describe patients on several dimensions simultaneously and thus offer a greater degree of complexity than the

81

The Psychobiology of the Depressive Disorders:
Implications for the Effects of Stress

endogenous–neurotic studies. These multidimensional analyses call attention to potentially useful subtypes of depression. In this chapter, we will concentrate on the evidence that there are several subtypes within the neurotic depression group, with a particular emphasis on the differences in anxiety within neurotic depression. However, we will also consider multidimensional analyses of psychotic patients because they provide evidence that a group of depressed patients exhibiting prominent anxiety symptoms spans both sides of the neurotic–psychotic dichotomy.

We will focus on the concept of anxious depression, not only because there is evidence to support its significance, but also because of its theoretical importance—especially to the concept of neurotic depression. It is widely assumed that anxiety is common to the etiology of the neuroses, and this view has been incorporated into the official diagnostic system in the United States (American Psychiatric Association, 1968). Given this presumed central role of anxiety in the neuroses, the question arises as to whether all neurotic depressions are to be viewed as anxious depressions, or whether anxious depression applies to only a subset of neurotic depressions. If, as will be argued in the following, anxious depression is only a subset of neurotic depressions, should it be grouped with or kept separate from the anxiety neuroses? Finally, how does anxious depression relate to the psychotic–neurotic distinction? An attempt will be made to answer these questions to the extent possible, given the current state of the literature.

MULTIDIMENSIONAL ANALYSES OF NEUROTIC DEPRESSION

A recent and major study by Paykel (1971, 1972a, b) provides the clearest evidence that subtypes of neurotic depression need to be distinguished. This study is important owing to the inclusion of a large group of outpatients, the use of cluster analysis to assign patients to mutually exclusive diagnostic categories, and the collection of additional evidence supporting the validity of the subtypes that were generated.

The subjects were consecutive patients with depression admitted to a number of different treatment facilities (Paykel, 1971): 100 outpatients, 30 day-hospital patients, 25 emergency-unit patients, and 65 inpatients. Thirty-five variables from standardized interviews and personality tests were used in a cluster analysis from which four nonoverlapping groups of patients were derived. Paykel (1971) labeled these four subtypes psychotic, anxious, and hostile depressed patients, and young depressed patients with personality disorder.

The psychotic patient group, which Paykel views as displaying symptoms typical of psychotic or endogenous depression, were the oldest, had ideas of guilt and hopelessness of delusional intensity, and had the highest scores on such typically endogenous symptoms as distinct quality of depression, anorexia, psychomotor retardation, and delayed insomnia. In addition they had low scores on a questionnaire about recent stressful life events (RLE) and on the Maudsley Personality Inventory (MPI) neuroticism scale.

The patients having anxious depression were the second oldest group and showed the highest scores on psychic and somatic anxiety, depersonalization, obsessional symptoms, and fatigue. In addition to the admixture of anxiety and neurotic symptoms, they were moderately depressed. They had the highest scores on suicidal tendencies, number of previous episodes of depression, and MPI neuroticism, but *low* scores on the RLE and reactivity to environmental events during the depression. The prominent neurotic features place this anxious depressed group in the neurotic depressive category, and the high number of previous episodes indicates a fairly chronic condition. They do not easily fit the reactive depressive stereotype, on the other hand, because they were relatively low scoring on reactivity during depression and on precipitating events. Thus, the picture emerges of an anxious depressed patient with moderate depression but strong suicidal tendencies, who tends to have recurrences in the absence of major stressors.

The two younger groups of patients shared many features and were less strikingly different than the older groups. The patients showing hostile depressive symptoms had particularly high scores on hostility and self-pity in relation to their scores on other symptoms, and showed only moderate depression. (The group having psychotic depressive symptoms also had high scores on these two items, but they had high scores on other items as well.) The young patients exhibiting both depression and personality disorders were the youngest group and had *high* MPI neuroticism scores, RLE scores, and reactivity (indicating fluctuations in the depressed mood related to concurrent environmental changes). They were mildly depressed and had a tendency to receive clinical diagnoses of personality disorders. Because of their high score on reactivity, they may represent a portion of patients traditionally classified as reactive.

The four group classification is somewhat consistent with—though more differentiated than—the psychotic–neurotic dichotomy. The psychotic group clearly corresponds to a psychotic or endogenous group. Paykel suggests that the other three groups may all be regarded as neurotic, in the sense of the absence of psychotic symptoms, in displaying some neurotic symptoms, and in having poor premorbid adjustment as evidenced by high scores on the MPI neuroticism scale.

Hospital diagnoses provided some support for this interpretation (Paykel, 1972a). The largest fraction of the patient groups, designated anxious depressive, hostile depressive and young depressive with personality disorder, was diagnosed as psychoneurotic depressive reaction, although 21% of the anxious depressive group was labeled psychotic. Very few patients in the hostile and young depressive groups (4.5% and 3.8%, respectively) were labeled psychotic, whereas a much larger fraction of patients in these groups (15.9% and 20.8%, respectively) were diagnosed as having personality disorders. The largest fraction of patients in Paykel's psychotic group was labeled psychotic depressive (40.9%), whereas a somewhat smaller fraction fell into the psychoneurotic depressive reaction category (27.3%). Although Paykel's four groups do not fall neatly into the traditional categories, it appears that psychotic depression bears a closer resemblance to the traditional psychotic diagnosis than any other group. Similarly, the other three groups are composed predominantly of patients exhibiting neurotic depressions, suggesting that they are primarily subtypes of neurotic depression. No explanation was offered for the relatively large minority (21%) of patients exhibiting anxious depression who were diagnosed as psychotic depressives. Regardless of the explanation for the results, they demonstrate that although the patients having anxious depression are predominantly found among the neurotic depressive group, a substantial minority typically are labeled psychotic.

A number of correlates of the four group typology provided some external validity for the groupings (Paykel, 1972a). Race, presence of hysterical traits, choice of treatment setting, chronicity of illness, and clinical diagnosis were the variables that were most useful in distinguishing among the four groups. Black patients were found to be underrepresented among the patient groups termed psychotic and anxious depressive, and overrepresented among the groups termed hostile depressive and young depressive with personality disorder. The young depressive with personality disorder group had patients showing the most evidence of hysterical personality traits, and the anxious depressive group had the least. With respect to treatment settings, the psychotic depressive group (from the four group typology) was admitted mostly to inpatient facilities; the anxious depressive group was mostly admitted to a day hospital, whereas the young depressive with personality disorder group comprised over 50% of the outpatients in the study. As already stated, the patient group termed anxious depressive had the most previous episodes and therefore may be considered the most chronic patients.

The tentative conclusions to be reached from Paykel's study are that

1. It is possible to develop a typology in which anxious depressed patients form one class.
2. Although these patients were more often labeled as neurotic, a significant minority were viewed as psychotic by the hospital staff.
3. The group labeled anxious depressive does not fit the stereotype of a reactive depressive group.
4. There are other depressed patients who are diagnosed as neurotic, some of whom do fit the stereotype of reactive depression.

Several studies employing multidimensional factor analysis have yielded results that, although not identical to Paykel's, are sufficiently overlapping to offer the hope that clearly defined subtypes might eventually be identified.

Both a retarded psychotic and an anxious depression factor or profile have been reported by several other investigators: among inpatient depressives by Overall, Hollister, Johnson, and Pennington (1966) and Grinker and Nunnally (1968); for samples described as psychotic depressives by Lorr, Pokorny, and Klett (1973). Friedman, Cowitz, Cohen, and Granick (1963) found a retarded depression factor but not an anxious depression factor among a population limited to psychotic depressives.

Grinker and Nunnally's (1968) anxious depression factor involved moderate depression, marked anxiety, low self-esteem, considerable guilt, and clinging demands for attention. One anxious depression profile was characterized by high scores on the obsessive–phobic and functional impairment factors, as well as the anxious depression factor (Lorr *et al.*, 1973). The second anxious depression profile (Overall *et al.*, 1966), found in four separate analyses, was characterized by high scores on depressive mood, anxiety, and tension. These authors state that this profile brings to mind (but is not identical with) terms such as "agitated," "reactive," and "neurotic," and that the most common diagnoses are "mixed anxiety and depression," "depressive reaction with anxiety," or "anxiety with depressive features [p. 947]." Elsewhere they comment that these patients constitute approximately 57% of a heterogeneous sample of carefully diagnosed inpatient depressives (Hollister, Overall, Shelton, Pennington, Kimbell, & Johnson, 1967) and that although most of the anxious depressed patients would be considered to have neurotic depressive reactions, "some of the more agitated . . . might fall into the 'agitated' group, though by no means all [Hollister & Overall, 1965, p. 362]." This description seems particularly consistent with Paykel's anxious depression group as it primarily consists of patients exhibiting neurotic depression but having a significant minority of patients viewed as psychotic (i.e., agitated).

Factors or subtypes identified with the hostile depressive group have also been found occasionally. Grinker and Nunnally's (1968) "Pattern D" was characterized by provocative, demanding, and hostile behavior similar to that shown by patients in Paykel's hostile depressive group. Similarly, both Lorr *et al.* (1973) and Overall *et al.* (1966) reported a hostile depressive profile. In the former study, limited to psychotic patients, this group was called "hostile-paranoid-depressive" and the authors hypothesized that they represented depression rather than paranoid schizophrenia or paranoid state. This group showed high scores on the anxious depression, functional impairment, hostile belligerence, and paranoid projection factors. Again, the hostile depression group described by Overall *et al.* (1966) was anxious and depressed as well as hostile, and they tended to blame others for their problems. This group is about half the size of the anxious depressive group

(Hollister *et al.*, 1967), and are said to bring to mind such adjectives as "reactive," "agitated," or "paranoid [Overall *et al.*, 1966]."

Hamilton and White (1959) found a factor they called psychopathic depression. These patients seemed younger and, judging from the case histories presented, were characterized by prominent antisocial behavior. They appear similar in some ways to Paykel's (1971) young depressed patients with personality disorders.

One additional subtype of depression has been reported in two studies, though it did not appear in Paykel's (1971) analysis. Friedman *et al.* (1963) described the subtype as demanding, complaining, agitated, irritable, and hypochondriacal, whereas Grinker and Nunnally's (1968) "Pattern C" subtype exhibited agitation, demanding behavior, and hypochondriasis. These may be similar to a nonpsychotic "clinging" form of depression discussed by Arieti (1974), but that is by no means clear since Friedman *et al.* included only psychotics.

Taken as a group, these studies support the earlier suggestion that several subtypes of depression may be discriminated and indicate that anxious depression is frequently one of these subtypes. The existence of a hostile depressive type is also fairly well supported, and a young depressive type with personality disorder is at least a possibility, as is an agitated, hypochondriacal type. While a precise analysis of the intersection of these divisions with the neurotic–psychotic dichotomy is impossible, it appears that a large percentage of all except retarded depression (and possibly the agitated hypochondriacal type) would be labeled neurotic, but that both anxious depression and hostile depression extend into the psychotic group.

Some additional evidence that finer subdivisions than the endogenous–neurotic distinction may prove useful is provided by studies assessing patient response to pharmacotherapy. Paykel (1972b) evaluated the response to 4 weeks of treatment with amitriptyline among patients classified according to his four-group typology (Paykel, 1971). The major finding was that psychotic depressed patients showed the greatest improvement whereas anxious depressed patients showed the least. Hostile depressed patients and young depressed patients with personality disorders were least severely ill initially and showed an intermediate response to amitriptyline. When the response to treatment was assessed after partialing out the effects of the initial severity of the illness, the anxious depressed patients stood out as showing the worst response to pharmacotherapy. In this study, then, the poor response of neurotics to a tricyclic antidepressant was attributable only to the anxious depressed patients. It should be noted that all patients received amitriptyline, thus precluding a control for placebo response or spontaneous remission, but also indicating that the anxious depressed patients were not good placebo responders.

A differential response to pharmacotherapy among the three depression subtypes described by Overall *et al.* (1966) has been well-established, with particularly strong differences between those patients having an anxious depression and those having a retarded depression. These investigators found that a phenothiazine produced a better response than a tricyclic antidepressant when treating anxious depression with the reverse being true for retarded depression. This result was obtained whether the comparison was between thioridazine and imipramine (Hollister and Overall, 1965) or between perphenazine and amitriptyline (Hollister et al., 1967). The superiority of patient response to amitriptyline when treating retarded depression versus anxious depression was replicated in yet another study (Hollister, Overall, Johnson, Shelton, Kimbell, & Brunse, 1966). Finally, the effectiveness of a phenothiazine (acetophenazine) in treating anxious depression was replicated in a study (Hollister, Overall, Pokorny, & Shelton, 1971) comparing it with a minor tranquilizer (diazepam). These drugs were equally effective overall and both produced results comparable to earlier studies using phenothiazines. It was also found that the phenothiazines were better for the small subgroup of patients having an anxious depression with an early onset and a history of alcohol abuse, whereas diazepam was better for the larger group of anxious depressed patients with a later onset and without a history of alcohol abuse. Throughout these studies the results for the hostile depressed patients were somewhat variable, but they generally showed a relatively good response to pharmacotherapy regardless of drug type (Hollister & Overall, 1965; Hollister et al., 1966; Hollister et al., 1967). In two of these studies (Hollister et al., 1966; Hollister et al., 1967) patients were excluded who responded to a 1 week placebo trial prior to the active drug administration, a procedure which resulted in a loss of over 50% of the patients (Hollister et al., 1966).

Some independent confirmation of the utility of the Overall et al. (1966) depression subtypes comes from the NIMH collaborative study, the results of which have been summarized by Raskin (1974). The group termed hostile depressive was found to be good placebo responders in both studies (Raskin, Schulterbrandt, Reatig, Crook, & Odle, 1974; Raskin, Schulterbrandt, Reatig, & McKeon, 1970). In the second study (Raskin, 1974; Raskin et al., 1974) the anxious depressive group did better on a minor tranquilizer (diazepam) than on a placebo and the hostile depressive group did worse on the same drug than on a placebo. The differential effects of phenothiazines and tricyclic antidepressants for the Overall subtypes of anxious and retarded depression were not supported in the first NIMH study (Raskin et al., 1970). On the other hand, imipramine was much better than chlorpromazine for the symptom of retardation and both drugs were better than a placebo for reducing the symptom of anxiety and tension. Patients having an anxious depression did poorly when treated with a placebo (Raskin et al., 1974).

Why these results were obtained for the symptoms of retardation and anxiety rather than for Overall's subtypes is not clear. One possibility is that

Overall's group excluded schizophrenics, as seems to be implied by the designation of these patients as "truly depressives" in contrast to a sample of schizophrenics (Hollister & Overall, 1965). The NIMH studies included schizophrenics with depression, and these were said to be overrepresented in the retarded subtype and underrepresented in the anxious depressive group (Raskin *et al.*, 1970). Another possibility is that the Overall subtypes included a more heterogeneous group of patients than did the symptom evaluations. In the first study (Raskin *et al.*, 1970) 64% of the patient sample was classified as having an anxious depression, 21% had a hostile depression, and 15% had a retarded depression. Finally, the Brief Psychiatric Rating Scale (BPRS) used in these studies was developed to include only a *single item* for each relatively independent factor previously discovered (Overall & Gorham, 1962), which may make it unusually difficult to use without extensive training in the precise meaning of each item. Assuming that one of these explanations is sufficient to permit the results with symptoms to be viewed as an independent replication of the results with Overall's subtypes, there is strong agreement between the two groups of studies: Patients having a hostile depression are good placebo responders, patients with a retarded depression respond well to tricyclic antidepressant therapy but poorly to phenothiazine therapy, and patients having an anxious depression improve when treated with either a phenothiazine or a minor tranquilizer but do not respond well to placebo. The only discrepancy was that patients with anxiety responded to imipramine therapy in the NIMH study. These conclusions are essentially identical to Raskin's (1974) own summary of the NIMH studies. It should be noted that approximately half of each Overall subtype received a clinical diagnosis of neurosis in the NIMH study (Raskin *et al.*, 1974), indicating that all three dimensions cut across the psychotic–neurotic dichotomy. On the other hand, the exact percentages may not agree with those from Overall's studies, since, as stated earlier, most of their patients termed anxious depressives were diagnosed as having neurotic depressive reactions (Hollister & Overall, 1965).

The strongest conclusion to be reached from these studies is that there have been consistent findings of an anxious depression group, the majority of whom are classified as neurotic depressions, but who do not fit the picture of neurotic depression developed in the preceding chapter. That is, they show a poor response to both a placebo and imipramine therapy and are not reactive with respect to either precipitants prior to the onset of illness or reactivity during the depression. This discrepancy suggests an important subdivision within the neurotic depressive group in which an anxious depressive group is separated from the rest. Although it is not completely clear, the basis for this distinction would appear to be prominent and severe anxiety without noteworthy hostility. The neurotic depressive group, excluding the anxious depressives, would include a large portion of the hostile depressive subtype and, if this group proves to be replicable, Paykel's young depressive with personality disorder subtype. Undoubtedly it would also include a variety of other patients with even less clearly defined symptom patterns.

Insofar as these studies emphasize patients having a retarded depression as showing a specific response to tricyclic antidepressant therapy and exclude those anxious and hostile depressed patients who are diagnosed as psychotic, the conclusion of the previous chapter that psychotic depressed patients respond to tricyclic therapy can be made more accurate by limiting it to a subgroup within the psychotic depressive type. Whether agitated psychotic depressed patients belong with the retarded group among the good responders to tricyclic therapy or with the anxious depressive group is ambiguous. Raskin and Crook (1976) suggest that imipramine helps to relieve the mood or affective component in agitated depression but that, with respect to motor symptoms, its mild energizing and euphoriant properties are more beneficial for retarded than agitated depression. In their view, then, imipramine is moderately effective in treating agitated depression. As reported in the previous chapter, agitation was associated with a good response to ECT. Consequently, it would be theoretically simpler to keep agitated and retarded depression grouped together. Perhaps the ultimate resolution of this problem will depend on a clarification of the distinction between agitation and anxiety among psychotic depressed patients (see pages 89–91).

It is worth stressing at this point that we make no claim that these are well-defined groups. The method variance in studies of this type can be quite large, including among others the populations being studied and methods of selecting them, the choice of symptoms to be rated, the control of rater bias, the type of statistical techniques employed, the precise rotation of factors, and the decision to define types as opposed to dimensions. Nevertheless, the evidence does seem promising enough to justify a continued interest in these subtypes, especially in anxious depression.

An issue that remains quite ambiguous is the relationship between anxiety and agitation, particularly among psychotic patients. Paykel (1971, 1972a) did not comment on agitation in his studies. Agitation and anxiety loaded on the demanding, hypochondriacal factor in two studies (Friedman et al., 1963; Grinker & Nunnally, 1968), suggesting that this factor is distinct from anxious depression. On the other hand, some studies have reported an association between anxiety and agitation. In a major factor analytic study, Hamilton (1967) reported that his second factor was bipolar, contrasting retarded versus anxious, agitated depression. The large majority of patients' symptoms were quite severe and many of the patients were selected because they had been referred for ECT (see Hamilton, 1967, p. 280; Hamilton & White, 1960, p. 1032). Assuming that these patients primarily were suffering from psychotic depression, these results indicate that anxiety is associated with the symptoms of agitated psychotic depression and are negatively

correlated with retarded, psychotic depressive symptoms. A similar association between anxiety and agitation apparently was found by Hollister and
Overall (1965). They comment that some of the more agitated patients in
their anxious depressive group may fall into the category of agitated depression. This observation supports the notion that very severe anxious depression includes agitation, a hypothesis consistent with Lorr, Klett, and
McNair's (1963) statement that their anxious intropunitive factor resembled
involutional psychotic reaction (one symptom of which is agitation).

One approach to interpreting these results is to draw on the clinical
impression that agitation may be viewed as an expression of anxiety
(Mayer-Gross, Slater, & Roth, 1969, p. 214), while simultaneously noting
that anxiety need not be accompanied by the motor symptoms of agitation.
Thus one might argue that the greater the percentage of agitated depressed
patients in a sample, the higher will be the correlation between anxiety and
agitation. Few articles specify to what extent agitation, in and of itself, might
be taken as an indication of anxiety. A second approach is to focus on the
similarity between neurotic and psychotic forms of agitation. Carney, Roth,
and Garside (1965) comment that it is difficult to discriminate between
neurotic and endogenous agitation and anxiety: "A state of anguished,
hand-wringing restlessness" is associated with psychotic depression and this
must be differentiated from "a much less specific form of anxiety with motor
unrest [which] is a common component of the neurotic form of depression
[p. 670]."

Still another source of confusion is the distinction between anxiety as a
symptom or state versus more traitlike and pervasive neurotic symptoms.
Hays (1964) argued that anxiety was found among all types of psychotic
depression once the depression was fully developed, but that only one
subgroup showed predominantly neurotic symptoms during the early stages
of the developing depression. This study will be discussed in more detail
later in the chapter, but in the present context it suggests that anxious
depression may refer to depression with a more neurotic substrate rather
than simply to anxiety in depression. This distinction might explain why
agitation is associated with a good response to ECT even though neurotic
symptoms predict a poor response, as reported in the previous chapter. In all
likelihood there is a difference between agitated psychotic depression and
anxious psychotic depression involving neurotic symptomatology.

It is apparent from the foregoing that more care is needed in specifying
the precise nature of anxious depression as observed in the studies reviewed
above. The most probable reading of the situation at present is that there is
an anxious depression that cuts across the neurotic-psychotic boundary,
involves neurotic symptomatology, and that is confused with but different
from agitated psychotic depression.

The studies reviewed in this section suggest that it is possible to subdivide
the depressive disorders into several subtypes. In addition to the classical

retarded depression, anxious, hostile, and agitated-hypochondriacal sub-types appear most consistently across studies. Young depressed patients with personality disorders form yet another group. The anxious depressed patients who are the focus of this review appear to fit primarily among the neurotic depressive group, but they share this label with other patients lacking such prominent anxiety and they are also found among the psychotic depressive group. Surprisingly, in view of their fairly strong association with neurotic depression, these patients' symptoms do not correspond to the picture of reactive depression from the endogenous–reactive literature. Rather, they have been found *not* to be particularly reactive to the environment during the depression and to have few precipitating events. They appear to have an early onset and a relatively chronic course of illness, as evidenced by the large number of previous admissions, and they respond poorly to treatment with antidepressants but well to treatment with phenothiazines and/or diazepam. Although it has been suggested that agitation is found in severe anxious depression, the relationship between agitation and anxiety, particularly among psychotic anxious depressed patients, is unclear and remains a question for further research.

THE CLINICAL DISTINCTION BETWEEN ANXIETY STATES AND NEUROTIC DEPRESSION

The conclusion that an anxious depressive group should be separated from the other neurotic depressions points to the need for clarification of another boundary: that between the neurotic depressions and other neuroses. In particular, it raises the questions of whether anxious depression can and should be differentiated from other neurotic disorders involving prominent anxiety and of the clinical significance of mixed anxiety and depression within each group. It is well-known that a large number of patients show both anxiety and depressive symptoms, and many theories have emphasized the close association between the two (e.g., Derogatis, Klerman, & Lipman, 1972; Roth, Gurney, Garside, & Kerr, 1972). The difficulty of separating anxiety and depression is illustrated by one study (Woodruff, Guze, & Clayton, 1972) that found half their sample of anxiety neurotics also were diagnosed as having secondary affective disorder; these patients were distinguishable from those diagnosed as having primary depressions only because of the preexisting anxiety neurosis, not because of differences in the depressive symptoms. Thus this is an extremely difficult problem and one, unfortunately, about which there is insufficient information. What is known comes from two groups of studies, one British and one American, with quite different approaches.

The Newcastle Studies

The British studies by the Newcastle group (Roth *et al.*, 1972; Gurney, Roth, Garside, Kerr, & Schapira, 1972; Kerr, Roth, & Schapira, 1974; Kerr, Roth, Schapira, & Gurney, 1972; Schapira, Roth, Kerr, & Gurney, 1972) assessed the background, demographic, and personality characteristics of 145 inpatients diagnosed as having "a primary mood disorder of anxiety and/or depression [Roth *et al.*, 1972]" and then went on to examine the course and outcome at an average of 3.8 years later. The major concern of these studies was whether there is a qualitative distinction between anxiety neuroses and depressive illnesses, both of which many British psychiatrists view as affective disorders. As no attempt was made to subdivide the two primary mood disorders, it is difficult to draw conclusions about specific subtypes. In spite of this, these studies provide valuable information.

The first problem is to determine how their division of patients relates to the subtypes discussed earlier. The authors repeatedly emphasize that there was considerable overlap between the two groups in terms of affective symptomatology, the group having anxiety states showing considerable depression and the depressive group showing considerable anxiety. They also state that depressive symptomatology was so pervasive among the anxiety state group that these patients are likely to be included in any studies of depression unless specifically excluded (Roth *et al.*, 1972, p. 157). It seems highly probable, therefore, that the anxiety state group includes a large proportion of patients of the anxious depressive subtype, although limited to those in which anxiety was the predominant affect since patients in whom anxiety and depression were equally prominent were diagnosed as "doubtful" (15 out of the 145 patients). The depressive group, then, would include all primary depressions, severe enough to require admission to hospital, in which anxiety was not equal to or greater than the depression. Thus the depressive group is probably too heterogeneous to be of much interest in the present context, but the anxiety state group appears to include a large number of patients of the anxious depressive subtype without including other depressive types. The degree to which patients in this anxious depressive group overlap with the anxious depression groups as defined by Paykel, Overall, Raskin, and others in the studies described earlier is difficult to determine, but will be discussed after the results of these studies are presented.

In spite of the considerable overlap between the groups, quite striking differences were found in presenting symptoms, personality characteristics, and course and outcome, leading these investigators to conclude that there are two distinct syndromes of anxiety and depression. Patients in the anxiety state group were characterized by a variety of anxiety and neurotic symptoms both at the time of hospitalization and in their past history, whereas those in the depressive group were characterized by symptoms of endogenous or psychotic depression (e.g., depression worse in the morning, early awakening, retardation, delusions, absence of precipitants, and older age of onset). Agitation failed to differentiate between the groups. Of interest was the success of distinguishing between episodic and persistent depression: Persistent depression was found among 65% of the patients in the depressive group, whereas episodic depression was characteristic of 65% of the patients in the anxiety state group with only 21% of them showing persistent depression (Roth et al., 1972). A similar distinction for tension did not discriminate as well, as episodic tension was the rule for both groups (69 and 72%), but there was an increased risk of persistent tension among the anxiety state group (31 versus 16%).

The earlier onset of illness in the anxiety state group and the poor premorbid personality associated with them suggests a more chronic illness, and this was confirmed by the follow-up data. Whether outcome was measured in terms of percentage of relapses, percentage improved at time of follow-up, or average adjustment during the entire follow-up period, the anxiety state group fared worse (Schapira et al., 1972). At the time of follow-up, anxiety and neurotic symptoms discriminated between the groups but depressive symptoms did not, and there was a consistent tendency for the anxiety state group to show greater frequency and severity in the entire range of symptoms. The failure of depressive symptoms to discriminate between the groups was attributed to both a reduction in depressive symptoms associated with the better outcome for the depressive group, and a tendency for long-standing anxiety states to develop prominent depressive symptoms over time. The latter finding is of considerable importance in the present context, as it shows that the anxiety state group with a chronic course increasingly resemble the depressive group.

Finally, Kerr et al. (1974) applied a multiple regression analysis separately to the two groups of patients to determine which features at the initial hospitalization predicted adjustment during the follow-up period. As would be expected from the endogenous–neurotic follow-up studies summarized in the preceding chapter, symptoms of anxiety were associated with a poor outcome within the depressive group. In the anxiety group, on the other hand, the two best predictors of a poor outcome were suicidal tendencies and agitation. The authors viewed agitation as an indication of the greater severity of the illness and suicidal tendencies were attributed to swings into depression associated with marked emotional lability. Thus, at least one depressive feature is associated with a poor prognosis among the anxiety state group.

At this point it is possible to note a number of points that suggest an overlap between Paykel's anxious depressive group and the more depressed of the anxiety group in the Newcastle study. As stated earlier, the authors of the Newcastle study, stressed that these patients would be included in studies of depression unless care were taken to exclude them. It has just been mentioned that suicidal tendencies and agitation were associated with poor outcome in the anxiety group and that those patients with a poor outcome tended to develop even more prominent depressive symptoms. Paykel's anxious depressives were the highest among the four groups on suicidal tendencies and second highest on agitation. The primary argument against assuming an overlap between the two studies is that Paykel (1971) required that the central feature be depressed affect and excluded patients in whom depression was secondary to other neurotic disorders, whereas anxiety was required to be the predominant symptom in the Newcastle studies. A possible argument in favor of overlap is that Paykel (1971) described these patients as "moderately depressed" (probably based on their Hamilton scale score), while simultaneously reporting that they had the highest scores on depressed feelings and suicidal tendencies. Consequently, a decision as to whether anxiety or depression is the predominant symptom may depend on whether one looks at the overall depression, which was moderate, or depressed feelings and suicidal tendencies, which were severe. Given this amount of ambiguity in titrating anxiety and depression, it is likely that the same type of patient was included in both studies. However, there is an even more compelling reason to generalize from one study to the other. Paykel's anxious depressive group was older (mean 39.74) than the Newcastle anxiety state group, whose median age of onset was probably in the early thirties (Roth *et al.*, 1972, Table VIII). As the anxiety state group with a poor prognosis look increasingly depressive over time, it is quite likely that they would be included in an anxious depressive group if hospitalized at a later age.

This line of thought requires that some depressed patients show an initial anxiety state that gradually becomes a severe depression. Support for this type of onset was reported by Hays (1964), who used case folders to study the onset of endogenous or psychotic depression. He found three types of onset:

1. A sudden-onset group that corresponded to what is now called bipolar affective disorder, differing from the other two groups with respect to having fewer precipitants, a rapid response to ECT, a high constitutional loading for affective disorder and evidence of cyclothymia or hypomania.
2. A second group showed a gradual onset involving depressive features from the beginning.
3. A third group showed a gradual onset with only neurotic features and prominent anxiety at the beginning.

The neurotic-onset group differed from the gradual (depressive) onset group in terms of a past history of neurotic illness or a premorbid personality that was notably anxious or obsessional. The neurotic-onset group also showed a poorer response to antidepressant therapy than did the gradual onset group based on blind ratings of a "definite response"—only 36 versus 68%. Hays stressed that all of these groups showed a typical endogenous depressive pattern once the depression was fully developed, implying little difference in presenting symptoms. However, his ratings were based on case history material and his interest was in mode of onset; it is quite possible that differences in presenting symptoms would be found with careful examination. In any event, his data reveal a form of psychotic depression preceded by an anxiety neurosis. It seems reasonable to include these patients among the psychotic anxious depressive group defined in the multidimensional studies and to equate them with the anxiety state group with depressive features and a chronic course who later developed prominent depression in the Newcastle study.

The issue raised by this analysis is to what extent the anxious depressive group may be viewed as more closely related to anxiety states, representing either a more severe and advanced illness, or a separate group within the anxiety states. Insofar as this should be the case, it strengthens the argument that the anxious depressive group should be separated from the other neurotic depressions, but weakens the case for a separate subtype as they would then be grouped with the anxiety states. It also implies that the ratio of anxiety to depression varies over time, with the result that a different diagnosis may be made depending on when the patient is first seen. Obviously the tentativeness of the assumption that the same type of patients were being studied in the two studies and the fact that many patients in the anxious depressive group were day hospital patients in Paykel's study precludes any firm conclusions, but it is a hypothesis worth considering in future studies.

The American Studies

In contrast to the Newcastle studies just reviewed, three American studies have focused more specifically on the question of whether a division can be made between anxious and depressed neurotics using outpatient populations. These studies have, for the most part, been limited to an evaluation of the clinical features of these groups without supplying additional information concerning course and outcome. Therefore, their major contribution has been to demonstrate that, despite the difficulty of the diagnosis because of the pervasiveness of mixed anxiety and depression, patients diagnosed as anxious versus depressed neurotics do differ in their symptomatology.

In the earliest of these studies Derogatis, Lipman, Covi, and Rickels (1972) administered the Symptom Check List (SCL), a 58-item self-rating scale, to 641 anxious neurotic outpatients and 251 depressed neurotic outpatients. They performed a separate factor analysis of the SCL for each of the two groups of patients to determine whether the factor structure was invariant across diagnostic groups (i.e., whether the same dimensions could be used in both groups). A similar factor structure was found for the dimensions of somatization, interpersonal sensitivity, and obsessive-compulsiveness, but important differences were found for the factors of anxiety, depression, and hostility. A clear anxiety factor was found for the anxious neurotic outpatients but not for the depressed neurotic outpatients. Similarly, a distinct hostility dimension emerged in the analysis of the depressed neurotic outpatients but was absent among the anxious neurotic outpatients. A depression dimension was found among both groups of outpatients but tended to be fused with the missing factor. That is, among anxious neurotic outpatients the depression factor contained some hostility symptoms, whereas among depressed neurotic outpatients the depression factor contained some symptoms associated with anxiety. Moreover, there were differences between the groups in the factor loadings of the depression items on the depression factor. The authors concluded that there are different symptom patterns in anxious as compared with depressed neurotic outpatients.

These results would appear to corroborate the findings reported earlier (i.e., the neurotic depression group contains both hostile depressive and anxious depressive symptom patterns). As these were not associated with a bipolar factor, there is no implication that these are mutually exclusive patterns and thus mixed symptoms can be expected. Nevertheless, many patients will have symptoms consisting predominantly of anxious or hostile depression within the neurotic depressive group. Similarly, the independence of the anxiety and depression-hostility factors within the anxiety neurosis group reveals that some anxious patients will also show significant depression whereas others will show only anxiety. Thus both groups are heterogeneous and include patients with symptoms of both anxiety and depression.

The study also shows that the groups differ in terms of factor structure. Although this demonstrates that clinicians are not making random assignments to diagnostic groups (which has been an important question), the qualitative differences in the factor structure cannot be interpreted as supplying validity for the division into anxious and depressed neurotic subtypes. This is because the rules used in making diagnosis probably will attenuate the range of some symptoms which, in turn, will influence the factor structure. For example, if the definition of depressive neurosis requires that symptoms of anxiety be no more severe than those of depression, the anxiety factor is likely to be attenuated and perhaps even merged with depression (higher levels of anxiety could only be included accompanied by higher levels of depression). As reported in this study, the factors most affected would be those used in the determination of diagnosis (i.e., anxiety and depression). Thus, this study demonstrates that anxious and depressed neurotic groups differ from each other and that patients with both anxiety and depression are found within each group. It does not provide external validity for the diagnosis.

Prusoff and Klerman (1974) also gave the SCL to neurotic outpatients subdivided into anxiety-neurotic versus depressed-neurotic groups. They were concerned with whether these clinically defined groups could be separated on the basis of self-report and, if so, whether they differ in the patterning of symptoms or only in severity. Using multiple regression, statistically significant discrimination of the groups was obtained, again indicating that the clinical diagnosis predicts differences in symptomatology. Somewhat surprisingly, the differences were based primarily on greater severity of overall symptomatology among the depressive neurotic group. Of the five factors in the SCL, four (*including anxiety*) were significantly more severe among the depressed neurotic group. The others were Depression, Obsessive-compulsive, and Interpersonal Sensitivity. Some support for the patterning hypothesis was found with the Somatization factor which, although not significantly different in a simple comparison of groups, was higher among the anxious neurotic group after correction for differences in severity of depression in the multiple regression analysis. The anxiety factor did not discriminate after the correction for the depression factor. Thus the depressive neurotic group differed from the anxiety neurotic group in depression but not in anxiety and generally exhibited more severe symptomatology. No reference was made to a hostile depressive group or other presumably less anxious, neurotic depressive patients. However, from the description of the procedures, it appears that all neurotic depressives were included.

Downing and Rickels (1974) provide an unusually close look at mixed anxious depressed patients. They examined only those neurotic patients with both anxious and depressed symptomatology. These patients were subdivided into two groups as a function of whether they were assigned by the treating physician for treatment with antidepressants or anxiolytics. Using the treating physicians' ratings of anxiety and depression, they found that anxiety was greater than depression for the anxiolytic group whereas the reverse was true for the antidepressant group. This difference can be attributed largely to differences in depression between the groups, as there was much more depression among the antidepressant group than among the anxiolytic group ($p < .001$) with only a trend ($p < .10$) toward greater anxiety for the anxiolytic group than the antidepressant group. Despite these group differences, only 26.8% of the antidepressant group were rated by physicians as showing more depression than anxiety, the vast majority of the remaining patients in this group (60.4% of the total) were rated as having equal amounts of depression and anxiety. The authors were able to correctly predict treatment group in 80.7% of the cases by predicting antidepressants if depression was rated as equal to or greater than anxiety, and predicting anxiolytics only if anxiety was rated as greater than depression. The authors stress that it is the relative, rather than the absolute, amount of anxiety and depression that predicts assignment to treatment. In addition, the antidepressant group was found to have received significantly more previous medication and responded less satisfactorily to it, suggesting a more chronic course than in the anxiolytic group.

This study demonstrated that, even within a mixed anxious-depressed neurotic group, distinctions were being made in assignments to treatment and that the amount of depression is more variable than the amount of anxiety, hence contributing more heavily to this choice. This latter finding is consistent with Prusoff and Klerman's (1974) finding that the groups differed in depression but not anxiety. Similarly, the greater severity of the symptomatology in the depressive group in their study was corroborated in the Downing and Rickels study by the more chronic course of the patients assigned to antidepressants. It should be noted that as the medical history was available to the physician at the time the patient was assigned to treatment, data from this source cannot be viewed as completely independent evidence in support of the clinical distinctions being made. Moreover, controlled drug trials comparing response to treatment with anxiolytics and antidepressants were not conducted; as a result an actual differential drug response was not demonstrated.

The picture which emerges from these American studies is that within the large group of outpatient neurotics many patients exhibit a mixed anxious-depression. These patients with a mixed anxious-depression are assigned diagnoses of either anxiety neurosis or depressive neurosis largely on the basis of the ratio of symptoms of depression to anxiety, equal amounts or depression more severe than anxiety being justification for a diagnosis of depressive neurosis, with depressive symptoms but not anxiety distinguishing between the groups. In general, the neurotic depressive group appear to be more severe, both in terms of presenting symptomatology and a more chronic course with poor response to treatment, although the evidence for a more chronic course is not strong. No study produced clear support for the assumption that dividing the mixed anxious-depressive group into anxiety neurotics versus depressive neurotics produced differences other than those that could be explained in terms of a greater severity of illness in the neurotic depressive group (although, due to the early stage of research on this topic, this assumption cannot be rejected either). However, in view of the suggestion that the ratio of depression to anxiety may change over time, just mentioned, and based on the British studies that the ratio of depression to anxiety may change over time, fairly strong evidence should be required for the validity of subdividing the mixed anxious depression group down the middle.

SUMMARY AND CONCLUSIONS

The American studies suggested that among outpatient neurotics the presence of prominent depressive symptoms combined with anxiety reflect a greater severity of illness and a more chronic course than for anxiety without depression. From the British studies with inpatients a similar conclusion may be drawn: Early symptoms of depression in anxiety states are predictive of a more chronic course with the development of more prominent depressive symptoms over time. It was argued that this pattern may overlap with the anxious depressive subtype reported frequently in the multidimensional studies. Considerable differences were found between anxious depression and other neurotic depressions in the section on multidimensional analyses. The studies reviewed in the present section point to at least an important quantitative difference between anxious depression and anxiety states without prominent depression. It is not possible to say more than that about differences between anxiety states and anxious depression because so little research has been conducted on this topic.

Anxious Depression and the
Endogenous–Neurotic Distinction

The preceding chapter reviewed evidence for the validity of the endogenous–neurotic distinction. It concluded that, although there is considerable support for this distinction, the conceptualization is far from clear and predictions based on it can stand an increase in precision. A recognition of the anxious depression group discussed in the present chapter should contribute to that increased precision. If the picture drawn is correct, these patients show a relatively chronic course, fewer precipitants, are unreactive to environmental events during the depression, and are less responsive to placebos than other neurotic depressed patients and less responsive to antidepressant therapy (and possibly ECT) than other psychotic depressed patients. The majority of the anxious depressive group are diagnosed as being neurotic but a large minority are viewed as psychotic. Keeping them separate from the neurotic depressive group should increase the extent to which the neurotic depressive group show greater reactivity during depression, a higher rate of precipitants, and a good response to placebo. Keeping anxious depressive type of patients separate from other psychotic depressive types should produce a more endogenous group showing good response to somatic treatments, no residual deficit after recovery, and fewer relapses. Elimination of the anxious depressive type from endogenous–neurotic comparisons should, therefore, result in larger differences between these groups. Though it is not being suggested that this addition represents a complete solution to the complexity of clinical depression, it does seem to be a step in the right direction that is worth trying.

The assignment of anxious depression to a separate group means that endogenous is necessarily a narrower concept than psychotic. As indicated in the factor analytic studies, endogenous refers especially to retarded depression. Which other patients should be included has been ambiguous. If it is possible to distinguish between agitated depression and anxious depression (e.g., in terms of a broader range of neurotic symptoms), then patients having agitated depression might be included within the endogenous group as well. The results have been much less clear for agitation than for retardation, but perhaps, as suggested, this is due to confusion between anxious depression and agitation. Endogenous depression still would presumably not include all remaining psychotic depressives (e.g., the hostile depressives).

Anxious Depression and the Anxiety States

Assuming that anxious depression is to be separated from the other depressions, there remains the question of the degree to which it overlaps the anxiety states. Specifically, should anxious depression be viewed as a severe form of an anxiety state or as qualitatively distinct from anxiety states? Alternatively, should anxious depression be subdivided into those related to anxiety states versus those more depressive in nature? Several positions can be seen in the studies already reviewed.

Most of the studies reviewed in this chapter have not spelled out exactly where the line was drawn between anxiety states with depressive features and depressions with anxiety when selecting depressed patients. The American studies on this particular issue have indicated that the ratio of depression to anxiety is probably a major determinant of this distinction, but the exact cutting point is likely to have varied from study to study. More importantly, there is little evidence for the validity of this cutting point. Most studies have simply taken it for granted. One study (Downing & Rickels, 1974) showed that physicians assigned patients to different drug therapies (anxiolytics or antidepressants) on the basis of the ratio of depression to anxiety, implying a differential drug response. However, as the groups received different drugs, direct comparisons were not possible. Moreover, the expected effectiveness of antidepressants with the more depressed of these anxious depressive group of patients appears to be inconsistent with the studies reviewed here, which showed a poor response to antidepressants among the anxious depressive group of patients. Clearly more work is needed to determine the utility of this subdivision of anxious depression.

Other studies have been cited as indicating continuity between the anxious-depressive patient group and a portion of anxious-neurotic patient group. Of particular importance in this regard are the Newcastle studies and the study by Hays (1964), which reported the development of prominent depressive symptoms among patients who previously had appeared to be anxiety neurotics. The numerical importance of this sequence is indicated by the finding of Woodruff et al. (1972) that half their patient sample diagnosed as anxiety neurotics showed severe depressive symptoms but were diagnosed as having secondary depression because the anxiety neurosis preceded the depression. This frequent development of depression from an anxiety neurosis raises the possibility that all anxious depressions might be viewed as being secondary to anxiety neurosis. This is an attractive notion in view of the good response of the anxious depressive group to treatment with diazepam. The parallel to depression secondary to physical disorders is also reasonable inasmuch as chronic anxiety is likely to be as debilitating as many physical disorders. On the other hand, it is not clear what portion of anxious depressions are preceded by an anxiety neurosis. If many are not, the diagnosis of secondary depression would have the effect of subdividing the anxious depressions and would, therefore, require studies demonstrating the validity of such a division. Studies comparing primary and secondary depressions as a whole would not serve this purpose, as any differences found might be due to patients other than anxious depressives (e.g., to retarded depressives).

Yet another possibility is that anxious depression is a distinct syndrome that is not secondary to anxiety neurosis. It could be that the early stages of anxious depression are variable: In some cases anxiety is more prominent, whereas depression is more prominent in others. If this were true, the primary–secondary distinction would reflect this insignificant variability rather than fundamental differences in etiology. A major argument against this position is that Hays (1964) did find a differential drug response for patients with early anxiety symptoms as compared to those with early depressive symptoms. Nevertheless, this hypothesis should be kept in mind.

It can be seen from this brief analysis that there is no consensus as to the boundary between anxious depression and anxiety neurosis. Perhaps the most important need is a clarification of the relationship between anxious depression as defined in terms of presenting symptoms, and secondary depression as defined in terms of the temporal relationship between anxiety and depression. If the vast majority of patients in the anxious depressive group are found to have suffered initially from anxiety neuroses, the concept of secondary depression would be supported. If, on the other hand, only a portion show a preexisting anxiety neurosis, then one must consider whether they should be subdivided on this basis or whether the hypothesis that they are secondary to anxiety neurosis should be rejected. In the latter case, anxious depression would be seen as qualitatively distinct from anxiety neurosis. It is hoped that this important question can be answered in the next few years.

Types Versus Dimensions

Before leaving this topic a comment is needed concerning underlying models. Even though we have repeatedly referred to subtypes and groups of patients, we do not intend to endorse a typological as opposed to a dimensional approach. Our predilection is for a dimensional approach in which factors or clusters of symptoms vary in severity. Insofar as these factors are not highly correlated (either negatively or positively), a substantial number of patients will manifest the symptoms of only one factor to a severe degree, making it possible to refer to groups or subtypes of patients showing anxious depression, neurotic depression, etc. This should not be taken to imply that mixed types are not found. However, we have not been concerned with evaluating the evidence for a dimensional versus a typological approach. It is difficult enough to identify gross distinctions among depressed patients at this point without attempting to specify the exact nature of the underlying parameters.

REFERENCES

Arieti, S. Affective disorders: Manic-depressive psychosis and psychotic depression. Manifest symptomatology, psychodynamics, sociological factors, and psychotherapy. In S. Arieti (Ed.), *American handbook of psychiatry* (Vol. 3). Basic Books, New York, 1974.

Carney, M. W. P., Roth, M., & Garside, R. F. The diagnosis of depressive syndromes and the prediction of ECT response. *British Journal of Psychiatry*, 1965, *111*, 659–674.

Derogatis, L. R., Klerman, G. L., & Lipman, R. S. Anxiety states and depressive neuroses. *The Journal of Nervous and Mental Disease*, 1972, *155*, 392–403.

Derogatis, L. R., Lipman, R. S., Covi, L., & Rickels, K. Factorial invariance of symptom dimensions in anxious and depressive neuroses. *Archives of General Psychiatry*, 1972, *27*, 659–665.

Downing, R. W. & Rickels, K. Mixed anxiety-depression—fact or myth? *Archives of General Psychiatry*, 1974, *30*, 312–317.

Friedman, A. S., Cowitz, B., Cohen, H. W., & Granick, S. Syndromes and themes of psychotic depression. *Archives of General Psychiatry*, 1963, *9*, 504–509.

Grinker, R. R. & Nunnally, J. C. The phenomena of depressions. In M. M. Katz, J. O. Cole, & W. E. Barton (Eds.), *The role and methodology of clarification in psychiatry and psychopathology*. Chevy Chase, Maryland, National Institute of Health, 1968.

Gurney, C., Roth, M., Garside, R. F., Kerr, T. A., & Schapira, K. Studies in the classification of affective disorders—The relationship between anxiety states and depressive illnesses— II. *British Journal of Psychiatry*, 1972, *121*, 162–166.

Hamilton, M. Development of a rating scale for primary depressive illness. *British Journal Society of Clinical Psychologists*, 1967, 6, 278–296.

Hamilton, M. & White, J. M. Factors related to the outcome of depression treated with E.C.T. *Journal of Mental Science*, 1960, 106, 1031–1041.

Hamilton, M. & White, J. M. Clinical syndromes in depressive states. *Journal of Mental Science*, 1959, 105, 985–998.

Hays, P. Modes of onset of psychotic symptoms. *British Medical Journal*, 1964, 2, 779–784.

Hollister, L. E. & Overall, J. E. Reflections on the specificity of action of anti-depressants. *Psychosomatics*, 1965, vi, 361–365.

Hollister, L. E., Overall, J. E., Johnson, M. H., Shelton, J., Kimbell, I., Jr., & Brunse, A. Amitriptyline alone and combined with perphenazine in newly admitted depressed patients. *The Journal of Nervous and Mental Disease*, 1966, 142, 460–469.

Hollister, L. E., Overall, J. E., Pokorny, A. D., & Shelton, J. Acetophenazine and diazepam in anxious depressions. *Archives of General Psychiatry*, 1971, 24, 273–278.

Hollister, L. E., Overall, J. E., Shelton, J., Pennington, V., Kimbell, I., & Johnson, M. Drug therapy of depression; amitriptyline, perphenazine, and their combination in different syndromes. *Archives of General Psychiatry*, 1967, 17, 486–493.

Kerr, T. A., Roth, M., & Schapira, K. Prediction of outcome in anxiety states and depressive illnesses. *British Journal of Psychiatry*, 1974, 124, 125–133.

Kerr, T. A., Roth, M., Schapira, K., & Gurney, C. The assessment and prediction of outcome in affective disorders. *British Journal of Psychiatry*, 1972, 121, 167–174.

Lader, M. The psychophysiology of anxious and depressed patients. In D. C. Fowles (Ed.), *Clinical applications of psychophysiology*. New York: Columbia Univ. Press, 1975.

Lorr, M., Pokorny, A. D., & Klett, C. J. Three depressive types. *Journal of Clinical Psychology*, 1973, 29, 290–294.

Lorr, M., Klett, C. J., & McNair, D. *Syndromes of psychoses*. Oxford: Pergamon, 1963.

Mayer-Gross, W., Slater, E., & Roth, M. *Clinical Psychiatry* (3rd ed.). Baltimore, Maryland: Williams & Wilkins, 1969.

Overall, J. E. & Gorham, D. R. The brief psychiatric rating scale. *Psychological Reports*, 1962, 10, 799–812.

Overall, J. E., Hollister, L. E., Johnson, M., & Pennington, V. Nosology of depression and differential response to drugs. *The Journal of The American Medical Association*, 1966, 195, 946–948.

Paykel, E. S. Classification of depressed patients: A cluster analysis derived grouping. *British Journal of Psychiatry*, 1971, 118, 275–288.

Paykel, E. S. Correlates of a depressive typology. *Archives of General Psychiatry*, 1972, 27, 203–209. (a)

Paykel, E. S. Depressive typologies and response to amitriptyline. *British Journal of Psychiatry*, 1972, 120, 147–156. (b)

Prusoff, B. & Klerman, G. L. Differentiating depressed from anxious neurotic outpatients. *Archives of General Psychiatry*, 1974, 30, 302–309.

Raskin, A. A guide for drug use in depressive disorders. *American Journal of Psychiatry*, 1974, 131, 181–185.

Raskin, A. & Crook, T. H. The endogenous–neurotic distinction as a predictor of response to antidepressant drugs. *Psychological Medicine*, 1976, 6, 59–70.

Raskin, A., Schulterbrandt, J. G., Reatig, N., Crook, T. H., & Odle, D. Depression subtypes and response to phenelzine, diazepam, and a placebo. (Results of a nine hospital collaborative study). *Archives of General Psychiatry*, 1974, 30, 66–75.

Raskin, A., Schulterbrandt, J. G., Reatig, N., & McKeon, J. J. Differential response to chlorpromazine, imipramine and placebo. A study of subgroups of hospitalized depressed patients. *Archives of General Psychiatry*, 1970, 23, 164–173.

Roth, M., Gurney, C., Garside, R. F., & Kerr, T. A. Studies in the classification of affective disorders—the relationship between anxiety states and depressive illnesses—I. *British Journal of Psychiatry*, 1972, *121*, 147–161.

Schapira, K., Roth, M., Kerr, T. A., & Gurney, C. The prognosis of affective disorders: The differentiation of anxiety states from depressive illnesses. *British Journal of Psychiatry*, 1972, *121*, 175–181.

Woodruff, R. A., Jr., Guze, S. B., & Clayton, P. J. Anxiety neurosis among psychiatric outpatients. *Comprehensive Psychiatry*, 1972, *13*, 165–170.

CHAPTER 5

The Conceptualization and Measurement of Stressful Life Events: An Overview of the Issues[1]

Bruce P. Dohrenwend and Barbara Snell Dohrenwend

INTRODUCTION

Studies of the effects of natural and man-made disasters—especially the disaster of war—have provided the most unequivocal evidence for the proposition that stressful events can produce psychopathology in previously normal personalities (Arthur, 1974; Cooper & Shepherd, 1970; Hocking, 1970; Kinston & Rosser, 1974). For example, when a systematic sample of the population in a rural section of Arkansas was interviewed shortly after the area was hit by a severe tornado, 90% reported "some form of acute emotional, physiological, or psychosomatic aftereffect [Fritz & Marks, 1954, p. 34]." Similarly, pervasive effects were implied by Star's (1949) finding, based on a series of studies during World War II using subscales from the Neuropsychiatric Screening Adjunct, that "the fear and anxiety implicit in combat

[1] This work has been supported by Research Grant MH 10328 and by Research Scientist Award K5 MH 14663 from the National Institute of Mental Health, U.S. Public Health Service. This chapter was also published in J. S. Strauss, H. M. Babigian, and M. Roff (Eds.), *Origins and Course of Psychopathology*. New York: Plenum Press, 1977. Pp. 93–115.

105

The Psychobiology of the Depressive Disorders:
Implications for the Effects of Stress

ISBN 0-12-211650-X

brought forth the psychosomatic manifestations in so many men that these [symptom scales] served less and less to discriminate between men who were labeled psychiatric casualties and those who were not [p. 455]."

Although elevation in symptom levels was not necessarily accompanied by a breakdown in performance, under some conditions such breakdowns became endemic. In a study of 2630 soldiers who had "broken down" during combat in the Normandy campaign of World War II, Swank estimated that the onset of combat exhaustion occurred, even in previously normal soldiers, when about 65% of their companions had been killed, wounded, or had otherwise become casualties (1949, p. 501). Swank emphasized that the men in this study had been highly selected for health and ability to cope. As Swank (1949) describes them: "They were of better than average stability and willingness by virtue of the fact that they had passed the various training tests (induction, overseas assignment, battle simulation exercises), had been selected for combat units, and had proved their mettle by remaining in combat varying lengths of time [p. 476]." And although men who were stable prior to combat remained in combat longer without experiencing a performance of breakdown (pp. 480, 500), such prior stability did not prevent the eventual onset of combat exhaustion (p. 507).

Nor are the symptoms caused by such situations of extreme stress limited to those included under the heading of traumatic war neurosis, combat fatigue, and combat exhaustion. There is evidence that psychotic symptoms can appear in the form of what have been called "3 day" psychoses (Kolb, 1973, p. 438). It is possible, in fact, that such extreme circumstances can play a major role in inducing outright psychotic disorder because, as Paster (1948) found, there is far less evidence of individual predisposing factors in combat soldiers who became psychotic than among soldiers who developed psychotic disorders in less stressful circumstances. It would seem that most of the varied signs and symptoms observed in psychiatric patients in civilian settings have also been observed as reactions to combat (e.g., Kolb, 1973, pp. 436–438). In this sense, war has been indeed "a laboratory which manufactures psychological dysfunction [Grinker & Spiegel, 1963, p. vii]."

The extent to which symptomatology and disturbance of functioning produced by such extreme situations in previously normal persons are transient and self-limiting is a matter of controversy (Kinston & Rosser, 1974). Most observers have emphasized the transience of the symptoms (Dohrenwend & Dohrenwend, 1969, pp. 110–130). At the same time, studies in which persons exposed to these extraordinary events have been examined years later have repeatedly found some individuals with more or less severe pathology that apparently began at the time the stressful experience occurred (Kinston & Rosser, 1974, pp. 445–448). Certainly at the extreme of exposure to the brutalities of Nazi concentration camps, there is strong evidence that not only does severe stress-induced psychopathology persist in the survivors (Eitinger, 1964), but also that the survivors are more prone to physical illness and early death (Eitinger, 1973).

THE PROBLEM

Natural and man-made disasters, fortunately, are rare occurrences whose devastating effects are limited to relatively small populations of exposed persons. Most people live their lives without experiencing any of these extraordinary events. Yet psychopathology and somatic disturbances are far from rare in peacetime populations relatively secure from war, flood, famine, and other disasters. If stressful situations play an etiologic role in these disorders, the events involved must be more ordinary, more frequent experiences in the lives of most people. It is for this reason that we turn our attention to things that happen to most people at one time or another— things such as marriage, birth of a first child, and death of a loved one. These are not extraordinary events in the sense of being of rare occurrence in most populations. But they are extraordinary occurrences in the lives of the individuals who experience them. They are the life events that most of us experience, in a greater or lesser number, over our allotted years.

Most of these life events, taken singly, are far less extreme than natural or man-made disasters. One reason is that a disaster is likely to entail as sequelae a number of events occurring simultaneously or closely spaced in sequence (e.g., injury, loss of home and other possessions, death of a loved one). It seems reasonable to assume that life events must show a cumulative pattern, a clustering in the lives of some people in otherwise more ordinary times, if they are to have a similarly stressful impact and similarly severe consequences. This is the strongest reason, we believe, for seeking information about the occurrence of a wide variety of life events and their relationship to one another in investigations of the possible etiologic significance of such events in physical and psychological disorders. If life events have an etiologic significance, the central question becomes: What kinds of life events, in what combination, over what period of time, and under what circumstances are causally implicated in various types of physical and psychiatric disorders?

To date, the results of research on the influence of these more ordinary life events on various types of physical and psychiatric conditions are far more equivocal than the results of research on the effects of natural and man-made disasters. We will, therefore, selectively review the results of this research and the controversies to which these investigations have given rise as a background to our attempt to set forth the major methodological issues that need to be resolved.

PREVIOUS RESEARCH ON
STRESSFUL LIFE EVENTS

The Correlates of Such Events

The greatest variety of correlates of life events have been described by Holmes and Masuda (1974). In addition to reporting that overall changes in health were related to life events, they cited studies showing the following specific correlates: heart disease, fractures, childhood leukemia, pregnancy, beginning of prison term, poor teacher performance, low college grade-point average, and football injuries. Among the specific somatic disorders, Hinkle (1974, p. 38) and Theorell (1974) have focused attention on coronary heart disease, both fatal and nonfatal in outcome.

Paykel (1974), Hudgens (1974), and Brown (1974) among them have added evidence that various types of psychiatric disorder may follow life events; specifically, acute schizophrenia, depression, suicide attempts, and neurosis. The range of correlates has been expanded to include associations with symptom scales that measure various types of psychological distress, rather than outright disorder. Markush and Favero (1974) found that relatively mild symptoms of depression, as well as a symptom scale of less specific psychological distress, were related to measures of life events. Uhlenhuth, Lipman, Balter, and Stern (1974) have reported similar findings. Myers, Lindenthal, and Pepper (1974) have shown with still another measure of symptomatic distress that symptom scores will fluctuate over time with fluctuations in the nature and number of life events experienced. In addition, Gersten, Langner, Eisenberg, and Orzek (1974) have shown that the associations between various symptom measures and life events hold for children, as well as for adults. Such evidence from recent clinical and epidemiological investigations is consistent with Hinkle's (1974) conclusion "that there would probably be no aspect of human growth, development, or disease which would in theory be immune to the influence of the effect of a man's relation to his social and interpersonal environment [p. 10]." It would seem that almost any disease or disability may be associated with these events.

Controversy about Interpretation

But "may" is not "will"; the important questions become: First, what is the probability or risk that disorder will actually follow life events? And second, if disorder does follow, why is it of one type rather than another? On these questions, we find ourselves in the realm of controversy.

Holmes and Masuda (1974), for example, appear to assume that a clustering in time of life events of sufficient magnitude will have strong etiologic implications for physical or psychiatric health that are relatively indepen-dent of the constitutional or other predisposing characteristics of the indi-vidual involved. They postulate that when more ordinary life events ac-cumulate to "crisis" proportions, these events will evoke "adaptive efforts by the human organism that are faulty in kind and duration, lower 'bodily resistance' and enhance the probability of disease occurrence [p. 68]." Such a "crisis" will have "etiologic significance as a necessary, but not sufficient, cause of illness and accounts in part for the time of disease onset [p. 48]." By contrast, Hinkle (1974) sees the role of predisposing factors as primary, with accumulations of stressful life events playing a very secondary part. Other investigators tend more or less explicitly to assign varied weights to life events as a threat to health in general or in the etiology of particular disorders (Dohrenwend & Dohrenwend, 1974). In general, the consensus that has grown up about the impact of extreme situations such as natural or man-made disasters has not extended to more ordinary stressful life events.

SOURCES OF CONTROVERSY

The basic difficulty is that the evidence currently available simply does not permit us to answer questions about how important stressful life events are in the etiology of the various types of symptomatology and disorder with which such events have been found to be associated. There are three sets of reasons for the ambiguities: The first has to do with the designs of most of the research in which such correlations have been found; the second con-cerns the ways the populations of stressful life events have been defined and sampled for purposes of these investigations; and the third involves the procedures used to assess the stressfulness of the life events independently of their relationship to the symptoms, illnesses, or disorders that are being investigated.

Design Limitations

The majority of the studies of the effects of stressful life events have involved case-control designs. That is, the investigators have started with a group or series of patients and then compared these cases with a group or series of controls, usually healthy persons matched to the clinical cases on some of the relevant background characteristics.

In the case-control studies, the frequent finding that, compared to their controls, the clinical cases tend to have an excess of stressful life events prior to illness onset suggests that such events are a factor in the etiology of the disorder. However, only studies of cohorts of persons who differ with respect

to the nature and number of stressful life events experienced provide information about the magnitude of the risk that illness will actually follow these
events. Although a few such studies of general health changes in special
groups of nonpatients have been published (Holmes & Masuda, 1974),
research on the relationship between diagnosed psychiatric disorders and
life events in nonpatient populations is barely beginning (e.g., Dohrenwend,
1974). Most of the published literature on the relationship between life
events and psychological problems in general populations contains reports
of results obtained using scales measuring psychological distress in general,
rather than for cases of psychiatric disorders. In addition, only a few such
studies provide data over time (e.g., Myers *et al.*, 1974). By and large,
therefore, there is no satisfactory way from the existing data to calculate the
magnitude of risk entailed in various types and numbers of life events for
physical illnesses (Dohrenwend & Dohrenwend, 1974, pp. 315–316) much
less for psychiatric disorders.

Problems in Sampling the Relevant Population
of Stressful Life Events

Especially when the role of life events in relation to psychopathology is
being examined, there is a problem not only about how to estimate the
magnitude of risk attached to the life events but, even more basic, whether
etiologic inferences from the correlations of these events with psychopathology are warranted in the first place. This problem resides less in
the research designs used to investigate the events than in how the events to
be studied have been defined and sampled.

Consider some of the general definitions of stressful life events used by
researchers who have investigated the relationship of various samples of
such events to physical and psychological symptoms and disorders. For
Holmes and Rahe (1967), extrapolating from the types of events they extracted from "life charts" recording case histories of patients admitted to
treatment for medical problems, stressful life events are those "whose ad-
vent is either indicative of or requires a significant change in the ongoing life
pattern of the individual [p. 217]." Brown and Birley (1968) focus on "events
which on common sense grounds are likely to produce emotional disturbance in many people . . . [and usually involve] either danger; significant
changes in health, status or way of life; the promise of these; or important
fulfillments or disappointments [p. 204]." Similarly, Myers and his colleagues (1972) define "crises" or "events" as "experiences involving role
transformations, changes in status or environment, or impositions of pain
[p. 399]." Antonovsky and Kats (1967) refer to "life crises" consisting of
"objective situations which, on the face of it, would seem to be universally

stressful" and involving "an experience which either imposed pain or neces-
sitated a role transformation [p. 16]."

These definitions indicate both broad agreement and some differences in
emphasis concerning what is important about life events. The agreement
centers on the idea that stressful life events include those that involve
change in the usual activities of most individuals who experience them. The
differences and the reasons for them are more varied. Some of the differences are straightforward in the sense that there are important events
specific and meaningful to some groups of subjects and not to others. For
example, it is meaningful to include "court martial" on lists of events to be
investigated among military personnel (Rahe, McKean, & Arthur, 1967) and
experience in Nazi concentration camps are meaningful in studies done in
Israel (Antonovsky & Kats, 1967). Other differences, however, reflect underlying issues of major theoretical and methodological importance that are
barely suggested by the contrasts in emphasis among the highly abstract and
imprecise general definitions of life events quoted above.

The first of these issues is partly evident in the distinction between
objective and subjective events made by some investigators (e.g., Thurlow,
1971). Subjective events (e.g., "sexual difficulties," "major change in
number of arguments with spouse," and "major changes in sleeping habits"
see Holmes & Masuda, 1974, pp. 48–49) are more likely to be manifestations
of, or responses to, underlying psychopathology than causes of such pathology. Moreover, the problem is not limited to "subjective" events as many
"objective" events (e.g., "divorce" or "being fired from work," see Holmes &
Masuda, 1974, pp. 48–49) contained on the lists of different researchers are
as likely to be consequences as causes of psychopathology. Determination of
whether objective events are consequences of or causes of psychopathology
depends on the investigator's ability to date their onset in relation to the
onset of the pathology, and to learn something about whether the events are
within or outside the control of the subject. By Hudgens' count (1974), for
example, 29 out of the 43 events on the list constructed by Holmes and Rahe
(1967) "are often the symptoms or consequences of illness [p. 131]." As
Brown (1974) and B. P. Dohrenwend (1974) have pointed out, this type of
bias in a sample of live events seriously limits the kinds of inferences that can
be drawn from a correlation between the number or magnitude of events
experienced and the illness. The limitation on causal inference in particular
is especially severe in investigations of psychiatric disorders that are often of
insidious onset and long duration.

Most samples of events also include major physical illness or injury—
understandably enough as these are negative events and entail serious
disruption of usual activities. However, it is a basic proposition of
psychosomatic medicine that physical disorders are accompanied by some
degree of emotional disturbance and emotional disorders by some degree of

somatic disturbance. There is no instance of which we are aware in which investigations of the relationship between physical illness and emotional disturbance have failed to report a strong positive correlation between the two (Lipowski, 1975). Additionally, as Hinkle (1974) points out with reference to various types of physical illness, "The presence of one disease may imply the presence of others and beget yet other diseases [p. 39]," a fact that accounts in part for his finding that the risk of disease is not randomly distributed in groups of similar people who share similar experiences over periods of from 10 to 20 years (Hinkle, 1974). Thus, once again, a sample of events that includes physical illness and injury—and most lists do—can lead to further problems of interpretation when the events are summed to provide scores for the amount of stress experienced by particular individuals. The additional problem of interpretation centers on the extent to which a positive correlation indicates the impact of the amount of change and hence the amount of stress on health. It may, instead, indicate a relation among physical illnesses or between physical and psychiatric symptomatology— important problems in their own right.

We have argued, therefore, that there are at least three distinct populations of life events that must be sampled and kept distinct for purposes of analysis (B. P. Dohrenwend, 1974; Dohrenwend & Dohrenwend, 1974). These are:

1. A population of events that are confounded with the psychiatric condition of the subject
2. A population of events consisting of physical illnesses and injuries to the subject
3. A population of events whose occurrences are independent of either the subject's physical health or his psychiatric condition.

As a general principle, the more a sample of events in a particular measure of stressful life events represents a summated mixture of these three event-populations, the more difficult it is to assess the etiologic implications of a relationship between such a measure and various types of psychopathology.

Nor is it likely that meaningful distinctions will end with specifications of these three main types of event-populations. Paykel (1974), for example, found in case-control studies that events involving the loss or exit of significant others from the immediate environment are conspicuous in the histories of the onset of depressive disorders. This is, of course, a theoretically relevant finding and it raises the intriguing possibility that other theoretically dictated distinctions may sharpen the specificity with which particular outcomes can be predicted for particular types of stressful life events.

It would seem, then, that it will be necessary to refine the largely commonsense definitions of stressful life events quoted previously if we are to build on available theory and completed research, while avoiding some of the problems and pitfalls involved in previous work. Such specification would be a prerequisite to deciding on the relevant populations of events to be sampled (e.g., physical illnesses and accidents, loss events outside the individual's control, and so on). Once the realms of events in which we are interested have been designated, it is also useful to get nominations from the subjects to be studied as to the composition of such event populations. We have found in our previous research that the respondents interviewed mentioned quite a number of events they deemed "major" but that we failed to include on our own "common sense" checklist of events (e.g., B. P. Dohrenwend, 1974). Our question to our respondents was "What is the last major event in your life that, for better or worse, interrupted or changed your usual activities?" As our own definitions of what constitutes stressful life events become more precise, we should be able to put increasingly precise questions to our subjects as we enlist their help in delimiting the relevant populations of life events to be sampled.

Once the realms of events to be sampled have been enumerated, the question becomes one of how to sample them in a particular study. There is no easy answer. Coverage of the total population of events experienced by a particular individual over the course of his or her lifetime runs into major practical obstacles; foremost among them is the problem of imperfect recall of remote events (Uhlenhuth, 1974). It is for this reason that focus is often on a recent time sample of events (e.g., during the past year). We strongly suspect, however, that the factors of primacy, frequency, and recency would affect the impact of life events, as they do most things (Horowitz, Schaefer, & Cooney, 1974). For example, if the loss reported in the past year is one in a cumulative pattern of losses over the preceding 5 years, it might be expected to have added weight, if other things remained constant. On the other hand, it is possible that early experience with some types of events may "protect" against adverse effects of recent events of the same kind. This appears to be the case in bereavement (Bornstein, Clayton, Halikas, Maurice, & Robins, 1973, p. 565). There is also evidence that early adversity may be a factor leading to superior performance later in life—at least among highly educated males selected for health (Vaillant, 1974, p. 19).

The problem is one of how to come to terms with the opposition between practicality and what is required on grounds of theoretically relevant research operations. There is never an easy answer to such a question. Our own suggestion is to focus on contemporary events but to study their relationship to psychopathology prospectively as well as retrospectively. In addition, we believe it necessary to also try to elicit from our subjects, by way of context, a history of certain more remote landmark events from the event populations in which we are most interested (B. P. Dohrenwend, 1974). Examples of the latter would be deaths or other major separations from parents or parent surrogates—something few adults will fail to remember about their childhood—and incapacitating physical injuries and illnesses—things likely to be remembered about one's history of physical problems.

Assessing the Stressfulness of Life Events

Let us assume for purposes of argument that the general design limitations and the general problems of defining and sampling the relevant population of stressful life events have been surmounted. This would be a long step toward being able to assess whether causal inferences from correlations between life events and various types of disorder and symptomatology were warranted. It should also take us part of the way to learning why different types of disorder follow stressful life events. Additional problems will have to be resolved, however, if we are to be able to specify the risk attached to life events for various types of disorders.

THE MAGNITUDE OF THE EVENTS

In laboratory stress experiments with animals, there is little difficulty in defining the magnitude of the stressful event to which the subjects are introduced. The experimental animals receive shocks of greater or lesser voltage, are exposed to heat or cold of varying temperature, are deprived of food for greater or lesser periods of time, and so on. Similarly, extreme situations appear to have self-evident indications of magnitude, for example: duration of time in combat; number of wounded in the soldier's company; and so on. For the more usual life events with which we are concerned here, however, things are by no means so clear cut. Is "marriage" more or less stressful than "divorce?" Is "birth of a first child" more or less stressful than "being laid off a job?" Are "marriage" and "divorce" together more or less stressful than "birth of a first child" and "being laid off a job?"

Holmes and Rahe (1967) have offered a very attractive simplification of the problem in the Schedule of Recent Events and the Social Readjustment Ratings that they have secured for purposes of scoring. As mentioned earlier, Holmes and Rahe constructed a list of events that they found were positively correlated with illness onset in large samples of medical patients. Their method of scoring these events followed S. S. Stevens' proposal that direct estimation procedures that had been found to produce a consistent quantitative relationship between physical stimuli and perceptual responses could also be used to measure psychological dimensions related to social stimuli.

A simple form of this procedure, magnitude estimation, involves designating a modulus with an assigned value and asking judges to rate other stimuli in relation to the modulus. Holmes and Rahe designated "marriage" as the modulus, assigned it a value of 500, and obtained quantitative judgments about the amount of change or "readjustment" in relation to it for each of the other 42 events on their list. Life-change Unit (LCU) scores based on these ratings have been presented as a measure of the stressfulness of the rated events just as, in psychophysical experiments, ratings of sounds provide a measure of their loudness. The argument of Holmes and his colleagues is that if we weight events in terms of their different LCU scores and pay attention to how these weights add up when a series of events occurs, the risk of illness attached to the life events will vary directly with the magnitude of the LCU scores.

Holmes in particular has emphasized the high level of consensus about the amount of change associated with each life event. He refers to correlations in the .80s and .90s between the mean rating for each event, obtained from such diverse status groups as Blacks, Japanese, and Whites. His argument for the universalism of perceptions of the amount of change entailed by and hence the stressfulness of particular life events, however, has been sharply criticized. Among others, two of Holmes' collaborators have pointed out that considerable group differences are masked by the reported correlations: Specifically, Rahe (1969) found that ratings secured in Sweden were consistently higher than Holmes' West Coast American ratings. And Masuda and Holmes (1967) pointed out that certain differences in ratings of events by Japanese and American judges seem to be related to differences between the two cultures. Other researchers have also reported cultural contrasts. Miller, Bentz, Aponte, and Brogan (1974) have found sharp differences in the way their sample of rural North Carolina judges and Holmes' and Rahe's urban West Coast sample ranked such events as "marriage" and "taking out a mortgage of greater than $10,000." In the urban sample, for example, marriage is ranked fourth versus twenty-first in the rural sample in terms of the amount of change involved. Miller *et al.* argue that these differences are meaningful in terms of contrasts in the norms and customs of the two samples. Hough, Fairbank, and Garcia (1976) have reported differences in the judged magnitude of life events corresponding to differences in the cultural backgrounds of their college student subjects. Still other critics such as Brown (1974) have pointed out large individual variability in the LCU ratings in Holmes' and Rahe's data.

It seems to us that there are, nevertheless, great virtues in the general procedure developed by Holmes and his colleagues. It makes sense that some events are, objectively, of greater magnitude than others. Who would argue, for example, that the "death of a pet" is inherently as large an event as the "death of a spouse?" Yet, it also seems to us that much further work on the scaling procedures themselves needs to be done (Hough, Fairbank, & Garcia, 1976). Individual variability can probably be reduced by providing less ambiguous descriptions of the events to be rated (e.g., instead of the event "change in responsibilities at work" supply two events, "change to more responsibility" and "change to less responsibility at work"). It may also be possible to simplify the rating task, and thereby improve reliability of judgments, by using categorization procedures rather than direct estimation of a value for each event in relation to a standard.

The problem of cultural differences in judgments about the events is interesting in its own right, as Holmes is aware. As Holmes points out, the LCU ratings "offer a powerful tool for delineating quantitatively and qualitatively cross-cultural differences [1974, p. 57]." If so, the procedure for dealing with such differences would be to secure ratings from members of each of the contrasting groups and compute LCU scores that are specific to each of the groups (Hough, Fairbank, & Garcia, 1976).

Moreover, it is possible to envision valuable extensions of the rating procedure. To date, the judgments have focused on the amount of change associated with the events. Yet, the general definitions of stressful life events quoted earlier mention other properties that might be scaled, such as the desirability or undesirability of the events; the amount of loss or gain involved; and, where illness or injury or crime are involved, the seriousness or severity of the event. Some important work of this kind has already been done on various physical illnesses by Wyler, Masuda, and Holmes (1968). In general, the extension of ratings beyond the single dimension of the amount of change would probably yield improved measures of the stressfulness of life events.

By and large, however, critics of the scaling procedures developed by Holmes and his colleagues have taken other tacks. Concern about the individual variability in judgments made regarding the magnitude of life events has led to two recent innovations in measurement. The first is a Subjective Life Change Unit scaling system developed by Rahe (1974, pp. 76–77). In this procedure, the same subjects who are asked about events that have occurred in their lives and about their illness experiences also rate the amount of change involved in the events they have experienced. Rahe has found that the resulting subjective LCU scores are better predictors of illness than the objective LCU scores. The second innovation has been developed by Brown (1974) and relies on interviewers to probe the circumstances surrounding each event experienced by the subject and rate them on a number of dimensions, of which he has found "contextual threat" to be the most useful.

Although both procedures have the virtue of being directed at real difficulties with the original LCU ratings, both innovations have problems of their own that are at least as severe. It is difficult to see, for example, what we learn on the basis of Rahe's subjective rating procedure if we find that a person who has suffered a heart attack after a particular event tends to rate that event as more stressful than a person who has not suffered such an attack. It seems highly likely that his experience with the heart attack would lead the subject to retrospectively place a negative halo around the event.

Surely such a rating tells us nothing about the antecedents of the illness that will add to our knowledge of etiology or aid in prevention.

Brown (1974), by contrast with Rahe, argues that his procedure for securing ratings of contextual threat by the interviewer is measuring objective circumstances rather than subjective perceptions of an event. The problem is that his method, at least as it has been developed and described to date, asks that we accept a certain mystification of measurement. We must rely upon a mystic acceptance because so much is left to the interviewer and to his training in this particular procedure that it is not explicit or readily replicable by others. Thus, we think that Brown is right in arguing that the circumstances of an event influence its impact. As so far developed, however, it is difficult to see how his global rating procedure advances our understanding of the nature of that influence. The problem, it seems to us, is to make explicit what is implicit in this approach so that its virtues and defects can be assessed.

MEDIATING FACTORS

In our opinion, the most valuable part of Brown's approach is that it draws attention to the fact that the stressfulness of an event or event combinations may be a function as much or more of the context in which they occur as of the magnitude of the events themselves. Brown (1974) points to contextual threat examined especially in terms of the social circumstances of the subjects of his research on schizophrenia and depression as a possible mediator of the impact of life events. Antonovsky (1974) theorizes about a wide variety of social and psychological "resistance resources" that mediate the impact of life events. And Hinkle (1974) who, as we pointed out earlier, differs most sharply from Holmes on the importance of life events by contrast with other predisposing factors in etiology, emphasizes "pre-existing illness or susceptibility to illness [p. 42]."

Let us try to clarify this central controversy over the relative importance of the stressful life events themselves by contrast with the myriad factors that mediate their impact. To do so, we will make use of a general paradigm of the stress response based on Selyé's (1956) formulations and translated by one of us into social and psychological terms (Dohrenwend, 1961). The paradigm consists of four main elements abstracted from Selye's formulations: (a) an antecedent stressor—often a toxic agent or electric shock in Selye's experiments with animals; (b) conditioning or mediating factors, such as climate or diet, that increase or decrease the impact of the stressor; (c) the General Adaptation Syndrome of nonspecific physical and chemical changes, indicating the intervening state of stress in an organism over time; and (d) consequent adaptive or, in cases where there is a "derailment" of the mechanism of adaptation, maladaptive responses in the form of what Selye calls "diseases of adaptation."

Figure 5.1

By stripping these four kinds of elements of particular examples, it is possible to arrive at the general paradigm of the individual organism's stress response shown in Figure 5.1. The elements of this general paradigm, in turn, can be translated into social and psychological terms. For example, stressors can range from extreme situations such as natural and man-made disasters to the more ordinary stressful life events that we have been considering. In addition, mediating factors can be expanded to include both inner resources (e.g., intellectual abilities, physical health) and external resources (e.g., material wealth, social support in the form of family and friends).

Whether there is a *General* Adaptation Syndrome of nonspecific physical and chemical changes has been questioned (Mason, 1975). Whether there is anything directly analogous to it in social and psychological terms is an open issue. We have, therefore, left out the adjective "general" in Figure 5.1. Certainly, however, social-psychological adaptation syndromes must have affective elements of adaptation rooted in the arousal responses of fear and anger; conative elements of adaptation involving change or re-emphasis in activities—abandoning some activities, taking up others, increasing or decreasing still other activities; and adaptation is also likely to involve changes in orientation involving the assimilation of new information, alteration of beliefs, and so on. Finally, when the adaptation fails or the mechanisms underlying it become "derailed," we can look for maladaptive responses in the form of transient or persistent psychopathology.

In the context of this paradigm, it is easy to see why the results of research on extreme situations, such as exposure to combat in wartime, have seemed so much more clear-cut than the results of research on more ordinary stressful life events. Not only are differentials in the severity of combat stressors self-evident (e.g., the casualty rate for a company; duration of combat), but also, these stressors have been shown to be more important than the internal and external mediating factors. Thus, while external mediating factors (e.g., leadership, troop morale) and internal mediating factors (e.g., prior psychiatric disorder) are important in determining, for example, how much combat can be withstood before combat exhaustion occurs, the severity of the combat situation will override the mediating factors (e.g., Swank, 1949).

Nothing of the sort has been shown to be the case with more usual stressful life events in peacetime civilian populations. Rather, major theoretical controversies occur for physical illness and psychiatric disorders regarding questions about the relative importance of life events versus the external and internal factors mediating their impact (Brown, 1974; B. P. Dohrenwend, 1974; Holmes & Masuda, 1974; Hinkle, 1974; Hudgens, 1974; Mechanic, 1974). There are unanswered empirical questions underlying this controversy. If we are to have better answers, we shall have to be able to measure the magnitude of the life events with something approaching the incisiveness with which we measure the magnitude of electric shock or exposure to combat.

CONCLUSION

Life events are eminently researchable. They happen to the people we study and are important to them. Life events are things that people know about, are interested in, and can tell us about. If environmentally induced stress is an important factor in psychopathology, then life events are strategic phenomena upon which to focus as possible major sources of such stress.

The problem, however, is to ask the right questions about life events and their effects under circumstances in which the answers will provide clear demonstrations of whether, and to what extent, they are causally related to psychopathology. As our analysis suggests, it is by no means clear that the research has demonstrated their importance either in the etiology of psychiatric disorders or of physical illnesses—though the fascinating tangle of correlations reported virtually demands increased research efforts toward clarification (Dohrenwend and Dohrenwend, 1974). In this chapter, we have described our views about some of the ingredients that we believe such efforts should have if advances are to be made in our understanding of the effects of life events on physical and emotional health.

REFERENCES

Antonovsky, A. Conceptual and methodological problems in the study of resistance resources and stressful life events. In B. S. Dohrenwend & B. P. Dohrenwend (Eds.), *Stressful life events. Their nature and effects*. New York: Wiley, 1974. Pp. 245–255.

Antonovsky, A. & Kats, R. The life crisis history as a tool in epidemiological research. *Journal of Health and Social Behavior*, 1967, 8, 15–21.

Arthur, R. J. Extreme stress in adult life and psychic and psychophysiological consequences. In E. K. E. Gunderson & R. H. Rahe (Eds.), *Life stress and illness*. Springfield, Illinois: Thomas, 1974. Pp. 195–207.

Bornstein, P. E., Clayton, P. J., Halikas, J. A., Maurice, W. L., & Robins, E. The depression of widowhood after thirteen months. *British Journal of Psychiatry*, 1973, 122, 561–566.

Brown, G. W. Meaning, measurement, and stress of life events. In B. S. Dohrenwend & B. P.

Dohrenwend (Eds.), *Stressful life events: Their nature and effects*. New York: Wiley, 1974. Pp. 217–243.

Brown, G. W., & Birley, J. L. T. Crises and life changes and the onset of schizophrenia. *Journal of Health and Social Behavior*, 1968, 9, 203–214.

Cooper, B. & Shepherd, M. Life change, stress and mental disorder: The ecological approach. In J. H. Price (Ed.), *Modern trends in psychological medicine* (Vol. 2). London: Butterworths, 1970. Pp. 102–130.

Dohrenwend, B. P. The social psychological nature of stress: A framework for causal inquiry. *Journal of Abnormal and Social Psychology*. 1961, 62, 294–302.

Dohrenwend, B. P. Problems in defining and sampling the relevant population of stressful life events. In B. S. Dohrenwend & B. P. Dohrenwend (Eds.), *Stressful life events: Their nature and effects*. New York: Wiley, 1974. Pp. 275–310.

Dohrenwend, B. P. & Dohrenwend, B. S. *Social status and psychological disorder*. New York: Wiley, 1969.

Dohrenwend, B. S. & Dohrenwend, B. P. (Eds.). *Stressful life events: Their nature and effects*. New York: Wiley, 1974.

Eitinger, L. *Concentration camp survivors in Norway and Israel*. London: Allen & Unwin, 1964.

Eitinger, L. A follow-up of the Norwegian concentration camp survivors' mortality and morbidity. *Israel Annals of Psychiatry and Related Disciplines*, 1973, 11, 199–209.

Fritz, C. E. & Marks, E. S. The NORC studies of human behavior in disaster. *Journal of Social Issues*, 1954, 10, 26–41.

Gersten, J. C., Langner, T. S., Eisenberg, J. G., & Orzek, L. Child behavior and life events: Undesirable change or change per se? In B. P. Dohrenwend & B. S. Dohrenwend (Eds.), *Stressful life events: Their nature and effects*. New York: Wiley, 1974. Pp. 159–170.

Grinker, R. R. & Spiegel, J. P. *Men under stress*. New York: McGraw-Hill, 1963.

Hinkle, L. E. The effect of exposure to culture change, social change, and changes in interpersonal relationships on health. In B. P. Dohrenwend & B. S. Dohrenwend (Eds.), *Stressful life events: Their nature and effects*. New York: Wiley, 1974. Pp. 9–44.

Hocking, F. Extreme environmental stress and its significance for psychopathology. *American Journal of Psychotherapy*, 1970, 24, 4–26.

Holmes, T. H. & Masuda, M. Life change and illness susceptibility. In B. P. Dohrenwend & B. S. Dohrenwend (Eds.), *Stressful life events: Their nature and effects*. New York: Wiley, 1974. Pp. 45–72.

Holmes, T. H. & Rahe, R. H. The social readjustment rating scale. *Journal of Psychosomatic Medicine*, 1967, 11, 213–218.

Horowitz, M. J., Schaefer, C., & Cooney, P. Life event scaling for recency of experience. In E. K. E. Gunderson & R. H. Rahe (Eds.), *Life stress and illness*. Springfield, Illinois: Thomas, 1974. Pp. 125–133.

Hough, R. L., Fairbank, D. T., & Garcia, A. M. Problems in the ratio measurement of life stress. *Journal of Health and Social Behavior*, 1976, 17, 70–82.

Hudgens, R. W. Personal catastrophe and depression: A consideration of the subject with respect to medically ill adolescents, and a requiem for retrospective life-event studies. In B. P. Dohrenwend & B. S. Dohrenwend (Eds.), *Stressful life events: Their nature and effects*. New York: Wiley, 1974. Pp. 119–134.

Kinston, W. & Rosser, R. Disaster: Effects on mental and physical state. *Journal of Psychosomatic Research*, 1974, 18, 437–456.

Kolb, L. C. *Modern clinical psychiatry*. Philadelphia: Saunders, 1973.

Lipowski, Z. J. Psychiatry of somatic diseases: Epidemiology, pathogenesis, classification. *Comprehensive Psychiatry*, 1975, 16, 105–124.

Markush, R. E. & Favero, R. V. Epidemiologic assessment of stressful life events, depressed mood, and psychophysiological symptoms—a preliminary report. In B. P. Dohrenwend & B. S. Dohrenwend (Eds.), *Stressful life events: Their nature and effects*. New York: Wiley, 1974. Pp. 171–190.

Mason, J. W. A historical view of the stress field. *Journal of Human Stress*, 1975, *1*, 6–12.

Masuda, M., & Holmes, T. H. Magnitude estimations of social readjustments. *Journal of Psychosomatic Research*, 1967, *11*, 219–225.

Mechanic, D. Discussion of research programs on relations between stressful life events and episodes of physical illness. In B. S. Dohrenwend & B. P. Dohrenwend (Eds.), *Stressful life events: Their nature and effects*. New York: Wiley, 1974. Pp. 87–97.

Miller, F. T., Bentz, W. K., Aponte, J. F., & Brogan, D. R. Perception of life crisis events. In B. P. Dohrenwend & B. S. Dohrenwend (Eds.), *Stressful life events: Their nature and effects*. New York: Wiley, 1974. Pp. 259–273.

Myers, J. K., Lindenthal, J. J., Pepper, M. P., & Ostrander, D. K. Life events and mental status: A longitudinal study. *Journal of Health and Social Behavior*, 1972, *13*, 398–406.

Myers, J. K., Lindenthal, J. J., & Pepper, M. P. Social class, life events, and psychiatric symptoms: A longitudinal study. In B. P. Dohrenwend & B. S. Dohrenwend (Eds.), *Stressful life events: Their nature and effects*. New York: Wiley, 1974. Pp. 191–205.

Paster, S. Psychotic reactions among soldiers of World War II. *Journal of Nervous and Mental Disease*, 1948, *108*, 54–66.

Paykel, E. S. Life stress and psychiatric disorder: Application of the clinical approach. In B. P. Dohrenwend & B. S. Dohrenwend (Eds.), *Stressful life events: Their nature and effects*. New York: Wiley, 1974. Pp. 135–149.

Rahe, R. H., McKean, J. D., & Arthur, R. J. A longitudinal study of life-change and illness patterns. *Journal of Psychosomatic Research*, 1967, *10*, 355–366.

Rahe, R. H. Multi-cultural correlations of life change scaling: America, Japan, Denmark, and Sweden. *Journal of Psychosomatic Research*, 1969, *13*, 191–195.

Rahe, R. H. The pathway between subjects' recent life changes and their near-future illness reports: Representative results and methodological issues. In B. P. Dohrenwend & B. S. Dohrenwend (Eds.), *Stressful life events: Their nature and effects*. New York: Wiley, 1974. Pp. 73–86.

Selye, H. *The stress of life*. New York: McGraw-Hill, 1956.

Star, S. A. Psychoneurotic symptoms in the army. In S. A. Stouffer, L. Guttman, E. A. Suchman, P. F. Lazarsfeld, S. A. Star, & J. A. Clausen (Eds.), *Studies in social psychology in World War II. The American soldier: Combat and its aftermath*. Princeton, New Jersey: Princeton Univ. Press, 1949. Pp. 411–455.

Swank, R. L. Combat exhaustion. *Journal of Nervous and Mental Disease*, 1949, *109*, 475–508.

Theorell, T. Life events before and after the onset of a premature myocardial infarction. In B. P. Dohrenwend & B. S. Dohrenwend (Eds.), *Stressful life events: Their nature and effects*. New York: Wiley, 1974. Pp. 101–117.

Thurlow, H. J. Illness in relation to life situation and sick-role tendency. *Journal of Psychosomatic Research*, 1971, *15*, 73–88.

Uhlenhuth, E., Balter, M. D., Lipman, R. S., & Haberman, S. J. Remembering life events. In J. S. Strauss, H. M. Babigian, & M. Roff (Eds.), *Origins and course of psychopathology*. New York: Plenum Press: 1977. Pp. 117–132.

Uhlenhuth, E. H., Lipman, R. S., Balter, M. B., & Stern, M. Symptom intensity and life stress in the city. *Archives of General Psychiatry*, 1974, *31*, 759–764.

Vaillant, G. E. Natural history of male psychological health: Some antecedents of healthy adult adjustment. *Archives of General Psychiatry*, 1974, *31*, 15–22.

Wyler, A. R., Masuda, M., & Holmes, T. H. Seriousness of Illness Rating Scale. *Journal of Psychosomatic Research*, 1968, *11*, 363–374.

PART III

The Interaction of Stress and Biologic Variables in the Depressive Disorders

One of the more challenging problems in attempting to understand the role of stress as an initiator of depressive disorders concerns the manner in which stress alters or modifies biologic predisposing variables. Research on this problem, particularly clinical research, is only in its initial stages. However, several significant trends exist that are important in their own right, as well as a model for future stress–biology interaction studies.

This section focuses in large part on the catecholamines. This group of neurotransmitters has been studied most extensively in the depressive disorders, and it is heavily implicated in their pathophysiology. Moreover, several peripheral indexes that reflect central catecholaminergic metabolism appear to exist, rendering the study of stress–catecholamine interactions possible.

Weiss and his colleagues lead off with a discussion of the relationship between psychological parameters and brain catecholamine metabolism in Chapter 6. Because their work is with animals, it is able to provide an understanding of the interaction of psychological and biologic variables thus far unattainable in clinical studies. Nevertheless, there are interesting clinical studies being conducted on stress and catecholamine metabolism.

Sweeney and Maas in Chapter 7 present their recent data on stress, anxiety, and urinary 3-methoxy-4-hydroxyphenylglycol (MHPG), which illustrates further the usefulness of this peripheral index of central norepinephrine metabolsim. Depue and Kleiman describe a new paradigm for assessing the effects of stress on catecholamine functioning in Chapter 8. They are employing cortisol as a peripheral index of catecholamine activity in the inhibitory modulation system of cortisol release. They are studying this index as a function of laboratory controlled stress conditions. Moreover, these studies are being conducted with persons at high risk for unipolar and bipolar disorders, and hence these researchers discuss the potential of their results for predicting risk of future depressive episodes. Stolk and Nisula complete the catecholamine discussion by examining the implications for stress factors in relation to genetic influences on catecholamine metabolism in Chapter 9.

Finally, in Chapter 10 Buchsbaum discusses his most recent findings on stimulus intensity modulation in polar disorders and interprets his work for the first time within a stress framework.

CHAPTER 6

Coping Behavior and Stress-Induced Behavioral Depression: Studies of the Role of Brain Catecholamines [1]

Jay M. Weiss, Howard I. Glazer,
Larissa A. Pohorecky, William H. Bailey, and
Linda H. Schneider

INTRODUCTION

Our laboratory did not set out to investigate how stressful conditions might produce depression; rather, research relevant to this issue developed from studies originally directed at other questions. This chapter will trace the development of this research. As our research has now evolved, we are presently focused on the problem of how stressful conditions affect brain monoamines and how these stress-induced neurochemical changes then in turn affect behavior. In other words, we are presently exploring one of the ways by which stressful situations can lead to behavioral change—through alteration of brain chemistry that is involved in behavior.

[1] This work was supported by research grant HL 19974 from the National Heart, Lung, and Blood Institute and MH30144 from the National Institute of Mental Health.

The Psychobiology of the Depressive Disorders:
Implications for the Effects of Stress

INVESTIGATING EFFECTS OF
PSYCHOLOGICAL VARIABLES IN
ANIMALS

Our explorations in the area of depression grew out of our interest in examining the role played by psychological factors in stressful situations. In particular, we were concerned with how psychological factors affected physiological responses that led to pathology. In considering how to carry out these studies, it became clear that it would be highly advantageous to use animal models that would permit us to produce actual pathology under experimental conditions, but we then were forced to deal with the difficult issue of how one could study the influence of psychological variables in laboratory animals. The procedure used in previous research had been to select some stressful agent (i.e., stressor) that, when applied to the animal, would seem to have caused pathological consequences because it was emotionally noxious or exciting to the animal. Unfortunately, assuming that any physical stressor produced pathology because of its psychological aspects was a dubious assumption that, in several cases, has even proved to be plainly erroneous.

To overcome this problem, we developed a somewhat more elaborate experimental design. To study effects of psychological factors on various pathologies, we exposed two (or more) animals simultaneously to exactly the same electric shocks while each of these subjects was in a different psychological condition; thus, any physiological differences that were consequently seen between such matched subjects would be attributable to the psychological difference between their respective conditions since the physical stressor of shock was identical in the two (or more) conditions. Initially, we concentrated most of our effort on how psychological factors affected the development of gastric lesions. (For a review of these studies, see Weiss, 1972, 1977.)

EFFECTS OF COPING BEHAVIOR ON
BRAIN NOREPINEPHRINE

Effects on Norepinephrine Level

One of the psychological factors under study in these first experiments was the ability or inability to cope with the stressor. In these studies, two animals received exactly the same shocks simultaneously through fixed tail electrodes. The experimental situation is shown in Figure 6.1. One of the animals, called the "avoidance–escape" animal, was allowed to perform a response to terminate the shocks that it received. This animal was also able

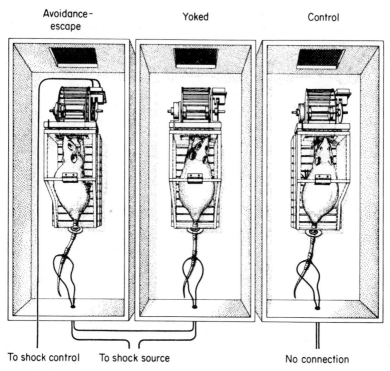

Figure 6.1   The figure illustrates a matched triplet in a study of coping behavior. At left is the avoidance–escape animal, whose wheel is wired to the shock control. At center is the yoked animal, whose tail electrodes are wired in series with the avoidance–escape subject and thus receives exactly the same shock but whose wheel turns have no effect on the shock. At right is the unshocked control subject.

to avoid shocks if it performed the same response before the shock began. In short, the avoidance–escape animal, by performing a specific response, could control the shock. A second animal, called a "yoked" animal, received the same shocks that the avoidance–escape animal received during the course of the stress session, but no response that the yoked animal made had any effect on the shocks. Thus, the yoked animal received the same shocks as its avoidance–escape partner and could perform all the same responses, but the behavior of the yoked animal had no effect on the shock; that is, it could not control the shock. Finally, a third matched subject, a nonshock control, was included in each experimental run so that a "baseline" condition would be available for comparison.

At the time these experiments were going on, Eric Stone became intensely interested in the role of brain catecholamines in behavior, and particularly in depression. He decided that we should use our experimental techniques to compare animals that could avoid and escape shock with animals that could not do so, measuring changes in the level of brain norepinephrine. In two experiments, we found that the animals able to avoid–escape shock showed a higher level of norepinephrine in the whole brain than did the nonshock control animals (Weiss, Stone and Harrell, 1969, 1970). In contrast, the yoked animals that received exactly the same shocks as the avoidance–escape animals but were unable to make any responses to affect the shocks did not show this change. In the first experiment where few shocks were given, these yoked animals showed no differences in norepinephrine level in comparison with control animals. In the second experiment where many shocks were given, yoked animals showed a lower norepinephrine level than controls, a result commonly found with the application of a severe stressor. Thus, whereas whole brain norepinephrine level rose in avoidance–escape animals, it either remained unchanged or was depleted in the case of yoked animals. As these studies completely equated the shock variable in the different conditions by using fixed electrodes, it rigorously demonstrated that a psychological–behavioral variable—the ability to avoid and/or escape shock versus being unable to do so—had a differential effect on brain norepinephrine levels. Similar results have been reported by other laboratories. Richardson, Scudder, and Karczmar (1970) and Fulginiti and Orsingher (1971) reported brain norepinephrine levels to be higher in animals able to avoid shock than in those receiving inescapable shock.

We subsequently studied the effects of this difference in coping behavior on norepinephrine levels in more specific brain regions. The results are shown in Figure 6.2. Again, animals able to avoid or escape shock showed overall higher norepinephrine levels than the yoked animals that were unable to control the same shocks. Yoked animals showed a larger norepinephrine depletion in the hypothalamus and a smaller depletion in the brainstem and cortex, whereas avoidance–escape animals showed no depletion in the hypothalamus and an elevation in brainstem and cortex.

In the experiments just described, the avoidance–escape animal controlled shock by performing some active response, such as jumping onto a platform or turning a wheel. In a subsequent experiment, we (J. Weiss, L. Pohorecky, D. Emmel, and N. Miller) obtained evidence that animals able to control shock show higher brain norepinephrine levels than do animals that cannot control shock, regardless of the skeletal activity involved in performance of the coping performance. For this particular experiment, half of the avoidance–escape animals were required to control shock by performing a typical active behavior (running) whereas the other half were required to adopt a passive motor response (not moving) in order to control shock. The apparatus used for this experiment is shown in Figure 6.3. As in the earlier studies, each avoidance–escape animal again controlled shock while a matched animal (the yoked animal) received exactly the same shocks as the avoidance–escape subject but could not control them.

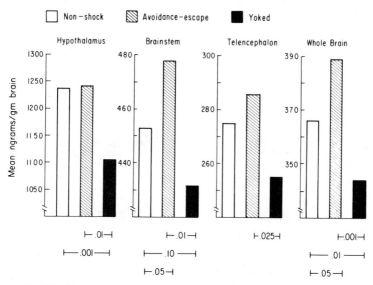

Figure 6.2 The figure shows the endogenous norepinephrine level in various brain areas. The experiment utilized matched triplets (3 animals) as shown in Figure 6.1, each consisting of an avoidance–escape animal whose responses controlled shock, a yoked subject who received exactly the same shocks while having no control over shock, and a nonshock control animal. The subjects of each triplet were exposed to their respective conditions for 20 hr prior to sacrifice for biochemical determinations. The results are based on 21 such matched triplets. At the bottom of the figure are shown the statistical confidence levels for differences between groups.

The results of this study are shown in Figure 6.3. As expected, the different avoidance–escape conditions produced a very large difference in activity: In the passive condition, avoidance–escape animals showed significantly less activity than yoked animals whereas, in the active condition, they showed significantly more activity than yoked animals. However, as can be seen from Figure 6.3, the effect on hypothalamic norepinephrine was similar in both conditions: avoidance–escape animals in both the active and the passive condition showed significantly higher levels than yoked animals.

Effects of Amine Turnover and Uptake

Up to this point, we had measured how the level of norepinephrine was affected by coping behavior. Of course, the level of any amine does not reflect the dynamic state of neurons. Therefore, we undertook experiments to compare a measure of turnover (synthesis and release) of amines in avoidance–escape and yoked animals. For these experiments, we adapted a

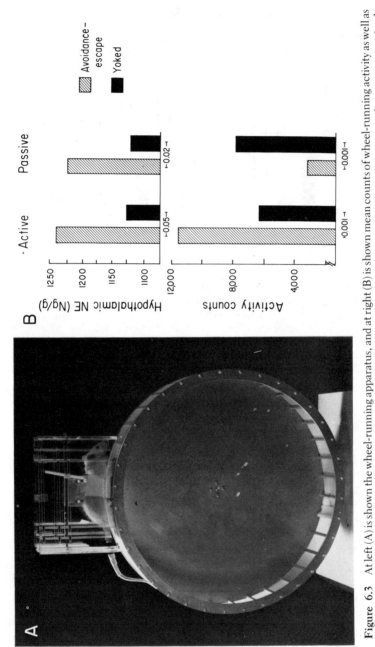

Figure 6.3   At left (A) is shown the wheel-running apparatus, and at right (B) is shown mean counts of wheel-running activity as well as hypothalamic norepinephrine level for avoidance–escape and yoked animals in active and passive conditions. Avoidance–escape animals controlled shock to their tails by running (active condition) or remaining inactive (passive condition) in the apparatus shown at the left, while matched yoked animals in an identical adjacent apparatus received the same shocks unrelated to their behavior. Results, shown at the right, are based on 24 matched avoidance–escape and yoked animals in the active condition and the same number in the passive condition. The subjects were exposed to their respective conditions for 24 hours prior to sacrifice for biochemical determinations. Below each set of data is the statistical confidence level for the difference between the two groups.

widely-used technique to assess turnover *in vivo*, which was to inject radioactively-labeled amines intraventricularly and follow their decline over time.

To perform these experiments, we developed a cannula that could be permanently implanted in the ventricular system prior to the infusion procedure. This cannula permitted us to quickly infuse the animal without using an anesthetic so that the results obtained with this cannula were not compromised by (*a*) operative or recovery trauma at the time of infusion, or (*b*) effects of anesthetic, two factors that were usually present in turnover experiments and may well affect amine systems (Bourgoin, Morot-Gaudry, Glowinski, & Hamon, 1973; Irwin, Criswell, & Kakolewski, 1973).

One week after surgery to implant the cannulas, the experiment was begun. A triplet of animals—an avoidance–escape animal, a yoked animal, and a nonshock control—were subjected to the experimental conditions for 20 hr. At the end of that time, each subject in a triplet was removed from its apparatus, infused with ^{3}H-norepinephrine, and returned to its apparatus. (The amount of infusion was 20 μl, delivered through a motorized syringe to insure constant speed of infusion. The entire infusion procedure, from removal of the animal to its replacement in the apparatus, took approximately 90 sec.) At either 10 min or 2 hr after the infusion, the three animals of the triplet were sacrificed.

The results are shown in Figure 6.4. The cannula in each rat was implanted in the cerebral aqueduct just anterior to the cerebellum, so that our primary objective was to study turnover in the brainstem region, which lay just below the cannula tip and posterior to it (direction of cerebrospinal fluid flow from the cannula tip would be in a posterior direction). It can be seen that the rate of decline in ^{3}H-norepinephrine in the brainstem was greater (and significantly so) in yoked animals than in either avoidance–escape animals or nonshock animals, indicating that the rate of release was greater in the yoked animals than in the two other groups. However, the most interesting finding was the considerable difference in the concentration of ^{3}H-norepinephrine in the brainstem evident 10 min after the infusion; the yoked subjects showed significantly higher ^{3}H-norepinephrine concentration than did the avoidance–escape or nonshock animals at this time. This result suggested that yoked subjects were showing greater norepinephrine uptake than avoidance–escape or nonshock subjects.

On the right side of Figure 6.4 are shown the concentrations of ^{3}H-norepinephrine found in the hypothalamic and telencephalic regions. Because of the cannula placement, these structures showed a lower ^{3}H-norepinephrine concentration and more variability than was seen in the brainstem; nevertheless, yoked animals still showed significantly greater initial uptake than did avoidance–escape animals in these areas as well.

Summarizing the experiments described up to this point, we found that when animals received inescapable shock, the level of norepinephrine in

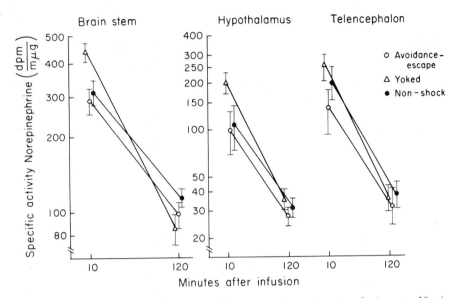

Figure 6.4 The mean specific activity of ³H-norepinephrine in various brain areas, 10 min and 2 hr after ventricular infusion is shown in this figure. The conditions represented by the three groups (avoidance–escape, yoked, nonshock) are the same as those of Figure 6.1. The results are based on 10 triplets at each time point.

various brain areas was depleted and reuptake of norepinephrine was increased, whereas neither of the changes occurred when animals received the same shocks in the course of avoiding or escaping.

COPING, BRAIN NOREPINEPHRINE, AND BEHAVIORAL DEFICITS

As stated earlier, our interest in brain norepinephrine metabolism stemmed from its potential involvement in behavior. Prior to our completing the experiments described above, investigators had reported that if brain norepinephrine were depleted by drugs, this led to a marked deficiency in avoidance–escape behavior (e.g., Moore, 1966; Rech, Bovys, & Moore, 1966; Seiden & Peterson, 1968). These findings suggested that noradrenergic activity might well be involved in the mediation of active avoidance–escape behavior. Therefore, it seemed to us that inescapable shock, which also could deplete norepinephrine level and increase reuptake as well, might well lead to a similar deficiency in behavior.

In considering this possibility, it was evident that relevant experiments had already been carried out. In a series of studies using dogs as subjects, a team of investigators at the University of Pennsylvania had shown that a highly stressful inescapable-shock condition did indeed produce a deficit in behavior (Overmier & Seligman, 1967). These investigators had shown that when the animals received a series of strong inescapable shocks, the dogs subsequently failed to learn a shuttle avoidance–escape response. Moreover, these investigators also found that, in contrast, animals that initially received the same shocks in the course of escaping and avoiding the shocks performed quite normally on the later avoidance test (Seligman & Maier, 1968). Thus, while we had found that yoked animals showed depletions of brain norepinephrine as well as augmented uptake whereas avoidance–escape animals did not show these changes, investigators at the University of Pennsylvania had found that yoked animals showed a marked deficit in behavioral responding in a shuttle box whereas avoidance–escape animals showed no deficit. It seemed to us that this behavioral difference produced by exposure to inescapable versus escapable shock could be the result of the neurochemical differences that we observed arising from these conditions, and we consequently proposed this explanation for their behavioral effect (Weiss, Stone, & Harrell, 1970).

Consistent with this view were the reports of how the dogs behaved after inescapable shock, for the behavior of these animals seemed quite compatible with the view that the avoidance–escape deficit was brought about by a stress-induced alteration in catecholamines. In these studies (Overmier & Seligman, 1967; Seligman & Maier, 1968), the test for the behavioral deficit was conducted in a shuttle box, which is a two-compartment apparatus in which the animal is placed in one compartment and required to jump a hurdle, thereby entering the opposite compartment in order to avoid or escape a shock to its feet. When the dogs were tested in this apparatus subsequent to inescapable shock, they responded to the initial shock(s) by moving around one side of the shuttle box without jumping the hurdle until they stopped moving about and simply howled for the remainder of the 60-sec trial. On succeeding trials, their activity progressively decreased until they were generally immobile throughout most of the time that the shock was on. Also, if one of these animals did jump the hurdle (thereby making an escape response), it failed to consistently repeat this success on subsequent trials. On the other hand, the animals that had been in the other conditions—either those that had been able to control shock or had received no shock—likewise moved around the box during the initial shock(s) but kept moving so that they eventually jumped the hurdle and quickly learned to do this whenever the signal and/or the shock occurred. Since there was considerable evidence that catecholamines were involved in the mediation of active motor behavior, the behavior pattern observed in dogs that received inescapable shocks seemed quite consistent with the view that their central catecholamines were disrupted, thereby reducing their ability to mediate a normal amount of motor activity, and thus bringing about the avoidance–escape deficit as described above.

However, our attempt to tie our neurochemical findings to the behavioral effect observed by Seligman, Maier, and co-workers initiated a controversy. When that group of investigators first showed that severe inescapable shock impaired subsequent shuttle avoidance–escape learning (Overmier & Seligman; Seligman & Maier, 1967), they had argued strongly that this avoidance–escape deficit occurred because the animals learned to be helpless during the inescapable shock. To be specific, those investigators suggested that during the inescapable shock the dogs learned that "nothing I do matters," and that this learned cognition, or attitude, then transferred to the subsequent shuttle test where the animal consequently failed to jump the hurdle because it quickly "gave up." This explanation they called the "learned helplessness" hypothesis.

Learned Helplessness or Transient Stress-induced Neurochemical Changes?

The question then arises: Which explanation, learned helplessness or stress-induced neurochemical changes, explains why inescapable shock leads to an avoidance–escape deficit? Of course, the first thing one might think of is that these two explanations are not incompatible. We would certainly agree that inherently there is no conflict between explaining a behavioral change (in this case, an avoidance–escape deficit) in terms of a neurochemical change, as we were considering, and explaining the same behavioral change by attributing it to a learned response, such as learned helplessness. These explanations could each be adequate ones that were simply formulated in different terms, with the neurochemical explanation describing events on a more molecular level than the "learning" explanation. However, with respect to the specific phenomenon in question here— the deficit caused by inescapable shock—such a reconciliation will not suffice. In this instance, the "stress-neurochemical change" explanation is fundamentally different from the learned helplessness hypothesis because it possesses different functional characteristics. Thus, the two explanations are not describing the same thing on different levels. Indeed, the "stress-neurochemical change" explanation was formulated as an alternative to learned helplessness because we saw learned helplessness as being, quite frankly, erroneous as an explanation for the phenomenon it attempted to explain.

We reached the conclusion that the learned helplessness hypothesis could not explain the poor performance seen in the dogs because it failed to account for a salient characteristic of that avoidance–escape deficit—the fact that the deficit was transient rather than permanent. In their original experiments, Seligman and his co-workers found that the deficit in avoidance–escape behavior was indeed present if 24 hr elapsed between the inescapable shock session and the avoidance–escape test, but absolutely no deficit was seen if 48 hr elapsed between the shock and the test. The deficit was similarly missing if 72 hr elapsed. This transience of the avoidance-escape deficit was replicated by Overmier (1968) who, in this case, found the deficit to be present 48 but not 72 hr after shock. This point is not a minor one, for permanence is one of the important functional characteristics by which any learned response, such as learned helplessness, is identified. It would be highly unusual for a learned response to be remembered and practiced 24 hr after the learning experience but totally forgotten 48 or 72 hr after the learning experience. As a result, we concluded that the deficit, in showing such transience, was not likely to have been based on any learned response. Moreover, the size of the deficit did not vary with the similarity or dissimilarity of the inescapable shock and test situation, i.e., there was no evidence for a gradient of generalization, as would be expected if the deficit were based on learning. (See Maier, Seligman, & Solomon, 1969; pp. 320–321.)

In contrast to the explanations that invoked learned responses, such as "learned helplessness," the fact that the shuttle avoidance–escape deficit after severe inescapable shock was not characterized by either a gradient of generalization or relative permanence presented no problem for an explanation that emphasized neurochemical disturbance. First, if the avoidance-escape deficit had been induced by a transient neurochemical change, then a gradient of generalization, being a characteristic of learned responses with no necessary relation to stress-induced neurochemical changes, consequently would not be expected at all. Second, and perhaps more important, the lack of permanence of the deficit, rather than being an anomaly, would be quite consistent with a disturbance of central catecholamines mediating the effect. Figure 6.5 shows results we have recently obtained examining the time course of changes in catecholamine levels following an inescapable shock treatment that impairs subsequent avoidance–escape performance. Note that levels of norepinephrine are significantly depressed for up to 24 hr after the shock but have returned to the normal range by 48 hr postshock. Thus, were the avoidance–escape deficit somehow related to depletion of brain norepinephrine level caused by the shock, the deficit would be expected to manifest itself at short time intervals after inescapable shock but not at 48 hr postshock.

BEHAVIORAL EFFECTS OF STRESSORS THAT DISTURB BRAIN NOREPINEPHRINE

Effects of Brief Cold Swim

The possibility that transient stress-induced neurochemical changes might have been responsible for the avoidance–escape deficit seen after

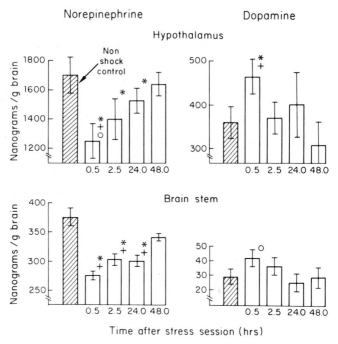

Figure 6.5 The figure illustrates mean levels of norepinephrine and dopamine in the hypothalamus and the brainstem at various time intervals following inescapable shock. Results are based on 8 subjects at each time point. Catecholamine determinations were made by the radioenzymatic method described by Coyle and Henry (1973). * denotes significant difference from Nonshock control; + denotes significant difference from 48-hr group; o denotes significant difference from 24-hr group.

inescapable shock led us to test this notion in a series of experiments (Glazer, Weiss, Pohorecky, & Miller, 1975; Weiss & Glazer, 1975; Weiss, Glazer, Pohorecky, Brick, & Miller, 1975). In the first experiments in this series, we attempted to produce an avoidance–escape deficit similar to that observed by Overmier and Seligman (1967) by exposing rats to a highly stressful situation that reduced brain noradrenergic activity. However, instead of using an inescapable shock, as had Overmier and Seligman, we selected a stressor whose effects could not easily be attributed to learned helplessness, namely, a brief swim in cold water.

The effects of a brief swim in cold water had been extensively investigated by Eric Stone. He had shown that this treatment rapidly leads to (*a*) lower norepinephrine level, and (*b*) higher concentrations of ^{3}H-norepinephrine after intracerebral injection of the labeled norepinephrine, suggesting decreased release (Stone, 1970a,b). Since both of these changes result in less neurotransmitter being available for neuronal release, the cold swim therefore produced a reduction in the receptor activation within noradrenergic neurons and, hence, a reduction in neuronal activity. As would be expected from any treatment that had these neurochemical effects, a cold swim also had behavioral effects and Stone reported that a cold swim indeed made animals hypoactive. Most importantly, Stone and Mendlinger (1974) also showed that such hypoactivity was not attributable to peripheral, debilitating effects of hypothermia induced by a cold swim by demonstrating that the infusion of norepinephrine directly into the brain would elevate activity without raising peripheral body temperature.

The procedure of our initial experiment in this series (which is explained here in some detail because various aspects of it, particularly the shuttle test, are common to many of the subsequent studies) was as follows: Two groups of animals were exposed to a cold swim, of 3.5-min duration for one group and of 6.5-min duration for the other. After 30 min, the avoidance–escape performance of these animals was tested in a shuttle box. Two other groups received exactly the same treatments except that they swam in warm water prior to avoidance testing. A fifth group received no swim before testing.

Figure 6.6 shows the average latency for each group to perform the correct response in the shuttle avoidance–escape test. The shuttle box used in this test was 12 in. long × 12 in. wide × 11 in. high. A barrier rising 2 in. from the floor divided the box into two chambers of equal size. The floor was

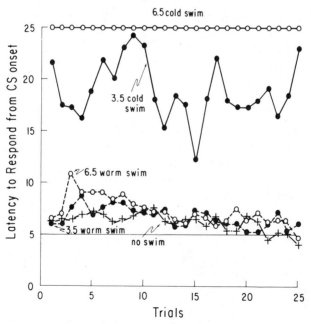

Figure 6.6 Mean latency (in seconds) to cross hurdle in the shuttle avoidance–escape test. The numbers appearing in the designations of the groups refer to the duration (in minutes) of the particular swim exposure, which was given 30 min before the shuttle avoidance–escape test. The number of subjects in each group was 6, which applies to all other experiments unless noted.

made of grid bars through which an electric shock could be delivered to the animal's feet. A 5-sec warning signal preceded the shock. If the animal jumped the 2-in. hurdle and entered the opposite chamber during this period, it terminated the warning signal and avoided the shock. If it did not respond in this period, the shock (1.0 mA intensity) was delivered and remained on until the animal responded or until 25 sec had elapsed, at which time the shock was terminated. Thus, in Figure 6.6, latencies of less than 5 sec represent avoidance responses, latencies longer than 5 sec denote escape (from shock) responses, and a latency of 25 sec indicates a failure to escape.

As can be seen in Figure 6.6, we found that the brief cold swim (3.5 or 6.5 min) markedly impaired avoidance–escape responding in the shuttle box 30 min after the swim. The same duration of forced swim in warm water, which Stone had shown did not reduce activity of noradrenergic neurons, had no deleterious effect on avoidance–escape behavior. Whereas the deficit produced by 6.5 min of a cold swim was very severe, the type of deficit produced by 3.5 min of swim in cold water was quite similar to that observed by Seligman and co-workers after they had given inescapable shocks to dogs. The rats given 3.5 min swim in cold water showed (a) long and variable latencies, and (b) no improvement over trials, characteristics that had earlier been said to indicate "helplessness" (Seligman, 1968). However, in the case of this avoidance–escape deficit produced by a cold swim, the deficit could not be explained easily by the "helplessness" hypothesis of Seligman and co-workers because the cold-swim stressor was (a) so brief that a pervasive sense of helplessness was not likely to have developed from this experience, and (b) the shuttle avoidance–escape test conditions were so different from the swim conditions that any learning taking place in the swim condition is not likely to have transferred to the avoidance–escape test.

The results therefore showed that a stressor condition that reduced central noradrenergic activity but was not likely to have produced learned helplessness could generate an avoidance–escape deficit similar to that observed by Overmier and Seligman in dogs. This is consistent with the possibility that these avoidance–escape deficits were mediated by reductions of central noradrenergic activity. In detail, this alternative hypothesis explains these stress-induced avoidance–escape deficits as follows: Because brain amines mediate active motor behavior, stressful conditions that interfere with these neurochemical systems (e.g., inescapable shock and cold swim) can result in an animal being unable to produce a normal amount of active behavior under appropriate stimulus conditions. In the 3.5-min cold-swim condition (and in the original dog experiments), the resulting neurochemical deficit was such that the animal could mediate only limited attempts to escape and avoid. Since the animal was tested in a task that required much motor activity to effectively learn and consistently perform (shuttle avoidance), the animal therefore failed to learn and perform the task adequately. This alternative explanation was called the "motor activation deficit" hypothesis.

In succeeding experiments, we further established that the avoidance-escape deficit produced by a cold swim was similar to that originally produced by inescapable shock in dogs. First, we showed that the deficit induced by cold swim was also transient, being completely absent if 48 hr were allowed to elapse between the cold swim and the shuttle avoidance-escape test. Next, we showed that the deficit induced by cold swim was also reduced considerably if the animals were first taught the shuttle avoidance–escape response before being exposed to the experimental procedure (i.e., swim followed by avoidance–escape test). That pretraining reduces the avoidance–escape deficit had been shown by Seligman, Maier, and Geer (1968) with respect to the effects of inescapable shock in dogs. In both cases, these findings can be explained on the basis that, as a result of pretraining in the shuttle task, the animal knows exactly what motor responses to perform in order to escape the shock and therefore is able to perform the correct response even after treatments (inescapable shock or cold swim) that have reduced central noradrenergic activity.

Relationship of Avoidance—Escape Deficit to Motor Activity Required

Having shown certain points of similarity between effects of a cold swim and inescapable electric shock, we attempted to define more precisely the nature of the deficit. According to the "motor activation deficit" hypothesis, the avoidance–escape deficit derives from the fact that brain amines play an important role in mediating active motor behavior, so that depletion of amines will impair responding in tasks where the animal is unable to initiate the necessary amount of motor activity to learn and/or perform the task. Thus, according to this view, a crucial factor in determining whether or not a behavioral deficit will occur is the amount of motor activity required to learn and/or perform the test response. To test whether severely stressed animals were particularly sensitive to the motor demands of the test task, we first examined the effects of raising the hurdle between compartments in the shuttle box from the usual height of 2 in. to 4 in. For normal animals, having to jump two additional inches of barrier height was trivial; this manipulation did not affect their performance at all. However, in animals exposed to a cold swim, performance was made significantly worse by this slight rise in the barrier height. Whereas animals in the cold-swim group who were tested with the 2-in. barrier failed to escape on an average of 8.7 trials of the 25-test trials (normal animals did not fail at all), the cold-swim animals tested with the 4-in. barrier failed on an average of 22.2 trials.

We then carried out an experiment which demonstrated the converse;

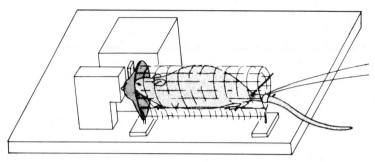

Figure 6.7 This figure shows the apparatus used in the "nosing" test. The animal shown above is performing the correct response, which was to place its nose through a small hole at the front of the tube in which it was confined. When the animal placed its nose through the hole, it disturbed an electronic field which activated a relay, thereby terminating the warning signal and/or shock.

namely, that the deficit induced by a cold swim could be reduced, in fact eliminated, by exposing animals to a test task requiring very little motor activity for adequate performance. In this case, we exposed animals to an avoidance–escape task in which the rat rested in a tube-shaped enclosure and simply had to poke its nose through a hole a short distance in front of its head in order to avoid or escape a shock to its tail. The test apparatus is shown in Figure 6.7. As can be seen in Figure 6.8, the cold-swim animals

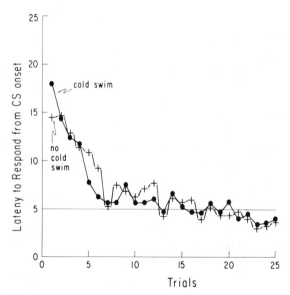

Figure 6.8 The mean latency to perform the correct response in the nosing avoidance–escape test. One group received a 3.5-min cold swim prior to testing in this avoidance–escape task, while the control group received no treatment (no cold swim) prior to the test.

showed no deficit in their ability to perform the low-activity nosing task. Taken together, the results of this and the previous experiment indicate that animals severely stressed by a cold swim were not incapable of learning a task but, rather, were extremely sensitive to the motor demands of tasks and performed poorly in tasks requiring a high output of motor activity.

Similar Behavioral Effects Produced by Inescapable Shock and Drugs

Up to this point, the behavioral experiments had exclusively studied the effects of a cold swim. Therefore, we conducted a fifth experiment which showed that inescapable shock did in fact produce a shuttle avoidance–escape deficit similar to that seen with cold swim. Equally important (and again paralleling the effects of cold swim), it was shown that severe inescapable shock did *not* impair avoidance–escape responding when animals were tested in the nosing task that required little motor activity. Thus, inescapable shock, like a cold swim, apparently did not impair the animal's ability to learn but, rather, its ability to perform tasks requiring considerable motor activity. These results are shown in Figure 6.9.

Next, we reasoned that if severe stressors interfered with active avoidance–escape behavior by depleting brain amines, then a similar behavioral deficit should be produced by drugs that deplete amines. First, we found that tetrabenazine (2 mg/kg, IP) indeed impaired responding in the shuttle avoidance–escape task but not in the low-activity nosing task. These results are shown in Figure 6.10. Figure 6.10 shows not only the effects of tetrabenazine on performance in the shuttle and nosing tasks but also shows the effects of the cold swim, which were replicated as part of this study to show the similarity of the effects of tetrabenazine and a cold swim. If one then compares these results with those shown in Figure 6.9, it can be seen that tetrabenazine, a cold swim, and inescapable shock all had a profile of similar effects on the two avoidance–escape tasks, which is what one would expect if the stressors (i.e., cold swim and inescapable shock) were producing their effects on responding by producing changes mimicked by tetrabenazine.

Preventing the Behavioral Deficit by Protecting Catecholamines

After these studies, we attempted to protect the animals against the adverse effects of a severe stressor by drug treatment. We reasoned that, according to the view that stress-induced changes in amines were responsible for the behavioral deficit, a drug which would prevent depletion of

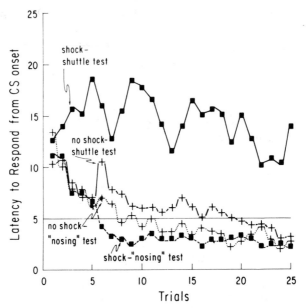

Figure 6.9 The mean latency to perform the correct response in either the shuttle or the nosing avoidance–escape test is shown here. One group received inescapable shock 30 min prior to the shuttle avoidance–escape test (shock-shuttle test) while another group received inescapable shock prior to the nosing avoidance–escape test (shock-"nosing" test). The third and fourth groups, both control conditions, received no shock prior to testing in either the shuttle test (no shock-shuttle test) or the nosing task (no shock-"nosing" test).

monoamines should therefore be able to protect the animal against the behavioral deficit that normally resulted from exposure to a severely stressful situation. For this important experiment, we chose to use a mono-amine-oxidase inhibitor since this type of drug seemed ideally suited to counteracting the effects of a stressor such as severe inescapable shock. Inescapable shock is likely to deplete norepinephrine by causing a high rate of release with which synthesis cannot keep pace. Depletion of the amine results because the released norepinephrine is metabolized, most of the metabolism being assumed to take place intraneuronally after reuptake. By blocking monoamine-oxidase (MAO), the enzyme responsible for this metabolism, this depletion should be prevented. Moreover, because the MAO inhibitor principally blocks catabolism of released amine, its action, particularly in an acute situation, would be largely restricted to counteracting deleterious consequences of a high rate of release without itself profoundly affecting release. In short, it seemed reasonable to hope that the drug would not result in nonspecific stimulation of control animals but, rather, would specifically protect animals receiving inescapable shock.

The results, which can be seen in Figure 6.11, bore this out quite well. First, the MAO inhibitor eliminated the behavioral deficit produced by

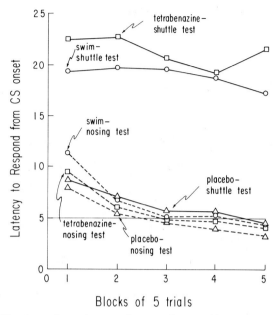

Figure 6.10   The figure shows the mean latency (shown in blocks of 5 trials) to perform the correct response in either the shuttle or the nosing avoidance–escape test. Two groups received tetrabenazine (2 mg/kg) 30 min prior to testing in the shuttle task (tetrabenazine-shuttle test) or the nosing task (tetrabenazine-nosing test). Two additional groups were 3.5-min cold swim prior to testing in the shuttle task (swim–shuttle test) or nosing task (swim-nosing test). The remaining two groups represented control conditions that received only a placebo injection prior to testing in the shuttle task (placebo-shuttle test) or the nosing task (placebo-nosing test).

inescapable shock, so that animals given the drug (pargyline, 100 mg/kg, IP) just before being exposed to inescapable shock subsequently performed in the shuttle avoidance–escape task as well as did nonshock control subjects. Second, control animals given the same dose of the drug did not perform any better than control animals not given the drug, indicating that the MAO inhibitor did not simply excite normal animals. Thus, the MAO inhibitor appears to have specifically counteracted the effects of the shock, suggesting that the neurochemical changes hypothesized to be taking place were indeed occurring.

Another type of experiment we carried out also points to the involvement of monoamines in the stress-induced avoidance–escape deficit. In these studies, which yielded perhaps the most interesting results in the series, we exposed animals to cold swim and inescapable shock repeatedly, rather than only once. To begin with, it is apparent that if animals showed a behavioral deficit after exposure to the stressful conditions we were investigating because they learned to be helpless, then exposing them to such stressful conditions repeatedly should make the behavioral deficit even worse. On the other hand, if the behavioral deficit arose because of stress-induced amine

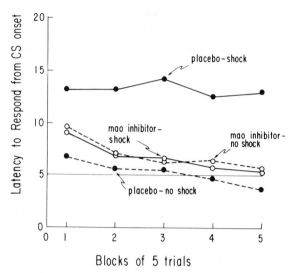

Blocks of 5 trials

Figure 6.11   Mean latency (in seconds) to cross hurdle in shuttle avoidance–escape test. One group received a MAO inhibitor (pargyline; 100 mg/kg) at the outset of a session of inescapable shock, followed 30 min after the shock session by the shuttle avoidance–escape test. A second group received only the MAO inhibitor without the shock session (MAO inhibitor–no shock). A third group received only a placebo injection at the outset of the shock session (placebo–shock) which, when compared with the fourth group that received only the placebo with no shock session, shows the usual effect of inescapable shock on shuttle avoidance–escape responding.

disruption, then repeated exposure to stressors should have the unusual effect of ameliorating the avoidance–escape deficit seen in the shuttle test. This is because repeated exposure to stressors produces a remarkable effect which might be called "neurochemical habituation." Zigmond and Harvey (1970) had shown that repeated exposure to stressors reduces stress-induced norepinephrine depletion. Repeated exposure to stressors elevates tyrosine hydroxylase activity, which probably accounts for this effect (e.g., Musacchio, Jalou, Kety, and Glowinski, 1969; Thoenen, 1970).

In this study, we exposed animals to either cold swim or inescapable shock 15 times. We then exposed all of these subjects to a session of shock or swim and subsequently tested them in the shuttle avoidance–escape apparatus. We compared these animals with animals that were simply exposed to shock or swim once and then tested (i.e., the usual procedure). The results are shown in Figure 6.12. The animals that had undergone repeated exposure to a stressor did not show an avoidance–escape deficit after the final stressor session whereas animals that received just the single stressor session showed the usual avoidance–escape deficit. Such results indicated that repeated exposure to stressors did in fact have the remarkable effect of reducing the avoidance–escape deficit.

We then conducted a separate experiment to measure neurochemical

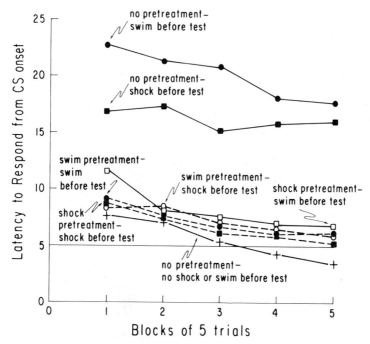

Figure 6.12 Mean latency (in seconds) to cross the hurdle in the shuttle avoidance–escape test. The term "pretreatment" in the designation of any group indicates that the group received 15 consecutive days of the stressor treatment indicated; "no pretreatment" refers to the absence of this repeated exposure to a stressor. The second part of each designation refers to the stressor condition ("shock" or "cold swim") administered to the animals 30 min before the shuttle avoidance–escape test, the results of which are shown in this figure.

changes from these treatments in order to relate the behavioral changes we had seen to the expected neurochemical changes. These results are shown in Figure 6.13. After animals received a single session of inescapable shock, they indeed showed a substantial depletion in norepinephrine level in both the hypothalamus and the cortex, a result consistent with the fact that such animals show an avoidance–escape deficit. Also consistent with behavioral effects, we observed that when animals that had been exposed to 15 sessions of inescapable shock were given the final session of inescapable shock (after which they do not show an avoidance–escape deficit), they subsequently showed (*a*) elevated tyrosine hydroxylase activity, and (*b*) no reduction in norepinephrine level in any brain region. However, when animals that had been repeatedly exposed to cold swim received the final session of inescapable shock (after which they also do not show an avoidance–escape deficit), these animals subsequently did *not* show higher tyrosine hydroxylase activity and consequently showed a reduction in brain norepinephrine level. But we also measured norepinephrine uptake in all animals, and this measure may have provided the answer to this inconsistency. Looking at uptake of

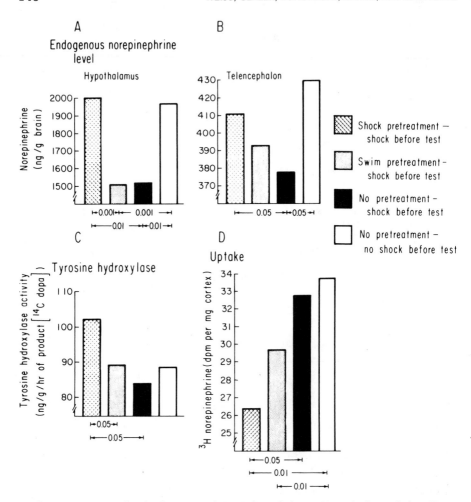

Figure 6.13 Mean levels of norepinephrine in hypothalamus (A) and telencephalon (B), as well as mean tyrosine hydroxylase activity (C) and norepinephrine uptake (D) in cortex. The designations for the various groups are explained in the legend to Figure 6.12. At the bottom of each section of the figure are indicated the statistical confidence levels for differences between various conditions.

[3]H-norepinephrine into slices of cortex *in vitro*, we observed that in both animals repeatedly exposed to inescapable shock and animals repeatedly exposed to cold swim, the amount of ^{3}H-norepinephrine taken up into cortical slices was less than in control animals. Animals given only one exposure to inescapable shock showed only a slight change in this direction. Such results suggest (*a*) that repeated exposure to severe stressors produces a reduction in uptake, and (*b*) that uptake changes may play an important role in the behavioral "habituation" effects produced by repeated exposure

as uptake changes were closely related to the behavioral results seen in these groups.

Behavioral Effects of Catecholamine-Depleting Brain Lesions

At this point, we should like to describe two experiments which have not been reported previously. These studies attempted to make clearer the nature of the avoidance–escape deficit we have been studying and also to specify more precisely the monoamines involved. As explained above, an avoidance–escape deficit similar to that brought about by stressful conditions could be produced by drugs that disrupted catecholamines. Linda Schneider therefore explored whether lesions of central catecholaminergic pathways would similarly affect performance in avoidance–escape tasks, paying particular attention to the motor-activity requirements of the task. She attempted to profoundly disrupt central catecholamines by making intracerebral lesions with 6-hydroxydopamine (6-OHDA) which were aimed at the nigrostriatal pathway and medial forebrain bundle.

Bilateral lesions were made in male albino rats (300–325 gm) by placing cannulas at the following coordinates: -5.1 mm posterior to the bregma, ±1.9 mm lateral to the midline, and 7.1 mm below the dura. Each subject was then infused with 4 μg 6-OHDA in 2 μl of solution through each cannula. After recovering from aphagia and adipsia, the animals were tested in three different avoidance–escape tasks that represented a range of motor-activity requirements. Animals were tested in the two tasks described thus far; that is, the standard shuttle avoidance–escape task which requires a considerable amount of motor activity, and the "nosing" avoidance–escape task which requires little activity. A third task, requiring an intermediate level of activity, was also administered. In the third test, the animals had to escape from shock (no avoidance was possible in this case) by turning a wheel mounted on the front wall of a small cage (for a picture of the apparatus, see Weiss, 1971). This escape response normally would not require a great deal of activity except that for this study the response requirement was increased to three-eighths of a turn of the wheel so that the activity requirement was moderate. The animals were tested serially in all three tasks, being tested for 2 days in each task. The order in which tasks were given was varied systematically across the animals in each group, but the results indicated that there was no apparent alteration of performance in any task based on the order in which the tasks were presented.

The behavioral results are shown in Figure 6.14. The tasks are shown in descending order with respect to the amount of motor activity required for successful performance, beginning (top) with shuttle avoidance–escape, the task requiring the most activity, to the nosing task (bottom) requiring the

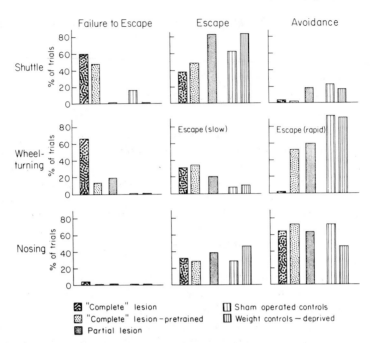

Figure 6.14 Performance of various groups with damage to central catecholaminergic pathways made by 6-hydroxydopamine as well as performance of nondamaged control groups. Performance is shown in shuttle, wheel-turning, and nosing avoidance–escape tasks, these tasks requiring (top to bottom) progressively less motor activity for successful performance. Performance is expressed as the mean percentage of trials on which subjects of a group failed to escape the shock at all, escaped (but did not avoid) the shock, or avoided the shock. (For the wheel-turning task where no avoidance was possible, the mean number of trials on which subjects escaped slowly [more than 2 seconds] or rapidly [faster than 2 seconds] is shown.) For explanation of the various groups, see text.

least. Performance in each task is expressed in three categories, each presenting the mean number of trials on which subjects (*a*) failed to escape at all, (*b*) escaped the shock, or (*c*) avoided the shock. For the wheel-turning task, in which no avoidance was possible, responding was expressed as "slow escape" (more than 2 sec) or "rapid escape" (less than 2 sec).

The subjects in the study were divided into five groups. First, two control groups were used, both sham-operated controls and also food- and water-deprived controls that had been matched to 6-OHDA-lesioned animals and subjected to the same food and water deprivation that occurred during recovery for the lesioned subjects. These matched controls also underwent the same intubation and delivery of food by intubation that was necessary to sustain the lesioned animals during their recovery.

Lesioned subjects were divided into three groups. First, one group received training in all three avoidance–escape tasks (2 days to each task) prior to the lesioning procedure; this group was included to determine if pretraining could counteract the effects of a catecholamine-depleting lesion, just as pretraining had been shown to counteract the effects of stressors. As this group proved to have complete lesions (see discussion immediately following), this group was designated as the "pretraining–complete-lesion" group. The other two groups consisted of lesioned animals that had not been pretrained. Whether an animal was placed into the "complete" or the "partial" lesion group was based on the amount of time the subject took to recover feeding and drinking behavior after surgery. Because it was well known that interruption of ascending dopaminergic pathways leads to feeding and drinking deficits (e.g., Ungerstedt, 1971; Zigmond & Stricker, 1972), the length of time to recover these functions was used as an indication of the extent of the lesion in each animal; in this way, the two lesioned groups were established prior to behavioral testing rather than post hoc.

After behavioral testing, when sacrifice occurred, the validity of the differentiation between "complete" and "partial" lesions was assessed biochemically. The results confirmed the differentiation. Measuring uptake of ^{3}H-amines in synaptosome-rich homogenate of brain regions, it was determined that all animals which had been assigned to the "complete lesion" group had severe damage to the forebrain catecholaminergic systems, with dopamine uptake in the striatum reduced in all cases to less than 20% of control values (mean for group = 7.7 ± 1.5% of control) and uptake of norepinephrine in the posterior cortex (i.e., nondopaminergic areas of cortex) also reduced to less than 20% of control in all cases (mean = 14.5 ± 1.9%). Damage was less extensive in the subjects that had been assigned to the partial lesion group, with dopamine uptake in the striatum averaging 56.9 ± 9.8% of control and norepinephrine uptake in the posterior cortex averaging 59.4 ± 18.8% of control. As stated, animals in the pretrained group proved to have "complete" lesions, according to recovery of feeding and drinking as well as uptake measurement.

Turning to the behavioral results of the study, the performance of normal animals in each task can be assessed by looking at the scores of the two control groups, which are shown on the right side in each segment of the graphs in Figure 6.14. Compared with these controls, animals having complete lesions performed very poorly in both the shuttle avoidance–escape task and in the wheel-turning task, showing many failures to escape shock at all. It can also be seen that, surprisingly, animals that had been pretrained before sustaining similar, extensive lesions were not greatly benefited by the pretraining when tested in the shuttle task. They were, however, markedly aided by pretraining in the wheel-turning task. Turning to the subjects with partial lesions, these animals, even without pretraining, showed no deficiency in the shuttle task and only a very slight (and nonsignificant) deficiency in the wheel-turning task, findings that are in agreement with the observation of other investigators who have found that partial lesions of catecholaminergic systems do not generate behavioral changes in many test responses. Finally, examining the results obtained in the low-activity nosing task, it can be seen that all groups in the study, regardless of condition, showed a similar pattern of responding. Thus, no matter how severe the lesions, animals could still perform the nosing task without deficiency.

Summarizing the findings of this study, the results showed, first, that deficits in avoidance–escape behavior deriving from lesions of catecholaminergic pathways were highly dependent on the level of motor activity required in the task. Animals with extensive lesions of these pathways performed quite poorly in tasks requiring considerable motor activity but were not deficient in the low-activity nosing task. Such a finding demonstrates a clear parallel between the lesion-induced avoidance–escape deficit and the deficit produced by highly stressful conditions.

On the other hand, there were certain differences between the deficit induced by the 6-OHDA lesions carried out in this study and the deficit brought about by stressful conditions. For one thing, the deficit in shuttle responding produced by 6-OHDA lesions was not ameliorated by pretraining as was the stress-induced deficit, suggesting that the lesion-induced deficit was more severe. This supposition is also supported by another observation. A few additional subjects who sustained "complete lesions" were tested in the nosing task within a few days after the lesioning, well before the recovery of feeding and drinking behavior. When tested at this time, these animals could not even escape in the nosing task, indicating that the initial undiminished effect of the lesion was to produce an extremely severe impairment of performance. Thus, the data from this experiment indicate that the deficit in avoidance–escape produced by extensive 6-OHDA lesions of noradrenergic and dopaminergic pathways is similar in nature to the deficit induced by highly stressful conditions but is more severe.

Do Stress-Induced Changes in Dopamine Play a Role in the Behavioral Deficit?

The experiment reported above clearly raises the question of whether dopaminergic alterations are involved in the avoidance–escape deficit. In an attempt to obtain more information about the relative importance of norepinephrine and dopamine in the "motor activation deficit," and in the hope of gaining insight into where in the brain behaviorally important changes in catecholamines were occurring, we carried out another study in which we exposed animals to the same inescapable shock that impairs shuttle avoidance–escape responding and measured levels of dopamine as well as of norepinephrine. A number of previous studies had examined the effects of stressors on the level of brain dopamine (e.g., Fuxe & Hanson, 1967; Corrodi, Fuxe, & Hökfelt, 1968; Welch & Welch, 1968; Engel, Hanson,

Roos, & Strombergsson, 1968; Bliss, Ailion, & Zwanziger, 1968; Bliss & Ailion, 1971) but only infrequently were changes in the level of this amine reported. However, in evaluating these data, it is evident that most of the dopamine in the brain (about 80%) is located in the striatum, so that changes in the level of dopamine that might occur within brain regions other than the striatum would be virtually impossible to detect if these regions were included for analysis in the same tissue sample as the striatum. As previous studies had indeed measured levels in whole brain or large parts of the brain, we thus knew very little of how stressors might be affecting dopamine levels in many discrete areas of the brain, particularly limbic dopaminergic regions thought to be important in mediating active motor behavior (e.g., Pijnenburg, Honig, & van Rossum, 1975; Costall & Naylor, 1975). In fact, analysis of how the level of norepinephrine changed in various regions of the limbic system as a result of exposure to stressors was not known either, so that this information could be gained as well from the study. In order to measure accurately the amount of both norepinephrine and dopamine present in small brain regions, we used a highly sensitive radioenzymatic method (Coyle & Henry, 1973) for this study.

In conjunction with the measurement of amines, this experiment also had a second purpose, which was to attempt to relate any stress-induced changes in amine level that were observed within various brain regions to deficits in active, motor behavior. If we could correlate the stress-induced deficit in behavior with a change in either norepinephrine or dopamine levels within a particular region of the brain, this would suggest that the particular amine in that brain region was involved in the deficit.

Therefore, in this experiment we exposed animals to inescapable shock and subsequently measured active motor behavior and brain catecholamine levels in a number of discrete brain regions, the intent being (a) to observe how the stressor affected catecholamine levels in the various brain regions, and (b) to observe a stress-induced depression of behavior and how this depression of behavior correlated with regional changes in catecholamine levels. The inescapable shock had the same parameters that we had found to produce the shuttle avoidance–escape deficit (e.g., Weiss & Glazer, 1975). Three different durations of the shock session were used (45, 60, 75 min), but to simplify for presentation here, this differentiation is ignored. For the subsequent behavioral test, which was given immediately after the shock, a 10-min measure of spontaneous motor activity was taken in a small enclosed box, activity being recorded electronically by a modification of the method described by Giulian and Silverman (1975). We chose the activity measure because it is evidently related to, and indicative of, the deficit we have studied, could be taken quickly, and also seemed unlikely to affect catecholamines.

The procedure described above suggests the use of two groups, one group receiving inescapable shock and the other being a nonshock control group, subsequently measuring spontaneous motor activity and then brain catecholamine levels in both groups. However, because we were going to correlate activity changes in individual animals with changes in brain amine levels, the best procedure was to measure activity prior to the stressful experience as well as afterward so that we could measure how an individual animal's activity changed from its own "baseline" activity. Thus, we were required to take two activity measures. Because we had to consider that taking even one activity measure might itself alter brain catecholamines in the animals that were not shocked, we added a third group that was not handled or disturbed in any way prior to sacrifice. The design is shown in Figure 6.15. Eighteen experimental runs consisting of one subject in each condition were conducted, so that each group consisted of 18 subjects.

After sacrifice, levels of catecholamines were measured in various parts of the limbic system (i.e., septum, amygdala, hippocampus) as well as the hypothalamus, brainstem, striatum, olfactory tubercle, and the anterior cortex. The results are shown in Table 6.1. First, it is obvious that the Activity control showed no significant difference from the No-disturbance control with respect to either catecholamine in any brain region. Thus, one can rule out the possibility that exposure to the activity tests produced the alterations in catecholamine levels seen in the shock group. Considering the changes in the shock group, levels of norepinephrine were markedly depleted (highly significant in all cases) in the brainstem, cortex, hippocampus, septum, amygdala, and hypothalamus. Depletions ranged from at least 20% to as much as 35% relative to control conditions in these brain regions.

Dopamine levels were more resistant to change than were norepinephrine levels. Virtually no change at all was found in dopamine levels in the striatum or the olfactory tubercle as a result of shock. In some brain areas, dopamine showed the tendency to rise (septum, amygdala, cortex), but the changes were not statistically significant. In the hypothalamus, however, a large rise in dopamine (+ 24% relative to No-disturbance controls) appeared that was statistically significant. Thus, in the same hypothalami where shock decreased norepinephrine levels by over 30%, the level of dopamine rose 24%. (It should be noted that a similar effect was also seen in another study, shown in Figure 6.5 on page 136).

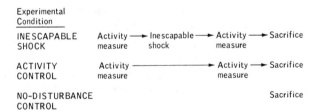

Figure 6.15 Design of experiment to study effects of inescapable shock on spontaneous motor activity and brain catecholamine levels in discrete brain regions.

Table 6.1
CATECHOLAMINE LEVELS IN VARIOUS BRAIN REGIONS

	Hypo-thalamus	Brain-stem	Striatum	Olfactory tubercle	Septum	Hippocampus	Amygdala	Cortex
	Norepinephrine (ng/g)							
Inescapable shock	1083.5* ± 68.3	235.1* ± 13.7	89.2 ± 16.5	426.6 ± 21.5	362.4* ± 28.4	204.6** ± 13.5	395.5* ± 21.8	177.6** ± 13.3
Activity control	1525.0 ± 69.4	295.4 ± 18.5	77.4 ± 25.2	445.0 ± 23.6	461.4 ± 30.7	236.4 ± 16.0	553.2 ± 33.8	212.9 ± 14.7
No-disturbance control	1570.3 ± 78.8	311.5 ± 17.2	83.6 ± 15.7	488.8 ± 29.8	486.1 ± 35.9	259.6 ± 17.6	583.3 ± 36.8	222.3 ± 9.1
r =	.60***	.70***	.15	.36	.32	.21	.29	.14
	Dopamine (ng/g)							
Inescapable shock	418.8* ± 24.2	42.2 ± 3.8	10,972.9 ± 317.2	5457.5 ± 170.0	509.9 ± 36.2	12.7 ± 3.0	563.9 ± 49.0	84.2 ± 9.3
Activity control	300.5 ± 11.9	33.9 ± 4.3	10,287.7 ± 340.4	5309.6 ± 147.2	411.1 ± 32.1	12.2 ± 5.3	453.4 ± 33.7	69.0 ± 2.8
No-disturbance control	336.9 ± 27.0	33.0 ± 4.0	11,061.2 ± 421.2	5690.6 ± 170.8	468.0 ± 38.4	10.9 ± 3.5	471.6 ± 46.9	73.3 ± 4.6
r =	.34	.46	.28	-.14	.01	.10	.03	.28

* Differs significantly ($p < .05$ or less) from both "Activity" control and "No-disturbance" control.
** Differs significantly ($p < .05$ or less) from "No-disturbance" control.
*** r Correlation between fall in motor activity and fall in catecholamine level within "Inescapable-shock" group ($p < .005$).

The most interesting results were found with regard to motor activity. First, application of the severe shock stressor produced a marked decrease in motor activity, as would be expected. On the second activity test, the Activity controls showed a 25% decline in activity relative to the first test, which was also expected as they habituated to the activity apparatus. However, for the Shock subjects, the decline in activity on the second test (postshock) relative to the first test was twice as large (50%), representing a highly significant decrease in motor activity produced by the shock stressor. Second, and perhaps the most important aspect of the study, was the finding of correlations between the extent to which activity was depressed by the shock and changes in brain catecholamine level produced by the shock. For each experimental animal, to measure how much activity fell as the result of shock, its activity after the shock was expressed as a percentage of its baseline activity before the shock. To measure how much catecholamine levels had changed in the animal, the levels measured after the shock were also expressed as a percentage of baseline. Obviously, a "pre-" measure of catecholamine level could not possibly have been taken, so that the baseline value was the level found in the matched "No-disturbance" control animal. The correlation coefficients obtained between these two values are also shown in Table 6.1. It can be seen that changes in the level of dopamine, which were obviously quite small as shock had no significant effects on dopamine level except in the hypothalamus, did not correlate highly with changes in motor activity. For norepinephrine, however, significant correlations were found in two brain regions: fall in motor activity correlated with the magnitude of the decline in the norepinephrine level of the hypothalamus (+ .60) and the brainstem (+ .70). These results, particularly the correlations, are quite interesting, but rather than discussing the findings by themselves, we shall at this point briefly summarize how the research on the general problem addressed throughout this chapter has progressed and, in the course of so doing, integrate the more recent results with those of previous experiments.

SUMMARY AND DISCUSSION

The studies presented throughout this chapter have indicated that highly stressful situations can lead to an impairment in the performance of certain behavioral responses. The impairment is seen in a variety of active behavioral tasks, and apparently is the result of a deficit in the animal's ability to mediate a normal amount of motor activity under challenging environmental conditions which require it. This "motor activation deficit" seems due to a disturbance of catecholamines produced by the highly stressful situation. A key role for catecholamines is indicated by several converging lines of evidence, including the production of a similar behavioral deficit by drug treatment that disrupts catecholamines and the amelioration of the deficit by either drug treatment or repeated exposure to stressors that protect against depletion of catecholamines. Of considerable clinical interest is the fact that both the catecholamine disturbances and the behavioral deficiency are dependent upon seemingly subtle psychological variables in the stressful situation, such as the inability of the animal to cope with the stressor. If an animal can cope effectively with the stressor, then neither the catecholamine disturbances nor the behavioral disturbances are observed even if the amount of the physical stressor the animal experiences is exactly the same as that experienced by an animal that is unable to cope.

The task that lies ahead is one of specifying more precisely which aspects of amine function are being altered by stressful situations so as to cause the behavioral deficit. Progress is being made here, though slowly. Of course, the intimate interrelations of the various amine pathways within the brain make it difficult, and perhaps logically impossible, to point to one aspect of amine function as being responsible for the behavioral deficit. Nevertheless, we can be quite certain that our efforts to date are well short of what can ultimately be said.

Throughout these investigations, we have entertained the possibility that a substance (a hormone or transmitter) was crucially involved in the production of the behavioral deficit we were studying if it satisfied two criteria: (a) the substance appeared important for mediating active motor behavior, and (b) stressors affected the substance in some way that might well interfere with this mediation. The first criterion immediately focuses one's attention on the catecholamines, and we have chosen, as a working hypothesis, to assign a potentially key role to brain norepinephrine. There is much evidence, some of the earliest of which has been cited previously, indicating that norepinephrine in brain satisfies the first criterion. It must be mentioned that during the recent past, debate has taken place regarding the possibility that dopamine rather than norepinephrine mediates motor activity. However, without attempting to analyze in detail the elements of this controversy, there is considerable evidence that argues against the exclusion of norepinephrine. As examples, (a) intracerebral infusion of norepinephrine potentiates motor activity even more than does infusion of dopamine (Geyer, Segal, & Mandell, 1972; Stone & Mendlinger, 1974), (b) the noradrenergic receptor stimulant clonidine augments motor activity following reserpine to a degree that cannot be achieved by dopaminergic receptor stimulants alone (Andén, Strömbom, & Svensson, 1973; Strömbom, 1975). and (c) brain lesions that destroy noradrenergic systems while sparing dopaminergic systems decrease spontaneous motor activity (Carey, 1976; Roberts, Zis, & Fibiger, 1975). Thus, it appears that while dopaminergic systems play a major, and perhaps dominant, role in mediating motor activity, noradrenergic systems mediate motor activity as well.

There is also evidence that norepinephrine satisfies the second criterion as well. A sizable body of research, including studies described in this paper, indicates that stressors reliably deplete norepinephrine level, which raises the possibility that the functional capacity of noradrenergic systems to respond is thereby diminished. To this reduction in norepinephrine level by stressors, we can now add some evidence that inescapable shock, the principal stressor with which we have been concerned, also augments reuptake. Whether either of these changes, or both acting in concert, actually serve to reduce depolarization of the postsynaptic membrane is the critical question that remains to be answered, but the observed changes certainly present the possibility clearly.

Turning our attention to dopamine, as stated earlier, the evidence very strongly supports this amine's importance in the mediation of motor behavior, indicating that it is even more significant in this regard than is norepinephrine. We have, in fact, been able to produce a shuttle avoidance–escape deficit similar to that produced by our inescapable-shock treatment by giving animals injections of haloperidol (200 and 500 μg/kg), a drug that predominantly blocks dopamine receptors. Thus, dopamine seems to satisfy the first criterion presented at the outset of this discussion.

With respect to the second criterion, there is presently only rudimentary evidence that stressors, even highly severe ones, produce changes in dopaminergic systems that would impair their functional capacity to respond normally. In fact, the final study described in this chapter contains one of the few indications that this might occur. In that study, we observed that the level of dopamine was elevated in the hypothalamus following inescapable shock. Although an elevation in the level of a transmitter would hardly seem to constitute prima facie evidence that neural activity might be reduced, the nature of dopaminergic neurons is such that this may well be true in the case of these particular neurons. Synthesis of dopamine appears to be inhibited by receptors located on the presynaptic terminals; thus, dopamine release stimulates these receptors and inhibits synthesis. As a result, reduction of dopaminergic transmission, which reduces activation of these receptors, thereby releases synthesis from inhibition and increases the level of dopamine, a change that has been observed in dopaminergic neurons following chemical blockade of receptors and transection of axons (e.g., Faull & Laverty, 1969; Stock, Magnusson, & Andén, 1973). Thus, our observation of increased dopamine levels in the hypothalamus following severe inescapable shock may indicate that dopamine release in this region is reduced.

However, with regard to this evidence, two comments are in order. First, Palkovits, Kobayashi, Kizer, Jacobowitz, and Kopin (1975) reported decreases rather than increases in the arcuate nucleus of the hypothalamus, and no changes elsewhere throughout the hypothalamus, as a result of three stressors—formalin injection, exposure to cold, and restraint. The discrepancy between these results and those reported here may derive from the anatomical region studied, or from differences in the intensity of the stressor used in our study; nevertheless, this discrepancy remains to be resolved. It is of interest to note that Kleim and Sigg (1977) have more recently reported results using restraint as a stressor that are in agreement with our findings (i.e., level of norepinephrine decreased and level of dopamine increased in hypothalamus). Second, whether altered dopamine release in the hypo-thalamus (presumably in the tubero-infundibular tract) is relevant to avoidance–escape responding also remains a question.

As the foregoing discussion makes evident, there are numerous ways in which amines might participate in the behavioral deficit. Up to this point, the discussion has dealt with the possibility that one amine—either norepi-nephrine or dopamine—could be responsible for the deficit. However, re-cent studies indicate that these amines may interact in such a way that both could be involved (e.g., Antelman & Caggiula, 1977). Most intriguing is the suggestion that norepinephrine acts to augment dopaminergic transmission (Donaldson, Dolphin, Jenner, Marsden, & Pycock, 1976a; Andén & Grabowska, 1976). Thus, according to this hypothesis, a decrease in norad-renergic transmission will diminish dopaminergic transmission. In regard to the behavioral deficit under discussion here, stressful events therefore might impair a noradrenergic maintenance of dopaminergic transmission to bring about the behavioral deficit under investigation. Were one to hypothesize that the avoidance–escape deficit came about in this manner, such an explanation would take into account the fact that stressful conditions seem to more readily affect norepinephrine than dopamine while the mediation of motor behavior seems more closely tied to dopamine.

Some of our own results presented in this chapter offer support for the preceding hypothesis, though this support is by no means unequivocal. The primary site for those noradrenergic cell bodies thought to facilitate dopaminergic neurons is the locus coeruleus (e.g., Donaldson, Dolphin, Jenner, Marsden, & Pycock, 1976b). Our "brainstem" region (see Table 6.1) included the locus coeruleus. Not only was a highly significant fall in norepinephrine level observed in this region as a result of inescapable shock, but the largest correlation between a fall in motor activity and a fall in norepinephrine level (+ .70) was also observed with respect to this region. However, as stated above, support for the hypothesis is not at all un-equivocal. In our data, those forebrain dopaminergic regions to which cells of the locus coeruleus project and which are thought relevant to avoidance–escape responding (striatum, olfactory tubercle) did not show an increase in dopamine levels as a result of inescapable shock. We would have expected to observe such an increase as an indication that the activity of forebrain dopaminergic neurons was indeed reduced. Thus, the results only partially support the proposed hypothesis. Another question that arises from our data is that the norepinephrine–dopamine interaction as hypothesized leaves unexplained the large correlation (+ .60) between the fall in motor activity and the fall in hypothalamic norepinephrine level as locus coeruleus is thought to make only meager projections to the hypothalamus. Thus, although intriguing hypotheses present themselves, there are numerous questions which await future answers.

REFERENCES

Andén, N.-E. & Grabowska, M. Pharmacological evidence for a stimulation of dopamine neurons by noradrenaline in the brain. *European Journal of Pharmacology*, 1976, 39, 275–282.
Andén, N.-E., Strömbom, U., & Svensson, T. H. Dopamine and noradrenaline receptor stimulation: Reversal of reserpine-induced suppression of motor activity. *Psychopharmacologia (Berl.)*, 1973, 29, 289–298.
Antelman, S. M. & Caggiula, A. R. Norepinephrine–dopamine interactions and behavior. *Science*, 1977, 195, 646–653.
Bliss, E. L. & Ailion, J. Relationship of stress and activity to brain dopamine and homovanillic acid. *Life Sciences*, 1971, 10, 1161–1169.
Bliss, E. L., Ailion, J., & Zwanziger, J. Metabolism of norepinephrine, serotonin, and dopamine in rat brain with stress. *Journal of Pharmacology and Experimental Therapeutics*, 1968, 164, 122–134.
Bourgoin, S., Morot-Gaudry, Y., Glowinski, J., & Hamon, M. Stimulating effects of short-term ether anesthesia on central 5-HT synthesis and utilization in the mouse brain. *European Journal of Pharmacology*, 1973, 22, 209–211.
Carey, R. J. Effects of selective forebrain depletions of norepinephrine and serotonin on activity and food intake effects of Amphetamine and Fenfluramine, *Pharmacology, Biochemistry, and Behavior*, 1976, 5, 519–523.
Corrodi, H., Fuxe, K., & Hökfelt, T. The effect of immobilization stress on the activity of central monoamine neurons. *Life Sciences*, 1968, 7, 107–112.
Costall, B. & Naylor, R. J. The behavioral effects of dopamine applied intracerebrally to areas of the mesolimbic system. *European Journal of Pharmacology*, 1975, 32, 87–92.
Coyle, J. T. & Henry, D. Catecholamines in the fetal and newborn rat brain. *Journal of Neurochemistry*, 1973, 21, 61–67.
Donaldson, I. M., Dolphin, A., Jenner, P., Marsden, C. D., & Pycock, C. The roles of noradrenaline and dopamine in contraversive circling behavior seen after unilateral electrolytic lesions of the locus coeruleus. *European Journal of Pharmacology*, 1976, 39, 179–191. (a)
Donaldson, I. M., Dolphin, A., Jenner, P., Marsden, C. D., & Pycock, C. Contraversive circling behavior produced by unilateral electrolytic lesions of the ventral noradrenergic bundle mimicking the changes seen with unilateral electrolytic lesions of the locus coeruleus. *Journal of Pharmacy and Pharmacology*, 1976, 28, 329–331. (b)
Engel, J., Hanson, L. C. F., Roos, B.-E., & Strombergsson, L.-E. Effect of electroshock on dopamine metabolism in rat brain. *Psychopharmacologia (Berl.)*, 1968, 13, 140–144.
Faull, R. L. & Laverty, R. Changes in dopamine levels in the corpus striatum following lesions in the substantia nigra. *Experimental Neurology*, 1969, 23, 332–340.
Fulginiti, S. & Orsinger, O. A. Effects of learning, amphetamine, and nicotine on the level and synthesis of brain noradrenaline in rats. *Archives Internationales de Pharmacodynamie et de Thérapie*, 1971, 190, 191–293.
Fuxe, K. & Hanson, L. C. F. Central catecholamine neurons and conditioned avoidance behavior. *Psychopharmacologia (Berl.)*, 1967, 11, 439–447.

Geyer, M. A., Segal, D. S., & Mandell, A. J. Effect of intraventricular dopamine and norepinephrine on motor activity. *Physiology and Behavior*, 1972, 8, 653–658.

Giulian, D. & Silverman, G. Solid-state animal detection system: Its application to open-field activity and freezing behavior. *Physiology and Behavior*, 1975, 14, 109–112.

Glazer, H. L., Weiss, J. M., Pohorecky, L. A., & Miller, N. E. Monoamines as mediators of avoidance–escape behavior. *Psychosomatic Medicine*, 1975, 37, 535–543.

Irwin, D. A., Criswell, H. E., & Kakolewski, J. W. Spontaneous whole brain slow potential changes during recovery from experimental neurosurgery. *Science*, 1973, 181, 1176–1177.

Kleim, K. L. & Sigg, E. B. Plasma corticosterone and brain catecholamines in stress: Effect of psychotropic drugs. *Pharmacology, Biochemistry and Behavior*, 1977, 6, 79–85.

Maier, S. F., Seligman, M. E. P., & Solomon, R. L. Pavlovian fear conditioning and learned helplessness. In B. A. Campbell & R. M. Church (Eds.), *Punishment and aversive behavior*. New York: Appleton-Century-Crofts 1969. Pp. 299–342.

Moore, K. Effects of α-methyltyrosine on brain catecholamines and conditioned behavior in guinea pigs. *Life Sciences*, 1966, 5, 55–65.

Musacchio, J. M., Jolou, L., Kety, S., & Glowinski, J. Increase in rat brain tyrosine hydroxylase activity produced by electroconvulsive shock. *Proceedings of the National Academy of Sciences, U.S.A.*, 1969, 63, 1117–1119.

Overmier, J. B. Interference with avoidance behavior: Failure to avoid traumatic shock. *Journal of Experimental Psychology*, 1968, 78, 340–343.

Overmier, J. B. & Seligman, M. E. P. Effects of inescapable shock upon subsequent escape and avoidance learning. *Journal of Comparative and Physiological Psychology*, 1967, 63, 23–33.

Palkovits, M., Kobayashi, R. M., Kizer, J. S., Jacobowitz, D. M., & Kopin, I. J. Effects of stress on catecholamines and tyrosine hydroxylase activity of individual hypothalamic nuclei. *Neuroendocrinology*, 1975, 18, 144–153.

Pinjenburg, A. J. J., Honig, W. M. H., & van Rossum, J. M. Inhibition of d-amphetamine-induced locomotor activity by injection of haloperidol into the nucleus accumbens of the rat. *Psychopharmacologia (Berl.)*, 1975, 41, 87–95.

Rech, R. H., Bovys, H. K., & Moore, K. Alterations in behavior and brain catecholamine levels in rats treated with α-methyltyrosine. *Journal of Pharmacology and Experimental Therapeutics*, 1966, 153, 412–419.

Richardson, D., Scudder, C. L., & Karczmar, A. G. Behavioral significance of neurotransmitter changes due to environmental stress and drugs. *Pharmacologist*, 1970, 12, 227.

Roberts, D. C. S., Zis, A. P., & Fibiger, H. C. Ascending catecholamine pathways and amphetamine-induced locomotor activity: Importance of dopamine and apparent non-involvement of norepinephrine. *Brain Research*, 1975, 93, 441–454.

Seiden, L. S. & Peterson, D. D. Blockade of L-dopa reversal of reserpine-induced conditioned avoidance response suppression by disulfiram. *Journal of Pharmacology and Experimental Therapeutics*, 1968, 163, 84–90.

Seligman, M. E. P. *Helplessness*. San Francisco: Freeman, 1976.

Seligman, M. E. P. & Maier, S. F. Failure to escape traumatic shock. *Journal of Experimental Psychology*, 1967, 74, 1–9.

Seligman, M. E. P., Maier, S. F., & Geer, J. The alleviation of learned helplessness in the dog. *Journal of Abnormal and Social Psychology*, 1968, 73, 256–262.

Stock, G., Magnusson, T., & Andén, N.-E. Increase in brain dopamine after axotomy or treatment with gamma-hydroxybutyric acid due to elimination of nerve impulse flow. *Naunyn Schmiedeberg's Archives of Pharmacology*, 1973, 278, 347–361.

Stone, E. A. Swim-stress-induced inactivity: Relation to body temperature and brain norepinephrine, and effects of d-amphetamine. *Psychosomatic Medicine*, 1970, 32, 51–59. (a)

Stone, E. A. Behavioral and neurochemical effects of acute swim stress are due to hypothermia. *Life Sciences*, 1970, 9, 877–888. (b)

Stone, E. A. & Mendlinger, S. Effect of intraventricular amines on motor activity in hypothermic rats. *Research Communications in Chemical Pathology and Pharmacology*, 1974, *7*, 549–556.

Strömbom, U. On the functional role of pre- and post-synaptic catecholamine receptors in the brain. *Acta Physiologica Scandinavica*, 1975, *Suppl. 431*.

Thoenen, H. Induction of tyrosine hydroxylase in peripheral and central adrenergic neurons by cold-exposure of rats. *Nature* (London), 1970, *228*, 861–862.

Ungerstedt, U. Adipsia and aphagia after 6-hydroxydopamine-induced degeneration of the nigrostriatal dopamine system. *Acta Physiologica Scandinavica*, 1971, *Suppl. 367*, 95–122.

Weiss, J. M. Effects of coping behavior in different warning signal conditions on stress pathology in rats. *Journal of Comparative and Physiological Psychology*, 1971, *77*, 1–13.

Weiss, J. M. Psychological factors in stress and disease. *Scientific American*, 1972, *226* (6), 104–113.

Weiss, J. M. Psychological and behavioral influences on gastrointestinal lesions in animals models. In J. Maser & M. E. P. Seligman (Eds.), *Psychopathology: Experimental models*. San Francisco: Freeman, 1977, 232–269.

Weiss, J. M. & Glazer, H. I. Effects of acute exposure to stressors on subsequent avoidance-escape behavior. *Psychosomatic Medicine*, 1975, *37*, 499–521.

Weiss, J. M., Glazer, H. I., Pohorecky, L. A., Brick, J., & Miller, N. E. Effects of chronic exposure to stressors on avoidance–escape behavior and on brain norepinephrine. *Psychosomatic Medicine*, 1975, *37*, 522–533.

Weiss, J. M., Stone, E. A., & Harrell, N. Coping behavior and brain norepinephrine level in rats. Paper presented at Eastern Psychological Association, Atlantic City, New Jersey, April, 1969.

Weiss, J. M., Stone, E. A., & Harrell, N. Coping behavior and brain norepinephrine level in rats. *Journal of Comparative and Physiological Psychology*, 1970, *72*, 153–160.

Welch, B. L. & Welch, A. S. Differential activation by restraint stress of a mechanism to conserve brain catecholamines and serotonin in mice differing in excitability. *Nature* (London), 1968, *218*, 575–577.

Zigmond, M. & Harvey, J. Resistance to central norepinephrine depletion and decreased mortality in rats chronically exposed to electric foot shock. *Journal of Neuro-Visceral Relations*, 1970, *31*, 373–381.

Zigmond, M. & Stricker, E. M. Deficits in feeding behavior after intraventricular injection of 6-hydroxydopamine in rats. *Science*, 1972, *177*, 1211–1214.

CHAPTER 7

Stress and Noradrenergic Function in Depression

Donald R. Sweeney and James W. Maas

INTRODUCTION

During the last several decades, the psychobiology of stress has received much attention from experimental and clinical researchers. Many studies have documented an association between exposure to stressful stimuli and autonomic or endocrinological changes in the organism under study. In studying humans, investigators such as Lazarus (1966) and Beck (1970) have emphasized the importance of cognitive variables in stress research as well as in the treatment of psychopathology.

Controversy persists regarding the definition of the term "stress." Mason (1975a, 1975b) has reviewed this problem, pointing out that "stress" has been defined in terms of stimulus variables, response variables, and stimulus–response interactions. Furthermore, the terminological boundaries between "stress," "anxiety," and "arousal" remain unclear, as is evident from a recent symposium on anxiety (Spielberger, 1972). In the present discussion, we shall not attempt to resolve these complexities surrounding definition.

The Psychobiology of the Depressive Disorders:
Implications for the Effects of Stress

Rather, where we review the studies of others, or where we present our own work, we shall attempt to specify the operations by which "stress" or "anxiety" are defined. Moreover, we shall incorporate animal literature only when it has critical relevance to the interpretation of human studies. Animal studies have contributed substantially to further understanding of the psychobiology of stress and of depression. However, there is no animal model in which the experiential component of the affective state is available to the researcher. As Lader (1974) points out, in examining relationships between catecholamines and anxiety, "the relationship between central states induced by the 'stressful' procedures in animals and anxiety in humans is unclear."

In discussing noradrenergic functioning, we shall focus on investigations that emphasize neurochemical events involving norepinephrine and its metabolites in the central nervous system (CNS). Along with its role as a neurotransmitter in the brain, norepinephrine is also the neurotransmitter for peripheral sympathetic neurons. Earlier reviews have covered the extensive literature on human emotion and peripheral noradrenergic changes (Frankenhaeuser, 1971, 1975; Levi, 1972). It is generally assumed that CNS mechanisms mediate the processes by which stimuli are interpreted as stressful and through which subsequent psychological and physiological coping mechanisms come into play. Thus, the possibility of approximating more closely some of these central processes offers substantial promise of significantly enhancing our knowledge of brain–behavior relationships.

NORADRENERGIC FUNCTION IN DEPRESSION

The "Catecholamine Hypothesis"

In the 1960s, the "catecholamine hypothesis" of the depressive disorders was proposed (Jacobsen, 1964; Schildkraut, 1965; Bunney & Davis, 1965; Schildkraut & Kety, 1967). This hypothesis holds that certain types of depressive disorders may be associated with a functional deficiency of norepinephrine at CNS synapses. The major support for this hypothesis stemmed from studies showing drugs that deplete norepinephrine centrally appear to produce depression in some individuals, whereas drugs that increase the synaptic availability of norepinephrine frequently alleviate symptoms of depression. The subsequent research on noradrenergic functioning in depression was focused on identifying the metabolite(s) of norepinephrine which might reflect central events.

Evidence for the Central Nervous System Origin of 3-Methoxy-4-Hydroxy-Phenethyleneglycol

At present, the available evidence from several mammalian species indicates that norepinephrine is degraded within the brain via oxidative and then reductive pathways to yield either 3-methoxy-4-hydroxy-phenethyleneglycol (MHPG) or dihydroxyphenethyleneglycol (DHPG). Depending upon the species, these glycols may leave the brain in free form or may be conjugated as the glucuronide or sulfate and then transported out of the brain. Subsequently they are excreted into urine (Maas & Landis, 1968; Maas, Landis, & Dekirmenjian, 1976; Meek & Neff, 1972; Sharman, 1969).

Lesioning and stimulation studies of the nucleus locus coeruleus provide further evidence that MHPG may be a major CNS metabolite of norepinephrine. Within the CNS, the locus coeruleus contains the highest density of cell bodies of norepinephrine-containing neurons (Dahlstrom & Fuxe, 1964). These cell bodies give rise to axons that provide diffuse innervation to the entire cerebral cortex and the cerebellum, as well as to limbic structures such as the hypothalamus and cingulate cortex. Lesions of the locus coeruleus produce decreased concentrations of both brain norepinephrine and MHPG (Arbuthnott, Christie, Crow, Eccleston, & Walter, 1973; Korf, Aghajanian, & Roth, 1973; Huang, Redmond, Snyder, & Maas, 1975) whereas stimulation of the locus coeruleus produces increases in brain MHPG (Korf et al., 1973). Earlier studies in the monkey produced estimates that 30–65% of the MHPG excreted in urine has its origin in the CNS. Subsequently, Maas and Landis (1971) obtained data from human subjects that raised the possibility that a fraction of urinary MHPG is derived from the CNS. Kopin (1976), also using an indirect technique, has reported that as much as 80% of human urinary MHPG originates in the CNS.

Clinical Studies of Urinary MHPG in Depression

With this evidence that urinary MHPG may reflect CNS norepinephrine metabolism, there was further opportunity to test the "catecholamine hypothesis" of depression. It has been found that diagnostically heterogeneous depressed patients excrete significantly less urinary MHPG than healthy comparison subjects (Maas, Fawcett, & Dekirmenjian, 1968). Because some depressed patients excrete normal or higher than normal amounts of urinary MHPG, there have been attempts to specify along clinical dimensions the subgroup(s) of depressed patients with low urinary MHPG. Schildkraut, Keeler, Papousek, and Hartmann (1973) have reported that patients with *bipolar* depression excrete lower amounts of MHPG than patients categorized as characterologically depressed, whereas Maas, Dekirmenjian, and Jones (1973) and Goodwin & Post (1975) have found lower urinary MHPG in bipolar depressives than in comparison subjects. Jones, Maas, Dekirmenjian, and Sanchez (1975) report that depressed patients with a diagnosis of a primary affective disorder (employing the diagnostic criteria of Feighner, Robins, Guze, Woodruff, Winokur, and Munoz (1972), regardless of whether they are subclassified as unipolar or bipolar, excrete significantly lower amounts of MHPG than comparison subjects. These results indicate that there may be a subgroup of depressed patients separable from other depressive groups or from normals on the basis of *baseline* urinary MHPG excretion.

Further biochemical separability of depressed patients may be possible on the basis of treatment response to tricyclic antidepressant medication. Three separate research groups have reported that low, baseline urinary MHPG predicts a favorable treatment response to imipramine, whereas normal or high baseline MHPG predicts a favorable treatment response to amitriptyline (Maas, Fawcett, & Dekirmenjian, 1972; Schildkraut, 1974; Beckmann & Goodwin, 1974). As these two tricyclic antidepressants affect noradrenergic and serotonergic systems somewhat differentially, there is further reason to propose that *baseline*, urinary MHPG excretion might form the basis for a biochemical or pharmacologic subgrouping of depressed patients (Maas, 1975).

NORADRENERGIC FUNCTION AND
STATE VARIABLES

In the previous discussion we have been careful to specify that much of the information available that relates MHPG excretion to depression is based on baseline measurements; that is, on urinary samples collected when patients or subjects are in a stable psychobiologic state, having taken no medications and having demonstrated no major mood changes for a period of usually at least 2 weeks prior to the collection itself. However, it is becoming increasingly important to examine the effects of psychobiologic state on urinary MHPG. On the one hand, if psychobiologic state changes have a significant influence on urinary MHPG excretion, and if measurement of MHPG is to provide a significant biochemical predictor, such psychobiologic state variables would need to be controlled just as diet is controlled in the study of metabolic diseases. Beyond issues of controlled observation, it may be that further information about which conditions produce transient changes in MHPG and on the relationship between these changes and variables such as diagnosis or baseline excretion, would aid significantly in increasing the specificity of the predictive value of urinary MHPG.

Much of the work to date on MHPG and psychobiologic state has focused on physical activity and "stress" as the state variables most worthy of study. Perhaps the reason for the attention given to these two variables is that it is now well documented that when bipolar patients (i.e., those patients who have periods of both mania and depression) are studied longitudinally, urinary MHPG is significantly higher during mania than during depression (Greenspan, Schildkraut, Gordon, Baer, Aronoff, & Durrell, 1970; Bond, Jenner, & Sampson, 1972; Jones, Maas, Dekirmenjian, & Fawcett, 1973; Post, Stoddard, Gillin, Buchsbaum, Runkle, Black, & Bunney, 1977). As manic or hypomanic states involve both increased physical activity as well as increased arousal, it has been suggested that the observed MHPG changes may relate to one or both of these variables.

Physical Activity and Urinary MHPG

With regard to physical activity, it has been reported that there are no differences in urinary MHPG between agitated and retarded depressed patients (Jones et al., 1975; Schildkraut, 1974). Moreover, young healthy males, exposed to strenuous physical exercise, showed no increase in urinary MHPG even though there were large increases in urinary norepinephrine, which is known to increase with exertion (Goode, Dekirmenjian, Meltzer, & Maas, 1973). However, Ebert, Post, and Goodwin (1972) reported significant increases in urinary MHPG after exposing six depressed patients to a 12-hr period of moderately increased physical activity. Examination of the individual data from this study shows that three of the patients demonstrated negligible changes in MHPG, whereas the other three showed significant increments. Implicit in these data, therefore, is a significant interaction between subjects and conditions that is not easily interpretable on the basis of increased physical activity alone.

Stress and Urinary MHPG

There are some studies which attribute urinary MHPG changes to "stress." In the study described earlier (Ebert et al., 1972), where six patients were exposed to regimens of increased physical activity, stress is considered to be a possible "nonspecific" factor affecting the results. However, the authors point out that they observed no mood changes during the period of increased physical activity.

Maas, Dekirmenjian, and Fawcett (1971) examined urinary catecholamine metabolites in six severely depressed patients and five healthy male subjects who were infused over 48 hr with labeled norepinephrine in a study designed to investigate central norepinephrine metabolism. During control periods, urinary MHPG levels were lower in depressed patients than in comparison subjects, but urinary levels of norepinephrine metabolites thought to be produced primarily in peripheral pools (i.e., metanephrine, normetanephrine, and vanillylmandelic acid) were similar in the two groups. The authors interpreted these data as providing evidence that the lower baseline levels of MHPG in depressed patients were not attributable to decreased *peripheral* activity of noradrenergic systems. During the infusion period, depressed patients showed increases in urinary MHPG such that their levels became normal. It was suggested that these increases were associated with the stress of the infusion period, but no data were available to allow a direct comparison of such MHPG increases with the intensity of experienced stress. However, the fact that these depressed patients showed urinary MHPG increasing to normal levels may be seen as a challenge to biologic "exhaustion" models of depression, which postulate that the functional depletion of norepinephrine in some depressive states results from a reduced or absent capacity to mobilize norepinephrine at central synapses.

Takahashi, Nakahara, and Sakurai (1974) studied eleven patients with histories of endogenous depression, three of whom were reported also to have histories of manic episodes. In the hope of identifying relatively enduring biochemical, psychophysiological, or psychological "trait" characteristics, perhaps indicative of factors associated with a vulnerability to depression, these patients were studied "during their complete recovery period." The authors do not specify the elapsed time between the study itself and the most recent illness period of the patients. Along with an age matched group of comparison subjects, the patients were exposed to a 6-hr protocol that included both control and stress periods. During control periods (scheduled before and after the stress period) subjects were allowed to relax and read magazines. The stress period consisted of a 15-min performance test involving continuous addition followed by the viewing of a 30-min film depicting scenes of traffic accidents and surgical operations. Measurements were made of urinary epinephrine, norepinephrine, and MHPG, along with self-rated anxiety and self-rated depression. Baseline (prestress) depression ratings did not differ significantly between patients and comparison subjects, but baseline urinary MHPG excretion was significantly lower in the patients.

Reemphasizing the fact that these patients were *recovered* from their depressions, this finding supports the notion that decreased urinary MHPG in depression may reflect, at least in part, a "trait" determined phenomenon. Both patient and comparison groups showed increases in self-rated anxiety during stress, but the only significant between-group difference in anxiety was during the poststress control period, where the patient scores were higher. However, urinary MHPG changes did not appear to reflect this difference. MHPG tended to increase during stress in the comparison group, but the recovered patients showed no change across control and stress conditions.

Rubin, Miller, Clark, Poland, and Arthur (1970) studied naval aviators and radar intercept officers during control periods, a simulated-aircraft-landing training procedure, and actual landings of aircraft on aircraft carriers. The landings themselves are reported to have the greatest risk of accident among naval aviation procedures. Thus, it is implied that the performance of these tasks would result in considerable stress on the assignees. Urines were collected during control and three experimental conditions, and assays for MHPG were performed. For both pilots and radar intercept officers, urinary MHPG was significantly elevated for day and night landings, but not for the simulated landings. Increases in MHPG ranged from 25 to 58% above levels in control periods and there were no observable MHPG adaptation effects across experimental conditions. However, it is reported that serum and urine corticosteroids decreased over time, that is, with increased frequency of exposure to the stressful situation. It is speculated that corticosteroids may reflect anticipatory anxiety that decreases with decreasing situational novelty, whereas MHPG may reflect the degree of attention or alertness required for the performance of a task. Between and within-individual relationships between "stress" and urinary MHPG are not reported in this study. Therefore, for example, it cannot be determined whether subjects experiencing the greatest "stress" also showed the greatest increases in urinary MHPG.

On the basis of the studies reviewed, it is difficult to reach general conclusions regarding stress and urinary MHPG. One problem is the lack of uniformity of the stressor used, along with the absence of measures to validate the stress. Although Rubin et al. (1970) studied a situation with a high degree of *face* validity as a stressor (i.e., aircraft landings), only Takahashi et al. (1974) present data that document the effect of their stressor (i.e., motion pictures). Maas et al. (1971) infer that stress resulted from an intravenous infusion procedure, whereas Ebert et al. (1972) employ a *possible* stressor (i.e., increased physical activity) without presenting data by which the effects of physical activity and stress might be separated.

A second problem is specifying the interaction between diagnostic group (depressed patients versus comparison subjects) and MHPG response to stress. Rubin et al. (1970) report that normal subjects show increased urinary MHPG under stress. The normal subjects in the study of Takahashi et al. (1974) showed a substantial mean increase in urinary MHPG with stress, but this increase was not statistically significant because the variability also increased, implying that, in *some* normals, urinary MHPG may have remained at baseline level or may even have decreased. Maas et al. (1971) found that normal subjects did not show increases in MHPG during stress, but that actively depressed individuals did show such increases. The *recovered* depressed subjects of Takahashi *et al.* (1974), on the other hand, showed no MHPG response to stress.

INVESTIGATIONS OF ANXIETY, PHYSICAL ACTIVITY, AND URINARY MHPG

Method

We have carried out some work that may begin to clarify some of the previous difficulties in interpreting relationships between state variables and urinary MHPG. Twenty-four female depressed patients ranging in age from 22 to 60 were studied. All patients were admitted with acute depressive symptoms to the research ward of the Connecticut Mental Health Center, and each patient gave informed consent to participate in the research. Upon admission, any medications a patient had been taking were discontinued and all patients were placed on a diet that excluded foods known to elevate urinary catecholamine metabolites. The data were collected during the third week of hospitalization, after at least 14 days without medication and on dietary control.

The study was designed to evaluate the effects of both "stress" and physical activity on urinary MHPG. Pilot studies had indicated that when a patient is asked either to increase or decrease general physical activity, *some* patients report increased anxiety whereas others report decreased anxiety. Thus, the "stressor" in the present study was an 8-hr period of either enhanced or restricted activity. In the enhanced activity condition, patients underwent a programmed schedule of walking, riding an exercycle, and playing table tennis or shuffleboard. In the restricted activity condition, patients reclined on their beds, arising only for bladder and bowel relief. One member of the ward staff was with the patient at all times throughout the protocol. Patients were assigned to either enhanced or restricted activity conditions in alternate fashion. (A cross-over design was not possible because of the resulting delay in instituting antidepressant treatment).

The protocol consisted of two control days, an experimental day during which the 8-hr period of enhanced or restricted activity took place, and two postexperimental days. On each of these five days, 8- and 16-hr urines were collected, the 8-hr samples corresponding to the time of the enhanced or restricted activity condition (7:30 A.M. to 3:30 P.M. for all of the patients studied). Each urine sample was assayed for creatinine by the method of Bonsnes and Taussky (1945) and for MHPG by the method of Dekirmenjian and Maas (1970). Urine samples were excluded in cases where research nurses had any question regarding completeness. Also excluded were any samples in which creatinine values suggested the possibility of incomplete collection.

During the five day protocol, mobility was monitored continuously by means of a telemetric system previously described by Kupfer, Detre, Foster, Tucker, and Delgado (1972). Essentially, the system involves subjects wearing a light-weight transmitter on the dominant wrist. Movement causes modulation changes in the transmitter frequency, these signals being received by antennae on the research ward and transformed into amplitude changes that are counted and punched on paper tape. This system provides an index of general mobility and has been used in previous studies of psychiatric patients (Kupfer, Weiss, Foster, Detre, Delgado, & McParland, 1974; Kirstein, Bowers, & Heninger, 1976; Heninger & Kirstein, 1977).

The measure of stress selected for the present study was the State Anxiety Inventory (Spielberger, 1970). This is a 20-item self-rating inventory consisting of statements such as "I am tense" and "I feel secure" with four response categories ranging from "not at all" to "very much so." This inventory has been employed in laboratory studies as well as in hospital settings (Spielberger, 1971). Additionally it may be used for repeated testing and was developed with a view toward a psychometric distinction between state and trait anxiety. This inventory was administered at 11:30 A.M. and 3:30 P.M. on each of the 5 protocol days.

Results

Only the data obtained during the 7:30 A.M. to 3:30 P.M. period during control, experimental, and post-experimental days are reported here. Analyses of 16- and total 24-hr data added no further information of help in evaluating the problems being investigated.

EFFECTS OF PHYSICAL ACTIVITY

Table 7.1 lists means and standard errors of urinary MHPG excretion for enhanced and restricted activity groups during each condition. Repeated measures analysis of variance showed no significant groups effect ($F = .81$, $df = 1/22$), no significant conditions effect ($F = .69$, $df = 2/44$) and no significant Groups × Conditions interaction ($F = .70$, $df = 2/44$). [1] Telemetered mobility data validated the induced activity procedure, showing significant reductions in mobility in the restricted activity group and significant increases in mobility in the enhanced activity group. Thus, the data yield no

[1] A complete analysis-of-variance summary table is available from the authors upon request.

Table 7.1

MEANS AND STANDARD ERRORS OF URINARY MHPG
EXCRETION (in μg) FOR ENHANCED AND RESTRICTED
ACTIVITY GROUPS

	Enhanced activity group (N = 11)		Restricted activity group (N = 13)	
	M	SE	M	SE
Control	361	37	366	40
Experimental	363	41	356	20
Postexperimental	362	45	333	28

evidence that changes in urinary MHPG excretion are produced by substantial changes in physical activity.

EFFECTS OF PHYSICAL ACTIVITY ON STATE ANXIETY

As it is possible that the induced activity conditions operated differentially in affecting state anxiety, analysis of state anxiety scores was carried out for enhanced and restricted activity groups. State anxiety means and standard errors are presented in Table 7.2. Six of the original 24 patients were unable to provide valid state anxiety ratings because of factors such as unwillingness to cooperate and cognitive disorganization. Repeated measures analysis of variance showed no significant groups effect ($F = .72$, $df = 1/16$), no significant conditions effect ($F = 1.63$, $df = 2/32$), and no significant interaction ($F = .36$, $df = 2/32$). These data demonstrate that the induced activity conditions did not have systematic effects on state anxiety.

RELATIONSHIPS BETWEEN STATE ANXIETY AND URINARY MHPG EXCRETION

Despite the absence of state anxiety changes associated with changes in physical activity, it was noted that *both* activity groups contained some patients who showed increases and others who showed decreases in their state anxiety during the experimental period. Considering only those patients who showed changes in their state anxiety, we compared data of a group of seven patients who showed a significant *increase* in their state anxiety ($t = 2.26$, $df = 6$, $p < .05$) and a group of seven patients who showed a significant *decrease* in their state anxiety ($t = 5.75$, $df = 6$, $p < .01$). Table 7.3 shows MHPG means and standard errors for the increased and de-

Table 7.2

MEANS AND STANDARD ERRORS OF STATE ANXIETY SCORES

	Enhanced activity group (N = 9)		Restricted activity group (N = 9)	
	M	SE	M	SE
Control	54.2	2.7	55.8	2.8
Experimental	48.6	3.8	54.6	5.4
Postexperimental	54.4	1.8	58.9	4.6

creased anxiety groups. Repeated measures analysis of variance showed no significant groups ($F = .38$, $df = 1/12$) or conditions ($F = 1.42$, $df = 2/24$) effects, but a highly significant interaction effect ($F = 9.09$, $df = 2/24$, $p < .01$). This interaction is accounted for by the significant *increase* in MHPG between control and experimental conditions in the *increased* anxiety group ($t = 4.14$, $df = 6$, $p < .01$), and the significant *decrease* in MHPG in the *decreased* anxiety group ($t = 5.12$, $df = 6$, $p < .01$). Moreover, the data suggest that those patients with increased anxiety and increased MHPG had lower *control* MHPGs than did those with decreased anxiety and decreased MHPG. This baseline difference does not achieve statistical significance ($t = 2.08$, $df = 12$), but allowing for the relatively small number of subjects in this analysis, it may generate some interesting hypotheses for future exploration.

The association between MHPG change and state anxiety change was also tested by correlational methods. The Pearson r between state anxiety change and MHPG change for 18 patients was .71 ($df = 16$, $p < .01$). When telemetered mobility data were partialled out, the partial correlation between changes in MHPG and state anxiety remained at .71. Because of difficulties

Table 7.3

MEANS AND STANDARD ERRORS OF URINARY MHPG EXCRETION (in μg)

	Increased anxiety group (N = 7)		Decreased anxiety group (N = 7)	
	M	SE	M	SE
Control	272	26	371	40
Experimental	359	29	320	37
Postexperimental	335	33	362	44

surrounding the reliability of change scores, these correlations should be interpreted with care. However, the evidence from this study suggests that within-individual changes in urinary MHPG covary with changes in anxiety, but not with changes in physical activity.

The relationship between these results and diagnostic considerations will not be examined in detail here. Each of the original group of 24 patients was suffering from acute depressive symptomatology. Included in this group were four bipolar depressed patients and four schizoaffective patients. The remaining 16 patients were suffering from unipolar depressive disorders of varying intensity. Diagnosis was not related systematically to the assignment to activity groups or to the state anxiety scores.

CONCLUSIONS

We have presented evidence demonstrating that urinary MHPG excretion covaries with state anxiety in a diagnostically heterogeneous sample of acutely depressed female inpatients. Combining these results with those of Rubin *et al.* (1970), who studied normal subjects, it appears that we are justified in concluding that urinary MHPG, thought to reflect *central* norepinephrine metabolism, is related to at least one common index of stress. Although these studies represent the first clear establishment of this relationship in humans, the findings are not surprising as it has been shown consistently in animals (Stone, 1975) that brain norepinephrine turnover increases under conditions such as foot-shock, treadmill running, or cold water swimming. Parenthetically, it might be noted that some of the stressors in animal experiments have also produced increased physical activity. We have shown here that urinary MHPG change appears to bear no relationship to physical activity per se but rather, to change in anxiety or arousal levels.

It should be emphasized that we find no association between MHPG and state anxiety under baseline conditions. In other words, we cannot predict high- or low-baseline MHPG from high- or low-baseline state anxiety. However, our data *suggest* that further detailed examination of baseline–change interactions may be crucial in the further understanding of human, central norepinephrine metabolism. Patients with lower baseline MHPGs seemed to be those whose MHPG increased and who showed increased anxiety, whereas those with higher baseline MHPG exhibited decreased MHPG and decreased anxiety. Because the directions of these changes are opposite, it is unlikely that this pattern reflects the psychophysiological "law of initial values." Nor do the data support an explanation based on a statistical regression effect. Rather, they may reflect two distinct modes of norepinephrine metabolism, possibly based on factors such as different feedback properties or different modulating effects of other neurotransmitters. The data supporting such speculations are preliminary, so that further hypothesis-testing studies are necessary.

A substantial segment of the research findings on baseline urinary MHPG and depression has been replicated and continues to be solidified. Not only do certain subgroups of depressed patients excrete less MHPG than other subgroups and comparison subjects, but baseline MHPG may predict psychopharmacologic treatment response, as noted earlier in this chapter. However, there is little information available on urinary MHPG as a potential measure of noradrenergic *reactivity*. Stated differently, we need to know more about the individual differences and about the specific conditions associated with a *change* in norepinephrine metabolism or disposition. Clinical studies will continue to depend upon relatively indirect measurements of norepinephrine metabolism such as urinary MHPG. Such studies are critical for the further development of reliable indices that might eventually provide substantial aid in the earlier alleviation of depressive symptomatology. We feel that it is quite possible that the application of "provocative" test models may be useful in the further pursuit of this goal. Our data suggest that anxiety and urinary MHPG are related, and further that baseline MHPG differences may be associated with differences in vulnerability to anxiety. It is a commonly held clinical belief that some individuals are more vulnerable to stress than others and that such vulnerability may be an important determinant not only of depression, but of other psychiatric syndromes as well. Further studies of noradrenergic reactivity may hold some promise of being able to identify vulnerable individuals and perhaps to develop prophylactic measures that would reduce or modify susceptibility to stress-related syndromes.

REFERENCES

Arbuthnott, G. W., Christie, J. E., Crow, T. J., Eccleston, D., & Walter, D. S. Lesions of the locus coeruleus and noradrenaline metabolism in cerebral cortex. *Experimental Neurology*, 1973, *41*, 411–417.

Beck, A. T. Cognitive therapy: Nature and relation to behavior therapy. *Behavior Therapy*, 1970, *1*, 184–200.

Beckmann, H. & Goodwin, F. K. Antidepressant response to tricyclics and urinary MHPG in unipolar patients. *Archives of General Psychiatry*, 1975, *32*, 17–21.

Bond, P. A., Jenner, F. A., & Sampson, G. A. Daily variations of the urine content of MHPG in two manic-depressive patients. *Psychological Medicine*, 1972, *2*, 81–85.

Bonsnes, R. W. & Taussky, H. H. On the colorimetric determination of creatinine by the Jaffe reaction. *Journal of Biological Chemistry*, 1945, *158*, 581–595.

Bunney, W. E., Jr. & Davis, J. M. Norepinephrine in depressive reactions. *Archives of General Psychiatry*, 1965, *13*, 483–494.

Dahlstrom, A. & Fuxe, K. Evidence for the existence of monoamine-containing neurons in the central nervous system. I. Demonstration of monoamines in the cell bodies of brain stem neurons. *Acta Physiologica Scandinavica*, 1964, 62 (232), 1–55.

Dekirmenjian, H. & Maas, J. W. An improved procedure of 3-methoxy-4-hydroxyphenyl-ethylene glycol determination by gas-liquid chromatography. *Analytical Biochemistry*, 1970, 35, 113–122.

Ebert, M. H., Post, R. M., & Goodwin, F. K. Effect of physical activity on urinary MHPG excretion in depressed patients. *Lancet*, 1972, 2, 766.

Feighner, J. P., Robins, E., Guze, S. B., Woodruff, R. A., Winokur, G., & Munoz, R. Diagnostic criteria for use in psychiatric research. *Archives of General Psychiatry*, 1972, 26, 57–63.

Frankenhaeuser, M. Experimental approaches to the study of human behavior as related to neuroendocrine functions. In L. Levi (Ed.), *Society, Stress and Diseases* (Vol. I). New York: Oxford Univ. Press, 1971. Pp. 22–35.

Frankenhaeuser, M. Experimental approaches to the study of catecholamines and emotion. In L. Levi (Ed.), *Emotions: Their parameters and measurement*. New York: Raven Press, 1975. Pp. 209–234.

Goode, D. J., Dekirmenjian, H., Meltzer, H. Y., & Maas, J. W. Relation of exercise to MHPG excretion in normal subjects. *Archives of General Psychiatry*, 1973, 29, 391–396.

Goodwin, F. K. & Post, R. M. Studies of amine metabolites in affective illness and in schizophrenia: A comparative analysis. In D. X. Freedman (Ed.), *Biology of the major psychoses: A comparative analysis* (Vol. 54). Association for Research in Nervous and Mental Disorders. New York: Raven Press, 1975. Pp. 249–332.

Greenspan, J., Schildkraut, J. J., Gordon, E. K., Baer, L., Aronoff, M. S., & Durrell, J. Catecholamine metabolism in affective disorders III: 3-methoxy-4-hydroxyphenylglycol and other catecholamine metabolites in patients treated with lithium carbonate. *Journal of Psychiatric Research*, 1970, 7, 171–183.

Heninger, G. & Kirstein, L. Effects of lithium carbonate on motor activity in mania and depression. *Journal of Nervous and Mental Disease*, 1977, 164, 168–175.

Huang, Y. H., Redmond, D. E., Jr., Snyder, D. R., & Maas, J. W. In vivo location and destruction of the locus coeruleus in the stumptail macaque (Macaca arctoides), 1975, 100, 157–162.

Jacobsen, E. The theoretical basis of the chemotherapy of depression. In E. B. Davies (Ed.), *Depression: Proceedings of the symposium held at Cambridge 22–26 September 1959*. London: Cambridge Univ. Press, 1964. Pp. 208–213.

Jones, F., Maas, J. W., Dekirmenjian, H., & Fawcett, J. A. Urinary catecholamine metabolites during behavioral changes in a patient with manic-depressive cycles. *Science*, 1973, 179, 300–302.

Jones, F., Maas, J. W., Dekirmenjian, H., & Sanchez, J. Diagnostic subgroups of affective disorders and their urinary excretion of catecholamine metabolites. *American Journal of Psychiatry*, 1975, 132, 1141–1148.

Kirstein, L., Bowers, M. B., Jr., & Heninger, G. CSF amine metabolites, clinical symptoms and body movement in psychiatric patients. *Biological Psychiatry*, 1976, 11, 421–433.

Kopin, I. Measuring turnover of neurotransmitters in man. Presented at the 15th annual meeting of American College of Neuropsychopharmacology. New Orleans, 1976.

Korf, J., Aghajanian, G. K., & Roth, R. H. Stimulation and destruction of the locus coeruleus: Opposite effects on 3-methoxy-4-hydroxyphenylglycol sulfate levels in the rat cerebral cortex. *European Journal of Pharmacology*, 1973, 21, 299–306.

Kupfer, D., Detre, T., Foster, G., Tucker, G. L., & Delgado, J. The application of Delgado's telemetric mobility recorder for human studies. *Behavioral Biology*, 1972, 7, 585–590.

Kupfer, D., Weiss, B. L., Foster, F. G., Detre, T. P., Delgado, J., & McParland, R. Psychomotor activity in affective states. *Archives of General Psychiatry*, 1974, 30, 765–768.

Lader, M. The peripheral and central role of the catecholamines in the mechanism of anxiety. *International Pharmacopsychiatry*, 1974, 9, 125–137.

Lazarus, R. S. *Psychological stress and the coping process*. New York: McGraw-Hill, 1966.

Levi, L. Stress and distress in response to psychosocial stimuli. Laboratory and real life studies on sympathoadrenomedullary and related reactions. *Acta Medica Scandinavica*, 1972, Supplement 528.

Maas, J. W. Biogenic amines and depression. *Archives of General Psychiatry*, 1975, 32, 1357–1364.

Maas, J. W., Dekirmenjian, H., & Fawcett, J. A. Catecholamine metabolism and stress. *Nature*, 1971, 230, 330.

Maas, J. W., Dekirmenjian, H., & Jones, F. The identification of depressed patients who have a disorder of norepinephrine metabolism and/or disposition. In E. Usdin & S. Snyder (Eds.), *Frontiers in catecholamine research*. New York: Pergamon Press, 1973. Pp. 1091–1096.

Maas, J. W., Fawcett, J. & Derkirmenjian, H. 3-Methoxy-4-hydroxyphenylglycol (MHPG) excretion in depressive states: A pilot study. *Archives of General Psychiatry*, 1968, 19, 129–134.

Maas, J. W., Fawcett, J. & Dekirmenjian, H. Catecholamine metabolism depressive illness and drug response. *Archives of General Psychiatry*, 1972, 26, 252–262.

Maas, J. W. & Landis, D. H. In vivo studies of the metabolism of norepinephrine in the central nervous system. *Journal of Pharmacology and Experimental Therapeutics*, 1968, 163, 147–162.

Maas, J. W. & Landis, D. H. The metabolism of circulating norepinephrine by human subjects. *Journal of Pharmacology and Experimental Therapeutics*, 1971, 177, 600–612.

Maas, J. W., Landis, D. H., & Dekirmenjian, H. The occurrence of free vs. conjugated MHPG in non-human and human primate brain. *Psychopharmacology Communications*, 1976, 2, 403–410.

Mason, J. W. A historical view of the stress field (Part I). *Journal of Human Stress*, 1975, 1, 6–12. (a)

Mason, J. W. A historical view of the stress field (Part II). *Journal of Human Stress*, 1975, 1, 22–36. (b)

Meek, J. L. & Neff, N. H. Acidic and neutral metabolites of norepinephrine: Their metabolism and transport from brain. *Journal of Pharmacology and Experimental Therapeutics*, 1972, 181, 457–465.

Post, R. M., Stoddard, F. J., Gillin, J. C., Buchsbaum, M., Runkle, D. C., Black, K. E., & Bunney, W. E., Jr. Alterations in motor activity, sleep and biochemistry in a cycling manic-depressive patient. *Archives of General Psychiatry*, 1977, 34, 470–479.

Rubin, R. T., Miller, R. G., Clark, B. R., Poland, R. E., & Arthur, R. J. The stress of aircraft carrier landings. II. 3-methoxy-4-hydroxyphenylglycol excretion in naval aviators. *Psychosomatic Medicine*, 1970, 32, 589–596.

Schildkraut, J. J. The catecholamine hypothesis of affective disorders: A review of supporting evidence. *American Journal of Psychiatry*, 1965, 122, 509–522.

Schildkraut, J. J. Catecholamine metabolism and affective disorders. In E. Usdin & S. Snyder (Eds.), *Frontiers in catecholamine research*. New York: Pergamon Press, 1974.

Schildkraut, J. J., Keeler, B. A., Papousek, M., & Hartmann, E. MHPG excretion in depressive disorders: Relation to clinical subtypes and desynchronized sleep. *Science*, 1973, 181, 762–764.

Schildkraut, J. J. & Kety, S. S. Biogenic amines and emotion. *Science*, 1967, 156, 21–30.

Sharman, D. F. Glycol metabolites of noradrenaline in brain tissue. *British Journal of Pharmacology*, 1969, 36, 523–534.

Spielberger, C. D. Trait-state anxiety and motor behavior. *Journal of Motor Behavior*, 1971, 3, 265–279.

Spielberger, C. D. (Ed.). *Current trends in theory and research* (Vol. 2). New York: Academic Press, 1972.

Spielberger, C. D., Gorusch, R. L. & Lushene, R. E. *The State-Trait Anxiety Inventory*. Palo Alto, California: Consulting Psychologists Press, 1970.

Stone, E. A. Stress and catecholamines. In A. Friedhoff (Ed.), *Catecholamines and Behavior– 2: Neuropsychopharmacology*. New York: Plenum, 1975. Pp. 31–72.

Takahashi, R., Nakahara, T., & Sakurai, Y. Emotional stress and biochemical responses of manic-depressive patients. *Psychoneuroendocrinology*. (Workshop Conference of the International Society of Psychoneuroendocrinology), Basel: Karger, 1974. Pp. 58–66.

CHAPTER 8

Free Cortisol as a Peripheral Index of Central Vulnerability to Major Forms of Polar Depressive Disorders: Examining Stress–Biology Interactions in Subsyndromal High-Risk Persons

Richard A. Depue and Ross M. Kleiman

INTRODUCTION

It is now relatively clear that most, if not all, psychopathologic disorders represent diseases whose etiologies involve some form of dysregulation within the central nervous system (CNS). This fact simultaneously poses one of the more vexing problems for psychopathologists, as well as one of the more exciting challenges to evolving an understanding of the behavioral disorders. The problem lies in not being able to assess CNS systems directly in intact humans, while the challenge involves developing indirect measures that reflect dynamic properties of CNS functioning. Much of the biologic research in psychopathology during the last decade may, indeed, be characterized as an attempt to find reliable and valid peripheral indexes that reflect the functioning of CNS variables. In research in the depressive disorders alone, the search for peripheral indexes has been particularly creative and has produced several workable peripheral models for studying CNS systems, including *in vivo* and *in vitro* erythrocyte models for examining lithium and sodium membrane transport dynamics (Ostrow, 1978), urinary MHPG as a

The Psychobiology of the Depressive Disorders:
Implications for the Effects of Stress

reflection of central norepinephrine metabolism (Sweeney & Maas, Chapter 7 of this volume), blood platelet models for enzyme activity determination (Buchsbaum, Coursey, & Murphy, 1976), and dynamic measures of neurotransmitter functioning derived from cerebrospinal fluid metabolite assays under the probenecid paradigm (Depue & Evans, 1979). The significance of this research cannot be overemphasized, for the development of assessable peripheral indexes of central variables not only allows the study of the pathophysiologies of clinical disorders, but it also provides a way of investigating the predispositional nature of biologic variables in persons at risk for particular disorders.

The latter process, of determining which variables may serve as predisposing factors in high-risk groups, is one of the most difficult and uncertain aspects of deriving explanations of disease, and no patent strategies exist as a guide for research. One of the most straightforward strategies is to begin work on a variable that has been reliably found to be dysfunctional in cases exhibiting full syndromal disorder. The problem with this strategy, of course, is that it is uncertain whether the specific dysfunction in question is primary to the disorder or only a secondary dysfunction, and whether it is predisposing in nature or only specific to the clinical state. One strong line of evidence suggesting that the dysfunction may be related to predisposition is its presence, even in a mild degree, in individuals in the remitted state (i.e., outside of the clinical episode). If this can be demonstrated, investigation of this variable in high-risk subjects provides the next logical test of a variable's relationship to predisposition (Gershon, 1978).

One example of this progression in research in psychopathology is the work by Buchsbaum et al. (1976) on blood platelet monoamine oxidase (MAO) activity. Starting with the evidence (albeit somewhat inconsistent) that MAO activity is lower in monozygotic twins discordant for schizophrenia, in the clinical states of schizophrenia, and in bipolar depressive disorder (Gershon, 1978), Buchsbaum successfully employed this enzyme to select individuals at varying risk for behavior disorder. Individuals selected from the general population with low MAO activity, and their relatives, exhibited significantly greater behavioral and social dysfunction than persons with high MAO activity levels. This is an important finding with respect to the preceding discussion for it suggests that this, or other biochemical strategies, may be profitably applied to milder, subsyndromal high-risk cases in the search for biologic predisposing variables.

Unfortunately, this strategy has not been systematically applied to the depressive disorders. Indeed, in reviewing the evidence on genetic markers of vulnerability to depressive disorders, Gershon (1978) urged researchers to shift their emphasis from research on patients during periods of illness to the investigation of the preonset state of persons at high risk for illness. But Gershon's review also made it clear that the evidence is, at best, only suggestive as to which direction this effort might take.

I wish to propose that the integrity of cortisol functioning is worth exploratory investigation as a peripheral index of central vulnerability to some
forms of depressive disorder. The argument follows these lines:

1. Cortisol functioning is altered in the clinical episode and appears to
   reflect failure of the normal CNS circadian inhibitory influence on
   hypothalamic–pituitary–adrenocortical (HPAC) activity.
2. The central, inhibitory modulation system of cortisol appears to be
   dependent in part upon the integrity of biogenic amine metabolism.
3. Because there appear to be functional alterations in some biogenic
   amines in some forms of depressive disorders, cortisol dysfunction may
   reflect this central amine problem.
4. There is preliminary evidence that cortisol, norepinephrine, and
   serotonin (5-HT) functioning may be disturbed in some patients after
   remission.

These points were summed up succinctly by Rubin and Kendler (1977)
when they stated:

> The theoretical relevance is that neuroendocrine responses are excellent tools
> for testing various neurochemical hypotheses about psychiatric disease. Since our
> knowledge of the neurochemical control of the pituitary hormone is increasing, it
> is now possible, given an established neuroendocrine abnormality in a psychiatric
> illness, to postulate to what degree the activity levels of neurotransmitters might
> be altered to cause that abnormality [p. 135].

CORTISOL FUNCTIONING DURING THE CLINICAL EPISODE

The evidence related to cortisol dysfunction in depression has been reviewed numerous times (Carroll, 1975, 1977, 1978; Carroll & Mendels,
1976). Therefore, findings will only be summarized here. There is very
consistent evidence that the production or secretion rate of cortisol over a
24-hr period is elevated in most, if not all, patients suffering from depression. Production rates run as high as 30 mg/day (Gibbons, 1964; Sachar,
Hellman, Roffwarg, Halpern, Fukushima & Gallagher, 1973), whereas in
normals this value rarely exceeds 20 mg/day. Moreover, a study assessing
plasma cortisol levels every 20 min over a 24-hr period characterized this
elevated production rate in detail (Sachar et al., 1973). Depressives significantly deviated from normals as follows:

1. The number of cortisol secretory episodes was greater than normal.
2. The peaks of the episodes were higher than normal.
3. The cortisol baseline did not fall to the low levels seen in normals, even
   in the late hours of the evening and early hours of sleep.

4. During the latter period, patients often had secretory bursts when normally secretion ceases.

Significantly, findings indicate that there is not a strong relationship between cortisol production rate and a patient's level of anxiety and psychotic disorganization (Carroll, 1976; Carroll & Mendels, 1976; Depue & Evans, 1979). The cortisol dysfunction is unlikely, therefore, to be simply a stress response.

Another large body of research supports the production-rate studies in a different manner by indicating that tissue exposure to cortisol is excessive in depressed patients. Plasma total-cortisol levels of depressed patients are usually elevated in depression over control or recovery values, especially during the evenings or night hours rather than in the early morning (6:00–9:00 A.M.). One interpretative difficulty with these findings is that the cortisol measure employed refers to the total circulating plasma-glucocorticoid-level (cortisol plus corticosterone) when fluorometric or competitive protein-binding assays are used, or to the total 17-hydroxycorticosteroid (OHCS) level (mainly cortisol alone) when colorimetric assays are employed (Carroll, 1972). It is well known, however, that less than 10% of the total plasma cortisol is free in the circulation (i.e., not bound to the protein, transcortin), and it is this small fraction that is considered to be responsible for the tissue effects of circulating glucocorticoids. It is of significance, then, that plasma free cortisol (PFC) levels in depression are higher than those of control psychiatric inpatients (Carroll, Curtis, & Mendels, 1976). This latter study also found cortisol levels in the cerebrospinal fluid (CSF) of depressed patients to be significantly higher than control, normal, or recovered values. Because cortisol levels in CSF bear a close relationship to PFC levels (Carroll, 1972) in general, and did so in depressed patients (Carroll et al., 1976), these findings are important. Finally, several studies found results for urinary free cortisol (UFC) in support of excessive tissue exposure to cortisol in depressed patients (Carroll, 1976; Ferguson, Bartram, Fowlie, Cathro, Bircholl, & Mitchall, 1964). The average depressive UFC value of 134 μg/day far exceeded that for schizophrenics (39 μg/day), as well as that for normal values (40 μg/day) reported by Murphy (1968).

By all of these measures (elevated PFC and total cortisol, elevated CSF cortisol, and elevated UFC excretion), the evidence points strongly to a significantly increased exposure of the tissues and CNS of depressed patients to active cortisol. The extent of this increase is considerable, often twice the normal value, but is not as great as that seen in diencephalic Cushing's disease.

As a large portion of the evidence in support of increased tissue exposure involves plasma cortisol levels, it should be noted that the increase for PFC could be due to a reduction of the plasma transcortin binding capacity. In the only investigation of this possibility, plasma transcortin levels were found in most cases to be essentially normal in value (King, 1973). As Carroll and Mendels (1976) suggest, further studies of this variable are in order, although it is not likely that major abnormalities will be found.

Other lines of evidence that illustrate cortisol dysfunction in depression come from the study of central regulatory mechanisms of HPAC function. One such line of evidence concerns the circadian profile of cortisol secretion. Under basal conditions in man, the HPA axis does not operate continuously with minute-to-minute feedback control. Instead, the system is activated in an episodic manner, with intervening periods of total adrenocortical quiescence. Half the daily cortisol production takes place at approximately the time of waking, whereas during late evening and night hours cortisol secretory episodes are rarely seen. Thus, there appears to be a "CNS program" for HPA activation throughout the circadian cycle; during most of the day the brain exerts an *inhibitory* influence on the HPA axis, with this inhibition being relaxed during the morning peak of cortisol secretory episodes (Carroll, 1972; Hellman, Nakada, Curti, Weitzman, Kream, Roffwarg, Ellman, Fukushima, & Gallagher, 1970; Krieger, Allen, Rizzo, & Krieger, 1971).

Most depressed patients do maintain a circadian rhythm of HPA activity (where rhythm is defined as morning values being higher than night values). There is, however, a circadian variation in the extent of HPA overactivity because night values are more abnormal than morning values. In fact, in some depressed patients, night values are so abnormal that the HPA circadian profiles cannot be distinguished from those seen in diencephalic Cushing's disease (Carroll, Curtis, Mendels, & Sugerman, 1976; Sachar *et al.*, 1973).

These data suggest that "*the essential neuroendocrine lesion in depression therefore appears to be a disinhibition of the HPA axis*, that is, a failure of the normal inhibitory influence of the brain on adrenocorticotrophic hormone (ACTH)–cortisol release (Carroll & Mendels, 1976, p. 204)." A failure of the normal CNS inhibitory modulation of ACTH–cortisol release may *result in* an abnormal drive from other limbic areas of the steroid-sensitive neurons of the hypothalamus (Carroll, Martin, & Davies, 1968). Support for such a notion comes from the dexamethasone suppression literature in depression. There appears to be one "critical period" (perhaps around midnight) of ACTH release within the 24-hr cycle. If the concentration of steroid within the nervous system at this critical time is sufficient to block ACTH release (i.e., about .5 mg dexamethasone given orally at midnight), cortisol secretory episodes in normal subjects are prevented for 28 hr, that is, until the next day's major secretory phase is expected (Krieger *et al.*, 1971). Escape from suppression is seen as the steroid is metabolized over the next 24 hr.

In summarizing the dexamethasone suppression literature in depression, Carroll (Carroll *et al.*, 1976; Carroll & Mendels, 1976) illustrated that depressed patients do not exhibit cortisol suppression for 28 hr. They do, in fact, show suppression, but they escape from suppression abnormally early.

This abnormality appears in a predictable sequence, occurring progressively earlier in the circadian cycle with the increasing severity of depression. The abnormal escape occurs in both unipolar and bipolar patients with an endogenormorphic symptom profile, but not in neurotic depressions. Patients in the manic phase apparently do not exhibit this abnormality, but do show early escape in the transition period prior to a switch into retarded depression (Carroll et al., 1976).

Although the circadian profile and dexamethasone suppression data suggest a disturbance of the inhibitory modulation system of ACTH–cortisol release, dysfunction may result from other factors. One factor is whether the adrenal cortex can respond normally to ACTH, but apparently depressed patients do show normal plasma cortisol responses, or similar responses during illness and recovery, to injections of synthetic ACTH (Carroll & Mendels, 1976). Thus, the increased cortisol secretion rates described above probably do reflect increased hypothalamic–pituitary activity. Another factor is whether the HPA feedback-control mechanism (cortisol feedback control of ACTH release) is functioning normally, but again there appears to be no significant impairment of the HPA response to metyrapone (a cortisol synthesis inhibitor in the adrenal cortex) in depressed patients (Carroll & Mendels, 1976).

Taken together, then, the literature on cortisol dysfunction in depressive disorders suggests that a quite abnormal disinhibition of circadian cortisol secretion is characteristic of the clinical episode of depression. The abnormality does not appear to be general to patients suffering depressed mood (i.e., neurotic depressives), but is more specific to unipolar and bipolar patients with an endogenomorphic symptom profile. Moreover, the dysfunction does not appear to be simply a stress response, nor can it be accounted for by factors outside of the central inhibitory modulation system (i.e., adrenal cortex response, a feedback mechanism, etc.). Therefore, the problem may well be located in the central modulation system itself. It may be, then, that the failure of the normal CNS modulation of ACTH–cortisol release is, as Sachar et al. (1973) suggested, another reflection of apparent limbic system dysfunction in depression, along with disturbances in mood, affect, appetite, sleep, aggressive and sexual drives, and autonomic nervous system activity.

THE ROLE OF BIOGENIC AMINES IN THE CENTRAL INHIBITORY MODULATION SYSTEM OF ACTH–CORTISOL RELEASE

The possibility that the cortisol dysfunction evidenced in depressed patients may be due to a failure of the central inhibitory modulation system of

ACTH–cortisol release itself raises questions as to which neurotransmitters are utilized in this system's neural pathways. Numerous reviews and studies addressing these questions have appeared, and they have focused on the role of norepinephrine (NE) and serotonin (5-HT) in particular.

The major portion of the animal evidence concerned with the role of NE in the regulation of ACTH release is quite consistent. Norepinephrine appears to exert a *tonic* inhibitory influence over ACTH release throughout the circadian rhythm, its influence being overridden during the major secretory episodes of ACTH (Carroll, 1972; Carroll & Mendels, 1976; Fuxe, Hokfelt, Johnsson, & Lidbrink, 1971; Fuxe, Hokfelt, Johnsson, Levine, Lidbrink, & Lofstrom, 1973; Ganong, 1971; Jones, Hillhouse, & Burden, 1976; Kizer & Youngblood, 1978; Van Loon, 1973). Norepinephrine also appears to inhibit the ACTH response to stress as well (Carroll, 1972; Fuxe *et al.*, 1973; Kizer & Youngblood, 1978; Van Loon, 1973). Moreover, Fuxe *et al.* (1973) have suggested that the pathway involved in the NE inhibitory influence is the ventral NE pathway to the hypothalamus and the preoptic area.

The evidence for an inhibitory effect of NE derives from several strategies. First, when NE content is *depleted* by reserpine, large increases in ACTH secretion occur if the reduction in NE content is at least 50%. The time course of NE depletion and corticotrophin releasing factor (CRF) increase are coincident in this case. Moreover, the reserpine effect on ACTH can be partially countered by drugs that potentiate the action of NE at the receptor, such as MAO inhibitors and imipramine.

Other strategies for reducing NE levels have had similar effects on ACTH release. Thus, administration of α-methyl-para-tyrosine (AMPT) (an NE synthesis inhibitor via inhibition of tyrosine hydroxylase) results in increased ACTH release, and this effect can be reduced by jointly administering dihydroxyphenylserine (which increases NE synthesis via a dopa to NE pathway, bypassing the dopamine step). AMPT also has been found to abolish the cortisol rhythm, where cortisol levels remain elevated.

These effects appear to be due to NE and not dopamine (DA) alterations (Fuxe *et al.*, 1973; Van Loon, 1973). For instance, whereas administration of fusaric acid (a dopamine-β-hydroxylase inhibitor) results in greatly increased cortisol levels, L-dopa loading is much less effective in this respect.

Various endocrine manipulations also implicate NE as an inhibitory influence in ACTH release. Administration of ACTH increases the activity of tyrosine hydroxylase in NE pathways and increases urinary 3-methoxy-4-hydroxy-phenylglycol (MHPG) in *man* (Hauger-Klevene & Moyano, 1973; Van Loon, 1973). Moreover, adrenalectomy increases fluorescence of catecholamines in the median eminence (Fuxe *et al.*, 1971, 1973), whereas hypophysectomy has been found to decrease NE turnover in some studies (Van Loon, 1973).

The data on cortisol stress response and NE also favor an inhibitory role for NE. In brief, pharmacologically induced increases in NE metabolism have resulted in a reduced cortisol stress response, whereas conversely stress-induced cortisol increases have been correlated with increased NE turnover (Carroll, 1972; Van Loon, 1973), although Fuxe *et al.* (1973) attribute the latter finding to a direct effect of ACTH on NE synthesis (short-loop feedback).

In contrast to the NE evidence, findings concerned with serotonin's roles in ACTH modulation are conflicting; some data suggest an inhibitory role for 5-HT (Carroll, 1972; Fuxe *et al.*, 1973; Rotsztein, Beaudet, Roberge, Labonde, & Fortier, 1977; Telegdy & Vermes, 1973, 1975; Vermes & Telegdy, 1972; Westermann, Maickel, & Brodie, 1962), whereas other evidence indicates that 5-HT is excitatory in action (Fuller, Snoddy, & Molloy, 1976; Naumenko, 1973; Popova, Maslova, & Naumenko, 1972; Rotsztein *et al.*, 1977). The reasons for this inconsistency are not yet known, but it may have to do with whether the parameter studied is circadian rhythm or ACTH stress response (Carroll, 1972; Fuxe *et al.*, 1973), which areas of the brain are manipulated (Carroll, 1972), which serotonergic neural pathways are affected (Fuxe *et al.*, 1973), or whether the experimental method involves local applications of transmitter agents or pharmacological manipulations (Carroll, 1972). Concerning the latter point, for instance, whereas local applications of transmitter agents have led to equivocal results in terms of NEs inhibitory role, pharmacological studies have been relatively consistent (Carroll, 1972). The same state of affairs may exist in the 5-HT literature.

When inhibitory effects for 5-HT have been found, they have often involved stress responses (Carroll, 1972; Fuxe *et al.*, 1973; Telegdy & Vermes, 1975). For instance, 5-HT synthesis inhibition by parachlorophenylalanine (PCPA) administration has resulted in increased and prolonged ACTH and cortisol secretion at both 8 A.M. and 8 P.M. under stress conditions. Also, when 5-HT content has been increased by an L-tryptophan loading strategy, decreased ACTH secretion has been found in man. Importantly, the decrease in ACTH secretion was less noticeable in nonstress conditions.

Other evidence of an inhibitory role for 5-HT involves endocrine manipulation studies. Adrenalectomy has been reported to decrease the activity of tryptophan hydroxylase (the rate-limiting enzyme for 5-HT synthesis) and 5-HT turnover in certain limbic and hypothalamic areas, whereas conversely increasing cortisol or corticosterone concentrations has been correlated with increased tryptophan hydroxylase activity and increased 5-HT turnover in certain amygdaloid, limbic, and hypothalamic areas (Telegdy & Vermes, 1973, 1975).

In all, the neuroendocrine literature suggests that the inhibitory influence of the modulation system of ACTH–cortisol release is, in part, dependent upon the integrity of biogenic amine metabolism. In particular, NE appears to exert a tonic inhibitory influence on ACTH release throughout the circadian rhythm of ACTH. The evidence related to 5-HT action is less clear, although some strong data suggest an inhibitory influence for 5-HT on ACTH–cortisol stress responses. A model incorporating these relationships and feedback loops discussed above may be viewed in Figure 8.1. However, a word of caution concerning both the NE and 5-HT literature is in order. The major portion of this data has been collected on animals, mainly rats. In the few cases where the role of NE and 5-HT in ACTH regulation has been investigated in man, the findings have confirmed the animal data. But the regulation of ACTH by central pathways involves exceedingly more complex interactions between transmitter systems than is implied in this discussion, and whether these interaction patterns are similar in man and rats is still open to question (Kizer & Youngblood, 1978).

BIOGENIC AMINES AND
DEPRESSIVE DISORDERS

The theoretical significance surrounding the fact that the central regulation of ACTH–cortisol release is dependent on the integrity of biogenic amine metabolism is greatly increased by the literature indicating a relationship between altered biogenic amine metabolism and depressive disorders. This literature has been reviewed numerous times and need not be repeated here. However, several points are worth noting. Although the catecholamine hypothesis of depressive disorders has come under attack as being a reductionistic oversimplification of a very complex biological state (Baldessarini, 1975), integrative reviews demonstrate that certain indexes of NE metabolism (particularly urinary MHPG) implicate a role for altered catecholamine metabolism in some forms of depression and in the switch process in bipolar disorder. Additionally such indices provide one means of subcategorizing depressed patients on the basis of biochemical-pharmacological criteria (Bunney, 1978; Maas, 1975; Schildkraut, 1978). Therefore, it does not seem unreasonable to suggest that excessive cortisol production in depression may represent a peripheral index of alterations in central NE metabolism in view of the evidence of an NE inhibitory modulation of ACTH–cortisol release.

A similar argument for 5-HT is less easily made. A review of the indoleamine hypothesis of affective disorders showed that the evidence for 5-HT is inclusive (Murphy, Campbell, & Costa, 1978). The strongest support for the hypothesis comes from the repeated demonstrations from different laboratories that CSF levels of 5-hydroxy-indoleacedic acid (5-HIAA), the major serotonin metabolite, are reduced approximately 30% in depressed patients, or at least in a subgroup of depressed patients, compared to controls. Some additional support comes from the slimmer evidence that brain 5-HT levels were found to be 11–30% lower in the three of six studies

Control of Cortisol Release

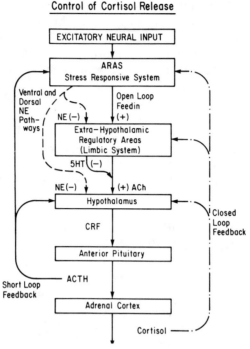

Figure 8.1. The figure represents a model of the modulation of the ACTH–cortisol release system. The solid center line represents the excitatory input by command pathways. The inner most hatched lines represent the inhibitory pathways that may utilize biogenic monoamines as transmitters, and are responsible for the modulation of ACTH–cortisol release.

finding differences between suicides and controls. Although the results from the brain 5-HT and brain 5-HIAA studies are both less uniform and more difficult to interpret because of the methodological problems inherent in postmortem investigations, the fact that, in all but one of these six brain 5-HT studies and in all four of the brain 5-HIAA studies, the values in suicides were lower than in controls can at least be considered compatible with the hypothesis. In addition, one of the most comprehensive CSF–5-HIAA studies has reported that the patient subgroup with low 5-HIAA levels had a higher incidence of suicide attempts (Asberg, Thoren, & Traskman, 1976), lending credence to the expectation of a connection between the suicide findings, depression, and low 5-HIAA levels. Furthermore, evidence for a contributory interaction of the brain 5-HT system with tricyclic and MAO-inhibiting drugs is becoming compelling.

There is substantial evidence for the efficacy of tricyclic drugs and some MAO inhibitors in treating depressed patients; given the small increment for possible improvement of their effects, the limited data suggesting enhancement by tryptophan cannot be disregarded. More persuasive is the apparent reversal of the therapeutic effects of imipramine and tranylcypromine by the 5-HT synthesis inhibitor PCPA (Shopsin, Friedman, & Gershon, 1976; Shopsin, Gershon, Goldstein, Friedman, & Wilk, 1975). If replicable, these results would implicate the 5-HT system in the mode of action of these drugs more clearly than any evidence previously available. These findings, as well as other data related to the specificity of action of certain tricyclics on 5-HT reuptake, have led to hypothesized subgroups of depression characterized by 5-HT system deficits (Maas, 1975; van Praag, 1977). Thus, the degree to which altered 5-HT metabolism, the central inhibitory modulation system of ACTH release, and cortisol dysfunction in depressed patients are associated remains an interesting but uncertain possibility.

CORTISOL AND BIOGENIC AMINES IN REMITTED DEPRESSED PATIENTS

Even if an association between cortisol dysfunction and altered, biogenic amine metabolism were established in depression, the extent to which either dysfunction can be viewed as predispositional in nature, and therefore likely to be observed in subsyndromal depressive cases, requires additional lines of evidence. One form of support for the existence of a predisposition would be to find altered functioning in the remitted state.

As far as cortisol, NE, and 5-HT are concerned, this form of evidence is minimal and indirect. As Gershon (1978) noted, perhaps the main reason for this lack is because this type of evidence is rarely sought. Concerning cortisol values, in the few studies that have reported data for both ill and recovered (not fully remitted, however) states, plasma cortisol values have generally been within normal limits, although Sachar et al. (1973) found that a few patients still exhibited slightly elevated levels. The problem with most of these studies is that they have measured total plasma cortisol (or the total urinary metabolite 17-OHCS) under steady-state conditions (i.e., conditions in which no demand is made on the ACTH–cortisol release system). As well as reviewed in detail later, total cortisol measures are insensitive to small but significant deviations between subjects, or with a subject across changing conditions, as are steady-state nondynamic measurement conditions. Therefore, the existing data on plasma total cortisol is largely uninformative with respect to cortisol functioning in depressed patients who are in the remitted state.

More sensitive cortisol measures have shown some depressed patients to have elevated values during remission, although no systematic study of patients in the remitted state has been done. Carroll and Mendels (1976, p. 197) assessed CSF cortisol levels in 13 depressed patients during illness and after recovery. The mean values were 13.1 ng/ml and 8.3 ng/ml, respectively. Although normal subjects were not studied, normal CSF cortisol values determined by the same technique are given by Murphy, Cosgrove, McIlquham, and Pattee (1967) as 4.0 ng/ml. The value for depressives after recovery was, therefore, slightly greater than twice the normal level. Because cortisol levels in CSF bear a close relationship to PFC levels (the biologically active cortisol in blood) and also indicate the exposure of the CNS to active cortisol, these findings, if replicable, are highly significant.

Carroll (1976) also studied the UFC values of 11 depressed patients before and after successful electroconvulsive therapy (ECT). This measure reflects the effective level of circulating plasma cortisol over time, and excreted free cortisol increases in direct proportion to the PFC level (Beisel, Cos, Horton, Chao, & Forsham, 1964). The mean value for patients was 134 μg/day before treatment and 79 μg/day after treatment. The mean excretion of normal subjects is 40 μg/day by the method used (Murphy, 1968), half the value found for depressed patients after ECT treatment.

Although these findings cannot be viewed as systematic follow-up remission values for depressed patients, it is significant that the most sensitive indices of cortisol functioning revealed cortisol values in patients considered ready for discharge to be twice that of normal subjects. A reasonable extension of these studies would be to use the more sensitive cortisol measures to assess cortisol functioning both in patients fully remitted (i.e., symptom free) and in subsyndromal depressive cases.

The recovery data for 5-HT come from one study but thus far they are systematic and highly encouraging. Van Praag (1977) found that slightly more than 50% of the patients who had low accumulations of CSF–5-HIAA (during probenecid administration) during the period of illness continued to exhibit low values on this measure 6 months after discharge at a time when patients were asymptomatic. Moreover, five of these patients with a highly recurrent disorder were followed and have responded well to a prophylactic regimen of 5-hydroxytryptophan (5-HTP) over a 1-year period. If these findings are replicated, they indicate that deficits in 5-HT metabolism are possibly predispositional in nature in some groups of depressed patients.

Overall, then, the recovery data on cortisol, NE, and 5-HT are minimal. The twofold increase in CSF cortisol values and UFC levels at time of recovery or improvement in clinical condition over published normal values, plus the CSF–5-HIAA findings of van Praag, are at least suggestive and encourage further investigation. The use of subsyndromal high-risk depressive cases in this research would help to circumvent the confounding factors associated with full syndromal disorder (e.g., chronic impairment and drug treatment, Depue & Monroe, 1978b). That this work might proceed with cases of subsyndromal levels of behavior disorder is supported by the MAO work of Buchsbaum et al. (1976). However, in using subsyndromal cases, it would seem crucial that any investigation of cortisol functioning employ the most sensitive cortisol measure available and dynamic test conditions.

INVESTIGATION OF CORTISOL
FUNCTIONING IN SUBSYNDROMAL
HIGH-RISK DEPRESSIVE DISORDERS

One logical extension of the cortisol research would be to investigate the existence of cortisol dysfunction in subsyndromal depressive cases (Gershon, 1978). Such investigation would help to establish whether cortisol dysfunction is specific to full syndromal disorder in the clinical episode or whether this dysfunction represents a more basic dysfunction of depressive disorder that is "observable" *outside* of the clinical episode. Furthermore, if the latter is the case, cortisol dysfunction in subsyndromal disorder may indicate, at a theoretical level, that alteration of biogenic amine metabolism is also a basic dysfunction (i.e., not specific to a clinical episode) characterizing the depressive disorders (Rubin & Kendler, 1977).

In studying cortisol in cases with subsyndromal level of severity, where dysfunction is likely to be of smaller magnitude than in full syndromal disorder, *steady-state* measures of *total* cortisol would probably be too insensitive to index alterations in the central, inhibitory modulation system of ACTH–cortisol release. For this purpose, a PFC measure would have several important advantages over "total" cortisol. First, over 90% of the total plasma cortisol is bound to a specific high-affinity protein, an alpha globulin called transcortin. The bulk of the total plasma cortisol, bound to transcortin, is not physiologically active, so that less than 10% of what is customarily measured is responsible for the biologic effects of circulating cortisol (Slaunwhite, Lockie, Back, & Sandberg, 1962). Thus, total plasma-cortisol level does not necessarily reflect the exposure of tissues to the active hormone.

A second, and more important, advantage of a free cortisol measure concerns sensitivity of measurement. Because the free portion is relatively very low in level under normal (nonstress) conditions, even small deviations in cortisol functioning between subjects, or within a subject across conditions, will represent differences of larger magnitude when groups are compared on free cortisol level rather than on total bound cortisol (Carroll, 1976). This increased sensitivity of the PFC measure may be significant in comparing the cortisol functioning of normal subjects with that of subsyndromal depressive cases, particularly if differences between these groups are of low magnitude.

Plasma free cortisol is a more sensitive measure than total cortisol in another way. The binding capacity of plasma transcortin is limited so that saturation normally occurs when the total plasma-cortisol level reaches 15–20 μg/100ml. Above this saturation level the relative amount of free cortisol in plasma increases sharply, and in a disproportionate manner to the increments of total plasma cortisol (Hamanaka, Manabe, Tanaka, Monden, Uozumi, & Matsumoto, 1970; Moor, Osinski, Decke, & Steeno, 1962; Murray, 1967; Sandberg, Slaunwhite, & Carter, 1960). As Mason (1975) has noted, because the average total cortisol concentration is about 10 μg/ 100ml, only a two-fold increase, on average, in total cortisol creates saturation of transcortin. This means that most stressors presented in the laboratory will generally produce a two-fold increase in total cortisol, after which a "ceiling" effect for total cortisol measures occurs (Mason, 1975). Free cortisol, however, will increase anywhere from 100 to 1000% after transcortin saturation, depending on the stress conditions.

For these various reasons, "there is no doubt that the *unbound plasma cortisol level is the most relevant parameter for psychoendocrine research* [Carroll, 1972, p. 52]." As PFC is sensitive to individual differences and stress manipulation, this measure may well provide a sensitive test of differences between normal and high-risk individuals in stress–biology interaction patterns. Moreover, in that free cortisol is potentially reflective of the functional activity of some biogenic amines, such a test may indirectly reflect the response characteristics of certain biogenic amines to stressful situations. Were these tests to show altered functioning in subsyndromal cases, one would have established a valuable first step in identifying a predispositional index to depressive disorder, as well as the nature of the interaction of this predisposition with stressors.

As a component of a larger research project on persons at risk for depressive disorders, we have recently begun to study the reactivity of PFC in subsyndromal high-risk individuals under varying laboratory stimulus conditions. However, before such studies could be undertaken, we (Depue, Slater, Goplerud, Kleiman, Wolfstetter-Kausch, 1979) were faced with the thorny problem of identifying, in an economical manner, subsyndromal cases at increased risk for major unipolar and bipolar disorders. We shall discuss our selection briefly before describing our cortisol paradigm further.

Identifying a Subsyndromal High-Risk Group

In the area of psychopathology, the process of identifying a group at risk for a certain disorder has taken three forms. Mednick and Schulsinger (1968), of course, identified their high-risk subjects on genetic grounds (i.e., selecting offspring of a biologic parent having the disease in question), as did Rosenthal, Wender, Kety, Schulsinger, Welner, & Ostergaard (1968). Mednick and Schulsinger (1968) completed the sequence just described by examining the validity and significance of what seemed to them, on theoretical grounds, to be a potential predisposing factor (autonomic reactivity and conditionability during stress).

Buchsbaum, Coursey, and Murphy (1976) approached the problem of identifying a group at risk from another vantage point. They selected, on theoretical and empirical grounds, a potential biochemical predisposing factor (i.e., the enzyme monoamine oxidase—MAO) and used this factor directly as a means of identifying subjects who were at-risk for behavior disorder. Although this approach to predicting risk was theoretically elegant and empirically successful, it does suffer currently from being uneconomical. The procedure requires the collection of blood samples from a large group of subjects, costly assays, and then the selection of individuals with low MAO activity as high-risk subjects. Fortunately, Buchsbaum's results provide the opportunity to develop more economical behavioral indices of risk that reflect variation in MAO activity. Moreover, Buchsbaum et al.'s results provide a crucial point concerning the study of high-risk subjects. Even though their high-risk subjects show only "mild" behavior disorder, a biochemical difference has, nevertheless, been associated with mild cases. This suggests that a biochemical approach to psychopathology is not necessarily limited to cases with disorder of full syndromal status.

The third method of identifying high-risk subjects is related to the promise held by Buchsbaum et al.'s findings, but is a mirror image of his approach. This method involves the assessment by self-report questionnaires of behaviors thought to reflect risk for a disorder, and then subsequent examination of selected risk subjects for predisposing factors chosen on theoretical grounds. This third approach has been explored only recently by Chapman, Chapman, and Raulin (1976). They developed a self-report questionnaire that attempts to identify individuals who are high in terms of physical anhedonia. This behavioral variation is thought to be indicative, on theoretical grounds, of one form of schizotypy. Hence, these individuals are viewed as being at high-risk for behavior disorder and/or schizophrenia. Once these subjects are identified, predisposing factors may then be investigated.

The rationale underlying this third method of identifying risk populations seems particularly valid for psychopathologic diseases. Because the pathophysiologies involved in these disorders are accompanied by patterns of profound behavioral variation, it is reasonable to assume that those individuals acquiring the geneticobiologic alterations of a particular disorder ought to evidence the associated pattern of behavioral variation, even if the biologic alterations are mild and the behavioral variations never achieve full syndromal status. Indeed, as far as understanding a particular disease is concerned, it is the milder, subsyndromal cases who are at increased risk, but who largely go undetected, and in whom predisposing factors may be studied unconfounded by variables accompanying chronic impairment of full syndromal disorder and treatment. This, of course, has been the rationale underlying the Chapman et al. work, and their initial findings appear to be promising (Chapman, Chapman, Raulin, & Edell, in press).

Although this third approach to identifying high-risk populations has not been developed for other psychopathologic categories, there is reason to believe that such an approach is needed in, and would be profitably applied to, the depressive disorders. This is so because within the less severe depressive conditions, there is a substantial subgroup of individuals who may be viewed as being at the greatest risk for developing the most severe forms of depressive disorders—the major unipolar and bipolar disorders (Depue & Monroe, 1978a, b). These individuals comprise the subsyndromal forms of unipolar and bipolar disorder. They have been variously labeled, but will be referred to here as dysthymia (subsyndromal unipolar disorder) and cyclothymia (subsyndromal bipolar disorder). The importance of these subsyndromal groups for high-risk research was shown by Akiskal, Djenderedjian, Rosenthal, and Khani (1977). Their data clearly showed that at least cyclothymic disorder lies along a continuum with the major bipolar disorders in that the subsyndromal cases shared crucial validating characteristics of the more typical or full syndromal forms of bipolar disorders. That is, they exhibited similar, albeit less severe, behavioral variations to full-syndromal cases; they came from families "loaded" with the same kind of affective illness as the classical polar disorders; the spontaneous risk for developing full-syndromal episodes of depression, hypomania, or mania was higher than that expected by chance and exceeded that of other personality disorders; and they showed drug response profiles comparable to the full-syndromal bipolar disorders.

Because the Akiskal *et al.* data illustrated qualitative similarity between sub- and full-syndromal cases in *behavioral variation* and geneticobiologic factors, it seemed reasonable to attempt to apply the third method of identifying high-risk cases (i.e., by identifying specific behavioral patterns by inventory) to the depressive disorders. Therefore, we initiated this effort by developing a case identification inventory (the General Behavior Inventory—GBI).

There are several theoretical positions that we adopted in developing the GBI, but because of their complexity, we can only cite these briefly in view of space limitations.

1. Although most of the behaviors comprising depressive symptoms probably range from normality to severe disturbance in a quantitative fashion, we were not interested solely in a *quantitative estimate* of an individual's disturbance. Rather, we were interested in gaining a *probability estimate* of an individual's likelihood of having a clinically significant disorder or of being a subsyndromal case. That is, we wanted the inventory to validly and reliably divide the population into "cases" and "normals."

2. This position dictated the manner in which items would be constructed. The establishment of a threshold point for separating "cases" and "normals" would be difficult and potentially subject to significant misclassification (both false positives and false negatives) if inventory items were constructed under a simple axis, quantitative severity model. Therefore, a compound definition of disturbance, including intensity (or severity), dura-

tion, and frequency, was employed in developing items. Therefore, although the behaviors characterizing cyclothymic and dysthymic disturbance may form a continuous dimension of intensity with the normal population, it was felt that combining more precise descriptions of behaviors with greater durations of experiencing the behavioral variation, and with more frequent occurrences of behaviors at a certain level of intensity and duration, would exclude normal subjects, and thus, produce a clearer threshold point for separating cases and noncases. We were aware that such a position might err in the direction of producing false negatives, but we were more concerned, from the standpoint of doing future research, in identifying by the GBI a subsyndromal case group as undiluted with false positives as possible. (This latter aim is particularly important for the study of biologic variables, which we are in the process of doing.)

3. The dimensions of intensity and duration were built into the wording of every question. Both dimensions were worded to describe a certain behavior or feeling definitely beyond the normal experience, but below the experience of full-syndromal depressive disorder. Even with intensity and duration built into items, the wording of the items alone did not appear to be discriminating enough to separate the normal from the subsyndromal experience of the behaviors. Therefore, a frequency dimension was added by having the subject mark each item on a scale of frequency-of-occurrence:

1	2	3	4
Never or hardly ever	Sometimes	Often	Very often

When the dimensions of intensity, duration, and frequency are combined, it is still possible for normal subjects to experience some of the items "Hardly Ever" or "Sometimes." But careful examination of the items indicates that rarely will normal subjects experience behaviors of such an intensity and duration as indicated by "Often" or "Very Often." This indicates that a large "conceptual distance" exists between Points 2 and 3 on the frequency scale. Indeed, the intensity and duration of each item were worded so as to create such a large distance. This was done because, in comparing several scoring methods for his self-report inventory, Goldberg (1972) found that a Case Scoring Method (where an item is counted in the total score only if it receives a frequency mark of 3 or 4) had the greatest power in discriminating "cases" and "normals." This scoring method has been used for the GBI.

4. A firm decision as to the content of the items was made at the outset of item development. Only those behaviors, feelings, and social and role dysfunction that form the core of characteristics defining the depressive disorders were selected. It was felt that these characteristics would best reflect the psychobiologic dysfunction associated with depressive disorders.

This procedure was followed for a methodological reason. Most serious medical and psychopathologic disorders are accompanied by feelings and cognitions of hopelessness, insecurity, inadequacy, etc. In addition, many "normals" have these experiences, especially those with feelings of low self-efficacy (Bandura, 1977). These types of experiences, therefore, may be considered secondary to a host of problems and not specific to depressive disorders. To include a good portion of them in the GBI could only serve to add unwanted heterogeneity to the group scoring high on the inventory.

Within the four guidelines just delineated, the 69-item GBI was developed to select relatively "pure" subsyndromal high-risk cases and normal comparison subjects. Our validation studies have found the inventory to be remarkably successful in this respect. Using empirically derived cut-off scores, the GBI identifies a subsyndromal case group from the general population with 94% accuracy (i.e., one false positive for every 35 "cases") and a normal comparison group with 97–100% accuracy. The identified subsyndromal cases not only report extreme behavioral variability in clinical interview, but they show clear behavioral instability and cyclicity relative to normals when both groups rate their behavioral patterns daily for 28 consecutive days (Goplerud, Depue, & Slater, 1979). Moreover, the first-degree relatives of the subsyndromal cases are highly significantly "loaded" with various forms of affective disorder relative to the normal comparison subjects.

Thus, we have employed the GBI as a first-stage, case identification procedure to select contrasting risk groups. Clinical interviews are then administered as a second-stage screening procedure, and, if subjects meet the research diagnostic criteria for cyclothymia or dysthymia (or are considered noncases), they are selected for our cortisol research.

A PARADIGM FOR STUDYING FREE CORTISOL AND STRESS

We have now initiated cortisol studies of subsyndromal cases and normals who are concordant on GBI score and interview diagnosis. A description of the paradigm and our concern with confounding factors follows, with the latter factors presented first.

Variables Affecting Cortisol Values: Subject Exclusion

There are a number of factors that affect either an individual's endogenous cortisol levels or the accuracy of cortisol assays. Consequently, any initially selected subject is replaced by another randomly chosen individual if any of the following confounding factors exists:

Factors Affecting Endogenous Cortisol Production
  1. Addison's disease
  2. Any form of Cushing's disease
  3. Adrenal hyperplasia
  4. Any other adrenal gland condition
  5. Any pituitary condition
  6. Any acute medical illness currently or recently experienced
  7. Smoking more than 1 pack of cigarettes per day

Factors Affecting Cortisol Assays
  1. Steroid therapy
  2. Estrogen therapy
  3. Other *heavy* drug use
  4. Pregnancy

**Variables Affecting Cortisol Values:
Control Procedures**

CIRCADIAN RHYTHM

In the earlier section on cortisol dysfunction in the clinical episode, it was noted that a circadian rhythm of cortisol secretion exists in man. Krieger (1975) and Krieger and Allen (1975) reported, in detail, on the various ACTH and cortisol episodes over a 24-hr period. Most of the daily cortisol secretion occurs between 4:00 A.M. and 9:00 A.M. Outside of that time period, there are a few cortisol episodes, with only rare secretion episodes during the late evening and night hours.

To study normal subjects and subsyndromal high-risk cases in the pre-noon hours would probably be an insensitive comparison due to the high, cortisol "noise" level from circadian influences. However, Krieger and Allen's (1975) data indicate that few secretory episodes occur between 1:00 P.M. and 4:00 P.M., and total plasma cortisol levels are relatively low then. Therefore, because the study's protocol involves a 3-hr "running" time, and because subjects are reluctant to participate for study in the late evening hours, all subjects are run between 1:00 P.M. and 4:00 P.M. This period was considered to be the best time period outside of late evening and night hours.

**Variables Affecting Cortisol Values:
Measurement Procedures**

There are two variables that *may* affect cortisol values that cannot be controlled but can be measured to assess their influence. Moreover, if subsyndromal cases are found to be different than normal subjects in cortisol functioning, it will be important to demonstrate that the difference is not due simply to these two variables.

LIFE STRESS

Cortisol values may fluctuate under normal circumstances with varying levels of life stress. Because subsyndromal cases may experience a greater number of stressors or perceive events as more distressing on average than normal subjects, a subanalysis compares the subsyndromal group's cortisol functioning with a normal subgroup matched on the extent of life stress. Life stress is assessed at the *end* of the study by having subjects check off on an inventory of life events those events that have occurred to them or a very close relative or friend in the last 6 months.

LEVEL OF DEPRESSED MOOD

It is well known that normal individuals experience transient states of depressed mood, but these are not accompanied by the behavioral–physiological components of the full depressive syndrome (Depue & Monroe, 1978a). It will be important to show that any cortisol differences between normal subjects and subsyndromal cases are the product of full depressive disorder and not just a depressed mood state. Therefore, all subjects complete the Beck Depression Inventory (Beck, 1967) just prior to the cortisol procedure. This inventory incorporates many items of cognitive and mood change typical in normals with transient depressed mood (Depue & Monroe, 1978a). A subanalysis compares the subsyndromal group's cortisol functioning with a normal subgroup matched on level of depressed mood.

Experimental Conditions

In planning the experimental conditions, two factors were considered: (a) that assessment of cortisol functioning under dynamic conditions will be more likely to reflect dysfunction of the central inhibitory modulation system of ACTH–cortisol release than will steady-state values, and (b) that assessment of cortisol response to and recovery from stress in subsyndromal cases would be of theoretical interest with respect to the stress–biology interaction hypotheses of onset of full syndromal depressive disorders.

The three experimental conditions span a 3-hour period (1:00–4:00 P.M.). During this entire period, continuous withdrawal of venous blood occurs at the rate of 5.00 cc per 5 min via a Cormed Inc. Constant Blood Withdrawal Pump.

Subjects are seated in a comfortable chair in a normally lit, furnished room located in a quiet area. However, because noise can result in cortisol responses, to assure that no unexpected alerting or distracting sounds reach the subject, subjects wear headphones throughout the 3-hr study. The headphones produce a faint, constant "hissing" sound of approximately 50 dB (measured at headphones).

The catheter tubing (nonthrombogenic) extends from the subject to an adjoining room where blood is collected at specific times as discussed below. Except during certain times in the stress condition, the experimenter and a nurse are located in an adjoining room.

REST CONDITION

After catheter placement, subjects are asked to rest for 60 min. During this time, subjects may read nonexciting magazines. The purpose of this condition is (a) to allow subjects to return to baseline cortisol values after the "stress" of venapuncture (to avoid excessive stress reactions to catheterization, subjects who state that they are extremely fearful of injections when initially approached about the study are excluded), (b) to allow adaptation to the experimenters and the experimental room, and (c) to assess the frequency and extent of fluctuations in baseline cortisol values over a prolonged rest period. Because it is unknown under which conditions differences between subsyndromal cases and normal subjects will appear (if they in fact do exist), the rest-condition assessment attempts to provide an index of "natural" variability of cortisol release, and therefore perhaps endogenous fluctuations in the activity of the central inhibitory modulation system, under *nonstimulus* conditions.

To assess this potential variability, blood samples (collected into vials in adjoining room) are taken every 15 min throughout the 60-min rest period (i.e., at 15, 30, 45, and 60 min after venapuncture).

STRESS CONDITION

It seemed equally important to assess cortisol response to stress. Such an assessment should reflect (a) the rate at which the central inhibitory modulation system is overridden (determined by the slope of the rise in cortisol levels, from baseline to maximum cortisol values), and (b) the peak magnitude of the cortisol stress response, which may reflect the extent to which the modulation system is overridden. Of course, from points (a) and (b), it will be impossible to know if any differences between normal subjects and subsyndromal cases reflect alterations in the modulation system per se or differences in the perception of the stressor. To partially assess these alternatives, subjects are asked to rate the degree of distress experienced on a 10-point scale immediately after the termination of the stressor.

Immediately after the final rest-condition blood sample is collected, the stress task begins. The stress task consists of three sets containing nine difficult math problems each. Each set is presented individually, and the subject has 10 min to complete each set. However, none of the sets can be completed in the 10-min period, despite the fact that all of the problems are only addition, multiplication, or division problems.

The stress in this task derives from three sources:

The Experimenter

The experimenter provides time-pressure instructions when Math Task 1 is introduced. Although subjects are told they have only 10 min to complete the nine math problems, they are also told this should be sufficient time if they work "extremely fast." After 5 min into Math Task 1, the experimenter reenters the room, looks at the subject's progress and says "We'd hoped you'd be further along. Do you think you could increase your speed." At the end of Math Task 1, the experimenter reenters and provides a failure comment. The subject is given Math Task 2, told he has 10 min, and is told to work "as fast as possible." After 5 min into the second set, the experimenter reenters, checks the subject's progress, and applies time pressure. At the end of Math Task 2, the experimenter reenters and gives encouragement so that the subject will not become discouraged and give up. Time pressure is again applied. After 5 min into Math Task 3, the experimenter enters, shakes his head in a discouraged manner, and says "Please, go faster if you can."

Distraction

During the entire 30-min stress period, distracting noise of normal voice level and variable thematic content is played through headphones via a tape recorder. The content of the noise changes frequently (approximately every 30 sec on average) and includes: music excerpts; the counting of numbers; text read in French; sounds of a lawn mower, a truck engine, and a flushing toilet; a food order being given at a Burger King restaurant; a cash register at work; etc.

Feelings of Failure

Subjects' feelings of having done poorly on the math tasks should result in a stressful experience. While the experimenter attempts to induce these feelings, he also attempts to encourage subjects so that they will not become too discouraged and give up, and so they will feel anxious to please the experimenter rather than be defiant and angry. These attempts are made in order to maintain the subject's commitment to all three math sets.

There were several specific reasons for constructing the stress condition as it is set up. First, it was important to construct a condition stressful enough to produce an increase in cortisol secretion of sufficient magnitude to saturate transcortin. After saturation occurs, the free cortisol value will increase disproportionately and will best reflect differences in stress response between normal subjects and subsyndromal cases. Other researchers have found that math problems completed under time pressure are quite stressful and lead to general physiological activation (Brod, 1960, 1970; Brod, Fencl, Hejl, & Jirka, 1959; Brod, Fencl, Hejl, Jirka, & Ulrych, 1960) as well as to cortisol elevations (Mason, 1975). The aspect of distracting noise seemed to be an important addition for assuring a stressful experience.

Second, saturation of transcortin is likely to be a function not only of stress intensity, but also of the duration of stress. Mason (1975) reported data showing that after 20 min of anticipation of intense physical exercise, subjects reached total plasma cortisol levels of at least 20 μg/100 ml. As this cortisol value represents the upper limit where saturation of transcortin occurs, it was felt that our stress task should be at least 20 min in duration. Therefore, in view of a lack of direct data on duration of stress and transcortin saturation, and to be more assured of achieving saturation, a 30-min stress task was chosen.

In an attempt to assess the cortisol response to stress, the first blood sample is collected 20 min following the initiation of the stress condition. Thereafter, 5 samples will be taken at 5-min intervals (i.e., at 25, 30, 35, 40, and 45 min after initiation of the stress condition). This time format for sampling seemed necessary in order to obtain the closest approximation of maximum cortisol response to stress.

RECOVERY CONDITION

After a cortisol response to stress has occurred, the central inhibitory modulation system becomes activated by the increasing concentration of ACTH in the blood, a short-loop feedback, and by the increasing concentration of cortisol in the blood, a closed-loop feedback (Van Loon, 1973). An assessment of free cortisol values after a stress experience and throughout a recovery period would appear to be a direct determination of how adequately the inhibitory modulation system is functioning to restore cortisol concentrations to more normal levels. If subsyndromal cases showed a slower return to more normal cortisol levels than normal subjects, this finding would indicate dysfunction in the modulation system. Whether the dysfunction is owing to the insensitivity of the feedback mechanism or to the inadequate operation of the system itself cannot be determined from such data. However, when the adequacy of the HPAC feedback control mechanism (cortisol feedback control of ACTH release) has been tested in full syndromal depressed patients, no significant impairment of the mechanism has been observed (Carroll & Mendels, 1976). This suggests that if slower recovery of cortisol is found in subsyndromal cases, it is likely to reflect inadequate operation of the inhibitory modulation system itself.

The beginning of the recovery period is defined here as occurring 30 min after the initiation of the stress condition and after the subject rates his distress. It begins with the experimenter's reentry after Math Task 3, at which time he says "Actually, you did fine on all three math sets. We had to stress you to see your hormone response. Relax now. You may read magazines for the next 90 min. I will come and get you then." This serves to relieve the subject's feelings of having done poorly.

A 90-min recovery period was chosen for a specific reason. The half-life of cortisol is 60–90 min (Carroll, 1972). Therefore, the 90-min period defines the outer limits of a biologically "meaningful" recovery period. Blood samples are taken throughout the recovery period.

Parameters of interest for the recovery period are: (a) rate of recovery (slope), and (b) magnitude of recovery expressed as the difference between the maximum cortisol value after initiation of stress and the lowest cortisol value reached during the recovery period.

CONCLUDING REMARKS

We have only recently initiated these studies and, although the preliminary data look promising, we can not yet judge if the findings will be reliable. It is our hope that the free cortisol studies on subsyndromal high-risk individuals will provide reliable indexes of central vulnerability to major forms of depressive disorders, as well as an initial illustration of the stress-responsiveness of central modulation systems in these disorders. If such indexes can be demonstrated, we plan to use these in combination with behavioral indexes of dysfunction, in a longitudinal manner, to test their predictive power. It is our firm belief, as suggested in Chapter 1 of this volume, that this form of research is the necessary first step in going beyond functional explanations of disease and in providing predictive explanations of the development of the major depressive disorders.

REFERENCES

Akiskal, H. S., Djenderedjian, A. H., Rosenthal, R. H., & Khani, M. K. Cyclothymic disorder: Validating criteria for inclusion in the bipolar affective group. American Journal of Psychiatry, 1977, 134, 1227–1233.
Asberg, M., Thoren, P., Traskman, L., Bertilsson, L., & Ringberger, V. "Serotonin depression"—A biochemical subgroup within the affective disorders? Science, 1976, 191, 478–480.
Baldessarini, R. J. Amine metabolism in relation to affective disorders. In F. F. Flach & S. Draghi (Eds.), The nature and treatment of depression. New York: Wiley, 1975.

Bandura, A. Self Efficacy: Toward a unifying theory of behavioral change. *Psychological Review*, 1977, *84*, 191–215.

Beck, A. *Depression: Clinical, experimental, and theoretical aspects.* New York: Harper & Row, 1967.

Beisel, W. R., Cos, J. J., Horton, R., Chao, P. Y., & Forsham, R. H. Physiology of urinary cortisol excretion. *Journal of Clinical Endocrinology and Metabolism*, 1964, *24*, 887–893.

Brod, J. Essential hypertension-hemodynamic observations with learning on its pathogenesis. *Lancet*, 1960, *i i*, 773.

Brod, J. Hemodynamics and emotional stress. *Bibliography in Psychiatry*, 1970, *144*, 13.

Brod, J., Fencl, V., Hejl, Z., & Jirka, J. Circulatory changes underlying blood pressure elevation during acute emotional stress (mental arithmetic) in normotensive and hypertensive subjects. *Clinical Science*, 1959, *18*, 269.

Brod, J., Fencl, V., Hejl, Z., Jirka, J., & Ulrych, M. General and regional hemodynamic pattern underlying essential hypertension. *Clinical Science*, 1962, *23*, 339.

Buchsbaum, M. S., Coursey, R. D., & Murphy, D. L. The biochemical high-risk paradigm. Behavioral and familial correlates of low platelet monoamine oxidase activity. *Science*, 1976, *194*, 339–341.

Bunney, W. E., Jr. Psychopharmacology of the switch process in affective illness. In M. A. Lipton, A. Di Mascio, & K. F. Killam (Eds.), *Psychopharmacology: A generation of progress*. New York: Raven Press, 1978.

Carroll, B. J. The hypothalamic-pituitary adrenal axis: Functions, control mechanisms, and methods of study. In B. Davies, B. J. Carroll, & R. M. Mowbray (Eds.), *Depressive illness: Some research studies*. Springfield, Illinois: Thomas, 1972.

Carroll, B. J. Review of clinical research strategies in affective illness. In J. Mendels (Ed.), *Psychobiology of depression*. New York: Spectrum, 1975.

Carroll, B. J. Limbic system-adrenal cortex regulation in depression and schizophrenia. *Psychosomatic Medicine*, 1976, *38*, 106–121.

Carroll, B. J. Psychiatric disorders and steroids. In E. Usdin, D. A. Hamburg, & J. D. Barchas (Eds.), *Neuroregulators and psychiatric disorders*. New York: Oxford Univ. Press, 1977.

Carroll, B. J. Neuroendocrine function in psychiatric disorders. In M. A. Lipton, A. DiMascio, & K. F. Killam (Eds.), *Psychopharmacology: A generation of progress*. New York: Raven Press, 1978.

Carroll, B. J., Curtis, G. C., & Mendels, J. Cerebrospinal fluid and plasma free cortisol levels in depression. *Psychological Medicine*, 1976, *6*, 235–244.

Carroll, B. J., Curtis, G., Mendels, J., & Sugerman, A. Neuroendocrine regulation in depression. *Archives of General Psychiatry*, 1976, *33*, 1039–1057.

Carroll, B. J., Martin, F. I., & Davies, B. M. Resistance to suppression by dexamethasone of plasma 11-OHCS levels in severe depressive illness. *British Medical Journal*, 1968, *3*, 285–287.

Carroll, B. J. & Mendels, J. Neuroendocrine regulation in depression. In E. Sachar (Ed.), *Hormones, behavior, and psychopathology*. New York: Raven Press, 1976.

Chapman, L. J., Chapman, J. P., & Raulin, M. L. Scales for physical and social anhedonia. *Journal of Abnormal Psychology*, 1976, *85*, 374–382.

Chapman, L. J., Chapman, J. P., Raulin, M. L., & Edell, W. S. Schizotypy and thought disorder as a high risk approach to schizophrenia. In G. Serban (Ed.), *Cognitive defects in the development of mental illness*. New York: Brunner-Mazel, in press.

Depue, R. A. & Evans, R. The psychobiology of depressive disorders. In B. A. Maher (Ed.), *Progress in experimental personality research* (Vol. 9). New York: Academic Press, 1979.

Depue, R. A. & Monroe, S. M. Learned helplessness in the perspective of the depressive disorders: Conceptual and definitional issues. *Journal of Abnormal Psychology*, 1978, *87*, 3–21. (a)

Depue, R. A. & Monroe, S. M. The unipolar–bipolar distinction in the depressive disorders. *Psychological Bulletin*, 1978, *88*, 1001–1030. (b)

Depue, R. A., Slater, J., Goplerud, E., Kleiman, R., & Wolfstetter-Kausch, H. The behavioral high risk paradigm: A procedure for identifying persons at risk for polar depressive disorders. Paper presented at the American Psychological Association Meetings, New York City, September 1–5, 1979.

Ferguson, A. C., Bartram, A., Fowlie, H. C., Cathro, D. M., Bircholl, K., & Mitchall, F. L. A preliminary investigation of steroid excretion in depressed patients before and after electroconvulsive therapy. *Acta Endocrinologie*, 1964, *47*, 58–68.

Fuller, R. W., Snoddy, H. D., & Molloy, B. B. Pharmacologic evidence for a serotonin neural pathway involved in hypothalamus-pituitary-adrenal function in rats. *Life Sciences*, 1976, *19*, 337–346.

Fuxe, K., Hokfelt, T., Johnsson, G., Levine, S., Lidbrink, P., & Lofstrom, A. Brain and pituitary-adrenal interactions: Studies on central monoamine neurons. In A. Brodiak & E. Redgate (Eds.), *Brain-pituitary-adrenal interrelationships*. Basel: Karger, 1973.

Fuxe, K., Hokfelt, T., Johnsson, G., & Lidbrink, P. Brain–endocrine interaction: Are some effects of ACTH and adrenocortical hormones on neuroendocrine regulation and behaviour mediated via central catecholamine neurons? In K. Lissak (Ed.), *Hormones and brain function*. New York, Plenum, 1971.

Ganong, W. F. Brain amines and ACTH secretion. In V. James & L. Martini (Eds.), *Hormonal steroids*. Amsterdam: Excerpta Medica, 1971.

Gershon, E. S. The search for genetic markers in affective disorders. In M. A. Lipton, A. DiMascio, & K. F. Killam (Eds.), *Psychopharmacology: A generation of progress*. New York: Raven Press, 1978.

Gibbons, J. L. Cortisol secretion rate in depressive illness. *Archives of General Psychiatry*, 1964, *10*, 572–575.

Goldberg, D. P. *The detection of psychiatric illness by questionnaire*. New York: Oxford Univ. Press, 1972.

Goplerud, E., Depue, R., & Slater, J. Longituding assessment of behavioral variability in persons at risk for polar depressive disorders. Submitted for publication, 1979.

Hauger-Klevene, J. H. & Moyano, M. ACTH—induced alterations in catecholamine metabolism in man. *Journal of Clinical Endocrinology and Metabolism*, 1973, *36*, 679–683.

Hamanaka, Y., Manabe, H., Tanaka, H., Monden, Y., Uozumi, T., & Matsumoto, K. Effects of surgery on plasma levels of cortisol, corticosterone, and nonprotein-bound cortisol. *Acta Endocrinologica*, 1970, *64*, 439–451.

Hellman, L., Nakada, F., Curti, J., Weitzman, E. D., Kream, J., Roffwarg, H., Ellman, S., Fukushima, D. K., & Gallagher, T. F. Cortisol is secreted episodically by normal man. *Journal of Clinical Endocrinology and Metabolism*, 1970, *30*, 411–422.

Jones, M. T., Hillhouse, E. W., & Burden, J. Effect of various putative neurotransmitters on the secretion of corticotrophin—releasing hormone from the rat hypothalamus *in vitro*—A model of the neurotransmitters involved. *Journal of Endocrinology*, 1976, *69*, 1–10.

King, D. J. Plasma cortisol-binding capacity in mental illness. *Psychological Medicine*, 1973, *3*, 53–65.

Kizer, J. S. & Youngblood, W. W. Neurotransmitter systems and central neuroendocrine regulation. In M. A. Lipton, A. DiMascio, & K. F. Killam (Eds.), *Psychopharmacology: A generation of progress*. New York: Raven Press, 1978.

Krieger, D. T. Rhythms of ACTH and corticosteroid secretion in health and disease and their experimental modification. *Journal of Steroid Biochemistry*, 1975, *6*, 785–791.

Krieger, D. T. & Allen, W. Relationship of bioassayable and immunoassayable plasma ACTH and cortisol concentrations in normal subjects and in patients with Cushing's disease. *Journal of Clinical Endocrinology and Metabolism*, 1975, *40*, 675–687.

Krieger, D., Allen, W., Rizzo, F., & Krieger, H. Characterization of the normal temporal pattern of plasma corticosteroid levels. *Journal of Clinical Endocrinology and Metabolism*, 1971, *32*, 266–284.

Maas, J. W. Biogenic amines and depression: Biochemical and pharmacological separation of two types of depression. *General Psychiatry*, 1975, 32, 1357–1361.

Mason, J. Assessment of psycho-endocrine profiles. In L. Levi (Ed.), *Emotions: Their parameters and measurement*. New York: Raven Press, 1975.

Mednick, S. A. & Schulsinger, F. Some premorbid characteristics related to breakdown in children with schizophrenic mothers. In D. Rosenthal & S. S. Kety (Eds.), *Transmission of schizophrenia*. New York: Pergamon, 1968.

Moor, P. D., Osinski, P., Decke, R., & Steeno, D. The specificity of fluorometric corticoid determinations. *Clinica Chimera Acta*, 1962, 7, 475–480.

Murphy, B. E. P. Clinical evaluation of urinary cortisol determinations by competitive protein-binding radioassay. *Journal of Clinical Endocrinology and Metabolism*, 1968, 28, 343–348.

Murphy, B. E. P., Cosgrove, J. B., McIlquham, M. C., & Pattee, C. J. Adrenal corticoid levels in human cerebrospinal fluid. *Canadian Medical Association Journal*, 1967, 97, 13–17.

Murphy, D. L., Campbell, I., & Costa, J. L. Current status of the indoleamine hypothesis of the affective disorders. In M. A. Lipton, A. DiMascio, & K. F. Killam (Eds.), *Psychopharmacology: A generation of progress*. New York: Raven Press, 1978.

Murray, D. Cortisol binding to plasma proteins in man in health, stress and at death. *Journal of Endocrinology*, 1967, 39, 571–591.

Naumenko, E. V. *Central regulation of the pituitary-adrenal complex*. New York: Consultants Bureau, 1973.

Ostrow, D. G. A heritable disorder of lithium transport in erythrocytes of a subpopulation of manic-depressive patients. *American Journal of Psychiatry*, 1978, 135, 1070–1078.

Popova, N. K., Maslova, L. N., & Naumenko, E. V. Serotonin structures in the pituitary-adrenal system. *Brain Research*, 1972, 47, 61–67.

Rosenthal, D., Wender, P. H., Kety, S. S., Schulsinger, F., Welner, J., & Ostergaard, L. Schizophrenics' offspring reared in adoptive homes. In D. Rosenthal & S. S. Kety (Eds.), *Transmission of schizophrenia*. New York: Pergamon Press, 1968.

Rotsztein, W. H., Beaudet, A., Roberge, A. G., Labonde, J., & Fortier, C. Role of brain serotonin in the circadian rhythm of corticosterone secretion and the corticotropic response to adrenalectomy in the rat. *Neuroendocrinology*, 1977, 23, 157–170.

Rubin, R. T. & Kendler, K. S. Psycho-neuroendocrinology: Fundamental concepts and correlates in depression. In G. Usdin (Ed.), *Depression: Clinical, biological and psychological perspectives*. New York: Brunner-Mazel, 1977.

Sachar, E. J., Hellman, L. Roffwarg, H., Halpern, F., Fukushima, D., & Gallagher, T. Disrupted 24-hour patterns of cortisol secretion in psychotic depression. *Archives of General Psychiatry*, 1973, 28, 19–24.

Sandberg, A. A., Slaunwhite, W. R., & Carter, A. C. Transcortin: A corticosteroid binding protein of plasma. III. The effects of various steroids. *Journal of Clinical Investigation*, 1960, 39, 1914–1926.

Schildkraut, J. J. Current status of the catecholamine hypothesis of affective disorders. In M. A. Lipton, A. DiMascio, & K. F. Killam (Eds.), *Psychopharmacology: A generation of progress*. New York: Raven Press, 1978.

Shopsin, B., Friedman, E., & Gershon, S. *Archives of General Psychiatry*, 1976, 33, 811–819.

Shopsin, B., Gershon, S., Goldstein, M., Friedman, E., & Wilk, S. *Psychopharmacology Communication*, 1975, 1, 239–249.

Slaunwhite, W. R., Lockie, G. N., Back, N., & Sandberg, A. A. Inactivity *in vivo* of transcortin-bound cortisol. *Science*, 1962, 135, 1062–1063.

Telegdy, G. & Vermes, I. Role of serotonin in ACTH release. In A. Brodiak & E. S. Redgate (Eds.), *Brain-pituitary-adrenal interrelationships*. Basel: Karger, 1973.

Telegdy, G. & Vermes, I. Effect of adrenocortical hormones on activity of the serotoninergic system in limbic structures in rats. *Neuroendocrinology*, 1975, 18, 16–26.

Van Loon, G. R. Brain catecholamines and ACTH secretion. In W. F. Ganong & L. Martini (Eds.), *Frontiers in neuroendocrinology*. New York: Oxford Univ. Press, 1973.

van Praag, H. M. Significance of biochemical parameters in the diagnosis, treatment, and prevention of depressive disorders. *Biological Psychiatry*, 1977, *12*, 101–131.

Vermes, I. & Telegdy, G. Effects of adrenocortical hormones on activity of the serotoninergic system. *Acta Physiologie Academie di Sci. Hungarie*, 1972, *42*, 49–59.

Westermann, E. O., Maickel, R. P., & Brodie, B. B. *Journal of Pharmacology and Experimental Therapeutics*, 1962, *138*, 208–217.

CHAPTER 9

Genetic Influences on Catecholamine Metabolism[1]

Jon M. Stolk and Bruce C. Nisula

INTRODUCTION

Among the various metabolic pathways presumed to form the biochemical basis of the organism's behavior in its environment, the catecholamine pathway has been one of the most extensively investigated. The observations to be reviewed in this chapter indicate that genetic composition plays a significant role in determining the biochemical parameters of catecholamine metabolism. This has been shown to apply not only to the basal state of the organism, but also to the state in which an adaptive response is evoked by an environmental stimulus. That there are genetic influences on the biochemical substrates of behavior seems to be a logical extension of the long accepted concept of genetic loading in schizophrenia (Kety, 1959) and in affective disorders (Leonhard, Korff, & Schulz, 1962). But, while it is intuitive that certain behavioral disorders may be determined

[1] Portions of the research outlined in this chapter were supported by USPHS Research Grants MH25601 and MH26913. We would also like to thank Dr. Ian C. Bush for his assistance in writing this chapter.

The Psychobiology of the Depressive Disorders:
Implications for the Effects of Stress

through genetic effects on brain biochemistry, it is obviously imprudent to conclude that all genetically determined changes in brain biochemistry result in behavioral changes or altered adaptive responses. Thus, a central theme of this chapter is that genetically determined biochemical changes in catecholamine pathways may be qualitatively or quantitatively divergent from strain to strain; and yet the behavioral responses to various environmental stimuli may be not only appropriate, but even identical. In essence, the biochemical parameters that form the substrates of the behavioral response are encoded in the genome.

The primary focus of this chapter will be on biochemical aspects of catecholamine function. Data pertaining to the genetic determination of basal enzyme levels in catecholamine-containing cells are summarized in the first section. Data pertaining to stimulus elicited changes in basal enzyme levels and potential genetic determinants of the diverse mechanisms for altering catecholamine function are discussed in the second section. Although most of the explicit studies have been conducted in animal species, human data have been introduced into the discussions wherever possible, as befits the specific focus of this volume.

GENETIC FACTORS DETERMINING BASAL ACTIVITY IN CATECHOLAMINE PATHWAYS

Data from Nonhuman Species

The significant influence of genetic factors on catecholamine metabolism has been inferred in different species from measures of several variables including tissue amine levels and, more appropriately, the concentration of enzymes specific for amine synthesis or degradation. Representative data are assembled in Table 9.1. The following text will concentrate on pertinent articles establishing genetic influences on catecholamine-containing systems, and those investigating specific biochemical mechanisms contributing to the observed genetic differences.

Mouse adrenal gland phenylethanolamine-N-methyltransferase (PNMT), the enzyme converting norepinephrine (NE) to epinephrine (E), has been the best studied aspect of catecholamine-containing systems subjected to genetic analysis in animals. Much of the relevant work was conducted by Ciaranello and his associates. Basal PNMT activity in adult male mice shows wide variations between inbred strains; for instance, a 2.5-fold difference was observed between the inbred strains with the lowest and highest PNMT activity (Ciaranello, Barchas, Kessler, & Barchas, 1972a). As adrenal weight and catecholamine concentration sorted independently of PNMT activity, it

Table 9.1

REPRESENTATIVE DATA SUPPORTING THE PRESENCE OF
GENETIC INFLUENCES ON CATECHOLAMINE-CONTAINING
SYSTEMS

Species	Comment	Reference
1. Tissue catecholamine concentration		
Mouse	Brain NE content recombinant inbred strains	Eleftheriou (1974)
	Adrenal NE and E content in inbred strains	Ciaranello et al (1972a)
Rat	Brain NE content in Sprague-Dawley rats obtained from different breeding stock	Miller, Cox, and Maickel (1968)
2. Tissue enzyme activity		
Mouse	Brain and adrenal TH activity in inbred strains	Kessler et al (1972)
	Adrenal TH, DBH, and PNMT in BALB sublines	Ciaranello et al (1974)
Rat	Serum DBH in different strains	Lamprecht et al (1974)
	Adrenal TH and DBH in different strains	Lovenberg et al (1973)
	Brain TH in inbred strains	Segal et al (1972)
Man	Serum DBH in families	Weinshilboum et al (1975)
	Platelet MAO in twins	Nies et al (1973)
	Erythrocyte COMT in siblings	Weinshilboum et al (1974)
3. Tissue catecholamine uptake and turnover		
Mice	Heart NE	Page, Kessler, and Vessell (1970)
4. Postsynaptic receptor mechanisms		
Mice	Brain cyclic AMP (cAMP) concentration in inbred strains	Orenberg, Renson, Elliott, Barchas, and Kessler (1975)
Rats	NE-stimulated cAMP production in brain in inbred strains	Skolnick and Daly, (1974)

appears unlikely that adrenal morphology is responsible for the enzyme differences. Hybridization of three inbred mouse strains revealed that the population variance in PNMT activity can be attributed primarily to genetically determined factors (Kessler, Ciaranello, Shire, & Barchas, 1972). Additionally, the absence of significant reciprocal differences indicated that pre- or postnatal factors in maternal environment, and X-linkage effects, are not important determinants of enzyme activity. Genes for PNMT activity carried by one of the three strains tested (CBA/J) are dominant and determine intermediate, rather than extreme, enzyme activity.

Ciaranello and Axelrod (1973) extended their genetic analysis of mouse adrenal PNMT using two BALB/c sublines. These sublines, BALB/cJ (Jackson) and BALB/cN (NIH), originally were derived from common stock but were propagated separately for about 25 years. BALB/cJ males had nearly twice the PNMT activity as BALB/cN subjects. Similarly, BALB/cJ adrenal glands required nearly twice as much anti-PNMT antiserum to neutralize enzyme activity, suggesting that the enzyme activity differences are due to changes in PNMT protein concentration. Hybridization studies again revealed an absence of reciprocal effects, thereby minimizing the potential effects of the environment or X-linkage. F1 and F2 offspring had identical PNMT levels that were intermediate to those of the parental strains; however, the F2 generation had a significantly greater population variance than did F1 offspring, indicating that the F2 mice were a heterogeneous population. Analysis of the F2 generation on the basis of a single gene model revealed three subgroups that were comparable to either the parental F1 hybrid strain (intermediate phenotype) or to one of the grandparental strains (high or low phenotype). Therefore, these data are consistent with a single gene model.

Biochemical studies revealed that both sublines synthesized PNMT protein molecules at similar rates. However, the turnover rate of PNMT protein in the BALB-cN subjects was nearly twice that of BALB/cJ mice; this alteration satisfactorily accounted for the differences in basal PNMT levels. The mutant allele, therefore, could be present in either (a) a gene controlling the activity or concentration of some product involved in degrading the enzyme, or (b) a structural gene that altered the properties of the enzyme as a substrate for degradation. Although studies on the crude enzyme from each subline showed similar physical (thermal stability, rate of degradation by trypsin, electrophoretic mobility) and biochemical properties (substrate and methyl-donor affinities), it was not possible to completely rule out a structural gene mutation. Thus, either alternative for determining the altered PNMT turnover rate remains viable.

An important extension of these studies was the demonstration that other enzymes involved in catecholamine biosynthesis are also under genetic control. Several studies show that the activity of tyrosine hydroxylase (TH), the presumed rate-limiting enzyme in the biosynthetic pathway, covaries with that of PNMT in most inbred mouse strains (Ciaranello et al., 1972a) and that genetic determinants of adrenal TH and PNMT are similar in three inbred strains (Kessler et al., 1972, see earlier). Using the BALB/c sublines described earlier, Ciaranello, Hoffman, Shire, and Axelrod (1974) found that single gene loci control the steady state levels of TH and dopamine-β-hydroxylase (DBH), as well as PNMT. A high correlation was observed in the activities of all three enzymes in parental and segregating generations. These findings suggested that the enzyme phenotypes are inherited in association rather than as independent traits. Phenotypic classification in the F2 offspring was analyzed against two possible models:

1. The gene for each enzyme resides on separate linkage groups that segregate independently.
2. The enzyme phenotypes are inherited in association owing to either

the linkage of three genes or to the control of all three enzymes by a single gene.

Results of this analysis suggested that Model 2 provided an adequate explanation of the data, whereas Model 1 did not. As independent mutation in each of three genes joined on the same linkage group is highly improbable, the data are more likely explained by common control of the enzymes through a single regulatory factor.

Data from Human Subjects

Adequate assessment of the potential effect of genetic factors on catecholamine metabolism in man was facilitated by the finding of Weinshilboum and Axelrod (1971) that DBH, one of the biosynthetic enzymes, is measurable in human serum. Early studies anticipated that serum DBH activity measurements would reflect sympathetic nervous system function, as the circulating enzyme was thought to be released from sympathetic nerve endings, along with NE, by exocytosis in response to neuronal discharge (Weinshilboum, Thoa, Johnson, Kopin, & Axelrod, 1971). At present the relationship between circulating DBH and sympathetic activity is controversial (cf. Kopin, Kaufman, Viveros, Jacobowitz, Lake, Ziegler, Lovenberg, & Goodwin, 1976); nonetheless, there is little doubt that the level of circulating DBH is genetically determined in man.

Ross, Wetterberg, and Myrhed (1973) studied plasma DBH activity in twins. Enzyme activity in dizygotic (DZ) twins revealed a high correlation coefficient, and differed significantly from a random distribution. Monozygotic (MZ) twins had a substantially greater concordance than DZ twins; the nearly complete concordance observed in MZ twins suggests that environmental factors are less important than genetic determinants of circulating DBH activity in DZ twins. Weinshilboum, Raymond, Elveback, and Weidman (1974) independently observed the sibling–sibling correlation in serum DBH activity. Frequency-distribution analyses provided evidence for two populations, one with very low and one with normal DBH activity. The latter finding subsequently was detailed further by the same group. Approximately 4% of children and 3% of the adult population tested had very low activity. Analysis of serum DBH activity in families of probands with very low activity was compatible with monogenic autosomal recessive inheritance of the phenotype. (Weinshilboum, Schrott, Raymond, Weidman, & Elveback, 1975.)

Two other enzymes involved in catecholamine metabolism and readily measured in man seem to be genetically determined. These enzymes are catechol-O-methyltransferase (COMT) and monoamine oxidase (MAO), both of which are involved in catecholamine degradation. Erythrocyte COMT activity reveals a bimodal frequency distribution in an unselected, adolescent school population (Weinshilboum et al., 1974). A highly significant correlation was found between COMT activity and members of sibling pairs. Thus, familial factors appear to be important determinants of erythrocyte COMT activity, although the contributions of the environment and the possible mechanisms of inheritance remain to be studied. Information available for MAO (Nies, Robinson, Lamborn, & Lampert, 1973) suggests that genetic factors are of importance in determining the platelet and plasma enzyme activity. Although the data did not reach significance, there was a strong trend for variance to decrease from control pairs to DZ twins to MZ twins. As multiple MAO-like enzymes have been described, a detailed analysis of potential inheritance must await appropriate methodologic development.

Evaluation of Genetically Determined Differences in Basal Enzyme Activity

   Information available from studies of several animal species clearly demonstrates that genetic composition determines the basal activity of the enzymes subserving catecholamine synthesis. Data obtained from mice studies suggest that linked genes, or a single control gene, determine enzyme protein concentration in the adrenomedullary biosynthetic pathway by regulating the degradation rates of TH, DBH, and PNMT. Results obtained from human subjects indicate that serum DBH is under single gene control, and that two circulating catabolic enzymes (MAO and COMT) also may have genetic determinants; specific details of the mechanisms regulating these circulating enzymes in man remain to be determined, however.

   The implications of genetic control of basal activity in catecholamine-containing systems can be viewed from several perspectives. On a molecular level, inherited factors provide a unique tool for studying fundamental regulatory mechanisms. For instance, Lovenberg, Yamabe, DeJong, and Hansen (1973) suggested that TH and DBH in rat adrenal glands were under separate genetic control, unlike the situation in mice (see pages 208–209). With respect to different tissues in the same organism, Kessler et al. (1972) provided evidence that the genetic determinants of brain TH differed from those of the adrenal enzyme. Kessler et al.'s observation emphasized the potential limitations attendant to functional correlations based upon genetically determined differences in a particular group of catecholamine-containing cells.

   Attaching functional relevance to the inherited differences in the levels of catecholamine metabolizing enzymes has been hampered by a lack of specific methodology for correlating sympathetic function with behavioral or physiologic function. Studies relating blood pressure and catecholamine

Table 9.2

INHERITED CONDITIONS ASSOCIATED WITH ABNORMALITIES IN
CATECHOLAMINE-CONTAINING SYSTEMS

Condition (Species)	Biochemical abnormality	Reference
Brindled mouse (mice)	Presumed deficit in brain DBH activity	Hunt and Johnson (1973)
Inherited diabetes insipidus (rats)	Elevated serum DBH activity	Wooten, Hanson, and Lamprecht (1975)
Spontaneous hypertension (rats)	Elevated brainstem PNMT activity	Saavedra et al (1975)
	Elevated serum and arterial DBH activity	Nagatsu et al (1976)
Familial dysautonomia (man)	Reduced plasma DBH activity	Weinshilboum and Axelrod (1971)
Down's syndrome (man)	Reduced serum DBH activity	Wetterberg, Gustavson, Backstrom, Ross, and Froden (1972)
Autosomal dominant torsion dystonia (man)	Elevated serum DBH activity	Wooten, Eldridge, Axelrod, and Stern (1973)

function provide an appropriate example. Human studies relating hypertension to serum DBH activity have produced conflicting data; for example, Schanberg, Stone, Kirshner, Gunnels, and Robinson (1974) reported a correlation, whereas Horowitz, Alexander, Lovenberg, and Keiser (1973) concluded that diastolic blood pressure and serum enzyme activity were unrelated. That serum DBH activity, although genetically determined, was unrelated to systolic or diastolic blood pressure is further confirmed by Weinshilboum et al. (1975). Similar observations were reported in various rat strains (Lamprecht, Eichelman, Williams, Wooten, and Kopin, 1974), including a spontaneously hypertensive (SHR) strain (Nagatsu, Kato, Numata, Ikuta, Umezawa, Matsuzaki, & Takeuchi, 1974). Although young SHR assessed prior to the development of hypertension do show increases in serum and vascular DBH activity (Nagatsu, Ikuta, Numata, Kato, Sano, Nagatsu, Umezawa, Matsuzaki, & Takeuchi, 1976) as well as in brainstem PNMT (Saavedra, Grobecker, & Axelrod, 1976), it is unclear whether observed changes are responsive to, or determinants of the physiological change.

Similarly, it is difficult to correlate behavioral variables with genetic differences in catecholamine metabolism. For instance, strain-related differences in brain TH activity (Segal, Kuczenski, & Mandell, 1972) bear no apparent relationship to various behavioral differences observed in an independent study using inbred rat strains obtained from the same stock (Ray & Barrett, 1975). Ciaranello, Lupsky, and Axelrod (1974), using the BALB/cJ and BALB/cN sublines described earlier in this chapter, observed parallelism between genetic determinants of both adrenal catecholamine synthesizing enzymes (TH, DBH, and PNMT) and isolation-induced attack behavior in male mice. These authors were cautious in interpreting this apparent association, however, and left the nature of the observed correlation unresolved. Consideration of specific characteristics of the particular behavior studied supports the authors' caution, as documented sex-related differences (i.e., female mice do not demonstrate the behavior) and the lack of a reliable correlation between adrenal enzymes and isolation-induced aggression across different inbred mouse strains, appears to rule against a specific genetic association. Therefore, broader conclusions concerning the functional correlates of genetically determined biochemical differences await more extensive data.

GENETIC FACTORS CONTROLLING STIMULUS-INDUCED CHANGES IN CATECHOLAMINE METABOLISM

Catecholamine Regulatory Mechanisms

Genetic determination of the parameters of catecholamine metabolism at the organism's basal state represents only one aspect of genetic regulation of catecholamine systems. The response of the catecholamine system to changes in the organism's internal or external environment represents another area where genetic factors can be operant. Mechanisms regulating the stimulus-induced changes in catecholamine metabolism have received intense study. Several general types of regulatory processes may be discerned. Synthetic enzyme activity (and thus, NE production) can be modified by (a) changes in the intraneuronal milieu (i.e., feedback inhibition of TH; Spector, Gordon, Sjoerdsma, & Udenfriend, 1967), and (b) changes in the quantity of enzyme protein (i.e., induction of TH and DBH in superior cervical ganglia after cold exposure; Thoenen, Kettler, Burkard and Saner, 1971). Each of these general regulatory processes may be effected in a variety of ways. For example, changes in the quantity of enzyme protein can result from altered rates of protein synthesis or degradation (i.e., increased TH synthesis after reserpine treatment; Mueller, Thoenen, & Axelrod, 1969), or at least for DBH, release of enzyme from nerve terminals by exocytosis (Gewirtz & Kopin, 1970). Finally, mechanisms for altering specific regulatory processes may be elicited through different pathways. For example, adrenal PNMT concentration can be altered by a hormonal messenger (i.e., ACTH: Wurtman & Axelrod, 1966), nerve impulse activity (Thoenen, Mueller, & Axelrod, 1970), or through a combination of mechanisms (Ciaranello, Dornbusch, & Barchas, 1972b, discussed in detail on p. 213). These considerations illustrate clearly the diversity underlying

catecholamine regulatory mechanisms. As these mechanisms may be subject to genetic determination, the potential for inherited factors to produce
diversity in catecholamine regulation is large. The following text will consider two aspects of this diversity: (a) inheritance of specific regulatory
features, and (b) genetic determination of qualitative, as well as quantitative,
response characteristics.

Potential Inheritance of Specific Regulatory Features

An important article by Ciaranello, Dornbusch, and Barchas (1972b)
describes, in detail, adrenal medullary PNMT induction by cold stress in
inbred mouse strains. They studied three strains (DBA/2J, C57BL/Ka,
CBA/J), all of which reveal a rapid increase in adrenal PNMT activity after
exposure to a 4°C environment. Although the strains increased PNMT at
different rates, the features of predominant importance were the variety of
routes by which PNMT induction proceeded in the face of the common
(4°C) stimulus. Glucocorticoids were specifically required for PNMT induction in CBA/J mice; while adrenocorticotropic hormone (ACTH) could
effect the change, induction was mediated via, and exclusively dependent
upon, glucocorticoids. The C57BL/Ka strain required ACTH to effect
PNMT induction; suppression of ACTH release and hypophysectomy
abolished the response, whereas inhibition of ACTH-mediated glucocor-
ticoid secretion by aminoglutethimide had no effect on induction. Finally,
PNMT induction in DBA/2J mice could be effected either by increased
afferent input into the adrenal or by glucocorticoids; ACTH alone was
ineffective in altering PNMT activity. A more detailed characterization of
the genetic factors, or of the specific intraneuronal biochemical features of
the induction (i.e., increased synthesis or decreased degradation of PNMT
protein; Ciaranello, Dornbusch and Barchas (1972) have demonstrated that
cold stress causes increased PNMT synthesis in C57BL/Ka mice), is not yet
available.

Genetic Determinants of Biochemical Response Diversity

That diverse biochemical events in catecholamine-containing systems
may accompany the same adaptive response in different subjects is integral
to the conceptual framework outlined in the introduction to this chapter.
Experiments being conducted in our laboratory will be used to illustrate this
point. We are analyzing biochemical events in catecholaminergic systems
using stressful environments. Our initial studies indicated that different,

inbred rat strains revealed marked variations in their biochemical responses when exposed to an identical cold environment (4 days at 4°C). The data for serum DBH activity in the control and cold-exposed animals are summarized in Table 9.3. Two strains reveal a significant increase in serum DBH activity, one strain shows no effect, and three strains have decreased enzyme activity during cold exposure. As sympathetic activation in response to cold exposure is well documented, and because rat serum DBH activity does not correlate with sympathetic function (Reid & Kopin, 1974, 1975), these results are representative of dissimilar biochemical changes accompanying successful organismic responses to an identical environment.

Breeding studies were conducted using a strain (LEW) with increased and another (WF) with decreased serum DBH activity in response to cold exposure to investigate potential determinants of the response. Initial results obtained in the F1 generation and summarized in Table 9.4 are consistent with X-linked dominant inheritance for increased serum DBH activity during cold exposure. Assuming that the LEW X gene (X_L) is dominant for increasing serum DBH activity, the data show nearly complete concordance (the homozygous WF female offspring just fail to reach significance, although the change is in the predicted direction). Current studies are being directed at evaluating potential environmental influences (reciprocal cross of WF sires with LEW dams), and at segregating F2 offspring (backcross analysis). We anticipate that the mechanism underlying these findings is

Table 9.3

THE EFFECT OF ENVIRONMENTAL COLD
STRESS ON SERUM DBH ACTIVITY IN SIX
INBRED RAT STRAINS

	Serum DBH activity	
Strain	Control	Cold stress
ACI/f Mai	11.57 ± 0.84	10.81 ± 0.97
LEW/f Mai	10.26 ± 0.45	12.43 ± 0.45[a]
WF/f Mai	7.35 ± 0.30	5.52 ± 0.44[a]
F344/f Mai	9.72 ± 0.20	7.53 ± 0.21[a]
BN/f Mai	10.50 ± 0.52	12.73 ± 0.33[a]
BUF/f Mai	12.31 ± 0.44	9.00 ± 0.32[a]

Note: Male rats of each strain were housed 5 per cage in a 4°C (cold stress) or a 20°C (Control) environment for 4 consecutive days. The values shown represent the mean enzyme activity, in units per ml, ±SEM, where units of activity are defined as nanomols of product formed per h incubation at 37°C.

[a] Indicates a significant change ($p < 0.05$) in serum DBH between cold stressed and control rats within a strain.

Table 9.4

ANALYSIS OF SERUM DBH RESPONSE TO COLD
STRESS AS AN X-LINKED DOMINANT TRAIT

F_1 parents Sire × dam	F_1 sex	X_L	Predicted	Observed
LEW × LEW	Male	Present	Increase	+17%
LEW × LEW	Female	Present	Increase	+19%
WF × WF	Male	Absent	Decrease	−21%
WF × WF	Female	Absent	Decrease	−11%
LEW × WF	Male	Absent	Decrease	−16%
LEW × WF	Female	Present	Increase	+30%
WF × LEW	Male	Present	Increase	Test Case

Note: Parentage, sex of F_1 offspring, presence of LEW derived X-chromosome (X_L), predicted and observed serum DBH response to cold exposure are compared. The values for observed serum DBH response are expressed as the percentage of change from control.

related to differences in the metabolism of serum enzyme effected by cold exposure; this working hypothesis predicts that the X_L gene dictates decreased serum DBH degradation.

Comments about Genetically Determined Diversity for Stimulus-induced Changes in Catecholamine-containing Systems

The examples previously discussed can be viewed as representative of the diversity of genetically determined response in catecholamine-containing systems. That the genetic control of basal function may be independent from the genetic control of induced-response function is of obvious importance in this respect. Evidence obtained in our laboratory indicates a separate control, with basal DBH activity determined by an autosomal gene (as observed in mice and humans, see Ciaranello *et al.*, 1974, Weinshilboum *et al.*, 1975), and alterations of serum DBH activity in response to stimuli mediated by an X-linked gene or genes. Whether these initial observations are applicable to other catecholamine-containing systems in rats, and whether independent genetic factors control basal and dynamic function in other species, is open to future experimentation.

Irrespective of any relationship to basal metabolism, genetically-determined response diversity is manifested in at least two ways. First, an observed response in different strains of the same species can be mediated through various mechanisms. Thus, the increased PNMT activity of CBA/J mice is dependent upon glucocorticoids, whereas the similar biochemical change in C57BL/Ka subjects required ACTH for expression. Therefore, we might anticipate that most of the regulatory mechanisms present in catecholamine-containing cells are governed by comparable inherited factors. Second, the qualitative nature of the induced biochemical change does not necessarily bear a distinctive relationship to successful adaptation. Thus, the X_L chromosome appears to determine whether serum DBH activity increases or decreases in response to cold stress; as either change accompanies successful adaptation (defining adaptation as the ability to survive), neither can be viewed as selectively advantageous. In a general sense, then, consideration of genetic diversity from either of these two perspectives reveals that inherited factors define necessary conditions for inducing change in catecholamine-containing systems, and specify the nature of that change. However, neither the conditions for, nor the nature of the change can be viewed as predictive of successful adaptation to the stimulus.

CONCLUDING COMMENTS

A consideration of the data bearing upon genetic factors influencing metabolism in catecholamine-containing systems leads to the following conclusions.

1. Basal levels of catecholamine synthesizing and degrading enzymes are determined by inheritance.
2. Genetic factors govern the mechanisms that induce metabolic change in catecholamine-containing cells, as well as specifying the qualitative nature of such change. More specifically, inheritance defines the necessary conditions for effecting metabolic change in response to an imposed challenge.
3. Neither basal nor induced metabolic parameters in catecholamine-containing systems appear to predict an organism's ability to respond successfully to an imposed challenge.

These conclusions form the basis of the conceptual framework outlined in the introduction of this chapter. One observation deriving from these conclusions is that it is improbable, if not impossible, to predict the metabolic response to a common stimulus in a genetically heterogeneous population. Although we have shown that it is an equally important consideration for a given species between strains, this observation is most obvious for a population composed of different species. For example, effects on catecholamine-containing systems that accompany social isolation in mice (Garattini, Giacolone, & Valzelli, 1969) are quite different from those in rats (Stolk, Conner, & Barchas, 1974). Therefore, hypothetical constructs for the behavioral significance of isolation-induced changes in catecholamine metabolism outlined for mice (Welch, 1967) do not apply for rats, and may not be relevant for other species.

In essence, the major implication of the conceptual framework developed in this chapter is that stereotyped biochemical changes need not accompany integrated behavioral responses either between different mammalian species, or between strains within the same species. It is clear, for instance, that initial hypotheses relating catecholamine metabolism to the affective disorders (Schildkraut & Kety, 1967) are unable to incorporate more recent biochemical observations made in appropriate human populations. While one explanation for such inconsistencies may lie in our inability to accurately assess synaptic metabolic events, the discordant data are no less valid than the results supporting the original hypothesis. Indeed, the biogenic amine models of affective illness have served well in structuring experimentation that now calls for modification of the theoretical model. We believe that a conceptual framework incorporating genetically determined diversity in the processes regulating catecholamine metabolism is important to further investigation of the biochemical basis of the affective disorders. By recognizing inherited diversity in adaptive biologic mechanisms, this framework can accommodate the variety of amine metabolic changes observed in human (or animal) experiments. Additionally, the concept of genetically determined variability in the biochemical accompaniments of affective illness appears to be consistent with "threshold models" of genetic liability to manifesting affective illness (Gershon, Baron, & Leckman, 1975). This framework, while adding complexities from an experimental viewpoint, suggests that future research emphasize longitudinal studies in individual subjects or in relatively genetically homogeneous populations of animals.

REFERENCES

Ciaranello, R. D. & Axelrod, J. Genetically controlled alterations in the rate of degradation of phenylethanolamine N-methyltransferase. *Journal of Biological Chemistry*, 1973, 248, 5616–5623.
Ciaranello, R. D., Barchas, R., Kessler, S., & Barchas, J. D. Catecholamines: Strain differences in biosynthetic enzyme activity in mice. *Life Sciences (I)*, 1972, 11, 565–572. (a)
Ciaranello, R. D., Dornbusch, J. N., & Barchas, J. D. Regulation of adrenal phenylethanolamine N-methyltransferase activity in three inbred mouse strains. *Molecular Pharmacology* 1972, 8, 511–520. (b)
Ciaranello, R. D., Dornbusch, J. N., & Barchas, J. D. Rapid increase of phenylethanolamine N-methyltransferase by environmental stress in an inbred mouse strain. *Science (Washington)*, 1972, 175, 789–790. (c)
Ciaranello, R. D., Lupsky, A., & Axelrod, J. Association between fighting behavior and catecholamine biosynthetic enzyme activity in two inbred mouse sublines. *Proceedings of the National Academy of Science USA*, 1974, 71, 3006–3008.
Ciaranello, R. D., Hoffman, H. J., Shire, J. G. M., & Axelrod, J. Genetic regulation of the

catecholamine biosynthetic enzymes. *Journal of Biological Chemistry*, 1974, 249, 4528–4536.

Eleftheriou, B. E. A gene influencing hypothalamic norepinephrine levels in mice. *Brain Research*, 1974, 70, 538–540.

Garattini, S., Giacolone, E., & Valzelli, L. Biochemical changes during isolation-induced aggressiveness in mice. In S. Garattini & E. B. Sigg (Eds.), *Aggressive Behavior*. Amsterdam: Exerpta Medica, 1969.

Gershon, E. S., Baron, M., & Leckman, J. F. Genetic models of the transmission of affective disorders. *Journal of Psychiatric Research*, 1975, 12, 301–317.

Gewirtz, G. P., & Kopin, I. J. Release of dopamine-β-hydroxylase with norepinephirne during cat splenic nerve stimulation. *Nature (London)*, 1970, 227, 406–407.

Horowitz, D., Alexander, D. W., Lovenberg, W., & Keiser, H. R. Human serum dopamine-β-hydroxylase: Relationship to hypertension and sympathetic activity. *Circulation Research*, 1973, 32, 594–599.

Hunt, D. M., & Johnson, D. R. An inherited deficiency in noradrenaline biosynthesis in the brindled mouse. *Journal of Neurochemistry*, 1972, 19, 2811–2819.

Kessler, S., Ciaranello, R. D., Shire, J. G. M., & Barchas, J. D. Genetic variation in activity of enzymes involved in synthesis of catecholamines. *Proceedings of the National Academy of Science, USA*, 1972, 69, 2448–2450.

Kety, S. S. Biochemical theories of schizophrenia. *Science (Washington)*, 1959, 129, 1528–1532.

Kopin, I. J., Kaufman, S., Viveros, H., Jacobowitz, D., Lake, C. R., Ziegler, M. G., Lovenberg, W., & Goodwin, R. K. Dopamine-β-hydroxylase; basic and clinical studies. *Annals of Internal Medicine*, 1976, 85, 211–223.

Lamprecht, F., Eichelman, B. S., Williams, R. B., Wooten, G. F., & Kopin, I. J. Serum dopamine-β-hydroxylase (DβH) activity and blood pressure response of rat strains to shock-induced fighting. *Psychosomatic Medicine*, 1974, 36, 298–303.

Leonhard, K., Korff, I., & Schulz, H. Die temperamente in den familien der monopolaren und bipolaren phasischen psychosen. *Psychiatrie Neurologie*, 1962, 143, 415.

Lovenberg, W., Yamabe, H., DeJong, W., & Hansen, C. T. Genetic variation of catecholamine biosynthetic enzyme activities in various strains of rats including spontaneously hypertensive rats. *Life Sciences*, 1973, 13, 104–106.

Miller, F. P., Cox, R. H., Jr., & Maickel, R. P. Intrastrain differences in serotonin and norepinephrine in discrete areas of rat brain. *Science (Washington)*, 1968, 162, 463–464.

Mueller, R. A., Thoenen, H., & Axelrod, J. Increase in tyrosine hydroxylase activity after reserpine administration. *Journal of Pharmacology and Experimental Therapeutics*, 1969, 169, 74–79.

Nagatsu, T., Kato, T., Numata, Y., Ikuta, K., Umezawa, H., Matsuzaki, M., & Takeuchi, T. Serum Dopamine-β-hydroxylase activity in developing hypertensive rats. 1974, *Nature (London)* 251, 630–631.

Nagatsu, T., Ikuta, K., Numata, Y., Kato, T., Sano, M., Nagatsu, I., Umezawa, H., Matsuzaki, M., & Takeuchi, T. Vascular and brain dopamine-β-hydroxylase activity in young spontaneously hypertensive rats. *Science (Washington)*, 1976, 191, 290–291.

Nies, A., Robinson, D. S., Lamborn, K. R., & Lampert, R. P. Genetic control of platelet and plasma monoamine oxidase activity. *Archives of General Psychiatry*, 1973, 28, 834–838.

Orenberg, E. K., Renson, J., Elliot, G. R., Barchas, J. D., & Kessler, S. Genetic determination of aggressive behavior and brain cyclic AMP. *Psychopharmacology Communications*, 1975, 1, 99–108.

Page, J. G., Kessler, R. M., & Vessell, E. S. Strain differences in uptake, pool size, and turnover rate of norepinephrine in hearts of mice. *Biochemical Pharmacology*, 1970, 19, 1381–1386.

Ray, O. S. & Barrett, R. J. Behavioral pharmacological and biochemical analysis of genetic differences in rats. *Behavioral Biology*, 1975, 15, 391–417.

Reid, J. L. & Kopin, I. J. Significance of plasma dopamine-β-hydroxylase as an index of sympathetic neuronal function. *Proceedings of the National Academy of Sciences, U.S.A.* 1974, *71*, 4392–4394.

Reid, J. L. & Kopin, I. J. The effects of ganglionic blockade, reserpine and vinblastin on plasma catecholamines and dopamine-β-hydroxylase in the rat. *Journal of Pharmacology and Experimental Therapeutics*, 1975, *193*, 748–756.

Ross, S. B., Wetterberger, L., & Myrhed, M. Genetic control of plasma dopamine-β-hydroxylase. *Life Sciences*, 1973, *12*, 529–532.

Saavedra, J. M., Grobecker, H., & Axelrod, J. Adrenaline-forming enzyme in brainstem, elevation in genetic and experimental hypertension. *Science (Washington)*, 1976, *191*, 483–484.

Schanberg, S. M., Stone, R. A., Kirshner, N., Gunnels, J. C., & Robinson, R. R. Plasma dopamine-β-hydroxylase a possible aid in the study and evaluation of hypertension. *Science (Washington)*, 1974, *183*, 523–525.

Schildkraut, J. J. & Kety, S. S. Biogenic amines and emotion. *Science (Washington)*, 1967, *156*, 21–30.

Segal, D. S., Kuczenski, R. T., & Mandell, A. J. Strain differences in behavior and brain tyrosine hydroxylase activity. *Behavioral Biology*, 1972, *7*, 75–81.

Skolnick, P. & Daly, J. W. Norepinephrine-sensitive adenylate cyclases in rat brain: Relation to behavior and tyrosine hydroxylase. *Science (Washington)*, 1974, *184*, 175–177.

Spector, S., Gordon, R., Sjoerdsma, A., & Udenfriend, S. End-product inhibition of tyrosine hydroxylase as a possible mechanism for regulation or norepinephrine synthesis. *Molecular Pharmacology*, 1967, *3*, 549–555.

Stolk, J. M., Conner, R. L., & Barchas, J. D. Social environment and brain biogenic amine metabolism in rats. *Journal of Comparative and Physiological Psychology*, 1974, *87*, 203–207.

Thoenen, H., Kettler, R., Burkard, W., & Saner, A. Neurally initiated control of enzymes involved in the synthesis of norepinephrine; are they regulated as an operational unit? *Naunyn-Schmiedebergs Archives of Pharmacology*, 1971, *270*, 146–160.

Thoenen, H., Mueller, R. A., & Axelrod, J. Neuronally dependent induction of phenylethanolamine N-methyltransferase by 6-hydroxydopamine. *Biochemical Pharmacology*, 1970, *19*, 669–673.

Weinshilboum, R. & Axelrod, J. Reduced plasma dopamine-β-hydroxylase in familial dysautonomia. *New England Journal of Medicine*, 1971, *285*, 938–942.

Weinshilboum, R. M. & Axelrod, J. Serum dopamine-β-hydroxylase. *Circulation Research*, 1971, *28*, 307–315.

Weinshilboum, R. M., Thoa, N. B., Johnson, G., Kopin, I. J., & Axelrod, J. Proportional release of norepinephrine and dopamine-β-hydroxylase from sympathetic nerves. *Science (Washington)*, 1971, *174*, 1349–1351.

Weinshilboum, R. M., Raymond, F. A., Elveback, L. R., & Weidman, W. H. Serum dopamine-β-hydroxylase activity: Sibling–sibling correlation. *Science*, 1973, *181*, 943–945.

Weinshilboum, R. M., Raymond, F. A., Elveback, L. R., & Weidman, W. H. Correlation of erythrocyte catechol-O-methyl-transferase activity between siblings. *Nature (London)*, 1974, *252*, 490–491.

Weinshilboum, R. M., Schrott, H. G., Raymond, F. R., Weidman, W. H., & Elveback, L. R. Inheritance of very low serum dopamine-β-hydroxylase activity. *American Journal of Human Genetics*, 1975, *27*, 573–585.

Welch, B. L. Discussion of the paper "Aggression, defense, and neurohumors" by A. B. Rothballer. In C. D. Clemente & D. B. Lindsley (Eds.), *Aggression and defense: Neural mechanisms and social patterns (brain function Vol. 5)*. Los Angeles: Univ. of California Press, 1967.

Wetterberg, L., Gustavson, K.-H., Backstrom, M., Ross, S. B., & Froden, O. Low dopamine-β-hydroxylase activity in Down's syndrome. *Clinical Genetics*, 1972, *3*, 152–153.

Wooten, G. F., Eldridge, R., Axelrod, J., & Stern, R. S. Elevated plasma dopamine-β-hydroxylase activity in autosomal dominant torsion dystonia. *New England Journal of Medicine*, 1973, 288, 284–287.

Wooten, G., Hanson, T., & Lamprecht, F. Elevated serum dopamine-β-hydroxylase activity in rats with inherited diabetes insipidus. *Journal of Neural Transmission*, 1975, 36, 107–112.

Wurtman, R. J. & Axelrod, J. Control of enzymatic synthesis of adrenaline in the adrenal medulla by adrenal cortical steroids. *Journal of Biological Chemistry*, 1966, 241, 2301–2305.

CHAPTER 10

Neurophysiological Reactivity, Stimulus Intensity Modulation and the Depressive Disorders

Monte S. Buchsbaum

INTRODUCTION

Environmental stress figures importantly in many theoretical models of biologic psychiatry as the most convenient explanation for the weak nature of the role of heritability in producing psychiatric illness. Although the contribution of genetic factors to the development of affective illness and schizophrenia is well established, the relatively low concordance rates in twin studies and the irregular patterns of appearance of symptomatic individuals in families are troublesome. Under the general heading of diathesis-stress, Rosenthal (1970) reviews a number of such models of interaction between a vulnerable central nervous system (CNS) and the environment. Underlying these models is the assumption that the vulnerable person might not decompensate if he did not encounter the stressful stimuli, but breaks down because the stimuli exceed some tolerable limit.

How do we know if a given environmental stimulus is stressful? Psychiatrists have traditionally concentrated on the meaning of the stimulus to the subject. Any stimulus can be anxiety provoking, arousing and/or evocative

221

The Psychobiology of the Depressive Disorders:
Implications for the Effects of Stress

ISBN 0-12-211650-X

of a stress response (e.g., the sound of footsteps behind you in a dark alley)—depending upon the setting and significance.

Physical parameters of the stimulus alone are insufficient to specify the possible response. A strong somatosensory stimulus may be less stressful than a weak one—in the case of a lover's bite and a drop of water in an oriental torture. Additionally, sensory stimulation can have stress effects relatively independent of its meaning; chronic pain, aircraft-noise exposure, and absence of windows are all examples. Such kinds of sensory stress, although typically used in animal experiments (e.g., chronic electric shock, noise, low temperature, crowding) where meaning is more difficult to assess, also are common, human, environmental stress components.

Either too much or too little sensory stimulation can be stressful. Too little sensory input appears to lead to permanent functional damage to the developing organism. Psychiatric reactions in adults including hallucinations, anxiety, change in body image, etc., have been reported with both sensory deprivation (see review by Zubek, 1973) and sensory overload (Gottschalk, Haer, & Bates, 1972; Ludwig, 1972). Continuous sensory stimulation at some optimal level seems necessary to maintain intellectual functioning and the feeling of psychological well-being (see Zuckerman, 1974). The optimum level may be sought by two means: (*a*) by approaching or avoiding environmental stimuli or (*b*) by modulating sensory input within the CNS by means of inhibitory or excitatory mechanisms. Defects in such central control mechanisms could reduce the flexibility of the organism in meeting sensory challenges and lead to, or exacerbate, the major behavioral disorders (see Lipowski, 1975; Ludwig, 1975; Ludwig & Stark, 1973; Miller, 1960).

This chapter reviews responses to sensory stimulation in relation to affective disorders. Could defects in sensory input homeostasis be a diathesis in affective illness? Might sensory input levels of everyday life be sensory deprivation to a manic patient or sensory overload for a schizophrenic patient? The powerful situational and affective conditions that give special personal significance to sensory stimuli are difficult to capture in a neurophysiological laboratory, so we have focused on the sensory aspects of stimulation. Similarly, as the conventional animal neurophysiologic or neuroanatomic techniques are inapplicable in man, we have used scalp-recorded, cortical, average evoked potential (EP) techniques to study responses to simple auditory, visual, and somatosensory stimuli in searching for abnormalities in inhibition, modulation, or the altering of incoming sensory signals.

The reader should be warned that this is, and for two reasons must be, a very speculative article. First, the wealth of sensory, perceptual, and attentional studies that exists for the schizophrenias simply does not exist for affective illness. Perhaps because of the colorful and dramatic symptoms of young schizophrenics or because of their higher prevalence rate, researchers have flocked to their sides with a tremendous repertoire of fascinating sensory tasks. Sad, middle-aged patients have tended to be ignored, or worse yet (for the present reviewer's purpose), lumped with three obsessives, four alcoholics, and an airplane hijacker into an "other patient" group. Second, where depressives are identified, psychotic–neurotic, agitated–retarded or other dichotomies are often used, rather than the unipolar–bipolar distinction so much in favor in biologic and genetic studies. Sensory and perceptual studies in affective illness may well reveal as many findings as have been reported in schizophrenia research and may greatly aid in the understanding of gene–environment interaction that is so badly needed.

SENSORY OVERLOAD, SENSORY DEPRIVATION AND PSYCHIATRIC ILLNESS

Environmental stress as a factor in mental illness has nearly universally been postulated, but is extremely illusive experimentally. Therefore, the report of vivid and cohesive visual hallucinations, delusions, and other perceptual changes in normal subjects undergoing sensory deprivation at McGill University (Bexton, Heron, & Scott, 1954) excited psychiatrists and stimulated both theories and experimental approaches to the major psychoses. Because of the appearance of hallucinations and perceptual changes, most of the early efforts centered on schizophrenia. Calling attention to the bizarre experiences of long-haul night truckers, antarctic explorers, and military sentinels, sensory deprivation was proposed as a model psychosis (e.g., Brawley & Pos, 1967; Rosenzweig, 1959). Strangely, in clinical trials, sensory deprivation was found not to exacerbate schizophrenia (e.g., Cleveland, Reitman & Bentinck, 1963) and even to cause symptomatic improvement in some studies (Gibby, Adams, & Carrera, 1960; Harris, 1959; Smith, Thakurdas, & Lawes, 1961). Suedfeld and Roy (1975) report case histories of the uncontrolled but apparently successful therapeutic application of isolation on disruptive inmates, some schizophrenic, and Suedfeld (1975) reviews the clinical relevance of reduced sensory stimulation. Sensory deficits such as prolonged deafness may also have a mitigating effect on schizoid characteristics (Cooper, Garside, & Kay, 1976). As sensory deprivation was studied intensively, it became apparent that the similarity between deprivation-induced visual phenomena and schizophrenic hallucinations was questionable. Quite apart from the issue that most schizophrenics have auditory, not visual hallucinations, the visual sensations of sensory deprivation seemed brief, impersonal, and without pathological significance (Zuckerman, 1969).

Furthermore, certain psychological features related to schizophrenia, such as personal disorganization and cognitive-intellectual impairment

(Gottschalk et al., 1972) seemed worsened by sensory overload. The impaired performance of schizophrenics produced by distracting stimuli (e.g., Buss, 1966) tended to point to inadequate, sensory filtering mechanisms in schizophrenia, not relative sensory deprivation. Furthermore, if schizophrenics were really in a state of sensory deprivation, homeostatic (Zuckerman, 1969) or sensoristatic theories (Schultz, 1965) suggest that they would go out and seek exciting sensory and social stimulation. Not only is this quite inconsistent with clinical observations, but on psychological tests, schizophrenics score low on stimulus-seeking behavior (e.g., Sidle, Acker, & McReynolds, 1963). McReynolds (1960) conceptualizes schizophrenia as resulting from an overload of unassimilated percepts, not a shortage of stimulation.

Homeostatic theories of sensory input might well implicate relative sensory deprivation in the etiology of bipolar affective disorder rather than schizophrenia. Could the active, thrill-seeking, expansive behavior of the manic patient be an adaptation to a relative sensory deprivation in everyday life? Are bipolar patients individuals with particularly high optimal levels of stimulation? Some evidence among normal subjects links affective state and sensory deprivation. Among normal individuals, high scorers on Zuckerman's Sensation Seeking Scale have high MMPI hypomania scores (Zuckerman, 1974). Myers (1969) concluded that quitters from isolation experiments tended to score higher on MMPI psychopathic deviate and hypomania scales. Zuckerman, Persky, Miller, and Levine (1970) found increases in feelings of depression on the multiple adjective checklist in normal volunteers exposed to sensory deprivation, but not in volunteers exposed to social isolation with sensory stimulation.

SENSORY DIFFERENCES IN AFFECTIVE DISORDERS

If the patient with bipolar affective disorder has a higher than usual optimal level of stimulation, we might speculate that measurement of sensory response at a neurophysiological level would tend to indicate increased reactivity and diminished filtering of incoming sensory stimulation. This could appear especially at higher intensities or for repetitious stimuli, situations where the CNS of individuals with lower optimal levels of sensory input might already be operating inhibitory mechanisms to prevent sensory overload. Changes in the optimal level of stimulation might precede switches into mania or depression, with a cycle of inhibitory release accompanied by sensory overload and subsequent overinhibition causing a slow unstable oscillation in behavior and neurochemistry. A suggestion of such cyclic triggering of manic episodes was observed in a patient who had unusually regular and rapid switches from mania to depression and was studied for 113 consecutive days. Sensory, evoked potential amplitude and amplitude–intensity slope decreased about 8–10 days before a switch from mania to depression (Buchsbaum, Post, & Bunney, 1977). Unipolar depressed patients might show chronic operation of inhibitory systems and thus reduced sensory reactivity accompanied by sensory deprivation and chronic depression.

Although it would be attractive to approach these speculations with direct neurophysiological studies of the sensory system, conventional neurophysiological approaches of single unit studies or an anatomical degeneration are clearly inapplicable. Scalp recorded evoked potentials (EPs), while lacking in some specificity, are entirely noninvasive, and furnish a measure of the specific CNS response at a particular cortical area.[1]

Evoked Potential Amplitude in Affective Disorders

Though there is general agreement that schizophrenic patients tend to have smaller amplitude EPs than normal subjects (see review by Buchsbaum, 1977), there are fewer studies available on patients with affective disorders. Problems of the remitting, or cyclic, nature of the disorder and variations in diagnostic categories from center to center over the last 10 years make the published findings especially difficult to review. Nevertheless, unlike the small EPs seen in schizophrenics, affective disorder patients appear to have EPs as big or bigger than those of normal subjects.

It is in the visual system that the most data are available. Larger amplitude visual EPs of N70 (III) and N140 (V) in endogenous depressed patients in comparison to age-matched normal subjects were reported by Vasconetto, Floris, and Morocutti (1971). Larger amplitudes (P100–N140) in bipolar patients than controls were found by Buchsbaum, Landau, Murphy, and Goodwin (1973). A small group of "manic-depressive" patients, thus probably bipolar, had larger amplitudes (N70 [OIII]) than schizophrenics or normal subjects but the manic-depressive–normal comparison was not significant (Speck, Dim, & Mercer, 1966).

Larger somatosensory EPs (Peaks 1–4) were found initially in psychotic depressions by Shagass and Schwartz (1963) and confirmed in some, but not all, subsequent studies (Shagass & Schwartz, 1966) in which subjects were matched for age and sex. Larger auditory EPs (N100–P200 [N1–P2]) were reported by Satterfield (1972), especially for long interstimulus intervals.

---

[1] For the purpose of uniformity in dealing with various EP studies individual components will be identified in the review that follows as Positive (P) or Negative (N) and their approximate latency from stimulus onset in milliseconds (e.g. N 140 is a negative component at 140 msec); the author's original peak nomenclature is usually given in following parentheses.

However, Levit, Sutton, and Zubin (1973) found auditory and visual EPs smaller in depressed subjects than normal subjects (N105–N125 [N1] to P320–P340 [P3]). Small and Small (1971) also report smaller contingent negative variation in manic patients in a flash–click reaction-time paradigm. Shagass and Schwartz (1965) stress the importance of age and sex in explaining variability in EP findings. They note age and sex interacting with EP amplitude and such personality variables as extraversion. These interactions are potentially important to studies of mania and depression. Perris (1974) notes an interhemispheric difference in psychotic depression with an EP diminution over the left hemisphere, suggesting that laterality and the verbal or nonverbal nature of a stimulus-related task may be important.

Stimulus Intensity and Evoked Potential Response in Depression

Under the speculative scheme discussed in the introductory section, intense stimuli may be stressful to the sensorially overloaded CNS and invoke inhibitory processes—or may be accepted by, and then activate the sensorially deprived CNS. Early results in the visual (Shagass, Schwartz, & Krishnamoorti, 1965) and somatosensory system (Shagass & Schwartz, 1963) suggested that depressed patients might show steeper EP amplitude-intensity slopes than controls, although depressed subjects alone were apparently not directly compared with control subjects. Depue and Fowles (1976) stress the importance of stimulus intensity in the psychophysiological response of patients.

Unusual EP amplitude–intensity relationships are not restricted to patients; normal volunteers show striking differences in their EP responses at high stimulus intensities—with certain individuals showing marked drops as the stimulus intensity increases. The slope of the EP amplitude–intensity function has been shown to be a relatively stable individual trait in normal subjects (Shagass & Schwartz, 1963; Buchsbaum & Pfefferbaum, 1971; Soskis & Shagass, 1974; Stark & Norton, 1974) as well as in patients with affective illness (Buchsbaum, Goodwin, Murphy, & Borge, 1971; von Knorring, 1974). Amplitude–intensity functions are partially set genetically, as suggested by twin studies (Buchsbaum, 1974) and family studies in normal and affective disorder pedigrees (Gershon & Buchsbaum, 1977). We have labeled people whose EP amplitudes decrease with increasing intensity "reducers," whereas those whose amplitudes increase with increasing intensity are termed "augmenters"—terms borrowed from Petrie (1967). The general concept underlying augmenting–reducing or stimulus intensity control is that individuals may be categorized according to whether they are augmenters or reducers. The empirical support for this concept comes both from EP studies and studies using Petrie's psychophysical procedure (see

Petrie, 1974). Despite methodological difficulties with both techniques, scores on the two procedures are correlated (see Schooler, Buchsbaum, & Carpenter, 1976). Buchsbaum and Silverman (1968) hypothesized that reducers might be hypersensitive to low intensity stimuli and require compensatory inhibitory mechanisms to protect them from sensory inundation at high levels. In support of this concept, EP reducers were found to have lower visual thresholds than EP augmenters (Silverman *et al.*, 1969) and larger EP amplitudes at low light levels (Buchsbaum & Pfefferbaum, 1971). The compensatory, protective aspects of reduction were illustrated in experiments that indicated that reducers were tolerant to pain and noise and showed that reduction increased in sensory overload conditions (Buchsbaum, 1976).

Individual differences in augmenting or reducing may reflect differences in the individuals' optimal level of sensory input. At the low end of the stimulus intensity scale, reducers might be expected to tolerate sensory deprivation better than augmenters because of their relative sensitivity to low levels of stimulation. This hypothesis is only weakly supported by Peters, Benjamin, Helvey, and Albright (1963) and Zubeck (1963), who found that pain-tolerant subjects (and therefore possibly reducers) endured reduced sensory input conditions longer. However, augmenting–reducing was not measured directly in these studies.

At the high end of the stimulus intensity scale, augmenters might be expected to seek stimulation to maintain their arousal level. Human, visual-EP augmenters were found to score high on the Sensation Seeking Scale (Zuckerman, Murtaugh, & Siegel, 1974), and "augmenting" cats (Hall, Rappaport, Hopkins, Griffin, & Silverman, 1970) were reported to have had more exploratory behaviors. Zuckerman *et al.* (1974) postulate that individuals differ "as to the level of reticulo-cortical (excitatory) activation which will trigger the cortico-fugal (inhibitory) feedback necessary to dampen and control further reticular arousal." Reducers, they postulate, possess a "low threshold for the initiation of cortico-fugal inhibitory processes" whereas augmenters "possess a neural set point which permits them to accept and process higher levels of stimulation before their cortico-reticular inhibitory threshold is reached."

We have investigated both visual and somatosensory EP amplitude–intensity slopes in a series of patients from the research wards of the National Institute of Mental Health at the Clinical Center in Bethesda, Maryland. Patients have been tested after withdrawal of psychoactive medication for at least 10 days. In an initial study (Buchsbaum *et al.*, 1971) bipolar patients (N = 55) were found to show larger amplitude increases in visual EPs with stimulus intensity than unipolar patients (N = 18) or matched normal controls (N = 20). Four intensities of light flashes from a Grass photostimulator were used and stimuli presented to the subject with closed eyes. Amplitude was measured from P100 to N140. Landau,

Buchsbaum, Carpenter, Strauss, and Sacks (1975) noted that 19 acute schizophrenics showed almost no increase in EP amplitude with increasing stimulus intensity as compared to 19 age- and sex-matched bipolar patients drawn from the previous study. In a replication series of 63 patients (Buchsbaum, Landau, Murphy and Goodwin, 1973), male and female bipolar patients had relatively greater rates of increase in amplitude with increasing stimulus intensity. Male, but not female, unipolar patients demonstrated a decrease in amplitude at high stimulus intensity.

Bipolar–unipolar differences were maintained even when patient groups were approximately matched for depression. In this study, visual stimuli were 500-msec pulses, presented with computer-controlled fluorescent tubes that were mounted behind a translucent screen and viewed by subjects with open eyes. The finding of the same result in both patient series mitigates against some artifact of eyelid thickness or eye movements explaining the effect. Experimental studies of the effect of pupillary diameter on EPs also tend to rule this out as an artifact (see Soskis & Shagass, 1974); this and other technical problems are discussed elsewhere (Buchsbaum, 1976; Buchsbaum, 1978).

Recently, using a new group of 26 bipolar patients and 49 age- and sex-matched normal controls and the same visual stimuli, we again confirmed bipolar–normal differences for the P100 component. Borge (1973) has also reported psychotic depressed patients to be visual EP augmenters. The report of Bruder, Sutton, Babkoff, Gurland, Yozawitz, and Fleiss (1976) that manic-depressive patients have lower sensitivity for detecting an auditory signal is consistent with our association of EP augmenting with poor auditory sensitivity (Silverman, Buchsbaum, & Henkin, 1969).

Somatosensory Evoked Potentials, Stimulus Intensity and Pain Response

As differences between bipolar and normal patient groups were largest at the highest stimulus intensities, we next examined EPs in relation to somatosensory stimuli, where stimulus intensity can be increased to high levels more easily than with visual stimuli. Electrical stimuli are also advantageous because no peripheral adjustment exists for the somatosensory system (such as the pupil or stapedius muscle in the visual or auditory system). Furthermore, the central modulation of pain stimuli in both the spinal cord and cerebral cortex is supported with neuroanatomic evidence (see Albe-Fessard & Fessard, 1975) and theoretical models (see Melzack and Wall, 1965). Because electrical stimuli can be delivered with great precision, good stimulus control, and can range from threshold to painful, critical tests of stress response, sensory overload, and pain tolerance and their relationship to EPs can be made.

Evoked potentials to electric shocks have been used in a number of psychophysical studies of pain (e.g., Moldofsky & England, 1975; Satran & Goldstein, 1973) and amplitude–intensity relationships have been related to pain response (Mushin & Levy, 1974).

We have previously reported that individuals who appear relatively pain tolerant (on the basis of signal detection analysis of their subjective pain ratings) show somatosensory AERs that increase in amplitude less rapidly with increasing stimulus intensity than those of relatively pain-intolerant subjects (Buchsbaum, 1975). Very similar visual EP results have also been reported (von Knorring, Espvall, & Perris, 1974; von Knorring, 1974) in a mixed group of patients with depressive illness. Audioanalgesia in normal subjects was also associated with a reduction in the amplitude–intensity slope for the EP (Lavine, Buchsbaum, & Poncy, 1976). All of these studies showed the reduced slope effect either for the P100 component or in the visual EPs for the largest component in the first 150 msec (probably P100–N140). Physostigmine, which causes analgesia in man, also diminished P100 (Sitaram, Buchsbaum, & Gillin, 1977). The P200 component tended to show habituation and order effects—suggesting the possibility of separating analgesia effects from effects due to fatigue or inattention.

Pain tolerance for heat (Hall & Stride, 1954; Hemphill, Hall, & Crookes, 1952), electric shock (von Knorring & Espvall, 1974) or pressure (Merskey, 1965) appears to be elevated in depressed patients. High intra-individual reliabilities (e.g., von Knorring and Espvall, 1974) and suitability for EP recordings led us to utilize electrical stimuli for studies comparing bipolar and unipolar patients and relating EPs to signal-detection pain procedures.

Brief electrical shocks, ranging from barely noticeable to painful were presented to the dorsum of the left forearm. Patients and age- and sex-matched normal subjects received a pain-rating psychophysical task (following a signal-detection paradigm) and an EP procedure in which shocks of four intensities were administered in a random order in a manner similar to our visual EP procedure. Both rating and EP procedures are described elsewhere (Lavine, Buchsbaum, & Poncy, 1976). Initially, all EPs have been measured using the same area integration techniques (see Lavine *et al.*, 1976) to allow comparability of the results.

In an initial study (Buchsbaum, Muscettola, & Goodwin, in preparation) 8 bipolar and 4 unipolar patients and 10 age- and sex-matched normal controls had visual and somatosensory EPs, and did a pain-rating procedure. During this session and during a comparison session of quiet relaxation, urinary 3-methoxy-4-hydroxy-phenyglycol (MHPG) excretion was measured. Visual and somatosensory EPs were recorded and analyzed as described elsewhere (Lavine *et al.*, 1976). In this study (despite the small numbers of patients) bipolar, unipolar, and normal EPs were significantly different, with bipolars showing marked amplitude increases—especially at the highest stimulus intensity. (This was confirmed by two-way analysis of variance (ANOVA) with quadratic trend intensity-by-group effects.) This augmenting effect was seen and statistically confirmed for somatosensory stimuli in a lateral somatosensory area lead (C4) and for visual stimuli over the occipital area (Oz).

The bipolar patients also had significantly higher pain criteria for the unpleasant–painful choice than unipolar or normal subjects. The normal groups as a whole showed increases in MHPG during the electric shock session (7 out of 10 subjects) whereas only 2 out of 12 patients showed an increase ($p < .05$, Fisher exact). The normal group also showed a significant correlation between somatosensory EP amplitude–intensity slope (for P100) and total urinary MHPG—consistent with our conception of the augmenter as pain tolerant. This correlation did not appear in the patient group, nor was the EP effective in predicting the magnitude of the urinary MHPG rise in either group. This and other correlational differences between the normal and patient groups suggested rather different patterns in responding to stress. Were the patients, largely bipolar, accepting the so-called stress session as a relief from the relative sensory deprivation of an inpatient ward? Might pain tolerance appear in the augmenting bipolar?

A larger study (Davis, Buchsbaum and Bunney, in press) on 28 bipolar and 41 normal controls studied pain tolerance and somatosensory EPs. All patients were off psychoactive medications at the time of testing. We found depressed male bipolar patients showing higher pain criteria and lower pain sensitivity than normal subjects. Male unipolar patients showed only lower pain sensitivity than controls. These results are clearly consistent with earlier studies showing pain tolerance in depressed patients. Eight patients (two males and six females) were tested while showing manic or hypomanic symptoms. These patients showed significantly lower pain sensitivity. This finding is especially intriguing in view of the recent report of elevated, endogenously occurring morphinomimetic peptides in the cerebrospinal fluid of manic patients (Terenius, Wahlstrom, Lindstrom, & Winderlov, 1976). EP results again confirmed EP augmenting in the bipolar patients, however (Figure 10.1). This contradiction of our earlier findings in normal subjects relating pain tolerance with EP parameters suggests different regulation of pain and/or stress response in bipolar patients. Although von Knorring et al. (1974) found EP-reducer depressed patients to be pain tolerant (consistent with our findings in a normal group), they used visual, not shock, stimuli and did not analyze data from bipolar patients separately. Confinement, boredom, and social isolation might be the most salient stress in this bipolar group. Psychophysiological pain procedures, often lengthy, may be stimulating, painful or boring, depending on testing details and previous patient experience.

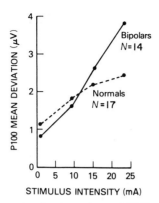

Figure 10.1 Somatosensory stimulus intensity and P100 amplitude in 14 male bipolar affective disorder patients off all medications and 17 age-matched normal male controls.

Stress of New Situations

Is coming into a computerized EEG laboratory, being wired up and exposed to a series of light flashes a stress, or is it a novel experience, relatively rich in sensory stimulation and information? A second session a week or more later would appear to be less stressful or to have less novelty. By comparing sensory EPs obtained on the first and second session in naive subjects, we can examine the effect of such novelty on affectively ill patients and normal subjects.

In an initial study of normal adult twin pairs reported elsewhere (Buchsbaum, 1974), we compared visual EPs obtained in the first and second sessions (N = 115). Visual EPs for the second session were significantly smaller both for the P100–N140 and N140–P200 components when measured peak-to-trough. However, the amplitude diminution was greater for EPs at the lowest intensity for P100–N140; N140–P200 showed equal diminution at all intensities. These effects were statistically confirmed in a two-way ANOVA with repeated measures and trend analysis (session effect, $F = 23.5$ and 49.2, for P100–N140 and N140–P200, respectively, $df = 1/114$; $p < .001$; Session × Intensity interaction, linear trend analysis, $F = 15.9$ and $.6$ for P100–N140 and N140–P200, $p < .025$ for P100–N140). Very similar amplitude–intensity effects were seen in a sample of 15 unrelated adults tested twice (Figure 10.2) using the area integration measure of P100, but were not statistically confirmed. Despite these session differences in augmenting–reducing, subjects maintained their ranking within the group; test–retest correlations on the amplitude–intensity slope measure were .63 and .69 in the twin and unrelated subject samples, respectively.

Genetic factors may have a small role in determining these session differences in EP amplitude. Differences in EP amplitude–intensity slopes be-

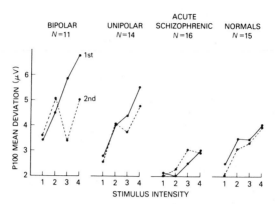

Figure 10.2 Visual EP amplitude for P100 and stimulus intensity in bipolar, unipolar, acute schizophrenic and normal individuals tested twice approximately 1–2 weeks apart. Note that bipolar patients show a large decrement in amplitude at high stimulus intensities on the second session; schizophrenics show no change, and normals show a small drop at the lowest intensity.

tween the first and second session had a product moment correlation of .42 ($p < .05$) for P100 (area measures) in male identical twins and $-.12$ in male fraternal twins. No correlations were significant in females.

A subsample of our patient population was tested on two occasions, 4–14 days apart, during their initial medication-free period. Figure 10.2 reveals that bipolar patients showed marked augmenting on their first session on P100 as compared to their second session. In comparison, age- and sex-matched normals showed a small, but not significant, change in amplitude–intensity slope. And, unlike the small, low intensity diminution seen in normals, bipolars showed a large, high intensity drop. Comparison of bipolar, unipolar, and schizophrenic patient groups in a three-way ANOVA (Group × Session × Intensity) confirmed the group differences seen in Figure 10.2 (three-way interaction, $p < .05$).

P100 appears to be relatively specific for this effect; no significant N140 effect of any kind was found and P200 showed only group differences in the mean EP amplitude (bipolars and normals with 5.0 μv and unipolars at 2.8 μv, averaging across session and intensities).

We have previously observed the high-amplitude diminution effect seen here in bipolars during audioanalgesia experiments that utilized music to affect somatosensory EPs (Lavine et al., 1976) or noxious 94-dB noise to affect visual EPs (Buchsbaum, 1976)—in both cases an effect specific to P100. We have identified this previously (Buchsbaum, 1976) as a protective inhibitory effect, evoked by unpleasant stimulation or facilitated by music. Selective attention effects on identically presented stimuli appear restricted to low, not high stimulus intensities (see Buchsbaum, 1976; Schechter & Buchsbaum, 1973) and affect N140 more than P100. Could the confinement and repetitiousness of electrophysiological recording be as noxious and stressful for bipolar patients as the punishing tone or electric shock is for normal subjects? Might the bipolar patient's overrapid adaptation to situational novelty lead to greater sensory deprivation, and ever more strenuous efforts to seek stimulation in bizarre, socially unacceptable, or destructive (e.g., painful) ways? A peculiar vulnerability to sensory deprivation and a defect in optimizing sensory input levels in the bipolar group would be consistent with these findings.

Sleep Deprivation

The effects of sleep deprivation have been interpreted both as a stress (Wilkinson, 1969) and as a modifier of optimal activation level (e.g., Taub & Berger, 1976). Viewed as a stress, sleep deprivation leads to physiological disturbance, fatigue, and poor performance. Sleep deprivation, as suggested by Post, Kotin, and Goodwin (1976), may mobilize a depressed patient in a manner similar to other nonspecific stresses (e.g., electroshock, insulin shock, and physical illness) that have been associated with a lessening of depressive symptoms. Viewed as a modifier of optimal activation, changes in sleep might modify arousal levels, moving a subject to higher or lower arousal levels. Overaroused, overactivated subjects might be pushed in this way toward more optimal levels of arousal, at least temporarily. This concept provides a framework for the observed improvement in affective disorder patients with sleep deprivation (Pflug & Tolle, 1971; Post et al., 1976). The finding that sleep deprivation decreases the threshold for photo-induced epileptic activity (e.g., Broughton, 1972) suggests that activation of certain components of the visual system could result from sleep deprivation as well. Consequently, investigation of the effect of sleep deprivation on stimulus intensity control in the visual system seemed of special interest.

In collaboration with R. Gerner and R. Post (in preparation) 22 normal volunteers and 16 affectively ill patients (11 bipolar, 5 unipolar) were studied with our visual EP augmenting–reducing procedure. Each subject was tested on the afternoon of three consecutive days—after normal sleep, after a night of sleep deprivation, and following a night of recovery sleep.

Primary affective disorder patients, especially bipolar patients, showed an increase in augmenting following sleep deprivation that was maintained following the "recovery" night. This effect of sleep deprivation was statistically confirmed in the patient group (two-way ANOVA, Intensity × Night interaction, quadratic effects $F = 4.36; df = 1/12; p < .05$). Normal subjects showed a small decrease in augmenting following sleep deprivation and a return toward normal on the recovery night (see Figure 10.3). This difference between patients and normals was confirmed in a three-way ANOVA (Night × Groups × Intensities, three-way interaction, $F = 3.58; df = 2/72;$

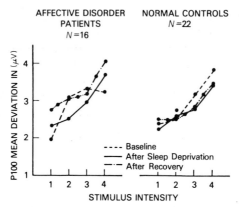

Figure 10.3   Effect of a night of sleep deprivation on visual EPs at four intensities in normal controls and patients with affective illness. Normal controls show a slight EP diminution on the day after sleep deprivation whereas affective patients show an amplitude increase, especially for intense stimuli.

$p < .05$). Bipolar patients showed this effect more strongly than unipolar patients but bipolar–unipolar differences could not be confirmed statistically.

Thus, sleep deprivation appeared to have a sensorially activating effect on the visual system. Could the mood-elevating effects reported elsewhere (Post *et al.*, 1976) result from the relief of sensory deprivation secondary to this activation? In contrast, normal subjects show minimal effects of sleep deprivation (no significant night or Night × Intensity effect in an ANOVA within the normal group).

ADRENOCORTICOTROPHIC HORMONES, CARBOHYDRATE-ACTIVE STEROIDS, AND EVOKED RESPONSE

Elevations in urinary steroid levels have been widely utilized as indicators of situational stress response. The balance of studies seems to indicate that cortisol excretion is elevated in affectively ill patients (Carroll & Mendels, 1976) and that high cortisol levels may fail to be suppressed on dexamethasone (Carpenter & Bunney, 1971; Stokes, Pick, Stoll, & Nunn, 1975). However, elevated levels are not universal and may not occur in many patients (Sachar, Hellman, Roffwarg, Halpern, Fukushima, & Gallagher, 1973). Bipolar patients may have lower 17-hydroxycorticosteroids (17-OHCS) than unipolar patients (Dunner, Goodwin, Gershon, Murphy, & Bunney, 1972) but this has not uniformly been found. Furthermore, available data on brains of suicide victims appear to indicate cortisol concentration at lower than normal levels (Carroll & Mendels, 1976).

Could EPs as indicators of CNS neurophysiological reactivity and as correlates of hypothalamic–pituitary–adrenal cortical axis function shed some light on these contradictory findings? In adrenalectomized patients (Buchsbaum & Henkin, 1976) EP amplitude is reduced, but Kopell, Wittner, Lunde, Warrick, and Edwards (1970) noted reduced EP amplitude in normal volunteers given adrenal corticosteroids. This suggests that a similar brain effect could occur both with too little or too much carbohydrate-active steroid.

Do spontaneous variations in 24-hr 17-OHCS excretion rates relate to these EP changes? Analysis of the data we collected from bipolar patients (Dunner et al., 1972) indicated that individuals with high, visual EP amplitude also had high levels of 24-hr excretion of 17-OHCS. Eight bipolar patients had both urine collections and visual EPs (technique described in Buchsbaum et al., 1971) done while taking placebo medication. The mean amplitude of P100–N140 (measured peak-to-trough) correlated .62 with 24-hr 17-OHCS excretion ($p < .05$, one-tailed). It is noteworthy, however, that in 18 active schizophrenic patients (patient population described in Landau et al., 1975) the same correlation was $-.43$ (both correlations are significant at the .05 level, one-tailed, and significantly different from each other at the .025 level, two-tailed).

Changes in adrenocorticotrophic hormones (ACTH) levels caused by administering steroids might also be important because direct effects of ACTH and ACTH-like peptides on the CNS that are not mediated through the adrenal gland have recently been reported. Kastin, Miller, Gonzalez-Barcena, Hawley, Dyster-Aas, Schally, Velasco de Parra, and Velasco (1971) administered MSH (melanocyte stimulating hormone) and reported that an increase in the N140–P100 component of somatosensory EPs paralleled improvements in attentional performance. Similar attentional improvements have been noted with short peptide fragments of ACTH (Sandman, George, Nolan, van Reizen, & Kastin, 1975), which are not adrenally active. A direct CNS effect of ACTH on EPs is also indicated by our study (Buchsbaum & Henkin, 1976) in which ACTH was administered to patients with adrenal cortical insufficiency while they were withdrawn from carbohydrate-active steroid replacement. Low P100 amplitudes and P100 amplitude–intensity slopes were observed for visual EPs, a pattern similar to that seen in unipolar patients (Buchsbaum et al., 1973). Peak N140, the component most conspicuously influenced by selective attention manipulation, was also the most markedly modified by ACTH.

The findings that pituitary–adrenal function related to EP indicators of selective attention and augmenting–reducing suggest that EP techniques may be useful in understanding the great individual differences in steroid stress response. As Mason (1975) points out, the interpretation of steroid levels or steroid stress response requires consideration of not only the stress but also the "evaluation of the style and effectiveness of the psychological defenses of the subject." Dunner *et al.* (1972) suggest that the preferential use of denial as a psychological defense by bipolars may reduce conscious awareness of anxiety and be associated with lower 17-OHCS excretion. The EP data showing low P100 amplitude and low amplitude–intensity slopes (reducing) to be associated, among bipolars, with low steroid levels ($r = .62$ and .49, respectively) seems consistent with this formulation: The more analytically inclined reader might conveniently link denial to the neurophysiological phenomena of reducing. Low anxiety and psychotic disorganization also appear to be correlated with low cortisol production in depressed patients (Sachar, Hellman, Fukushima, & Gallagher, 1970). Any speculation about the EP–steroid findings must be tempered by the opposite direction of the correlations in schizophrenics and the fact that large extra-adrenal effects of ACTH have been reported. Data relating dexamethasone suppression to EP findings collected in varying mood states are an essential element in further verifying these contradictions.

RECOVERY CYCLES IN THE EVOKED POTENTIAL AND DEPRESSION

The recovery cycle paradigm examines the changes in CNS sensory responsiveness brought about by an initial stimulus, and the time course of return to baseline. One expects to observe a second stimulus, closely following the initial stimulus, to encounter a state of relative unresponsiveness associated with the refractoriness of neurons in sensory systems. Typically, recovery functions are measured by administering pairs of stimuli close together (often every 10 msec) and comparing the amplitude of the second stimulus to that of the first. Because the EPs may overlap in time and confound EP measurement, special techniques are necessary to assess recovery. A second series of single stimuli, spaced in time so as not to overlap, is presented. The EPs obtained in this way are subtracted from the EPs of the paired stimuli, yielding an unconfounded second response.

Within the framework of this chapter, such a paradigm may be useful in examining a sensory homeostasis. A stimulus is presented (the stress) and changes in CNS responsiveness assessed. The overloaded nervous system might be expected to recover more slowly—and the underloaded or sensorially deprived one to recover more rapidly or even be facilitated.

In general, recovery cycle studies have shown reduced recovery in psychotic patients, both in schizophrenia and with psychotic depression (see summary by Shagass, 1976). However this reduction in recovery at short (10–30 msec) intervals seems greater in schizophrenic than depressive subjects (see Vasconetto *et al.*, 1971) and greater in schizophrenic patients than in patients with "neurosis with anxiety and depression [Shagass and Schwartz, 1965]." Patients with psychotic depression showed diminished somatosensory recovery, especially for the initial component, particularly during the first 20 msec (Shagass & Schwartz, 1966). Many individuals, however, actually show facilitation of the response to the second stimuli, especially for weak stimuli (as illustrated in 1968 by Shagass for a manic-depressive patient).

Further complications are the finding that sex-related differences in these measurements among a patient sample were in the reverse direction from those in nonpatients, and that these reversals were strongest with the weak stimuli (Shagass, 1976). These low intensity facilitatory effects and their sex-related differences are intriguing from the viewpoint of sensory deprivation–sensory overload theories of affective disorders, well known to be sexually dimorphic (e.g., Weissman and Klerman, 1977). However, separate comparisons of bipolar and unipolar patients with an equivalent sample of normal subjects regarding recovery cycles are not currently available. Consequently, we cannot evaluate the possibility of facilitatory effects in bipolars directly.

SUMMARY

Stress may occur with the intense overstimulation of electric shock or the understimulation of solitary confinement: It may be as depressing to be burned as bored. Eric Fromm, in *The Anatomy of Human Destructiveness* (1975), discusses the need for stimulation to prevent chronic depressive boredom. Investigators of stress should note that the sensory sameness of a hospital ward or "home cage" may be a stress as much as any "experimental" condition planned for patient or animal. In the homeostatic model discussed in this chapter individuals with high requirements for stimulation may seek out exciting activity and adapt by minimally inhibiting incoming sensations centrally; special insensitivity at low sensory levels may be part of this pattern. Individuals with low optimal levels of sensation may accept weak stimuli but inhibit strong ones with powerful cortico-fugal output. The bipolar patient, relatively insensitive at very low stimulus levels but with large EPs for intense stimuli, appears to have a high setting on his sensori-stat. The schizophrenic's small EPs at high intensity levels stand in contrast. The bipolar patient's diminution of EP amplitude on repeated testing and reduced recovery cycle may be examples of defective balancing of stimulatory need and inhibitory processes. Pain tolerance may be another pathological example of stimulatory need and disturbed stimulus–intensity modulation. Such inbalances could form a basis for the oscillations seen in bipolar illness and their imperfect linkage to environmental stress.

The neurophysiology of control of ascending sensory flow to conscious and unconscious centers by descending cortical and cortico-cortical pathways is beginning to be understood. Experimental approaches in humans to these processes using EPs may be more tractable than memory or cognitive processes and may aid in the search for the "Holy Grail" of biologic psychiatry—the biologically homogeneous subgroup of patients.

REFERENCES

Albe-Fessard, D. & Fessard, A. Recent advances on the neurophysiological bases of pain sensation. *Acta Neurobiologiae Experimentalis*, 1975, 35, 715–740.

Bexton, W. H., Heron, W., & Scott, T. H. Effects of decreased variation in the sensory environment. *Canadian Journal of Psychology*, 1954, 8, 70–76.

Borge, G. F. Perceptual modulation and variability in psychiatric patients. *Archives of General Psychiatry*, 1973, 29, 760–763.

Brawley, P., & Pos, R. The informational underload (sensory deprivation) model in contemporary psychiatry. *Canadian Psychiatric Association Journal*, 1967, 12, 105–124.

Broughton, R. Sleep and neurological states. In M. H. Chase (Ed.), *The sleeping brain*. Los Angeles, California: Brain Information Service, Brain Research Institute, Univ. California at Los Angeles, 1972.

Bruder, G. E., Sutton, S., Babkoff, H., Gurland, B. J., Yozawitz, A., & Fleiss, J. L. Auditory signal detectability and facilitation of simple reaction time in psychiatric patients and nonpatients. *Psychological Medicine*, 1976, 5, 260–272.

Buchsbaum, M. S. Average evoked response and stimulus intensity in identical and fraternal twins. *Physiological Psychology*, 1974, 2, 365–370.

Buchsbaum, M. S. Average evoked response augmenting/reducing in schizophrenia and affective disorders. In D. X. Freedman (Ed.), *Biology of the major psychoses: A comparative analysis*, New York: Raven Press, 1975.

Buchsbaum, M. S. Self-regulation of stimulus intensity: Augmenting/reducing and the average evoked response. In G. E. Schwartz & D. Shapiro (Eds.), *Consciousness and self-regulation*, New York: Plenum Press, 1976.

Buchsbaum, M. S. The middle evoked response components and schizophrenia. *Schizophrenia Bulletin*, 1977, 3:93–104.

Buchsbaum, M. S. The average evoked response technique in the differentiation of bipolar, unipolar and schizophrenic disorders. In H. Akiskal (Ed.), *Psychiatric diagnosis: Exploration of biological criteria*. New York: Spectrum, 1978.

Buchsbaum, M. S., Goodwin, F., Murphy, D., & Borge, G. AER in affective disorders. *American Journal of Psychiatry*, 1971, 128, 19–25.

Buchsbaum, M. S. & Henkin, R. I. Effect of carbohydrate active steroids and ACTH on visual evoked responses in patients with adrenal cortical insufficiency. *Neuroendocrinology*, 1976, 19, 314–322.

Buchsbaum, M. S., Landau, S., Murphy, D. L., & Goodwin, F. Average evoked response in bipolar and unipolar affective disorders: Relationship to sex, age of onset and monoamine oxidase. *Biological Psychiatry*, 1973, 7, 199–212.

Buchsbaum, M. S. & Pfefferbaum, A. Individual differences in stimulus intensity response. *Psychophysiology*, 1971, 8, 600–611.

Buchsbaum, M. S., Post, R. M., & Bunney, W. E., Jr. AER in a rapidly cycling manic-depressive patient. *Biological Psychiatry*, 1977, 12, 83–99.

Buchsbaum, M. S. & Silverman, J. Stimulus intensity control and the cortical evoked response. *Psychosomatic Medicine*, 1968, 30, 12–22.

Buss, A. H. *Psychopathology*. New York: Wiley, 1966.

Carpenter, W. T. & Bunney, W. E., Jr. Adrenal cortical activity in depressive illness. *American Journal of Psychiatry*, 1971, 128, 31–40.

Carroll, B. J. & Mendels, J. Neuroendocrine regulation in affective disorders. In E. J. Sachar (Ed.), *Hormones, behavior, and psychopathology*. New York: Raven Press, 1976.

Cleveland, S. E., Reitman, E. E., & Bentinck, C. Therapeutic effectiveness of sensory deprivation. *Archives of General Psychiatry*, 1963, 8, 455–460.

Cooper, A. F., Garside, R. F., & Kay, D. W. K. A comparison of deaf and nondeaf patients with paranoid and affective psychoses. *British Journal of Psychiatry*, 1976, 129, 532–538.

Davis, G. C., Buchsbaum, M. S., & Bunney, W. E., Jr. Analgesia to painful stimuli in affective illness. *American Journal of Psychiatry* (in press).

Depue, R. A. & Fowles, D. C. Electrodermal activity and schizophrenia: The problem of stimulus intensity modulation. *Psychological Bulletin*, 1976, 83, 192–193.

Dunner, D. L., Goodwin, F. K., Gershon, E. S., Murphy, D. L., & Bunney, W. E., Jr. Excretion of 17-OHCS in unipolar and bipolar depressed patients. *Archives of General Psychiatry*, 1972, 26, 360–363.

Fromm, E. The anatomy of human destructiveness. New York: Fawcett, 1975.

Gershon, E. S. & Buchsbaum, M. S. A genetic study of average evoked response augmentation/reduction in affective disorders. In C. Shagass, S. Gershon, & A. J. Friedhoff (Eds.), *Psychopathology and brain dysfunction*. New York: Raven Press, 1977.

Gibby, R. G., Adams, H. B., & Carrera, R. N. Therapeutic changes in psychiatric patients following partial sensory deprivation. *Archives of General Psychiatry*, 1960, 3, 33–42.

Gottschalk, L. A., Haer, J. L., & Bates, D. E. Effect of sensory overload on psychological state changes in social alienation-personal disorganization and cognitive-intellectual impairment. *Archives of General Psychiatry*, 1972, 27, 451–457.

Hall, R. A., Rappaport, M., Hopkins, H. K., Griffin, R., & Silverman, J. Evoked response and behavior in cats. *Science*, 1970, 170, 998–1000.

Hall, K. R. L., & Stride, E. The varying response to pain in psychiatric disorders: A study in abnormal psychology. *The British Journal of Medical Psychology*, 1954, 27, 48–60.

Harris, A. Sensory deprivation and schizophrenia. *Journal of Mental Science*, 1959, 105, 235–237.

Hemphill R. E., Hall, K. R. L., & Crookes, T. G. A preliminary report on fatigue and pain tolerance in depressive and psychoneurotic patients. *The Journal of Mental Science*, 1952, 98, 433–440.

Kastin, A. J., Miller, L. H., Gonzalez-Barcena, D., Hawley, W. D., Dyster-Aas, K., Schally, A. V., Velasco de Parra, M. L., & Velasco, M. Psycho-physiologic correlates of MSH activity in man. *Physiology and Behavior*, 1971, 7, 893–896.

von Knorring, L. An intraindividual comparison of pain measures, averaged evoked responses and clinical ratings during depression and after recovery. *Acta Psychiatrica Scandinavica*, 1974, 255, 109–120.

von Knorring, L. & Espvall, M. Experimentally induced pain in patients with depressive disorders. *Acta Psychiatrica Scandinavica*, 1974, 255, 121–133.

von Knorring, L., Espvall, M., & Perris, C. Averaged evoked responses, pain measures, and personality variables in patients with depressive disorders. *Acta Psychiatrica Scandinavica*, 1974, 255, 99–108.

Kopell, B. S., Wittner, W. K., Lunde, D., Warrick, G., & Edwards, D. Cortisol effects on averaged evoked potential, alpha rhythm, time estimation, and two-flash fusion threshold. *Psychosomatic Medicine*, 1970, 32, 39–49.

Landau, S. G., Buchsbaum, M. S., Carpenter, W., Strauss, J., & Sacks, M. Schizophrenia and stimulus intensity control. *Archives of General Psychiatry*, 1975, 32, 1239–1245.

Lavine, R., Buchsbaum, M. S., & Poncy, M. Auditory analgesia: Somatosensory evoked response and subjective pain rating assessment. *Psychophysiology*, 1976, 13, 140–148.

Levit, R. A., Sutton, S., & Zubin, J. Evoked potential correlates of information processing in psychiatric patients. *Psychological Medicine*, 1973, 3, 487–494.

Lipowski, Z. J. Sensory and information inputs overload: Behavioral effects. *Comprehensive Psychiatry*, 1975, 16, 199–221.

Ludwig, A. M. "Psychedelic" effects produced by sensory overload. *American Journal of Psychiatry*, 1972, *128*, 114–117.

Ludwig, A. M. Sensory overload and psychopathology. *Diseases of the Nervous System*, 1975, *36*, 357–360.

Ludwig, A. M. & Stark, L. H. Schizophrenia, sensory deprivation and sensory overload. *Journal of Nervous and Mental Disease*, 1973, *157*, 210–216.

Mason, J. W. Psychologic stress and endocrine function. In E. J. Sachar (Ed.), *Topics in Psychoendocrinology*, New York: Grune and Stratton, 1975.

McReynolds, P. Anxiety, perception and schizophrenia. In D. D. Jackson (Ed.), *The etiology of schizophrenia*. New York: Basic Books, 1960.

Melzack, R. & Wall, P. D. Pain mechanisms: A new theory. *Science*, 1965, *150*, 971–980.

Merskey, H. The effect of chronic pain upon the response to noxious stimuli by psychiatric patients. *Journal of Psychosomatic Research*, 1965, *8*, 405–419.

Miller, J. G. Information input overload and psychopathology. *American Journal of Psychiatry*, 1960, *116*, 695–704.

Moldofsky, H. & England, R. S. Facilitation of somatosensory average-evoked potentials in hysterical anesthesia and pain. *Archives of General Psychiatry*, 1975, *32*, 193–197.

Mushin, J. & Levy, R. Averaged evoked response in patients with psychogenic pain. *Psychological Medicine*, 1974, *4*, 19–27.

Myers, T. I. Tolerance for sensory and perceptual deprivation. In J. P. Zubek (Ed.), *Sensory deprivation: Fifteen years of research*. New York: Appleton Century Crofts, 1969.

Perris, C. Averaged evoked responses (AER) in patients with affective disorders. *Acta Psychiatrica Scandinavica*, 1974, *255*, 89–97.

Peters, J., Benjamin, F. B., Helvey, W. M., & Albright, G. A. Study of sensory deprivation, pain and personality relationships for space travel. *Aerospace Medicine*, 1963, *34*, 830–837.

Petrie, A. *Individuality in pain and suffering*. Chicago: Univ. of Chicago Press, 1967.

Petrie, A. Reduction or augmentation? Why we need two "planks" before deciding. *Perceptual and Motor Skills*, 1974, *39*, 460–462.

Pflug, B. & Tolle, R. Disturbance of the 24-hour rhythm in endogenous depression and the treatment of endogenous depression by sleep deprivation. *International Pharmacopsychiatry*, 1971, *6*, 187–196.

Post, R. M., Kotin, J., & Goodwin, F. K. Effects of sleep deprivation on mood and central amine metabolism in depressed patients. *Archives of General Psychiatry*, 1976, *33*, 627–632.

Rosenthal, D. *Genetic theory and abnormal behavior*. New York: McGraw-Hill, 1970.

Rosenzweig, N. Sensory deprivation and schizophrenia: some clinical and theoretical similarities. *American Journal of Psychiatry*, 1959, *116*, 326–329.

Sachar, E. J., Hellman, L., Fukushima, D. K., & Gallagher, T. F. Cortisol production in depressive illness. *Archives of General Psychiatry*, 1970, *23*, 289–298.

Sachar, E. J., Hellman, L., Roffwarg, H. P., Halpern, F. S., Fukushima, D. K., & Gallagher, T. F. Disrupted 24-hour patterns of cortisol secretion in psychotic depression. *Archives of General Psychiatry*, 1973, *28*, 19–24.

Sandman, C. A., George, J. M., Nolan, J. D., van Riezen, H., & Kastin, A. J. Enhancement of attention in man with ACTH–MSH 4–10. *Physiology and Behavior*, 1975, *15*, 427–431.

Satran, R. & Goldstein, M. Pain perception: Modification of threshold of intolerance and cortical potentials by cutaneous stimulation. *Science*, 1973, *180*, 1201–1202.

Satterfield, J. H. Auditory evoked cortical response studies in depressed patients and normal control subjects. In T. A. Williams, M. M. Katz, & J. A. Shield, Jr. (Eds.), *Recent advances in the psychobiology of the depressive illnesses*. Washington, D. C.: U. S. Govt. Printing Office, DHEW Pub. (HSM) 70–9053, 1972.

Schechter, G. & Buchsbaum, M. The effects of attention, stimulus intensity and individual differences on the average evoked response. *Psychophysiology*, 1973, *10*, 392–400.

Schooler, C., Buchsbaum, M. S., & Carpenter, W. T. Evoked response and kinesthetic measures of augmenting or reducing in schizophrenics: Replications and extensions. *Journal of Nervous and Mental Disease*, 1976, *163*, 221-232.

Schultz, D. P. *Sensory restriction*. New York: Academic Press, 1965.

Shagass, C. Averaged somatosensory evoked responses in various psychiatric disorders. In J. Wortis (Ed.), *Recent advances in biological psychiatry*. New York: Plenum Press, 1968.

Shagass, C. An electrophysiological view of schizophrenia. *Biological Psychiatry*, 1976, *11*, 3-30.

Shagass, C. & Schwartz, M. Cerebral responsiveness in psychiatric patients. *Archives of General Psychiatry*, 1963, *8*, 87-99.

Shagass, C. & Schwartz, M. Age, personality and somatosensory cerebral evoked responses. *Science*, 1965, *148*, 1359-1361.

Shagass, C. & Schwartz, M. Somatosensory cerebral evoked responses in psychotic depression. *British Journal of Psychiatry*, 1966, *112*, 799-807.

Shagass, C., Schwartz, M., & Krishnamoorti, S. Some psychotic correlates of cerebral responses evoked by light flash. *Journal of Psychosomatic Research*, 1965, *9*, 223-231.

Sidle, A., Acker, M., & McReynolds, P. "Stimulus-seeking" behavior in schizophrenics and non-schizophrenics. *Perceptual and Motor Skills*, 1963, *17*, 811-816.

Silverman, J., Buchsbaum, M. S., & Henkin, R. Stimulus sensitivity and stimulus intensity control. *Perceptual and Motor Skills*, 1969, *28*, 71-78.

Sitaram, N., Buchsbaum, M. S., & Gillin, J. C. Physostigmine analgesia and somatosensory evoked responses in man. *European Journal of Pharmacology*, 1977, *42*, 285-290.

Small, J. G. & Small, I. F. Contingent negative variation (CNV) correlations with psychiatric diagnosis. *Archives of General Psychiatry*, 1971, *25*, 550-554.

Smith, S., Thakurdas, H., & Lawes, T. G. G. Perceptual isolation in schizophrenia. *Journal of Mental Science*, 1961, *107*, 839-844.

Soskis, D. & Shagass, C. Evoked potential tests of augmenting-reducing. *Psychophysiology*, 1974, *11*, 175-190.

Speck, L. R., Dim, B., & Mercer, M. Visual evoked responses of psychiatric patients. *Archives of General Psychiatry*, 1966, *15*, 59-63.

Stark, L. H. & Norton, J. C. The relative reliability of AER parameters. *Psychophysiology*, 1974, *11*, 600-602.

Stokes, P. E., Pick, G. R., Stoll, P. M., & Nunn, W. D. Pituitary-adrenal function in depressed patients: Resistance to dexamethasone suppression. *Journal of Psychiatric Research*, 1975, *12*, 271-281.

Suedfeld, P. The clinical relevance of reduced sensory stimulation. *Canadian Psychological Review*, 1975, *16*, 88-103.

Suedfeld, P. & Roy, C. Using social isolation to change the behaviour of disruptive inmates. *International Journal of Offender Therapy and Comparative Criminology*, 1975, *19*, 90-99.

Taub, J. M. & Berger, R. J. The effects of changing the phase and duration of sleep. *Journal of Experimental Psychology: Human Perception and Performance*, 1976, *2*, 30-41.

Terenius, L., Wahlstrom, A., Lindstrom, L., & Widerlov, E. Increased CSF levels of endorphines in chronic psychosis. *Neuroscience Letters*, 1976, *3*, 157-162.

Vasconetto, C., Floris, F., & Morocutti, C. Visual evoked responses in normal and psychiatric subjects. *Electroencephalography and Clinical Neurophysiology*, 1971, *31*, 77-83.

Weissman, M. M. & Klerman, G. L. Sex differences and the epidemiology of depression. *Archives of General Psychiatry*, 1977, *34*, 98-111.

Wilkinson, R. Some factors influencing the effect of environmental stressors upon performance. *Psychological Bulletin*, 1969, *72*, 260-272.

Zubek, J. P. Pain sensitivity as a measure of perceptual deviation tolerance. *Perceptual and Motor Skills*, 1963, *17*, 641-642.

Zubek, J. P. Behavioral and physiological effects of prolonged sensory and perceptual deprivation: A review. In J. E. Rasmussen (Ed.), *Man in isolation and confinement*. Chicago:
Aldine, 1973.

Zuckerman, M. Hallucinations, reported sensations and images. In J. P. Zubek (Ed.), *Sensory
deprivation: Fifteen years of research*. New York: Appleton Century Crofts, 1969.

Zuckerman, M. The sensation seeking motive. *Progress in Experimental Personality Research*,
1974, *7*, 80–148.

Zuckerman, M., Murtaugh, T., & Siegel, J. Sensation seeking and cortical augmenting-
reducing. *Psychophysiology*, 1974, *11*, 535–542.

Zuckerman, M., Persky, H., Miller, L., & Levine, B. Sensory deprivation versus sensory
variation. *Journal of Abnormal Psychology*, 1970, *76*, 76–82.

PART IV

Psychosocial Aspects of Stress and the Depressive Disorders

The concept of initiation of disease generally involves two foci: (a) the dimensions of psychosocial stimuli that are most importantly related to the onset of human disorders, and (b) psychological characteristics that predispose an individual to disease. The significance of these issues in relation to the development of depressive disorders has been hotly debated for decades, but recently substantive data have begun to predominate over the polemics.

Part 4 presents the latest statements on these two issues by researchers of depression. Paykel and Brown discuss their most recent data on, and models of, the impact of the psychosocial environment on the initiation of depressive episodes. Brown also discusses several factors that increase an individual's vulnerability to depressive disorder, such as social support, childhood loss, and family size. Moreover, Averill contributes a specific discussion on stimulus and response parameters that modulate the impact of stressors.

Lewinsohn and his colleagues present new and exciting data on the measurement of daily positive and negative experiences and the impact of these experiences on the onset of depression. Their discussion of the data within a reinforcement framework provides a unique conception of the relevant aspects of psychosocial stimuli for depression.

Finally, Becker, and Judy Garber and her colleagues both discuss psychological characteristics that may predispose individuals to depressive disorders. These are difficult variables to delineate and measure, but these two chapters are remarkable in their clarity and exciting in their findings, in spite of the difficulties. They both focus on factors that can exert a persuasive influence on the perception of the environment, and it is of interest that Brown has come to focus on similar factors as a result of his findings on stress and the onset of depressive episodes.

CHAPTER 11

Recent Life Events in the Development of the Depressive Disorders[1]

E. S. Paykel

INTRODUCTION

The relationship between illness and life events is one of the great issues in twentieth-century psychiatry. The debate in the earlier literature particularly crystalized around depression. Discussions were fraught with as much in the way of polemics as any of the other schismatic controversies. It is only recently that an accumulating body of empirical research has taken some of the heat out of the question by producing some reasonably consistent findings.

The two contrasting positions in the debate are well known. One side points to the subjective distress that frequently in normal life follows certain unwanted events and the common occurrence of similar stressful events at the onset of depression. The other side, noting that the events involved are often quite everyday in their occurrence, and that there is a large genetic

---

[1] Studies reported in this chapter were carried out collaboratively with a number of authors, particularly Selby Jacobs, Gerald L. Klerman, Jerome Myers, Brigitte Prusoff, and E. H. Uhlenhuth.

The Psychobiology of the Depressive Disorders:
Implications for the Effects of Stress

component in many illnesses, suggests that the events observed are either coincidental or, at most, mere precipitants contributing only a trivial element to causation.

This chapter will review some of the findings from a series of studies carried out with colleagues, mainly in New Haven, Connecticut although now continuing in London. The results, in general, strongly support the role of events in the development of depression, but they also make it clear that the contribution is a partial one in which other elements are important.

The basic technique used in these studies was that of the retrospective elicitation of life events and comparison with matched controls. Retrospective studies present certain well-known difficulties such as distortions of recall due to illness, and the fact that illness itself may produce new events (Paykel, 1974; Brown, Sklair, Harris & Birley, 1973a). Attention to reporting, therefore, becomes of crucial importance. The technique used in these studies involves a list of 61 events (condensed for some purposes to 33), each carefully defined. Information is obtained from the patient by a trained research assistant. The interview is semistructured: Every event is asked for, unless clearly inapplicable, by an initial question that is followed by further enquiry to establish full details. The interview is postponed until acute psychiatric disturbance has subsided, to diminish reporting distortions. The time period for which events are recorded is carefully defined as that period immediately prior to the symptomatic onset of illness.

COMPARISON WITH GENERAL
POPULATION CONTROLS

The first study was a controlled comparison of depressive onset (Paykel, Myers, Dienelt, Klerman, Lindenthal, & Pepper, 1969). The subjects were 185 depressed patients obtained from surveying a representative variety of treatment facilities in New Haven, Connecticut. About half were outpatients, the remainder being treated in inpatient units and day hospitals. The controls were derived from a concurrent, general population, epidemiological survey, sampling one adult in each of 938 households (Myers et al., 1971). From this large sample a subsample of 185 subjects was obtained, each matched with a depressed patient on sociodemographic variables.

The depressed patients received an initial psychiatric assessment, but this did not cover life events. Some weeks later, after symptoms were much improved, patients received the life events interview. The time period concerned was the 6 months before symptom onset. General population controls were interviewed in their homes, regarding the 6-month period prior to interview. Overall, depressives experienced many more events than the general population, reporting 1.69 events from the list per person, as opposed to 0.59 in controls.

This pattern was paralleled by an increased frequency of most of the individual events in the list. For eight events the differences reached statistical significance. These were increased arguments with spouse, marital separation, change to a new type of work (which here included starting work for the first time or after a long absence), death of immediate family member, serious illness of a family member, departure of a family member from home, serious personal physical illness, and a substantial change in work conditions. Most of the other events were also reported more frequently in the depressed group, but they occurred too infrequently for differences to achieve statistical significance.

In order to explore for differential effects, events were grouped into categories according to several alternative, but partly overlapping, sets of criteria. For each category frequencies were calculated in terms of the numbers of individuals reporting at least one event from that category.

One way of looking at events was by using a value dimension, based on cultural norms and social desirability. In terms of generally shared values, some events are regarded as undesirable, and other events as desirable. In our event list, only a few, clearly desirable events had been included. A much larger group of events was clearly undesirable. As shown in Table 11.1, when depressives were compared with the control group, undesirable events were reported much more frequently by the depressives. By contrast, there were no significant differences between the two groups regarding desirable events. Indeed, although not significant, the pattern was reversed, with the control group reporting more desirable events than the depressives. Here was clear indication of differential effects: Only certain types of events appeared to precede depression.

A second and more specific categorization referred to 10 events that involved changes in the immediate social field of the subject. Two classes of events were defined. Entrances referred to those events that involved the introduction of a new person into the social field, and exits referred to those events that clearly involved a departure from the social field. The findings are also shown in Table 11.1. Exits were much more frequently reported by depressed patients. Entrances, although reported with almost equal frequency overall, were equally distributed between the two groups. Exits from the social field correspond closely to a familiar psychiatric concept in relation to depression, that of loss.

Not all such categorizations discriminated between events. Grouping by area of activity—work, marital relationships, health, family, etc.—failed to do so. One additional category did provide striking results. The original life events list contained several items which referred to arguments or difficulties in interpersonal relationships. These were omitted from the final list of

Table 11.1

FREQUENCIES OF EVENT CATEGORIES IN DEPRESSED PATIENTS
AND CONTROL GROUP[a]

Event category	Depressed patients (N = 185)	Controls (N = 185)	Significance[b]	Events in category
Desirable	6	10	None	Engagement Marriage Promotion
Undesirable	82	31	< .01	Death of family member Separation Demotion Serious illness of family member Jail Major financial problems Unemployment Court appearance Son drafted Divorce Business failure Fired Stillbirth
Entrance	21	18	None	Engagement Marriage Birth of child New person in home
Exit	46	9	< .01	Death of close family member Separation Divorce Family member leaves home Child married Son drafted

[a] Number of individuals reporting at least one event in category.
[b] X^2 with Yates' Correction.

events on which the two groups of subjects were compared, as it was felt that
the patient group might report these more readily as a result of their recent
experience of psychiatric treatment. We did, however, examine them separately (Paykel, 1974). Ninety patients reported at least one event from this
category, as opposed to five controls. It seemed unlikely that all this difference could be due to interview artifact. Clinically, these interpersonal
arguments appear to be a common antecedent of depression in the outpatient clinic.

Overall these findings strongly supported the role of life events in the
onset of clinical depression. Moreover, they suggested some degree of

specificity in that exits and undesirable events appear particularly related to depression, whereas their opposites, entrances and desirable events, were not implicated.

How specific is this relationship? At best it can only be considered partial. A highly specific hypothesis would propose that there are certain classes of events that produce depression, and only depression. The evidence does not indicate such a degree of specificity. The excess among depressives included almost every event in our list, except entrances and desirable events. Many subjects reported a cluster of events, which suggested a cumulative model of stress.

OTHER PATIENT GROUPS

Adequate investigation of the degree of specificity also requires attention to the other side of the question, the disturbances produced. The same kind of event may produce a variety of illnesses. In later studies, similar techniques were applied to record the events experienced by 50 first-admission schizophrenics in the 6 months before onset of illness (Jacobs, Prusoff, & Paykel, 1974; Jacobs & Myers, 1976) and to 53 suicide attempters in the 6 months prior to the attempt (Paykel, DiMascio, Haskell, & Prusoff, 1975).

Table 11.2 summarizes the findings for all these samples. Sample charac-

Table 11.2

PERCENTAGE BY PATIENT GROUP REPORTING EVENTS IN CATEGORY AT LEAST ONCE IN 6 MONTHS

	Suicide attempters	Depressed	Schizo-phrenics	General population controls
Number of events reported[a]	3.3	2.1	1.5	.8
Exits	21[b]	25[b]	14[b]	9
Entrances	34[b]	13	16	11
Undesirable	60[b]	40[b]	42[b]	21
Desirable	15	4	8	11
Interpersonal events (full event list)	75[b]	62[b]	18[b]	3
Major upset	68[b]	45[b]	—	23
Intermediate upset	53[b]	26[b]	—	4
Minor upset	49[b]	45[b]	—	25
Uncontrolled	66[b]	40[b]	—	21
Controlled	34[b]	32[b]	—	17

[a] Mean number of events in 6 months.
[b] The patient group reports event-category significantly more frequently than general population.

teristics differed somewhat in the original groups, and the findings shown for depressives are based on a more comparable subsample. Published reports for the schizophrenics used slightly different event lists, but the findings shown are based on the standard list.

All patient groups reported significantly more events than did the general population. There was a rank order from suicide attempters, who reported the most events, to depressives, to schizophrenics, to the general population. These differences presumably reflect, retrospectively, the degree to which recent events are involved in the genesis of the illness.

With regard to the categories of events included in Table 11.1, the same findings for depression tended to hold for the other disorders, with the same rankings as before. Exits, undesirable events, and interpersonal arguments were reported to excess in all conditions, desirable events in none. Entrances were also reported excessively before suicide attempts, and exits were barely excessive before the symptomatic onset of schizophrenia, so that the exit–entrance distinction tended to be more specific for depression.

Findings in two additional categories were also available for suicide attempters and depressives. Regarding the first category, we divided events into three groups (i.e., major, intermediate, and minor) by scores from another study in which subjects had scaled the degree to which each of the events was upsetting (Paykel et al., 1971). Both patient groups tended to report more events than the general population controls in all three categories: Suicide attempters showed more events of the major and intermediate (but not minor) types than did the depressed patients. The second categorization was by the degree of control or choice the respondent might exert over the initiation of the event. Some events, such as the serious illness of a family member, are likely to be outside his control; other events, such as marriage, may be within it. In both these categories depressives also reported more events than the general population subjects. Suicide attempters reported significantly more uncontrolled events than depressives, but not more controlled events. It was particularly the more threatening categories of events, scaled as major or intermediate in terms of upset, events outside the respondent's control, and undesirable events that suicide attempters reported as occurring more frequently than depressives.

In a further study (Uhlenhuth & Paykel, 1973) we utilized a sample of mixed neurotic patients. Within the limited spectrum of this sample, there were no differences between patients with predominantly depressive symptoms and other symptom pictures regarding types of events experienced. Overall, it is fairly clear from this series of comparisons with other conditions that specificity is, at best, weak and that the same event can be followed, in different subjects, by a variety of different disturbances. These disturbances would include somatic as well as psychiatric disorders (Rahe, 1968).

TIMING

The month of occurrence of each event was recorded for suicide attempters, depressives and general population subjects, but not schizophrenics. Figure 11.1 shows the mean number of events reported in each of the 6 months. For general population subjects, there was a fairly even spread of events over the entire 6-month period. However, suicide attempters showed a marked peaking of events in the month before the attempt, indicating a particularly immediate reaction. Depressed patients exhibited a mild peaking of events in the month before onset. The excess of events the depressed group reported as compared with the general population subjects was, however, spread over most of the 6 months and might have extended even earlier. These findings are similar to those reported by Brown, Harris, and Peto (1973b).

FOLLOW-UP STUDY

Another kind of control, which has been little used, is the within-patient control provided by follow-up study. This deals with the possibility that events reported by depressives at the onset of illness are primarily reflections of personality disturbances and habitual, unstable life patterns, and therefore might be reported just as frequently at any other time.

We carried out a short-term 9-month follow-up of a small sample of 30 depressives (Paykel, 1974). Over the last 6 months of the follow-up, frequencies for entrances and desirable events remained low. Those for exits and undesirable events fell considerably to about half the frequency at onset, from 25 to 10% for exits, 45 to 23% for undesirable events. They still

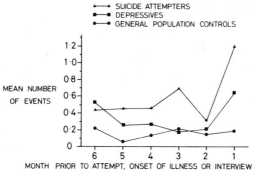

Figure 11.1 Mean number of events reported during each 1-month period prior to attempted suicide, onset of illness, or interview. ▲: Suicide attempters. ■: Depressives. ●: General population controls. [From Paykel *et al.*, 1975.]

remained a little higher than control values—10 versus 5% for exits, 23 versus 16% for undesirable events. Some other events, particularly those related to work, increased in frequency. Many of these were changes arising from the recent illness and recovery. We are hoping to analyze data from a longer follow-up to establish a clear period of freedom from illness and its effects. Within these limits, the follow-up study did confirm the relationship between depression and the major classes of exits and undesirable events.

RELAPSE

If events are important in depression, they would also be expected to produce effects in situations other than onset of illness. One such, commonly met with in practice, is that of relapse after apparent recovery. Another study (Paykel & Tanner, 1976) enabled us to test the hypothesis that events also produce relapse. Subjects were depressed women who responded to initial treatment with amitriptyline and then received maintenance treatment for 8 months in a factorial design. Life event occurrence was recorded concurrently. We took 30 patients who underwent a relapse of their depression during the follow-up period and matched them on demographic variables and treatment group with 30 patients from the study who did not relapse. Table 11.3 indicates the mean number of events reported in each month, counting backward from the month of relapse or the comparable month for controls. In the first month, that is, the month before relapse,

Table 11.3

OCCURRENCE OF EVENTS IN RELAPSING AND
NONRELAPSING DEPRESSED PATIENTS
DURING FOLLOW-UP

Months prior to relapse	Mean number of events		Significance of difference[a]
	Relapsers (N = 30)	Matched nonrelapsers (N = 30)	
First month	1.00	.47	< .05
Second month	1.13	.83	None
Third month	.93	.57	None
Fourth month[b]	.75	.54	None
Fifth month[c]	.71	.64	None
3 months prior to relapse, combined	3.07	1.87	< .05

[a] Wilcoxon matched-pairs signed-ranks test, two-tailed.
[b] N = 24
[c] N = 14

there was a significant elevation of events in "relapsers". The difference was suggestive in the second and third months, but in earlier months the two groups were fairly comparable.

The sample was too small to examine the types of events, however, we did find a significant excess of undesirable events but not desirable events and the findings for exits were suggestive. The pattern of findings for the onset of illness seemed similar to those shown in relapse.

PERCEPTIONS OF LIFE EVENTS

So far, we have found strong evidence that events are involved in the onset of depression and relapse. Depressives report more events than schizophrenics, but fewer than suicide attempters. Certain kinds of events are particularly involved, but they are not very specific. The same event, such as an exit, may precede a variety of illnesses: Any illness can be preceded by a variety of events.

What does emerge is that different types of events differ in their general propensity to produce illness. This is particularly apparent where groups of events can be contrasted with their opposites, such as desirable and undesirable events, exits and entrances. There seems to be something pathogenic about certain events which operates over a range of disorders.

Further evidence that this is so comes from perceptions of life events. In another set of studies, we modified the technique of Holmes and Rahe (1967) to scale the stressfulness of our list of 61 events. Subjects were asked to rate, on a 0–20 equal-interval scale, the degree to which each of these events was regarded as upsetting. The first study was carried out in an American sample of psychiatric patients and relatives (Paykel, Prusoff, & Uhlenhuth, 1971). Subsequently the scale was given to 183 English patients and relatives at St. George's Hospital (Paykel, McGuiness, & Gomez, 1976). Results were closely comparable in both studies.

The primary purpose of this scaling study was to provide weighting scores for use in other applications. However, the scores also reveal which events are perceived as stressful and they were found to be perceived in much the same way as they relate to psychiatric illness. Events were divided into categories, and mean scores were calculated for each group of events as a whole. The findings are shown in Table 11.4. Exits were scored much higher than entrances. In fact, when individual events were examined, there was scarcely any overlap; almost all exits were scored high and all entrances low. Undesirable events were rated as much more upsetting than desirable events. This is not altogether surprising, although the concepts of upset and undesirability are not identical: Some undesirable events are trivial and score low on the upset scale. In addition uncontrolled events were scored higher than controlled ones. The categories of major, intermediate, and

Table 11.4

MEAN SCALED DEGREE OF UPSET
FOR EVENT CATEGORIES[a]

Category	Mean score	
	American study	English study
Exit	13.1	13.2
Entrance	6.2	6.5
Undesirable	13.9	14.1
Desirable	4.7	4.7
Uncontrolled	13.6	13.5
Controlled	7.4	7.2

[a] Scores are corrected for a systematic difference
in levels of all events, with English scores being
higher.

minor events are not shown in the table, as they were derived from the upset
scale.

These findings should be interpreted a little cautiously, as selection
among the events included in the list might influence the findings. However
they do indicate a universality in the meaning and implications of these
events that extends beyond their precipitation of illness in the normal realm.
This universality is further supported by the cross-cultural similarity.

ENDOGENOUS DEPRESSIONS

In further analyses of the 185 depressives from the controlled study, we
sought evidence of endogenous depressions, in the sense of a depression
unrelated to life stress (Paykel, 1974). Using the 33-item event list employed
for the controlled studies, 19% of the depressives reported no events in the 6
months preceding onset of symptoms, but on the full 61-item list, only 7%
did so. However, some of the events were trivial and probably unrelated to
depression. Counting events is not a very useful way of looking at the data as
it ignores the kind of event. One alternative way of proceeding was by
clinical judgment, using narrative summaries and case histories. Using this
approach, about 15% of illnesses appeared to be unprecipitated. The majority involved at least some element of life stress.

The judgment as to whether a depression is endogenous or reactive,
although it features prominently in the literature, is difficult to answer with
a clear-cut yes or no. Often there are some events, but they are not
sufficiently overwhelming to be the sole cause of the depression, and the

situation is one of partial and ambiguous precipitation. This kind of circumstance requires a quantitative, rather than categorical, approach.

The weights shown previously were applied to the events reported by the depressed patients. The main tool was a summed score, the total stress score derived for each patient by adding weights for all the events that he reported. To avoid dependence on the assumption of additivity of events, a maximal event score was also derived by taking the single weight for the highest event reported by the patient. In fact, the two scores gave closely similar results. Distributions of both these scores were continuous, without any hint of bimodality that would have indicated a clearly separate endogenous group. Confirming the earlier impressions, only a small proportion of patients fell within the range where stress could be regarded as low (Paykel, 1974).

As usually employed, the concept of endogenous depression involves additional issues. Patients having an endogenous depression are considered to be distinguished not only by the absence of precipitant stress, but also by certain specific symptom features, and by non-neurotic premorbid personalities (Klerman, 1971). A number of studies have used factor analysis to explore this issue (Mendels & Cochrane, 1968). One problem is that presence of precipitants is usually recorded as an inadequate yes–no judgment, and made by the same rater who rates symptoms and personality, so that it is easy for rater bias to produce a spurious correlation.

We employed the quantified measures of precipitant stress, and used separate raters. Symptoms were rated by a psychiatrist at an initial interview, without knowledge of life event material. Then, a principal component analysis was carried out on the symptom data alone (Paykel, Klerman & Prusoff, 1970). The first factor showed positive loadings on almost all items and appeared to be a severity factor. The second factor was bipolar, contrasting negative loadings on a pattern of retardation, depression worsening in the morning, and quality of depression different from the usual experience, against positive loadings on irritability, anxiety, reactivity, initial and middle of the night insomnia, self-pity, and depersonalization. This closely resembled the bipolar factors contrasting endogenous and neurotic depression reported by Kiloh and Garside (1963) and Carney, Roth and Garside (1965). The third factor was also bipolar. It appeared to contrast negative loadings on typical depressive symptoms and hostility with positive loadings on anxiety and hypochondriasis.

The second factor in this analysis provided strong evidence that the symptoms of endogenous and neurotic depression tended to cluster together so as to form two contrasting patterns. To examine the relationship of this symptomatic distinction to stress, correlations were computed between factor scores on the three factors and the two alternative stress scores (Paykel, 1974). These are shown in Table 11.5. The total stress score correlated

Table 11.5

CORRELATIONS BETWEEN STRESS
SCORES ON UPSET SCALE AND
SYMPTOM FACTORS

Factor	Total stress score	Maximal event score
1 Severity	−.08	.04
2 Neurotic (+) versus endogenous (−)	.15*	.07
3 Anxious (+) versus depressed (−)	−.14	−.15*

* $p < .05$

significantly with Factor 2 in the predicted direction, which was that patients with endogenous symptom pattern reported less life stress, but the correlation, .15, was so low as to account for little variance, and there was an almost significant correlation with Factor 3. For the maximal event score, the correlation was only with Factor 3, and equally as low. Thus, the relationship between stress and symptom pattern, although in the predicted direction, was so weak as to be trivial and was not entirely specific to the endogenous–neurotic symptom dimension. The neurotic factor did, however, correlate (.35) with premorbid neuroticism as measured by the neuroticism scale of the Maudsley Personality Inventory (Eysenck, 1959).

Further analysis of these data, using cluster analysis techniques for grouping individuals showed evidence of four groups, rather than two (Paykel, 1971). One group corresponded closely to the usual concept of psychotic depression, and was reflected in clinical diagnoses made by treating clinicians. The remaining three groups all appeared to be neurotic, and on the basis of the most prominent features, were labeled "anxious depressives," "hostile depressives," and "young depressives with personality disorder." Here too stress scores were only weak differentiators. The flavor of the results is perhaps best illustrated by the flawed clinical judgment. In terms of this, 20% of psychotic depressives were regarded as showing no evidence of a precipitant, as opposed to 36% of anxious depressives (a neurotic group), 8% of hostile depressives and 4% of young depressives with personality disorder.

Similar findings, with respect to the presence of precipitants in severe psychotic depressions, have been reported by Leff, Roatch, and Bunney (1970). Stress appears to be only a weak differentiator in clinical classification. Clinical syndromes can readily be delineated, but they are predominantly on a symptomatic basis. When assessed separately, the presence or absence of precipitant stress relates only very weakly. Although some depressions appear entirely endogenous, they are a relatively small proportion of the total. We are currently re-examining the role of events in a new sample of neurotic depressives to see if the nature and amount of stress can usefully be related to personality among them.

The absence of a relationship between stress and clinical syndromes has additional implications for psychobiologic research. Psychotic or endogenous depressions form a particular focus for biologic investigations. There is also evidence that they respond better to electro-convulsive therapy and tricyclic antidepressants, and poorly to monoamine oxidase inhibitors. Closer scrutiny of this work suggests that most studies depend on symptom pattern rather than life stress. The findings have validity, provided they are accepted in these terms, and divorced from implications of precipitant stress. The terms psychotic and endogenous have been used almost synonymously in the literature. The former may be preferable in that it lacks any implication of absence of precipitants, although the word endogenous is probably embedded too firmly in the literature for any useful purpose to be gained by trying to remove it.

MAGNITUDE OF EFFECT

A more telling argument against the role of life events as the sole determinant of depression can be derived by focussing not on unprecipitated depressions, but on those in which events are implicated. It has often been pointed out that close scrutiny of the events reported by patients suggests that they can, at best, only be partial causes. Most of the events reported in our studies were in the range of everyday experience, rather than catastrophic. It seems probable that in most cases these events are negotiated without illness so that some other factors must contribute to the development of depression. It is particularly easy to lose sight of the importance of base rates for the population. When the prevalence of a disease state is relatively low, single events will be of limited value in explaining it if they occur with moderate frequency in the general population. A simple calculation for exits illustrated this point. Based on the findings from the controlled study, and assuming a hypothetical annual incidence of depression of 4%, it was easy to show that about 9% of the exits would be followed by depression (Paykel, 1974). This calculation made a number of assumptions, and in particular, the relationship would be closer if we used a higher incidence for depression. However the general point remains that most stressful events are not followed by psychiatrically treated depression. Some are followed by other psychiatric disorder (for which however incidences are considerably lower), or by somatic disorders, but many do not lead to any disorder at all.

This is not a very good way of looking at the relationship: the event can still be important in determining onset in spite of these figures. Another approach is the "brought-forward time" of Brown et al. (1973b), corresponding to the amount of time by which the events may be considered on the average to have advanced the expectation of a spontaneous onset. Applying the formula to our findings for exits they obtained a brought-forward time of 2.7 years, quite close to values found by Brown *et al.* in a similar study. The brought-forward time does not translate very easily into real terms and it is not immediately apparent what would be a high or low value. We have found it easier to use an established epidemiologic concept, that of relative risk. This is the ratio of the disease rate among those exposed to a causative factor to the rate among those not exposed, that is, it is a measure of the degree to which the factor increases the disease rate. In a case control study of an illness in which the numbers of persons affected is small as compared to the number unaffected, the relative risk can be calculated approximately, as shown here (McMahon & Pugh, 1970), without actual knowledge of the rates.

Cause	Cases	Controls
Present	a	b
Absent	c	d
Relative risk	$\dfrac{ad}{bc}$	

Table 11.6 shows relative risks computed for depression, with those for suicide attempts and schizophrenia (from unpublished data) for comparison. An exit event increases the risk of depression 6.5-fold in the next 6 months. The occurrence of any event on our list increases the risk of depression on average by 5.4 times. Figures for suicide attempts are a little higher, whereas those for schizophrenia are rather lower. Computations from the studies of Brown and colleagues (Brown *et al.*, 1973b; Brown, Ni Bhrolchain, & Harris, 1975) give figures for markedly threatening events associated with the onset of depression that are of comparable order to those shown for exits (Paykel, 1978). The effects of life events in the genesis of depression are important in magnitude, but it is clear that they are very far from the sole determinants. Something else is important in producing illness. It falls under the general rubric of vulnerability or predisposition.

Table 11.6

RELATIVE RISKS

Illness	Exits in last 6 months	All events in last 6 months
Depression	6.5	5.4
Suicide attempts	6.7	6.3
Schizophrenia	3.9	3.0

A MODEL FOR
THE EFFECTS OF LIFE EVENTS

We can now attempt to formulate a model for the effects of life events. The event must be regarded as interacting with a host of other factors in determining whether the outcome is an illness, and which specific illness. It is not merely the event, but also the soil into which it falls. Figure 11.2 is an attempt to specify some of the factors between event and consequence.

At the start, the event itself may be regarded as incorporating modifying factors. Events appearing to be the same, may differ in circumstances, and in the variety of implications they carry. Next, other stresses and supports in the social environment may modify the consequences. These modifiers would include such factors as outside employment, confiding relationships, presence of several young children in the home, and lower social class, identified by Brown *et al.* (1975) as affecting the likelihood that life events in women will be followed by depression. Chronic stresses, which have tended to be ignored in life event research, may sometimes have this modifying effect and may sometimes act like new events.

Nearer to the core, we must assume that there are a large number of personal factors reflecting vulnerability to events. There may be personality factors leading to greater vulnerability to events in general, such as are hypothesized in work on the neurotic constitution (Slater, 1953). On the other hand, specific vulnerabilities seem likely; for instance obsessional personalities might be expected to be particularly sensitive to events involving major changes in their life pattern and routine. Such personal vulnerabilities might be genetic or environmental in origin. There is mounting evidence that early loss may predispose to the effects of subsequent loss in inducing depression (Brown *et al.*, 1975) or suicide attempts (Levi, Fales, Stein, & Sharp, 1966). In this sense all earlier life events may be seen as having persisting influences of lesser degree, both pathogenic, and protective, in the learning of coping behavior. Equally, the psychological effects of events, translated into their neurophysiological substrates, must interact with other neurochemical, physiological and pharmacologic aspects of central nervous system function, for instance in the pathways regulating mood, which thus become a final common pathway for depression.

However, depression is not the only possible consequence of life events. We must also envisage personal vulnerability factors relating to the onset of specific diseases. These might include, for affective disorder, such elements as habitual psychological defense mechanisms and reaction patterns, cyclical changes in function, enzyme defects in monoamine pathways, and variations in metabolic pools of transmitter substances. More generally they include all sorts of deficits of biologic structures and functions, exposure to

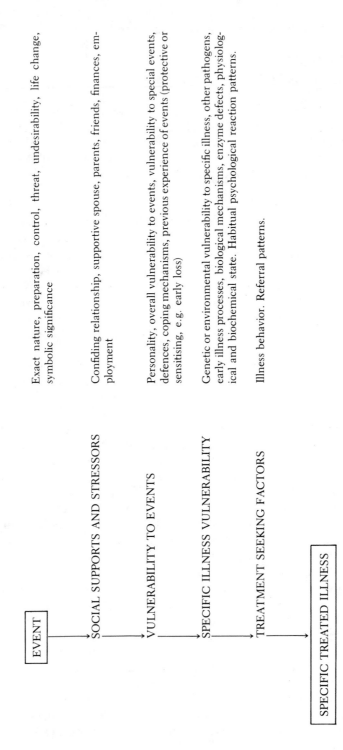

EVENT

↓

SOCIAL SUPPORTS AND STRESSORS — Exact nature, preparation, control, threat, undesirability, life change, symbolic significance

↓

VULNERABILITY TO EVENTS — Confiding relationship, supportive spouse, parents, friends, finances, employment

↓

SPECIFIC ILLNESS VULNERABILITY — Personality, overall vulnerability to events, vulnerability to special events, defences, coping mechanisms, previous experience of events (protective or sensitising, e.g. early loss)

↓

TREATMENT SEEKING FACTORS — Genetic or environmental vulnerability to specific illness, other pathogens, early illness processes, biological mechanisms, enzyme defects, physiological and biochemical state. Habitual psychological reaction patterns.

↓

SPECIFIC TREATED ILLNESS — Illness behavior. Referral patterns.

Figure 11.2 Modifying factors between event and illness.

pathogens, and incipient disease processes, including whatever abnormality of central nervous system function is found to underlie schizophrenia, and such diverse factors as the extent of coronary atheroma, and exposure to carcinogens or the virus of the common cold.

Lastly the factors of illness behavior (Mechanic, 1976) will determine whether or not an individual regards himself as ill and seeks professional treatment. Furthermore, referral patterns may also determine whether psychiatric treatment is required, for those countries where there are nonpsychiatric primary givers of care. Such factors may be of great importance if, as some evidence suggests, there is a high prevalence of untreated depression in the community (Brown et al., 1975; Richman, 1974). It is of course easy to specify some of these modifying factors in broad outline, but most have been little investigated, and many more detailed studies are required. Prospective studies of single events have advantages in this context.

The kind of causative chain that is indicated by this model is a multifactorial one, in which many factors converge on the final state, even in a single case. Rigid criteria for a reactive depression (Jaspers, 1923) and rigid separation into reactive and endogenous types, become inappropriate. Most depressions may be, to some extent, reactive and to some extent, endogenous. Although this kind of multifactorial etiology may, in its complexity and absence of clear-cut separation, be less logically satisfying than the apparently precise distinctions posited by earlier views, it is more in keeping with empirical data and our knowledge of the complexity of psychological relationships and brain mechanisms in general.

REFERENCES

Brown, G. W., Harris, T. O., & Peto, J. Life events and psychiatric disorders Part 2: Nature of causal link. *Psychological Medicine*, 1973, 3, 159–176.(b)

Brown, G. W., Ni Bhrolchain, M., & Harris, T. Social class and psychiatric disturbance among women in an urban population. *Sociology*, 1975, 9, 225–254.

Brown, G. W., Sklair, F., Harris, T. O., & Birley, J. L. T. Life events and psychiatric disorders, Part 1: some methodological issues. *Psychological Medicine*, 1973, 3, 74–87.(a)

Carney, M. W. P., Roth, M., & Garside, R. F. The diagnosis of depressive syndromes and the prediction of E. C. T. response. *British Journal of Psychiatry*, 1965, 111, 659–674.

Eysenck, H. S. *The manual of the Maudsley Personality Inventory*, Univ. London Press, 1959.

Holmes, T. H. & Rahe, R. H. The social readjustment rating scale. *Journal of Psychosomatic Research*, 1967, 11, 213–218.

Jacobs, S. & Myers, J. Recent life events and acute schizophrenic psychosis: a controlled study. *Journal of Nervous and Mental Disease*, 1976, 162, 75–87.

Jacobs, S., Prusoff, B. A., & Paykel, E. S. Recent life events in schizophrenia and depression. *Psychological Medicine*, 1974, 4, 444–453.

262   E. S. PAYKEL

Jaspers, K. General psychopathology (J. Hoenig & M. W. Hamilton, trans.) Manchester Univ. Press, 1923.
Kiloh, L. G. & Garside, E. F. The independence of neurotic depression and endogenous depression. British Journal of Psychiatry, 1963, 109, 451–463.
Klerman, G. L. Clinical research in depression. Archives of General Psychiatry, 1971, 24, 305–319.
Leff, M. J., Roatch, J. F., & Bunney, W. E. Environmental factors preceding the onset of severe depression. Psychiatry, 1970, 33, 293–311.
Levi, L. O., Fales, C. H., Stein, M., & Sharp, V. H. Separation and attempted suicide. Archives of General Psychiatry, 1966, 15, 158–165.
MacMahon, B. & Pugh, T. F. Epidemiology: Principles and methods. Boston: Little Brown, 1970.
Mechanic, D. Stress, illness and illness behaviour. Journal of Human Stress, 1976, 2, 2–6.
Mendels, J. & Cochrane, C. The nosology of depression: The endogenous–reactive concept. American Journal of Psychiatry, 1968, 124 (May supp.) 1–11.
Myers, J. K., Lindenthal, J. J., & Pepper, M. P. Life events and psychiatric impairment. Journal of Nervous and Mental Disease, 1971, 152, 149–157.
Paykel, E. S. Classification of depressed patients: A cluster analysis derived grouping. British Journal of Psychiatry, 1971, 118, 275–288.
Paykel, E. S. Recent life events and clinical depression. In E. K. Gunderson & R. H. Rahe (Eds.), Life stress and illness. Springfield, Illinois: Thomas, 1974.
Paykel, E. S. Environmental variables in the aetiology of depression. In F. C. Flach & S. Draghi (Eds.), The nature and treatment of depression. New York: Wiley, 1975.
Paykel, E. S. Contribution of life events to causation of psychiatric illness. Psychological Medicine, 1978, 8, 245–253.
Paykel, E. S., DiMascio, A., Haskell, D., & Prusoff, B. A. Effects of maintenance amitriptyline and psychotherapy on symptoms of depression. Psychological Medicine, 1975, 5, 67–77.
Paykel, E. S., Klerman, G. L., & Prusoff, B. A. Treatment setting and clinical depression. Archives of General Psychiatry, 1970, 22, 11–21.
Paykel, E. S., McGuiness, B., & Gomez, J. An Anglo-American comparison of the scaling of life events. British Journal of Medical Psychology, 1976, 49, 237–247.
Paykel, E. S., Myers, J. K., Dienelt, M. N., Klerman, G. L., Lindenthal, J. J., & Pepper, M. P. Life events and depression: A controlled study. Archives of General Psychiatry, 1969, 21, 753–760.
Paykel, E. S., Prusoff, B. A., & Uhlenhuth, E. H. Scaling of life events. Archives of General Psychiatry, 1971, 25, 340–347.
Paykel, E. S. & Tanner, J. Life events, depressive relapse and maintenance treatment. Psychological Medicine, 1976, 6, 481–485.
Rahe, R. H. Life-change measurement as a predictor of illness. Proceedings of the Royal Society of Medicine, 1968, 61, 1124–1128.
Richman, N. The effects of housing on pre-school children and their mothers. Developmental Medicine and Child Neurology, 1974, 16, 53–58.
Slater, E. Psychotic and neurotic illnesses in twins. Her Majesty's Stationary Office: London, 1953.
Uhlenhuth, E. H. & Paykel, E. S. Symptom configuration and life events. Archives of General Psychiatry, 1973, 28, 743–748.

CHAPTER 12

The Social Etiology of Depression—London Studies[1]

George W. Brown

INTRODUCTION

Psychiatry has not given a great deal of serious attention to the role of the current social environment in the etiology of mental disorder. Although every clinician will know of major depressive illnesses that have followed a tragic event, the possibility of an important etiologic link is easily ignored. Why is it that so few develop clinical depression after such events? Surely something else must be at work: Have the events merely triggered illnesses that would have occurred before long in any case?

These are legitimate and important questions. They also display some hint of a misconception. The idea of predisposition is usually evoked with a "genetic," "constitutional," or "personality" factor in mind. Yet there is no reason why some social factor *other* than the event itself could not increase the risk of depression in the presence of an event.

In this chapter, I will review a program of research that I believe begins to

[1] The research was supported by the Medical Research Council, the Social Science Research Council, and the Foundations' Fund for Research in Psychiatry.

263

The Psychobiology of the Depressive Disorders:
Implications for the Effects of Stress

make a reasonably convincing case for the position that the social environment plays a crucial role in the etiology of depression—both as a provoking and predisposing factor. But this, and similar research in New Haven by Eugene Paykel and his colleagues, is quite recent and there will naturally be skepticism. In any case, no profession is likely to be pleased to see its problems explained in everyday terms. And the notion of environmental stress does have an uncomfortably obvious ring about it. But there is some solace. These obvious notions have not proved easy to unravel and already appear to be complex enough for psychiatry to feel some shelter in the intricacies.

The program of research has been carried out at the Social Research Unit at Bedford College of the University of London, although we have always collaborated with psychiatric colleagues at the Institute of Psychiatry. My colleagues and I started the research in 1968 and are at present devoting several years to the development of a new set of family measures to pursue some of the results outlined here. The work has concentrated on the role of the current environment in the etiology of clinical depression in women between 18 and 65—although some men have been seen and we have also devoted some attention to the issue of the course taken by the disorder. We have looked at two series of women living in Camberwell, an inner borough in South London. First, 114 women treated by psychiatrists either as inpatients or outpatients for depression and second, those found to be depressed among a random sample of 458 women. In planning the research we were influenced by earlier work in Camberwell on the role of life events and family relationships on the course of schizophrenic disorders (e.g., Brown & Birley, 1968; Brown, Birley, & Wing, 1972).[2]

METHODOLOGICAL CONSIDERATIONS

Where direct observation is possible, no one doubts that it is the social investigator who should undertake the job of measurement. But often, he cannot observe—he cannot be present when a wife learns of her husband's infidelity; he can only ask about what happened. Under these circumstances there is a common and curiously illogical belief that the respondent should take over the main task of measurement by the use of some form of "standard questionnaire." The Midtown Manhattan study of psychiatric disorder followed the pattern of large-scale social surveys by asking "When

[2] The first stage of the research was carried out in 1968–1972 and has been published in a series of papers (Brown, Sklair, Harris, & Birley, 1973a; Brown, Harris, & Peto, 1973b; Brown, 1974; Brown, Ní Bhrolcháin, & Harris, 1975). A further stage involving a second community survey was completed in 1975 (Brown, Harris, & Copeland, 1977). The present chapter summarizes the main findings of both stages. A full account is published in Brown and Harris (1978).

you were a teenager, did you have disagreements with your parents—
—often, occasionally, rarely, never?" This kind of "test" question has come,
for many in the social sciences and psychiatry, to be equated with sound
measurement. Somehow, the fact that everyone is asked the same thing in
the same way will rule out dangerous "subjectivism." For the most part, this
approach has not worked. Standard questions do not provide standard
stimuli: The meaning of a question depends on its significance for the
individual respondent and this in turn depends on a host of contingent
factors, such as the individual's biography and what has already been said in
the interview. There is also a good deal of evidence now that such
"standard" questions do not provide accurate data—at least when dealing
with material of any complexity or emotional significance (e.g., Brown &
Rutter, 1966; Edmonds, 1967; Rutter & Brown, 1966; Yarrow, Campbell, &
Burton, 1968). Moreover, they are usually open to serious methodological
criticism. The association of past "stresses" with psychiatric disorder in the
Midtown Manhattan study cannot provide convincing evidence of a causal
link. It is obviously possible that someone who is psychiatrically ill will report
his past in a more unfortunate light just because he is disturbed. This
possible contamination comes, I believe, largely because the job of deciding
whether "disagreements" had occurred was left entirely to the respondent.
Similarly, the Holmes-Rahe Schedule of Recent Experiences (SRE) asks in
a standard way whether "events" such as "change in health of family
member" have occurred (Holmes & Rahe, 1967). Their description is so
brief and ambiguous that it is highly likely that the disorder itself (or some
long-term "personality" factor related to it) will influence replies.

The significance of an event for a person can never be said to be entirely
settled: It is always open to reinterpretation. Someone whose wife has
developed a major depressive illness may exaggerate the degree to which she
had been upset by a recent illness of her sister as a means of making some
sense of her depression. Such "effort after meaning" is particularly likely
about the time of major crises. Because the SRE leaves it open to the
respondent to decide *what* is worth reporting (should a hernia operation be
included as a "change of health"?) and *who* should be covered (is a mother-
in-law a "family member"?), there can be no control over this; and it is just
one of a number of sources of bias that are possible, even within a longitudinal design (Brown, 1974).

There are therefore two tasks: (*a*) to increase accuracy and (*b*) to control
sources of bias that can vitiate all hope of causal enquiry. For both reasons
we chose to keep the task of measurement firmly in the hands of the
investigator-interviewer, using a flexible method of interviewing and rating
scales to deal with the resulting material that might occur at any point in a
lengthy interview. The approach was also systematic. Like other instruments measuring life events, we asked whether various incidents had occurred by going through a standard list of possible events. (In our case we

covered the year before interview.) In this list, we attempted to include incidents that were likely to be at all emotionally arousing, including events such as changing jobs, moving house, and getting married (where feelings might well be largely pleasant). If, at any point in going through this list, the interviewers believed there was any hint that the event had occurred, they went on to establish this by further questioning. They then collected a good deal of information about it, including the date it occurred. This material was used to complete some 30 rating scales about each event. The scales covered past experience of the event (or ones like it), immediate reaction, its implications, and anything in a person's past and present that might be relevant to his reaction to it. However, it was quite insufficient for the respondent to mention an incident in our list. Before the main study began we defined, in considerable detail, just what events should be included. Although we asked about accidents to children, a positive answer was not enough for the incident's inclusion as an event. Every event had to meet certain minimal criteria—that, for instance, the child received emergency treatment after the incident. Once an event met these criteria it was included, whatever the respondent (or interviewer) felt about it. We ignored what the respondent said the event meant for him.

Our purpose in drawing up these definitions was to take out of the hands of both interviewer and respondent what should be included as an event; although, as I have emphasized, the interviewer had complete responsibility (after a lengthy training period) to obtain the information on which the decision about inclusion could be made. In his interviewing he had to be thoroughly conversant with the information required for a decision. This procedure allowed us to rule out many methodological objections (e.g., the respondent had exaggerated the distress caused by an event). But it left us dissatisfied.

Although the approach had been successfully used in our earlier work on schizophrenia, it depended on treating all events as alike. This was not a position on which we felt we could base a research program on depression. We needed to deal with the fact that apparently similar events have a variety of meanings and not lose our methodological gains. We did this by adding a second stage to our measurement procedure. We reasoned that meanings need not be seen as irrevocably linked to a respondent's account of her feelings—how a woman *said* she felt about a particular event. Clearly we would like to have used this information but, as it might bring bias, we had to seek another way of introducing meaning into our measures.

We argued that, if we could find out about a person's plans or goals relevant to the event, we could make a reasonable estimate of its meaning without taking into account how she felt about it. We further argued that we could make an accurate enough assessment of such plans and goals by finding out about past behavior and current circumstances. Once we knew that the mother always made sure her son had a hot meal before she went out in the evening, that she set his alarm clock every evening, that she had no other children or any other relatives or friends she could confide in—in short that her life revolved around him—we could make what, on common sense grounds, would be regarded as a reasonable guess that she would be very threatened by his departure for Canada. And such a guess, as it would not be based on the woman's own report of her feelings, would avoid the kind of bias that vitiates the hope of etiologic research. In this procedure we used ourselves to assess what Schutz has called "typical patterns of actor's motives and ends [Schutz, 1962]." The investigator's judgment was crucial: In reacting to a good deal of biographical material, he judged what most women would have felt if they had had the same event in similar circumstances.

To summarize: To put these ideas into practice, we asked each respondent whether they had been involved in specific events within a specific time period; and if so, who was involved, whether they'd had any previous experience of the same or similar events, their day-to-day routines and how they had changed, etc. We encouraged women to talk at length in their own terms. But although this usually gave us information about whether or not they had experienced an event and what their circumstances were at the time, we were not of course out of trouble. The fact that women still reported on the significance of the event to them could mean that our attempts to establish a causal link between the event itself and a subsequent depressive disorder could have been contaminated by the post hoc meaning she attached to it in the light of her subsequent depression. One patient, for example, said she had been terribly upset when she saw her new baby because it reminded her of a baby she had intended to adopt but who had been taken away from her. She might, for instance, have only had this thought after she had become depressed and given it some post hoc significance, or on the other hand, she might only have had such a thought because she was depressed.

I believe we largely overcame these difficulties (and also other problems not dealt with here) by the use of a rather simple procedure based on the argument I have just outlined. After the interview had been done, taking into account past and present circumstances, other members of the research team made a judgment about the degree of threat of each event on a 4-point scale running from "severe" to "none." However, in making this assessment of threat for the woman's future, the raters were given no information at all about what the women said themselves about the severity of the threat—that is, her feelings about the event. We believe this device largely overcame the problem of reworking of meaning by ignoring what the women had said they felt. For example, we rated the birth I have mentioned low on threat; there was no obvious reason why the woman should have found it particularly threatening in terms of the future as it had been planned, she had a reasonably successful marriage, etc. We rated the event of the birth by how we thought most women would have felt, given a particular set of biographic circumstances and the plans implicit in them. We relied on the investigator's judgment about meaning, but now only after taking into consideration a good deal of the idiosyncrasy of each woman's life. We dealt with personal meaning in a contextual sense and then translated it into our own terms.

We made two of these *contextual threat* ratings according to the time perspective involved. The consequences of events, such as unexpectedly witnessing a stranger being killed by a car, are likely to be largely resolved within a week. Others, such as discovering that one's husband is planning to leave home to live with another woman, have much longer implications. We rated *short-term* threat in terms of the threat implied on the day the event occurred and *long-term* threat in terms of the threat implied one week after its occurrence. This, as will be seen, turned out to be a critical distinction.

The interviewers had three aids in rating the contextual scales:

1. There was a series of anchoring examples to illustrate the 4 points on each scale.

2. Although ratings were made independently, they were followed by a discussion about any discrepancies, and a final rating was agreed upon. Inter-rater agreement was high, and these discussions undoubtedly helped to establish and maintain this.

3. Fairly standard ratings were applied to events such as death and childbirth. These were not subtle, and we usually required quite major reasons to change a standard rating. For example, we had a convention that childbirths were not rated high on long-term threat unless they occurred in markedly overcrowded or otherwise poor housing, or in an obviously difficult social situation (for instance, to a woman who had recently separated from her husband or was unmarried). All deaths of close relatives were rated on the highest scale point (except for one mother who was 80, lived in South America, and had not been seen for 20 years).

LIFE-EVENTS AND ONSET OF DEPRESSION

The women in our study lived in Camberwell in South London. The 114 receiving psychiatric care as inpatients and outpatients had all been given a diagnosis of primary depression (and this was confirmed by a research psychiatrist). The 458 selected at random from the Camberwell population were given the same interview as the patients. This included a clinical type interview using the Present State Examination (PSE) developed at the Institute of Psychiatry (Wing, Cooper, & Sartorius, 1974). We also developed a reliable means of recording the onset of psychiatric disorder in the year before interview (Brown, Sklair, Harris, & Birley, 1973a). The PSE is based on a lengthy list of questions about symptoms, but allows for such further questioning as the interviewer thinks is necessary. For women in the general community, we made a further overall rating about the presence of psychiatric disorder. Seventy-six of the 458 women were judged to have suffered from a definite psychiatric disorder (17%) in the year and were termed *cases*.[3] Thirty-seven (8%) were *recent cases* who had had an onset in the year before the interview and 39 (9%) were *chronic cases* who had been disturbed continuously for over a year.

All 76 cases were suffering from an affective disorder of some kind, most with predominantly depressive features. They were not defined by depressed mood alone, however severe. All 76 women reported *clusters* of symptoms such as loss of weight, lack of energy, various features of sleep disturbance, and heightened anxiety. The rating of *caseness* is therefore a clinical one: However, our general definition is that the women should be broadly comparable to women seen for affective disorder in outpatient clinics and, if they appeared in one, they would be readily accepted as in need of treatment. A further 87 women (19%) were rated as *borderline cases*: Although they had definite psychiatric symptoms, they were not considered severe enough to be rated as cases. They were of a severity that would be expected to be seen in a psychiatric clinic only rarely, although such women are often treated by general practitioners.

There is evidently an arbitrary element in choosing a cut-off point between borderline and case. The important point is that the criteria, despite its arbitrariness, could be applied consistently and reliably. Descriptions of caseness and borderline caseness were drawn up and used as anchoring examples.[4] In general I will refer to noncases as *normals*—that is, the term normal will usually include borderline conditions as well as those considered relatively asymptomatic.

The occurrence of depressive conditions is highly related to the presence of what we have called *severe* life events in the histories of patients and recent cases in the general population before the onset of illness. Because of the methodological safeguards outlined earlier, I believe that a reasonable case can be made for the causal role that these severe events play in the onset of depression. The events were rated "marked" and "moderate" threat on the *long-term* contextual threat scale as long as they were also focused on the woman herself.[5] A quarter of the total 458 women in the community

[3] In other publications, we have referred to disorder occurring in the 3 months before interview: 15% of the women were cases within this period.

[4] Psychiatrists from the Institute of Psychiatry visited most of the women that the nonmedical interviewers had considered to be cases or borderline cases and also a random subsample of the remaining women. Of the women rated as a case or borderline case by either nonmedical or medical interviewers, there was an 84% agreement about who was a case and who was a borderline case. Agreement about who was normal was even higher. In a recent larger study agreement was only a little lower (Cooper *et al.*, 1977; Wing *et al.*, 1977). Some of the disagreement in both studies could clearly be attributable to *real* changes in the condition between the dates of the two interviews.

[5] An illustration may make the rating of "focus" clear. Take the example of a car accident,

sample had at least one such severe event in the 9 months before interview, compared with 61% of the patients in a comparable period before onset of their depressive disorder.[6] Some of these severe events would be expected to occur by chance before the onset of depression. Applying a correction formula which allows for this, the proportion (x) of patients with a severe event of causal importance is 49%. Using the same correction, 53% of the recent cases in the general community had a severe event of causal significance.[7] The distinctive feature of the great majority of severe events is the experience of actual or threatened major loss. We defined loss broadly to include threat of, or actual, separation from a key figure (e.g., separation from husband), an unpleasant revelation about someone close forcing a major reassessment of the relationship, a life-threatening illness to someone close, a major material loss or disappointment or threat of it, and, finally, miscellaneous crises involving events such as redundancy after a long period of steady employment. Most of the events involved actual, rather than threat of, loss.

It is *only* these long-term threatening events that play a role in depression for either patients or recent cases. *Severe, short-term threatening events play no role whatsoever in the onset of depression* once the occurrence of severe long-term threat has been allowed for. This, of course, is just what would be expected if loss was an important element in depression. It is important to note that severe short-term threat (without long-term threat) could be extremely upsetting and involve major changes in routine and way of life. However, this does not appear enough to produce depression. This is confirmed by the fact that none of the other scales we used to describe events was related to the onset of depression once severe long-term threat had been taken into account.

THE SIGNIFICANCE OF THE CAUSAL
LINK WITH EVENTS—
THE BROUGHT-FORWARD TIME

In 1970 investigators in St. Louis criticized the evidence for a causal link between life events and depression on the grounds that they obtained a low

---

the event would be rated as subject-focused if the respondent was in the accident, either alone or with another person; it would not be rated as subject-focused if, for example, the respondent's husband was involved but she herself was not.

[6] The 9 months for patients was an average figure. Because the time between the onset of the depression and first outpatient attendance or admission varied between patients, the length of time between the beginning of the year and onset (i.e., the time to be covered for events of possible causal importance).also varied.

[7] The formula is $x = (h - p)/(1 - p)$ where h is the proportion of patients with at least one event in the period and p is the proportion of the total general population sample having an event in the same period. See Brown, Harris, and Peto (1973b) for a full account. Note, for the recent cases, p is still based on the total population of 458 women.

level of agreement between the patients and the people who knew them well about what event had occurred (Hudgens, Robins, & Delong, 1970). Their failure, however, was almost certainly due to poor measurement (Brown, 1972; Brown *et al.*, 1973a). In our study, a patient and a relative were seen by separate interviewers about events occurring in a 12-month period. When specific events are considered, there was a 79% agreement between patient and relative about an event reported by either and a 92% agreement about the occurrence of a severe event. This level of agreement is simply a matter of suitable intensive interviewing and sensitive criteria of what incidents should count as events. More fundamental criticism relates to sources of bias. I have discussed some of the ways we have attempted to meet these, and the reader must judge how far we have managed to do this in the light of fuller accounts of what we have done.

A third criticism accepts that there is a causal link between events and onset but dismisses it as of little significance. An event may act by merely *triggering* a depressive disorder that was about to occur in any case. In this view it would, at most, bring forward the onset of illness by a short period of time. Predispositional (probably nonsocial) factors are emphasized and the influence of events played down. An alternative view is that events are of *formative* importance and that the depression would not have occurred at all, or for a long period of time, without the event. Onset is either substantially advanced in time, or brought about altogether by the event. We have argued that it is possible to chose between these views by using the data we collected. However, as the argument is quite complicated and has already been published in full, I will give only a brief summary (Brown, Harris & Peto, 1973b).

We assume that individuals are potentially "depressive" (or "schizophrenic," etc.) for genetic, constitutional, or other reasons and that the onset of psychiatric disorder can occur because of these or current environmental factors in varying degrees—we accept, in other words, a multifactorial view of etiology and do not see the influences as at all incompatible. We refer to any onset not brought about by an observed event in the previous 9 months as "spontaneous," even though the onset might be due to an unobserved event or social factors (e.g., long-term difficulties, loneliness, and the like). The model we have developed views each person as having an overall onset rate for a particular psychiatric condition. *Onset rate* refers to the probability of onset occurrence in a short period of time. We see the overall onset rate as having two components: one stemming from the influence of particular life events and the other, from a spontaneous process.

Thus, a person might have a chance of developing a disorder in adolescence, this chance increases slightly as he grows older but is much increased after his mother's death when he is 30. We assume that after such an event there is a definite probability it will cause an onset of illness—although the onset itself may not follow for months or even years. For any one person we cannot establish whether an onset was "provoked" or "spontaneous," as we have no idea of the spontaneous rate for any one individual; but it is relatively simple to calculate for a group of patients the proportion of onsets that were provoked. I have already referred to this as x, which takes account of the chance juxtaposition of event and onset.

We believe it follows that in the study of life events we must estimate both: (a) the proportion of onsets that have been brought about by events— this is really what I have been dealing with until now, and (b) the average time after such a provoked onset when a spontaneous onset would have occurred had onset not been provoked by the event. This second estimate, the time from provoked to spontaneous onset is what we call the *brought-forward time*.

The brought-forward time is a minimal estimate of the average length of time between onset provoked by an event and spontaneous onset had no event occurred. We call this the brought-forward time because we believe that it gives an estimate of the average amount of time by which events have brought forward the onset of illness. Its length is greater the rarer the event is in the general population and the greater the proportion of patients with an event. The length of the brought-forward time allows us to choose between two rival causal hypotheses—and it was for this that it was designed. If it is long, for example, a year, we believe that a triggering effect is untenable. It is incompatible with our definition of such an effect as bringing about an illness that probably would have occurred before long anyway. Therefore, if the time given is implausibly long, a formative effect is indicated. I want again to emphasize that the time is likely to be a very conservative one; we have chosen to base our calculations on various conservative assumptions as this allows us to be confident about any claims we make for the existence of a formative effect.

I will not attempt to summarize the argument justifying the calculation of the brought-forward time itself. The time for patients is 1.95 years and for recent cases 2.18 years; therefore, a formative effect is clearly indicated for both groups of depressed women. As the estimates are extremely conservative, it follows that those with a severe event of causal significance would not have developed depression for a lengthy period of time, if at all, without the event.[8]

DIFFICULTIES

Most life-event measures have included some persistent difficulties in their list of "events" (e.g., "major financial difficulties" in Paykel, 1974; p.

---

[8] The brought-forward time for schizophrenic patients with a life event before the onset of illness is, on average, 10 weeks and no more than a triggering effect can therefore be claimed for such patients.

139). Instead of muddling them with events in this way, we developed a separate measure aimed to cover most difficulties. We followed as closely as possible the same procedure used for events. We had, however, to rely on a number of general questions about what women had found difficult in particular areas such as housing and employment, as well as more specific questions about particular difficulties. We did this as we found that we could not develop, in the same way as we had for events, an exhaustive list of questions about possible specific difficulties that did not become impossibly cumbersome. We rated each difficulty on a 6-point scale of severity using a scale similar to that used to rate the contextual threat of events. Each woman in Camberwell had an average of four difficulties—most were comparatively minor. Comparing patients and onset cases with normal women, we found that only about 10% of the difficulties were of a type that were capable of playing an etiologic role (i.e., had a raised rate before onset). These were difficulties rated on the top 3 points of contextual severity, that had lasted at least 2 years and did *not* involve health. We call these *major* difficulties. We found little to suggest that other types of difficulty played a causal role among the patients, although for recent cases there was some suggestion that major difficulties lasting from 1 to 2 years might play a causal role. However, I have included only difficulties lasting 2 years or more in the present analysis.

The issue of validity is somewhat more complex than with events, as women were directly asked about the difficulties they had. However, we found no serious evidence of bias. If patients and cases were "over-reporting" their difficulties it would be reasonable to assume they would also report more health difficulties and more difficulties of lesser severity. As neither of these was more common among patients and recent cases than normal women, a general tendency to over-report because of depression seems unlikely. If the presence of a causal link is accepted as likely, the results for difficulties can be added to those for events. Using the same formula to obtain a corrected proportion for *either* a severe event or major difficulty of causal importance (x), 61% is obtained for patients and 83% for recent cases (see Tables 12.1 and 12.2). Major difficulties therefore, although of lesser importance than events, do appear to play an etiologic role along with events in both groups of depressed women.

VULNERABILITY AND SOCIAL CLASS

I want now to deal with the role of social class in the etiology and course of depressive disorder. As we have evidence that, in Camberwell at least, class is related to who received psychiatric care the matter can only unequivocally be studied in our random sample of 458 women from Camberwell.

The two most important background variables relating to the rate of

Table 12.1

PROPORTION WITH AT LEAST ONE
SEVERELY THREATENING EVENT OR AT
LEAST ONE MAJOR DIFFICULTY IN THE
PERIOD BEFORE ONSET FOR PATIENTS
AND RECENT CASES VERSUS "NORMAL"
AND "BORDERLINE" WOMEN[a]

	Patients (N = 114) (%)	Recent cases (N = 37) (%)	"Normal" and "borderline" women (N = 382) (%)
Severe event alone	30	41	13
Severe event and major difficulty	32	24	6
Major difficulty	14	24	11
Total	76	89	30
No severe event or major difficulty	25	11	70

[a] The period before onset was, on average, 38 weeks for patients and recent cases: A comparison of 38 weeks before interview was therefore taken for "normal" women. Chronic cases were excluded: 20 of the 39 had a severe event or major difficulty.

psychiatric disturbance (i.e., caseness) are social class and whether or not women have a child living at home. In the 3 months before interview 23% (55 of 240) of working-class and 6% (14 of 218) of middle-class women were recent or chronic cases.[9] Working-class women with a child under 6 at home were particularly likely to be depressed. The obvious explanation of this large class difference in the rate of depression is that more working-class women experience severe events and major difficulties; factors we have shown to be capable of provoking clinical depression. Working-class women do in fact have more, particularly when they have children. (They have over half again as many as middle-class women.) But the question remains: Can differences in the rate of severe events and major difficulties explain the differential rates of psychiatric disorder *between* the social classes? The

[9] Our measure of social class was based largely on the occupational head of the household—in most instances the husband. We have used Goldthorpe and Hope's recent development of the RGO occupational classification: Their occupational groups 1–22 have been called "middle class" and 23–35 "working class" (Goldthorpe & Hope, 1974, pp. 134–143). When related to the prevalence of psychiatric disorder among women, this scale gives almost identical results to the more complex measure of social class used in previous analyses (Brown et al., 1975).

Table 12.2

CORRECTED VALUE (X) FOR THE PROPORTION
INVOLVED IN THE CAUSAL EFFECT[a]

	Patients (%)	Recent cases (%)
Based on severe events alone	49	53
Based on severe events and major difficulties	61	83

[a] See Brown et al., 1973b, p. 162 for account of the X correction.

answer is *no*. Table 12.3 shows that working-class women with children who lived in Camberwell still had a much greater chance of developing psychiatric disorder when only those with a severe event and major difficulty are considered. In fact, standardization for the proportions having a severe event or major difficulty only reduces the working–middle class ratio in disturbance rate by one-fourth. The table shows incidentally that the presence of an event or difficulty raises the risk of developing psychiatric disorder by a factor of 10. At this stage of our analysis we were reasonably convinced that our data was unlikely to reveal further factors capable of producing psychiatric disorder. We therefore reasoned that there were likely to be factors that, in themselves, were not capable of producing depression, but in the presence of a severe event or major difficulty, greatly increased the risk of developing a psychiatric disorder.

As sociologists, the obvious place to start to look for such *vulnerability*

Table 12.3

PERCENTAGE OF WOMEN DEVELOPING A
PSYCHIATRIC DISORDER BY SOCIAL CLASS
AND WHETHER PRECEDED BY A SEVERE
EVENT OR MAJOR DIFFICULTY (CHRONIC
CASES EXCLUDED)

	Severe event or major difficulty in year	No severe event or major difficulty in year
Women with children		
Working-class	31% (21/67)	1% (1/68)
Middle-class	8% (3/36)	1% (1/80)
Total	23% (24/103)	1% (2/148)
All women		
Working-class	25% (24/97)	2% (2/112)
Middle-class	13% (9/67)	1% (2/143)
Total	20% (33/164)	2% (4/255)

factors was in the support received from social relationships. For this, we developed a measure of the closeness and intimacy of a woman's contacts with other adults, taking into account the frequency and quality of personal contacts in general. Although we developed the measure during the analysis, all its components had been collected systematically at the time of interview. Each respondent was asked to name people to whom she could talk about things that were troubling her, and we call the persons mentioned, if any, *confidants*. The scale is a 4-point one: The high point *a* is used only for women considered to have a close, intimate, and confiding relationship with their husband, boyfriend, or in exceptional cases, a woman with whom they live. A relationship with a husband or boyfriend was rated *a* if the respondent mentioned him as a confidant, provided that there was nothing in the overall account based on evidence from the whole interview that contradicted this answer. We also occasionally placed in an *a* relationship a husband who had not been named as a confidant in this way but where the overall account made it clear he was treated as such.[10]

There is, of course, the possibility that women who were psychiatrically disturbed might give a more jaundiced view of their close ties. In this respect we can only state that a "non-*a*" rating was given to such women only when there was convincing evidence that the lack of closeness had clearly antedated the onset of the disorder. (In a third of the women rated "non-*a*" the problem did not arise as they had no husband or boyfriend.) The second point (*b*) was kept for women without such an intimate tie (in practice almost always with a husband or boyfriend) but who nevertheless had a confiding relationship with someone else (e.g., mother, sister, or friend whom they saw at least weekly). The third point (*c*) covered all women having a confidant who was seen less than once a week and the final point (*d*) encompassed those women who mentioned no confidant at all.

Intimacy acts as a powerful mediator between a severe event or major difficulty and the onset of depression. In the community, Table 12.4 shows that of the women with an event or a difficulty only 1 in 10 with an *a* relationship developed a psychiatric illness in the year in comparison with 1 in 3 of those with a "non-*a*" relationship. The table also suggests that having a *b* relationship does offer some degree of protection compared with those having a *c* or *d* rating. (In our first Camberwell survey we were only able to show that an *a* relationship was protective.) Table 12.4 also makes the

[10] We tended, if anything, to place women in an *a* relationship on too little evidence. The reported level of general discussion between husband and wife often appeared sparse but, in the absence of a specific report that either held things back from the other, we rated the marriage as *a* as long as the husband had been mentioned as a confidant. In some cases we felt that we were only able to do this because the relationship had not been tested by a recent crisis. However, this doubt was not really important. It is precisely for women with a severe event or major difficulty that we wished to know whether an intimate relationship was protective.

Table 12.4

PERCENTAGE OF WOMEN EXPERIENCING
ONSET OF ILLNESS IN YEAR BY WHETHER
THEY HAD A SEVERE EVENT OR MAJOR
DIFFICULTY AND BY INTIMACY CONTEXT
(CHRONIC CASES EXCLUDED)

	a (high)	b	c or d (low)
Severe event or major difficulty	10% (9/88)	26% (12/47)	41% (12/29)
No severe event or major difficulty	1% (2/193)	3% (1/39)	4% (1/23)

important point that the *lack* of an intimate tie *without* an event or a difficulty does not in itself provoke the onset of illness.

The intimacy context forms part of the explanation of the higher rate of vulnerability to events and difficulties of working-class women relative to their middle-class counterparts. One in 3 of the working-class women have a "non-*a*" relationship, compared with 1 in 4 of middle-class women; and this difference is greatest among women with young children. Working-class women, therefore, are particularly at risk because they have a greater chance of experiencing a severe event or major difficulty at the same time as having a "non-*a*" relationship.

Our measure of intimacy is obviously open to bias (although we have some arguments in its favor—see Brown, Ní Bhrolcháin, & Harris, 1975:p236). Therefore, it is important that we found three "hard" measures that acted as vulnerability factors in the presence of severe events or major difficulties: the loss of a mother before age 11, having three or more children at home who are 14-years old or less, and lack of full- or part-time employment. As with low intimacy they do not raise chance of onset in the absence of an event or difficulty. An index formed by these three items gives a similar result to that of intimacy.

Because their association with depression is far less likely to be due to biased reporting, they greatly support the general case for the presence of social vulnerability factors and make the particular case for the role of intimacy more plausible. When the four factors are considered as a whole, working-class women are much more likely to have more than one of them and, in statistical terms at least, this explains the entire class difference in the risk of developing depression that is not accounted for by the greater frequency of severe events and major difficulties among working-class women.

Although vulnerability factors appear to play an etiologic role among the patients, the differences are less striking. In order to account for this, we have suggested that vulnerability factors act in *two* ways. They increase the chances of developing depression, but once onset has occurred they *reduce* chances of contacting a psychiatrist (Brown, Ní Bhrolcháin, & Harris, 1975). For instance, a woman with young children, once she has developed depression, is less likely to see a psychiatrist—perhaps because she has less time and opportunity to go through the various stages involved in reaching a psychiatric outpatient clinic. A woman having an intimate tie with a husband is less likely to develop depression, but, if she does, he is more likely to encourage her to seek help. However, evidence of such a two-way effect is indirect and speculative and it is bound to be a more complex process than these illustrations suggest. A hint of the complexity is suggested, for instance, by the fact that there was no class difference in the rate of depression among our patients.

SYMPTOM FORMATION FACTORS

I have presented, so far, a two-factor causal model of depression: I will now deal with the issue of early loss, particularly in childhood and adolescence, and in doing so add a third, symptom-formation factor, to the model (Brown *et al.*, 1977 gives full details).

There has been a curious failure to establish that loss of a parent in childhood or adolescence plays *any* etiologic role in depression, despite a widespread conviction to the contrary. Empirical findings have been inconsistent and frequently negative, and Granville-Grossman's conclusion in 1968 that there is no unambiguous evidence on the etiologic role of early environment in depression was clearly correct. And yet, as already mentioned, we found the early loss of a mother (i.e., before age 11) did increase the risk of depression among women in Camberwell. Among the 458 women, 22% of the *cases* had lost a mother before age 11, in comparison with 6% of *normal* women ($p < .01$). We considered loss by death , separation of parents, or any separation from either of more than a year's duration. Loss of mother *after* age 11 and loss of father were *not* related to an increased risk of depression. I have already discussed the role of loss of mother before age 11 as a vulnerability factor and this is shown in Table 12.5. The early loss of a mother only leads to the onset of depression in the presence of a severe event or major difficulty: None of the women with an early loss, but without an event or difficulty became cases in the year (Table 12.5). Table 12.5 also shows that, once the loss of a mother is allowed for, the early loss of a father does not increase the risk of developing depression.

However, for depressed *patients* there is no greater rate of loss of either parent when compared with the total Camberwell population. Although this is just the comparison made by previous studies, it is, of course, important to

Table 12.5

PERCENTAGE OF WOMEN SUFFERING AN ONSET OF
PSYCHIATRIC DISORDER BY WHETHER THEY HAD A SEVERE
EVENT OR MAJOR DIFFICULTY AND BY THE PRESENCE OF LOSS
OF MOTHER OR LOSS OF FATHER BEFORE AGE 11 (CHRONIC
CASES EXCLUDED)

	Loss of mother before age 11		Loss of father before age 11 (excluding women with a loss of mother)	
	Yes	No	Yes	No
Severe event or major difficulty	47* (7/15)	17* (26/140)	20 (3/15)	17 (23/135)
None	0 (0/15)	2 (4/240)	0 (0/17)	2 (4/222)

* $p < .01$. Other differences are not significant.

exclude depressed women from the general population group, and the
failure to do this is probably one reason for the many negative results. When
exclusion occurs, the loss of a mother before age 11 does appear of some
importance, although the difference between normal women and patients is
still much less than that between the former and recently developed cases
and does not reach statistical significance (10.5% of the patients and 6.0% of
normal women).

This apparent inconsistency between the results for recent cases and
patients is, of course, just what would be expected from the published
literature, which has been entirely based on studies of depressed *patients*.
We believe the difference is most likely to be due to the possibility I
discussed earlier—that the vulnerability factors influence selection into
psychiatric treatment. In this instance the loss of a mother before age 11 not
only increases the chances of developing psychiatric disorder, but is also
correlated with other factors that tend to *lower* the chances of contacting a
psychiatrist. Therefore, patients would be expected to have a somewhat
lower proportion with early loss of a mother than cases in the general
community (Brown *et al.*, 1975, p. 239). For example, the correlation
between the loss of a mother before age 11 and a lack of an intimate
relationship with a husband or boyfriend was .60 (gamma).

So far I have dealt with the loss of parents before age 11; we also looked at
the loss of a sibling before age 17, loss of a child at any age through death
(including stillborn) and adoption, and loss of a husband by death. We bore
in mind the need to exclude *past losses* that might have been brought about
by an earlier psychiatric episode, and a woman's loss of a husband by
separation or divorce was therefore excluded. In order to avoid contamination with the onset of the recent disorder, any loss within 2 years of the date

of the interview was also ignored. In almost all instances the past loss apparently preceded the first onset of depression.

In our random sample of women in Camberwell 37% had at least one such past loss. In general such a past loss plays, at most, a small role in the etiology of depression once the loss of a mother before age 11 is allowed for. (Table 12.5 on loss of father illustrates the kind of analysis on which this conclusion is based.[11]) However, the existence of such a past loss has an effect on *symptom formation*, although (except for the loss of a mother before age 11) it does *not* increase the risk of developing depression.

We divided our patients into "psychotic" or "neurotic" groups on the basis of the clinical material, taking into account criteria such as the presence of early morning waking, which have fairly general acceptance in the literature as distinguishing features of the two forms of depression. Sixty-three patients were considered psychotic, and 49 neurotic (2 with some manic symptoms were excluded). We next took all the *clinical* material, excluding such factors as age and history of prior treatment, and by using a discriminant function analysis obtained the weighted clinical items that best separated the two groups classified as psychotic and neurotic. Using these scales, we divided patients for certain purposes into the "most" psychotic and "least" psychotic.

There has been an increasing tendency to equate the concepts of *neurotic* and *reactive* depression on the assumption that they are far more highly related to environmental stress than *psychotic* or *endogenous* depression (Beck, 1967, p. 79). Systematic research has given no support to this view (Paykel, 1974; Leff *et al.*, 1970). Our own material confirms this lack of association: Almost equal proportions of the patients considered to be psychotic and neurotic had a provoking life event in the 9 months before onset. Nor were the two types of depression related to the presence of the four vulnerability factors.[12]

The two forms of depression were, however, highly related to *past loss*. Psychotic patients were more likely to have had such losses than neurotic patients (66% as opposed to 39%). Furthermore, if the psychotic patients are divided into a "most psychotic" and a "least psychotic" half (on the basis of the scores derived from the discriminant function analysis), this association is increased (e.g., 77%, 55%, and 39%, respectively, of the three groups had a past loss as indicated by the dotted line in Figure 12.1—$p < .01$).

These differences are increased still further if the loss due to death is distinguished from other kinds of loss (e.g., separation of parents, adoption of the woman's child). This index shows that loss *through death* and through factors *other than death* are both strongly related to the threefold clinical

---

[11] The frequency of past loss was related to social class and age and this has been allowed for in our calculations (Brown *et al.*, 1977, p 3).

[12] This material is about to be published (Brown, Ní Bhrolcháin, & Harris, 1979).

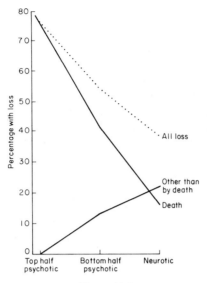

Figure 12.1.

classification but related in opposite ways: 77% of the most psychotic, 42% of the least psychotic, and 16% of the neurotic group had had a past loss through death ($p < .01$). By contrast, none of the most psychotic, 13% of the least psychotic, and 22% of the neurotic group have had a past loss other than by death ($p < .01$). In other words, although the incidence of past loss is not a very potent etiologic factor, as I have argued above, it may well be a most powerful influence on what form her symptoms will take when a woman *does* get depressed: loss by death predisposing to psychotic depression and other forms of loss to neurotic depression.

An independent check on these results was possible using patients who had been classified as psychotic and neurotic depressives in a way similar to our patients (Kendell, 1968). Using hospital notes to obtain details of past losses, very similar results were obtained (Brown *et al.*, 1977, Tab. 8). We found that a past loss also played a role in determining the severity of depression once the degree of psychotic and neurotic features was controlled (Brown *et al.*, 1977, Tab. 7 and Fig. 3). Finally, although we found as others have done that our psychotic patients were older, there is no suggestion that age affected our results (Brown *et al.*, 1977, Tab. 9).

There is, therefore, a large association between past losses and the type and severity of depressive symptoms in women. However, this only emerges when one distinguishes (*a*) the severity of the depression at admission, (*b*) the predominance of neurotic and psychotic features, (*c*) four kinds of loss (of siblings, child, and husband—not just of parents) and (*d*) whether the loss was due to death or other reasons. Although this has not been done before, a few studies have looked at the loss of a parent during childhood and adolescence and the severity of depression. As these studies ignored the other three distinctions, only a modest association between loss and severity could be expected. In general they confirm these results. Birtchnell (1970), for example, provides results for women with a loss before age 19 and there is a close similarity with our material when the same simple twofold distinction is made—38% of the most and 22% of the least depressed patients had lost a parent in childhood or adolescence compared with 37 and 23% in our series.[13] It seems unlikely than an artifact is involved: In the link between past loss and symptom formation, there is no reason to believe that there is much error in recording major losses, nor that the measurement of the variables was in some way confounded. Moreover, there is no suggestion that age, previous admissions, or social class are biasing factors and it seems unlikely that constitutional or genetic factors have produced a spurious association. We therefore find it difficult to conceive of an interpretation that does not largely depend on environmental, rather than on constitutional and genetic, factors.

SOME INTERPRETATIONS

So far I have dealt with the use of our measures to build a 3-factor etiologic model of depression using provoking agents (severe event and major difficulties), vulnerability factors (e.g., low intimacy) and symptom-formation factors (e.g., type of past loss). Only the loss of a mother before age 11 is capable of acting in more than one of these three ways, as a vulnerability factor and as a symptom-formation factor.[14]

I have not dealt with the issue of chronicity. Half the women in Camberwell with psychiatric disorder had had the symptoms for more than a year. Such chronicity is highly related to social class and a provisional case can be made for the role of social factors (Brown et al., 1975, p. 241). I have also ignored borderline conditions; 20% of the women in Camberwell suffered from these. There was some suggestion that the onset of symptoms in the borderline group was also related to severe events and difficulties. Working-class women were not more likely to have had an onset of a borderline condition, but they were much more likely to have a chronic borderline state.

---

[13] See Beck, Sethi, & Tuthill, 1963; Sethi, 1964; Munro, 1966; Abrahams & Whitlock, 1969; Wilson, Alltop, & Buffaloe, 1967; and Forrest, Fraser, & Priest, 1965. The study by Sethi (1964) includes loss of a sibling; however, the inclusion of nondepressed patients in his "no or low depression" group confuses the issue of the role of loss and symptom formation in depression.

[14] I assume that the loss of a mother before age 11 very rarely provokes clinical depression in a child (Graham, 1976). It should also be noted that an event can act both as a provoking agent and vulnerability factor when there is loss of a husband with whom there was an a relationship. This occurred only rarely in our study (Brown et al., 1975, p. 236).

Our results suggest that social factors play a powerful role in the etiology of all forms of depression (perhaps excluding the rare bipolar conditions we did not study). However, a causal model is only one part of the scientific task. We also need a theory to tell us something about what is happening. Consider employment and its protective role for women. Does this occur because work improves her economic circumstances, alleviates her boredom, keeps her occupied, brings her a greater variety of social contacts or enhances her sense of personal worth? And just why should any of these aspects play a protective role? A causal model is not enough: Theory is needed to explain what is happening. Theory, unfortunately, takes longer than a causal model to develop and to test. Any theory concerning the etiology of depression has to deal with two crucial "facts" provided by our model. First, although on the whole life-events that provoke illness mainly involve major losses (if this term is allowed a certain licence to include events such as learning of a husband's infidelity), major difficulties and threats of loss can also at times bring about a depressive disorder. Something more than loss must be involved. Second, in the absence of a vulnerability factor, such provoking agents rarely bring about depression. In other words, no matter how catastrophic a loss, depression will tend not to follow without the presence of at least one vulnerability factor.

We have speculated that low self-esteem is the common feature behind all four vulnerability factors and it is this speculation that makes sense of our results. It is not the loss itself that is important but rather the capacity of a woman to hope for better things once an event or difficulty has occurred. In response to a provoking agent relatively specific feelings of hopelessness are likely to occur: The person has usually lost an important source of value— something that may have been derived from a person, a role or an idea. If this develops into a *general* feeling of hopelessness it may form the central feature of the depressive disorder itself. For as Aaron Beck has suggested, in depression there is a central cognitive triad, accompanied by varying combinations of characteristic affective and somatic symptoms (Beck, 1967). We believe that it is crucial to determine whether the specific feelings of hopelessness develop into three feelings—that the world is meaningless, the self worthless and the future hopeless. These feelings are crucial to a person's ongoing self-esteem, their sense of their ability to control their world and thus to repair damage, and their confidence that, in the end, alternative sources of value will become available. If self-esteem is low *before* the onset of any depression, a woman is less likely to be able to imagine herself emerging from her privation. We suggest that vulnerability factors play a crucial etiologic role because they limit a woman's ability to develop an optimistic view about controlling the world in order to regain some source of value. Of course, an appraisal of hopelessness is often entirely realistic: the future for many woman *is* bleak. But given a particular event or difficulty, ongoing low self-esteem will increase the chance of such an interpretation. Therefore, loss as such is not central: Hopelessness and not grief is the crucial element. (Others have also believed that loss itself is not central—e.g., Gaylin, 1968, pp. 16–22). Major loss events are very often involved in the onset of depression as they are the most common way in which important sources of value are threatened.

I need to stress that these are as yet largely speculative ideas, although they are based on some observation. We were, for instance, particularly interested in a few of these women in our sample who took up employment a few weeks *after* the occurrence of a severe event, none of whom developed psychiatric disturbance. Their comments suggest that a sense of achieve-ment might be crucial. One working class woman who had previously not worked for 6 years, commented that "the money was not much" but that it gave her "a great boost" and "greater self-esteem." And, of course, loss of self-esteem has long been recognized as a critical component in depression itself, although the psychoanalyst Bibring (1953) seems to have been the first to argue clearly for its direct role in etiology.

Although at present we place most weight on the production of hopeless-ness, we do believe that loss, at times, can play a more direct role through a second mechanism. Adjustment to major loss is likely to involve "grief work" if the person is to come to terms with the situation (e.g., Marris, 1974). The loss of another person will often mean the loss of someone who valued and appreciated the depressed person; but loss may involve not only a lost *object* but also a lost *role* (Averill, 1968). A sense of purpose can be lost when with the loss of a person, the performance for which identity has been fabricated and sustained ceases to have meaning (Becker, 1962).

Many have pointed out the adverse consequences of failing to do such "grief work" (e.g., Bowlby, 1963; Parkes, 1964; Engel, 1967). In a recent discussion of "reactive depression," it has been suggested that many of the depressive symptoms the patient forms may be regarded as helping him *avoid* experiencing painful loss, and in particular helping to deny the fact of loss and the significance of the loss (Sachar *et al.*, 1968, pp. 24–25). Along somewhat similar lines we suggest that low self-esteem, stemming from any source, can at times hinder a woman "recognizing" a recent loss. This failure in turn can lead to the development of a depressive disorder. The loss cannot be fully faced because it is just one more painful blow to feelings of self-regard.

We have therefore speculated that the common feature of the vulnerabil-ity factors is that they are associated with low self-esteem. Because three of them concern the present (i.e., lack of intimacy with husband, three or more children under age 14 at home, and lack of employment), it follows that is the *current environment* that most powerfully influences the risk of depression. However, the effect of the loss of a mother before age 11 indicates that the past can also play a role and may well do so by lowering self-esteem. We have seen that such loss of a mother has two special features. First, the loss of any *other* close relative does not increase the risk, and second, loss *after* the age of 11 plays no role. The first feature can probably be explained by the fact that the mother will usually be the largest source of appreciation and support. A father's or sibling's disappearance is likely to be a less painful experience. Second, until a child is about 11-years old, his main means of controlling the world is likely to be his mother. The earlier she is lost, the more the child is likely to be set back in his or her learning of mastery of the environment; and a sense of mastery is probably an essential component of high self-esteem. The loss of a mother before age 11 may well permanently lower a woman's feelings of mastery and self-esteem, and hence act as a vulnerability factor by interfering with the way she deals with grief in adulthood.

One important recent account is Seligman's (1975) comparison of depression with "learned helplessness." Using animal experiments, he has shown that uncontrollable and unpredictable trauma tends to lead to a passive resignation—what he calls learned helplessness. He sees this as primarily a cognitive disposition that, once established, greatly increases the chance of an animal passively undergoing a traumatic situation (such as receiving electric shocks) rather than seeking a solution. Seligman (1975) notes about absence of mother that "stimulus deprivation, and nonresponsive mothering all contribute to the learning of uncontrollability . . . . Since helplessness in an infant, however, is the foundational motivational attitude which later motivational learning must crystallise, its debilitating consequences will be more catastrophic [pp. 150-151]."

We do not believe (as Seligman argues) that the loss of a mother before age 11 is specifically related to so-called "reactive" or "neurotic" depression. Nor do we believe that "learned helplessness" is a model for clinical depression itself. It is, we believe, akin in status to our vulnerability factors and the loss of a mother before age 11, like the other three vulnerability factors, raises the chance of developing *any* form of depression. However, as whether past loss occurs by death or other means also influences the *form and severity* of the depression, the loss of a mother before age 11 plays a double role: as a vulnerability factor and as a symptom-formation factor. Other types of past loss influence only symptom formation.

The results concerning past loss and symptom formation suggest some form of enduring cognitive influence. It is possible that loss by death may be related to psychotic-like symptoms because it tends to lead to a very general attitude that one's own efforts are useless; that loss of any kind becomes like death, irreversible and there is nothing that can be done. Such an attitude may be particularly linked to the denial of the implications of a loss and to greater "bodily" expression of symptoms. A person who has lost a parent through separation and knows they are still alive will be likely to feel the situation less irredeemable. It is not as if an outside fate had removed them. This may give them a less passive cognitive set than a person whose parent has died (Brown *et al.*, 1977, pp. 15–16).

About three-fourths of the recent provoking events among the patients involved a clear-cut loss: Psychotic patients were no more or less likely to have had such a clear-cut loss than neurotic patients. (And if age is allowed for, they were only a little more likely to have a loss by death.) Moreover, a woman who had had a recent loss by death was no more likely to have had a past loss brought about by death. The lack of an association between the types of past and recent loss is just what would be expected if cognitive schemes influence reactions to a severely threatening event. For a woman who has earlier lost an important person by death, the emigration of her child may be seen to have deathlike qualities.

Figure 12.2 summarizes our model and theoretical interpretations. A good deal more research is required to check on our model, test some of the implications of our theory and to see how far either can be generalized to other communities.

However, our results suggest that by conceptualizing recent and past loss in different ways and paying attention to methodological issues, a plausible case can be made for their vital role both in bringing about depression and in determining its severity and form. To this must be added the role of long-term difficulties and vulnerability factors. The implication of the three-factor model for current psychiatric views of depression need not be stressed. The general survey of women in Camberwell has wider implications. It suggests, with a number of other recent studies, that all is not well with women in our cities (for London see Richman, 1974; Rutter & Quinton, 1977; Rutter, Yule, Quinton, Rowlands, Yule, & Berger, 1975). We also begin to spell out in intensive studies some of the underlying structural problems women face in our society, problems that may well be at the root

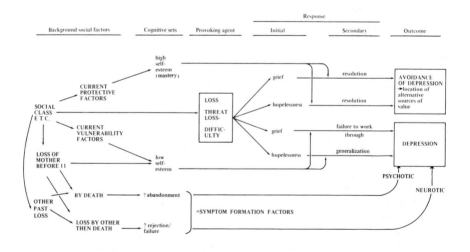

Figure 12.2.

of a good deal of the psychiatric disorder seen in general practice and outpatient clinics (for London see Oakley, 1974; Ginsberg, 1976).

Psychiatry is not in a position to deal directly with the great number of women involved; and it is difficult to believe that primary care, at least as presently organized in either England or the United States, can deal adequately with the problem. Without more knowledge it is futile to suggest specific solutions: But it is clear that we cannot rule out the need for a broader, partly preventive approach that is best implemented *outside* the medical sphere.

ACKNOWLEDGMENTS

The research I have reported has been the work of a team. Tirril Harris has been closely involved with most stages of the work, Freda Sklair made important contributions in the early developmental work and the study of patients, Julian Peto was closely involved in the work on the "brought-forward time," and Máire Ní Bhrolcháin has done much invaluable work in the analysis of data. Janet Cabot, Sue Davidson, Jenny Frankland, Marie Moyer, Sue Pollock, and Sue Ulrich, between them, carried out a good deal of the work on the task of interviewing. The work has also involved collaboration with psychiatric colleagues at the Institute of Psychiatry of the University of London. John Copeland did most of the psychiatric interviews with patients and, with John Cooper and Michael Kelleher, cooperated with us in the rating of psychiatric disorder in the first community series. John Wing and Julian Leff and Sheila Mann collaborated with us in the second series.

REFERENCES

Abrahams, M. J. & Whitlock, F. A. Childhood experience and depression. *British Journal of Psychiatry*, 1969, *115*, 883–888.
Averill, J. R. Grief: Its nature and significance. *Psychological Bulletin*, 1968, 70, 721–748.
Beck, A. T. *Depression: clinical experimental and theoretical aspects*. New York: Harper & Row, 1967.
Beck, A. T., Sethi, B. B., & Tuthill, R. W. Childhood bereavement and adult depression. *Archives of General Psychiatry*, 1963, 9, 295–302.
Becker, E. Towards a comprehensive theory of depression. *Journal of Nervous and Mental Diseases*, 1962, *135*, 26–35.
Bibring, E. The Mechanism of Depression. In P. Greenacre (Ed.), *Affective disorders*. New York: International Univ. Press, 1953.
Birtchnell, J. Depression in relation to early and recent parent death. *British Journal of Psychiatry*, 1970, *116*, 299–306.
Bowlby, J. Pathological mourning and childhood mourning. *Journal of American Psychoanalytical Association*, 1963, *11*, 500–641.
Brown, G. W. & Birley, J. L. T. Crises and life changes and the onset of schizophrenia. *Journal of Health and Social Behaviour*, 1968, 9, 203–214.
Brown, G. W., Birley, J. L. T., & Wing, J. K. Influence of family life on the course of schizophrenic disorders: A replication *British Journal of Psychiatry*, 1972, *121*, 241–258.
Brown, G. W. & Rutter, M. The measurement of family activities and relationships—a methodological study. *Human Relations*, 1966, *19* (3), 241–263.

Brown, G. W. Meaning, measurement and stress of life-events. In B. S. Dohrenwend & B. P. Dohrenwend (Eds.), *Stressful life-events: Their nature and effects.* New York: Wiley, 1974.

Brown, G. W., Sklair, F., Harris, T. O., & Birley, J. L. T. Life-events and psychiatric disorder: 1. Some methodological issues. *Psychological Medicine*, 1973, 3, 74–87. (a)

Brown, G. W., Harris, T. O., & Peto, J. Life-events and psychiatric disorder: 2. Nature of causal link. *Psychological Medicine*, 1973, 3, 159–176. (b)

Brown, G. W. Life-events and psychiatric illness: some thoughts on methodology and causality. *Journal of Psychosomatic Research*, 1972, 16, 311–320.

Brown, G. W., Ni Bhrolcháin, M., & Harris, T. O. Social class and psychiatric disturbance among women in an urban population. *Sociology*, 1975, 9, 225–254.

Brown, G. W., Ní Bhrolcháin, M., & Harris, T. O. Psychotic and neurotic depression. Part 3. Aetiological and background factors. *Journal of Affective Disorders*, 1979, 1, (In press).

Brown, G. W., Harris, T. O., & Copeland, J. R. Depression and loss. *British Journal of Psychiatry*, 1977, 130, 1–18.

Brown, G. W., & Harris, T. O. *Social origins of depression.* London: Tavistock Press; New York: Free Press, 1978.

Cooper, J. E., Copeland, J. R. M., Brown, G. W., Harris, T., and Gourley, A. J. Further studies in interviewer training and inter-rater reliability of the present state examination (P.S.E.). *Psychological Medicine*, 1977, 7, 517–523.

Edmonds, V. H. Marital conventionalisation: definition of measurement. *Journal of Marriage and Family Living*, 1967, 23, 681–688.

Engel, G. L. A psychological setting of somatic disease: The giving up, given up complex. *Proceedings of the Royal Society of Medicine*, 1967, 60, 553–555.

Forrest, A. D., Fraser, R. H., & Priest, R. G. Environmental factors in depressive illness. *British Journal of Psychiatry*, 1965, 111, 243–253.

Gaylin, W. (Ed.). *The meaning of despair.* New York: Science House, 1968.

Ginsberg, S. Women, Work and Conflict. In N. Fonda & P. Moss (Eds.), *Mothers and employment.* Brunel University Press, 1976.

Goldthorpe, J. H., & Hope, K. *The social grading of occupations–a new approach and scale.* London: Oxford Univ. Press, 1974.

Graham, P. Management in child psychiatry: Recent trends. *British Journal of Psychiatry*, 1976, 129, 17–108.

Granville-Grossman, K. L. The early environment of affective disorder. In A. Coppen & A. Walk (Eds.), *Recent developments in affective disorders.* London: Headley, 1968.

Holmes, T. H. & Rahe, R. H. The social readjustment rating scale. *Journal of Psychosomatic Research*, 1967, 11, 213–218.

Hudgens, R. W., Robins, E., & Delong, W. B. The reporting of recent stress in the lives of psychiatric patients. *British Journal of Psychiatry*, 1970, 117, 635–643.

Kendell, R. E. The classification of depressive illness. *Institute of Psychiatry Monographs* (18). Oxford Univ. Press, 1968.

Leff, M. J., Roatch, J. F., & Bunney, W. E. Environmental factors preceding the onset of severe depression. *Psychiatry*, 1970, 33, 293–311.

Marris, P. *Loss and change.* London: Routledge & Kegan Paul, 1974.

Munro, A. Parental deprivation in depressive patients. *British Journal of Psychiatry*, 1966, 112, 443–457.

Oakley, A. *The sociology of housework.* London: Martin Robertson, 1974.

Parkes, C. M. Recent bereavement as a cause of mental illness. *British Journal of Psychiatry*, 1964, 110, 198–204.

Paykel, E. S. Recent life-events and clinical depression. In E. K. E. Gundeson & R. H. Rahe (Eds.), *Life stress and illness.* St. Louis: Thomas, 1974.

Richman, N. The effects of housing on pre-school children and their mothers. *Developmental Medicine and Child Neurology*, 1974, 16, 53–58.

Rutter, M. & Brown, G. W. The reliability and validity measures of family life and relationships in families containing a psychiatric patient. *Social Psychiatry*, 1966, *1*, 38–53.

Rutter, M. & Quinton, D. Psychiatric disorder—ecological factors and concepts of causation. In H. McGurk (Ed.), *Ecological factors in human development*. North Holland, Amsterdam, 1977.

Rutter, M., Yule, B., Quinton, D., Rowlands, O., Yule, W., & Berger, M. Attainment and adjustment in two geographical areas: III—Some factors accounting for area differences. *British Journal of Psychiatry*, 1975, *126*, 520–533.

Sachar, E. J., Mackenzie, J. M., Binstock, W. A., & Mack, J. E. Corticosteroid responses to the psychotherapy of reactive depression. *Psychosomatic Medicine*, 1968, *30*, 23–44.

Schutz, A. Concept and theory formation in the social services. In M. Natason & A. Schutz (Eds.), *Collected papers 1. The problem of social reality*. Amsterdam: Martinbus Nijhoff, 1962.

Seligman, M. E. P. *Helplessness: On depression, development, and death*. San Francisco: Freeman, 1975.

Sethi, B. B. Relationship of separation to depression. *Archives of General Psychiatry*, 1964, *10*, 486–496.

Wilson, I. C., Alltop, L., & Buffaloe, W. J. Parental bereavement in childhood: MMPI profiles in a depressed population. *British Journal of Psychiatry*, 1967, *113*, 761–764.

Wing, J. K., Cooper, J. E., & Sartorius, N. *The Measurement and Classification of Schizophrenic Symptoms: an instruction manual for the present state examination and CATEGO Programme*. London: Cambridge Univ. Press, 1974.

Wing, J. K., Nixon, M., Mann, S. A., & Leff, J. P. Reliability of the PSE (9th edition) used in a population survey. *Psychological Medicine*, 1977, *7*, 505–516.

Yarrow, M. R., Campbell, J. D., & Burton, R. V. *Child Rearing–An Inquiry into Research and Methods*. California: Jossey-Bass, 1968.

CHAPTER 13

Reinforcement and Depression[1]

Peter M. Lewinsohn, Mary Ann Youngren, and
Sally J. Grosscup

INTRODUCTION

The purpose of this chapter is to clarify hypotheses concerning the relationship between reinforcement and depression and to present data consistent with such hypotheses.

AN OPERATIONAL DEFINITION OF DEPRESSION

Within the context of this chapter, the term "depression" is used to refer to the syndrome of behaviors that have been identified in descriptive studies of depressed individuals (e.g., Grinker, Miller, Sabshin, Nunn, & Nunnally, 1961). This syndrome includes verbal statements of dysphoria, self-depreciation, guilt, material burden, social isolation, somatic complaints,

[1] This research was supported, in part, by U.S. Public Health Service Grant MH 24477 from the National Institute of Mental Health.

291

The Psychobiology of the Depressive Disorders:
Implications for the Effects of Stress

and a reduced rate of behavior. We assume depression to be a continuous variable that can be conceptualized as a "state" (which fluctuates over time) and as a "trait" (i.e., some people, "depressives," may be more prone to becoming depressed than others). Operationally, we have used a two-stage screening process involving cutoff scores on selected MMPI scales and on interviewers' ratings on the depression factors identified by Grinker *et al.* (1961). To be included as a "depressive," a person had to meet the following three criteria:

1. An MMPI D-scale score of at least 80 *or* D of at least 70, with D being greater than other clinical scales.
2. A Grinker Factor I (Dysphoria) score of at least 1.0 and mean of all Grinker factor (Dysphoria, Material Burden, Guilt, and Social Isolation) scores of at least .70.
3. Depression rated as the major presenting problem by the intake interviewer.

Individuals with serious health problems, alcoholism, and manic-depressive disorder were excluded. The depressives upon whom our results are based were all outpatients, not psychotic, relatively "pure" depressives, and generally could be classified as "unipolar, neurotic."

It has seemed important to us that investigators whose conclusions are based upon differences between depressed and nondepressed groups include a "psychiatric control" group as well as a normal control group. The inclusion of a "psychiatric control" group (i.e., individuals for whom anxiety or other problems, but not depression, constitute the major psychopathology) permits attribution of observed group differences to depression (depressed not being equal to psychiatric control and normal control) rather than to the deviation hypothesis (depressed and psychiatric control not being equal to normal control). Selection criteria for psychiatric controls were: An MMPI D-scale of not more than 70; any other clinical MMPI scale (except *Mf*, *Ma*, and *Si*) at least 70; and a Grinker Factor I score of less than 70. Criteria for inclusion as a "normal control" were: All MMPI clinical scales less than 70; mean Grinker factor score no more than .35; and no Grinker factor equal to or greater than .70.

The results obtained for four separate samples will be presented. All participants in Sample 1 and the nondepressed control groups in Sample 3 were recruited through announcements soliciting paid participation in psychological research. The depressives in Samples 2, 3, and 4 consisted of patients receiving treatment at the University of Oregon Psychology Clinic. Patients participated in a variety of treatment outcome studies, with treatment duration varying from 4 weeks to 12 weeks. Patients were reassessed on the basis of the MMPI and Grinker interview ratings at the end of treatment and at 1- or 2-month intervals thereafter. As we are not concerned with treatment in this chapter, the specifics of the treatment programs will not be discussed. However, patients as a group showed very substantial and significant changes in depression level from pre- to posttreatment. The MMPI-D scores at various assessment times (Ts) and the age and sex distribution of patients are shown in Table 13.1. Because there were large individual differences in the amount of improvement shown by patients, the depressives were dichotomized, and, in one instance, trichotomized, into more and less improved subgroups on the basis of MMPI-D residual gain scores (T_1 to T_2 in Samples 2 and 4; T_1 to T_4 in Sample 3). The use of residual gain scores ensures that the more and less improved groups are fairly well matched in regard to initial depression level. As can be seen in Table 13.1, the residual gain scores were quite successful in this regard.

THE CONCEPT OF REINFORCEMENT

Although the important effect reinforcement has on behavior is generally recognized, the theoretical status of reinforcement is probably the most central, unresolved issue in psychology (Estes, 1972). Still a subject of controversy is the question of whether the occurrence of reinforcement is necessary for learning to occur; it probably is not. Furthermore, there is no consensus about the underlying processes whereby some consequences serve to increase the probability of the occurrence of the behavior they follow. Drive reduction has been seen as crucial by some (e.g., Dollard & Miller, 1950; Hull, 1943), whereas others argue that the effect of reinforcement is mediated by expectancies (e.g. Tolman, 1949). Some have focused on the motivational aspects of reinforcement, whereas others have emphasized information feedback, which presumably modifies the individual's expectations.

As an empirical generalization, the concept of reinforcement is quite straightforward. It prescribes the relationship between behavior and its consequences. Glaser (1971) defines a reinforcer as "an event, stimulus, or state of affairs that changes subsequent behavior when it temporally follows an instance of that behavior [p. 1]." Throughout the various theoretical interpretations of reinforcement mechanisms, this description of reinforcing situations has remained relatively consistent. It is this operational definition that we will use. Some consequences increase the probability of the behavior they follow (positive reinforcers); others reduce the probability of the behavior they follow (aversive events). Whether an event has positive or negative reinforcing properties is inferred from its empirical effect on the behavior. As used by us, this concept of reinforcement refers to person–environment interactions. In broad terms, such person–environment interactions may be thought of in three general categories: (a) interactions serving to strengthen the behavior (i.e., increase the probability of its future occurrence); (b) events having a negative reinforcing impact (i.e., decrease

Table 13.1

MEAN AGE, SEX DISTRIBUTION AND MMPI-D SCORES FOR SAMPLES

	Sample 1			Sample 2 (depressed)			Sample 3				Sample 4 (depressed)	
	Depressed (N = 85)	Psychiatric control (N = 71)	Normals (N = 89)	Most improved (N = 14)	Intermediate (N = 13)	Least improved (N = 14)	Depressed More improved (N = 24)	Depressed Less improved (N = 23)	Psychiatric control (N = 25)	Normal (N = 29)	More improved (N = 9)	Less improved (N = 9)
Mean age	30.0	29.7	30.0	28.5	32.9	40.0	31.0	41.3	26.0	30.0	29.0	30.1
Percentage female	58%	56%	58%	65%	71%	62%	81%	81%	59%	51%	44%	44%
MMPI-D	85.1	59.0	49.2						57.5	50.5		
T_1				86	86	87	88.1	89.6			92.9	91.6
T_2				59	66	85	72.6	79.2			56.4	82.8
T_3				59	66	83	58.8	78.3			71.4	83.8
T_4							52.6	79.4				

the probability of the future occurrence of the behavior); and (c) those events not having an impact upon the future occurrence of the behavior.

Nonlaboratory investigations of reinforcement are beset with difficulties not encountered in laboratory research. In the laboratory, it has been a relatively straightforward procedure to arrange behavior-contingent stimulus events that serve to increase or decrease the probability of a future occurrence of the behavior (e.g., Ferster & Skinner, 1957). However, in nonlaboratory situations, defining reinforcement in an analagous manner requires continuous observation and coding of an individual's behavior and covarying stimulus events over a long period of time (e.g., Libet, Lewinsohn, & Javorek, 1973; Patterson, 1974; Patterson & Cobb, 1971). Such practical problems probably account for the fact that most investigators who have attempted to identify reinforcers (e.g., Cautela & Kastenbaum, 1967) are primarily concerned with the individual's preferences for a variety of "positive" stimuli—on the assumption that such preferences sample events that have reinforcing properties for the individual. Thus, despite the fact that reinforcing events have consistently been defined in terms of their functional relationship to behavior, there has been a persistent tendency to equate reinforcers with rewards (i.e., stimuli that on a priori grounds are assumed to be reinforcers). The important role of cognitive factors (e.g., attention, appraisal, awareness) further complicates investigations of reinforcement in the natural environment. For example, the effectiveness of reinforcement has been shown to be vastly enhanced when the individual is aware of the contingencies to which his responses will lead (Bandura, 1969).

In order to cope with some of the practical problems involved in identifying events with reinforcing properties for depressed individuals, we have developed several psychometric instruments. The model instrument is the Pleasant Events Schedule (MacPhillamy & Lewinsohn, 1971), on which we have done extensive developmental work demonstrating its good psychometric (reliability, validity) properties. Work on the Unpleasant Events Schedule (Lewinsohn, 1975) and the Interpersonal Events Schedule (Youngren, Zeiss, & Lewinsohn, 1975) is less advanced, but our preliminary findings suggest that these instruments also have good psychometric properties, including construct validity.

The Pleasant Events Schedule (PES) consists of a list of 320 events that were reported to be sources of pleasure by a highly diverse sample of people. The schedule calls for two responses to each item. The subject is first asked to rate the frequency of the event's occurrence during the past month on a 3-point scale: (a) has not happened in the past 30 days (rated 0); (b) has happened a few times (1–6) in the past 30 days (rated 1); and (c) has happened often (7 or more) in the past 30 days (rated 2). Second, the subject is asked to rate the subjective enjoyability of the event on a 3-point scale: (a) unpleasant (rated 0); (b) somewhat pleasant (rated 1); and (c) very pleasant (rated 2). The frequency ratings are assumed to reflect the rate with which the events on the schedule occurred during the past month. The enjoyability ratings are assumed to reflect the potential reinforcing value of the events. The product of the frequency and enjoyability ratings for all the events is assumed to provide an approximate measure of response-contingent positive reinforcement obtained over a specified period of time. A multiplicative function was chosen so that a response of either zero frequency or no enjoyability would yield a zero cross-product score. Since an attempt was made to sample exhaustively from the domain of pleasant events, and since the items on the Pleasant Events Schedule (PES) primarily refer to events in which an individual would have to actively participate, the pleasures reported on the PES are assumed to be largely of a response-contingent nature. The general rationale, reliability, validity, and internal structure of the PES have been reported previously (MacPhillamy & Lewinsohn, 1971, 1973).

The Unpleasant Events Schedule (UES) was constructed in a completely analogous fashion. The UES consists of 320 items selected after an extensive search of the universe of unpleasant events. The frequency scores are assumed to reflect the frequency of occurrence of the events; the aversiveness ratings are assumed to reflect potential for aversiveness or the potential negative reinforcing value of the events; and the cross-product scores are assumed to reflect the total amount of aversiveness experienced during the past month.

The Interpersonal Events Schedule (IES) consists of 160 items, all of which involve interpersonal activities or cognitions concerning such interactions. The items are grouped into eight rationally derived scales: Social Activity, Assertion, Cognition, Conflict, Give Positive, Receive Positive, Give Negative, and Receive Negative. Frequency, impact, and cross-product scores are computed separately for each scale. The frequency scores (based on a 3-point scale identical to the PES frequency scale) are assumed to reflect the rate with which the events occurred during the past month. The impact scores, unlike those for the PES and UES, are based on a 5-point scale indicating the subjective comfort–discomfort associated with each event: very uncomfortable or upset (rated 0); somewhat uncomfortable or upset (rated 1); neutral (rated 2); fairly comfortable or good (rated 3); very comfortable or good (rated 4). Impact scores are assumed to reflect the potential positive or negative reinforcing value of the events. The cross-product scores are assumed to provide an approximate measure of response-contingent, positive social reinforcement or of interpersonal aversiveness experienced during the past month.

For all three instruments, the mean pleasantness, aversiveness, and impact ratings may be said to constitute something about the reinforcing–aversiveness value of the particular event in the population at large; how specific individuals answer the items presumably reflects something about the potency of these events for them.

We have used another related, but somewhat different, strategy to identify events that have reinforcing properties, namely, having people monitor the occurrence of specified events and complete mood ratings on a daily basis. Specifically, we have had groups monitoring in four different ways: (a) on 160 pleasant events; (b) on 160 unpleasant events; (c) on 80 pleasant and 80 unpleasant events; and (d) on 160 interpersonal events. By studying correlations between the occurrence of events and mood level, we have been able to show covariations between feeling good and the occurrence of pleasant events (mean rate is .36 for Sample 1, .38 for Sample 2, .48 for Sample 3, and .56 for Sample 4, all of which are significant at the .01 level) and between feeling bad and the occurrence of certain aversive events (mean rate is .28 for Sample 3 and .42 for Sample 4, both of which are significant at the .01 level). Events which are correlated with mood in a substantial proportion of the sample (mood-related events), signify something about the reinforcement value of such events in the population at large. On the other hand, by looking at event–mood correlations for an individual, we are able to identify specific events that have reinforcing value for that person. The assumption is that events which are followed by good feeling have positive reinforcing value, whereas events followed by dysphoria have a negative reinforcing value. This assumption may be traced back historically to Thorndike (1935) whose law of effect concerned the relationship between pleasure and behavior. Thorndike postulated that responses accompanied or closely followed by satisfaction are more likely to reoccur whereas those accompanied or closely followed by discomfort will be less likely to occur. Our inference that mood-related events have reinforcing value is also consistent with the work by Olds and Milner (1954) supporting the postulated relationship between pleasure and positive reinforcement.

THE RELATIONSHIP BETWEEN
DEPRESSION AND REINFORCEMENT

In previous publications (Lewinsohn, Weinstein, & Shaw, 1969; Lewinsohn, 1974) we have advanced several general hypotheses about the relationship between positive reinforcement and depression, focusing on the effect a reduction in the rate of response-contingent positive reinforcement is assumed to have on the behavior of the individual. Lewinsohn, Weinstein, and Shaw (1969) have argued that feelings of dysphoria are directly due to a reduction in the rate of response-contingent positive reinforcement. Dysphoria is assumed to occur when there is either little reinforcement, or when available reinforcers are not contingent on the person's behavior. Thus, a low rate of response-contingent positive reinforcement acts as an eliciting stimulus for dysphoria. It has also been hypothesized that a low rate of response-contingent positive reinforcement constitutes a sufficient explanation for other aspects of the depressive syndrome, such as a low rate of behavior; the depressed individual is assumed to be on a prolonged extinction schedule.

Lewinsohn (1974) has suggested three ways in which a low rate of response-contingent positive reinforcement may occur. First, events that are contingent on behavior may not be reinforcing. This could be, as Costello (1972) has suggested, because of a loss of reinforcer effectiveness. Second, events that are reinforcing may become unavailable. For example, incapacitating physical injury may prevent individuals from engaging in sports and social activities that have previously been significant factors in maintaining their behavior. Third, reinforcers may be available, but because of the lack of necessary repertoires, the individual is unable to elicit them. This last possibility is particularly important in the area of social behavior. An individual who lacks requisite social skills may fail to attain social reinforcement otherwise available. These possibilities are, of course, not mutually exclusive.

On the basis of the previously mentioned assumptions, the following specific predictions may be made:

1. The rate of response-contingent positive reinforcement will be less in depressed than in nondepressed control groups.
2. The rate of positive reinforcement will increase as a function of the improvement in the clinical depression level.
3. The increase in the rate of response-contingent positive reinforcement will be greater in patients who improve more, than in those who improve less.

In previous publications (Stewart, 1968; Lewinsohn, Lobitz, & Wilson, 1973; Libet, Lewinsohn, & Javorek, 1973) we have also presented data consistent with the hypothesis that depressed individuals are more sensitive to aversive contingencies. In these studies it was shown that depressed individuals respond with a larger autonomic response (GSR) to an aversive stimulus (e.g., mild electric shock); the behavior of depressed individuals in a social situation was found to be consistently more attenuated by a behavior from an "aversive" person than that of nondepressed subjects; and the latency of response (time between reaction by another person to the subject's verbalization and subsequent action by the subject in a group situation) was significantly longer for depressed than nondepressed subjects following the incidence of a negative social reaction (e.g., being criticized, disagreed with). The "sensitivity to aversiveness" hypothesis is also supported by the finding of Schless, Schwartz, Goetz, & Mendels (1974) who found that aversiveness ratings assigned to specific life events by depressed individuals were higher than ratings by the control group.

On the basis of the above findings, we were interested in testing predictions about the relationship between the occurrence of aversive events and depression. We assumed that aversive events were events that had a negative reinforcing value (i.e., they cause people to reduce behavior, avoid situations, withdraw, not participate, etc.). The specific predictions were as follows:

4. The rate of experienced aversiveness in depressed individuals will be higher than in nondepressed control groups.
5. The rate of experienced aversiveness will diminish as clinical depression level decreases.
6. The decrease in experienced aversiveness will be greater in depressives who improve more, than in depressives who improve less.

The process by which the occurrence of aversive events leads to depression deserves some attention. A plausible paradigm for how aversive events can result in depression has been developed by Seligman (1975) in his learned-helplessness theory of depression. Seligman has based his reasoning upon the effects of uncontrollable shock on animals (passivity in the face of later trauma, retarded learning, lack of aggressiveness and competitiveness, weight loss and undereating—collectively called "learned helplessness") and on the similarities between the symptoms of learned helplessness and depression. Specifically, he has suggested that uncontrollable aversive events (i.e., the probability of the occurrence of an aversive event is the same whether the organism emits or does not emit a behavior) constitute a critical antecedent condition for the occurrence of depression.

A more parsimonious explanation, paralleling our hypothesis about the relationship between positive reinforcement and depression, would be that a high rate of occurrence of aversive events leads to the attenuation of behavior. We would expect the individual who experiences many aversive events to be less likely to initiate interactions and more likely to withdraw from situations that otherwise have potential for positive reinforcement. In other words, the prediction is that a high rate of occurrence of aversive events leads to a low rate of behavior. A second prediction would be that the occurrence of aversive events elicits dysphoria; thus, we are postulating a covariation between the rate of occurrence of aversive events and mood level, as we did for the pleasant activities. There is another possible mechanism, however. The occurrence of aversive events may reduce the enjoyment (potential reinforcement value) of behaviors and events that occur in temporal proximity to aversive events. For example, the person who has just received some distressing news is hypothesized to derive less enjoyment from a subsequent social interaction than he would if he had not been given the bad news. Based upon this third hypothesis, we made the following specific prediction:

7. A high rate of occurrence of aversive events is negatively related with the experienced pleasantness of pleasant events.

RESULTS CONSISTENT WITH
HYPOTHESES

PREDICTION 1: *The rate of response-contingent positive reinforcement will be less in depressed than in nondepressed control groups.*

Table 13.2 shows PES results for the four samples. As can be seen, depressives are consistently lower than nondepressed controls on the cross-product score (assumed to be proportional to the total amount of response-contingent positive reinforcement) at the initial point of assessment. Depressives are consistently lower in frequency (rate of engagement in the activities on the schedule); in enjoyability ratings (potency of reinforcers); and, hence, in the cross-product scores.

The IES T1 results for Sample 3 are shown in Table 13.3. Of particular relevance to Prediction 1 are the results for the three "positive" scales (scales for which mean impact scores for all groups equalled or exceeded 2): Social

Table 13.2

**PLEASANT EVENTS SCHEDULE (PES) SCORES
FOR SAMPLES 1–4.**

	Sample 1			
		Psychiatric		
	Depressed	control	Normals	
PES variable	(N = 85)	(N = 71)	(N = 89)	F
Mean frequency	.711	.800	.792	9.4*
Mean enjoyability	.985	1.089	1.113	8.2*
Mean cross-products	.882	1.107	1.107	14.3*

		Sample 2					
		Depressed					
		Most	Inter-	Least	F		F
		improved	mediate	improved	(Between	F	(Inter-
PES variable	T	(N = 14)	(N = 13)	(N = 14)	groups)	(Across Ts)	action)
Mean	1	.663	.568	.662	1.8	11.9*	1.6
frequency	2	.800	.686	.702			
	3	.770	.678	.670			
Mean	1	.959	.926	.922	1.6	8.7*	1.4
enjoyability	2	1.131	1.124	.961			
	3	1.129	1.105	.934			
Mean	1	.805	.679	.745	2.6****	17.7*	1.3
cross-products	2	1.149	.969	.879			
	3	1.124	.895	.850			

Table 13.2

(*Continued*)

		Sample 3						
		Depressed						
PES variable	T	More improved (N = 21)	Less improved (N = 21)	Psychiatric control (N = 21)	Normals (N = 25)	F (between groups)	F (across Ts)	F (Inter-action)
Mean	1	.714	.620	.867	.789	5.5**	1.3	2.8**
frequency	2	.713	.684	.835	.754			
	3	.738	.610	.807	.776			
	4	.765	.583	.789	.764			
Mean	1	1.023	.918	1.094	1.075	2.3	5.0**	1.7
enjoyability	2	1.098	.987	1.120	1.092			
	3	1.166	.956	1.165	1.155			
	4	1.229	.910	1.115	1.126			
Mean	1	.893	.743	1.165	1.066	4.6**	< 1	2.8**
cross-products	2	.975	.877	1.154	1.007			
	3	1.040	.775	1.131	1.107			
	4	1.128	.691	1.086	1.055			

		Sample 4				
		Depressed				
PES variable	T	More improved (N = 9)	Less improved (N = 9)	F (between groups)	F (across Ts)	F (Inter-action)
Mean frequency	1	.708	.611	4.0***	9.0*	1.7
	2	.828	.649			
	3	.707	.589			
Mean enjoyability	1	1.033	.923	3.8****	3.2***	1.8
	2	1.250	.919			
	3	.987	.856			
Mean cross-products	1	.887	.650	7.1***	6.5**	1.9
	2	1.303	.767			
	3	.902	.644			

* $p \leq .001$
** $p \leq .01$
*** $p \leq .05$
**** $p \leq .10$

Activity Scale, Give Positive Scale, and Receive Positive Scale. Included content areas on the Social Activity Scale are: engaging in conversations (e.g., "talking with a stranger of the same sex"); engaging in an activity with another person (e.g., "having lunch or a coffee break with friends"); and being in a situation where other people are invariably present (e.g., "going to a service, civic, special interest, or social club meeting"). The Social Activity Scale clearly discriminated the depressives from nondepressed control groups on frequency, impact ratings, and cross-product scores. Depressed individuals are much less active socially, are less comfortable while engaging in social interactions, and derive less positive reinforcement from such interactions.

Items on the IES Give Positive Scale all explicitly refer to giving a positive response to another person (e.g., "complimenting someone on their skill or creativity" and "smiling at someone"). Items on the Receive Positive Scale explicitly refer to receiving positive responses from others (e.g., "being praised by someone I admire" and "having someone show interest in what I have said"). On both the Give Positive and Receive Positive Scales, depressives are clearly lower in frequency, and their impact ratings are less positive; hence, the total positive reinforcement obtained from giving and receiving positive interpersonal responses is lower for depressives than for nondepressed controls.

Thus, results obtained with relevant IES scales, as well as the PES results, strongly support Prediction 1.

PREDICTION 2: *The rate of positive reinforcement will increase as a function of improvement in clinical depression level.*

Depressives who were treated and who showed significant decreases in depression level show a corresponding increase in PES cross-product scores (Table 13.2). Although there were some differences between samples on PES frequency changes (i.e., frequency increased in Samples 2 and 4 but not in Sample 3), there was consistent improvement in the enjoyability ratings.

The results on the IES Social Activity, Give Positive, and Receive Positive Scales also provide strong support for Prediction 2 (Table 13.3). On all three scales, depressives who showed significant improvement in depression level also clearly showed increases on cross-product scores (Table 13.3).

PREDICTION 3: *The increase in the rate of response-contingent positive reinforcement will be greater in patients who improve more than in those who improve less.*

There was a consistent tendency for more improved depressives to show the largest changes in PES cross-product scores (Table 13.2). At the last assessment, the most improved patients in Samples 2, 3 and 4 are very close or identical to the normal control-group values. The less improved groups, on the other hand, continue to show values which are substantially below those of the control groups.

The more improved depressed patients also showed the largest increases

Table 13.3

INTERPERSONAL EVENTS SCHEDULE (IES) SCALE SCORES FOR SAMPLE 3

	(T 1 Data Only)			
IES variable	Depressed (N = 64)	Psychiatric control (N = 61)	Normal (N = 74)	F (between groups)
Social activity				
Mean frequency	.605	.865	.850	23.5*
Mean impact	2.125	2.781	2.781	33.6*
Mean cross-products	1.491	2.692	2.609	39.9*
Assertion				
Mean frequency	.619	.763	.692	3.1***
Mean impact	1.568	1.890	1.846	10.5*
Mean cross-products	1.120	1.689	1.516	12.2*
Cognition				
Mean frequency	1.046	.811	.604	24.7*
Mean impact	.602	.878	.961	12.0*
Mean cross-products	.457	.621	.544	1.4
Conflict				
Mean frequency	.465	.490	.415	1.6
Mean impact	.759	.958	.951	1.9
Mean cross-products	.348	.558	.468	4.0***
Give positive				
Mean frequency	.871	1.143	1.125	15.8*
Mean impact	2.700	3.078	3.067	12.9*
Mean cross-products	2.630	3.729	3.644	18.7*
Receive positive				
Mean frequency	.816	1.089	1.080	13.5*
Mean impact	2.987	3.367	3.286	9.9*
Mean cross-products	2.582	3.743	3.618	16.2*
Give negative				
Mean frequency	.448	.462	.391	1.6
Mean impact	.848	1.008	.993	< 1
Mean cross-products	.406	.518	.458	< 1
Receive negative				
Mean frequency	.462	.461	.373	3.4***
Mean impact	.638	.793	.806	1.1
Mean cross-products	.268	.392	.338	1.1

* $p \leq .001$
** $p \leq .01$
*** $p \leq .05$

(Continued)

Table 13.3

(Continued)

IES variable	T	Depressed More improved (N = 21)	Less improved (N = 22)	Psychiatric control (N = 21)	Normal (N = 25)	F (between groups)	F (across Ts)	F (inter-action)
				Sample 3 (T 1–T 4)				
Social activity								
Mean	1	.618	.576	.939	.834	4.6**	1.5	4.7*
frequency	2	.695	.549	.852	.814			
	3	.850	.601	.802	.769			
	4	.835	.604	.846	.813			
Mean impact	1	2.183	2.059	2.789	2.844	9.3*	3.9**	1.6
	2	2.405	2.101	2.679	2.759			
	3	2.528	2.206	2.787	2.904			
	4	2.780	2.219	2.715	2.917			
Mean	1	1.481	1.423	2.937	2.632	8.7*	3.6***	4.8*
cross-products	2	1.834	1.477	2.570	2.519			
	3	2.262	1.652	2.523	2.593			
	4	2.426	1.618	2.526	2.710			
Assertion								
Mean	1	.655	.544	.795	.614	3.1***	1.6	1.8
frequency	2	.637	.473	.670	.614			
	3	.763	.494	.670	.570			
	4	.716	.470	.719	.566			
Mean impact	1	1.703	1.458	1.910	1.822	5.8*	3.3***	< 1
	2	1.742	1.377	1.910	1.920			
	3	1.843	1.464	2.002	1.945			
	4	2.059	1.485	1.951	1.959			
Mean	1	1.197	.954	1.773	1.337	5.8*	1.4	2.4***
cross-products	2	1.286	.840	1.553	1.444			
	3	1.568	.961	1.583	1.420			
	4	1.577	.875	1.651	1.354			

in IES cross-product scores on the Social Activity, Give Positive, and Receive Positive Scales (Table 13.3). Following treatment this group's frequency scores were comparable to those for normals; they were only slightly lower in terms of positive reinforcement obtained from social activity and from giving and receiving positive interpersonal responses. The less improved group, on the other hand, changed very little and remained substantially below the control groups on all three scales.

PREDICTION 4: *The rate of experienced aversiveness in depressed individuals will be higher than in nondepressed control groups.*

Table 13.3

(Continued)

		Sample 3 (T 1–T 4)						
		Depressed						
IES variable	T	More improved (N = 21)	Less improved (N = 22)	Psychiatric control (N = 21)	Normal (N = 25)	F (between groups)	F (across Ts)	F (inter-action)
Cognition								
Mean	1	1.064	.990	.760	.562	4.5**	15.9*	3.1*
frequency	2	.976	.762	.719	.534			
	3	.770	.666	.665	.497			
	4	.653	.663	.714	.498			
Mean impact	1	.665	.597	.973	.962	3.1***	2.8***	1.7
	2	.609	.622	1.008	1.020			
	3	.794	.623	1.035	.926			
	4	1.063	.773	.939	1.016			
Mean	1	.436	.468	.650	.496	1.6	< 1	1.3
cross-products	2	.364	.463	.787	.494			
	3	.512	.428	.648	.414			
	4	.646	.467	.671	.416			
Conflict								
Mean	1	.500	.421	.476	.364	1.7	1.5	< 1
frequency	2	.463	.337	.412	.356			
	3	.502	.352	.445	.328			
	4	.501	.325	.453	.323			
Mean impact	1	.931	.649	.988	.866	2.4	1.1	1.1
	2	.783	.520	1.093	.960			
	3	.876	.657	1.121	.810			
	4	1.039	.755	1.030	.919			
Mean	1	.410	.281	.569	.378	3.2***	< 1	1.3
cross-products	2	.397	.223	.650	.464			
	3	.488	.336	.592	.338			
	4	.553	.311	.616	.342			

The UES data are shown in Table 13.4. The UES was administered only to Sample 3 and 4 subjects. As can be seen, Prediction 4 was very strongly supported in that the total amount of aversiveness (cross-product score) was substantially higher for the depressed group than for the two control groups. Upon inspection of the frequency and aversiveness means, however, it becomes clear that this difference is largely contributed by the substantially elevated aversiveness scores of the depressives. During the month preceding the initial assessment, depressed individuals do not have a larger number of aversive events happening to them, but they are apparently experiencing such events as much more aversive. This finding suggests that the greater potency of aversive events is what is responsible for the increased aversive-

Table 13.3

(*Continued*)

		Sample 3 (T 1–T 4)						
		Depressed						
		More improved	Less improved	Psychiatric control	Normal	F (between	F (across	F (inter-
IES variable	T	(N = 21)	(N = 22)	(N = 21)	(N = 25)	groups)	Ts)	action)
Give positive								
Mean	1	.900	.809	1.212	1.082	7.0*	2.1	3.1*
frequency	2	.958	.700	1.079	1.038			
	3	1.162	.823	1.057	1.028			
	4	1.076	.780	1.118	.998			
Mean impact	1	2.745	2.711	3.126	3.100	5.4**	< 1	< 1
	2	2.987	2.576	2.919	3.082			
	3	2.986	2.578	3.066	3.134			
	4	3.052	2.625	2.987	3.181			
Mean	1	2.638	2.504	3.964	3.550	6.7*	2.9***	2.5**
cross-products	2	3.056	2.139	3.326	3.420			
	3	3.626	2.519	3.519	3.588			
	4	3.403	2.441	3.584	3.515			
Receive positive								
Mean	1	.888	.726	1.169	1.022	6.3*	3.3**	2.7**
frequency	2	.904	.712	1.052	1.060			
	3	1.167	.795	1.071	1.028			
	4	1.123	.795	1.097	1.043			
Mean impact	1	2.900	3.118	3.348	3.360	3.4***	< 1	1.0
	2	3.153	2.864	3.081	3.292			
	3	3.143	2.896	3.225	3.318			
	4	3.209	2.882	3.143	3.384			
Mean	1	2.669	2.399	3.967	3.512	6.4*	4.5**	2.2***
cross-products	2	2.893	2.196	3.260	3.588			
	3	3.721	2.548	3.637	3.702			
	4	3.568	2.518	3.572	3.738			

ness experienced by depressed persons. Values for Sample 4 are in the same general range.

The IES Scales relevant to Prediction 4 are those showing clearly negative (less than or equal to 1) impact scores: The Cognition Scale, the Conflict Scale, the Give Negative Scale, and the Receive Negative Scale (Table 13.3). For these scales, the differential scaling of the frequency ratings (low to high) and impact ratings (negative to positive) results in noninterpretable cross-product scores (i.e., the high frequency multiplied by the more negative impact is similar or equal to the low frequency multiplied by the less negative impact). Therefore, it is more meaningful to jointly examine frequency and impact scores for these scales.

The Cognition Scale items all explicitly refer to negative thoughts and

Table 13.3

(*Continued*)

		Sample 3 (T 1–T 4)						
		Depressed						
IES variable	T	More improved (N = 21)	Less improved (N = 22)	Psychiatric control (N = 21)	Normal (N = 25)	F (between groups)	F (across Ts)	F (inter-action)
Give negative								
Mean	1	.483	.389	.455	.332	1.9	2.2	< 1
frequency	2	.465	.323	.360	.342			
	3	.440	.306	.389	.294			
	4	.500	.300	.438	.291			
Mean impact	1	1.036	.667	1.038	.960	2.2	1.3	< 1
	2	.838	.602	1.169	1.048			
	3	.943	.717	1.145	.954			
	4	1.129	.800	1.128	1.015			
Mean	1	.507	.257	.521	.374	1.8	1.9	1.2
cross-products	2	.460	.270	.586	.490			
	3	.395	.264	.493	.354			
	4	.607	.261	.621	.343			
Receive negative								
Mean	1	.498	.417	.460	.342	1.6	3.2***	< 1
frequency	2	.452	.342	.355	.328			
	3	.452	.299	.394	.322			
	4	.472	.295	.418	.320			
Mean impact	1	.848	.528	.805	.720	1.9	< 1	1.3
	2	.628	.417	.950	.850			
	3	.783	.556	.958	.658			
	4	.911	.620	.886	.780			
Mean	1	.350	.216	.419	.300	1.8	< 1	< 1
cross-products	2	.262	.193	.457	.346			
	3	.355	.237	.411	.224			
	4	.425	.230	.476	.267			

* $p \leq .001$
** $p \leq .01$
*** $p \leq .05$

feelings concerning personal interactions (e.g., "feeling rejected by someone" and "knowing someone is forming an unfavorable impression of me"). As shown in Table 13.3, depressives—and to a lesser extent, psychiatric controls—have such cognitions more frequently than normals. Impact scores are clearly lower (i.e., more negative) for the depressives than for the controls. Therefore, we infer that the total experienced aversiveness associated with negative cognitions is greater for depressed individuals than for the nondepressed controls.

Table 13.4

UNPLEASANT EVENTS SCHEDULE (UES) SCORES FOR SAMPLES 3
AND 4

	Sample 3 (T 1 data only)			
UES variable	Depressed (N = 76)	Psychiatric control (N = 61)	Normals (N = 75)	F (between groups)
Mean frequency	.586	.626	.548	3.3***
Mean aversiveness	1.117	.957	.908	5.6**
Mean cross-products	.604	.475	.368	15.2**

		Sample 4 (T 1–T 3)				
		Depressed				
UES variable	T	More improved (N = 9)	Less improved (N = 9)	F (between groups)	F (across Ts)	F (inter-action)
Mean frequency	1	.571	.617	< 1	11.6*	< 1
	2	.456	.508			
	3	.474	.494			
Mean aversiveness	1	1.032	1.073	< 1	< 1	< 1
	2	1.143	1.030			
	3	1.016	.972			
Mean cross-products	1	.609	.683	< 1	8.6*	< 1
	2	.419	.497			
	3	.444	.470			

$* \ p \leq .001$
$** \ p \leq .01$
$*** \ p \leq .05$
$**** \ p \leq .10$

The IES Conflict Scale items refer explicitly to arguing (e.g., "having an
argument with my spouse"); criticizing or being criticized (e.g., "being
criticized by my boss"); or substantive disagreement with another person
(e.g., "expressing an opinion that differs from that of the person I am talking
with"). The Give Negative Scale consists of items which refer to giving
negative responses to others (e.g., "frowning or scowling at someone" and
"ignoring someone"). The Receive Negative Scale items all involve receiving negative responses from others (e.g., "being yelled at by someone important to me"). On all three scales, both depressed and psychiatric controls
showed a slightly elevated frequency of occurrence relative to normals,
suggesting that differences in the frequency for negative interpersonal ex-
changes may be attributed to the deviation hypothesis rather than to depression. However, the obtained frequency differences were not statistically
significant. Depressives' impact scores for all three scales were lower (i.e.,

Table 13.4

(Continued)

		Sample 3 (T 1–T 4)						
		Depressed						
UES variable	T	More improved (N = 24)	Less improved (N = 23)	Psychiatric control (N = 25)	Normal (N = 29)	F (between groups)	F (across Ts)	F (inter-action)
Mean	1	.621	.523	.633	.543	1.7	15.8*	< 1
frequency	2	.570	.497	.586	.486			
	3	.563	.460	.581	.487			
	4	.530	.456	.571	.485			
Mean	1	1.140	1.057	.929	.934	2.1****	8.3*	2.4**
aversiveness	2	1.136	1.055	.898	.978			
	3	1.020	1.010	.912	.919			
	4	.988	.960	.916	.937			
Mean	1	.667	.487	.478	.378	4.4**	22.3*	3.6*
cross-products	2	.573	.439	.420	.342			
	3	.524	.363	.403	.325			
	4	.419	.352	.401	.339			

* $p \leq .001$
** $p \leq .01$
*** $p \leq .05$
**** $p \leq .10$

more negative) than controls' scores but these differences also were not significant. Thus, it appears that only one "negative" IES Scale, the Cognition Scale, provides firm support for Prediction 4.

On the face of it, these results seem to contradict those of Paykel, Myers, Dienelt, Klerman, Lindenthal, & Pepper (1969), Brown, Ní Bhrolcháin, & Harris (1975), and others who have found an increased incidence of the occurrence of aversive events in depressed individuals during the 6-month period preceding the onset of depression. Fortunately, we had administered the Social Readjustment Rating Scale (Holmes & Rahe, 1967) to Sample 3; our results were consistent with those of previous investigators in showing the incidence of aversive events to be elevated in the depressives. What needs to be kept in mind is that the Social Readjustment Rating Scale includes some very aversive but low frequency events (e.g., the death of a close relative). Although this type of event is included on the UES, the low rate of occurrence of such events means that they do not contribute very much to the total UES frequency score. The UES was intended to sample the universe of aversive events much more broadly than current, life-events schedules. When these very aversive, low frequency events are given weight comparable to that of the life change units used by Holmes and Rahe (1967), then we do obtain results consistent with those found in other studies.

PREDICTION 5: *The rate of experienced aversiveness will diminish as clinical depression decreases.*

Consistent with this prediction, there is a decrease in reported incidence of aversive events (UES) with improvement in the clinical depression level in Samples 3 and 4. However, inspection of the UES data for Sample 3 indicates that this decrease is also shown by the control groups and, therefore, seems to represent a general tendency for people to check fewer events on the UES over a series of repeated administrations. There was a significant tendency for the depressives in Sample 3, but not for the control groups, to decrease their aversiveness ratings over the four time intervals (Interaction: Groups multiplied by the Time-intervals, $F = 2.4$, $p < .01$). In contrast, there was very little change in the aversiveness ratings for Sample 4. On the cross-product score there is a significant decrease for the depressives in Samples 3 and 4 across the time intervals. The UES data are interpreted as supporting Prediction 5.

PREDICTION 6: *The decrease in experienced aversiveness will be greater in depressives who improve more than in depressives who improve less.*

The results relevant to this prediction are equivocal. Consistent with the prediction, the "more improved" group in Sample 3 showed the greatest decrease in the UES cross-products score. For Sample 4, however, the more and less improved groups showed comparable decreases.

PREDICTION 7: *A high rate of occurrence of aversive events is negatively related with the experienced pleasantness of pleasant events.*

The participants in Sample 4 recorded the occurrence of 80 pleasant and 80 unpleasant events on a daily basis and rated each event, when it occurred, on a 3-point scale of pleasantness (1 = pleasant; 2 = neutral; 3 = unpleasant). To test Prediction 7, we computed the correlation between the number of unpleasant events, which both occurred and were rated as unpleasant, and the mean pleasantness rating of the pleasant events which occurred. This correlation was computed across days ($N = 42$) and separately for each participant. The mean of these correlations (averaged across subjects) was $-.41$. The null hypothesis ($r = 0$) was strongly rejected ($t = 4.5$, $p < .001$).

These results are discussed in greater detail elsewhere (Grosscup & Lewinsohn, In Press). As the results are based on a small sample, they need to be cross-validated. The obtained results tentatively suggest that a high rate of occurrence of aversive events decreases the potency of positive reinforcers. Thus, an empirical bridge is provided between the occurrence of aversive events, positive reinforcement, and depression.

THE NATURE OF
DEPRESSION-RELATED
REINFORCEMENT

If, as the data seem to indicate, depression is uniquely associated with reinforcement in the sense that the occurrence of depression is associated with reduced positive reinforcement and elevated aversiveness, then we may ask if there are specific types of events that are of special importance for the occurrence of depression. In the case of the pleasant events, they would be those that are *not* being engaged in by depressed individuals; in the case of aversive events, they would be those that have heightened aversiveness for depressives. Two competing hypotheses may be formulated. The intensity hypothesis states that depressed individuals engage in fewer pleasant activities and have greater experienced aversiveness in regard to *all* events on the schedules. The configural hypothesis, on the other hand, postulates the existence of a specific subset of events in all three schedules that are associated with the occurrence of depression. Such a subset of events, were it to exist, would be especially important in terms of understanding the nature of depression. But at a more general level, such events might also have some implications for reinforcement.

We had two ways of defining such subsets: (*a*) on the basis of the most discriminating items; and (*b*) on the basis of "mood-related" items.

The discriminating item method involves examining the individual items on each schedule and selecting those clearly discriminating depressed individuals from both psychiatric and normal controls (i.e., those pleasant events clearly occurring with decreased frequency and those aversive events occurring with elevated frequency). The disadvantage of this method is that it capitalizes on chance and the composition of a most discriminating item set would be expected to be a function of sample size and to vary somewhat across samples.

The second method of defining subsets of depression-related events is on the basis of mood-related items, that is, events that were found to be associated significantly with mood in at least 10% of the population. A set of 49 such items were identified on the PES; these items have been published previously (Lewinsohn & Graf, 1973). We were also able to identify 59 mood-related items from the daily monitoring of 58 subjects on the UES (Lewinsohn & Talkington, 1976). A smaller sample of depressed subjects (N = 19) completed daily monitoring on the IES; 58 IES items were found to covary with dysphoria for 10% of the sample. To clarify the dimensionality of these events, the cross-product scores for the three sets of mood-related activities were separately submitted to principal-components factor analysis and rotated to a simple structure according to the varimax criterion. Eight factors were retained in each factor analysis.

The Pleasant Events Schedule
Mood-Related Factors

By inspecting items with high factor loadings, several clearly interpretable factors emerged. Factor 1 is interpreted as a "sex" factor having the highest loadings (at least .6) on kissing, petting, necking, having sexual relations, and being told that "I am loved" and a loading of over .5 on "being with someone I love." Factor 2 is interpreted as a "positive social interactions" factor having the highest loadings (more than .5) on going to a party, being with friends, being popular at a gathering, and being with happy people and a loading of more than .4 on seeing old friends. Factor 3 is interpreted as a "passive outdoor" factor with loadings over .5 on being in the country, watching wild animals, and seeing beautiful scenery, and a loading of over .4 on sitting in the sun. Factor 4 is interpreted as a "solitude" factor with loadings of more than .6 on being relaxed and more than .5 on having spare time and having peace and quiet. Factor 5 is interpreted as a "competence" factor with loadings of more than .5 on planning or organizing something and over .4 on having a frank and open conversation, doing a job well, learning to do something new, doing a project my own way, being asked for my help or advice, and having people show interest in what the individual said. Factors 6, 7, and 8 had few positive loadings so that no easily interpretable pattern emerged for these factors.

The Unpleasant Events Schedule
Mood-Related Factors

This factor analysis yielded three clearly interpretable factors. Factor 1 is interpreted as a "work hassle" factor with loadings of over .6 on having too much to do, working on something when I am tired, and working under pressure and a loading of greater than .5 on being rushed. The second UES mood-related factor is interpreted as a "marital discord" factor with loadings of over .6 on arguments with spouse, being dissatisfied with my spouse, and having my spouse dissatisfied with me. Factor 3 is interpreted as a "receive negative" factor with a loading of more than .6 on having someone criticize or evaluate me and loadings of over .5 on having someone disagree with me, being insulted, doing "something I don't want to in order to please someone else," and talking with an unpleasant person. The other five UES mood-related factors had few large loadings and no easily interpretable pattern emerged.

The Interpersonal Events Schedule
Dysphoria-Related Factors

Five readily interpretable factors emerged here. Factor 1 is interpreted as a "social activity" factor with highest loadings (over .6) on "introducing myself to someone," talking with a stranger of the same sex, talking with a stranger of the opposite sex, joining a friend or friends for a social activity, and helping a friend. It should be noted that there are significant differences between depressed and nondepressed controls on both the frequency and impact on these items; depressed persons engage in these social interactions less frequently and feel much more uncomfortable when doing so.

The second IES mood-related factor is interpreted as a "projected negative" factor (i.e., one's perception that another person is negatively evaluating him/her). The highest loading (over .6) occurred on being ignored by someone; loadings of more than .5 occurred on "being afraid I will say or do the wrong thing," feeling "I am boring someone," and "knowing someone is forming an unfavorable impression of me." Factor 3 is an artifact having a loading of over .4 on only one item: "talking with my husband or wife" and having its highest loading on marital status.

Factor 4 involves "striving via negative assertion" with highest loadings (more than .6) on "contradicting someone when I think I might hurt them by doing so" and "telling someone how I feel if they have done something that is unfair to me" and a loading of more than .4 on "telling someone that they have disappointed me or let me down." Factor 5 is a "feeling one down" factor with loadings of more than .6 on feeling exploited or pushed around by others, feeling unpopular at a social gathering, and worrying that "people who are important to me won't think very much of me."

Factor 6 is a "seeking and being helped" factor with loadings of more than .6 on being helped by someone and asking someone for help or advice; a loading of over .5 on asking for clarification when confused about what someone has said; and a loading of over .4 on interrupting someone to ask them to repeat something not heard clearly. It is of considerable interest that seeking and receiving help apparently is associated with dysphoria for depressed persons.

We are suggesting that these are the types of events bearing a critical relationship to the occurrence of depression. When the good ones (PES) occur at low rates and the negative ones (UES, IES) occur at high rates, the individual is likely to feel depressed. We also hypothesize that these are the major types of events that act as reinforcers for people; occurrence of the ones that are negatively associated with dysphoria serve to maintain our behavior, and occurrence of events that are positively associated with dysphoria reduces our rate of behavior. We are currently exploring this whole issue of the dimensionality of reinforcement by identifying a matched set of

nonmood-related PES and UES items (which we assume to be less important for the occurrence of depression and less important as sources of
reinforcement for people in general). We plan to submit all of these items to
factor analysis with the expectation that the mood-related PES and UES
items will define bipolar factors. The positive pole of each factor is
hypothesized to be defined by the occurrence of events that act as positive
reinforcers and the negative pole, by events within the same cluster, but
qualitatively different in that they reduce the probability of future behavior.
Other possible future directions involve testing hypotheses about individual
differences in regard to the potency of specific dimensions of reinforcement
and subsequently making predictions about the occurrence of depression.
Thus, we would expect an individual who has high positive potency for
social interaction and high negative aversiveness potency for negative social
interactions to become depressed when positive social events decrease and
negative social events increase. Similar kinds of projections can be made in
regard to the other dimensions.

CONCLUDING COMMENTS

We subscribe to a multicausation model for depression in which different
kinds of antecedent conditions may be sufficient but not necessary for the
occurrence of depression. The reinforcement model appears to be a useful
framework, generating data consistent with the hypothesized relationship
between reinforcement and depression. This model also has clear treatment
implications (e.g., Lewinsohn, Biglan, & Zeiss, 1976). At the same time,
along with Akiskal and McKinney (1973), we believe that there may be other
developmental, biochemical, genetic, and cognitive factors that can either
cause an individual to become depressed or make him more vulnerable to
becoming depressed in situations in which there are significant alterations in
reinforcement contingencies. Brown, Ní Bhrolcháin, and Harris (1975), for
example, have identified a number of factors which appear to increase a
person's vulnerability to depression: (a) support and quality of interpersonal
relationships; (b) loss of mother by death or separation before the age of 11;
(c) having three or more children aged 14 or less at home; and (d) lack of full-
or part-time employment.

Cause and effect relationships between reinforcement and depression
have not yet been established. Much of our work has been based upon the
assumption that a low rate of reinforcement leads to depression. It is equally
plausible that the presence of depression leads to alterations in the reinforcement potential. The two causal hypotheses lead one to postulate different antecedent conditions. The reinforcement to depression hypothesis
leads one to focus on social skill, anxiety level, the occurrence of aversive
events, and the presence of support systems. The second causal hypothesis

(depression as related to decreased reinforcement potential) leads one to search for biochemical antecedents. However, it is important to note that these are by no means mutually exclusive hypotheses. Both hypotheses could very well be true, putting the person in a vicious circle where a low rate of reinforcement leads to depression which, in turn, alters the biochemical substrates of reinforcement potential, thereby further reducing reinforcement and intensifying depression.

REFERENCES

Akiskal, H. S., & McKinney, W. T. Depressive disorders: Toward a unified hypothesis. *Science*, 1973, *182*, 20–29.

Bandura, A. *Principles of behavior modification*. New York: Holt, 1969.

Brown, G. W., Nı Bhrolcháin, M. & Harris, T. Social class and psychiatric disturbance among women in an urban population. *Sociology*, 1975, *9*, 225–254.

Cautela, J. R. & Kastenbaum, R. A Reinforcement Survey Schedule for use in therapy, training, and research. *Psychological Reports*, 1967, *20*, 1115–1130.

Costello, C. G. Depression: Loss of reinforcer or loss of reinforcer effectiveness. *Behavior Therapy*, 1972, *3*, 240–247.

Dollard, J. B. & Miller, N. E. *Personality and psychotherapy*. New York: McGraw-Hill, 1950.

Estes, W. K. Reinforcement in human behavior. *American Scientist*, 1972, *60*, 723–729.

Ferster, C. B. & Skinner, B. F. *Schedules of reinforcement*. New York: Appleton, 1957.

Glaser, R. (Ed.). *The nature of reinforcement*. New York: Academic Press, 1971.

Grinker, R. R., Miller, J., Sabshin, M., Nunn, R., & Nunally, J. C. *The phenomena of depressions*. New York: Harper, 1961.

Grosscup, S. J. & Lewinsohn, P. M. Unpleasant and pleasant events and mood. *Journal of Clinical Psychology* (In Press).

Holmes, T. H. & Rahe, R. H. The social readjustment rating scale. *Journal of Psychosomatic Research*, 1967, *11*, 213.

Hull, C. L. *Principles of behavior*. New York: Appleton Century-Crofts, 1943.

Lewinsohn, P. M. Clinical and theoretical aspects of depression. In K. S. Calhoon, H. E. Adams, & K. M. Mitchell (Eds.), *Innovative methods in psychopathology*. New York: Wiley, 1974.

Lewinsohn, P. M. *The unpleasant events schedule: A scale for the measurement of aversive events*. Eugene, Oregon: Univ. Oregon, 1975.

Lewinsohn, P. M. & Graf, M. Pleasant activities and depression. *Journal of Consulting and Clinical Psychology*, 1973, *41*, 261–268.

Lewinsohn, P. M., Biglan, T., & Zeiss, A. Behavioral treatment of depression. In P. Davidson, (Ed.), *Behavioral management of anxiety, depression and pain*. New York: Bruner-Mazel, 1976.

Lewinsohn, P. M., Lobitz, W. C., & Wilson, S. "Sensitivity" of depressed individuals to aversive stimuli. *Journal of Abnormal Psychology*, 1973, *81*, 259–263.

Lewinsohn, P. M. & Talkington, J. Studies on the measurement of unpleasant events and relations with depression. *Applied Psychological Measurement*, 1979, *3*, 83–101.

Lewinsohn, P. M., Weinstein, M., & Shaw, D. Depresssion: A clinical-research approach. In R. D. Rubin & C. M. Frank (Eds.), *Advances in behavior therapy, 1968*. New York: Academic Press, 1969.

Libet, J. M., Lewinsohn, P. M. & Javorek, F. *The construct of social skill: An empirical study of several behavioral measures on temporal stability, internal structure, validity and situational generalizability*. Unpublished mimeograph, Univ. Oregon, 1973.

MacPhillamy, D. J. & Lewinsohn, P. M. *Pleasant events schedule.* Unpublished mimeograph, Univ. Oregon, 1971.

MacPhillamy, D. J. & Lewinsohn, P. M. *A scale for the measurement of positive reinforcement.* Unpublished mimeo, Univ. Oregon, 1973.

Olds, J. & Milner, P. Positive reinforcement produced by electrical stimulation of the septal area and other regions of the rat brain. *Journal of Comparative and Physiological Psychology,* 1954, 47, 419–427.

Patterson, G. R. A basis for identifying stimuli which control behaviors in natural settings. *Child Development,* 1974, 45, 900–911.

Patterson, G. R. & Cobb, J. A. A dyadic analysis of "aggressive" behaviors. In J. P. Hill (Ed.) *Minnesota symposia on child psychology* (Vol. 5). Minneapolis, Minnesota: Univ. Minnesota Press, 1971.

Paykel, E. S., Myers, J. K., Dienelt, M. N., Klerman, G. L., Lindenthal, J. J., & Pepper, M. P. Life events and depression: A controlled study. *Archives of General Psychiatry,* 1969, 21, 753–760.

Schless, A. P., Schwartz, L., Goetz, C., & Mendels, J. How depressives view the significance of life events. *British Journal of Psychiatry,* 1974, 125, 406–410.

Seligman, M. E. P. *Helplessness.* New York: W. H. Freeman, 1975.

Stewart, R. C. *The differential effects of positive and negative social reinforcement upon depressed and nondepressed subjects.* Unpublished master's thesis. Univ. Oregon, 1968.

Thorndike, E. L. *The psychology of wants, interests, and attitudes.* New York: Appleton Century-Crofts, 1935.

Tolman, E. C. There is more than one kind of learning. *Psychological Review,* 1949, 56, 144–155.

Youngren, M. A., Zeiss, A., & Lewinsohn, P. M. *Interpersonal events schedule.* Unpublished mimeograph, Univ. Oregon, 1975.

CHAPTER 14

Vulnerable Self-Esteem as a Predisposing Factor in Depressive Disorders

Joseph Becker

INTRODUCTION

Although vulnerable self-esteem has been regarded as a central feature of clinical depression by leading theorists, the construct has been largely ignored in research on depression. While depression and self-esteem (Wells & Marwell, 1976; Wylie, 1974) are somewhat nebulous constructs, they appear to have meaningful referents.

In some depressives, chronically low self-esteem seems to operate like a classical trait disposition: the cognition-affect is broadly transituational and relatively independent of identifiable events. In other depressives, diminished self-esteem is triggered by a broad range of situations so that low self-esteem acts like a widely generalized stress response. In still other depressives, there seem to be complex interactions between self-esteem and particular events: in some, these stressors elicit a generalized deflation in self-esteem, whereas others experience a circumscribed deflation. Unfortunately, there are no data to substantiate the validity of these clinically derived distinctions.

317

The Psychobiology of the Depressive Disorders:
Implications for the Effects of Stress

This chapter reviews theory, observations, and speculations on the developmental determinants of self-esteem, on aspects of the premorbid socialization of depressives that appear to be relevant to self-esteem regulation and on the socialization practices of depressed parents whose children are at 10 times greater risk for depression than the general population. It is assumed that stress adaptiveness, moderately high self-esteem, and resistance to psychogenic depression have common antecedents.

Clinical depression is probably an endpoint for multiple causal factors. Variable susceptibility to depression may be due to biologic factors alone, or in combination with differing socialization histories, competencies, attribution processes (Wortman & Coates, 1977), or support systems (Miller, Ingham, & Davidson, 1976). The extent to which personality factors are primary components of a depressive diathesis versus epiphenomena or orthogonal, additive, interactive, or reactive to biologic factors is undetermined. Familial concordance rates, the tendency of unipolar and bipolar affective disorders to breed true within families plus the psychopharmacologic response specificity of depressive subtypes, support the probability of a significant genetic factor in many depressions. Although this chapter stresses the depressive's premorbid socialization experiences, there is no intent to minimize the probable etiologic significance of biologic factors.

THE CONSTRUCT OF SELF-ESTEEM

Epstein's (1976) studies of self-esteem fluctuation in college students indicate that lowered self-esteem is accompanied by increased feelings of unhappiness, anger, sense of threat, fatigue, withdrawal, tension, disorganization, feelings of constraint, conflict, and inhibition. Increased self-esteem is accompanied by increased feelings of integration, freedom, positive emotions, and availability of energy.

Much of the research literature on self-esteem predates concern with interindividual differences in trait consistency (Bem & Allen, 1974), and interactions between traits and situations as more adequate predictors of behavior than either alone (Mischel, 1973). Wylie's (in press) contention that self-referential constructs like self-esteem may be useful is buttressed by Markus' (1977) study of self-schematas. As Markus notes, rigorous construct-validation studies of self-schematas have been rare. She defines self-schematas as "cognitive generalizations about the self, derived from past experience that organize and guide the processing of the self-related information contained in an individual's social experience [p. 63]." Information retrieval, judgments and decisions, actions, inferences, and predictions are selectively influenced by schematas. Counterschematic information is resisted. The stronger the schemata, the greater the tendency to make inferences from minimal, fragmentary data. The methodology of her study is beyond the scope of this chapter, but it provides a promising paradigm for testing assumptions about self-referential schematas.

Self-esteem is a cognitive-affective product of self-evaluation processes. Whether it is meaningful to conceptualize self-esteem as a general, global trait or as an interactionist, situation-specific attribute is a crucial issue. Most studies of self-esteem have used global, self-esteem measures that assess conscious self-concept and are thus susceptible to social desirability biases (Crandall, 1973), as are self-esteem measures derived from self- versus ideal-self discrepancy. The complexities of determining causal relationships between a global concept of self-esteem and several discrete indices of competence are well demonstrated by Bachman and O'Malley (1977). They report on a longitudinal study of relationships among self-esteem, educational, and occupational attainment. The investigators expected to find that self-esteem assessed in the tenth grade would relate positively to subsequent educational and occupational attainment, and that such attainments would increase initial differences in self-esteem.

Path analysis was used to determine causal directionality. Parents' socioeconomic level, the student's intellectual ability, and academic performance prior to 1966 were determined as "background" variables. Initial self-esteem levels in high school had negligible *direct* effect on subsequent educational and occupational attainment *despite sizable correlations among them*. The latter were due to the effects of background variables on all three factors.

Though Bachman and O'Malley define self-esteem as a relatively enduring global dimension, they contend that the constituents and weighting of factors determining self-esteem shift over time. For example, the limited relationship between tenth grade self-esteem and subsequent achievements may reflect a generalized developmental trend (factors like competitive achievement may contribute centrally to self-esteem at age 16, but this may be less true by age 23), or a transient cultural shift (the rampant alienation and disenchantment with conventional values related to Vietnam and Watergate). Longitudinal study of a single cohort often entails such interpretive problems.

Antecedents of Self-Esteem

The most extensive research on the *antecedents* of self-esteem is Coopersmith's (1967). The subjects were 10- to 12-year olds. These findings relate positive self-esteem to parental warmth, acceptance, respect, and clearly defined limit-setting. Parents who set clear limits also set age-appropriate limits, allow more deviation from conventional behavior and greater individual expression, use less severe punishment, and expect better academic performance. Parents of high self-esteem children are active, poised, relatively self-assured, on good mutual terms, and have major sources of gratification outside the family. Appropriate limit-setting by the parents provides a basis for realistic self-appraisal of performance, facilitates accurate perception and judgment, and provides a guide to societal expectancies, demands, and taboos; they render the environment more predictable, hence, more manageable. In turn, self-definition is enhanced by clearcut differentiation of wishes and environmental contingencies. Children reared with realistic limits are more independent and creative than children reared more permissively. The former are more able to express opinions and to accept criticism, and are more accepted by peers as leaders and associates. When limit-setting standards are ambiguous, children tend to remain dependent or to withdraw. High parental self-esteem goes strongly with acceptance of the child, and limit-definition goes with respect for the child. Parental acceptance is strongly related to the internalization of parental values by the child.

Coopersmith hypothesized that self-esteem reflects the extent to which performances are perceived as matching aspirations. The impact of such matching on self-esteem is weighted by the value of the aspirations. Regardless of their level of self-esteem, middle-class preadolescents value achievement and social success most highly; social norms become internalized as self-values that determine self-judgments. These self-judgments are more influenced by the appraisals of others within the "immediate effective interpersonal environment" than by "general public standards." Competence relative to one's own group and parental acceptance are the crucial determinants of perceived success. Personal norms are less significant in judging self-worth than the norms of personal groups.

High and low self-esteem children differ little in public goals, but markedly in personal aspirations. Those with high self-esteem set higher personal goals. The level of personally significant standards is determined more by expectancy of success than by hope; low self-esteem results in anticipated failure and pessimism which decreases motivation and lowers personal aspirations.

Self-Esteem as an Aspect of Implicit Self-Theory

Epstein (1976) redefines self-concept as an implicit self-theory consisting of a hierarchy of postulates. The chief function of self-theory is to provide a positive, pleasure–pain emotional balance. A favorable emotional balance depends on the effective assimilation of new data that enhance self-esteem and increase the prospects for self-esteem enhancement. The integrative and regulatory functions of self-theory can disintegrate if a major postulate is invalidated, if it cannot assimilate the data of experience, or if it fails to maintain a sufficient level of self-esteem; hence invalidating data tend to be resisted.

Self-esteem regulation derives from infantile dependency on the support and approval of the parents. Internalization of the parents' value system increases the likelihood of gaining approval and avoiding punishment. But with the internalization of values comes the capacity for self-disapproval. This self-evaluative function becomes the principal source of positive or negative feelings, including generalized positive or negative evaluations. "A person with high self-esteem carries, in effect, a loving parent within him [Epstein, 1976, p. 3]."

Internalization of self-evaluations that provide meager self-enhancement results in a weak and vulnerable self-system. Self-esteem reflects a balance of forces: the generalized self-image influences the perception of events toward congruency with itself, but the need for realistic assimilation minimizes chronic, excessive distortion. The extreme unpleasantness of abrupt drops in self-esteem likewise foster the maintenance of realistic trait levels of self-esteem.

The self-system is chiefly modified by reinforced learning. If stress cannot be mastered in this fashion, reality avoidant or distorting defenses are resorted to. If these measures prove insufficient, self-concept disorganization may ensue. A stable, adaptable self-theory contains widely generalized postulates firmly embedded in experience and difficult to invalidate. Epstein cites, "I am a worthy, competent person" as such a desirable postulate. Such postulates must be buffered by less general and more specific postulates that can be invalidated without jeopardizing the system.

Assimilation is more likely to occur if stress is faced rather than defended against. These reaction tendencies reflect learned value systems. External factors that affect assimilation versus defensiveness are magnitude of stimulation and rate of stimulus input. The closer a person is to their asymptote for arousal tolerance, the less the increase in stimulation required to evoke anxiety. Sudden increases in unexpected stimulation against a background of high arousal may induce pathological reactions such as phobias, which are rather common among depressives and "wax and wane" with major depressive symptoms. Dysphoric arousal is generated by threat, frustration, and high levels of unpleasant stimulation. Sufficient arousal may induce cortical inhibition with impaired integration.

Epstein's data indicate a similar pattern of response to one's self and to others following particular kinds of experience. For example, after an unpleasant experience, a substantial proportion of subjects report self-punitive tendencies (23%), whereas after pleasurable activities, an even higher proportion (62%) report self-indulgent tendencies. These findings accord well with those reported on children (Mischel, Ebbesen, & Zeiss, 1973).

In sum, Epstein's data (1976) suggest that dysphoric emotions evoke "avoidance of stimulation, both social and otherwise; negative reactions toward self and others; and either reassessment of basic values or increased defensiveness [p. 45]." As the section on parental depression indicates, the instigation to dysphoric emotions within families containing depressed parents is very high.

Self-Perception

Self-referent schematas and implicit theories derive from observational learning. Bem's (1972) functional analysis of self-perception notes that children are taught to label private events just as they do public ones. The observer infers and labels the state of the actor's thoughts and feelings largely on the basis of the actor's behavior and its context. The actor infers his internal state by applying labels acquired from observers to inferences based on observations of his own behavior and its context. The critical contextual factors are those that appear to control the behavior. Self-evaluation develops from such processes and from the actor's inferences about the observer's attitudes toward him.

If significant others or observers have badly skewed biases in their inferences, serious damage can result to the evolving self-referential schematas. Highly dysphoric parents are unlikely to perceive and label the affective state, intent, and expectancies of their children accurately.

Self-Efficacy

Bandura's concept of self-efficacy appears to be crucially related to the level and regulation of self-esteem. The construct of self-efficacy is related to the initiation and persistence of coping behavior. Efficacy expectancies entail beliefs about one's capacity to obtain desired outcomes. Mastery of previously threatening situations increases the sense of self-efficacy and reduces defensiveness. Expectancies of personal efficacy ultimately derive from observational learning, performance achievements, vicarious experiences, verbal persuasion, and physiological states. Behavioral change is postulated to arise from altered self-efficacy.

Motivation results from the cognitive representation of future outcomes. Prior reinforcement is chiefly effective via this indirect cognitive route which entails goal-setting and self-evaluating reactions. Anticipated satisfactions or dissatisfactions act as incentives to performance. People tend to avoid situations in which outcomes are important but in which their expectations of efficacy are low; conversely, they tend to engage in activities when expectations of efficacy are high. Adequate component skills, incentives, and positive expectancies are the principal determinants of persistence under stress.

Expectancies of efficacy vary in how broadly they are generalized, in how strongly they are held, and to what level of difficulty they apply. Performance accomplishments are the most effective way of strengthening efficacy expectations as they tend to extinguish fear, as well as to strengthen skills. Occasional failures may strengthen expectancies of mastery, depending on their timing, frequency, and the total context of experience. High states of emotional arousal interfere with performances and arouse anticipatory fear, hence aversive arousal diminishes perceived self-efficacy. Vicious cycles can occur in which the avoidance of stressful activities prevents the development of coping skills, and thus provides a realistic basis for fear and a low sense of self-efficacy.

Low expectancies of self-efficacy acquire protective functions that are not easily countered by successful experience; their alteration requires multiple successful experiences under varied circumstances. Bandura's prescription for durable and favorable changes in self-efficacy is analogous to those involved in skillful limit-setting during socialization. Self-efficacy is most readily altered by models who are perceived as creditable, prestigeful, trustworthy, expert, and self-assured. Atttibution of aversive arousal to situational factors is less likely to diminish expectancies of self-efficacy than attributions to personal inadequacies.

CLINICAL THEORY LINKING
DEPRESSION AND SELF-ESTEEM

Orality, Attachment, and Undue
Dependency

Fenichel (1945) contended that depressives are (orally) fixated on a need for external supplies (typically approval) to maintain their self-esteem. But chronic frustration of these needs engenders rage which conflicts with their attempted use of ingratiation and submissiveness as a means of gaining dependency gratifications. Depressives' great need to be loved, but inability to reciprocate, renders them constantly vulnerable to lowered self-esteem.

Chodoff (1974) and Fenichel suggest two personality types among depressives: (a) a more passive-dependent type whose self-esteem is regulated largely by feelings of being loved; and (b) a more obsessional type whose self-esteem is regulated largely by feelings of having done the right thing. Nonpathological drops in self-esteem are attributed to threatened loss or prolonged deprivation of dependency gratifications, and depression or melancholia is attributed to despair about regaining them.

However, as Chodoff (1974, p. 182) notes, some depressives seem to eschew dependency gratifications. They may have conflicts about such gratification, lack skill in obtaining them, or have a biologic deficiency in their "reward" center (Akiskal & McKinney, 1975). In most traditional psychodynamic theory, adequate levels of dependency gratification are necessary for the maintenance of self-esteem. However, depressives seem to have varied combinations of difficulty in obtaining, accepting, experiencing, recalling, and anticipating such gratification. These difficulties may be linked to mood-state dependent learning and recall (Weingartner, Miller, & Murphy, 1977).

Bowlby's (1977) attachment theory combines psychodynamic theory with ethology, social-learning theory, and cognition in accounting for many of the observations of psychodynamic theorists, but without the use of instinctual energy or drive concepts. Bowlby resembles social-learning theorists in his emphasis on observational learning in the acquisition of attachments, but he continues to weight the importance of early self- and object-representations heavily, especially in explanations of psychopathology (p. 209).

According to Bowlby, the chief parenting functions are the provision of secure love and understanding, and the fostering of individuation via encouragement to explore the environment and to acquire alternative sources of gratification. Frustration of these needs engenders anxiety and anger. If expression of the anger is difficult and resentment underlies a defensively acquired pseudocompulsive self-reliance, then a high vulnerability to depression results. Such persons anticipate rejection or coercion into a caretaker role. Such parental coercion fosters an overly conscientious, guilt-ridden individual. Depressed mothers are especially likely to induce such a self-system.

Unattainable Ego Ideals

Bibring (1953) contends that ego states reflect the extent to which the ego perceives itself as living up to its vital aspirations. He posits a developmental sequence of phase-specific aspirations that are vital to the maintenance of self-esteem. Bibring agrees that most depressives are excessively dependent on external love, care, and support: Aspirations that are specific to the first developmental phase of narcissistic aspirations. However, he contends that depressions can also result from a perceived inability to attain subsequent aspirations related to mastery and successful competitiveness.

Predisposers to depression include constitutional intolerance of persistent frustration, severe and prolonged helplessness, and developmental deficiencies in skill acquisition. These deficiencies are enhanced by the ego ideals which tend to be high and rigidly adhered to by depressives.

Self–Object Differentiation and Cathectic Balance

Jacobson (1975) argues that Bibring unduly minimizes the role of aggression in depression. She stresses the importance of the balance between the libidinal and aggressive cathexes of the self-representations and of the object-representations, and the independence of self-representations from object-representations as prime determinants of self-esteem. The greater the proportion and balance of the libidinal cathexis and the more differentiated the self- from the object-representations, the higher and more stable the self-esteem. Jacobson contends that depression does not necessarily accompany affects and cognitions of helplessness, much depends on attribution processes; only if the individual turns aggression against himself by blame and guilt does depression ensue. She contends that depressives' protestations about their inability to fulfill their aspirations often mask their ambivalence toward frustrating objects. Jacobson (1971, p. 180) subscribes to Mahler's (1966) notion that impaired self-esteem results from a socialization history that involved a lack of acceptance and emotional understanding of the child. The child becomes ambivalent and coercive before turning aggression inward and feeling helpless. Fluctuations in self-esteem both index and regulate the relative balance of libidinal and aggressive cathexes of the self and objects. Generalized guilt about aggressive impulses diminishes the discrete signal function of conscience and leads to pathological mood slumps or states.

Many predepressives view themselves as weak or dependent, whereas their love or attachment objects are highly idealized. But the imbalance in these relations can shift readily. Much defensive energy is needed to maintain chronic over- or underestimations. If the self is devalued, then successes must be selectively ignored or discounted, and conversely if the attachment object is overvalued, many of its attributes have to be ignored. When defenses break down, massive shifts in libidinal and aggressive energy occur, along with reversion to splitting and fusion of objects. The primary depressive disturbance occurs when the self and the attachment object are both aggressively devalued.

Autonomous Gratification Deficiencies

In Bemporad's (1971) interpersonal approach, the essence of a depressive predisposition is viewed as an inability to seek "autonomous gratification." The predepressive has been coerced into conformity with an idealized parental model which reflects values espoused, but not exemplified, by the dominant parent. The predepressive is socialized to believe that only compliance with these values makes life worthwhile. The depressive repeatedly projects these internalized values within subsequent significant relationships.

Bemporad addresses the paradox of why many depressives display pathological dependency yet sustain high levels of achievement. So long as pursuits are compatible with the internalized values of the "dominant other," depressives may be highly productive, but attempts at autonomous gratification evoke intense "pleasure anxiety." Depressives are reputedly unaware of their dependent tendencies. They are very resistant to social influence attempts that entail values incompatible with their own. Often they espouse values like self-reliance that are at variance with aspects of their behavior.

Bemporad contends that the families of depressives are often cohesive, pretentious, and dominated by one parent. They overvalue achievement and material success, provide little sexual or social information, and are socially isolated. The predepressive is often exploited emotionally by a depressed, ego-centric mother. The depressive fails to internalize an androgynous sexual identity that combines a healthy blend of masculinity and femininity.

Negative Bias against the Self

Beck (1976) views a negatively skewed cognitive bias toward self, world, and future as the central feature in most depressions. Affective and motivational aspects of depression are regarded as inevitable secondary resultants. For example, the depressive's pervasive pessimism fosters a sense of passive resignation or active avoidance of stressors. Their self-devaluation leads them to think of themselves as unworthy of pleasure, which further contributes to low self-regard. According to Beck, this self-devaluation stems from early parental deprivation and peer rejection. These early experiences result in schematas or cognitive templates that selectively filter subsequent experience in a negative manner.

Contributions from General Behavioral Theory

Bandura (1969) argues that depressives may have excessively high standards for self-reinforcement, and Baron (1966) states that persons are motivated to maintain customary levels of social reinforcement standards. Thus, if the depressive was deprived of much dependency gratification in early life and developed chronically low self-esteem, he would tend to maintain such expectancies. According to Seligman's concept of learned helplessness (Abramson & Seligman, 1977), animals and humans exposed to uncontrollable reinforcement, positive or negative, acquire a cognitive set of helplessness.[1]

Earlier notions that vulnerability to depression might be linked to an exceptionally high incidence of parental deprivation in childhood have not been well supported. However, deprivation has typically been defined in terms of death or absence only. It appears that repeated transactions between a child and significant others over a prolonged period affect personality functioning more than interactions during any particular critical phase (Clarke & Clarke, 1976).

This chapter does not extensively review the burgeoning literature generated by Seligman's concept of learned helplessness and Lewinsohn's operant-interpersonal approach (1974). Most of these studies are conducted on college students and many assess the transient effects of elevating or reducing scores on self-report measures of depression. The relevance of these findings for clinical depression is unclear as yet. As Blaney (1977) notes, these experimental designs often confound the effects of self-esteem with the constructs ostensibly measured. For example, attempting to induce learned helplessness by telling the subject that a task is solvable when it is not, may induce a state confounded by any possible combination of lowered self-regard, frustration, disinterest, or disdain (Wortman & Brehm, 1975). When changes in anxiety and hostility, as well as depression, have been assessed, the former usually increase at least as much as depression.

Perhaps the most significant difference between Beck's position and Seligman's is Beck's contention that depressives hold themselves unduly

---

[1] A reformulation of learned helplessness theory arrived as this chapter was being completed. Abramson, Seligman, and Teasdale (1978) address the issue of learned helplessness (LH) and self-esteem for the first time and quite interestingly. This reformulation of LH introduces a set of attributional concepts that are invoked when independence of response and outcome occur. The principal dimensions are global–specific, stable–unstable, and external–internal. They contend that only internal or personal attributions of responsibility for response-outcome independence result in lowered self-esteem (pp. 37–38). In depressive individuals personal attributions usually accompany global, stable ones. The Abramson et al. paper reflects an excellent and stimulating conceptual advance. However, like other social psychological approaches to depression, it fails to acknowledge the pervasive ambivalence that is so characteristic of depressive thought. It is my impression that people generally, and depressive ones especially, do not tend to make mutually exclusive, logically consistent attributions under natural circumstances. Logical external attributions for adverse outcomes frequently seem to spill over into self-derogation in depressive individuals and, as Epstein's data suggest, in normals as well. Survivors of catastrophic events such as concentration camps may clearly identify the logical source as external but be full of self-loathing as well. Probably the belief in a just world hypothesis (Lerner & Miller, 1978; Wortman & Dintzer, 1978) could partly explain such illogicality.

responsible; whereas Seligman argues that depression results from a perceived lack of control of reinforcers. Blaney summarized a number of studies that suggest that depressives hold themselves responsible for failures, but allow themselves no credit for successes, and Abramson and Sackeim (1977) review evidence for the apparent paradox of helplessness and self-blame.

IMPACT OF PARENTAL DEPRESSION ON THEIR CHILDREN

Systematic observations on interactions between depressed parents and their children have been fragmentary; but largely clinical accounts suggest very damaging effects on the nondepressed spouse and children. Although it is generally accepted that maternal deprivation is likely to result in personality disturbances in their offspring, it remains unclear as to whether specific kinds of deprivation result in specific forms of psychiatric disturbance in the child. Findings on depressed mothers have been summarized by Weissman and Paykel (1974, pp. 103–121). Disturbed children are most likely to occur when the parent has a chronic or recurrent depression. Many writers have noted marked maternal oscillation between "murderous hostility" and extreme inhibition. Children of depressed parents are reputedly much more disturbed than those of schizophrenic or normal control parents. Apparently children of schizophrenics can more readily discriminate the inappropriateness of their parents' behavior, and other adults respond more readily to the children's needs for support.

Previous pilot studies by investigators associated with Klerman indicated that depressed mothers frequently felt emotionally ungratified and abandoned by their grown children ("empty nest syndrome"). Working class, full-time housewives with multiple young children and unsympathetic husbands are especially vulnerable to depression (Brown, Ní Bhrolcháin, & Harris, 1975). Disparate role expectancies within the depressive's family generate considerable conflict; for example, once depressed, the mother is often unable to fulfill normal housekeeping functions, but others are very reluctant to assume them. As many investigators have observed, the patient's subjective role impairment often greatly exceeds her objective impairment.

Weissman and Paykel studied 40 depressed, mostly lower socioeconomic class, married women with intact families who responded favorably to antidepressant drug therapy and matched nonpsychiatric controls. Data on interactions between the depressed women and their children were based on the patient's self-reports and on case descriptions that often included home observations.

The depressed mothers were divided according to so-called family life-cycle stages based on the ages of their children (which resulted in very small sample sizes). Most serious impairment was found in children whose mothers were depressed during the post-partum phase, infancy, or adolescence. The adolescents of depressed mothers showed increased rebellion and withdrawal, and exploration of the social and material environment was much inhibited. The depressed mothers communicated poorly, were fractious and withdrawn, worried, guilty, and were often envious and competitive with their adolescent children. Common problems among their adolescent children included truancy, school dropout, drug abuse, theft, and promiscuity. Whereas younger children were typically supportive of depressed mothers, adolescents were often sadistic and rejecting, especially if the nondepressed spouse supported the child against the mother. The maternal depressions were not the result of problems with their adolescents, though they may have been aggravated by them. Usually these mothers had had depressive episodes prior to their children's adolescence during which the children had not been overtly disturbed. Improvement in maternal depression usually resulted in improved adolescent adjustment. The increased ability of the depressed mother to set limits, negotiate, and display genuine interest, seemed highly beneficial.

Numerous clinical investigators have speculated that much adolescent and childhood acting-out masks depression (Connors, 1976; Malmquist, 1975; Weiner, 1975). Clinical trials on antidepressants and lithium carbonate have yielded encouraging results (e.g., Gallemore & Wilson, 1972) with such acting-out adolescents. Malmquist (1975) speculated that much aggressiveness by the adolescent children of depressed mothers reflects the adolescent's attempt to counter his own depressed feelings. These feelings stem from loss due to the parent's withdrawal, and may serve to provoke punishment and assuage guilt for his anger toward the depressed parent. The mother's conflict between her feelings of deprivation and need to receive support versus her need to cope with heavy maternal role-demands that she provide other family members with support recurs in the literature.

Rashkis (1968) contends that depression in middle-aged parents is often reciprocally related to behavioral disturbances in their adolescent offspring. In the commonest constellation, the adolescent's conflicts reactivate unresolved adolescent conflicts in the parents. Typically, the parents have opted or been coerced into a somewhat repressive, conservative, secure life/style that prevents gratification of many sexual and aggressive impulses. The middle-aged parent is stressed "from above" by aging, illness, and death of parents; "from below" by their adolescent's conflicts; "from within" by physiological changes and their subjective impact; and "from without" by socioeconomic constraints. Overloads in any of these areas may precipitate depression. The parent may project his difficulties onto the child and the children's perception of parental distress may elevate their own insecurity.

Adolescents may respond by acting out their own and their parent's repudiated sexual and aggressive impulses, and/or they may become depressed themselves.

Hogan and Hogan (1975) recently reviewed their extensive experience in family therapy with depressives; their findings are similar to those of Meyersburg, Ablon, and Kohn (1974). These writers contend that much depressive behavior results from an acquired powerless–grandiose polarity. The depressed mother views her offspring's difficulties as indications of her inadequacy, rather than as cues to solvable problems. These mothers respond to many of their children's difficulties with anger and/or withdrawal. A young child's sense of self-value and interpersonal effectiveness is thought to depend heavily on its ability to elicit maternal nurturance. Infantile communications are primarily affective; therefore, adequate maternal responses to these communications require accurate inferences about the sources of distress and appropriate actions toward their relief. These are often not forthcoming from depressed mothers. The lack of an adequate maternal response hampers the child's use of speech for more precise and active specification of needs. As a result, many depressive adults have difficulty with directly expressing and responding to needs; direct requests are perceived as demands. In families of depressives, "Real love is expressed by understanding and responding to the needs . . . in the absence of clear verbal communication [Hogan & Hogan, 1975, p. 205]." Feelings of powerlessness are thus enhanced.

Efforts toward increased independence are frequently undermined; the child's striving for autonomy is often criticized and "guilt-evoking blame" is used to imply that he should have known better than to engage in such behavior. Compliance with the mother's threats and demands strengthens the child's identification with the maternal aggressor. This strong identification with the aggressor impedes individuation. The child's *prime responsibility* is to be concerned with the needs and feelings of others, just as he is to expect to have his own needs met by others. This pattern reinstates the infantile sense of powerlessness.

Strong affects, especially anger, are discouraged. Anger endangers nurturance. Depressives frequently have very ambivalent beliefs about anger: that it is futile (powerless) on the one hand, or enormously destructive (grandiose) on the other. Interference with direct affective expression often results in indirect expressions via somatization, acting-out, or symbolic symptoms. Depressives have particular difficulty in coping with loss because it triggers their feelings of powerlessness and their capacity for direct affective communication has been obstructed.

The predepressive's fears about his lack of value to, and impact on, others tend to be pervasive. This leads to giving up too easily without seeking alternative ways and means of gratification, or to excessive concern with manipulating or controlling others who are perceived as potential sources of gratification. Self-esteem is not increased by achievements, as the latter are often perceived as "selling out" to gain others' approval. Unsuccessful manipulations detract from self-esteem because the resultant anger gets turned against the powerless self. Anger cannot be effectively turned outward because of its perceived futility or destructiveness. Once depressed, others' approval is unhelpful because their support is seen as extracted rather than spontaneously given. The depressive repeatedly projects his grandiose, harsh, internalized parent onto others and feels he cannot meet their expectations.

The interactions of depressives foster depression in all participants. Depressives may achieve some feeling of effectiveness by reducing others to the same sense of impotence they experience. This end is achieved by rejecting others' helpful efforts, and then responding to their frustration with even more self-devaluation.

Anthony's study (1975) of children at high risk for developing psychopathology provides a graphic clinical description of the impact of bipolar parents on their children. Anthony stresses the importance of the interaction between the developmental phase of the child and the timing of the parental disturbance. The parental disturbance is not simply modelled or imitated by the child, but is assimilated and reacted to, so that some children appear to be relatively unaffected, others emulate the affected parent, and still others show opposite or complementary inclinations. Many of these children feel "transmogrified" by the parental illness. These children report struggles between becoming just like the affected parent or just the opposite.

The basic issues Anthony describes resemble those discussed by the Hogans: These high-risk children often oscillate between feelings of omnipotence and impotence, and between blaming and hating their disturbed parent and hating themselves for their parent's affliction as well as their own. Anthony (1976), like Jacobson, contends that self-esteem and esteem for the parents run parallel courses. If the parent is drastically devaluated, so is the child's self-regard; if the parent is defensively overidealized, then the child's ego ideals and super-ego development are arrested at a relatively primitive state which results in excessively high, rigid standards that are punitively enforced for failures and transgressions.

Anthony draws heavily on the mother–child observations and theorizing of Mahler (1966) and Benedek (1975). He especially cites Benedek's concept of the "depressive constellation" in which the unmet needs of the youngster stirs hatred toward the depressed mother which reactivates the mother's ambivalence toward her own mother. Aggression becomes "defused" and the child may be treated as a projection of the mother's bad self and her bad mother. The child's confidence is sapped; it becomes apathetic; and there is no energy for pleasure or environmental exploration.

IMPLICATIONS

To paraphrase the conclusion of Smith's (1968) excellent paper on competence and socialization, there should be no neat summary that reflects greater theoretical integration or empirical data than our state of knowledge permits. Nonetheless, to cast matters in contemporary terminology, this paper implicitly suggests that many depressives are socialized under regimens that strongly predispose them toward "illusions of incompetence" (Langer, in press) and/or "learned helplessness" (Abramson et al., 1978) as a result of being "programmed" toward controlled information processing (Schneider & Shiffrin, 1978) biased toward rendering cues salient (Taylor & Fiske, 1978) that engender depressogenic attributions and expectancies.

At this point, promising leads for the investigation of antecedents and effective intervention (Becker, 1977) appear to be in the realm of self-reinforcement standards as exemplified in the work of Bandura (1977), Kanfer (1977), and Rehm (1977); in self-referent schematas as exemplified in the concerns of Beck (1976) and Markus (1977); and in mood-state and dependent-verbal associations (Weingartner, Miller, & Murphy, 1977). The conceptual model and research paradigms associated with "egoistical relative deprivation" or equity theory (e.g., Crosby, 1976) may provide a fruitful source of research hypotheses and treatment strategies. Considerable leverage in the prevention of depression might be gained if children at especially high risk for depression could be detected early and discretely monitored for prodromal signs such as highly vulnerable self-esteem. Some extensions of Buchsbaum's work (Chapter 9) on differentiating psychopathological entities by distinctive evoked potential patterns may pick up those who are especially vulnerable because of genetic predisposition (Becker, Buffington, MacGregor, & Martin, 1979).

REFERENCES

Abramson, L. Y. & Sackeim, H. A. A paradox in depression: Uncontrollability and self-blame. *Psychological Bulletin*, 1977, 84, 838–851.

Abramson, L. Y., Seligman, M. E. P. & Teasdale, J. D. Learned helplessness in humans: Critique and reformulation. *Journal of Abnormal Psychology*, 1978, 87, 49–75.

Akiskal, H. S. & McKinney, W. T. Overview of recent research in depression. *Archives of General Psychiatry*, 1975, 32, 285–305.

Anthony, E. J. The influence of a manic-depressive environment on the developing child. In E. J. Anthony & T. Benedek (Eds.), *Depression and human existence*. Boston: Little, Brown, 1975.

Bachman, J. C. & O'Malley, P. M. Self-esteem in young men: A longitudinal analysis of the impact of educational and occupational attainment. *Journal of Personality and Social Psychology*, 1977, 35, 365–381.

Bandura, A. *Principles of behavior modification*. New York: Holt, Rinehart, & Winston, 1969.

Bandura, A. Self-efficacy: Toward a unifying theory of behavioral change. *Psychological Review*, 1977, 84, 191–216.

Baron, R. M. Social reinforcement effects as a function of social reinforcement history. *Psychological Review*, 1966, 73, 527–539.

Beck, A. T. *Cognitive therapy and the emotional disorders*. New York: International Univ. Press, 1976.

Becker, J. *Affective disorders*. Morristown, New Jersey: General Learning, 1977.

Becker, J., Martin, D. C., Buffington, V., & MacGregor, B. Evoked potential patterns of alcoholics with familial histories of affective disorders. In R. W. Pickens & L. L. Heston (Eds.) *Psychiatric factors in drug abuse*. New York: Academic Press, in press.

Bem, D. Self-perception theory. *Advances in Experimental Social Psychology*, 1972, 6, 1–62.

Bem, D. J. & Allen, A. On predicting some of the people some of the time: The search for cross-situational consistencies in behavior. *Psychological Review*, 1974, 81, 506–520.

Bemporad, J. R. New views on the psychodynamics of the depressive character. In S. Arieti (Ed.), *The world biennial of psychiatry and psychotherapy*, 1971, 1, 219–244.

Benedek, T. Ambivalence and the depressive constellation in the self. In E. J. Anthony & T. Benedek (Eds.), *Depression and human existence*. Boston: Little, Brown, 1975.

Bibring, E. The mechanism of depression. In P. Greenacre (Ed.), *Affective disorders*. New York: International Univ. Press, 1953.

Blaney, P. H. Contemporary theories of depression: Critique and comparison. *Journal of Abnormal Psychology*, 1977, 86, 203–223.

Bowlby, J. The making and breaking of affectional bonds. *British Journal of Psychiatry*, 1977, 130, 201–210.

Brown, G. W., Ní Brolcháin, M., & Harris, T. Social class and psychiatric disturbance among women in an urban population. *Sociology*, 1975, 9, 225–254.

Chodoff, P. The depressive personality: A critical review. In R. J. Friedman & M. M. Katz (Eds.), *The psychology of depression: Contemporary theory and research*. Washington, D.C.: V. H. Winston, 1974.

Clarke, A. M. & Clarke, A. D. B. (Eds.). *Early experience: Myth and evidence*. New York: Free Press, 1976.

Conners, C. K. Classification and treatment of childhood depression and depressive equivalents. In D. M. Gallant & P. G. M. Simpson (Eds.), *Depression*. New York: Spectrum, 1976.

Coopersmith, S. *The antecedents of self-esteem*. San Francisco, California: Freeman, 1967.

Crandall, R. The measurement of self-esteem and related constructs. In J. P. Robinson & P. R. Shaver (Eds.), *Measures of social psychological attitudes*. Ann Arbor, Michigan: Survey Research Center, Institute for Social Research, 1973.

Crosby, F. A model of egoistical relative deprivation. *Psychological Review*, 1976, 83, 85–113.

Epstein, S. Anxiety, arousal and the self-concept. In I. G. Sarason & C. D. Spielberger (Eds.), *Stress and anxiety* (Vol. 3). Washington, D.C.: Hemisphere, 1976.

Fenichel, O. *The psychoanalytic theory of neurosis*. New York: Norton, 1945.

Gallemore, J. L. & Wilson, W. P. Adolescent maladjustment or affective disorder? *American Journal of Psychiatry*, 1972, 129, 608–612.

Hogan, P. & Hogan, B. K. The family treatment of depression. In F. F. Flach & S. C. Draghi (Eds.), *The nature and treatment of depression*. New York: Wiley, 1975.

Jacobson, E. The regulation of self-esteem. In E. J. Anthony & T. Benedek (Eds.), *Depression and human existence*. Boston: Little, Brown, 1975.

Kanfer, F. H. Self-regulation and self-control. In H. Zeier (Ed.), *The psychology of the 20th century* (Vol. 4), Zurich: Kindler Verlag, 1977.

Langer, E. J. The illusion of incompetence. In L. Perlmutter & R. Monty (Eds.), *Choice and perceived control*. Hillsdale, N.J.: Erlbaum, in press.

Lerner, M. J. & Miller, D. T. Just world research and the attribution process: Looking back and ahead. *Psychological Bulletin*, 1978, 85, 1030–1051.

Lewinsohn, P. M. A behavioral approach to depression. In R. J. Friedman & M. M. Katz

(Eds.), *The psychology of depression: Contemporary theory and research*. Washington, D.C.: V. H. Winston, 1974. Pp. 157–179.

Mahler, M. Notes on the development of basic moods. In R. M. Loewenstein, L. M. Newman, M. Schur, & A. J. Solnit (Eds.), *Psychoanalysis: A general psychology*. New York: International Univ. Press, 1966. Pp. 152–168.

Malmquist, C. P. Depression in childhood. In F. F. Flach & S. C. Draghi (Eds.), *The nature and treatment of depression*. New York: Wiley, 1975. Pp. 73–99.

Markus, H. Self-schemata and processing information about the self. *Journal of Personality and Social Psychology*, 1977, *35*, 63–78.

Meyersburg, H. A., Ablon, S. L., & Kotin, J. A reverberating psychic mechanism in the depressive processes. *Psychiatry*, 1974, *37*, 372–386.

Miller, P. M., Ingham, I. G., & Davidson, S. Life events, symptoms and social support. *Journal of Psychosomatic Research*, 1976, *20*, 515–522.

Mischel, W. Toward a cognitive social learning reconceptualization of personality. *Psychological Review*, 1973, *80*, 252–283.

Mischel, W., Ebbesen, E. B., & Zeiss, A. R. Selective attention to the self: Situational and dispositional determinants. *Journal of Personality and Social Psychology*, 1973, *27*, 129–142.

Rashkis, H. A. Depression as a manifestation of the family as an open system. *Archives of General Psychiatry*, 1968, *19*, 57–63.

Rehm, L. P. *A behavioral self-control approach to depression*. Paper presented at the Loyola Symposium on Depression, Chicago, 1977.

Schneider, W., & Shiffrin, R. M. Controlled and automatic human information processing: I. Detection, search, and attention. *Psychological Review*, 1977, *84*, 1–66.

Smith, M. B. Competence and socialization. In J. A. Clausen (Ed.), *Socialization and society*. Boston: Little, Brown, 1968. Pp. 271–320.

Taylor, S. E., & Fiske, S. T. Salience, attention, and attribution: Top of the head phenomena. In L. Berkowitz (Ed.), *Advances in experimental social psychology*, Vol. II. New York: Academic Press, 1978. Pp. 249–288.

Weiner, I. B. Depression in adolescence. In F. F. Flach & P. S. C. Draghi (Eds.), *The nature and treatment of depression*. New York: Wiley, 1975. Pp. 99–119.

Weingartner, H., Miller, H., & Murphy, D. Mood-state-dependent retrieval of verbal associations. *Journal of Abnormal Psychology*, 1977, *86*(3), 276–284.

Weissman, M. M. & Paykel, E. S. *The depressed woman: A study of social relationships*. Chicago: Univ. Chicago Press, 1974.

Wells, L. E. & Marwell, G. *Self-esteem: Its conceptualization and measurement*. Beverly Hills, California: Sage Publications, 1976.

Wortman, C. B. & Brehm, J. W. Responses to uncontrollable outcomes: An integration of reactance theory and the learned helplessness model. In L. Berkowitz (Ed.), *Advances in experimental social psychology* (Vol. 8). New York: Academic Press, 1975.

Wortman, C. B. & Coates, D. *Social psychological perspectives on depression*. Paper presented at the Loyola Symposium on Depression, Chicago, 1977.

Wortman, C. B. & Dintzer, L. Is an attributional analysis of the learned helplessness phenomenon viable: A critique of the Abramson-Seligman-Teasdale reformulation. *Journal of Abnormal Psychology*, 1978, *87*, 75–90.

Wylie, R. C. *The self-concept: A review of methodological considerations and measuring instruments* (Vol. 1). Lincoln, Nebraska: Univ. Nebraska Press, 1974.

Wylie, R. C. *The self-concept* (Vol. 2) (Rev. ed.). Lincoln, Nebraska: Univ. of Nebraska Press (in press).

CHAPTER 15

Learned Helplessness, Stress, and the Depressive Disorders[1]

Judy Garber, William R. Miller, and
Stephen F. Seaman

INTRODUCTION

This chapter will focus on the relationship between learned helplessness, stress, and depression. We propose, on the basis of similarities in symptoms, cause, treatments, and prevention, that learned helplessness provides a model of depression. As with any model of psychopathology, the usefulness of the learned helplessness model lies in its potential for enhancing the experimental testability of hypotheses about depression and for sharpening the definition of the clinical phenomenon.

Before formally presenting the evidence for the learned helplessness model of depression and discussing its relationship to stress, we will carefully delimit our use of the term depression and clearly define learned helplessness. A great deal of confusion has arisen in the literature due to the tendency to use the term depression in a number of different ways, depres-

[1] Preparation of this chapter was supported in part by a National Institute of Mental Health Grant (MH-19604) to M. E. P. Seligman.

The Psychobiology of the Depressive Disorders:
Implications for the Effects of Stress

sion having been variously defined as a mood, a symptom, a syndrome, and a nosological entity.

We refer to depression here as a syndrome, that is, a group or cluster of symptoms that tend to co-occur. The symptoms of depression fall into four general classes: emotional, motivational, cognitive, and somatic (Beck, 1967). It is not necessary that any one of these symptoms, or even that a certain number of these, be present for an individual to be labeled as having the syndrome of depression. It is the nature of the clinical phenomenon that there are no *necessary* characteristics by which it is defined.

Confusion over terminology is compounded by the presence of numerous classification systems for depression. Many of the important issues in classification have been discussed elsewhere in this volume (see Chapters 1–4). We are primarily concerned with unipolar depressions, that is, those syndromes of depression without a personal or family history of mania or hypomania.

In the present chapter we will review the experimental evidence supportive of learned helplessness as a model of depression. We will then examine the role of stress in the production of learned helplessness and depression. Finally, we will particularly emphasize the importance of the *expectation* of lack of control over stress as a sufficient condition for the development of depression.

LEARNED HELPLESSNESS

The term "learned helplessness" was first used to describe the interference with avoidance responding in dogs produced by inescapable shock, and also as a shorthand to describe the process believed to underlie the behavior. Overmier and Seligman (1967) and Seligman and Maier (1967) found that dogs given inescapable shocks in a Pavlovian harness were subsequently poorer at escaping shock in a shuttle-box than dogs given escapable shock or no prior shock at all. The "inescapable-shock" animals seemed to give up and passively accept the shock, and even when they occasionally did escape shock in the shuttle box, they failed to learn. These dogs failed to profit from exposure to the barrier-jumping, shock-termination contingency.

The main behavioral symptoms of learned helplessness are failure to initiate responses, and difficulty learning that responding is effective. Seligman, Maier, and Solomon (1971) postulated that these behavioral symptoms result from the organism's learning about the independence between outcomes and responding (the uncontrollability), and forming expectations about its ability to control outcomes in subsequent situations. An outcome is said to be uncontrollable only if the probability of the outcome given a response is equal to the probability of the outcome given the absence of that response, and if this is true of all voluntary responses. Thus, an organism is helpless with respect to an outcome when the outcome occurs independently of all his voluntary responses. Note that this noncontingency may be a function of the situation (i.e., no individual possesses the controlling responses), or of the individual (i.e., the individual lacks the requisite controlling responses which are available to other people). A more detailed discussion of the difference between "universal helplessness" and "personal helplessness" may be found in Abramson, Seligman, and Teasdale (1978).

Learning that outcomes are uncontrollable has three major effects:

1. A motivational effect that reduces the probability that the subject will initiate responses to escape, because part of the incentive for making such responses is the expectation that responses will bring relief
2. A cognitive effect, that involves learning that responding and the shock are independent. This makes it more difficult to learn that responding *does* produce relief, when the organism makes a response which actually terminates shock.
3. An emotional effect, occurring when an uncontrollable, traumatic stimulus is introduced into a situation. It causes a heightened state of emotionality including fear, anxiety, and depression.

The debilitating consequences of uncontrollable events have been demonstrated in a variety of situations, with a variety of uncontrollable events, and in a variety of species, including fish (Frumkin & Brookshire, 1969; Padilla, 1973; Padilla, Padilla, Ketterer, & Giacolone, 1970), cats (Masserman, 1971; Seward & Humphrey, 1967; Thomas & Dewald, 1977), rats (Maier, Albin, & Testa, 1973; Maier & Testa, 1975; Seligman & Beagley, 1975; Seligman, Rosellini, & Kozak, 1975), and men (Fosco & Geer, 1971; Gatchel & Proctor, 1976; Glass & Singer, 1972; Hiroto, 1974; Hiroto & Seligman, 1975; Klein, Fencil-Morse & Seligman, 1976; Klein & Seligman, 1976; Krantz, Glass, & Snyder, 1974; Miller & Seligman, 1975; Racinskas, 1971; Rodin, 1976; Roth, 1973; Roth & Bootzin, 1974; Roth & Kubal, 1976; Thornton & Jacobs, 1971). In addition to passivity and retarded response–relief learning, the following characteristics are also associated with learned helplessness:

1. Helplessness in dogs has a time course (Overmier & Seligman, 1967; Overmier, 1968).
2. Helpless animals show reduced aggression (Maier, Anderson, & Lieberman, 1972; Powell & Greer, 1969).
3. Uncontrollable shock results in weight loss and anorexia (Mowrer & Viek, 1948; Linder, 1968; Weiss, 1968).
4. Placing monkeys in an inescapable, aversive setting produces deficits in social and sexual behavior (Harlow, Harlow, & Suomi, 1971; Suomi & Harlow, 1972).
5. Whole brain norepinephrine is depleted in helpless animals (Weiss, Glazer, & Pohorecky, 1975; Weiss, Stone, & Harrell, 1970).

6. Septal activation is associated with learned helplessness (Thomas & Balter, in press).
7. Inescapable noise with humans produces self-reported affect changes, with increases in sadness, anxiety, and hostility (Miller & Seligman, 1975; Gatchel, Paulus, & Naples, 1975; Roth & Kubal, 1976), and physiological changes (Gatchel & Proctor, 1976).

These, then, are the basic learned helplessness effects found in animals and humans.

A number of alternative explanations for the etiology of the learned helplessness effects have been advanced. These hypotheses have been limited to examining the effects of uncontrollable shocks in animals, rather than attempting to explain learned helplessness in man. A description of these alternative theories may be found in Anisman and Waller (1973), Bracewell and Black (1974), Glazer and Weiss (1976a,b) and Weiss et al. (1975). We believe, however, that only the learned helplessness hypothesis (Maier & Seligman, 1976; Maier, Seligman, & Solomon, 1969; Seligman, 1975; Seligman et al., 1971), which has received the most experimental support, provides the most unified theoretical framework integrating the animal and human data.

LEARNED HELPLESSNESS MODEL OF DEPRESSION

Etiology

Historically, the learned helplessness model of depression was proposed by Seligman (1974) on the basis of gross similarities between the behaviors characteristic of learned helplessness and symptoms of depression. Learned helplessness is caused by learning that responding is independent of reinforcement; so the model suggests that the cause of depression is the expectation that action is futile. Seligman argues that experience with uncontrollability is similar to the experiences thought to be precipitants of depression (e.g., loss of a loved one, loss of a job). The depressed person believes or has learned that he cannot control those elements of his life that relieve suffering, bring gratification, or provide nurturance. In short, he believes he is helpless. Such events as failure at work or school, rejection or separation from loved ones, physical disease, financial difficulty, or growing old, are often interpreted as meaning that the person's efforts have been in vain; his responses have failed to bring about desired gratification; or he can no longer control a significant source of gratification and support. What these frequently depressing situations have in common is that the person believes he no longer has control of those aspects of his life that are important to him.

Other theorists of depression emphasize the centrality of helplessness and hopelessness in the etiology of depression. Bibring (1953), arguing from a dynamic viewpoint, sees the ego's shocking awareness of its helplessness as a central theme of depression. Melges and Bowlby (1969) suggested that the depressive feels he is incapable of obtaining his goals and believes that his plans of action are no longer effective, though his goals remain relatively unchanged. Lichtenberg (1957) also believes that the depressive feels hopeless about attaining his goals, and he stresses that depressed people blame themselves for their failures. Schmale (1958) and Engel (1968) have indicated that hopelessness and helplessness make a person more susceptible to depression, as well as to illness and death. Beck (1967, 1976) sees depression primarily as a cognitive disorder resulting from depressed individuals' negative cognitive set, particularly about their inability to change their situation. Depressed people are characterized by the "cognitive triad": They view their world, themselves, and their future in a negative way.

The evidence which has accumulated over the past few years, showing parallels between the symptoms of learned helplessness and depression, increases the confidence in the etiologic significance of the model. Such research allowed direct experimental manipulation of the events considered by the learned helplessness model to be etiologically significant in depression. Studies by Miller and Seligman (1975, 1976) and Klein et al. (1976) all involved the same 3 × 2 (controllability × depression) design—depressed and nondepressed subjects were first exposed to controllable outcomes, uncontrollable outcomes, or no pretreatment and then asked to perform on a test task where the outcome was controllable. In all three studies, strikingly similar test-task performance deficits were found for depressed subjects who had no pretreatment and for nondepressed subjects who had uncontrollable pretreatment. With a slightly different design, Klein and Seligman (1976) obtained parallel results. Clearly, the fact that noncontingent reinforcement results in behavioral deficits similar to those of naturally occurring depression does not *prove* that the depression was also produced by experiences with uncontrollable reinforcement. However, if experiments using the 3 × 2 design continue to demonstrate a variety of similarities in the effects of helplessness and depression, the hypothesis that learned helplessness and depression are parallel phenomena with a similar etiology will be strengthened.

Symptoms

Table 15.1 summarizes the symptom similarities of learned helplessness and depression, and it shows that most of the behavioral and physiological

Table 15.1

SYMPTOM SIMILARITIES OF LEARNED HELPLESSNESS AND
DEPRESSION

Learned helplessness	Depression
Absence of, or slowness in, responding	Passivity (Miller, 1975)
Difficulty learning that responses produce relief	Cognitive distortions (Beck, 1967)
Dissipates in time	Time course (Lundquist, 1945; Paskind, 1929, 1930)
Reduced aggression	Introjected hostility (Freud, 1917)
Weight loss, appetite loss, social and sexual deficits	Weight loss, appetite loss, social and sexual deficits (Beck, 1967)
Norepinephrine depletion and cholinergic activity	Norepinephrine depletion (Schildkraut, 1965)
Increased self-reported depression, anxiety, and hostility	Dysphoria (Beck, 1967)

characteristics of learned helplessness have parallels in human depression. Thus, the symptoms of learned helplessness and depression have a great deal in common.

The following review will focus on the experimental tests of the model, giving only brief mention to the similarities that have been discussed in earlier presentations of the model (Miller, Rosellini, & Seligman, 1977; Seligman, 1974, 1975; Seligman, Klein, & Miller, 1976). To date, symptom and therapy parallels between learned helplessness and depression have received the most experimental attention. Nondepressed subjects made helpless with unsolvable problems or inescapable noise subsequently show large deficits in solving anagrams (Klein et al., 1976; Miller & Seligman, 1975) and in escaping noise in a shuttle-box task (Klein & Seligman, 1976), as do depressed controls.

According to the learned helplessness model, the *central* cause of the deficits associated with helplessness and depression is the belief that outcomes are independent of responding. The method used to assess this belief is derived from Rotter and his associates (James, 1957; James & Rotter, 1958; Phares, 1957; Rotter, Liverant, & Crowne, 1961). These investigators demonstrated that verbalized expectancies for future success change more when reinforcement is perceived as response-dependent (skill determined) than when it is perceived as response-independent (chance determined). In other words, expectancies for future success change little when the outcome is perceived as beyond personal control.

Using this method, Miller & Seligman (1973) examined cognitive functioning in college students and found that depressed subjects showed smaller expectancy changes than nondepressed subjects when compared in a skill task but not in a chance task. Also, the depth of depression signi-ficantly correlated with the smaller expectancy change in skill, but did not correlate with expectancy changes in chance. Miller, Seligman, and Kur-lander (1975) replicated these results using a different set of tasks. Further-more, they found no consistent differences in expectancy changes between anxious and nonanxious subjects who were matched for level of depression. They concluded, therefore, that the belief in response-outcome indepen-dence in skill was specific to depression. Abramson, Garber, Edwards, and Seligman (1978) further examined the specificity question using a popula-tion of markedly depressed inpatients. They found that hospitalized, unipo-lar depressives exhibited significantly smaller expectancy changes in skill than did normal controls, and both depressed and nondepressed schizo-phrenics. Finally, Klein and Seligman (1976) and Miller and Seligman (1976) tested the prediction that experience with uncontrollability produces a belief in response-outcome independence. Both studies found that normal sub-jects exposed to inescapable noise reacted similarly to depressed subjects given no noise by showing smaller changes in expectancy in skill than nondepressed subjects given no noise.

These experimental findings support the contention that both helpless-ness induced by uncontrollable events and naturally occurring depression (mild and severe) have a negative cognitive set in common: The belief that outcomes are independent of responses. This negative cognitive set also produces the failure of both depressed controls and nondepressed subjects made helpless with inescapable noise (Miller & Seligman, 1975) or unsolv-able problems (Klein et al., 1976) to see the pattern on an anagram task. Not only are depressed and helpless subjects slower to solve anagrams, but they are also slower to pick up the pattern common to all the anagrams.

Recent data (Garber & Hollon, in press) suggest that the cognitive distortion associated with depression is specific to depressive's view of themselves, rather than a general belief in the independence between all responses and outcomes. Garber and Hollon asked depressed and nondepressed subjects to estimate either the probability of their own future success, or the probability of another person's success in the skill–chance situation. They replicated the finding that depressed subjects, estimating future success for them-selves, show small expectancy changes. However, depressed subjects, simi-lar to nondepressed subjects, show large expectancy changes when estimat-ing the probability of another person's success in the same skill task. Garber and Hollon concluded that depressed individuals view themselves as per-sonally helpless in a skilled situation, but do not view the situation itself as universally uncontrollable.

In addition to these cognitive deficits, physiological changes induced by exposure to uncontrollability have been assessed. Gatchel and Proctor (1976) reported that subjects pretreated with inescapable tones demon-strated impaired performance in solving anagrams relative to the other subjects. Moreover, the helpless group demonstrated lower tonic skin-conductance levels, smaller phasic skin-conductance responses, and more spontaneous electrodermal activity relative to the group pretreated with escapable tones. These are symptoms that some researchers (Greenfield, Katz, Alexander, & Roessler, 1963; McCarron, 1973) have claimed to be associated with clinical depression (see Lewinsohn, Lobitz, & Wilson, 1973, for contrary results). Gatchel and Proctor (1976) viewed the lower tonic and phasic skin-conductance responses as correlates of the decreased task involvement and motivation found in learned helplessness and depression.

There are also a number of features of depression that have only recently been investigated in learned helplessness. Pre-eminent among these are many of the subjective symptoms that go into the clinical diagnosis of depression and cannot be investigated in animals: dejected mood, feelings of self-blame, loss of self-esteem, loss of mirth, feelings of worthlessness and apathy. For example, affective similarities in naturally occurring depression and laboratory induced helplessness have been demonstrated. Miller and Seligman (1975) exposed three groups of depressed and nondepressed subjects to escapable, inescapable, or no noise. All subjects received the Multiple Affect Adjective Check List (Zuckerman & Lubin, 1965) both before and after pretreatment. As expected, the depressed subjects had higher depression scores than the nondepressed subjects. As a result of experience with uncontrollable noise, the nondepressed subjects became significantly more depressed, anxious, and hostile. Similarly, Gatchel et al. (1975) replicated the finding that nondepressed subjects exposed to inescapable noise become significantly more depressed, anxious, and hostile than nondepressed subjects receiving escapable noise. Roth and Kubal (1976) found that subjects exposed to unsolvable problems, perceived as reflecting intellectual ability, reported more feelings of depression, incompetence, stress, frustration, anger, and fatigue than controls. Klein et al. (1976) also found that unsolvable problems increased self-rated anger, though they found no differences in ratings of depression.

Finally, in a study assessing the effects of controllability and predictability in the physical and psychological well-being of the institutionalized age, Schulz (1976) found that subjects who received either predictable or controllable visits from college students, showed more positive affect than did the unpredictable-visit and no-treatment subjects. Thus, experience with uncontrollability does produce emotional changes in humans.

Recently, a number of investigators have suggested that the perception of the causes of one's helplessness may be an important determinant of many of the other subjective symptoms of depression (Abramson, Seligman, & Teasdale, 1978; Miller, 1977; Wortman & Brehm, 1975). Abramson, Seligman, and Teasdale (1978) distinguished between personal and universal helplessness and suggested that individuals who believe that outcomes are not contingent on responses in their own repertoire, but are contingent for others (personal helplessness) will show lower self-esteem than individuals who believe that desired outcomes are neither contingent on responses in their or other's repertoire (universal helplessness). Wortman and Brehm (1975) predicted that individuals who attribute failure to exert control to their own short-comings would react more intensely and show greater "psychological disturbance" than those who made external attributions of causality. Wortman, Panciera, Shusterman, and Hibscher (1976) tested this prediction and found that subjects who attributed their failure to their own incompetence rated themselves as significantly more helpless, upset, frustrated, angry, and aroused than subjects who made situational attributions. Interestingly, the inadequate ability groups performed *better* on a subsequent cognitive task than all other groups. Similarly, others have found that subjects who are forced to attribute their failures during training to their own lack of ability performed better on a subsequent task than all other groups. Thus, although attributions to personal inadequacy lead to emotional and self-esteem deficits associated with depression and helplessness, they do not always lead to cognitive and motivational deficits.

Before leaving this section on symptom parallels between learned helplessness and depression, it is useful to examine *differences* between the two. Even though the symptoms of learned helplessness and depression have a great deal in common, there are substantial gaps. In the first place, there are two symptoms found with uncontrollable shock that may or may not correspond to depression. Stomach ulcers occur more frequently and severely in rats receiving uncontrollable shock than controllable shock (Weiss, 1968; 1971a,b,c). We know of no study examining the relationship of depression to stomach ulcers. Second, uncontrollable shock produces more anxiety (measured subjectively, behaviorally, and physiologically) than controllable shock (see Seligman, 1975, for a review). The question of whether depressed people are more anxious than others does not have a clear answer. Beck (1967) reported that although both depression and anxiety can be observed in some individuals, only a small positive correlation existed over a population of 606 inpatients. However, Mendels, Weinstein, and Cochrane (1972) found high positive correlations between self-report measures of anxiety and depression with psychiatric inpatients. In addition, Miller *et al.* (1975) found very few depressed college students who were not also anxious. So, both depression and helplessness may also be associated with anxiety.

In summary, then, there are a number of direct symptom parallels between learned helplessness and depression. The helplessness model of depression predicts that any symptom displayed by depressed people under naturally occurring circumstances should be exhibited by nondepressed people who experience uncontrollable events and acquire an expectation of response-outcome independence. Parallels in behavioral (failure to escape noise; failure to solve anagrams), cognitive (distorted beliefs concerning the effects of skilled responding; difficulty in detecting patterns in cognitive problems), affective (lowered mood), and physiological (lower skin conductance responses) symptoms have been experimentally produced. Further, the central feature of learned helplessness, belief in independence between outcomes and skilled responding, is specific to depression and is present in severely depressed inpatients, as well as mildly depressed college students. Thus, a large body of experimental evidence exists that confirms many predictions of the learned helplessness model of depression.

Treatment

According to the learned helplessness hypothesis, a helpless animal fails to escape shock because it expects that no response it emits will produce shock termination. If the animal is forcibly exposed to the fact that its responding produces shock termination (i.e., positive response reinforcement), this expectation should be changed. Seligman, Maier, and Geer (1968) and Seligman, Rosellini, and Kozak (1975) found that animals required repeated, forced exposure to the response–shock termination contingency before they could learn to escape on their own.

There is, as yet, no scientifically established panacea for depression. Left alone, depression often dissipates in a few weeks or months. But there are therapies that are reported to alleviate depression and are consonant with the learned helplessness model. A detailed discussion of parallels between therapy for learned helplessness and those therapies that work for depression is presented in Seligman et al. (1976).

Recently, therapeutic parallels between learned helplessness and depression have been examined in the laboratory. Klein and Seligman (1976) tested the prediction that experience with controllable events reverses the belief in response-outcome independence. They found that depressed subjects and nondepressed helpless subjects who receive experience with solvable cognitive problems, subsequently show adequate escape performance and normal expectancy changes. Similarly, Miller and Seligman (1975) found that depressed individuals exposed to *escapable* noise performed better on anagrams than depressed individuals exposed to no noise. Using a direct cognitive intervention, Klein et al. (1976) found that depressed individuals instructed to attribute failure on an unsolvable task to the difficulty of the task performed better on a subsequent anagrams task than depressed individuals instructed to attribute failure to their own incompetence. Thus, changing the expectation of uncontrollability appears to ameliorate deficits characteristic of helplessness and depression.

Prevention

Behavioral immunization has been demonstrated to be an easy and effective means of preventing learned helplessness in dogs (Seligman & Maier, 1967), rats (Hannum, Rosellini, & Seligman, 1976; Seligman et al., 1975), and humans (Douglas & Anisman, 1975; Jones, Nation, & Massad, 1977; Thornton & Powell, 1974). The helplessness viewpoint suggests a way to immunize organisms against the effects of uncontrollable events. Initial experience with escapable shocks, for example, should interfere with learning that responding and shock termination are independent and should allow the animal to discriminate between the situation where shocks are escapable and where they are inescapable. In a relevant experiment, Seligman and Maier (1967) demonstrated that giving dogs 10 escape–avoidance trials in the shuttle box before they received inescapable shock in the hammock eliminated interference with subsequent escape–avoidance behavior. More recently, lifelong immunization against helplessness has been found. Rats given escapable shock at weaning, did not become helpless when given inescapable shock as adults (Hannum et al., 1976).

Immunization has also been demonstrated in man. Douglas and Anisman (1975) found that initial success on a task prevents the deficits normally produced by exposure to uncontrollable events. Subjects first exposed to contingent success on one task and then given an unsolvable task, performed better on a third problem-solving task than subjects exposed to the unsolvable task with no prior contingency training. Similarly, Jones et al. (1977) found that subjects exposed to a 50% immunization schedule performed significantly better than helpless subjects without immunization.

So, learned helplessness can be prevented if the subject first masters outcomes before being exposed to uncontrollability. Can depression be prevented? Almost everyone at sometime loses control over significant reinforcers in his life—loved ones die; failures occur. Most people also become at least mildly and transiently depressed at times. Why are some people hospitalized for long periods and others resilient? The data on immunization against helplessness may provide some clues.

The life histories of those individuals who are particularly resistant to or resilient from depression may have been filled with mastery. These people may have had experience controlling and manipulating the sources of reinforcement in their lives, and may, therefore, have the expectation that they will be able to do so in the future. Those people who are particularly susceptible to depression may have had lives filled with situations in which they were unable to influence their sources of suffering and gratification. In the remaining sections we will discuss further this relationship between stressful life experiences and helplessness and depression.

It seems reasonable that extensive experience controlling reinforcement might make one more resistant to depression, though some experience with uncontrollable events is desirable to allow the development and use of coping responses against failure. Successful therapy procedures should provide the patient with a wide repertoire of coping responses that he can use when, in future situations, he finds he cannot control reinforcement by his usual responses. In this way therapy can be seen as preventative, by arming the patient against future depressions.

STRESS, LEARNED HELPLESSNESS, AND DEPRESSION

What is the role of stress in the production of learned helplessness and depression? Obviously stress factors can be identified in many of the experiments previously referred to. However, the role of stress in learned helplessness has never been specifically detailed. Examination of the learned helplessness model of depression suggests that the following core concepts should be evaluated: uncontrollability, stress, uncontrollable stress, perceptions of noncontingency, and expectancies. Although previous statements of the model have emphasized all five of these concepts, their relative importance for learned helplessness and depression has not yet been adequately delineated. We will argue here (on the basis of experimental, clinical, and anecdotal evidence) that the *expectancy* of an inability to control stress is a sufficient condition for the full range of behavioral, cognitive, and affective deficits of learned helplessness and depression.

The learned helplessness model of depression maintains that when an organism is faced with an outcome that is independent of its responses, it learns that responding is futile. What makes learned helplessness an important phenomenon is that it generalizes beyond the training situation. In new situations the organism has the expectation that responding and outcomes are still independent (i.e., there is an expectancy of an inability to control outcomes).

How do we know, however, that learned helplessness results from being unable to control a physical trauma, and not merely from experiencing the trauma? A simple and elegant experimental design has been used in a number of studies to isolate the effects of controllability from the effects of the stimulus being controlled. Briefly, this triadic design involves three groups: (a) one group receives escapable trauma; (b) a second group is yoked to the first group and, thus, receives uncontrollable trauma; and (c) a third group is not exposed to the trauma at all.[2] The final result is that only those subjects who receive uncontrollable trauma exhibit the behaviors associated with learned helplessness. Studies using the triadic design have

---

[2] See Church (1964) and Levis (1976) for a critique of the yoked design.

consistently found that it is not trauma per se that produces interference with subsequent adaptive responding but rather, it is the expectation of not having control over trauma (Hiroto & Seligman, 1975; Maier, 1970; Seligman & Maier, 1967) that produces performance deficits.

Another related issue, however, must be considered. Does the uncontrollability increase the degree of stress and do these higher levels of stress lead to learned helplessness? Evidence in the animal literature suggests that uncontrollability does produce emotional changes. Mowrer and Viek (1948) found that rats who received uncontrollable shock while they ate, subsequently ate less than the rats who could control the shock. Moot, Cabulla, and Crabtree (1970) and Weiss (1968; 1971a,b,c) have shown that lack of control over stressors in a wide variety of situations results in significantly more stomach ulceration in rats than do the same stressors when they are controllable.[3] If the amount of ulceration is viewed as an indicator of the level of stress to which the subject has been exposed, then these data suggest that uncontrollability increases the degree of stress in animals.

In the human literature, however, the relationship between behavior control and stress is more complex. This is partially due to a lack of agreement on the definition of the terms. Control has been used to mean: control over stressor nature (regulation); temporality of onset (self-administration) and offset (escape); probability (avoidance); and consequences (mitigation) (Hollon, 1977). Stress can be measured behaviorally, subjectively, or physiologically, and at a variety of times (i.e., before, during, after, or continuously across exposure intervals).

In a comprehensive review of controllability and stress, Miller and Seligman (1977) examined the evidence in terms of instrumental, self-administration, and potential control. *Instrumental control* refers to conditions in which the individual is able to make a response that modifies the aversive event. A number of studies have demonstrated that instrumental control is preferred (Elliot, 1969), decreases anticipatory arousal as measured by ratings of anxiety (Bowers, 1968; Gatchel, McKinney, & Koebernick, in press; Houston, 1972; Szpiler & Epstein, 1976), and as measured physiologically by nonspecific phasic skin conductance responses (Gatchel & Proctor, 1976; Geer, Davison, & Gatchel, 1970; Geer & Masel, 1972; Sandman, 1975; Szpiler & Epstein, 1976). Additionally, it reduces the impact of the stressor as measured physiologically (Champion, 1950; Corah & Boffa, 1970; DeGood, 1975; Geer et al., 1970; Geer & Masel, 1972; Hokanson, DeGood, Forrest, & Brittain, 1971; Staub, Tursky, & Schwartz, 1971), and subjectively (Bowers, 1968; Corah & Boffa, 1970; Glass, Singer,

---

[3] On the other hand, the well-known study by Brady, Porter, Conrad, and Mason (1958) found that monkeys with control over shock (executive monkeys) were more prone to ulceration than those monkeys who had no control but were exposed to shocks of the same duration and intensity. However, this result may have been an artifact of the group assignment procedure (see Maier & Seligman, 1976, for a more complete discussion of this issue).

Leonard, Krantz, Cohen, & Cummings, 1973; Staub *et al.*, 1971). In contrast, a few studies have found no difference between controllability and uncontrollability on measures of anxiety (Averill & Rosenn, 1972; Elliot, 1969), anticipatory arousal (Glass *et al.*, 1973), impact arousal (Bendler, Madras, & Bim, 1968; Bowers, 1968; Gatchel & Proctor, 1976; Glass *et al.*, 1973), and subjective ratings of pain (Averill & Rosenn, 1972; Sandman, 1975; Szpiler & Epstein, 1976).

Self-administration refers to conditions in which the individual can deliver the aversive stimuli to himself. In general, self-administration tends to be preferred (Pervin, 1963; Ball & Vogler, 1971), reduces anticipatory arousal (Haggard, 1943; Stotland & Blumenthal, 1964), tends to reduce anticipatory anxiety (Pervin, 1963), and reduces the physiological arousal upon impact (Bjorkstrand, 1973). Some investigators, however, have been unable to demonstrate a differential effect of self-administration upon anticipatory arousal (Bjorkstrand, 1973) or on subjective ratings of pain (Pervin, 1963; Staub *et al.*, 1971).

Potential control studies induce the individual to believe that some controlling response is available to him, but he is asked to refrain from using it. These studies have demonstrated reduced anticipatory arousal (Glass, Reim, & Singer, 1971), lower impact arousal (Corah & Boffa, 1970), and reduced pain ratings (Corah & Boffa, 1970; Glass, Singer, & Friedman, 1969). However, Glass *et al.* (1971) found no difference on measures of impact arousal. Thus, while the evidence is not conclusive, it suggests that, for humans, control is preferred and results in lower stress-related arousal than the absence of control.

A number of theories have been proposed to explain this complex and inconsistent relationship between controllability and stress, including relevant feedback theory (Weiss, 1971a,b,c), survival value (Averill, 1973), interruption theory (Mandler & Watson, 1966), feelings of helplessness (Glass & Singer, 1972), learned helplessness (Seligman, 1975), minimax theory (Miller & Seligman, 1977), and expectancy theory (Hollon, 1977). It is beyond the scope of this chapter, however, to discuss these theories in detail. In general, many of these theories are consistent with Averill's (1973) conclusion that the stress-inducing and stress-reducing properties of personal control depend upon the meaning and the context of the control response for the individual, and not simply upon its effectiveness in preventing or mitigating the impact of the stressor.

If, as the evidence seems to suggest, uncontrollable events are more stressful, it is possible that the deficits associated with learned helplessness demonstrated by subjects given uncontrollable pretreatments are owing to these subjects being exposed to more stress, rather than owing to the uncontrollability itself. This argument might predict that subjects in the escape (controllable) group would perform worse than no pretreatment subjects, as escape subjects receive levels of stress intermediate between no pretreatment and uncontrollable subjects. The evidence clearly indicates, however, that subjects in the escape group perform at least as well as subjects in the no pretreatment group.

It might be argued, however, that an inverted U-shaped function is involved. That is, with mild to moderate stress subjects perform better on subsequent tasks than with minimal or no stress and that performance deteriorates with increases in stress to higher levels. This position would lead to the prediction that if stress were increased sufficiently, at some point the controllable subjects would receive enough stress to render them helpless. As yet, there is no good evidence for or against this hypothesis. However, the results of other studies argue against the view that stress is sufficient to produce learned helplessness.

As mentioned earlier, Seligman et al. (1968) and Seligman et al. (1975) found that helpless animals forced to experience the shock escape contingency were no longer helpless. Also, the studies by Hannum et al. (1976), Seligman and Maier (1967), Seligman et al. (1975), Douglas and Anisman (1975), and Jones et al. (1977) showing the efficacy of prior escape training as an immunization against helplessness, cast doubt upon the notion that stress per se is sufficient to produce the helplessness effect. If helplessness is due entirely to exposure to stress, it is difficult to imagine why additional exposure to stress, even if it were escapable, should either break up the helplessness effect or prevent its later appearance. In sum, the existing evidence does not support the hypothesis that stress in itself will produce learned helplessness; rather, it is the lack of control over outcomes which is important.

But, must the uncontrollable outcome be stressful? Can experience with uncontrollable positive events produce the deficits of learned helplessness? Early statements of the model focused only on the importance of uncontrollability of outcomes, and gave little attention to the valence of the outcomes. Situations involving noncontingent positive reinforcement were considered analogous, in terms of uncontrollability, to situations involving noncontingent aversive stimulation. In both cases, there is nothing the individual can do to affect outcomes. Seligman (1975) noted the similarities of these situations and speculated that "not only trauma occurring independently of response, but noncontingent positive events can produce helplessness and depression."

Experimental studies with animals have demonstrated that exposure to noncontingent food interferes with the acquisition of a response to escape shock (Goodkin, 1976; Rosellini & Bazerman, 1977). The effects of experience with uncontrollable positive outcomes in humans, however, is less clear. Eisenberger, Kaplan, and Singer (1974) demonstrated that noncontingent social approval leads to subsequent performance decrements in children on an approval-contingent task. MacGriffith (1976) found that individuals given noncontingent success performed significantly worse on anagrams than subjects given contingent success. Other studies, however, (Benson & Kennely, 1976; Eisenberger, Park, & Frank, 1976) have demonstrated improved performance following *contingent* positive feedback but have failed to demonstrate helplessness effects associated with *noncontingent* positive feedback.

Thus, the evidence regarding the effects of experience with uncontrollable positive outcomes on subsequent performance is inconclusive. Our position is that uncontrollable positive events may, under certain conditions, lead to the motivational and cognitive deficits associated with helplessness. However, we believe that the valence of the outcome is important in producing the third component of learned helplessness—emotionality. A recent statement of the model (Maier & Seligman, 1976) suggested that changes in emotionality result "when the outcome is traumatic." In the reformulated learned helplessness model, Abramson *et al.* (1978) specify that "only those uncontrollable outcomes where the estimated probability of the occurrence of a desired outcome is low or the estimated probability of the occurrence of an aversive outcome is high are sufficient for depressed affect." MacGriffith (1976) examined the effects of noncontingent outcomes on mood and found that the noncontingent failure group showed an increase in depression, whereas the noncontingent success group showed a decrease, demonstrating that the valence of the outcome may determine mood change. Therefore, the emotional component of depression will be produced only in those cases where the expectation of response-outcome independence concerns the absence of a highly desired outcome or the presence of a highly aversive one.

According to the theory of helplessness, then, having the expectation that an outcome (regardless of the valence) is independent of responding reduces the motivation to control that outcome and interferes with learning that responding controls future outcomes. Changes in emotionality result from the expectation of a lack of control over stressful events (i.e., a negative outcome that can be neither avoided nor escaped, or a positive outcome that cannot be obtained). Thus, the expectation of a lack of control over stressful events is seen as the primary condition for the full range of deficits associated with learned helplessness and depression.

The discussion above has focused on factors identified as important in producing learned helplessness in laboratory experiments. How do these laboratory findings relate to learned helplessness and depression in the real world? In reviewing the learned helplessness experiments we found that controllable stress does not lead to the behavioral deficits of learned helplessness or to the affective symptoms of depression, whereas uncontrollable stress does. However, it should be noted that all of the human helplessness studies have used mild stressors. Although we indicated earlier that there is no *experimental* support for the view that learned helplessness is a function of the level of stress, the possibility that depression might follow from experience with more intense stresses (such as those in the natural environment) should be considered.

Studies by a number of researchers have suggested that environmental stresses may precipitate depressive episodes. Investigators have consistently found significantly more stressful life events (including death or separation from a loved one, job loss, a major move, etc.) in the recent history of depressed patients when compared with other psychiatric patients or the general population (Forrest, Fraser, & Priest, 1952; Leff, Roatch & Bunney, 1970; Paykel, Myers, Dienelt, Klerman, Lindenthal, & Pepper, 1969). Many of these studies, however, are correlational in nature and consequently do not firmly establish the causal chain between stress and depression. However, there does appear to be evidence to support the notion that depression is often preceded by life stressors. This issue is dealt with more directly in a number of other chapters in this volume.

One final point concerning studies of stress in the real world, is that these studies often confound the variables of stress and uncontrollability. A stressful event has been defined here as an aversive event you cannot avoid or escape, or a positive outcome you cannot obtain—that is, an undesirable outcome over which you have no control. Whereas not all uncontrollable outcomes are undesirable or for that matter stressful, all undesirable and stressful outcomes are by definition uncontrollable (if you could avoid or escape the outcome, you would). Without an experimental procedure similar to the triadic design used in learned helplessness studies, it is difficult to separate the effects of uncontrollability and stress in the real world. We suggest that when stress in the natural environment is followed by depression, that uncontrollability is typically the mediator. Life stresses such as the death of a loved one or the loss of a job (Forrest et al., 1965; Paykel et al., 1969) are *uncontrollable* stresses, and are therefore more likely to lead to the expectation of a lack of control over important events in the future, and thus to depression.

EXPECTANCY OF A LACK OF CONTROL OVER STRESS

Another difficulty with applying the results of laboratory experiments on learned helplessness to depression is the observation that experience with an uncontrollable stressor in the real world is not a perfect predictor of subsequent depression. In fact, all of us routinely encounter some uncontrollable stress without necessarily developing depression (e.g., traffic jams, financial losses). This observation might lead us to believe that only certain uncontrollable stressors will lead to depression. However, even given exposure to a particular uncontrollable event, one individual may develop a depression whereas another may not. How then do we account for these observations?

Recall that our formulation of the learned helplessness model of depression suggests that *the expectancy of inability to control stress* is a sufficient condition for learned helplessness and depression.[4] Given this condition, it may seem more clear why *experience* with uncontrollable stress does not always result in helplessness or depression, and also explain why the same uncontrollable stressor may result in depression in some individuals and not in others. The review of the learned helplessness experiments suggested that experience with uncontrollability, and perhaps uncontrollable stress, produces the deficits associated with learned helplessness. However, the *expectancy* of a future lack of control over stress is presumed to be the causal agent; experience with actual lack of control (objective noncongingency) is only predicted to lead to symptoms of helplessness if and only if the expectation of a lack of control (noncontingency) is formed. It may be that uncontrollable stress in one situation will lead to the expectancy of a lack of control, whereas in other situations it will not. Actual *experience* with uncontrollability has a higher probability than other experiences for producing an expectancy of a lack of control in the future. The model does not require, however, that such an expectancy must follow from every exposure to uncontrollable stress, nor does it exclude the possibility that the expectancy may result from other types of experiences as well.

An experiment by Glass and Singer (1972) highlights the fact that it is the expectation, not the objective conditions of controllability, that is the crucial determinant of helplessness. They found that merely telling an individual about controllability duplicates the effects of actual controllability. They attempted to simulate the stress of the urban environment by having their subjects (college students) listen to a very loud melange of sound. Subjects who could actually turn off the noise by pushing a button (first group) were more persistent at problem solving, found the noise less irritating, and did better at a proof-reading task than a group of yoked subjects (second group). A third group was presented with the same uncontrollable noise as the yoked group. However, this group had a "panic button" and was told that they could terminate the noise by pressing the button, although it was preferred for them not to do it. None of the subjects attempted to turn off the noise. These subjects had only the false belief that they had potential control over the noise, yet they performed just as well as the people who actually controlled the noise. So, objective controllability and objective uncontrollability can produce identical expectations. It is only in the condi-

---

[4] We recognize, of course, that postpartum conditions, hormonal states, chemical depletions, genetic predispositions, etc., can result in depression also. We emphasize, though, that the majority of depressions, which cannot be explained by these various other factors, result from the expectation of uncontrollability over important outcomes.

tion where subjects acquire the expectation of uncontrollability that performance deficits emerge.

The Glass and Singer (1972) study demonstrates that uncontrollability itself does not necessarily lead to helplessness. Additional studies suggest that other factors are important in determining when an exposure to uncontrollability will and will not produce the expectation of a future lack of control. One such factor is prior experience with controllability. The immunization studies described previously show that exposure to contingent outcomes interferes with the production of learned helplessness following an exposure to noncontingency (Douglas & Anisman, 1975; Hannum et al., 1976; Jones et al., 1977; Seligman et al., 1975). In addition, Seligman and Groves (1970) found that cage-reared dogs, who had a life characterized by a general lack of control, were more susceptible to learned helplessness than dogs who had had more numerous prior experiences with control. Previous experiences with controllability should lead to the expectation of future control and thus interfere with the later acquisition of an expectation of a future lack of control.

Another factor affecting the generalization of the expectation of learned helplessness is the attribution one makes about the causes of the uncontrollability. When people find that they are helpless, they often ask why. Abramson et al., (1978) recently suggested that the causal attributions people make for their helplessness will determine its generality and chronicity. Attribution theorists (Weiner, Frieze, Kukla, Reed, Rest, & Rosenbaum, 1971) postulate that the perceived causes of outcomes can be subsumed within two basic causal dimensions: stability (the relative endurance of the cause over time) and locus of control (causes are either internal or external to the individual). Abramson, Seligman & Teasdale (1978) suggested an additional dimension of globality-specificity to describe the relative endurance of a cause from situation to situation. Using these attributional dimensions, Abramson, Seligman, and Teasdale (1978) hypothesized that an attribution to *global* factors predicts that the expectation of helplessness will recur when the situation changes. An attribution to *specific* factors predicts that the expectation of helplessness need not recur when the situation changes. An attribution to *stable* factors predicts that the expectation of helplessness will recur even after a lapse of time, whereas an attribution to *unstable* factors predicts that the expectation need not recur after a lapse of time. Therefore, whether the expectation recurs across situations and time determines whether the helplessness will recur. The attribution may predict the recurrence of the expectations; the expectation of a lack of control determines the occurrence of helplessness and depression.

Carol Dweck and her associates (Dweck, 1976; Dweck & Repucci, 1973; Dweck, Davidson, Nelson, & Enna, 1976; Dweck, Goetz, & Strauss, 1977) have demonstrated the effects of differential attributions for failure on subsequent performance. Dweck et al. (1977) found that grade-school girls tended to attribute their failure to a lack of ability (a global attribution) and performed badly on a subsequent cognitive task, whereas grade-school boys tended to attribute their failure to a lack of effort (an unstable and probably more specific attribution) and performed well on the subsequent task. Furthermore, when students were specifically instructed to attribute their failure to "not trying hard enough," rather than to a lack of ability, they subsequently performed better (Dweck, 1976). It appears that attributions to stable factors for one's helplessness (i.e., lack of ability) are more likely to lead to the expectation of helplessness on subsequent tasks, thus producing performance deficits. Finally, Dweck and Repucci (1973) reported discriminative control over helplessness in school children. Children exposed to uncontrollability in the presence of one teacher, but not with another, subsequently exhibited performance deficits only with the teacher who had been associated with uncontrollability. Here, uncontrollability is seen as leading to the expectation of a lack of control only under specific conditions. Under other conditions, this expectation is not present.

Discriminative control over helplessness may also result from just being told—particularly by someone "who should know"—that a given event is uncontrollable. This information may create an expectation that the event is uncontrollable, even without experiencing the contingency. Conversely, just being told that an event is controllable will also short-circuit experiencing the contingency. Recall that merely telling people they have a "panic button" that will turn off loud noise, even if they do not use it, is enough to prevent helplessness.

In summary, the expectation of a future lack of control will be affected by individuals' prior experience with control, by their attributions about the causes of outcomes, and by information about the controllability of outcomes even in the absence of direct experience with noncontingency. The following anecdotes illustrate the main points relating to uncontrollability, expectation, and depression.

Consider the case of a middle-aged woman whose husband leaves her for another woman after 20 years of marriage. The wife feels that her husband's leaving was independent of anything she did or did not do. It was totally beyond her control. (Whether or not the husband's actions were in fact independent of what the wife did is not the issue. The research cited above indicated that uncontrollability exerts its effect when a situation is simply *perceived* as uncontrollable.) She now feels unable to take care of herself and fears the future. She anticipates being unhappy and lonely and cannot imagine how she will manage without him. She thinks she will never find another man like him and sees her future as hopeless. She cries a great deal. Small chores now seem very difficult. The things she used to enjoy no longer bring her pleasure. On her bad days she cannot even bring herself to get out of bed. She is depressed.

Consider a second case with an almost identical set of circumstances. A middle-aged woman's husband leaves her for another woman after 20 years of marriage. Again, the woman perceives his leaving as totally beyond her control. She is disappointed and disturbed that someone she loved has left her. She anticipates having to go through a period of adjustment where she will have to begin doing more for herself. She knows she may be lonely at times but also expects to continue her present friendships as well as develop new ones. She continues to function as before he left and gradually adjusts to this new set of circumstances. She is not depressed.

The precipitating events for these two individuals are objectively identical. They both experienced an uncontrollable and undesirable stressful event. However, their cognitions about the consequences of the event (i.e., their expectations for the future) differ tremendously. How is it that the same event can affect people so differently? How does one come to develop the kinds of negative expectations that lead to depression, whereas the other manages to cope in the face of the same adversity?

People develop expectancies on the basis of experience, instructions, and observation (Bandura, 1969). Learned helplessness predicts that repeated experience with uncontrollable events will lead to the expectation that future events will be uncontrollable. It may be that the first woman had a lifetime of experiences with uncontrollable outcomes and therefore developed the expectancy that she would not be able to control her future. Alternatively, it is possible that she developed the expectancy without actually experiencing noncontingency in the past. For instance, she may have acquired the belief that a woman cannot live happily without a man because all the single women she knows are unhappy, or because as a young girl her mother told her that a woman cannot get along without a man. Because she now finds herself in the predicament of being a woman without a man, she automatically assumes she will not be able to manage.

Learned helplessness is a cognitive model of depression and suggests that merely the experience of an uncontrollable stressful event (i.e., a loss) is not sufficient to cause depression. Only when this experience produces the expectation that one will be unable to control future stresses will the person be depressed. Thus, the expectation that one cannot control important outcomes in one's life is a sufficient cause of depression.

SUMMARY AND CONCLUSIONS

We have reviewed the animal and human experiments that demonstrate the phenomenon of learned helplessness. These studies suggest that experience with uncontrollable events leads to two primary deficits: (a) reduced motivation to respond in new situations where outcomes are controllable; and (b) impaired ability to learn about contingencies in new situations. Furthermore, experience with uncontrollable aversive events has been shown to be associated with a number of additional characteristics: (*a*) time course; (*b*) reduced aggression; (*c*) weight loss and anorexia; (*d*) deficits in social and sexual behavior; (*e*) whole brain norepinephrine depletion; (*f*) septal activation; and (*g*) increased sadness, anxiety, and hostility.

It was noted that there are close parallels between the behavioral signs of learned helplessness following uncontrollable aversive events and the symptoms of depression. On the basis of these parallels, it has been suggested that learned helplessness may serve as a model of unipolar depression. Possible similarities between learned helplessness and depression in the areas of etiology, therapy, and immunization were also examined.

We have considered the role that uncontrollability and stress play in producing learned helplessness and depression. Although both uncontrollability and stress are present in the paradigmatic learned helplessness experiment, we have suggested that *neither* factor in itself is the crucial determinant of depression. Rather, we have suggested that the *expectation* of a lack of control over stress is a sufficient condition for depression.

Learned helplessness experiments have occasionally examined expectancy notions. However, the suggested role of the expectation of a future lack of control over stress in producing learned helplessness and depression needs to be tested further experimentally. We would like to consider here two potential, experimental tests of this view of the learned helplessness model.

1. Measurement of expectancy: Clearly, one way to test the expectancy hypothesis is to directly assess the expectancy of control over stress for helpless and/or depressed subjects. Typically a questionnaire or other forms of self-report instruments are used in such assessments. However, a caveat is in order here. Subjects cannot always reliably and accurately report or verbalize their own internal states and cognitions. Consequently the investigator must often resort to indirect measures of factors such as expectancies. The skill–chance studies referred to previously are an example of indirect measures of expectancy. Such measures can be used to further investigate whether helpless and depressed individuals have the expectancy of a future lack of control over stress.

2. Manipulation of expectancy: The learned helplessness model predicts that inducing the expectancy of a lack of control leads to learned helplessness and depression. To date, learned helplessness experiments have utilized uncontrollable aversive events to produce the deficits associated with helplessness. In more powerful tests, the model would entail a variety of procedures, including treatments other than uncontrollable aversive events, that would be predicted to produce such an expectancy. Therefore, if a variety of pretreatments, all of which lead to the expectancy of future inability to control stress, produce learned helplessness and depression then the model is strengthened. Further, the model predicts that procedures

either inhibiting the formation of the expectancy or changing an expectancy of no control to one of control over future stress, would prevent or reverse learned helplessness and depression. Note that the production of this change need not entail actual experience with control, as in the usual learned helplessness therapy and immunization experiments. Any procedure which changes the expectancy should suffice.

The above discussion suggests that depression entails the expectancy of a lack of control over stress and that uncontrollable aversive events are likely to produce such an expectancy. However, it should be clear that events other than uncontrollable aversive events may lead to the expectancy, and therefore to depression. As a reading of this volume indicates, there are a variety of views as to the factors or events that produce depression. Each view has received at least some experimental support. What we have attempted to identify, by means of a learned helplessness model of depression, is the variable that mediates between apparent etiologic factors and subsequent depression. We believe that experience with uncontrollability is an important cause of depression. But more importantly, we believe that what links the various etiologic viewpoints is that a number of different types of events may lead to the same *expectancy*, the expectancy that one cannot control the stresses in one's life.

REFERENCES

Abramson, L. Y., Garber, J., Edwards, N. B., & Seligman, M. E. P. Expectancy changes in depression and schizophrenia. *Journal of Abnormal Psychology*, 1978, 87, 102–109.

Abramson, L. Y., Seligman, M. E. P., & Teasdale, J. Learned helplessness in humans: critique and reformulation. *Journal of Abnormal Psychology*, 1978, 87, 49–74.

Anisman, H. & Waller, T. G. Effects of inescapable shock on subsequent avoidance performance: Role of response repertoire changes. *Behavioral Biology*, 1973, 9, 331–335.

Averill, J. R. Personal control over aversive stimuli and its relationship to stress. *Psychological Bulletin*, 1973, 80, 286–303.

Averill, J. R. & Rosenn, M. Vigilant and nonvigilant coping strategies and psycho-physiological stress reactions during the anticipation of electric shock. *Journal of Personality and Social Psychology*, 1972, 23, 128–141.

Ball, J. S. & Vogler, R. E. Uncertain pain and the pain of uncertainty. *Perceptual and Motor Skills*, 1971, 33, 1195–1203.

Bandler, R. J., Madras, G. R., & Bim, D. J. Self-observation as a source of pain perception. *Journal of Personality and Social Psychology*, 1968, 9, 205–209.

Bandura, A. *Principles of Behavior Modification*. New York: Holt, 1969.

Beck, A. T. *Depression: Clinical, Experimental, and Theoretical Aspects*. New York: Harper, 1967.

Beck, A. T. *Cognitive Therapy and the Emotional Disorders*. New York: International Univ. Press, 1976.

Benson, J. S. & Kennelly, K. J. Learned helplessness: The result of uncontrollable reinforcement or uncontrollable aversive stimuli. *Journal of Personality and Social Psychology*, 1976, 34, 138–145.

Bibring, E. The mechanism of depression. In P. Greenacre (Ed.), *Affective Disorders*. New York: International Univ. Press, 1953. Pp. 13–48.

Bjorkstrand, P. A. Electrodermal responses as affected by subject versus experimenter-controlled noxious stimulation. *Journal of Experimental Psychology*, 1973, 97, 365–369.

Bowers, K. S. Pain, anxiety, and perceived control. *Journal of Consulting and Clinical Psychology*, 1968, 32, 596–602.

Bracewell, R. J. & Black, A. H. The effects of restraint and noncontingent pre-shock on subsequent escape learning in the rat. *Learning and Motivation*, 1974, 5, 53–69.

Brady, J. V., Porter, R. W., Conrad, D. G., & Mason, J. W. Avoidance behavior and the development of gastroduodenal ulcers. *Journal of the Experimental Analysis of Behavior*, 1958, 1, 69–72.

Champion, R. A. Studies in experimentally induced disturbances. *Australian Journal of Psychology*, 1950, 2, 90–99.

Church, R. M. Systematic effect of random error in the yoked control design. *Psychological Bulletin*, 1964, 62, 122–131.

Corah, N. & Boffa, J. Perceived control, self-observation, and response to aversive stimulation. *Journal of Personality and Social Psychology*, 1970, 16, 1–4.

DeGood, D. E. Cognitive control factors in vascular stress responses. *Psychophysiology*, 1975, 12, 399–401.

Douglas, D. & Anisman, H. Helplessness or expectation incongruency: Effects of aversive stimulation on subsequent performance. *Journal of Experimental Psychology*, 1975, 1, 411–417.

Dweck, C. S. Children's interpretation of evaluative feedback: The effect of social cues on learned helplessness. In C. S. Dweck, K. T. Hill, W. H. Reed, W. M. Steihman, & R. D. Parke, (Eds.), The impact of social cues on children's behavior. *Merrill-Palmer Quarterly*, 1976, 22, 83–123.

Dweck, C. S., Davidson, W., Nelson, S., & Enna, B. *Sex differences in learned helplessness: (II) The contingencies of evaluative feedback in the classroom and (III) an experimental analysis*. Unpublished manuscript, Univ. Illinois at Urbana-Champaign, 1976.

Dweck, C. S., Goetz, T., & Strauss, N. *Sex differences in learned helplessness: (III) An experimental and naturalistic study of failure generalization and its mediators*. Unpublished manuscript, Univ. Illinois at Urbana-Champaign, 1977.

Dweck, C. S. & Repucci, N. D. Learned helplessness and reinforcement responsibility in children. *Journal of Personality and Social Psychology*, 1973, 25, 109–116.

Eisenberger, R., Kaplan, R. M., & Singer, R. D. Decremental and non-decremental effects of noncontingent social approval. *Journal of Personality and Social Psychology*, 1974, 30, 716–722.

Eisenberger, R., Park, D. C., & Frank, M. Learned industriousness and social reinforcement. *Journal of Personality and Social Psychology*, 1976, 33, 227–232.

Elliot, R. Tonic heart rate: Experiments on the effects of collative variables lead to an hypothesis about its motivational significance. *Journal of Personality and Social Psychology*, 1969, 12, 211–228.

Engel, G. A life setting conducive to illness. The giving-up—given-up complex. *Bulletin of the Menninger Clinic*, 1968, 32, 355–365.

Forrest, A. D., Fraser, R. H., & Priest, R. B. Environmental factors in depressive illness. *British Journal of Psychiatry*, 1952, 43, 33–41.

Fosco, R. & Geer, J. H. Effects of gaining control over aversive stimuli after differing amounts of no control. *Psychological Reports*, 1971, 29, 1153–1154.

Freud, S. Mourning and melancholia, in *Collected Works*, London: Hogarth, 1917.

Frumkin, K., & Brookshire, K. H. Conditioned fear training and later avoidance learning in goldfish. *Psychonomic Science*, 1969, 16, 159–160.

Garber, J. & Hollon, S. D. *Universal versus personal helplessness: Belief in uncontrollability or incompetence? Journal of Abnormal Psychology*, in press.

Gatchel, R. J., McKinnery, M. E., & Koebernick, L. F. Learned helplessness, depression and physiological responding. *Psychophysiology*, 1977, (in press).

Gatchel, R. J., Paulus, P. B., & Maples, C. W. Learned helplessness and self-reported affect. *Journal of Abnormal Psychology*, 1975, 84, 589–620.

Gatchel, R. J. & Proctor, J. D. Physiological correlates of learned helplessness in man. *Journal of Abnormal Psychology*, 1976, 85, 27–34.

Geer, J., Davison, G. C., & Gatchel, R. J. Reduction of stress in humans through nonveridical perceived control of aversive stimulation. *Journal of Personality and Social Psychology*, 1970, 16, 731–738.

Geer, J. H. & Maisel, E. Evaluating the effects of the prediction-control confound. *Journal of Personality and Social Psychology*, 1972, 23, 314–319.

Glass, D. C., Reim, B., & Singer, J. E. Behavioral consequences of adaption to controllable and uncontrollable noise. *Journal of Experimental Social Psychology*, 1971, 7, 244–257.

Glass, D. C., Singer, J. E., & Friedman, L. N. Psychic cost of adaptation to an environmental stressor. *Journal of Personality and Social Psychology*, 1969, 12, 200–210.

Glass, D. C. & Singer, J. E. *Urban stress: Experiments on noise and social stressors*. New York: Academic Press, 1972.

Glass, D. C., Singer, J. E., Leonard, H. S., Krantz, D., Cohen, S., & Cummings, H. Perceived control of aversive stimulation and the reduction of stress response. *Journal of Personality*, 1973, 41, 577–595.

Glazer, H. I. & Weiss, J. M. Long-term and transitory interference effects. *Journal of Experimental Psychology: Animal Behavior Processes*, 1976, 2, 191–201. (a)

Glazer, H. I. & Weiss, J. M. Long-term interference effect: An alternative to "learned helplessness," *Journal of Experimental Psychology: Animal Behavior Processes*, 1976, 2, 202–213. (b)

Goodkin, F. Rats learn the relationship between responding and environmental events: An expansion of the learned helplessness hypothesis, *Learning and Motivation*, 1976, 7, 382–393.

Greenfield, N., Katz, D., Alexander, A., & Roessler, R. The relationship between physiology and psychological responsivity: Depression and galvanic skin response. *Journal of Nervous and Mental Disease*. 1963, 136, 535–539.

Haggard, E. A. Experimental studies in affective processes: I. Some effects of cognitive structure and active participation on certain autonomic reactions during and following experimentally induced stress. *Journal of Experimental Psychology*, 1943, 33, 257–284.

Hannum, R., Rosellini, R. A., & Seligman, M. E. P. Learned helplessness in the rat: Retention and immunization. *Developmental Psychology*, 1976, 12, 449–454.

Harlow, H. F., Harlow, M. K., & Suomi, S. J. From thought to therapy: Lessons from a primate laboratory. *American Scientist*, 1971, 59, 538–549.

Hiroto, D. S. Locus of control and learned helplessness. *Journal of Experimental Psychology*, 1974, 102, 187–193.

Hiroto, D. S. & Seligman, M. E. P. Generality of learned helplessness in man. *Journal of Personality and Social Psychology*, 1975, 31, 311–327.

Hokanson, J. E., DeGood, D. E., Forrest, M. S., & Brittain, T. M. Availability of avoidance behaviors in modulating vascular-stress responses. *Journal of Personality and Social Psychology*, 1971, 19, 60–68.

Hollon, S. D. Prediction, control, and subsequent stress: An expectancy-based theory. Unpublished manuscript, Florida State Univ., 1977.

Houston, B. K. Control over stress, locus of control, and response to stress. *Journal of Personality and Social Psychology*, 1972, 21, 249–255.

360 GARBER, MILLER, AND SEAMAN

James, W. H. *Internal versus external control of reinforcement as a basic variable in learning theory.* Unpublished doctoral dissertation, Ohio State Univ., 1957.

James, W. H. & Rotter, J. B. Partial and 100% reinforcement under chance and skill conditions. *Journal of Experimental Psychology*, 1958, 55, 397–403.

Jones, S. L., Nation, J. R., & Massad, P. Immunization against learned helplessness in man. *Journal of Abnormal Psychology*, 1977, 86, 75–83.

Klein, D. C., Fencil-Morse, E., & Seligman, M. E. P. Learned helplessness, depression, and the attribution of failure. *Journal of Personality and Social Psychology*, 1976, 33, 508–516.

Klein, D. C. & Seligman, M. E. P. Reversal of performance deficits and perceptual deficits in learned helplessness and depression. *Journal of Abnormal Psychology*, 1976, 85, 11–26.

Krantz, D. S., Glass, D. C., & Snyder, M. L. Helplessness, stress level, and the coronary prone behavior pattern. *Journal of Experimental Social Psychology*, 1974, 10, 284–300.

Leff, M. J., Roatch, J. F., & Bunney, W. E., Jr. Environmental factors preceding the onset of severe depressions. *Psychiatry*, 1970, 33, 293–311.

Levis, D. J. Learned helplessness—reply and an alternative S-R interpretation. *Journal of Experimental Psychology: General*, 1976, 105, 47–65.

Lewinsohn, P. M., Lobitz, W. C., & Wilson, S. "Sensitivity" of depressed individuals to aversive stimuli. *Journal of Abnormal Psychology*, 1973, 81, 259–263.

Lichtenberg, P. A. A definition and analysis of depression. *Archives of Neurology and Psychiatry*, 1957, 77, 519–527.

Lindner, M. *Hereditary and environmental influences upon resistance to stress.* Unpublished doctoral dissertation, Univ. Pennsylvania, 1968.

Lundquist, E. Prognosis and course in manic depressive psychosis, a follow-up study of 319 first admissions. *Acta Psychiatrica et Neurologica*, Copenhagen, 1945, 35, 95.

MacGriffith, S. *Effects of noncontingent success and failure on mood and performance: Learned helplessness and competence.* Unpublished manuscript, 1976.

Maier, S. F. Failure to escape traumatic shock: Incompatible skeletal motor responses of learned helplessness? *Learning and Motivation*, 1970, 1, 157–170.

Maier, S. F., Albin, R. W., & Testa, T. J. Failure to learn to escape in rats previously exposed to inescapable shock depends on the nature of the escape response. *Journal of Comparative and Physiological Psychology*, 1973, 85, 587–592.

Maier, S. F., Anderson, C., & Lieberman, D. A. Influence of control of shock on subsequent shock-elicited aggression. *Journal of Comparative and Physiological Psychology*, 1972, 81, 94–100.

Maier, S. F. & Seligman, M. E. P. Learned helplessness: Theory and evidence. *Journal of Experimental Psychology: General*, 1976, 105, 3–46.

Maier, S. F., Seligman, M. E. P., & Solomon, R. L. Pavlovian fear conditioning and learned helplessness. In B. A. Campbell & R. M. Church (Eds.), *Punishment*, New York: Appleton-Century-Crofts, 1969.

Maier, S. F. & Testa, T. J. Failure to learn to escape by rats previously exposed to inescapable shock is partly produced by associative interference. *Journal of Comparative and Physiological Psychology*, 1975, 88, 554–564.

Mandler, G. & Watson, D. L. Anxiety and the interruption of behavior. In C. D. Spielberger (Ed.), *Anxiety and Behavior*, New York: Academic Press, 1966.

Masserman, J. H. The principle of uncertainty in neurotegenesis. In H. D. Kimmel (Ed.), *Experimental Psychopathology*, New York: Academic Press, 1971.

McCarron, L. J. Psychophysiological discriminants of reactive depression. *Psychophysiology*, 1973, 10, 223–230.

Melges, F. T. & Bowlby, J. Types of hopelessness in psychopathological process. *Archives of General Psychiatry*, 1969, 20, 690–699.

Mendels, J., Weinstein, N., & Cochrane, C. The relationship between anxiety and depression. *Archives of General Psychiatry*, 1972, 27, 649–653.

Miller, S. M. & Seligman, M. E. P. *Controllability and stress*. Unpublished manuscript, Univ. Pennsylvania, 1977.

Miller, W. R. *The construct of control in depression research*. In M. E. P. Seligman (Chair), *Current issues and applications of the construct of control*. Panel discussion presented at the 84th Annual Convention of the American Psychological Association, Washington, D.C., September, 1976.

Miller, W. R. Psychological deficit in depression. *Psychological Bulletin*, 1975, 82, 238–260.

Miller, W. R., Rosellini, R. A., & Seligman, M. E. P. Depression and learned helplessness. In J. J. Maser & M. E. P. Seligman (Eds.), *Psychopathology: Experimental models*. San Francisco: Freeman, 1977.

Miller, W. R. & Seligman, M. E. P. Depression and the perception of reinforcement. *Journal of Abnormal Psychology*, 1973, 82, 62–73.

Miller, W. & Seligman, M. E. P. Depression and learned helplessness in man. *Journal of Abnormal Psychology*, 1975, 84, 228–238.

Miller, W. R. & Seligman, M. E. P. Learned helplessness, depression, and the perception of reinforcement. *Behavior Research and Therapy*, 1976, 14, 7–17.

Miller, W. R., Seligman, M. E. P., & Kurlander, H. M. Learned helplessness, depression and anxiety. *Journal of Mental and Nervous Disease*, 1975, 161, 347–357.

Moot, S. A., Cebulla, R. P., & Crabtree, J. M. Instrumental control and ulceration in rats. *Journal of Comparative and Physiological Psychology*, 1970, 71, 405–410.

Mowrer, O. H. & Viek, P. An experimental analogue of fear from a sense of helplessness. *Journal of Abnormal and Social Psychology*, 1948, 43, 193–200.

Overmier, J. B. Interference with avoidance behavior: Failure to avoid traumatic shock. *Journal of Experimental Psychology*, 1968, 78, 340–343.

Overmier, J. B. & Seligman, M. E. P. Effects of inescapable shock upon subsequent escape and avoidance learning. *Journal of Comparative and Physiological Psychology*, 1967, 63, 23–33.

Padilla, A. M. Effects of prior and interpolated shock exposures on subsequent avoidance learning by goldfish. *Psychological Reports*, 1973, 32, 451–456.

Padilla, A. M., Padilla, C., Ketterer, T., & Giacolone, D. Inescapable shocks and subsequent avoidance conditioning in goldfish (Carrasius auratus). *Psychonomic Science*, 1970, 20, 295–296.

Paskind, H. A. Brief attacks of manic-depressive depression. *Archives of Neurology and Psychiatry*, 1929, 22, 123–134.

Paskind, H. A. Manic-depressive psychosis in private practice: Length of attack and length of interval. *Archives of Neurology and Psychiatry*, 1930, 23, 789–794.

Paykel, E. S., Myers, J. K., Dienelt, M. N., Klerman, G. L., Lindenthal, J. J., & Pepper, M. P. Life events and depression: A controlled study. *Archives of General Psychiatry*, 1969, 21, 753–760.

Pervin, L. A. The need to predict and control under conditions of threat. *Journal of Personality*, 1963, 31, 570–587.

Phares, E. J. Expectancy changes in skill and chance situations. *Journal of Abnormal and Social Psychology*, 1957, 54, 339–342.

Powell, D. A. & Greer, T. L. Interaction of developmental and environmental variables in shock-elicited aggression. *Journal of Comparative and Physiological Psychology*, 1969, 69, 219–225.

Racinskas, J. R. *Maladaptive consequences of loss or lack of control over aversive events*. Unpublished doctoral dissertation, Waterloo Univ., Ontario, Canada, 1971.

Rodin, J. Density, perceived choice, and response to controllable and uncontrollable outcomes. *Journal of Experimental Social Psychology*, 1976, 12, 564–578.

Rosellini, R. A. & Bazerman, N. H. *Exposure to noncontingent food interferes with the acquisition of response to escape shock*. Unpublished manuscript, Univ. Pennsylvania, 1977.

Roth, S. *The effects of experimentally induced expectancies of control: Facilitation of controlling behavior or learned helplessness?* Unpublished doctoral dissertation, Northwestern Univ., 1973.

Roth, S. & Bootzin, R. R. The effects of experimentally induced expectancies of external control: An investigation of learned helplessness. *Journal of Personality and Social Psychology*, 1974, 29, 253–264.

Roth, S. & Kubal, L. The effects of noncontingent reinforcement on tasks of differing importance: Facilitation and learned helplessness effects. *Journal of Personality and Social Psychology*, 1976, 32, 680–691.

Rotter, J. B., Liverant, S., & Crowne, D. P. The growth and extinction of expectancies in chance controlled and skill tasks. *Journal of Psychology*, 1961, 52, 161–177.

Sandman, C. A. Physiological response during escape and nonescape from stress in field-independent and field-dependent subject. *Biological Psychology*, 1975, 2, 205–216.

Schmale, A. H. Relationship of separation and depression to disease: I. A report on a hospitalized medical population. *Psychosomatic Medicine*, 1958, 20, 259–277.

Schulz, R. Effects of control and predictability on the physical and psychological well-being of the institutionalized aged. *Journal of Personality and Social Psychology*, 1976, 33, 563–573.

Seligman, M. E. P. Depression and learned helplessness. In R. J. Friedman & M. M. Katz (Eds.), *The psychology of depression: Contemporary theory and research*, Washington, D. C.: V. H. Winston, 1974.

Seligman, M. E. P. *Helplessness. On depression, development, and death.* San Francisco: Freeman, 1975.

Seligman, M. E. P. & Beagley, G. Learned helplessness in the rat. *Journal of Comparative and Physiological Psychology*. 1975, 88, 534–541.

Seligman, M. E. P. & Groves, D. Non-transient learned helplessness. *Psychonomic Science*, 1970, 19, 191–192.

Seligman, M. E. P., Klein, D. C., & Miller, W. R. Depression. In H. Leitenberg (Ed.), *Handbook of behavior modification and behavior therapy*. Englewood Cliffs, New Jersey: Prentice Hall, 1976.

Seligman, M. E. P. & Maier, S. F. Failure to escape traumatic shock. *Journal of Experimental Psychology*, 1967, 74, 1–9.

Seligman, M. E. P., Maier, S. F., & Geer, J. The alleviation of learned helplessness in the dog. *Journal of Abnormal and Social Psychology*, 1968, 73, 256–262.

Seligman, M. E. P., Maier, S. F., & Solomon, R. L. Unpredictable and uncontrollable aversive events. In F. R. Brush (Ed.), *Aversive Conditioning and Learning*. New York: Academic Press, 1971.

Seligman, M. E. P., Rosellini, R. A., & Kozak, M. Learned helplessness in the rat: Reversibility, time course, and immunization. *Journal of Comparative and Physiological Psychology*, 1975, 88, 542–547.

Seward, J. & Humphrey, G. L. Avoidance learning as a function of pretraining in the cat. *Journal of Comparative and Physiological Psychology*. 1967, 63, 338–341.

Staub, C., Tursky, B., & Schwartz, G. E. Self-control and predictability: Their effects on reactions to aversive stimulation. *Journal of Personality and Social Psychology*, 1971, 18, 157–162.

Stotland, E. & Blumenthal, A. The reduction of anxiety as a result of the expectations of making a choice. *Canadian Journal of Psychology*, 1964, 18, 139–145.

Suomi, S. J. & Harlow, H. F. Depressive behavior in young monkeys subjected to vertical chamber confinement. *Journal of Comparative and Physiological Psychology*, 1972, 80, 11–18.

Szpila, J. A. & Epstein, S. Availability of an avoidance response as related to autonomic arousal. *Journal of Abnormal Psychology*, 1976, 85, 73–82.

Thomas, E. & Balter, A. Learned helplessness: Amelioration of symptoms by cholinergic blockade of the septum. *Science*, (in press).

Thomas, E & Dewald, L. Experimental neurosis. In J. Maser & M. E. P. Seligman (Eds.), *Psychopathology: Experimental models*, San Francisco: Freeman, 1977.

Thornton, J. W. & Jacobs, P. D. Learned helplessness in human subjects. *Journal of Experimental Psychology*, 1971, 87, 369–372.

Thornton, J. W. & Powell, G. D. Immunization to and alleviation of learned helplessness in man. *American Journal of Psychology*, 1974, 87, 351–367.

Weiner, B., Frieze, I., Kukla, A., Reed, L., Rest, S., & Rosenbaum, R. M. *Perceiving the causes of success and failure*. Morristown, New Jersey: General Learning Press, 1971.

Weiss, J. M. Effects of coping response on stress. *Journal of Comparative and Physiological Psychology*, 1968, 65, 251–260.

Weiss, J. M. Effects of coping behavior in different warning signal conditions on stress pathology in rats. *Journal of Comparative and Physiological Psychology*, 1971, 77, 1–13. (a)

Weiss, J. M. Effects of punishing the coping response (conflict) on stress pathology in rats. *Journal of Comparative and Physiological Psychology*, 1971, 77, 14–21. (b)

Weiss, J. M. Effects of coping behavior with or without a feedback signal on stress pathology in rats. *Journal of Comparative and Physiological Psychology*, 1971, 77, 22–30. (c)

Weiss, J. M., Glazer, H. I., & Pohorecky, L. A. Coping behavior and neurochemical changes: An alternative explanation for the original "learned helplessness" experiments. In G. Serban & A. Kling (Eds.), *Animal models in human psychobiology*. New York: Plenum Press, 1976.

Weiss, J. M., Stone, E. A., & Harrell, N. Coping behavior and brain norepinephrine in rats. *Journal of Comparative and Physiological Psychology*, 1970, 72, 153–160.

Wortman, C. B. & Brehm, J. W. Responses to uncontrollable outcomes: An integration of reactance theory and the learned helplessness model. In L. E. Berkowitz (Ed.), *Advances in experimental social psychology*. New York: Academic Press, 1975.

Wortman, C. B., Panciera, L., Shusterman, L., & Hibscher, J. Attributions of causality and reactions to uncontrollable outcomes. *Journal of Experimental Social Psychology*, 1976, 12, 301–316.

Zuckerman, M. & Lubin, B. *Manual for the multiple affect adjective check list*. San Diego, California: Education and Industrial Testing Service, 1965.

CHAPTER 16

A Selective Review of Cognitive and Behavioral Factors Involved in the Regulation of Stress[1]

James R. Averill

INTRODUCTION

Stress has been widely implicated in the etiology of depression. The regulation of stress is, therefore, an important consideration in the prevention and treatment of this disorder. This fact provides the rationale for the present chapter, which focuses on the role of information—about the stressor and about potential coping responses—in the regulation of stress. The reason for this focus will be explained shortly. But first, it will be helpful to consider briefly the nature of stress as viewed from the standpoint of this chapter.

THE NATURE OF STRESS

The concept of stress has no settled meaning. Although numerous suggestions have been made regarding its use, no single proposal has met

[1] Preparation of this chapter was supported, in part, by a grant (NH22299) from the National Institute of Mental Health.

The Psychobiology of the Depressive Disorders:
Implications for the Effects of Stress

with universal, or even widespread, acceptance. Some (e.g., Hinkle, 1974) have even suggested that the concept has outlived its usefulness and should be abandoned. In view of this controversy, no attempt will be made here to give a precise definition of stress. However, there are two traditions of stress research that deserve brief comment, namely, the physiologic and the psychological. Hans Selyé is the founding father and guardian angel of the physiological tradition. "For scientific purposes," Selyé (1976) states, "stress is defined as *the nonspecific response of the body to any demand* [p. 55]." Somewhat less scientifically, Selyé believes that the study of stress "touches closely upon the essence of life and disease" and that it can give us "a new philosophy to guide our actions in conformity with natural laws [p. 3-4]." But whatever its broader philosophical implications, the study of stress as envisioned by Selyé places emphasis on nonspecific hormonal responses, especially those of the pituitary and adrenal glands. The nature of the stressor agent ("any demand") is given relatively little attention.

Within the psychological tradition of stress research, by contrast, the most emphasis has been placed on how a person (or infrahuman animal) comes to judge a situation as threatening, and hence stressful. Considerably less attention has been devoted to the nature of the stress response. Indeed, within this tradition, "stress" has been used as a generic term to cover almost any response to a situation that taxes the individual's adaptive resources. This covers such specific states as fear, anger, etc., as well as such diffuse affective experiences as anxiety and depression.

In a sense, then, the physiological and psychological traditions complement one another—the former concentrating on response mechanisms and the latter concentrating on eliciting conditions. But the relationship between these two traditions may be closer than even this statement indicates. In concluding an extensive review of endocrine response patterns, Mason (1968) has pointed out that many of the "physical stressors" used by physiological researchers (e.g., prolonged cold, physical injury, and the like) produce little effect on the endocrine system unless they are part of a psychological or emotion-inducing context. He goes on to ask what is undoubtedly one of the most fundamental questions in contemporary stress research:

> In the light of present knowledge of the keen sensitivity of the pituitary–adrenal cortical system to psychological influences, is it not disturbing to consider that most, if not all, of the situations described by Selyé very likely involve some degree of *emotional reaction, discomfort, or pain as well as the designated "nocuous stimuli?"* Does the widely occurring pituitary–adrenal cortical response, then, reflect a "general adaptive" or a "nonspecific" endocrine response to many different "nocuous" stimuli or does it reflect a specific response to a single type of stimulis (psychological) which these various unpleasant situations share in common [p. 800]?

By these rhetorical questions, Mason does not mean to imply that the pituitary–adrenal cortical system responds only to psychological stimuli. What he does suggest is that the term "nonspecific" may be misleading when applied to physiological stress reactions. Even more importantly from the standpoint of the present chapter, he suggests that most physiological stress reactions may be the result, at least in part, of a psychological process, namely, the *appraisal* of threat (Mason, 1975).

The notion of appraisal was introduced systematically into the psychology of stress and emotion by Arnold (1960) and R. S. Lazarus (1966, 1968). In its broadest sense, appraisal refers to the psychological processes by which an event is assimilated into a cognitive structure (i.e., a set of ideas, beliefs, and expectations), and thus given meaning. The importance of the concept of appraisal is that it focuses attention on the interaction between the individual and the environment in the production of stress. In the normal course of affairs few events are inherently threatening. To become a source of stress, an event must be appraised as potentially harmful to the individual; and what may be appraised as harmful by one person may be appraised as benign by another, or by the same individual at some later time.

Figure 16.1 presents a schematic diagram of a typical stress syndrome viewed from a psychological perspective. For reasons which will become clear in the following discussion, two factors important to the appraisal of threat are distinguished in the figure: (*a*) knowledge of the stressor (its physical characteristics, etc.) and (*b*) knowledge of its immediate (sensory) impact. The appraisal of threat leads, in turn, to three types of coping mechanismas: (*a*) physiological reactions, including the endocrine and autonomic responses described by Selyé and others; (*b*) overt behavior, including instrumental responses intended specifically to alter the nature of the stressor or one's relation to it; and (*c*) cognitive activities (i.e., symbolic

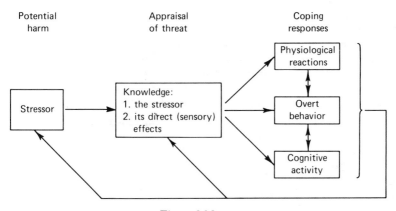

Figure 16.1

attempts to alter the meaning of the threat). Through feedback loops, these three types of coping mechanisms influence one another, the appraisal of threat, and often the external stressor. But despite this mutual interaction, there is also considerable autonomy among the various kinds of coping responses, so that each may be manipulated or influenced semiindependently of the others.

INFORMATION AND
THE REGULATION OF STRESS

Because the nature of stress is complex, the regulation of stress is necessarily also complex. This poses a difficulty: How can we, in a brief chapter, review all the relevant factors involved in the regulation of stress? The answer, of course, is that we cannot. Some simplifying assumptions and limitations must be made. The major limitation we will make is to focus on the role of information and knowledge as a regulating factor. The reason for this limitation is twofold: First, there is considerable evidence that information by itself (i.e., even in the absence of any kind of direct behavioral control) is an extremely important factor in the regulation of stress; and, second, in many situations information is the simplest—if not the only— factor that can be varied. Frances Bacon is credited with the observation that knowledge is power. This aphorism is true in more ways than Bacon realized.

The potential importance of information in the regulation of stress is easily demonstrated. For example, in a now classic study, Janis (1958) observed that patients who thought about their impending operations (i.e., who did the "work of worrying") made better postsurgical recoveries than did patients who avoided any thought about the surgery. Following up this lead, Egbert, Battit, Welch, and Bartlett (1964) prepared a group of patients for surgery by providing them with information regarding the impending operation, the reactions they might experience during recovery, and how they might cope with the situation (e.g., by doing pain-relieving exercises). Patients who received such instruction required less medication and were discharged earlier than patients who received no preparation. In a similar vein, H. R. Lazarus and Hagens (1968) found that psychological preparation prior to open-heart surgery reduced the postoperative psychotic-like symptoms (hallucinations, disorientation, inappropriate emotional reactions, etc.) by approximately one half—from 33 to 14%.

Other investigators have reported findings similar to the above, although the results have by no means been completely uniform or unequivocal (Chapman, 1969; Cohen & Lazarus, 1973; Elms & Leonard, 1966; Goldstein, 1973; Healy, 1968; Langer, Janis & Wolfer, 1975; Lindeman, 1972; Lindeman & Airman, 1971; Sime, 1976). Without going into detail, it would appear from these studies that the relationship between information and the regulation of stress is complicated by a variety of factors, such as: (*a*) the personality or preferred coping style of the individual; (*b*) the source of the information; (*c*) the time interval between the receipt of information and the occurrence of the threatening event; (*d*) the degree of threat; and (*e*) the kind of information provided. In the present chapter, we will review evidence related to the last variable, the kind of information provided.

Referring back to Figure 16.1 (p. 367), five kinds of information may be relevant to the regulation of stress. Two of these pertain to the appraisal of threat, and three to the types of coping responses. As previously stated, the appraisal of threat may be influenced by information about (*a*) the physical properties or "objective" characteristics of the stressor, and (*b*) the sensations and feelings that may be experienced as a result of the stressor. To illustrate these two kinds of information, consider a patient suffering from cancer. He might be informed about the nature of the tumor, how cancer cells proliferate, the type of treatment possible, etc. But he might also be informed about whether the cancer will produce pain, what the treatment will feel like, and so forth. Although this latter kind of information is "subjective" in the sense that it refers to sensations and feelings, it is nevertheless factual and can be consensually validated.

Information also may be provided with regard to each of the three types of coping responses depicted in Figure 16.1. To continue with our previous example, a patient suffering from cancer may be informed that at certain times he is likely to experience particular bodily symptoms—not as an immediate consequence of the stressor, but as a result of his own emotional (coping) reactions. He may also be instructed to take certain instrumental actions to alleviate his condition. Finally, he may be instructed in problem–solving techniques or encouraged to engage in other cognitive activities (such as denial) designed to alleviate the stress.

In the remainder of this chapter, we will examine how each of the above kinds of information may be involved in the regulation of stress. Our approach will be largely empirical rather than theoretical. The reason for this will become apparent as we proceed. Although often dramatic, the relationship between information and the regulation of stress is extremely complex. Too often, one hears ex cathedra pronouncements, based upon broad theoretical assumptions, that patients should be informed about this or that for their own good. As we shall see, however, information can sometimes increase rather than decrease stress. Therefore, generalizations in this area must be made with some care. But there is one theoretical assumption that pervades the entire chapter, and perhaps it should be made explicit at the outset. A human being is not a passive information-processing machine. Each person *informs* (imposes meaning on) the environment, as well as vice versa. And in order for a person to impose meaning on events, he must possess some model or cognitive structure that represents the environment and his place within it. Borrowing an analogy from George Kelly (1955), these cognitive structures may be compared to spectacles through which an individual views his world. Any information given to the individual must be filtered through these mental prisms before it can be acted upon. Some implications of this fact will be examined in the conclusion to the chapter, after we have reviewed the empirical research.

INFORMATION ABOUT
THE POTENTIAL HARM

Information about the nature of a threat can emphasize the physical or other "external" properties of the stressor or the reactions to the stressor that may be experienced by the person. These two kinds of information were manipulated independently in an experiment by Staub and Kellet (1972). Specifically, subjects were faced with the threat of electric shock and were given information about the characteristics of the shock (e.g., the nature of the delivery apparatus and its safety features, transfer of electricity, and the like) and/or about the types of sensations they would experience when the shock was delivered. Subjects who received both types of information were willing to accept more intense shocks before evaluating them as painful than were subjects who received either type of information by itself. The latter subjects, in fact, did not differ in pain tolerance from those who received no information at all. The no-information subjects, however, did express more worry or anxiety than those who had either kind of information.

In a series of studies using ischemic pain as a stressor, Johnson (1973) and Johnson and Rice (1974) also found that information about the procedure used to produce the pain (i.e., the inflation of a cuff around the upper arm, thus cutting off circulation to the muscles) did not reduce ratings of distress. In these studies, however, information about sensory experiences (e.g. tingling and numbness of the hand, aching, blueness) was sufficient *by itself* to reduce stress. Following up these laboratory findings in a field setting, Johnson and Leventhal (1974) found that informing patients of the specific sensations they would experience during an endoscopic examination reduced the amount of stress exhibited. Information about the procedures had no prophylactic effect except when combined with sensory information. Similar results were obtained with children during the removal of an orthopedic cast (Johnson, Kirkhoff, & Endress, 1975).

In discussing these findings, let us consider first why information about the objective or physical aspects of the threatening events did not lead to reduced stress. This is perhaps due to the fact that neither the laboratory experiments (mild electric shock, ischemic pain) nor the medical procedures (endoscopy and cast removal) posed any real danger to the subjects. Moreover, ethics and good medical practice dictated that all subjects be given a minimal amount of information about the procedures so that they could give their informed consent. Under such conditions of safety and prior information, it is possible that further descriptions of the procedures did not add a great deal to subjects' knowledge or expectations.

Numerous studies could be cited which in fact have demonstrated that providing subjects with information about a noxious stimulus can help reduce stress (for reviews, see Averill, 1973; Lazarus, 1968; Lazarus, Averill, & Opton, 1974). Some of these studies will be described later in this chapter. For the moment, suffice it to say that objective information about a stressor may have little effect unless it (a) increases predictability, (b) facilitates certain modes of coping with the threat, and/or (c) results in a more benign appraisal of the threat.

With appropriate modification, each of the above three principles can also help explain the stress-reducing effects of sensory information. Let us begin by considering increased predictability. Johnson (1975) has argued that sensory information leads the individual to form accurate expectations about what will be experienced, and that the congruency between expected and experienced sensations results in decreased stress during the encounter with the noxious stimulus. Although her own data are not definitive in this regard, it might be noted that other studies have found that predictable noxious stimuli generally produce less stress than do unpredictable stimuli (Glass & Singer, 1972; Weiss, 1971a). Perhaps the same is true of painful or unpleasant sensations.

Increased predictability cannot be the entire explanation, however. Consider a recent study by Fuller, Endress, & Johnson (1978). Fuller et al. provided sensory information to women who were about to undergo a pelvic examination (emphasizing the experiences women typically have during such an examination, together with the temporal order of events). Another group of women received information on how to cope behaviorally with the procedure (e.g., by relaxing the abdominal muscles). The women who received the sensory information showed fewer overt signs of distress and lower physiological arousal during the examination than did those who received behavioral instruction. Moreover, the latter did not differ significantly from a control group that received general health information emphasizing the importance of pelvic examinations.

At first, this study by Fuller et al. might appear to be just another demonstration of the ameliorative effects of sensory information. However, the interpretation of the findings is complicated by the fact that all of the women studied had previously had pelvic examinations (over four times, on the average). Thus, they all knew from direct experience what sensations to expect. It would appear that the receipt of sensory information did more than just increase predictability.

A second possible explanation for the stress-reducing effects of sensory information is that the information suggests, or facilitates, certain modes of coping. The most intriguing version of this type of explanation has been advanced by Leventhal (1976). By way of background, Leventhal (1970, 1974) has postulated that information can be processed in at least two different ways: (a) an objective or analytical way, which aims at a veridical (reality-oriented) view of events; and (b) a subjective or affective way, which generates an emotional experience in connection with events. Leventhal assumes that these two modes of information processing are somewhat antagonistic, and that they may even be mediated by different neural mechanisms (located in the left and right hemispheres, respectively). If the above assumptions are correct, it follows that if persons could be induced to adopt an analytical mode of information processing, then stress and emotional reactions would be reduced. An analytical approach might be induced directly through instructions or indirectly through the provision of information. In several studies using the cold-pressor test (immersion of the hand in ice water), Leventhal (1976) found that simply asking subjects to attend to their sensations in an objective fashion had the same stress-reducing effect as providing accurate sensory information. By contrast, providing accurate sensory information accompanied by instructions designed to block an analytical set (by facilitating emotional arousal) had no ameliorative effect.

Leventhal's ideas with regard to different modes of information processing are based largely on research in cognitive psychology. It is instructive, however, to relate his ideas to some more familiar notions derived from clinical research. Within the clinical tradition, it is common to distinguish between two broad categories of defense mechanisms. On the one hand, there are defenses related to repression and denial, where thought processes tend to be unreflective, constricted, and accompanied by unmodulated affect. This kind of defense may thus involve what Leventhal calls a subjective or affective mode of information processing. At the other pole are defenses related to intellectualization (sensitization, isolation, externalization, etc.), where thought processes can best be described as analytical.

Laboratory research has demonstrated that if subjects are given an orientation that facilitates intellectualization and related defenses, then stress may be reduced. It is also reasonable to assume, as Leventhal does, that providing subjects with information about sensations might also facilitate the adoption of an analytical approach akin to intellectualization. It does not follow, however, that an analytical approach is necessary for the reduction of stress. On the contrary, the encouragement of repressive and denial-like defense strategies can be just as effective in reducing stress as is intellectualization (Lazarus, 1968).

In short, sensory information may have beneficial effects because of the mode of information processing or defense mechanisms it encourages. By the same token, however, a lack of information may encourage opposite, but equally effective coping strategies (e.g., repression, denial, avoidant thinking). We shall return to this issue shortly.

Let us consider now a third possible explanation for the ameliorative effects of sensory information, namely, that such information results in a more benign appraisal of the threat. On the basis of an early series of studies, Johnson (1973) argued that the effects of sensory information cannot be explained in this fashion, as subjects who received information did not evaluate the procedure (cutting off circulation to produce ischemic pain) as less dangerous than did subjects who received no information. However, the appraisal of threat depends not only on an evaluation of the objective danger, but also on an assessment of one's own ability to cope (by whatever means). Other things being equal, stress will be reduced in proportion to the confidence that a person has in his or her ability to overcome or withstand the danger.

In most studies that have investigated the effects of sensory information, subjects have been told explicitly that the expected sensations were *typical*. And even when such a message was not explicit, it has been implicit. (How could a person be informed of what sensations to expect if those sensations were not typical?) Thus, receipt of sensory information also provides subjects with a normative frame of reference. It says, in essence, "Others have had the same experiences as you and have done just fine." Having such a standard of comparison can greatly enhance one's tolerance for stress (e.g., Harvey, 1965; Krupat, 1974; Orne, 1965).

To summarize briefly, the finding that information about sensory experiences can lead to reduced stress appears to be quite robust. The explanation for this finding is not, however, clear. Increasing predictability and encouraging an analytical attitude are two of the ways in which sensory information could have such an effect. However, in the majority of cases, the explanation is probably much simpler. Sensory information, especially if accompanied by assurances from someone in authority (e.g., the experimenter, physician), provides the subject with a frame of reference in which to interpret his ongoing experiences. Confidence in one's ability to cope with the threat may thereby be increased and stress reduced.

I have devoted so much space to a discussion of these three possible explanations for the effects of sensory information because the same principles can also be used to explain the effects of other kinds of information, as will be discussed below. But before leaving the present topic, an important caveat must be added. It would be wrong to leave the impression that sensory information always has a beneficial effect. As noted above, denial-like or repressive coping strategies can also be effective in reducing stress, and such strategies may actually be hindered by providing a person with too much information. This fact is well illustrated in a study by Langer *et al.* (1975). These investigators provided patients about to undergo major surgery with either of two kinds of information. One kind encouraged denial-like coping strategies (selective attention, emphasis on positive outcomes, calming self-talk, and the like). The other kind of information described, in an objective fashion, the probable pains and discomforts that would be experienced, and it reassured the patients about the high quality of the medical care. It was expected that the latter (sensory-oriented) information might arouse moderate levels of anticipatory fear, but that postoperative recovery would nevertheless be facilitated. The first but not the second part of this expectation was confirmed. That is, patients who received realistic information about the surgical experience evidenced more anticipatory stress than did subjects who received no information or who received information describing coping procedures. Contrary to expectations, however, information about the surgical experience had no positive effect on reactions to the surgery or on the speed of recovery.

It is difficult to say why ostensibly similar procedures were beneficial in the studies reported by Johnson and her colleagues (Johnson, 1975; Fuller et al., 1978), and ineffective in the study by Langer et al. (1975). One possible factor is the degree of threat. The patients studies by Langer et al. were anticipating major surgery, whereas those studied by Johnson were anticipating more benign procedures. Research by Goldstein (1973) indicates that if a person is going to effectively utilize information regarding an impending harm, there must be an initial set for the appraisal of threat, based either on specific situational cues or on a person's characteristic cognitive style. Often, this initial set may involve a moderate degree of stress or emotional arousal. However, if the initial stress is too great, as might have been the case among the patients studied by Langer et al. (1975), then coping responses may be directed at the emotional arousal itself and not toward the potential threat.

INFORMATION ABOUT PHYSIOLOGICAL (EMOTIONAL) REACTIONS

In his Inaugural Address of 1933, Franklin Roosevelt warned the nation, then deep in an economic depression, that "the only thing we have to fear is fear itself." This is one variant of a very ancient theme, namely, that our own emotional reactions to an impending threat may be more harmful than the actual threat. In the present section, we will review some recent research relevant to the control of emotional reactions. As much of this research stems from the theory of emotion proposed by Stanley Schachter (1964, 1971), we shall begin with a brief summary of his position.

According to Schachter, emotions are a joint product of two factors: physiological arousal and cognitive appraisals regarding the source of that arousal. The feedback from physiological arousal provides a nondiscriminative affective tone to the experience, whereas the cognitive appraisal determines which, if any, emotion will be experienced. Thus, precisely the same state of physiological arousal might be experienced as joy, anger, sadness, or perhaps as no emotion at all, depending upon how the individual appraises the situation. It follows that if, for example, a person were given an appropriate nonemotional explanation for any physiological reactions experienced in a potentially frightening situation, then the tendency to regard the experience as emotional would be diminished. Moreover, if a reaction were not considered emotional, then disruptive behavior might be reduced and more adaptive coping responses facilitated.

In one test of the above implications, Nisbett and Schachter (1966) asked subjects to undergo a series of increasingly intense electric shocks. Presumably, most subjects in such a situation experience the kind of physiological reactions normally associated with mild fear. In this experiment, some of the subjects were given a placebo pill before the shock trials, and were told that the pill might produce hand tremors, heart palpitations, and other fear-like reactions. These subjects therefore had a nonemotional explanation for any physiological reactions they might experience. Other subjects were given a list of inaccurate (nonfear-like) symptoms to expect; hence, these subjects had no alternative explanations available for any fear-like reactions they might experience. As predicted, the subjects who received accurate information about potential physiological reactions, and who were able to attribute those reactions to a nonemotional source (the pill), were willing to tolerate more shock than were subjects who received an inaccurate list of symptoms.

The preceding findings have been essentially replicated by Ross, Rodin, and Zimbardo (1969). These investigators gave subjects, who also were faced with the threat of electric shock, either accurate or inaccurate information about potential physiological reactions. Subjects who received accurate information, and who were persuaded to attribute their arousal to an irrelevant source (a distracting noise), spent less time trying to avoid the shock and more time working for a monetary reward, than did subjects who received inaccurate information. In a similar vein, Dienstbier (1972) found increased cheating behavior (through the reduction of guilt), and Storms and Nisbett (1970) facilitated the onset of sleep among insomniacs (through the reduction of presleep anxiety), by providing subjects with accurate information about potential physiological reactions and a nonemotional source to which the reactions could be attributed.

The preceding studies raise two important issues for the regulation of stress. The first issue has to do with the misattribution of symptoms to an irrelevant source (e.g., a placebo); the second has to do with the effect of providing accurate information about symptoms, regardless of the source to which the symptoms are attributed. Beginning with the first issue, it will be noted that the effects reported are opposite to the traditional placebo effect: That is, when a person is given an irrelevant treatment (the placebo) and told that it will produce a certain reaction, then the likelihood of that reaction is typically increased. However, consider the study by Storms and

Nisbett (1970), which offers a good illustration of the reverse effect. One group of insomniacs was given a placebo pill and told that it would produce arousal symptoms. It was reasoned that if the subjects could attribute their arousal to the pill, then they would feel less emotionally upset and would fall asleep faster. Such a "reverse placebo" effect was observed. Another group of insomniacs was given the placebo and told that it would reduce arousal. It was reasoned that these subjects, experiencing some arousal *despite* the pill, would become more upset and have even greater difficulty in falling asleep. This prediction, too, was confirmed.

Several attempts to replicate the findings of Storms and Nisbett (1970) with insomniacs have produced the traditional placebo effects: Subjects who were given a pill and a list of arousal symptoms stayed awake longer than usual, whereas subjects who were given a pill and a list of symptoms indicative of relaxation fell asleep more rapidly than usual (Bootzin, Herman, & Nicassio, 1976; Kellogg & Baron, 1975). This indicates that considerable caution must be exercised before applying the reverse placebo phenomenon to actual clinical problems. There is no doubt that the misattribution of physiological reactions to a neutral or irrelevant source can often facilitate adaptive behavior. However, it is not clear under what conditions such an effect will be obtained, and under what conditions the suggested symptoms might actually exacerbate an existing problem.

Let us now turn to the second issue raised by the above studies. In each study, subjects were given accurate information about possible symptoms *and* a neutral or irrelevant source (e.g., a placebo) to which the symptoms could be attributed. Are both these conditions necessary for the reduction of stress? Several recent studies (Calvert-Boyanowsky & Leventhal, 1975; Rodin, 1976) have found that accurate information about physiological reactions is, by itself, sufficient to facilitate adaptive behavior. In the study by Calvert-Boyanowsky and Leventhal, for example, subjects were faced with the threat of electric shocks. Those who were given accurate information about possible physiological reactions (hand tremors, heart palpitations, general visceral upset, etc.) showed less avoidance behavior than did those who received a list of irrelevant symptoms. This was true regardless of whether the reactions were attributed to the actual source (threat of shock) or to a neutral source (distracting noise).

Why would information about physiological reactions lead to reduced stress? The same three mechanisms discussed previously with regard to sensory information (see p. 371 ff) may be involved here also. That is, information about physiological reactions may provide a normative frame of reference, thus altering the appraisal of threat; it may lead to accurate expectations; and/or it may induce an analytic mode of thought. It is impossible to say at the present time which of these mechanisms is the most consequential, as all, of course, may be important.

In summary, it would seem that accurate information concerning potential physiological reactions may be an important factor in the regulation of stress, especially if the individual is led to attribute those reactions to some neutral (nonemotional) source. Information about physiological reactions may be especially important for states such as anxiety and depression, where the nature of the response is often diffuse and the source of the symptoms ambiguous. In these cases, the individual may be at a loss to explain his own reactions. This could, in turn, result in a misinterpretation that lends meaning to the experience but also exacerbates the stress. For example, the depressed patient who feels miserable and fatigued for reasons he does not understand might conclude that he is a bad person who deserves to be punished. A vicious cycle could then be established, where feeling bad or worthless leads to even greater misery and depression. Such a sequence of events has frequently been observed (Beck, 1976).

INFORMATION ABOUT OVERT (INSTRUMENTAL) BEHAVIOR

We come now to the second response category depicted in Figure 16.1 (p. 367), namely, overt behavior. The present discussion will be confined to behavior that has some direct effect on the environment (e.g., by preventing or modifying the potential harm). Three types of information are relevant to such instrumental coping responses: (a) that a response is possible, (b) how to make the response, and (c) the outcome of the response.

Information That a Response Is Possible

Simply knowing that a coping response is possible, even though that response is never made, can greatly influence the stressfulness of a situation. This has been well demonstrated in a series of experiments by Glass and Singer (1972), who required subjects to work on a task while being subjected to unpredictable blasts of noise. Following this rather noxious procedure, subjects were asked to work on several additional tasks (e.g., proofreading) that involved considerable attention and frustration. Prior exposure to unpredictable noise had a detrimental effect on these tasks—but only if the subjects believed they had no control over the noise. The detrimental effect did not appear if subjects were told that they could stop the noise simply by pressing a button. None of the subjects actually used the button, but the information that an instrumental coping response was possible evidently helped to alleviate the stressfulness of the situation. (Similar beneficial effects were observed if the noise was presented on a fixed rather than random schedule, thus allowing predictability.)

Numerous other studies could also be cited illustrating that the mere knowledge of a potential coping response may mitigate the impact of a stressful stimulus (for reviews, see Averill, 1973; Lefcourt, 1976; Leventhal, 1970; Seligman, 1975). However, one must be cautious about generalizing these results to all situations. On occasions, knowledge of a potential response may actually increase rather than decrease stress reactions. For example, in a study by Orne and Scheibe (1964), subjects were instructed that they could terminate a sensory deprivation (isolation) experiment at any time. All they had to do was press a button, thus signaling the experimenter. Subjects receiving these instructions exhibited greater stress than did subjects who underwent the same amount of isolation without the availability of an escape response.

The study by Orne and Scheibe illustrates an important point often overlooked in discussions of coping and stress; namely, that the stress-reducing (or stress-inducing) properties of a coping response are not simply a function of the effectiveness of the response. The meaning of the response for the individual is of central importance. If the response is suggestive of stress or fear (as most avoidance responses are), then the exercise of that response may be stressful. Moreover, the mere availability of such a response may suggest that the situation *is* more dangerous than is actually the case.

A study by Leventhal and Watts (1966) further illustrates how the meaning of a coping response may interact with stress reactions. These investigators showed motion pictures dealing with smoking and lung cancer to visitors at a state fair. The movies were designed to elicit high, medium, or low fear, and two types of instrumental responses were assessed: Immediately after the films, subjects had the opportunity to obtain chest x-rays and, 5 months later, a questionnaire was sent to all subjects to determine whether or not they had reduced their smoking. The number of smokers taking x-rays actually *decreased* as fear arousal increased. However, on the follow-up questionnaire, smokers exposed to the high-fear message reported greater success in reducing the amount they smoked. Because an x-ray might have revealed cancer, it was an anxiety-arousing procedure in its own right. Therefore, subjects who were already highly aroused avoided this type of response. A reduction of smoking, on the other hand, was a way of coping that would not further increase the large amount of stress already induced in the high-fear condition.

Information about How to Make a Response

As the study by Leventhal and Watts (1966) indicates, an individual will not always utilize a coping response (such as taking a chest x-ray), even when that response is readily available. Indeed, one of the major problems for preventive medicine is to get people to do something for their own good, and depressed patients particularly may lack the initiative to cope with their situation. It is therefore important to consider the conditions under which a person will undertake a particular coping response.

Perhaps the most common strategy to encourage a coping response is to increase motivation. However, as we have just seen, such a strategy can backfire if the coping response is itself stressful. Another, more cognitively oriented approach, is to provide sufficient information so that making the coping response becomes very easy and natural. The efficacy of this latter approach was demonstrated in a study by Leventhal, Singer, and Jones (1965). The coping response they wished to encourage was obtaining an innoculation against tetanus. The subjects were students at Yale University. The motivation to be innoculated was manipulated by describing the effects of tetanus in either a highly threatening or a neutral fashion. Information about how to obtain innoculations was also manipulated, being either very general or quite specific. Twenty-nine percent of the subjects in both the high- and low-fear groups obtained innoculations if they received specific coping instructions, whereas only 3% of the subjects obtained innoculations when the instructions were very general.

These results are rather surprising as the relevant coping response (obtaining an innoculation) was quite simple, and all students knew how to get to the University health center. However, the specific instructions indicated to the students how they might obtain innoculations during the course of their daily routines. In discussing these and similar findings from other studies. Leventhal (1970) concludes that "to some degree the success of instructions appears to depend primarily on a careful analysis of the individual's daily action pattern, locating natural chunks or subdivisions for the introduction of new behaviors, and locating the specific cues that initiate the action sequences that are to be eliminated [or encouraged] [p. 155]." In other words, information about potential coping responses, like any other kind of information, must be incorporated into a person's cognitive structure or "scheme of action" if it is to be acted upon.

Information about the
Outcome of a Response

Even if a coping response is made and the response is effective in eliminating or preventing the source of threat, it cannot be assumed that stress will automatically be reduced. Weiss (1968; 1971a; 1971b; 1971c) has found that, in animals, stress increases proportionately with the number of coping responses emitted, but inversely with the amount of positive feedback regarding the success of the response. The most stressful conditions appear to be those in which many responses are demanded, but the responses result in negative or inconsistent feedback (the traditional conflict situation); also stressful are situations where the animal must wait to learn the outcome of its response or rely on difficult discriminations.

In the case of human beings, information regarding the outcome of a response may be delayed almost indefinitely provided the individual has confidence in eventual success. Thus, much of our everyday behavior is meant to cope with some possible future contingency. We save money for a "rainy day," go to college to prepare for a career, stop smoking to lessen the risk of cancer, etc. As long as we can assume that such behavior ultimately will be rewarded, then little stress may be generated. Such confidence presumes the existence of cognitive systems that bridge the gaps of time, and allow intermediate (and sometimes negative) outcomes to be interpreted as signs of future success. These cognitive systems may be quite circumscribed, if the time span to be bridged is short. That is, they may consist of little more than specific beliefs, based on past experience, regarding the efficacy of a particular response. However, the longer the time span to be bridged and the more indeterminate the intermediate results, then the more encompassing and firm must be the cognitive system. On the broadest level, such a system may represent a set of religious or philosophical beliefs. Within such a complex system, even profound misfortune may be taken as a sign of ultimate satisfaction (e.g., in some future existence).

If confidence that our efforts eventually will be rewarded is called into question, then many of our daily activities may become a source of stress. In the extreme, the result might bear close resemblance to a depressive syndrome. In fact, the lack of feedback, either actual or assumed, can be considered a special case of the noncontingency of reward and punishment, that, as Seligman (1975) has shown, can produce many of the symptoms of depression.

INFORMATION ABOUT COGNITIVE COPING RESPONSES

In many situations, there is no action that a person can reasonably take to eliminate the potential harm, either because the harm has already occurred (as in bereavement or injury) or because, like death and taxes, the harm is inevitable. In such situations, the individual must rely on cognitive or intrapsychic devices in order to cope. There are two main schools of thought that deal with cognitive coping strategies. The first is psychoanalysis, with its "ego-functions" and "defense mechanism." The second is more recent and has been called by various names: "constructive alternativism (Kelly, 1955)," "rational-emotive therapy (Ellis, 1962)," "cognitive-behavior modification (Miechenbaum, 1976)," and—most simply—"cognitive therapy (Beck, 1976)." Both psychoanalysis and these newer cognitive therapies emphasize the use of conceptual tools and psychological devices to regulate stress. But, whereas psychoanalysis attempts to unravel the symbolic transformations that presumably conceal the source of stress (often a traumatic event occuring in early childhood), the newer cognitive therapies emphasize more traditional problem-solving techniques (e.g., logical reasoning and the accurate testing of assumptions about the immediate situation). According to Beck (1976): "the cognitive therapist induces the patient to apply the same problem-solving techniques he has used throughout his life to correct his fallacious thinking [p. 20]."

There obviously is not space here to review the methods or findings of these cognitively oriented psychotherapies. However, one point does need to be emphasized briefly in order to tie up some loose threads left hanging from previous sections. Throughout this chapter, we have been emphasizing the role of information in the regulation of stress. On several occasions, we have noted in passing that information about a potential harm and/or about one's own coping responses may sometimes increase rather than decrease stress. It would follow that, on some occasions, one way to reduce stress would be to *ignore* relevant information. As knowledge can be power, so too may ignorance be bliss.

The study by Langer *et al*. (1975), described previously, illustrates this last point. As will be recalled (p. 373), these investigators compared the effectiveness of two types of preparatory instructions on postoperative recovery. One type of instruction, consisting of information about the impending operation along with reassurances about the high quality of the medical care, was relatively ineffective in reducing stress. The second type of instructions were directed primarily at assisting the patient to control his or her own emotional reactions. It was explained to the patients that events themselves rarely cause stress; rather, it is the view people take of the events. Through numerous examples, patients were instructed to focus on the positive aspects of their operations (e.g., the beneficial outcome, the opportunity to relax) whenever they started to feel upset or frightened about surgery. In the words of Langer *et al*. (1975), this coping strategy involved "the cognitive reappraisal of anxiety-provoking events, calming self-talk, and *intentional cognitive control through selective attention* [p. 155, italics added]."

Patients who received such coping instructions requested fewer pain relievers and sedatives following surgery than did patients who received detailed information about the operation and its consequences. The former patients also required less hospitalization, although this trend did not reach traditional levels of statistical significance. Langer *et al*. (1975) conclude that "focusing on expected suffering [e.g., by the group who received detailed information about their operation] may be a less effective means, so far as tolerating temporary postoperative pains is concerned, than focusing on something else, and thereby not 'noticing' the pain as much [p. 163]."

There is little doubt that diverting attention from the source of threat, or from one's own emotional reactions, can be an extremely important means of regulating stress. This is especially true when there are no instrumental responses available for dealing directly with the potential harm (Averill, O'Brien, & DeWitt, 1977). Attention diversion may also account for the observation that people under stress often engage in a great deal of activity, much of it routine and only indirectly related to the source of threat. After an extensive review of the literature on the relationship between such activity and stress, Gal and Lazarus (1975) conclude that "the stress-reducing effects of activities unrelated to the cause of the stress probably can best be explained by viewing these activities as distracting or diverting the person's attention from the stress cues [p. 17]." This conclusion might even be extended to some of the stress-reducing effects of coping responses *directly* related to the cause of stress. That is, while attacking, feeling, or otherwise attempting to cope with a threat, attention may be diverted and stress reduced. This would help account for the commonplace observation that stress may be experienced more intensely after a danger has passed than while a person is actively coping with the danger.

The fact that attention diversion can momentarily reduce stress is hardly surprising; but the fact that it can also facilitate long-range recovery from surgery, as in the Langer *et al.* study, would seem to run counter to the findings cited earlier on the beneficial effects of sensory and physiological information. Unfortunately, it is difficult to compare directly the results from different studies. Subtle differences in atmosphere, varying degress of threat, and many other personal and situational factors might influence the results.

Because of these conflicting results, one point does require emphasis. There is presently a tendency to assume that persons faced with an aversive event should be fully and accurately informed. This may be true from a broad social or ethical standpoint, but it is not necessarily true from the standpoint of the individual undergoing a stressful experience. It is evident that information about—and even personal control over—an aversive event may sometimes have harmful as well as beneficial results. In a recent book on personal control, Lefcourt (1976) has quoted from a sermon by Reinhold Niebuhr: "Oh God, give us the serenity to accept what cannot be changed, courage to change what should be changed, and wisdom to distinguish the one from the other." This prayer has been adopted by Alcoholics Anonymous, and it certainly is good advice for anyone concerned with the cognitive and behavioral regulation of stress.

CONCLUDING OBSERVATIONS

It would be nice if the preceding discussion could be summarized by more than a prayer. But that would be difficult. For every study demonstrating the stress-reducing properties of a particular kind of information, counter-examples can generally be found, or numerous qualifications must be added. Perhaps the safest generalization that can be made about this topic is: *Don't generalize.* But even that is unacceptable, for it is the purpose of research—clinical as well as experimental—to formulate general principles that will help guide future practice.

One solution to this dilemma is to go beyond such simple (or simplistic) questions as: Is information about a threatening event helpful or harmful? A question such as this has no answer; at least, not until some prior questions have been resolved. Thus, with regard to the nature of the threat, it must first be asked: Is it mild or severe? Is it an isolated event, or is it likely to be repeated? And are the long-term consequences likely to be beneficial or harmful? With regard to the coping response, it must be asked: Is it inherently stressful, e.g., because it involves pain or effort? Does it focus attention on the threat, or does it help divert attention away? And does it lead to an unambiguous outcome? Finally, with regard to the nature of the individual, it must be asked: What kind of events does this person find threatening? What kind of resources does he have for coping with the threat? And what are his characteristic or preferred modes of coping?

Despite the above qualifications, there is one general fact that does emerge from the research we have reviewed. That is, the appraisal of threat, the meaning of one's own coping responses, and hence the experiences of stress, are determined in large part by the conceptualizations or cognitive structures that an individual brings to the situation. As stated in the introduction to this chapter, a person *informs* (imposes meaning on or structures) his environment, as well as vice versa.

This fact is, of course, hardly novel. Piaget (1952), for example, speaks of perceptual and motor "schemata," Kelly (1955) of "cognitive constructs," Parkes (1971) of "assumptive worlds," and Marris (1975) of "structures of meaning." Whatever the terminology, the basic idea is the same. Events are meaningful only to the extent they can be assimilated into some existing cognitive model or structure. If they cannot be assimilated, then the relevant cognitive structures must be altered to accommodate the environmental input. What this means in practical terms is that the regulation of stress may require a two-stage process. The first stage involves the creation of an appropriate frame of reference, and the second stage is the presentation of specific information or instructions with regard to the nature of the threat, possible coping responses, etc. These two stages often are not distinguishable in practice. In cases where the individual already has the necessary conceptualizations available, the presentation of information (stage two) may be sufficient to evoke the appropriate cognitive structures (stage one).

In many cases, however, considerable preliminary work may have to be done before an individual is ready to assimilate and properly use the information that might be needed in order to cope optimally with threat. For example, a phobic may realize perfectly well that the object of his fear (e.g., a small spider, or open spaces) cannot cause any harm, yet he is still afraid; the person who knows that smoking is dangerous to his health, and who sincerely wants to stop smoking, may still continue to inhale carcinogenic agents; and the depressed individual may know that things are not all *that* bad, but still feel sad and helpless. Simply providing further information in such cases is likely to be of little value. It is not enough for the depressed, addicted, or phobic individual to "know" better, he must also "be" better; and being better may require the development of cognitive structures in which the desired attitudes and behaviors become part of the individual's own self- and object-world.

Any fundamental changes in a person's cognitive structures may, of course, be a source of severe stress and resistance. There is not space in the present chapter to discuss this source of stress and related issues of behavioral change and depression. For discussions of these topics, the interested reader must be referred elsewhere (e.g., Averill, 1976, 1979; Marris, 1975; Meichenbaum, 1976; Sarbin & Adler, 1971).

REFERENCES

Arnold, M. B. *Emotion and personality* (2 vols.). New York: Columbia Univ. Press, 1960.

Averill, J. R. Personal control over aversive stimuli and its relationship to stress. *Psychological Bulletin*, 1973, 80, 286–303.

Averill, J. R. Emotion and anxiety: Sociocultural, biological, and psychological determinants. In M. Zuckerman & C. D. Spielberger (Eds.), *Emotion and anxiety: New concepts, methods and applications*, New York: LEA-John Wiley, 1976.

Averill, J. R. The functions of grief. In C. Izard (Ed.), *Emotions in personality and psychopathology*, New York: Plenum, 1979.

Averill, J. R., O'Brien, L., & DeWitt, G. The influence of response effectiveness on the preference for warning and on psychophysiological stress reactions. *Journal of Personality*, 1977, 45, 395–418.

Beck, A. T. *Cognitive therapy and the emotional disorders*. New York: International Univ. Press, 1976.

Bootzin, R. R., Herman, C. P., & Nicassio, P. The power of suggestion: Another examination of misattribution and insomnia. *Journal of Personality and Social Psychology*, 1976, 34, 673–679.

Calvert-Boyanowsky, J. & Leventhal, H. The role of information in attenuating behavioral responses to stress: A reinterpretation of the misattribution phenomenon. *Journal of Personality and Social Psychology*, 1975, 32, 214–221.

Chapman, J. S. Effects of different nursing approaches upon psychological and physiological responses. *Nursing Research Report*, 1969, 5, 1–7.

Cohen, F. & Lazarus, R. S. Active coping processes, coping dispositions, and recovery from surgery. *Psychosomatic Medicine*, 1973, 35, 375–389.

Dienstbier, R. A. The role of anxiety and arousal attribution in cheating. *Journal of Experimental Social Psychology*, 1972, 8, 168–179.

Egbert, L. D., Battit, G. E., Welch, C. E., & Bartlett, M. K. Reduction of postoperative pain by encouragement and instruction of patients. *New England Journal of Medicine*, 1964, 270, 825–827.

Ellis, A. *Reason and emotion in psychotherapy.* New York: Lyle Stuart, 1962.

Elms, R. R. & Leonard, R. C. Effects of nursing approaches during admission. *Nursing Research*, 1966, 15, 30–48.

Fuller, S. S., Endress, M. P., & Johnson, J. E. The effects of cognitive and behavioral control on coping with an aversive health examination. *Journal of Human Stress*, 1978, 4, 18–25.

Gal, R. & Lazarus, R. S. The role of activity in stress. *Journal of Human Stress*, 1975, 4–20.

Glass, D. C. & Singer, J. E. *Urban Stress.* New York: Academic Press, 1972.

Goldstein, M. J. Individual differences in response to stress. *American Journal of Community Psychology*, 1973, 1, 113–137.

Harvey, O. J. Cognitive aspects of affective arousal. In S. S. Tomkins & C. E. Izard (Eds.), *Affect, cognition, and personality.* New York: Springer, 1965.

Healy, K. M. Does preoperative instruction make a difference. *American Journal of Nursing*, 1968, 68, 62–67.

Hinkle, L. E. The concept of "stress" in the biological and social sciences. *International Journal of Psychiatry in Medicine*, 1974, 5, 335–357.

Janis, I. L. *Psychological stress.* New York, Wiley, 1958.

Johnson, J. E. Effects of accurate expectations about sensations on the sensory and distress components of pain. *Journal of Personality and Social Psychology*, 1973, 27, 261–275.

Johnson, J. E. Stress reduction through sensation information. In I. G. Sarason & C. D. Spielberger (Eds.), *Stress and anxiety* (Vol. 2). Washington D. C.: Hemisphere, 1975.

Johnson, J. E., Kirchoff, K. T., & Endress, M. P. Altering childrens' distress behavior during orthopedic cast removal. *Nursing Research*, 1975, 24, 404–410.

Johnson, J. E. & Leventhal, H. Effects of accurate expectations and behavioral instructions on reactions during a noxious medical examination. *Journal of Personality and Social Psychology*, 1974, 29, 710–718.

Johnson, J. E & Rice, V. H. Sensory and distress components of pain: Implications for the study of clinical pain. *Nursing Research*, 1974, 23, 203–209.

Kellogg, R. & Baron, R. S. Attribution theory, insomnia, and the reverse placebo effect: A reversal of Storms and Nisbett's findings. *Journal of Personality and Social Psychology*, 1975, 32, 231–236.

Kelly, G. A. *The psychology of personal constructs.* (2 vols.). New York: Norton 1955.

Krupat, E. Context as a determinant of perceived threat: The role of prior experience. *Journal of Personality and Social Psychology*, 1974, 29, 731–736.

Langer, E. J., Janis, I. L., & Wolfer, J. A. Reduction of psychological stress in surgical patients. *Journal of Experimental Social Psychology*, 1975, 11, 155–165.

Lazarus, H. R. & Hagens, J. H. Prevention of psychosis following open-heart surgery. *American Journal of Psychiatry*, 1968, 124, 1190–1195.

Lazarus, R. S. *Psychological stress and the coping process.* New York: McGraw-Hill, 1966.

Lazarus, R. S. Emotions and adaptation: Conceptual and empirical relations. In W. Arnold (Ed.), *Nebraska symposium on motivation* (Vol. 16). Lincoln, Nebraska: Univ. Nebraska Press, 1968.

Lazarus, R. S., Averill, J. R., & Opton, E. M., Jr. The psychology of coping: Issues of research and assessment. In G. V. Coelho, D. A. Hamburg, & J. E. Adams (Eds.), *Coping and adaptation: Interdisciplinary perspectives.* New York: Basic Books, 1974.

Lefcourt, H. M. *Locus of control.* Hillsdale, New Jersey: Lawrence Erlbaum, 1976.

Leventhal, H. Findings and theory in the study of fear communications. In L. Berkowitz (Ed.), *Advances in experimental social psychology* (Vol. 5). New York: Academic Press, 1970.

Leventhal, H. Emotions: A basic problem in social psychology. In C. Nemeth (Ed.), *Social psychology: Classic and contemporary integrations*. Chicago: Rand McNally, 1974.

Leventhal, H. *A theory for studies of subjective and objective information processing. Paper presented at the meeting of the American Psychological Association, Washington, D. C.*, 1976.

Leventhal, H., Singer, R. E. & Jones, S. Effects of fear and specificity of recommendations. *Journal of Personality and Social Psychology*, 1965, 2, 20–29.

Leventhal, H. & Watts, J. C. Sources of resistance to fear arousing communications on smoking and lung cancer. *Journal of Personality*, 1966, 34, 155–175.

Lindeman, C. A. Effectiveness and efficiency of group and individual preoperative teaching—phase two. *Nursing Research*, 1972, 21, 196–209.

Lindeman, C. A. & Airman, B. V. Nursing intervention with the presurgical patient: The effects of structured and unstructured preoperative teaching. *Nursing Research*, 1971, 20, 319–334.

Marris, P. *Loss and change*. Garden City, New York: Doubleday, 1975.

Mason, J. W. "Over-all" hormonal balance as a key to endocrine organization. *Psychosomatic Medicine*, 1968, 5 (Part 2), 791–808.

Mason, J. W. A historical view of the stress field. Parts I and II. *Journal of Human Stress*, 1975, 1, 6–12, 22–36.

Meichenbaum, D. Toward a cognitive theory of self control. In G. Schwartz & D. Shapiro (Eds.), *Consciousness and self-regulation: Advances in research*. New York: Plenum, 1976.

Nisbett, R. E. & Schachter, S. Cognitive manipulation of pain. *Journal of Experimental Social Psychology*, 1966, 2, 227–236.

Orne, M. T. Psychological factors maximizing resistance to stress: With special reference to hypnosis. In S. Z. Klausner (Ed.), *The quest for self-control*. New York: Free Press, 1965.

Orne, M. T. & Scheibe, K. E. The contribution of nondeprivation factors in the production of sensory deprivation effects: The psychology of the "panic button." *Journal of Abnormal and Social Psychology*, 1964, 68, 3–12.

Parkes, C. M. Psychosocial Transitions: A field for study. *Social Science and Medicine*, 1971, 5, 101–115.

Piaget, J. *The origins of intelligence in children*. New York: International Univ. Press, 1952.

Rodin, J. Menstruation, reattribution, and competence. *Journal of Personality and Social Psychology*, 1976, 33, 345–353.

Ross, L., Rodin, J., & Zimbardo, P. G. Toward an attribution therapy: The reduction of fear through induced cognitive-emotional misattribution. *Journal of Personality and Social Psychology*, 1969, 12, 279–288.

Sarbin, T. R. & Adler, N. Self-reconstitution processes: A preliminary report. *Psychoanalytic Review*, 1971, 57, 599–616.

Schachter, S. The interaction of cognitive and physiological determinants of emotional state. In L. Berkowitz (Ed.), *Advances in experimental social psychology* (Vol. 1). New York: Academic Press, 1964.

Schachter, S. *Emotion, obesity, and crime*. New York: Academic Press, 1971.

Seligman, M. E. P. *Helplessness: On depression, development, and death*. San Francisco: Freeman, 1975.

Selye, H. *The stress of life* (Rev. ed.), New York: McGraw-Hill, 1976.

Sime, A. M. Relationship of preoperative fear, type of coping, and information received about surgery to recovery from surgery. *Journal of Personality and Social Psychology*, 1976, 34, 716–724.

Staub, E. & Kellett, D. S. Increasing pain tolerance by information about aversive stimuli. *Journal of Personality and Social Psychology*, 1972, 21, 198–203.

Storms, M. D. & Nisbett, R. E. Insomnia and the attribution process. *Journal of Personality and Social Psychology*, 1970, 16, 319–328.

Weiss, J. M. Effects of coping responses on stress. *Journal of Comparative and Physiological Psychology*, 1968, *65*, 251–260.

Weiss, J. M. Effects of coping behavior in different warning signal conditions on stress pathology in rats. *Journal of Comparative and Physiological Psychology*, 1971, *77*, 1–13. (a)

Weiss, J. M. Effects of punishing the coping response (conflict) on stress pathology in rats. *Journal of Comparative and Physiological Psychology*, 1971, *77*, 14–21. (b)

Weiss, J. M. Effects of coping behavior with and without a feedback signal on stress pathology in rats. *Journal of Comparative and Physiological Psychology*, 1971, *77*, 22–30. (c)

PART V

Models of Stress—Biology Interactions: Theoretical and Research Strategies

A major goal of this text is to stimulate an integration of the notions presented in the biological and psychosocial sections in future research. This form of integration is required if a comprehensive theory of the development of depressive disorders is to be achieved. However, such integration in depression research is noticeably lacking at present. This situation may be largely due to the lack of integrative models that delineate research strategies and testable hypotheses.

Most chapters in this text contribute to working models of stress—biology interactions. However, the final section of this volume specifically attempts to stimulate thinking on integrative models and research strategies. Erlenmeyer-Kimling discusses a novel behavior—genetic strategy that provides a test of the impact of the psychosocial environment on psychopathology; and, as the concluding chapter to the text, Akiskal provides a most creative integration of psychosocial findings, on the one hand, and biologic data on the other.

CHAPTER 17

Advantages of a Behavior–Genetic Approach to Investigating Stress in the Depressive Disorders

L. Erlenmeyer-Kimling

INTRODUCTION

As the preceding chapters and a considerable body of earlier work abundantly document, life stresses appear to be critical components in the etiology of the depressive disorders, acting in the capacity of both immediate precipitants and long-term "vulnerabilizers." Most people do not develop a depressive disorder, however, even though stress of many kinds is the common experience of nearly every human—nor do they necessarily succumb to alternatives, such as schizophrenia, peptic ulcer, coronary disease, and other conditions in which stress is thought to be implicated. Life events are obviously handled, or mishandled, in very different ways by different people.

There are several reasons for this phenomenon. First, there is a question of what one calls "stress." Stress situations differ not only in intensity, quantity, duration, and predictability but also in *perceived* intensity, quantity, duration, and predictability, as well as in contextual meaning for the individual. Second, there are large differences in the potency of the psy-

The Psychobiology of the Depressive Disorders: Implications for the Effects of Stress

chosocial supports that different people are able to rally to help them over difficult times. These aspects of variability in responses to stress have already been discussed by other authors in this book. But the third, and perhaps most important source of variation, is that people differ in genetic constitution and in the experiences they have already undergone. This chapter is concerned with the development of stress vulnerability and, ultimately, a depressive disorder, as the outcome of interactions between such genetic and environmental variables.

GENE-ENVIRONMENT INTERACTION, STRESS AND DEPRESSION

It is obvious that organisms enter the world with differences in their genetic makeup that may produce differences in their sensitivity and responsiveness to various kinds of environmental input. A large body of data from animal research, mostly on mice and dogs, demonstrates genotype-dependent responsiveness to early experiences, as well as to later treatments (Erlenmeyer-Kimling, 1972; Fuller, 1973). There also is ample evidence that humans differ from each other in temperament and receptivity to environmental stimulation from earliest infancy, presumably as a function of genetic differences or the interaction of genetic and prenatal factors (Berger & Passingham, 1973; Hersh, 1977). Some babies appear to notice very little in their environments, whereas others are aware of nearly everything—some seeming to reach out to each new experience and others responding negatively. Even relatively major events do not elicit the same responses in all human infants: The depressive syndrome described by Spitz (1947) in infants separated from their mothers actually occurred in only 15% of the infants, although the subsequent literature has tended to lose sight of the fact that the syndrome occurs with this moderate rarity, rather than universally, following loss of the mother. In addition, although reports on infant monkeys separated from their mothers have also tended to generalize a pattern of agitation and despair as applying to all subjects under study, not every investigator has shown behavioral homogeneity. In Kaufman and Rosenblum's (1967) study of pigtail macaques, one of the four infants observed failed to show a depression phase, and Spencer-Booth and Hinde (1971) and Lewis, McKinney, Young, and Kraemer (1976), studying infant rhesus monkeys, were impressed with the high degree of variability of behavior in response to separation from the mother.

Although the animal work clarifies the importance of genotype with respect to the impact early experience variables will have on later behavior, such research also testifies to the powerful influence of the early treatment itself in the development of adult behavior. Two mouse strains subjected to identical conditions of handling postnatally may diverge in, for example, adult activity level. However, the behavior of different samples of a single strain may also diverge after exposure to different early experiences. For humans, experimental evidence varying genotype and environment is rare and restricted mainly to such "natural" situations as the investigation of the developmental outcomes of treatment versus nontreatment of inborn metabolic disorders (e.g., phenylketonuria). Nonetheless, it is clear that for humans, as for other animals, gene–environment interactions play a major part in shaping behavior and in establishing a response set that helps to determine the nature of future responses.

Vulnerability to stress entails an interaction between an initial genetic diathesis—which, for simplicity, we can regard as a propensity to respond more or less strongly and more or less negatively to the environment—and the events that mark the life of the individual. Thus, one's degree of vulnerability is not a static, enduring condition but, instead (at any specified moment in the life span), it reflects a cumulative feedback relationship that has taken place between one's genetic predisposition and one's entire history. The feedback relationship is such that the genetically tailored response threshold is constantly altering, making the individual increasingly sensitive to further environmental insults following chronic or recurrent stress, and perhaps reducing sensitivity consequent to extended positive reinforcement.

Consider the following example. Child A and child B both have genotypes that result in a relatively low initial response threshold, so that they start out in life with the same potential for developing a high degree of vulnerability to stress. Child A experiences a great deal of stress in childhood (perhaps the loss of a parent, an abusive parent and chaotic home situation, or many changes of residence with attendant losses of peer attachments and status). These environmental events interacting with the genetic predisposition cause the child to become increasingly vulnerable to succeeding stresses. Child B, however, passes through a relatively well-buffered and unstressful childhood, and so attains adulthood with a much lower vulnerability than child A. Child C, whose genotype is associated with a relatively high initial threshold, also undergoes many adverse circumstances as a child. Child C's vulnerability may increase as a consequence of childhood stress, but child C will be far less vulnerable than child A for the same amount of exposure to stress. Or stress may actually serve as a strength-building process in the individual with a high genetic threshold, thereby developing a considerable degree of invulnerability.

Being vulnerable to stress does not necessarily mean that one is vulnerable to the development of a depressive disorder, of course. Stress appears to play an etiologic role in a variety of somatic and psychological conditions in addition to depression, and neither the kind of stress nor the amount is specific to any one condition. Genotypes, though, are specific in terms of the physiological response system that is affected. One stress-vulnerable person becomes depressed and another a victim of coronary disease because their different genotypes represent lesions in different response systems. This does not mean that all persons who develop a depressive disorder have the same genetic defect—indeed, family studies and other evidence point to genetic heterogeneity at least between the unipolar and bipolar forms of disorder and possibly within each disorder as well. However, although there may be several genotypes involving different genetic lesions, it is not unreasonable to suppose that they all ultimately channel stress responses through a common final pathway (Akiskal & McKinney, 1973).

Goodwin and Bunney (1973) have suggested two possible ways in which a genetic defect and stress may interact to produce a depressive disorder. First, the lesion might lie in one of the systems that normally serves to increase the biogenic amines in response to stress. If this were the case, the stores of critical biogenic amines could eventually become depleted during chronic or recurrent stress, thereby leading to a clinical state of retarded depression. Alternatively, assuming that, under stress, the normal response is to increase biogenic amine synthesis, the genetic error could be in the form of a defective feedback control mechanism so that amine synthesis does not decrease, as it should, when stress and the need for excess neurotransmitters have passed. Consequently, the individual would be left with excess amines or an excess amine-synthesizing capacity after recurrent or chronic stress. As Goodwin and Bunney (1973) note, such a neurochemical consequence might contribute to agitated depression or mania. It can be seen how, for either of these possible mechanisms, exposure to chronic or recurrent stress would lead eventually to a heightened vulnerability to further stress.

Akiskal and McKinney (1973), in attempting to integrate current behavioral and biochemical models of depression, have further pointed out how the interaction of certain genetic defects, object losses, and interpersonally induced states of helplessness could ultimately result in a depletion of the biogenic amines of the neurophysiological substrates of reinforcement—thus leading to failure to respond to reinforcement and then to the development of depression. Other possibilities of interactions between various genetic lesions and life stresses have been considered elsewhere. It seems clear, therefore, that reasonable models can be constructed to explain gene–environment interaction in the depressive disorders, but little attention has been devoted to research strategies designed to study such interaction.

Traditionally, genetic studies have focused on the estimation of morbidity risks in twins, other biological relatives, or adoptive relatives of affected probands. Such studies have been conducted for the purpose of (a) establishing that genetic factors do contribute to the predisposition to depressive disorders generally, or to a particular form of disorder; (b) analyzing the mode of genetic transmission underlying the predisposition; and (c) endeavoring to clarify nosology. Recently, other investigations have attempted to look for genetic linkage or various biochemical markers in the families of affected probands. Research to date has succeeded in amassing an impressive amount of evidence in support of the involvement of genetic factors in the depressive disorders and has contributed support to other lines of evidence indicating a nosological separation between unipolar and bipolar illness (Gershon, Bunney, Leckman, Van Eerdewegh, & DeBauche, 1976). Thus far, however, the genetic mode (or more likely, modes) of transmission must be considered uncertain for both the unipolar and the bipolar conditions, and no genetic or biochemical markers have been unequivocally established.

There has been almost no cross-fertilization between research on genetic factors in depression and research on life events. Studies concerned with morbidity risk data in relatives of depressed patients rarely obtain systematic information about stressful experiences in the lives of the patients or other family members. Studies centering on the relationship of stress to depressive disorders usually ignore the collection of genetic data, and often fail entirely to allow for a possible genetic contribution to stress-vulnerability in their interpretation of the significance of life events. Furthermore, if vulnerability to present stress does represent the interaction of genotype and previous environmental history, research on precipitating factors needs to incorporate knowledge about earlier experiences, as well as about the genetic background of the subjects, into some type of contingency analysis if information on the role of precipitants is to be meaningful. No studies have yet attempted to do this.

BEHAVIOR GENETIC STRATEGIES FOR STUDYING STRESS AND DEPRESSION

I will discuss here several possible research strategies that might be undertaken in a beginning effort to study the interaction of genetic diathesis, earlier life history, and recent precipitating events. These strategies are not highly developed. They offer, for the most part, only first steps to the solution of what we need to know about depressive disorders. Most of the strategies, for example, do not include the biochemical investigations that would be necessary to answer questions about the true nature of the genetic diathesis. I suggest them, however, to indicate how the behavior–genetic, interactive approach might be helpful in studying the role of stress in the depressive disorders.

Adaptation of a Social Stress versus Social Selection Model

The first strategy I want to discuss has been developed by Dohrenwend, Erlenmeyer-Kimling, and Rainer (unpublished) in connection with schizophrenia. I mention it by way of illustration because it is easy to see how a similar strategy can be adapted for the study of depressive disorders. This approach calls for the construction of a set of predictions using family risk data and a life events history to test two specific, contrasting hypotheses. The hypotheses to be tested in the case of schizophrenia are those that have been advanced to explain the fact that the incidence of schizophrenia is inversely related to social class. One hypothesis contends that the heavier concentration of schizophrenia in the lower classes is attributable to greater amounts of social stress in the lower classes, whereas the other hypothesis states that genetically predisposed individuals either drift down to or fail to rise out of the lower social classes.

The social stress versus social selection issue—around which sharp controversy has developed—has been carefully reviewed by Dohrenwend and Dohrenwend (1969, 1977) who have proposed one important step toward its resolution. The Dohrenwends argue that diametrically opposite predictions can be derived from the two hypotheses concerning the relative rates of schizophrenia expected in disadvantaged ethnic groups compared to advantaged ethnic groups of the *same* social class. Under the social stress hypothesis, it would be predicted that higher rates of schizophrenia are to be found in the disadvantaged ethnic group than in the same-class members of the advantaged group and that, within each ethnic group, higher rates would of course be found in the lower social class. Under the social selection (or social drift) hypothesis, however, it would be expected that the greater social pressure and discrimination experienced by the disadvantaged ethnic group would result in more of their healthier members being kept in the lower social class, thereby diluting the lower class's rate of schizophrenia in that group; in the advantaged ethnic group, by contrast, healthy members would be free to rise to or remain in higher social classes, so that a relatively undiluted pool of disabled persons would remain in the lower classes. Thus, the social selection hypothesis would lead to the expectation of higher schizophrenia rates in the *advantaged* groups than in the disadvantaged ethnic group of the same social class, with, again, the higher rates occurring in the lower class within each ethnic group. Table 17.1 summarizes the Dohrenwends' predictions for a test of the two hypotheses.

The strategy proposed by the Dohrenwends entails the collection, by personal interview, of incidence and life history data in cohorts of ethnically advantaged and disadvantaged groups of both higher and lower social classes. This strategy can be expanded to provide a more rigorous test of the social stress and social selection hypotheses by collecting data on the psychiatric status and environmental events of first-degree relatives and spouses of schizophrenic probands and matched normal controls for each of the four cohorts shown in Table 17.1. The inclusion of the genetic data allows an additional series of opposing predictions to be generated for the two hypotheses. For convenience, the predictions under each hypothesis are laid out side-by-side in Table 17.2, where it can be seen that some of the

Table 17.1

HYPOTHETICAL SUPPORT FOR SOCIAL
SELECTION HYPOTHESIS VERSUS SOCIAL
STRESS HYPOTHESIS IN RELATIVE RATES
OF SCHIZOPHRENIA ACCORDING TO
CLASS AND ETHNIC STATUS (1 = LOWEST
RATE OF SCHIZOPHRENIA; 4 = HIGHEST
RATE)[a]

	Ethnic group status	
Class status	Advantaged rate of schizophrenia	Disadvantaged rate of schizophrenia
Support for social selection hypothesis		
Higher	2	1
Lower	4	3
Support for social stress hypothesis		
Higher	1	2
Lower	3	4

[a] From Dohrenwend, Dohrenwend, and Levav (1977).

predictions (numbers 4, 5 and 9 in Table 17.2) involve direct tests of assumptions about gene–environment interactions in addition to testing the social stress versus the social selection hypothesis.

A similar strategy of collecting family risk data and stress scores on probands, controls, first-degree relatives, and spouses can be used in research on the depressive disorders. As the frequency of depression is not usually considered to be inversely related to social class, a social selection hypothesis is not advanced to compete with a social stress hypothesis, as is the case for schizophrenia. But suppose the hypotheses are simply stress-is-important versus stress-is-not-important? Then, looking at Table 17.2 and substituting "not important" for "social selection" and "depression" for "schizophrenia," we can retain Predictions 1, 4 (omitting the second sentence in the "not important" column), 5, 7, and 9. Further, we can change Prediction 6 to read "Depressive probands and controls have similar stress scores" under the "not important" column and to "Depressive probands have higher stress scores" under the "stress" column. In this manner we would have six pairs of opposed predictions, giving us a rather powerful tool for testing the two hypotheses concerning the importance of stress. Of course, for "stress" in the broad sense, specific kinds of stressful events might be substituted, and their presence and absence could then be contrasted in a set of similar predictions.

Table 17.2

SUMMARY OF ADDITIONAL PREDICTIONS UNDER SOCIAL SELECTION AND SOCIAL STRESS HYPOTHESES INCLUDING GENETIC FACTORS[a]

Group	Social selection	Social stress
First-degree relatives of schizophrenic probands	1. The schizophrenia rate in relatives is expected to be 8–15% (i.e., same as reported in literature for relatives of schizophrenics).	1. The schizophrenia rate in relatives is expected to be lower, because probands include many acute and transient cases.
	2. Schizophrenic relatives are expected to be found in lower social classes, as are probands. Nonschizophrenic relatives are expected to be found in higher classes than proband.	2. Relatives are expected to be in the same social classes as probands regardless of psychiatric status of the relatives.
	3. Schizophrenic relatives are expected to have the same distribution over ethnic–social class cells as do probands (see Table 17.1, Selection hypothesis).	3. Schizophrenic relatives are expected to have the same distribution over ethnic–social class cells as do probands (see Table 17.1, Stress hypothesis).
	4. A low correlation between stress scores and schizophrenia is generally expected. Higher stress scores are expected in probands with no family history of schizophrenia.	4. Stress scores are expected to be higher in probands and schizophrenic relatives than in nonschizophrenic relatives.
Spouses of schizophrenic probands	5. The schizophrenia rate in spouses is expected to be low (unless there is a significant tendency toward assortative mating, but this has not been demonstrated).	5. (a) The schizophrenia rate in spouses is expected to be higher than in general population. (b) The schizophrenia rate in spouses is possibly higher than in first-degree relatives of probands. (c) Stress scores are expected to be higher in schizophrenic than in nonschizophrenic spouses.
Matched general population controls and their relatives	6. Schizophrenic probands expected to show greater evidence of downward social mobility.	6. Schizophrenic probands are not expected to be more downwardly mobile than controls.

Table 17.2

(*Continued*)

Group	Social selection	Social stress
Matched general population controls and their relatives	7. The schizophrenia rates in relatives of controls are expected to be similar to the rates in the general population and much lower than the rates in relatives of probands.	7. The schizophrenia rate is expected to be somewhat higher in relatives of probands than in relatives of controls, but not as large a difference as is expected under the selection hypothesis.
	8. Schizophrenic relatives of controls are expected to be found in lower social classes than are controls and nonschizophrenic relatives.	8. Relatives of controls are expected to be in the same social classes as controls regardless of the psychiatric status of the relatives.
	9. A low correlation between stress scores and schizophrenia is expected in relatives of controls.	9. Stress scores are expected to be higher in schizophrenic relatives of controls than in controls and nonschizophrenic relatives.

a From Dohrenwend, Erlenmeyer-Kimling, and Rainer (unpublished).

Subgroup Strategy

A strategy that has been used in some studies of psychiatric disorders is that of classifying patients into subgroups based on a selected criterion and searching for differences between the subgroups with respect to other variables. The presence or absence of a family history of mental illness has frequently been used, either as the classifying criterion, or as a dependent variable. One mistake frequently made in this connection is the assumption that patients with a negative family history are necessarily *phenocopies*, that is, cases without a genetic predisposition. Some may be phenocopies, but others are genetically predisposed individuals. Under polygenic models, which may be applicable to at least some forms of depressive disorder, a substantial proportion of affected individuals would be expected to have no ill first-degree relatives. A single major locus model can also accommodate a large number of "sporadics." Unfortunately, there are at present no means for distinguishing between phenocopies, which may be quite rare, and genetically predisposed individuals who have no family history of illness. It seems likely, however, that the comparison between patients with a positive (FH+) versus a negative family history (FH−) is more often a comparison between cases of greater versus lesser genetic loading, rather than a comparison between genetic versus strictly environmentally-caused disorders.

In fact, environmental factors have not often been found to differentiate well between patients with FH+ and patients with FH− for depressive disorder. Woodruff, Pitts, and Winokur (1964) found no differences in clinical course, incidence of recent personal losses through death, or presence of a physical illness at the time of admission in FH+ and FH− patients. Thomson and Hendrie (1972) reported no differences in life-change events for FH+ versus FH− patients, for bipolar versus unipolar patients, or for patients with reactive depression versus endogenous depression. Angst and Perris (1972) were also unable to find bipolar–unipolar differences in the frequency of precipitating events or in childhood bereavement—which occurred in both groups at the same rate as in the relevant (i.e., Swiss and Swedish) general populations, although bipolar and unipolar patients have been shown to differ with respect to family history.[1] On the other hand, Pollitt (1972) noted that the morbidity risk for depressive disorders among relatives of unipolar patients who had suffered a *psychological* stress preceding the illness was significantly higher than the risk among relatives of patients who had undergone a *physical* stress prior to the onset of the illness. To Pollitt, these findings suggested that, in persons with a higher degree of genetic susceptibility, psychological factors constitute sufficient stress to precipitate a breakdown whereas, in persons with a lesser degree of genetic susceptibility, the stronger, more unmodifiable impact of physical illness is required. Nevertheless, it is difficult to account for the apparent contradiction between Pollitt's findings and those of the other investigating groups mentioned.

One other study is of interest here. Cadoret, Winokur, Dorzab, and Baker (1972) used age-at-onset to separate unipolar patients into an early onset (before age 40) and a later onset (after age 40) group. The groups did not differ in childhood bereavement experience, or in the incidence of physical illness within the 6 months prior to onset, or in recent deaths of relatives or friends. The early onset group, however, had a significantly higher frequency of real or personal losses in the year preceding onset than did the later onset group. This latter finding appears to give some indirect support to Pollitt's (1972) results in regard to a higher morbidity rate among relatives of patients suffering psychological stresses as precipitating factors, in view of the fact that a number of investigators (Angst, 1966; Hopkinson, 1964; Hopkinson & Ley, 1969; Kay, 1959; Mendlewicz, Fieve, Rainer, & Fleiss, 1972; Pollitt, 1972; Schulz, 1951; Winokur & Clayton, 1967) have reported a greater incidence of FH+ cases in early onset patients (or vice versa)

---

[1] Bipolars have more affected relatives and have both bipolar and unipolar relatives, whereas unipolars have fewer affected relatives and have only unipolar relatives (Angst & Perris, 1972; Leonhard, Korff, & Schulz, 1962; Winokur & Clayton, 1967).

compared to later onset patients. The picture might be thought to be one in which early onset results from a high genetic vulnerability coupled with psychological stresses that represent real or threatened loss. However, the relationship between psychological stress and family history would have to apply only in unipolar depression, as only Pollit and Cadoret *et al.* could find evidence for such a relationship, and they confined themselves to unipolar patients. Angst and Perris (1972) and Thomson and Hendrie (1972) also considered unipolar and bipolar patients separately, though, and did not find differences in precipitating factors. Thus, the picture is unclear.

Moreover, the causal role of personal losses remains uncertain, because, as Cadoret *et al.* (1972) observed, when individuals whose depressive symptoms preceded the personal loss were removed from the analyses, the incidence of losses was only slightly and nonsignificantly higher in the early onset group than in their healthy relatives. The authors concluded, therefore, that stressful events might be more likely to precipitate hospitalization in people who were already depressed than to precipitate the depression itself.

The classification strategy under discussion can scarcely be said to have yielded clearcut results across studies, except for the finding of an association between FH+ and early onset. There are methodological differences among the studies that may be responsible for the discrepancies, most important of which may be (*a*) differences in the nosological composition of the samples and (*b*) differences in the measurement and classification of the stress. The strategy remains potentially valuable if future investigators are willing to pay attention to the diagnostic homogeneity of their samples or separate analysis of homogeneous subgroups within the sample, classification of stress into carefully defined categories, early life events other than childhood bereavement, and age at onset.

Prospective Research

More definitive answers about the interaction of a genetic predisposition, early life events, and later stress may come from prospective studies of well-chosen target populations. The subjects under study in prospective research are not yet psychiatrically ill at the time of initial observation or, at least, were not ill at the time of the occurrence of the stressful event (e.g., early loss of a parent) which is being used as the basis for drawing the target population. A particular target population is selected because there is reason to believe that members of that group will eventually develop depressive disorders at a higher rate than do members of the general population. The target population may be selected on genetic grounds, as is the case in most of the ongoing prospective studies of schizophrenia, which examine children of schizophrenic parents because they are presumed to be at high genetic risk and because they are known to be at high empirical risk for manifesting schizophrenia in adulthood (Erlenmeyer-Kimling, 1975; Garmezy, 1974). A variety of environmental factors thought to be important in the development of the depressive disorders may also be used as a key to selecting a target population, although it is likely that, compared to genetically-selected target populations, environmental selection will require much larger sample sizes to yield an appreciable number of individuals who ultimately have a depressive disorder. Because base rate data are lacking on the general population frequency of many of the variables that the investigator will want to explore, careful attention to the selection of a control population is also essential.

The obvious value of prospective research is that it avoids the problems inherent in the retrospective recall of earlier events. A less apparent advantage is that the opportunity of observing events as they happen may engender hypotheses about idiosyncratic occurrences that the investigator would not have thought to inquire about in a retrospective probe. Nevertheless, prospective studies are burdened with a distinct disadvantage dictated by the length of time that the investigator may have to wait to find out which members of the target population will become ill. The average age of overt onset of illness is in the thirties for bipolar disorders and in the forties for unipolar depressions. Thus, if a target population of young children is selected, the investigator may have to wait for 20–40 years to learn whether predictions based on early observations are borne out. A compromise solution is to conduct quasiprospective studies, in which subjects are followed for shorter periods of the life span with reliance on retrospective reporting of previous history. Another alternative is to identify cohorts of adults who are known to have experienced a particular type of stress, either recently or in the past, and to track them forward.

Offspring of parents with depressive disorders are an important target group because their risk of becoming ill in adulthood is about 15% (Zerbin-Rüdin, 1967)—probably higher for children of bipolar parents and somewhat lower for children of unipolar parents. At least one prospective study is now being conducted on the offspring of parents with a (bipolar) depressive disorder, and others are being planned. Moreover, data are obtained on such children in some of the studies of children of schizophrenic parents, where the children of depressive parents were originally included mainly as a comparison group. Almost all of the high-risk studies of schizophrenia and, now, of the depressive disorders have elected to follow up children from relatively young ages, despite the attendant dangers mentioned earlier. There is some recent evidence, however, that, in the offspring of parents with depressive disorders, symptoms which may be precursors of the adult psychopathology appear during childhood (Cytryn & McKnew, personal communication; McKnew, Cytryn, Efron, Gershon, & Bunney, 1976; Weissman & Kidd, personal communication).

The thrust of most of the ongoing prospective research is to describe high-risk children clinically, psychologically, socially, etc., with relatively little effort going toward a systematic documentation of environmental events. Yet the prospective examination of children of affected parents offers one of the best possibilities for evaluating the role of stress and its interaction with genetic predisposition in the development of psychiatric disorders, provided that careful attention is given to the recording of life events. Several types of control or comparison populations are possible, including comparisons of outcomes in siblings exposed to similar environmental stresses, but a general population group is essential for base rate data on life histories.

Other personal characteristics of individuals, besides their family histories, may be used to select a target population. For example, just as Dweck (1975) was able to select children manifesting the trait of helplessness for a short-term experiment, investigators adhering to the learned helplessness model of depression might identify adults or children showing this trait for prospective study. Genetic and background environmental data would have to be collected on the target population and on subjects not displaying the trait, and subsequent stress and psychiatric outcome histories would be necessary to evaluate the part played by learned helplessness in depressive disorders. Personality characteristics of other types might also be used in selecting target and control populations. It must be recalled, however, that most researchers have been unable to demonstrate distinctive premorbid personality traits in persons who later have a depressive illness. Moreover, a large scale prospective study by Hagnell (1966) failed to find much relationship between personality traits assessed at the initial interview and the development of mental disorder by the time of re-interview 10 years later. It is possible, of course, that the follow-up studies of children of affected parents will pinpoint a specific (though not necessarily pathognomic) cluster of personality traits that can be utilized in screening large populations for persons at potential risk for developing depressive disorders.

Buchsbaum, Coursey, and Murphy (1976) and Buchsbaum, Murphy, Coursey, Lake, and Ziegler (1978), have recently advanced a biochemical approach to the identification of high-risk individuals. Platelet monoamine oxidase (MAO) activity was used as a biochemical indicator to locate a target population at potentially high risk for developing psychiatric illnesses. MAO activity was chosen as an indicator because previous research had shown (a) lower activity in chronic schizophrenia and in bipolar depressive disorder (although this result has not been obtained consistently), (b) association between activity level and personality test differences, and (c) genetic control of activity level. Additionally, the suggestion of deviant MAO activity is consistent with both the transmethylation and the dopamine hypotheses of biochemical defects in psychiatric disorders. College students and employees were screened for MAO activity level, and the high-MAO and low-MAO individuals took part in further examinations which included perceptual and cognitive tasks, average evoked response measures, personality tests, and an interview covering personal and family history. The low-MAO subjects reported having received psychiatric or psychological counseling twice as often as the high-MAO subjects. When males only were compared, the low-MAO males had a combined incidence of psychiatric hospitalization, suicide attempts, jail, and convictions for offenses (other than traffic offenses) more than three times greater than the incidence of these problems in high-MAO males. Also, it is important to note that the relatives of low-MAO males showed these problems more than three times as often as the relatives of the high-MAO males. Low-MAO subjects displayed a pattern on psychological test measures that was consistent with bipolar disorder (Buchsbaum *et al.*, in press). The authors (Buchsbaum *et al.*, 1976) reported that the low-MAO and high-MAO groups showed no "overall difference in incidence of childhood adjustment problems, family stress, or medical or neurological illness." It is not clear, though, from the published reports whether there may be differences in stressful life events between low-MAO subjects who have and those who have not experienced psychiatric problems. Although the clinical significance of low-MAO activity in this group of subjects remains to be evaluated after longitudinal follow-up, the significance of stressful life events, too, can only be assessed as differential outcomes become apparent in the potentially high-risk (i.e., low-MAO) subjects.

Although the foregoing suggestions concerning target populations rely on characteristics of the individuals to be studied, it is also possible to select target populations based on events that individuals have experienced. For example, cohorts of people who passed through their early years during World War II, when the risk of parental separation and loss was relatively high, might be screened to yield a target population with early loss of a parent and controls without parental loss. Similarly, the target population might be composed of persons who have undergone recent losses or other traumatic events. As Paykel (1973) has noted "much might be gained from careful prospective studies of moderate-sized samples of subjects who have experienced a variety of events." To understand why certain experiences result in psychiatric disorder in some subjects and not in others, however, such studies will have to pay attention to genotypic factors as well.

PSYCHIATRIC ASSESSMENT IN RELATIVES

The strategies I have outlined are all alike in that they call for meticulous attention to the collection of experiential data over the life span and for an estimation of the genotypic background of the individuals under study. The estimation of genotypic background is, clearly, the weak link in these strategies because there are at present no genetic markers or other biological indicators that permit us to say "individual A's genotype is one that produces a susceptibility to a depressive disorder but individual B's genotype does not." Until better indicators become available, the only clue possible is the individual's family history. I have already pointed out that family history is a poor guide to a person's genotype. It leads to both false positives (i.e., individuals who have affected relatives but who do not inherit the implicated gene(s) themselves) and a considerable number of false negatives (i.e., individuals without a family history of psychiatric disorder but with a faulty genotype). Because family history is, nevertheless, the closest approximation to information about genotypes currently within reach, it is especially important that the collection of psychiatric data on relatives be as painstaking and as exhaustive as possible. In advocating the gathering of family histories, I do not mean simply that an informant should be asked about other family members but that as many first-degree relatives as possible should be interviewed about their own psychiatric and medical status and about those relatives that cannot be studied directly. Information about second-degree relatives would also be of value.

In recent years, there has been a growing concern about the diagnostic criteria used in the assessment of psychiatric disorders and, particularly, about the expansion of criteria to include a spectrum of related conditions that are believed to share a common genetic etiology but differ in their expression and in the degree of severity. Attention to spectrum states that are not fully expressed as a depressive illness may significantly increase the sensitivity of family history data. For example, it might be useful to treat probands whose relatives show a spectrum condition, rather than a clear depression or manic-depressive disorder, as doubtful family history cases, separate and apart from probands with a clearly positive or negative family history.[2] The validity of the relationship between a so-called spectrum condition and a given type of depressive disorder can be partially checked by examining the incidence of the condition in families that have more than one member with the depressive disorder. What I am suggesting here is that, initially, in the collection of the family history data a coarse net be used to help ensure against false negatives. The net can then be pulled tighter by testing the applicability of spectrum conditions against other evidence, and especially against psychiatric outcome in probands.

The strategies proposed in this chapter are far from ideal because of our current inability to ascertain genetically predisposed individuals with a great

---

[2] Some investigators have begun to take this approach (Thomson & Hendrie, 1972).

degree of accuracy. They may, however, help to advance our understanding of the development of depressive disorders in response to the interaction of genetic predisposition and stressful life events.

REFERENCES

Akiskal, H. S. & McKinney, W. T., Jr. Depressive disorders: Toward a unified hypothesis. *Science*, 1973, *182*, 20–29.

Angst, J. *Zur Atiologie und Nosologie endogener depressiver Psychosen*. New York: Springer, 1966.

Angst, J. & Perris, C. The nosology of endogenous depression. Comparison of the results of two studies. *International Journal of Mental Health*, 1972, *1*, 145–158.

Berger, M. & Passingham, R. E. Early experience and other environmental factors: An overview. In H. J. Eysenck (Ed.), *Handbook of abnormal psychology* (2nd ed.). London: Pittman, 1973.

Buchsbaum, M. S., Coursey, R. D., & Murphy, D. L. The biochemical high-risk paradigm: Behavioral and familial correlates of low platelet monoamine oxidase activity. *Science*, 1976, *194*, 339–341.

Buchsbaum, M. S., Murphy, D. L., Coursey, R. D., Lake, C. R., & Ziegler, M. G. Platelet monoamine oxidase, plasma dopamine-beta-hydroxylase and attention in a "biochemical high risk" sample. *Journal of Psychiatric Research*, 1978, *14*, 215–224.

Cadoret, R. J., Winokur, G., Dorzab, J., & Baker, M. Depressive disease: Life events and onset of illness. *Archives of General Psychiatry*, 1972, *26*, 133–136.

Dohrenwend, B. P. & Dohrenwend, B. S. *Social status and psychological disorder: A causal inquiry*. New York: Wiley, 1969.

Dohrenwend, B. P., Dohrenwend, B. S., & Levav, I. *Social stress–social selection and psychiatric disorders*. USPHS grant number MH30710, 1977.

Dohrenwend, B. P., Erlenmeyer-Kimling, L., & Rainer, J. D. Unpublished.

Dweck, C. S. The role of expectations and attributions in the alleviation of learned helplessness. *Journal of Personality and Social Psychology*, 1975, *31*, 674–685.

Erlenmeyer-Kimling, L. Gene-environment interactions and the variability of behavior. In L. Ehrman, G. S. Omenn, & E. Caspari (Eds.), *Genetics, environment, and behavior*. New York: Academic Press, 1972.

Erlenmeyer-Kimling, L. A prospective study of children at risk for schizophrenia: Methodological considerations and some preliminary findings. In R. Wirt, G. Winokur, & M. Roff (Eds.), *Life history research in psychopathology* (Vol. 4). Minneapolis, Minnesota: Univ. Minnesota Press, 1975.

Fuller, J. L. Genetics and vulnerability to experiential deprivation. In J. P. Scott (Ed.), *Separation and depression*. Washington, D.C.: American Association for the Advancement of Science (Publication No. 94), 1973.

Garmezy, N. Children at risk: The search for the antecedents of schizophrenia. Part II: Ongoing research programs, issues, and intervention. *Schizophrenia Bulletin*, 1974, *9*, 55–125.

Gershon, E. S., Bunney, W. E., Jr., Leckman, J. F., Van Eerdewegh, M., & DeBauche, B. A. The inheritance of affective disorders: A review of data and of hypotheses. *Behavior Genetics*, 1976, *6*, 227–261.

Goodwin, F. K. & Bunney, W. E., Jr. Psychobiological aspects of stress and affective illness. In J. P. Scott (Ed.), *Separation and depression*. Washington, D.C.: American Association for the Advancement of Science (Publication No. 94), 1973.

Hagnell, O. *A prospective study of the incidence of mental disorder*. Copenhagen: Munksgaard, 1966.

Hersh, S. P. Epilogue: Future considerations and directions. In J. G. Schulterbrandt & A. Raskin (Eds.), *Depression in childhood*. New York: Raven, 1977.

Hopkinson, G. A genetic study of affective illness in patients over 50. *British Journal of Psychiatry*, 1964, *110*, 244–254.

Hopkinson, G. & Ley, P. A genetic study of affective disorder. *British Journal of Psychiatry*, 1969, *115*, 917–922.

Kaufman, I. C. & Rosenblum, L. A. Depression in infant monkeys separated from their mothers. *Science*, 1967, *155*, 1030–1031.

Kay, D. Observations on the natural history and genetics of old age psychoses. *Proceedings of the Royal Society of Medicine*, 1959, *52*, 791–794.

Leonhard, K., Korff, I., & Schulz, H. Die Temperamente in den Familien der monopolaren und bipolaren phasischen Psychosen. *Psychiatria et Neurologia*, 1962, *143*, 416–434.

Lewis, J. K., McKinney, W. T., Jr., Young, L. D., & Kraemer, G. W. Mother-infant separation in rhesus monkeys as a model of human depression. *Archives of General Psychiatry*, 1976, *33*, 699–705.

McKnew, D. H., Jr., Cytryn, L., Efron, A., Gershon, E. S., & Bunney, W. E., Jr. *Offspring of manic-depressive patients*. Paper read at annual meeting of the American Psychiatric Association, Miami, Florida, May 12, 1976.

Mendlewicz, J., Fieve, R. R., Rainer, J. D., & Fleiss, J. L. Manic-depressive illness: A comparative study of patients with and without a family history. *British Journal of Psychiatry*, 1972, *120*, 523–530.

Paykel, E. S. Life events and acute depression. In J. P. Scott (Ed.), *Separation and depression*. Washington, D.C.: American Association for the Advancement of Science (Publication No. 94), 1973.

Pollitt, J. The relationship between genetic and precipitating factors in depressive illness. *British Journal of Psychiatry*, 1972, *121*, 67–70.

Schulz, B. Auszählungen in der Verwandtschaft von nach Erkrankungsalter und Geschlecht gruppierten Manisch-Depressiven. *Archiv für Psychiatrie und Nervenkrankheiten*, 1951, *186*, 560–576.

Spencer-Booth, Y. & Hinde, R. A. The effects of 13 days maternal separation on infant rhesus monkeys compared with those of shorter and repeated separation. *Animal Behavior*, 1971, *19*, 595–605.

Spitz, R. A. Anaclitic depression: An inquiry into the genesis of psychiatric conditions in early childhood. II. *The Psychoanalytic Study of the Child*, 1947, *2*, 313–343.

Thomson, K. C. & Hendrie, H. A. Environmental stress in primary depressive illness. *Archives of General Psychiatry*, 1972, *26*, 130–132.

Winokur, G. & Clayton, P. Family history studies. I. Two types of affective disorders separated according to genetic and clinical factors. In J. Wortis (Ed.), *Recent advances in biological psychiatry*. New York: Plenum Press, 1967.

Woodruff, R., Pitts, F. N., Jr., & Winokur, G. Affective disorder: II. A comparison of patients with endogenous depressions with and without a family history of affective disorder. *Journal of Nervous and Mental Disorders*, 1964, *139*, 49–52.

Zerbin-Rüdin, E. Endogene psychosen. In P. E. Becker (Ed.), *Humangenetik (Handbuch)* (Vol. 2). Stuttgart: Thieme, 1967.

CHAPTER 18

A Biobehavioral Approach to Depression[1]

Hagop S. Akiskal

INTRODUCTION

Psychological medicine has made significant advances during the past decade in delineating the pathogenetic mechanisms of the more serious disorders that afflict the mind. For the first time in the history of psychological medicine, potent and rather specific therapeutic strategies are available for these disorders. Much of this progress, however, has occurred within specialized frames of reference representing various schools of thought. Despite the widespread use of eloquent concepts such as "systems theory," "psychobiology," and "eclecticism," a comprehensive framework for understanding psychopathology does not prevail. Instead, disciplinary fragmentation and semantic controversies have obscured much of the progress made by modern psychiatry. This situation has created serious paradoxes for both clinical practice and research (GAP, 1975). Therefore,

[1] The author thanks Dr. Ted L. Rosenthal for his critical comments in the preparation of this chapter.

The Psychobiology of the Depressive Disorders: Implications for the Effects of Stress

one of the major tasks to be accomplished in the area of mental disorders over the next decade is to build conceptual bridges that combine research findings from diverse theoretical positions.

In this chapter, I will develop a biobehavioral model of the depressive disorders in order to provide a heuristic conceptual framework for the stress–biology and stress–psychology literature reviewed in previous chapters of this volume. The extensive literature supporting such an integrative approach for understanding depressive phenomena has been documented elsewhere (Akiskal & McKinney, 1973a, 1975), therefore, I will largely focus on new lines of evidence which specifically illustrate the nature and mechanism of interaction between life events and neurobiology in the genesis of depressive disorders. However, let us first briefly examine those factors that have prevented the development of a biobehavioral approach to mental disorders.

HISTORICAL AND PHILOSOPHICAL IMPEDIMENTS TO THE EMERGENCE OF A BIOBEHAVIORAL POSITION

Much of the current polarization in psychiatry and the behavioral sciences can be understood in terms of William James' (1907) contrast between "tough-minded" and "tender-minded" approaches to the world of experience. As elaborated elsewhere (Akiskal & McKinney, 1973b), these two modes of perceiving reality have created a wide schism in current approaches to human behavior. This schism roughly corresponds to the biologic versus psychological dichotomy and is represented by several theoretical schools. Political rivalries between the various theoretical camps have unfortunately accentuated the schism by creating an atmosphere of ideological intolerance. Value judgments have been attached to the activities of each of these camps. Thus, biologic psychiatrists are often labeled as a "reactionary" group which its opponents believe represents a threat to human liberty; likewise, behaviorists are accused of being "mechanistic" and no lesser a threat to human liberty; whereas, existentialists and the groupologists officially designate themselves as being "humanistic." Another version of biased labeling contrasts the "scientific" nature of the behavior therapies with the "unscientific" nature of psychoanalysis and the "medical model." In still another version, researchers are regarded as being incapable of the "empathy" seen among the clinician-types. The perpetuation of such stereotypes has naturally precluded serious attempts to mutually examine the scientific bases of these various approaches to psychopathology.

Rasmussen (1975) has shown how Cartesian dualism served the useful function of breaking the power of the church over the human body and the natural sciences important for its study. Also, scientists could henceforth study molecular function without the need to be concerned with the totality of man as a psychobiologic unit. Thus, the mind–brain dichotomy epitomized a theoretical position that provided a comfortable scientific strategy. Unfortunately, in modern days, the Cartesian position has prevented the development of an integrative approach to mental disorders. In its extreme form, it finds expression in Torrey's (1974) version of reductionism: Psychiatry is proclaimed to be dead, as psychiatric phenomena are seen as being reducible to either "brain diseases" or "problems of living."

Such authors, who denounce psychological medicine, fail to appreciate the arbitrary nature of the Cartesian position. Descartes believed that the soul and body communicated occasionally through the pineal gland. Modern science is sufficiently advanced to provide us with more sophisticated interactional models between human neurobiology and life events. A major challenge for psychological medicine, then, is to construct conceptual bridges that unite the insights developed from opposite positions of the arbitrary Cartesian dichotomy.

HETEROGENEITY OF DEPRESSIVE PHENOMENA

A source of serious confusion in the realm of depression arises because different clinicians and researchers use the term with different meanings. Some investigators, for instance, do not distinguish between clinical depression and unhappiness: The depressed individual is seen merely as the victim of oppressive life circumstances (Becker, 1964). Others regard depression as the expression of a masochistic life style that serves the purpose of obtaining interpersonal rewards (Bonime, 1966). Finally, some clinicians restrict the term to those melancholic states of depression that can be justifiably regarded as maladies (Kiloh, Andrews, Neilson, & Bianchi, 1972). The failure to distinguish between the different concepts of depression has so blurred the boundaries of the depressive phenomena that it is often difficult to compare the data of different researchers. This situation is partly due to the "antinosological" climate that prevails in many academic departments of psychology and psychiatry (Meehl, 1973). It is ironical that investigators and clinicians who denounce nosology either in the name of "humanism" or "science" fail to realize that undue emphasis on the uniqueness of the individual precludes the use of accumulated scientific wisdom in alleviating the suffering of that individual (Akiskal, 1978; Kendell, 1975; Spitzer, 1976). Furthermore, such a stance is heuristically sterile.

The distinction between transient or symptomatic depressive states and clinical depression is extremely important from a methodological standpoint (Klerman, 1971), for the etiologic significance of life events may be quite different in the two conditions. It is, therefore, useful to distinguish between four meanings of depression (Robins & Guze, 1972; Whybrow & Parlatore, 1973; Friedman, 1974; Akiskal & McKinney, 1975).

Normal Depression

Depression as a normal mood or affect is part of the fabric of everyday life. It is a universal adaptive response to stress, frustration, and loss and ordinarily lasts hours to days. Normal depression is not only seen as a response to specific life events (e.g., temporary separation from family and other loved objects) but also as a concomitant of more complex psychobiologic states such as the premenstrual phase (Dalton, 1964) or following delivery (Pitt, 1973). Additionally, certain periods of the year, such as major holidays, can be associated with depressive responses because of their symbolic meaning or evocation of past memories (Schuyler, 1972). Thus one can speak of "menstrual blues," "maternity blues," and "Christmas blues," respectively.

Situational Depression

Situational or so-called "reactive" depression is continuous with the transient states of depression described above, but tends to last longer—usually from several weeks to several months. It has been said that some degree of reactive depression in certain life situations is not only normal, but reflects good reality testing in our present state of the world (Fenichel, 1945). Grief, defined as an understandable response to the death of a loved object, is probably the most often quoted model for reactive depression (Freud, 1917). Such depressive responses are ordinarily self-limited and rarely lead to seeking psychiatric help (Clayton, Desmarais, & Winokur, 1968). Parkes (1972) has argued that preoccupation with the image of the lost object (sometimes to the point of hallucinosis), anxiety, agitation, somatic symptoms, and difficulty falling asleep—rather than depression per se—constitute the symptomatological hallmarks of such separation responses in grief as well as in other responses to loss. Although Spitz's (1942) and Bowlby's (1961) observations on human infants, and experimental work on infrahuman primates (McKinney, Suomi, & Harlow, 1971), have delineated a biphasic protest–despair (i.e., agitation–depression) sequence in separation syndromes, various mixtures of anxiety and depression seem to characterize what is usually observed in the human adult (Clayton et al., 1968; Lindemann, 1944; Parkes, 1972).

Another example of situational depression is nostalgia (Rosen, 1975), but it has not been studied systematically. Nor have other forms of situational depression been subjected to rigorous study. The prevalence of such mild depressions is quite high in general population surveys (Blumenthal, 1975;

Comstock & Helsing, 1976), but their relationship to clinical depression is obscure. Moreover, it is unwise to generalize from studies of grief to other forms of depression elicited by separation. For instance, there is little evidence that romantic break-ups per se predispose to clinical depression. Indeed, the available data indicate that the depressive conditions seen in divorcing individuals are often the cause, rather than the result, of divorce (Briscoe & Smith, 1975).

Whatever the nature and actual prevalence of situational depressions, individuals experiencing them seek psychiatric treatment. This is not to say that it is always easy to distinguish clinically between a transient depressive response to life events and clinical depression. This brief discussion on situational depression is included here because the Meyerian concept of depression as a response to life situations has played an important role in generating research aimed at elucidating the relationship between life stressors and depressive disorders.[2] From a clinical standpoint, it is important to note that grief carries a modest risk of developing into a clinical depression. The risk is about 15% in children (Spitz, 1942), but not more than 5% in adults (Parkes, 1972). Thus, bereavement appears to be a precipitant rather than a cause of clinical depression, and the challenge for research is to identify the factors contributing to the increased vulnerability of those who succumb under such stress.

Secondary Depression

Secondary depression is analogous to situational depression, except that it is usually an understandable response to a serious medical or psychiatric disorder. What is commonly observed in lifelong psychiatric disorders is a state of demoralization (Klein, 1974)—a state of hopelessness and helplessness stemming from the intermittent but unpredictable exacerbations of illness, the uncertainties regarding causation and treatment–response, as well as the social and interpersonal costs of the illness. Such iatrogenic factors as chronic incarceration in a mental institution (Goffman, 1961), the stigmatizing sequelae of being labeled "mentally ill" (Scheff, 1963), and neuroleptic-induced anergy, amotivation, and apathy may further contrib-

---

[2] The fashionable diagnostic rubric of "neurotic depression" is often used synonymously with "situational depression." The current usage of the concept of "neurotic depression," however, has generated much confusion. The author and his associates (Akiskal, Bitar, Puzantian, Rosenthal, Walker, 1978) recently conducted an operational study on the diagnostic usage of this nosologic rubric and found that, in addition to situational depression, it referred to: neurotic syndromes with secondary depression, characterological depression, bipolar II disease (depression in cyclothymic individuals) and to nonpsychotic forms of primary unipolar depression. Hence, although Meyer's teachings have stimulated research in social stressors, unwarranted extensions of the diagnostic boundaries of the depressive reaction types has generated considerable nosological confusion.

ute to the pathogenesis of secondary depressive states. Erosion of self-esteem, extinction of social skills, and marginal social existence are often the final common pathways in the demoralized states that occur as secondary complications of nonaffective psychiatric disorders.

In contrast, many medical disorders that cause disfigurement (e.g., rheumatoid arthritis, extensive burns, radical surgery for cancer) lead to profound changes in body image, as well as imposing economic strains and serious limitations on one's usual social roles or modes of interpersonal reinforcement (Lipowski, 1975). Furthermore, involvement of the brain by the disease process (as in systemic lupus), the endocrine effects of the illness (e.g. hypothyroidism), or treatment side-effects (e.g. with corticosteroid therapy) may further contribute to the genesis of depressive mood states. Unfortunately, no systematic data are available to explain why some individuals are vulnerable to the depressionogenic impact of a given medical disorder and why some illnesses such as lupus have high incidence of depressive morbidity.

Despite the enormous magnitude of psychobiologic stress confronting this group of secondary depressives, their dysphoria generally parallels the vicissitudes of the underlying disorder (Guze, Woodruff, & Clayton, 1971; Woodruff, Murphy, & Herjanic, 1967) and rarely attains melancholic proportions (Winokur, 1972). It would therefore appear that even such adverse life circumstances as an affliction with a serious illness are usually insufficient by themselves to cause the states of melancholy to be depicted under "primary depression."

Primary Depression

As distinguished from situational and secondary depressions, primary depressions either arise without pre-existing or concurrent nonaffective disorders, or else appear to be grossly out of porportion to any life events that may have preceded them. Yet, it is in primary depression that one frequently finds the development of the full syndrome, with dysfunction manifested at emotional, cognitive, psychomotor, and vegetative levels (Beck, 1967). Of special significance are the abundance of signs and symptoms (Table 18.1) reflecting limbic-diencephalic dysfunction (Pollitt, 1965; Kraines, 1966); such as impairment of pleasure mechanisms (Akiskal & McKinney, 1973a; Klein, 1974) and neuroendocrine indices reminiscent of diencephalic Cushing's disease (Carroll, Curtis, & Mendels, 1976). The ancients recognized the "chemical" nature of clinical depression when they coined the term "melancholia." Indeed, deficiency of limbic norepinephrine, the "black bile" of modern psychobiology, may be etiologically related to the behavioral, vegetative, and endocrine disturbances of clinical depression (Ettigi & Brown, 1977). Furthermore, melancholic depression has all the attributes of a disease state (i.e. disruption of psychomotor and vegetative functions, considerable morbidity and mortality, autonomous course,

Table 18.1

SIGNS AND SYMPTOMS INDICATIVE OF LIMBIC-DIENCEPHALIC
DYSFUNCTION IN PRIMARY AFFECTIVE ILLNESS

1. Diurnal shifts in mood and activity
2. Disruption of sleep rhythm, appetite and libido
3. Anhedonia: Inability to experience pleasure
4. Inability to respond to reinforcement
5. Psychomotor retardation to the point of stupor
6. Menstrual disturbances
7. Excessive cortisol secretion which is resistant to dexamethasone suppression

and favorable response to specific pharmacological interventions (Prange, 1973). Unless interrupted by somatic treatment, melancholia tends to persist for 6–12 months (Winokur, 1970). The term "endogenous," still applied by some clinicians to such states of depression, should be discarded as it implies etiologic independence from environmental influences—a position that is no longer tenable on either philosophical or scientific grounds (Heron 1965).

Recent studies (Angst, 1966; Leonhard, 1966; Perris, 1966; Winokur, Clayton, & Reich, 1969) strongly suggest that affectively ill patients who develop hypomanic or manic episodes suffer from a genetically distinct kind of disorder (bipolar) when compared to those who only experience single or recurrent depressions (unipolar)—though not all investigators agree (Gershon, Baron, & Leckman, 1975). Bipolar conditions afflict about 1% of the general population, whereas unipolar depressions are at least five times more common (Winokur, 1970).

The remainder of this chapter seeks to clarify why most people facing everyday stresses undergo transient and adaptive oscillations in mood, but 5% of the men and 10% of the women (Helgason, 1964) make one or several descents into the abyss of despair. In other words, in an attempt to explore the mechanisms of stress–biology interaction in depressive illness, I will outline the confluence of pathogenetic factors that appear to differentiate primary depressions of melancholic depth from their situational and secondary counterparts.

ETIOLOGIC FACTORS THAT CONVERGE IN THE PATHOGENESIS OF MELANCHOLIA[3]

For at least 50 years, debate has persisted: Are melancholic depressions fundamentally different from other depressions that appear as psy-

[3] Throughout this chapter, melancholia, clinical depression, and depressive illness are used as interchangeable synonyms. When unqualified, however, the word depression is employed in a more generic sense to refer to all varieties of depressive conditions.

chologically understandable responses to life events, or do they form a continuum? The issues have been well summarized in a review by Kendell (1976). The position taken here is that, whether one subscribes to a dichotomous or a continuum model, sufficient clinical justification exists to separate primary depressions of melancholic depth from "problems-of-living" depressions. The failure to make such a differentiation can lead to clinical disasters. Whether or not melancholia represents accentuation of normal unhappiness, the end stage has all the attributes of an illness, and an individual so afflicted requires the care of a physician. A melancholic patient suffers from serious somatic dysregulation and is simply too ill to derive benefit from verbal therapies alone; somatic methods of intervention are needed to restore patients to a state where they can respond to interpersonal reinforcement.

In conceptualizing the various pathogenetic influences that impinge on the human organism to produce melancholia, one must consider the epidemiologic dictum that the most common causes are neither necessary nor sufficient—they are contributory (Susser, 1973). Accordingly, any viable theory of melancholia should consider genetic and developmental factors, along with interpersonal and acquired physiological causes. The discussion that follows will largely focus on factors that have the merit of providing psychobiologic bridges in the genesis of such melancholic states.

Multiple Social Stressors

If adverse life circumstances can cause situational depression, then one can logically extrapolate from this fact that perhaps a confluence of extremely unfavorable life events may so overwhelm the adaptive skills of the organism as to push the individual into a state of melancholic despair. Enormous methodological problems exist in life event research and are well summarized by Rabkin and Struening (1976). Yet, sufficiently rigorous data are now available to convincingly argue for the etiologic significance of life events in clinical depression (Brown, Harris, Copeland, 1977; Brown, Sklair, Harris, & Birley, 1973a; Paykel, Myers, Dienelt, Klerman, Lindenthal, & Pepper, 1969). The events are generally "undesirable" in the areas of health, finances, marital relationships, or represent "exits" from the social scene (e.g. deaths, separations, divorces).

The weight of evidence favors the view that the depressionogenic impact of life events is additive and peaks during the 6-month period preceding the depression; thus depressives experience, on the average, 3–4 times more aversive life circumstances than general population controls. It would therefore appear that a series of life stressors is cumulatively perceived to threaten the psychological homeostasis of the person. Nevertheless, cases illustrating so-called "success depressions" or "paradoxical" depressions associated with nominally "desirable" events do occur (Beck, 1974), even though they are statistically rare events. Such "paradoxical" depressions suggest that the stressful impact of life events may additionally reside in the adaptive demands placed on the individual as he attempts to cope with major departures from his usual life style (Holmes & Rahe, 1967). It is important to note, however, that life events do not seem to account for more than 25–30% of the variance in the causation of depressive disorders.[4] Furthermore, the causal link between life events and depression is not always etiologic. The complexity of the interactional patterns between life events and psychopathology can be illustrated by taking separation as a paradigm for "exit" type events:

1. Separation is not a sufficient cause for depression, because a depressive response of clinical proportions (i.e. primary depression) is not observed in more than 10% of those who experience it (Paykel et al., 1969).

2. Separation is not a necessary cause for depression, because many depressions develop in its absence (Paykel, 1976).

3. Separation is not a specific cause for depression, as it precedes the onset or exacerbation of other forms of psychiatric disorder (Brown et al., 1973a; Jacobs, Prusoff, & Paykel, 1974). Interestingly, bereavement (a specific type of separation) is associated with the onset or precipitation of nonpsychiatric medical disorders (Schmale, 1973), notably coronary thrombosis (Parkes, 1972).

4. Separation may result from clinical depression and, therefore, it may aggravate or maintain a pre-existing depressive condition. Depressive symptoms are often poorly tolerated by spouses who may not even be aware of the "psychiatric" nature of their marital problems. Indeed, marital failure is quite common in both bipolar (Perris, 1966) and unipolar depressive illness (Briscoe, Smith, Robins, Marten, & Gaskin 1973; Briscoe & Smith, 1975).

5. Finally, separation may precipitate hospitalization rather than the depressive disorder (Hudgens, Morrison, & Barchha, 1967; Morrison, Hudgens, & Barchha, 1968). The individual who experiences deepening of depressive symptoms as a consequence of separation may subsequently suffer mounting life pressures (e.g., losing one's job, or social status, financial hardships) that further aggravate the depressive condition; hospitalization may then become unavoidable.

Another important question is the relationship of life events to subtypes of affective illness. Cadoret, Winokur, Dorzab, and Baker (1972) have presented data suggesting that the etiologic role of social stressors may be more

---

[4] Brown, Harris & Peto (1973b) have developed a strategy for separating "formative" influences (i.e., without the stressor events the depressive condition would not have occurred) from "precipitating" influences (i.e., the depressive condition would have occurred anyway, but appeared earlier in time because of life stress). Although conceptually sound, the empirical application of this model presents methodological difficulties.

relevant to early-onset unipolar depressions (so-called "unipolar spectrum disease" where alcoholism and sociopathy are common in male biologic kin), and depressions that complicate the tempestuous life styles of sociopathy, hysteria, and alcoholism (Winokur, Cadoret, Dorzab, & Baker, 1971).

In summary, then, life events seem to enter the etiologic chain of depressive disorders at various junctures; they may have greater relevance to certain subtypes of depression than to others; more importantly, they do not account for the major variance in the genesis of depressive disorders. The failure of social stressors to cause primary depression by themselves, is analogous to the paradigm of secondary depression where, despite the multiplicity of social stresses generated by nonaffective psychiatric or medical illness, the depressive condition generally remains low-grade in intensity. It is therefore necessary to consider those mediating factors that augment the depressionogenic impact of life events.

Lack of Social Support

Individuals who affiliate with a cohesive group (e.g., extended family, ethnic subcultures) and who share common values and life styles may receive emotional sustenance from other group members during times of life crisis. Such a support system serves as a protective emotional buffer that may considerably attenuate the pathogenic impact of adverse life circumstances. Studies on bereavement suggest that the absence of emotional support during grief may indeed play a "permissive" role in the progression of grief to melancholia. Thus, in the Madison and Walker study (1967) widows who developed protracted depressive responses to bereavement reported unsatisfactory interpersonal support systems. Clayton and associates (1968) found that the only factor auguring a poor outcome in bereavement was the nonavailability of grownup children within the immediate geographic vicinity of the widow's home. Likewise, the syndrome of anaclitic depression does not develop in children separated from their mothers if appropriate mothering is substituted (Robertson & Robertson, 1971). It is therefore reasonable to conclude that the noxious effects of at least one major type of life event depend upon the nonavailability of protective interpersonal buffer systems. However, the absence of such support does not, in itself, produce depression.

The life event research reviewed earlier suggests that separation events figure prominently among the precipitating factors in depressive illness. One is therefore tempted to speculate that the reported rise in the incidence of depressive disorders in the United States is partially attributable to the dissolution of attachment bonds between members of the extended family, a situation that is further compounded by the high rate of geographic mobility characteristic of American society (Rome, 1973).

Deficient Social Skills

Whether separations and losses will leave an individual in a state of helpless despair also depends on one's ability to engage in activities that can provide substitute gratification for one's personal and social needs. Those who have a narrow range of interests and, therefore, possess a limited response repertoire—rarely displaying behavior that is positively reinforced by the environment—can be operationally characterized as lacking "social skills." The environment may fail to provide adequate supplies of reinforcement, placing such people on prolonged extinction schedules. For these individuals withdrawal of environmental reinforcement is of critical importance, because they lack the requisite social skills that would have provided them with substitute sources of gratification. Lewinsohn and associates (1974) have demonstrated in single-case experimental designs that social skill deficits are indeed associated with depressive states.

According to Seligman (1974), however, it is not the loss of reinforcement that is depressionogenic, but rather the provision of reinforcement noncontingently. In other words, persons lacking certain types of social skills may continue to receive rewards from the environment that are not contingent upon their responses or skills. A familiar example is the middle aged housewife who has lost her social role as a mother following the departure of her last child, yet continues to receive social rewards from her husband (i.e., the so-called "empty-nest" syndrome; Deykin, Jacobson, Klerman, & Solomon, 1966). Other examples include persons who receive financial assistance from welfare or after retirement, but are not required to perform personally or in a socially meaningful fashion.

The behavioral conceptualization of depression would predict that social classes and subcultures deficient in social skills would have a higher incidence of depression. Indeed, surveys on nonpsychiatric populations indicate that, contrary to the stereotype in the literature, depressive symptoms are most prevalent in the lowest social classes (Comstock & Helsing, 1976; Schwab, Bialow, Holzer, Brown & Stevenson, 1967). Furthermore, some clinicians postulate that depressive behavior, once released, can be maintained in certain hysteroid personalities through the rewards of the "sick role."

Behavioral formulations have the merit of delineating factors that can be manipulated in therapeutic intervention with individual cases. Unfortunately, the behavioral explanation of depressive phenomena is largely derived from studies on "problems-of-living" (situational) depression. Therefore, the concept of deficient social skills only refers to a general susceptibility: It identifies a population at risk, but it lacks specificity for depressive illness and may have little etiologic relevance for the melancholic states of despair under consideration here (Wolpe, 1971; Lazarus, 1968).

In summary, deficient social skills define the social context in which depression manifests itself. However, there is increasing realization that the individual may play a role in creating the life conditions that provide fertile soil for the genesis of depression; or that individuals may suffer from an *intrinsic* deficiency, possibly of biologic origin, influencing their response to interpersonal reinforcement (Akiskal & McKinney, 1973a).

Developmental Object Loss

Psychoanalytical theory traces maladaptive behavior to childhood events that interfere with the emergence of adult coping skills: The individual is thereby believed to be sensitized to events in adult life that somehow revive the childhood traumata. Thus, according to Bowlby (1961), failure to mourn in the face of object loss during childhood provides the behavioral predisposition for adult depression. Epidemiologic evidence based on human studies has been generally inconclusive in providing support for this hypothesis (Granville-Grossman, 1968). On the other hand, the sensitizing influence of early loss is supported by experimental work in infrahuman primates. For instance, one Wisconsin study (Young, Suomi, Harlow, & McKinney, 1973) found that 2-year-old monkeys' response to separation depended on whether or not they had undergone traumatic separation earlier during infancy (at the age 3–6 months): Those with a history of separation manifested increased self-centered behavior and social withdrawal, as compared with control subjects without a history of separation during infancy.

Although the human data do not provide evidence for a direct causal connection between childhood object loss and adult depression, several relationships of major clinical importance have been uncovered (Heinicke, 1973):

1. Perris (1966) noted, for instance, the mean age of onset for the first episode in unipolar psychotic depressives was 10 years earlier if they had experienced object loss during childhood.
2. Beck, Sethi, and Tuthill (1963) reported that the severity of depression, as measured by the Beck Inventory, was positively correlated to childhood object loss.
3. Other investigators demonstrated that suicide attempts in a depressive population were more frequent in the group with a history of object loss sustained during the developmental period in childhood (Hill, 1969; Levi, Fales, Stein, & Sharp, 1966).

4. Finally, the author and his associates (Akiskal, Strauss, & Rosenthal, 1979) found that developmental object loss predicted the adult occurrence of unstable characterological features of "hostile dependency" in a heterogeneous population of depressives. Furthermore, these characterological traits predicted chronicity and unfavorable social outcome.

These findings illustrate specific ways in which developmental object loss can modify the epidemiology and manifestations of clinical depression. It is likely that the depressionogenic potential of developmental object loss is translated into actual affective illness through the intermediary of a characterological component. Hostile dependency may be derived from unsatisfactory early object relationships (Abraham, 1911). Therefore, the characterological propensity towards hostile dependency may prepare a fertile soil of interpersonal friction that facilitates the expression of depressive illness at an earlier age. In fact, such interpersonal friction may actually create the life events that precipitate the depressive illness (Weissman & Paykel, 1974). Finally, these hostile dependent characterological traits may give rise to new life events that could augment the aversive social consequences of the depressive condition, once it occurs, with consequent chronic depressive sequelae and social incapacitation.

Another plausible mechanism relating early object loss to adult depression is through the character trait of "learned helplessness" (Seligman, 1974). The classical studies of the Harlows (1966) have demonstrated that attachment behavior is a primary reinforcer and the disruption of attachment bonds in the primate constitutes a major loss of reinforcement inducing a behavioral state characterized by helplessness and a breakdown of motivated behavior. Specifically, the loss of contact comfort (i.e. fondling and tactile intimacy) with a parent precludes the development of environmental exploration and coping skills in general. Thus, early separation from parent(s) without adequate substitute(s), may prevent the development of a sense of mastery over the environment (Bowlby, 1977). Such children will then be more likely to develop depression when faced with aversive life events as an adult. The mere presence of parents, however, does not immunize against learned helplessness, because developing a sense of control over one's fate requires suitable role models, as well as the opportunity to master a series of life events of increasing complexity (Rosenthal & Bandura, 1979).

The social and interpersonal data reviewed thus far suggest that depression is characterized by alterations in cognitive operations whereby individuals give up hope in their ability to cope with environmental reinforcers. The behavioral counterpart of such negative self-concepts is usually manifested in impaired motivation to obtain consummatory reward from interpersonal reinforcement. Whatever the nature of the life events eliciting or precipitating such states of helpless despair, melancholia is often accompanied by a temporary disruption in the individual's interpersonal, vocational, and ideologic bonds. The dissolution of such bonds may precede the depressive illness and thus play a precipitating role in its causation, or it may result from the depressive state, thereby perpetuating the maladaptive withdrawal from relationships. As noted earlier, in primate species, lack of secure attachment to significant others increases the adaptive demands placed on the individual in stressful situations and thereby lowers the threshold for developing psychological decompensation. With the expansion of our knowledge of the neurochemical substrates of reinforcement, concepts derived from primate research may help in developing conceptual bridges between biologic and psychological models of depression.

Monoamine Depletion

An impressive volume of animal literature indicates that many of the life events (including separation), which are postulated to precipitate depression in humans, can induce significant alterations in the brain levels of neurotransmitters. The most relevant of these studies (reviewed by Akiskal & McKinney, 1975; Goodwin & Bunney, 1973) for the present discussion are the following: (a) acute stress raises brain levels of both serotonin and norepinephrine; (b) inescapable aversive events deplete brain norepinephrine; and (c) chronic stress depletes brain serotonin. Norepinephrine and serotonin are monoamine neurotransmitters concentrated in the diencephalon and their action modulates the very functions that are impaired in melancholia: sleep, appetite, motivation, reward, pleasure, libido, and reinforcement in general (Crow, 1973, Heath, 1964; Olds & Milner, 1954; Stein, 1968). Thus, social stressors appear to produce chemical changes in the very centers one would have expected given the clinical picture of melancholia described earlier. It is unknown whether developmental events, which signal the cognitive state of learned helplessness, are accompanied by changes in monoamines. However, the Chapel Hill group (Prange, Wilson, Knox, McClane, Breese, Martin, Alltop, & Lipton, 1972) has presented data suggesting that prolonged stress may so "exhaust" the synaptic mechanisms in the diencephalon as to impair the postsynaptic receptor sensitivity leading to a compensatory increase in presynaptic norepinephrine. Consequently, as stresses accumulate, such an individual will not be able to synthesize functionally adequate levels of norepinephrine. Therefore, depending on the "dynamic" state of the synapse (Mandel, Segal, Kuczenski, Knapp, 1972), social stressors may lead to *functional* impairment at a diencephalic level (whether the absolute level of norepinephrine is decreased or increased).

If the diencephalic centers of reinforcement are intimately involved as the neurochemical pathways of melancholia, then one would predict that monoamine depleting drugs would produce alterations of behavior and mood in the direction of depression. Psychopathology induced in animals by treating them with reserpine, as well as with such selective monoamine-depletors as alphamethylparatyrosine (AMPT), 6-hydroxydopamine (6-HODA) and parachlorphenylanine (PCPA), indicates that behavioral syndromes in the expected direction do occur in many, but not all, of the studies conducted so far (Redmond, Maas, Kling, & Dekirmenjian, 1971; Akiskal & McKinney, 1973a). However, as pointed out in a provocative review of chemically-induced depressive states (Mendels & Frazer, 1974), there are many inconsistencies in a monoamine theory of depression. These inconsistencies become even more troublesome when one considers the few studies with monoamine-depleting drugs conducted in humans (summarized in Table 18.2).

Reserpine-depression is the best known paradigm for a monoamine-depletion theory of depression in man. It occurs in 15% of people treated with the rauwolfia drug in doses of at least .5 mg/day over several months (Goodwin & Bunney, 1971). In a third of these cases, the clinical picture is indistinguishable from a naturally-occurring state of melancholia. The remaining two-thirds, however, are best described as "pseudodepression." The latter condition probably reflects the sedative and activity-suppressant side effects of reserpine and it therefore lifts with drug withdrawal; the melancholic depression, on the other hand, does not remit upon withdrawal of the drug and assumes an autonomous course.

The question, then, is what factor(s) differentiate between the two groups? The available data favor the hypothesis that a monoamine-depleting drug, such as reserpine, can induce melancholic depression only in individuals predisposed to depressive illness. This interpretation rests on evidence that hypertensive patients receiving this drug and developing melancholia have a significantly higher percentage of either prior personal history of depressive episodes or family history for affective disorder (Goodwin & Bunney, 1971). Other hypothetical explanations, untested in the human, include: (a) the suggestion that "true" depression is more likely to occur in persons whose self-esteem depends on psychomotor activity and mental alertness, since they will poorly tolerate the sedative side effects of monoamine-depleting drugs; and (b) the possibility that the depressionogenic potency of monoamine-depleting drugs is augmented by stressful life events. Indeed, some animal data support this second hypothesis: thus AMPT, the selective inhibitor of catecholamine synthesis, in dosages which have no noticeable behavioral effects has been found to amplify the "despair" phase of the monkey syndrome induced by separation (Kraemer & McKinney, 1979).

As with social stressors, a chemical stressor alone does not appear to account for the occurrence of depressive illness. The stressor seems to impinge on a vulnerable central nervous system. Hence, the inconsistencies

Table 18.2

SELECTIVE INHIBITION OF BIOGENIC AMINE SYNTHESIS IN HUMAN SUBJECTS[a]

Inhibitor	Mechanism	Subjects	Response
Parachlorphenylalanine (PCPA)	Inhibits indoleamine synthesis	Normal controls Carcinoid syndrome	Fatigue Anxiety, agitation, confusion, and paranoia
Alphamethylparatyrosine (AMPT)	Inhibits catecholamine synthesis	Normal controls Depressed subjects Manic subjects	Fatigue and sedation Sedation (worse?) Better (?)
Fusaric acid	Inhibits norepinephrine synthesis	Hypomanic subjects Manic subjects	No change Worse

[a] Summarized from Mendels and Frazer (1974) and Sack and Goodwin (1974).

noted in the literature probably stem from simple-minded reductionistic attempts to equate chemistry with behavior.[5] If multiple factors are required for the production of a complex syndrome like melancholia, one cannot single out any one factor, whether chemical or social, to account for the entire variance.

It is also possible that distinct biologic vulnerabilities exist, as suggested by the genetic data on bipolar and unipolar depressions. Therefore, different biochemical types of depression (Schildkraut, 1965) may account for some of the inconsistencies in the literature. The following evidence for "Type A" and "Type B" depression is summarized from Maas' (1975) and Schildkraut's (1976) work:

1. *Type A* depressions are characterized by a norepinephrine deficit.

   a. They have a low pretreatment level of urinary 3-methoxy-4-hydroxyphenylethelene glycol (MHPG), the central metabolite of norepinephrine.
   b. They display an initial positive response to dextroamphetamine, a sympathomimetic drug.
   c. They show favorable therapeutic response to imipramine, a drug that is biotransformed to the noradrenergic metabolite desimipramine.
   d. They fail to respond to amitriptyline, the indoleaminergic tricyclic.

2. *Type B* depressions, on the other hand, are conceivably characterized by low levels of brain serotonin.

   a. The pretreatment level of urinary MHPG is normal.
   b. No appreciable mood elevation is seen with dextroamphetamine.
   c. They show favorable treatment response to the indoleaminergic amitriptyline.
   d. They do not respond to drugs, such as imipramine, that are biotransformed to noradrenergic metabolites.

In summary, then, reserpine-precipitated depression is the most familiar clinical example of monoamine-depletion depression in humans. Such depletion, though not demonstrated in man as a response to life stressors, may conceivably occur as a secondary phenomenon in depressive states that are precipitated by "exit" events. However, as neither chemical, nor life stressors alone account for the occurrence of melancholic depression, it is necessary to define the biologic vulnerabilities that predispose to monoamine depletion.

[5] For further discussion of the philosophical pitfalls of the "chemistry producing behavior" position, the reader is referred to earlier work by the author where this issue is extensively reviewed (Akiskal & McKinney, 1975).

Rising Levels of Monoamine Oxidase
(MAO) with Advancing Age

Treated depressive disorders are more common after age 40 (Winokur, 1970), and this is especially true for unipolar conditions. As for bipolar disorders (which often begin before age 30), the frequency of attacks increases with advancing age; moreover, manic episodes become less common whereas depressive episodes increase in frequency (Angst, 1966). In the United States, the upward trend in the incidence and recurrence of depressive illness is paralleled by a steady rise in completed suicide: For women, the peak is reached in the 50s and declines gradually, but for men the steady rise continues until the 80s (Schuyler, 1972). Heredity seems to be less important in such late onset depressive conditions (Hopkinson & Ley, 1969). It is therefore tempting to link such statistics to the rising incidence of incapacitating physical illness, the net decline of reinforcement, and the gradual erosion of adaptive social skills all of which are associated with increasing age. Unfortunately research findings have generally failed to specifically link depressive conditions arising in the senium with such factors (Post, 1977).

Another plausible explanation for the rise in depressive disorders in later life is the increasing level of the enzyme monoamine oxidase with age (Robinson, Davis, Nies, Ravaris, & Sylvester, 1971). This enzyme participates in the oxidative breakdown of monoamines in the brain. Therefore, a relative increase in the activity of MAO may lead to decreased levels of monoamines in the brain. If an optimally functioning diencephalic reward system depends on adequate levels of monoamine neurotransmitters, then a decline of such transmitters with age will render the organism more vulnerable to frustration, loss, and other life stressors that are expected to increase adaptive demands. These data regarding MAO provide one possible explanation for the higher incidence of depressive conditions in women because MAO levels are consistently higher in women throughout adult life.[6]

Borderline Hypothyroid Function

Whybrow, Prange, and Treadway (1969) demonstrated that although depression of melancholic proportion occurred with frank hypothyroidism, hyperthyroidism in its entire range seemed to protect against depressive

---

[6] The etiologic significance of increasing levels of MAO activity with age seems more germane to unipolar disorder, as some bipolar patients have been found to possess very low levels of MAO activity (Murphy & Weiss, 1972). However, even in bipolar patients, MAO tends to increase from its low baseline value with advancing age, with women showing the higher values.

illness. Moreover, subclinical hypothyroidism was associated with a higher risk for developing the cognitive and emotional manifestations of depressive illness. The relevance of these findings is more germane to women as their hypothalamothyroid axis appears more susceptible to hypofunction or hyperfunction under conditions of increased adaptive demands imposed by the environment, and a certain percentage of unipolar depressed females display borderline hypothyroid indices (Prange, Wilson, Rabon, & Lipton, 1969). As expected, such women recover faster when triiodothyronine (T_3) is added to the standard dose of the tricyclic antidepressant.

These findings on unipolar women can be linked to the monoaminergic synapses of the diencephalon. Synaptic function is determined by the availability of monoamines released from the presynaptic pools, as well as on the receptivity of the postsynaptic membrane; this receptor functions optimally when T_3 is available to modulate the neurotransmitter functions of the monoamines. The woman with borderline hypothyroidism is at high risk for developing a depressive condition because her diencephalic "reward" system might be functioning at a lower level of efficiency. Compensatory increase in monoamine production, as discussed earlier, may suffice for a while, but one would expect "exhaustion" under stressful conditions that tax adaptive mechanisms. These findings and extrapolations from the thyroid data provide yet another plausible explanation for the increased vulnerability of women to depression.

The Impact of the Puerperium

As contrasted with unipolar women, bipolar women have a modest, but nevertheless increased, risk for experiencing both depressive and manic episodes immediately following delivery (Reich & Winokur, 1970). The reasons for this are not entirely clear. Whether increased risk is related to sleep disturbance, to profound changes in the hormonal homeostosis or to the psychodynamic impact of an "entry" type life event—or combinations thereof—there is little doubt that the postpartum period merely precipitates an episode in a person vulnerable to bipolar disorder.

Alcoholism

The relationship of alcoholism to depression is complicated. A common stereotype in the literature is that depression underlies many forms of alcoholism; even when clearcut evidence for overt clinical depression is lacking, the dual concepts of "masked depression" and "depressive equivalents" are often invoked (Lesse, 1974). These concepts find some support in "depressive spectrum disease" (Winokur et al., 1971) where women suffer from depression, whereas their male relatives manifest alcoholism and sociopathy.

There is little disagreement about the occurrence of "alcoholism" in both recurrent unipolar and bipolar patients, but it has been known since the days of Kraepelin (1921) that alcoholic complications in these conditions take the form of dipsomania (i.e. episodic excessive drinking).

A more provocative relationship between alcoholism and depression is the reverse possibility, that is, alcoholism may itself induce depressive illness (Freed, 1970). Chronic and intermittent forms of alcoholism occur in the context of various ill-defined "character disorders" of which sociopathy is the only rigorously defined category (Cadoret & Winokur, 1975). There is increasing evidence that alcoholic populations, without a history of pre-existing depressive disorder, are at greater risk for developing depression. The data are as follows:

1. Alcoholics are at high risk for committing suicide. This is not merely the outcome of losing loved objects or social status because of chronic alcoholism (Murphy & Robins, 1967), as the risk for successful suicide increases with sustained alcoholic inebriation and withdrawal (Palola, Dorpat, & Larson, 1972; Mayfield & Montgomery, 1972).

2. Although alcohol consumption is subjectively experienced as anxiolytic, objective measurements have verified the occurrence of depressive affect and behavior during alcoholic binges (McNamee, Mello, Mendelson, 1968; Tamerin & Mendelson, 1969; Nathan, Titler, Lowenstein, Solomon, & Rossi, 1970). Such depressive states may be accentuated during alcohol withdrawal (Butterworth, 1971; Gibson & Beckes, 1973).

Recent work (Keeler, Miller, & Taylor, 1977) has challenged the relationship of alcohol to clinical depression; for instance, it has been suggested that much of what is considered "depression" on "objective" psychometric tests reflects nonspecific somatic and autonomic effects associated with alcoholism. Nevertheless, the possibility that alcohol may induce clinical depression or aggravate pre-existing depression is of great theoretical interest. Alcohol is known to produce intracellular sodium accumulation (Beard & Knott, 1968). An increase in brain sodium has been demonstrated in alcoholic suicides (Shaw, Frizel, Camps, & White, 1969).

Familial and Genetic Factors

Primary affective disorders run in families (Kallman, 1954; Kraepelin, 1921). Biologic relatives of both bipolar and unipolar probands have, respectively, morbidity risks of 50% and 28%[7] for affective disorder compared to

---

[7] Averaged from the risk figures in the literature.

5-9% in the general population (Cadoret & Winokur, 1975). A recent adoption study (Mendelewicz & Rainer, 1977) provides convincing evidence for attributing the increased familial incidence to genetic factors; in this study, an increased risk for affective disorder was found in the biologic relatives of affectively ill adoptees, the risk being negligible in the adoptive parents. A wide difference in concordance rates between monozygotic and dizygotic twin pairs (70 versus 19%) suggests that heredity plays a major role in the etiology of affective disorders, contributing at least 50% of the total variance (Gershon, Dunner, & Goodwin, 1971). As heritability is computed from large samples with familial and nonfamilial types of depression, the heritability estimate is the mean value, with probably higher weight provided by bipolar disorder. Furthermore, bipolar disorder is distributed in two consecutive generations and, in some families, is transmitted with traits carried on the X-chromosome (Mendlwicz & Fleiss, 1974; Winokur, 1973).

Such data favor the hypothesis that at least one type of bipolar illness is inherited as an X-linked dominant trait, whereas polygenic inheritance appears to be the more likely explanation for unipolar depression (Baker, Dorzab, Winokur, & Cadoret, 1972; Gershon et al., 1971). However, a spectrum of affective conditions which includes alcoholism, affective personalities[8] and both unipolar and bipolar disorders has been proposed (Gershon et al., 1975). In this "spectrum model," bipolar conditions are considered to be the severer form of the affective disorders—having an earlier onset because of high penetrance or a larger complement of genes.

Although heredity seems to account for much of the variance in the etiology of affective disorders, the familial nature of the disorder probably significantly influences its actual expression. As suggested elsewhere (Akiskal & McKinney, 1973a), the child reared in a family with primary affective disorder suffers from a dual disadvantage: genetic vulnerability to affective disturbance plus object loss from parental suicide, parental separation or divorce, or more subtle forms of deprivation related to the interaction of parents when one member is affectively disturbed. The relationship of developmental object loss to the severity of depressive disorders has been discussed earlier. Perhaps children exposed to suicide-prone, impulsive parents may learn to model such behavior during adult situations of stress in order to gain interpersonal rewards.

The metabolic defect which translates the genetic potential into actual clinical disorder is unknown. However, sufficient data have now accumulated to justify formulating tentative hypotheses about the possible neurochemical loci of dysfunction (reviewed by Akiskal & McKinney, 1975).

[8] Affective personalities refer to subclinical forms of affective disorder. Thus cyclothymic personalities suffer from mood swings, in both the depressive and hypomanic directions, without reaching the clinical severity of bipolar manic depressive disorder (Akiskal, Djenderedjian, Rosenthal, Khani, 1977). Likewise, some depressive personalities, who are habitually gloomy, pessimistic, anhedonic, etc., may well represent milder stages of the unipolar disorders, but the evidence is less compelling here (Fieve & Dunner, 1975).

One of these, impaired sensitivity of the postsynaptic receptor, has already been mentioned: Should such impairment exist on a genetic basis, the organism will then be particularly vulnerable to acquired thyroid deficits. The presynaptic membrane is another plausible site of neurochemical abnormality and has attracted great attention recently. This membrane could be genetically "leaky," permitting intraneuronal accumulation of sodium and extraneuronal leakage, and ultimate depletion of, biogenic amines. The hypothesis is supported by reports of increased residual sodium in states of depression and mania (Coppen & Shaw, 1963; Shaw, 1966), as well as evidence for an impaired "membrane pump" in the red blood cells of manic-depressive patients (Mendels & Frazer, 1973; Naylor P., Dick, E., Dick, D., Le Poidevin, D. & White, S. F. 1973; Hokin-Nyverson, Spiegel, & Lewis, 1974).[9] This second hypothesis about "leaky" presynaptic membrane is probably more relevant to manic-depressive conditions than to unipolar depressions.

MELANCHOLIA AS A FINAL COMMON PATHWAY

Different types of clinical depression are often difficult to distinguish on symptomatological grounds. Such homogeneity of clinical characteristics is in marked contrast to the increasing evidence for genetic and chemical heterogeneity; likewise, the clinical picture of melancholia, once attained, is the same whether precipitated by object loss, reserpine, or facilitated by borderline hypothyroidism. Such observations, along with the diencephalic "quality" of signs and symptoms, have led to the hypothesis that melancholia is the final common pathway (Whybrow & Parlatore, 1973) of various processes converging in the diencephalon as a functional derangement of the neurophysiological substrates of reinforcement (Akiskal & McKinney, 1973a; Klein, 1974). Concomitantly, profound disturbances in arousal mechanisms occur, despite behavioral "depression" (Whybrow & Mendels, 1969). The resultant breakdown in psychological and vegetative functions is experienced as hopelessness, with added psychic turmoil leading to heightened arousal and a vicious cycle of further impairment of diencephalic circuits.

Melancholia, then, is the culmination of various etiologic factors that conceivably converge in areas of the diencephalon that modulate arousal, mood, motivation, and psychomotor functions. Variation in the clinical expression of the syndrome may result from the interactional patterns of two or more of the factors outlined in Figure 18.1.

[9] It is believed that residual sodium represents total body sodium in the intracellular compartment, including the intraneural compartment, and that the RBC membrane is very similar to the neuronal membrane with regard to enzyme kinetics.

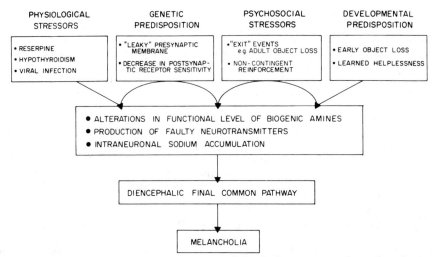

Figure 18.1. Diagrammatic representation of the final common pathway hypothesis of melancholia.

In summary, melancholia is conceptualized as a psychobiologic state that represents the final common pathway of various processes involving: (*a*) life events or chemical stressors that so overwhelm the adaptive skills of the affectively ill that they see themselves as losing control over their destiny; (*b*) escalating levels of subjective turmoil; (*c*) heightened neuronal excitability and arousal with interplay of genetically or developmentally vulnerable neuronal circuits in the diencephalon; (*d*) impaired monoaminergic transmission; (*e*) derangement of the neurochemical substrates of reinforcement; (*f*) further breakdown in coping mechanisms; and (*g*) a vicious cycle of more turmoil, arousal and hopelessness. This chain of etiologic events relates to the diencephalic centers of mood, reward, and arousal through interoceptive and exteroceptive circuits. For this reason, I agree fully with Becker's view that "dramatic breakthroughs seem less likely than a gradual clarification of how basic bio-psycho-social mood determinants interactively relate to depression [1974, p. 198]." The challenge for future research is to elucidate further the mechanisms whereby the 10 classes of determinants discussed in this chapter, and novel determinants yet to be discovered, interact.

REFERENCES

Abraham, K. Notes on the psychoanalytic investigation and treatment of manic-depressive insanity and allied conditions (1911). In *Selected papers on psychoanalysis*. New York: Basic Books, 1960. Pp. 137–156.

Akiskal, H. S. & McKinney, W. T., Jr. Depressive disorders: Toward a unified hypothesis. *Science*, 1973, *182*, 20–29. (a)

Akiskal, H. S. & McKinney, W. T., Jr. Psychiatry and pseudopsychiatry. *Archives of General Psychiatry*, 1973, 28, 367–373. (b)

Akiskal, H. S. & McKinney, W. T., Jr. Overview of recent research in depression: Integration of ten conceptual models into a comprehensive clinical frame. *Archives of General Psychiatry*, 1975, 32, 285–305.

Akiskal, H. S., Djenderedjian, A. H., Rosenthal, R. H., Khani, M. K. Cyclothymic disorder: Validating criteria for inclusion in the bipolar affective group. *American Journal of Psychiatry*, 1977, 134, 1227–1233.

Akiskal, H. S. The joint use of clinical and biological criteria for psychiatric diagnosis: I. A historical and methodological review. In H. S. Akiskal & W. L. Webb, Jr. (Eds.), *Psychiatric diagnosis: Exploration of biological predictors*. New York: Spectrum, 1978.

Akiskal, H. S., Bitar, A. H., Puzantian, V. R., Rosenthal, T. L, & Walker, P. W. The nosological status of neurotic depression: A prospective 3–4 year follow-up examination in the light of the primary–secondary and the unipolar–bipolar dichotomies. *Archives of General Psychiatry*, 1978, 35, 756–766.

Akiskal, H. S. *et al*. In preparation, 1979.

Angst, J. *Zur Atiologie and Nosologie Endogener Depressiver Psychosen*. Berlin: Springer Verlag, 1966.

Baker, M., Dorzab, J., Winokur, G., & Cadoret, R. Depressive disease: Evidence favoring polygenic inheritance based on an analysis of ancestral cases. *Archives of General Psychiatry*, 1972, 27, 320–327.

Beard, J. & Knott, D. Fluid and electrolyte balance during acute withdrawal in chronic alcoholic patients. *Journal of the American Medical Association*, 1968, 204, 135–139.

Beck, A., Sethi, B., & Tuthill, R. Child bereavement and adult depression. *Archives of General Psychiatry*, 1963, 9, 295–302.

Beck, A. T. *Depression: Cases and Treatment*. Philadelphia: Univ. Pennsylvania Press, 1967.

Beck, A. T. The development of depression: A cognitive model. In R. J. Friedman & M. M. Katz (Eds.), *The psychology of depression: Contemporary theory and research*. New York, John Wiley & Sons, 1974.

Becker, E. *The revolution in psychiatry*. London: Free Press of Glencoe, Collier-Macmillan Ltd, 1964. Pp. 108–135.

Becker, J. *Depression: Theory and research*. New York: Wiley, 1974.

Blumenthal, M. D. Measuring depressive symptomatology in a general population. *Archives of General Psychiatry*, 1975, 32, 971–978.

Bonime, W. The psychodynamics of neurotic depression. In S. Arieti (Ed.), *American handbook of psychiatry* (Vol. 3, 1st ed.). New York: Basic Books, 1966.

Bowlby J. Childhood mourning and its implication for psychiatry. *American Journal of Psychiatry*, 1961, 118, 481–498.

Bowlby, J. The making and breaking of affectional bonds—I. Aetiology and psychopathology in the light of attachment theory. *British Journal of Psychiatry*, 1977, 130, 201–10.

Briscoe, C. W. & Smith, J. B. Depression in bereavement and divorce. *Archives of General Psychiatry*, 1975, 32, 439–443.

Briscoe, C. W., Smith, J. B., Robins, E., Marten, S., & Gaskin, F. Divorce and psychiatric disease. *Archives of General Psychiatry*, 1973, 29, 119–125.

Brown, G. W., Harris, T., & Copeland, J. R. Depression and loss. *British Journal of Psychiatry*, 1977, 130, 1–18.

Brown, G. W., Harris, T. O., & Peto, J. Life events and psychiatric disorders—Part 2: Nature of causal link. *Psychological Medicine*, 1973, 3, 159–176.. (b)

Brown, G. W., Sklair, F., Harris, T. O., & Birley, J. L. T. Life-events and psychiatric disorders—Part 1: Some methodological issues. *Psychological Medicine*, 1973, 3, 74–87..

Butterworth, A. Depression associated with alcohol withdrawal. *Quarterly Journal of Studies on Alcohol*, 1971, 32, 343–348.

Cadoret, R., Winokur, G., Dorzab, J., & Baker, M. Depressive disease: Life events and onset of illness. *Archives of General Psychiatry*, 1972, 26, 133–136.

Cadoret, R. & Winokur, G. Genetic studies of affective disorders. In F. F. Flach & S. C. Draghi (Eds.), *The nature and treatment of depression*. New York: Wiley, 1975.

Carroll, B. I., Curtis, G. C., & Mendels, J. Neuroendocrine regulation in depression—I. Limbic system–adrenocortical dysfunction. *Archives of General Psychiatry*, 1976, 33, 1039–1044.

Clayton, P., Desmarais, L., & Winokur, G. A study of normal bereavement. *American Journal of Psychiatry*, 1968, 125, 64–74.

Comstock, G. W. & Helsing, K. J. Symptoms of depression in two communities. *Psychological Medicine*, 1976, 6, 551–563.

Coppen, A. & Shaw, D. Mineral metabolism in melancholia. *British Medical Journal*, 1963, 2, 1439–1444.

Crow, T. Catecholamine-containing neurones and electrical self-stimulation: II. A theoretical interpretation and some psychiatric implications. *Psychological Medicine*, 1973, 3, 66–73.

Dalton, K. *The premenstrual syndrome*. Springfield, Illinois: Thomas, 1964.

Deykin, E. Y., Jacobson, S., Klerman, G., & Solomon, M. The empty nest: Psychosocial aspects of conflict between depressed women and their grown children. *American Journal of Psychiatry*, 1966, 122, 1422–1426.

Ettigi, P. G. & Brown, G. M. Psychoneuroendocrinology of affective disorder: An overview. *American Journal of Psychiatry*, 1977, 134, 493–500.

Fenichel, O. *The psychoanalytic theory of neurosis*. New York: Norton, 1945.

Fieve, R. R. & Dunner, D. D. Unipolar and bipolar affective states. In F. F. Flach & S. C. Draghi (Eds.), *The nature and treatment of depression*. New York: Wiley, 1975. Pp. 145–160.

Freed, E. X. Alcoholism and manic-depressive disorders: Some perspectives. *Quarterly Journal of Studies on Alcohol*, 1970, 31, 62.

Freud, S. (1917) Mourning and melancholia. In *Standard Edition of the complete psychological works of Sigmund Freud*. Transl & ed by J. Strachey (Vol. 14). London: Hogarth Press, 1957.

Friedman, R. J. The psychology of depression: An overview. In R. J. Friedman & M. M. Katz (Eds.) *The psychology of depression: Contemporary theory and research*. Washington, D. C.: U.S. Gov. Printing Office, 1974, Pp. 281–298.

GAP (Group for the Advancement of Psychiatry). *Pharmacotherapy and Psychotherapy: Paradoxes, problems, and progress*. New York: Mental Health Materials Center, 1975.

Gershon, E. S., Baron, M., & Leckman, J. F. Genetic models of the transmission of affective disorders. *Journal of Psychiatric Research*, 1975, 12, 301–317.

Gershon, E., Dunner, D., Goodwin, F.: Toward a biology of affective disorders: genetic contributions. *Archives of General Psychiatry*, 1971, 25, 1–15.

Gibson, S. & Beckes, J. Changes in alcoholics' self-reported depression. *Quarterly Journal of Studies on Alcohol*, 1973, 34, 829–836.

Goffman, E. *Asylums: Essays on the social situation of mental patients and other inmates*. Garden City, New York: Doubleday, 1961.

Goodwin F. & Bunney, W. E., Jr. Depression following reserpine, a reevaluation. *Seminars in Psychiatry*, 1971, 3, 435–448.

Goodwin, F. & Bunney, W. E., Jr. A psychobiological approach to affective illness. *Psychiatric Annals*, 1973, 3, 19–53.

Granville-Grossman, K. The early environment in affective disorder. In A. Coppen, & A. Wak (Eds.) *Recent developments in affective disorders*. London: Headley Brothers, 1968. Pp. 65–79.

Guze, S. B., Woodruff, R. A., & Clayton, P. J. Preliminary communication–secondary affective disorder: A study of 95 cases. *Psychological Medicine*, 1971, 1, 426–428.

Harlow, H. & Harlow, M. Learning to love. *American Science*, 1966, 54, 244–272.

Heath, R. (Ed.). *The role of pleasure in behavior*. New York: Harper, 1964.

Heinicke, C. Parental deprivation in early childhood. In J. Scott & E. Senay (Eds.), *Separation and depression: Clinical and research aspects*. Washington, D. C.: Am. Assoc. Advance. Sci., 1973. Pp. 141–160.

Helgason, T. Epidemiology of mental disorders in Ireland: A psychiatric and demographic investigation of 5395 Irelanders. *Acta Psychiatrica Scandinavica (suppl 173)*, 1964.

Heron, M. J. A note on the concept endogenous–exogenous. *British Journal of Medicine and Psychology*, 1965, *38*, 241–245.

Hill, O. The association of childhood bereavement with suicidal attempt in depressive illness. *British Journal of Psychiatry*, 1969, *115*, 301–304.

Hokin-Nyverson, M., Spiegel, D., & Lewis, W. Deficiency of erythrocyte sodium pump activity in bipolar manic depressive psychosis. *Life Science*, 1974, *15*, 1739–1748.

Holmes, T. H. & Rahe, R. H. The social readjustment rating scale. *Journal of Psychosomatic Research*, 1967, *11*, 213–218.

Hopkinson, G. & Ley, P. A genetic study of affective disorder. *British Journal of Psychiatry*, 1969, *115*, 917–22.

Hudgens, R., Morrison, J., & Barchha, R. Life events and onset of primary affective disorders. *Archives of General Psychiatry*, 1967, *16*, 134–145.

Jacobs, S. C., Prusoff, B. A., & Paykel, E. S. Recent life events in schizophrenia and depression. *Psychological Medicine*, 1974, *4*, 444–453.

James, W. *Pragmatism: A new name for some old ways of thinking*. New York: Longmans, Green, 1907.

Kallmann, E. J. Genetic Principles in Manic-Depressive Psychosis. In P. H. Hoch & J. Zubin (Eds.), *Depression*. New York: Grune & Stratton, 1954. Pp. 1–24.

Keeler, M. H., Miller, W. C., & Taylor, C. I. Are all recently detoxified alcoholics depressed? *Scientific Proceedings of Amer. Psychiatric Association*, 1977.

Kendell, R. E. *The role of diagnosis in psychiatry*. Oxford: Blackwell, 1975.

Kendell, R. E. The classification of depressions: A review of contemporary confusion. *British Journal of Psychiatry*, 1976, *129*, 15–28.

Kiloh, I. G., Andrews, G., Neilson, M., & Bianchi, G. N. The relationship of the syndromes called enogenous and neurotic depression. *British Journal of Psychiatry*, 1972, *121*, 183–96.

Klein, D. Endogenomorphic depression: A conceptual and terminological revision. *Archives of General Psychiatry*, 1974, *31*, 447–454.

Klerman, G. Clinical research in depression. *Archives of General Psychiatry*, 1971, *24*, 305–319.

Kraemer, G. W. & McKinney, W. T. Interactions of pharmacological agents which alter biogenic amine metabolism and depression. An analysis of contributing factors within a primate model of depression. *Journal of Affective Disorders*, 1979, *1*, 33–54.

Kraepelin, E. (1921) *Manic-depressive insanity and paranoia*. New York: Arno Press, 1976.

Kraines, S. H. Manic depressive syndrome: A physiologic disease. *Diseases of the Nervous System*, 1966, *27*, 3–19.

Lazarus, A. Learning theory and the treatment of depression. *Behavior Research & Therapy*, 1968, *6*, 83–89.

Lessee, S. *Masked depression*. New York: Jason Aronson, 1974.

Leonhard, K. *Aufteilung der Endogenen Psychosen*. Berlin: Akademie-Verlag, 1966.

Levi, L. D., Fales, G. H., Stein, M., & Sharp, V. H. Separation and attempted suicide. *Archives of General Psychiatry*, 1966, *15*, 158–164.

Lewinsohn, P. A behavioral approach to depression. In R. Friedman & M. Katz (Eds.), *The psychology of depression: Contemporary theory and research*. New York, John Wiley & Sons, 1974.

Lindemann, E. Symptomatology and management of acute grief. *American Journal of Psychiatry*, 1944, *101*, 141–148.

Lipowski, Z. J. Psychiatry of somatic disease: Epidemiology, pathogenesis, classification. *Comprehensive Psychiatry*, 1975, *16*, 105–124.

Maas, J. W. Biogenic amines and depression. *Archives of General Psychiatry*, 1975, *32*, 1357–1361.

Maddison, D.& Walker, W. L. Factors affecting the outcome of conjugal bereavement. *British Journal of Psychiatry*, 1967, *113*, 1057–1067.

Mandell, A. J., Segal, D. S., Kuczenski, R. T., & Knapp, S. Etiological agent and defense in biological psychiatry. In J. Cole, A. Freedman, & A. Friedhoff (Eds.), *Psychopathology and Psychopharmacology*. Baltimore: Johns Hopkins Press, 1972, Pp. 251–271.

Mayfield, D., Montgomery, D. Alcoholism, alcohol intoxication and suicide attempts. *Archives of General Psychiatry*, 1972, *27*, 349–353.

McKinney, W. T., Jr., Suomi, S., & Harlow, H. Depression in primates. *American Journal of Psychiatry*, 1971, *127*, 1313–1320.

McNamee, H. B., Mello, N. K., & Mendelson, J. H. Experimental analysis of drinking patterns: Concurrent psychiatric observations. *American Journal of Psychiatry*, 1968, *124*, 1063.

Meehl, P. E. *Psychodiagnois—selected papers*. Minneapolis, Minnesota: Univ. Minnesota Press, 1973. Pp. 225–302.

Mendlewicz, J. & Fleiss, J. L. Linkage studies with X-chromosome markers in bipolar (manic-depressive) and unipolar (depressive) illness. *Biological Psychiatry*, 1974, *9*, 261–294.

Mendelewicz, J. & Rainer, J. D. Adoption study supporting genetic transmission in manic depressive illness. *Lancet*, 1977, *268*, 327–329.

Mendels, J. & Frazer, A. Intracellular lithium concentration and clinical response: Towards a membrane theory of depression. *Journal of Psychiatric Research*, 1973, *10*, 9–18.

Mendels, J. & Frazer, A. Brain biogenic amine depletion and mood. *Archives of General Psychiatry*, 1974, *30*, 447–451.

Morrison, J., Hudgens, R., & Barchha, R. Life events and psychiatric illness. *British Journal of Psychiatry*, 1968, *114*, 423–432.

Murphy, G. E. & Robins, E. Social factors in suicide. *Journal of the American Medical Association*, 1967, *199*, 81–86.

Murphy, D. & Weiss, R. Reduced monoamine oxidase activity in blood platelets from bipolar depressed patients. *American Journal of Psychiatry*, 1972, *128*, 1351–1357.

Nathan, P. E., Titler, N. A., Lowenstein, L. M., Solomon, P., & Rossi, A. M. Behavioral analysis of chronic alcoholism. *Archives of General Psychiatry* 1970, *22*, 419.

Naylor, G., Dick, D., Dick, E., Le Poidevin, D., & Whyte, S. F. Erythrocyte membrane cation carrier in depressive illness. *Psychological Medicine*, 1973, *3*, 502–508.

Olds, J., Milner, P. Positive reinforcement produced by electrical stimulation of septal area and other regions of rat brain. *Journal of Comparative Physiology & Psychology*, 1954, *47*, 419–427.

Palola, E. G., Dorpat, T. L., & Larson, W. R. Alcoholism and suicidal behavior. In D. J. Pittman & C. R. Snyder (Eds.), *Society, culture and drinking patterns*. New York: Wiley, 1972.

Parkes, C. M. *Bereavement: Studies of grief in adult life*. New York: International Univ. Press, 1972.

Paykel, E. S. Life stress, depression, and attempted suicide. *Journal of Human Stress*, September, 1976, 3–12.

Paykel, E. S., Myers, J. K., Dienelt, M. N., Klerman, G. L., Lindenthal, J. J., & Pepper, M. P. Life events and depression—a controlled study. *Archives of General Psychiatry*, 1969, *21*, 753–760.

Perris, C. A study of bipolar (manic-depressive) and unipolar recurrent depressive psychoses. *Acta Psychiatrica Scandinavica*, 1966, *42*, 7–188.

Pitt, B. Maternity blues. *British Journal of Psychiatry*, 1973, *122*, 431–433.

Pollitt, J. D. Suggestions for a physiological classification of depression. *British Journal of Psychiatry*, 1965, *3*, 489–495.

Post, F. Diagnosis of depression in geriatric patients and treatment modalities appropriate for the population. In D. M. Gallant & G. M. Simpson (Eds.), *Depression: Behavioral, biochemical, diagnostic, and treatment concepts*. New York: Spectrum, 1977. Pp. 205–231.

Prang, A. The use of drugs in depression: Its theoretical and practical basis. *Psychiatric Annals*, 1973, 3, 55–75.

Prange, A. J., Wilson, I. C., Knox, A. E., McClane, T. K., Breese, G. R., Martin B. R., Alltop, L. B., & Lipton, M. A. Thyroid–imipramine clinical and chemical interaction: Evidence for a receptor deficit in depression. *Journal of Psychiatric Research*, 1972, 9, 187–205.

Prange, A., Wilson, L., Rabon, A., & Lipton, M. A. Enhancement of imipramine antidepressant activity by thyroid hormone. *American Journal of Psychiatry*, 1969, 126, 457–468.

Rabkin, J. G. & Struening, E. L. Life events, stress, and illness. *Science*, 1976, 194, 1013–1020.

Rasmussen, H. Medical education—revolution or reaction? *Pharos*, 1975, 38, 53–59.

Redmond, D., Maas, J., Kling, A., & Dekirmenjian, H. Changes in primate social behavior after treatment with alpha-methyl-para-tyrosine. *Psychosomatic Medicine*, 1971, 33, 97–113.

Reich, T., Winokur, G. Postpartum psychoses in patients with manic-depressive disease. *Journal of Nervous and Mental Diseases*, 1970, 151, 60–68.

Robertson, J. & Robertson, J. Young children in brief separation: A fresh look. *Psychoanalitic Study of the Child*, 1971, 26, 264–315.

Robins, E. & Guze, S. Classification of affective disorders: The primary–secondary, the endogenous–reactive, and the neurotic–psychotic dichotomies. In T. A. Williams, M. M. Katz, & J. A. Shield (Eds.), *Recent advances in the psychobiology of the depressive illnesses*. Washington, D. C.: U. S. Government Printing Office, 1972.

Robinson, D. S., Davis, J. M., Nies, A., Ravaris, C. L., & Sylvester, D. Relation of sex and aging to monoamine oxidase activity of human brain, plasma, and platelets. *Archives of General Psychiatry*, 1971, 24, 536–539.

Rome, H. Depressive illness: Its sociopsychiatric implications. In P. Kielholz (Ed.), *Masked depression*. Bern: Huber, 1973.

Rosen, G. Nostalgia: A "forgotten" psychological disorder. *Psychological Medicine*, 1975, 5, 340–354.

Rosenthal, T. L. & Bandura, A. Psychological modeling. In S. L. Garfield & A. E. Bergin (Eds.), *Handbook of Psychotherapy and behavior change* (rev. ed.). New York: Wiley, 1979.

Sack, R. L. & Goodwin, F. K. Inhibition of dopamine-β-hydroxylase in manic patients. *Archives of General Psychiatry*, 1974, 31, 649–654.

Scheff, J. J. The role of the mentally ill and the dynamics of mental disorder: A research framework. *Sociometry*, 1963, 26 , 436–453.

Schildkraut, J. Catecholamine hypothesis of affective disorders. *American Journal of Psychiatry*, 1965, 122, 509–522.

Schildkraut, J. J. The current status of biological criteria for classifying the depressive disorders and predicting responses to treatment. *Psychopharmacological Bulletin*, 1976, 10, 5–25.

Schmale, A. H. Adaptive role of depression in health and disease, In J. P. Scott & E. Senay *Separation and depression*. Washington, D. C.: Amer. Assoc. Advance. Sci., 1973.

Schuyler, D. Holiday blues. *Mental health matters*. Rockville Maryland: U. S. Govt. Printing Office, 1972.

Schwab, J. J., Bialow, M., Holzer, C. E., Brown, J. M. & Stevenson, B. E. Sociocultural aspects of deprssion in medical inpatients—I. Frequency and social variables. *Archives of General Psychiatry*, 1967, 17, 533–538.

Seligman, M. Learned helplessness and depression. In R. Friedman & M. Katz (Eds.), *The psychology of depression: Contemporary theory and research*. Washington, D. C., U. S. Gov. Printing Office, 1974. Pp. 83–113.

Shaw, D. Mineral metabolism, mania, and melancholia. *British Medical Journal*, 1966, 2, 261–267.

Shaw, D. Frizel, D., & Camps, F., White S. Brain electrolytes in depressive and alcoholic suicides. *British Journal of Psychiatry*, 1969, *115*, 69–79.

Spitz, R. Anaclitic depression: An inquiry into the genesis of psychiatric conditions in early childhood. *Psychoanalytical Study of the Child*, 1942, *2*, 313–342.

Spitzer, R. L. More on pseudoscience in science and the case for psychiatric diagnosis. *Archives of General Psychiatry*, 1976, *33*, 459–470.

Stein, L. Chemistry of reward and punishment. In D. Efron, (Ed.), *Psychopharmacology: A review of progress 1957–1967.* Washington, D. C.: U. S. Gov. Printing Office, 1968. Pp. 105–123.

Susser, M. *Causal thinking in the health sciences: Concepts and strategies of epidemiology.* New York: Oxford Univ. Press, 1973.

Tamerin, J. S. & Mendelson, J. H. The psychodynamics of chronic inebriation. *American Journal of Psychiatry*, 1969, *125*, 886.

Torrey, E. F. *The death of psychiatry.* Randor: Chilton, 1974.

Weissman, M. & Paykel, E. S. *The depressed woman: A study of social relationships.* Chicago: Univ. Chicago Press, 1974.

Whybrow, P. & Mendels, J. Toward a biology of depression: Some suggestions from neurophysiology. *American Journal of Psychiatry*, 1969, *125*, 45–54.

Whybrow, P. & Parlatore, A. Melancholia, a model in madness: A discussion of recent psychobiologic research into depressive illness. *International Journal of Psychiatry in Medicine*, 1973, *4*, 351–378.

Whybrow, P. C., Prange, A. J., & Treadway, C. R. Mental changes accompanying thyroid gland dysfunction. *Archives of General Psychiatry*, 1969, *20*, 48–63.

Winokur, G., Clayton, P. J., & Reich, T. *Manic depressive illness.* St. Louis, Missouri: Mosby, 1969.

Winokur, G. The natural history of the affective disorders (manias and depressions). *Seminars in Psychiatry*, 1970, *2*, 451–463.

Winokur, G., Cadoret, R., Dorzab, J., & Baker, M. Depressive disease: A genetic study. *Archives of General Psychiatry*, 1971, *24*, 135–144.

Winokur, G. Family history studies VIII. *Diseases of the Nervous System*, 1972, *33*, 94–99.

Winokur, G. Diagnostic and genetic aspects of affective illness. *Psychiatric Annals*, 1973, *3*, 7–15.

Wolpe, J. Neurotic depression: Experimental analog, clinical syndrome, and treatment. *American Journal of Psychotherapy*, 1971, *25*, 367–368.

Woodruff, R. A., Murphy, G. E., & Herjanic, M. The natural history of affective disorders—I. Symptoms of 72 patients at the time of index hospital admission. *Journal of Psychiatric Research*, 1967, *5*, 255–263.

Young, L., Suomi, S., Harlow, H., & McKinney, W. T., Jr. Early stress and later response to separation in rhesus monkeys. *American Journal of Psychiatry*, 1973, *130*, 400–405.

Subject Index